Nor

Channel Islands

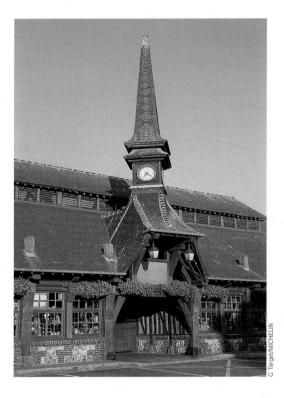

G Target/MICHELIN

Travel Publications

Hannay House, 39 Clarendon Road
Watford, Herts WD17 1JA, UK
☎ 01923 205 240 - Fax 01923 205 241
www.ViaMichelin.com
TheGreenGuide-uk@uk.michelin.com

Manufacture française des pneumatiques Michelin
Société en commandite par actions au capital de 304 000 000 EUR
Place des Carmes-Déchaux – 63 Clermont-Ferrand (France)
R.C.S. Clermont-Fd B 855 200 507

Typesetting: APS/Chromostyle, Tours
Printing and Binding: I.M.E., Baume-les-Dames

Cover design: Carré Noir, Paris 17ᵉ arr.

THE GREEN GUIDE
Spirit of Discovery

Leisure time spent with The Green Guide is also a time for refreshing your spirit, enjoying yourself, and taking advantage of our selection of fine restaurants, hotels and other places for relaxing: immerse yourself in the local culture, discover new horizons, experience the local lifestyle. The Green Guide opens the door for you.

Each year our writers go touring: visiting the sights, devising the driving tours, identifying the highlights, selecting the most attractive hotels and restaurants, checking the routes for the maps and plans.

Each title is compiled with great care, giving you the benefit of regular revisions and Michelin's first-hand knowledge. The Green Guide responds to changing circumstances and takes account of its readers' suggestions; all comments are welcome.

Share with us our enthusiasm for travel, which has led us to discover over 60 destinations in France and other countries. Like us, let yourself be guided by the desire to explore, which is the best motive for travel: the spirit of discovery.

Contents

Kharbine-Tapador/PHOTONONSTOP

A milkmaid of yore
in the traditional Norman headress

B. Kaufmann

Flags fly for peace in front
of Le Mémorial de Caen

Maps and plans

Thematic maps

Monuments

Local maps for touring

Town plans

Bayeux tapestry.
11C

Courtesy of the city of Bayeux

The inviting façade
of the Maison Saint-Amiens (Rouen)

Bernard Régent/PHOTONONSTOP

Michelin maps

Michelin products are complementary: for each of the sites listed in The Green Guide, map references are indicated which help you find your location on our range of maps. The image below shows the maps to use for each geographic area covered in this guide. To travel the roads in this region, you may use any of the following:

● the **regional maps** at a scale of 1:200 000 nos 231 and 232, which cover the main roads and secondary roads, and include useful indications for finding tourist attractions. They show castles, churches and other religious edifices, scenic view points, megalithic monuments, swimming beaches on lakes and rivers, swimming pools, golf courses, race tracks, air fields, and more.

● the **detailed maps** are based on the regional map data, but with a reduced format (about half a region), which makes them easier to consult and fold. For Normandy, use maps 52, 54, 55, 59, 60 and 63.

● the **departmental maps** (at a scale of 1:150 000, an enlargement of the 1:200 000 maps) are very easy to read, and make it easy to travel on all of the roads in the following departments: Calvados (4014), Eure (4027), Eure-et-Loire (4028) and Sarthe (4072). They come with a complete index of place names and include a plan of the towns which serve as administrative seats (préfectures).

And remember to travel with the latest edition of the **map** of France n° 989 (1:1 000 000), also available in atlas format: spiral bound, hard back, and the new mini-atlas – perfect for your glove compartment.

Michelin is pleased to offer a route-planning service on the Internet: **www.ViaMichelin.com.** Choose the shortest route, a route without tolls, or the Michelin recommended route to your destination; you can also access information about hotels and restaurants from The Red Guide, and tourists sites from The Green Guide. *Bon voyage!*

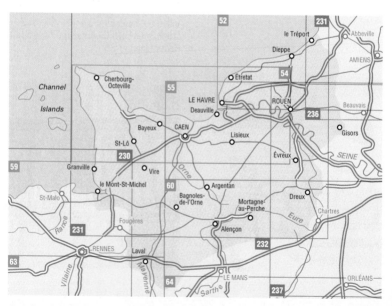

Using this guide

● The **summary maps** on the following pages are designed to assist you in planning your trip: the **Map of principal sights** identifies major sights and attractions, the **Map of regional driving** tours defines selected itineraries.

● We recommend that you read the **Introduction** before setting out on your trip. The background information it contains on history, the arts and traditional culture will prove most instructive and make your visit more meaningful.

● The main towns and attractions are presented in alphabetical order in the **Sights** section. In order to ensure quick, easy identification, original place names have been used throughout the guide. The clock symbol ⊙, placed after monuments or other sights, refers to the **Admission times and charges** section at the end of the guide.

● The **Practical information** section offers useful addresses for planning your trip, seeking accommodation, enjoying outdoor activities and more. Consult this section for the opening hours and admission prices for monuments, museums and other tourist attractions; festival and carnival dates; suggestions for thematic tours on scenic railways and through nature reserves etc.

● We have selected **hotels and restaurants**, and other places for **entertainment** in many of the towns in this guide. Turn to the pages bordered in blue.

● The **Index** lists attractions, famous people and events, and other subjects covered in the guide.

Let us hear from you. We are interested in your reaction to our guide, in any ideas you have to offer or good addresses you would like to share. Send your comments to Michelin Travel Publications, 39 Herts WD17 IJA, U.K. or by e-mail to thegreenguide-uk@uk.michelin.com.

G. Targa/MICHELIN

Key

Selected monuments and sights

⊙ ⇒	Tour - Departure point
🛉 ⚱	Catholic church
🛉 ⚱	Protestant church, other temple
✡ ▣ ☪	Synagogue - Mosque
▣	Building
■	Statue, small building
⚱	Calvary, wayside cross
◎	Fountain
●━━	Rampart - Tower - Gate
✕	Château, castle, historic house
∴	Ruins
⌣	Dam
✿	Factory, power plant
☆	Fort
⋂	Cave
▱	Troglodyte dwelling
⊓	Prehistoric site
▾	Viewing table
♈	Viewpoint
▲	Other place of interest

Sports and recreation

🏇	Racecourse
⛸	Skating rink
≋ ⊿	Outdoor, indoor swimming pool
🎥	Multiplex Cinema
⛵	Marina, sailing centre
⌂	Trail refuge hut
▯■■■▯	Cable cars, gondolas
▯++++▯	Funicular, rack railway
🚂	Tourist train
◇	Recreation area, park
⛹	Theme, amusement park
𝚼	Wildlife park, zoo
❀	Gardens, park, arboretum
◉	Bird sanctuary, aviary
🚶	Walking tour, footpath
☺	Of special interest to children

Abbreviations

A	Agricultural office (Chambre d'agriculture)
C	Chamber of Commerce (Chambre de commerce)
H	Town hall (Hôtel de ville)
J	Law courts (Palais de justice)
M	Museum (Musée)
P	Local authority offices (Préfecture, sous-préfecture)
POL.	Police station (Police)
🛡	Police station (Gendarmerie)
T	Theatre (Théatre)
U	University (Université)

Highly recommended	Sight	Seaside resort	Winter sports resort	Spa
Recommended	★★★	立立立	✳✳✳	‡‡‡
Interesting	★★	立立	✳✳	‡‡

Additional symbols

i		Tourist information
═══	═══	Motorway or other primary route
❶	**❶**	Junction: complete, limited
⊨═══	═══	Pedestrian street
I═════I		Unsuitable for traffic, street subject to restrictions
⊡⊡⊡⊡	- - -	Steps - Footpath
🚆	🚆	Train station - Auto-train station
🚌	SNCF	Coach (bus) station
·—·—·		Tram
🅜		Metro, underground
P/**R**		Park-and-Ride
♿		Access for the disabled
✉		Post office
☎		Telephone
▧		Covered market
·ˣ·		Barracks
△		Drawbridge
⌣		Quarry
✕		Mine
B	**F**	Car ferry (river or lake)
⛴		Ferry service: cars and passengers
⛴		Foot passengers only
③		Access route number common to Michelin maps and town plans
Bert (R.)...		Main shopping street
AZ B		Map co-ordinates

Hotels and restaurants

20 rooms: 38,57/57,17€	Number of rooms: price for one person/ double room
half-board or full board: 42,62€	Price per person, based on double occupancy
⊐ 6,85€	Price of breakfast; when not given, it is included in the price of the room (i.e., for bed-and-breakfasts)
120 sites: 12,18€	Number of camp sites and cos for 2 people with a car
12,18€ lunch- 16,74/38,05€	Restaurant: fixed-price menus served at lunch only- mini/maxi price fixed menu (lunch and dinner) or à la carte
rest. 16,74/38,05€	Lodging where meals are serve mini/maxi price fixed menu or la carte
meal 15,22€	"Family style" meal
reserv	Reservation recommended
⊘	No credit cards accepted
P	Reserved parking for hotel patrons

The prices correspond to the higher rates of the tourist season

Principal Sights

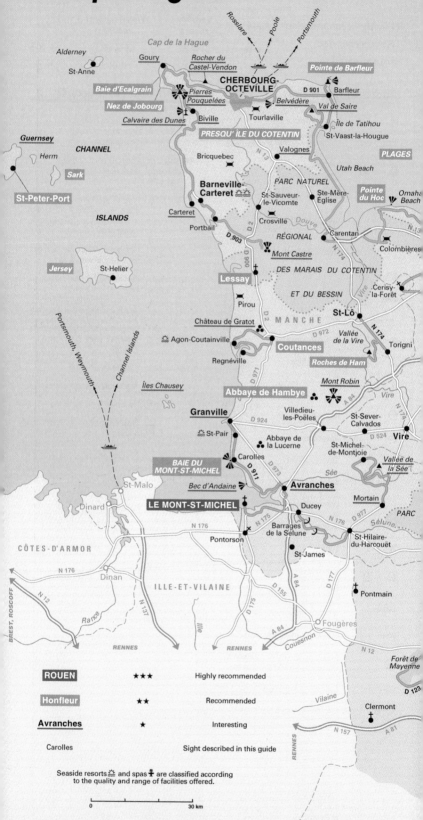

Rosslare · Poole · Portsmouth

Cap de la Hague

Alderney
St-Anne

Goury

Rocher du
Castel-Vendon

**CHERBOURG-
OCTEVILLE**

Pointe de Barfleur

D 901 · Barfleur

Baie d'Ecalgrain
Pierres
Pouquelées
Nez de Jobourg
Calvaire des Dunes

Belvédère
Val de Saire

Biville · Tourlaville

Île de Tatihou
St-Vaast-la-Hougue

PRESQU' ÎLE DU COTENTIN

Guernsey
Herm

CHANNEL

Valognes

PLAGES

Bricquebec

Utah Beach

Sark

St-Peter-Port

**Barneville-
Carteret**

St-Sauveur-
le-Vicomte

PARC NATUREL

Ste-Mère-
Eglise

**Pointe
du Hoc**

Omaha
Beach

ISLANDS

Carteret

Douve

Carentan

N 13

Portbail

Crosville

RÉGIONAL

Colombières

D 903

Mont Castre

Jersey
St-Helier

D 900

DES MARAIS DU COTENTIN

Cerisy-
la-Forêt

Lessay

ET DU BESSIN

Portsmouth, Weymouth

Channel Islands

Pirou

Vire

MANCHE

St-Lô

Torigni

Château de Gratot

D 972

Vallée
de la Vire

Agon-Coutainville

Îles Chausey

Regnéville

Coutances

Roches de Ham

D 971

Abbaye de Hambye

Mont Robin

Granville

Villedieu-
les-Poêles

St-Sever-
Calvados

Vire

St-Pair

A 84

Vire

D 924

Abbaye de
la Lucerne

D 524

Carolles

St-Michel-
de-Montjoie

Vallée de
la Sée

**BAIE DU
MONT-ST-MICHEL**

D 911

D 973

Avranches

Sée

Mortain

Bec d'Andaine

LE MONT-ST-MICHEL

PARC

Ducey

St-Malo

Dinard

N 175

N 176

D 977

N 176

Barrages
de la Sélune

Sélune

St-Hilaire-
du-Harcouët

Pontorson

St-James

CÔTES-D'ARMOR

N 176

D 177

Pontmain

N 12

Dinan

D 155

A 84

Rance

N 137

Ille

ILLE-ET-VILAINE

D 175

Fougères

Forêt de
Mayenne

RENNES

RENNES

Coueснon

N 12

D 123

Brest, Roscoff

N 12

Vilaine

Clermont

RENNES

N 157

A 81

ROUEN	★★★	Highly recommended
Honfleur	★★	Recommended
Avranches	★	Interesting
Carolles		Sight described in this guide

Seaside resorts ⌂ and spas ✝ are classified according
to the quality and range of facilities offered.

0 _____ 30 km

Driving Tours

See the pages following for a description of each tour

Cap de la Hague

Port Racine

Goury

Rocher du Castel-Vendon

Cap Lévy

Alderney

Baie d'Ecalgrain

Rocher du Castel

Nez de Joubourg

Baie d'Ecalgrain

Nez de Joubourg

Poole

Portsmouth

Pointe de Barfleur

Pointe de Bar

CHERBOURG-OCTEVILLE

D 116

Belvédère

Barfleur

Cherbourg-Octeville

Calvaire

Biville

Pierre Pouquelée

PRESQU'ÎLE DU COTENTIN

St-Vaast-la-

St-Vaast-la-Hou

Quettehou

Guernsey

Herm

CHANNEL

Sark

les Pieux

Bricquebec

Valognes

D 902

1

D 902

UTAH BEA

N 12

D 17

Ste-Mère-Église

Ste-Mère-Église

Pointe

St-Peter-Port

Barneville-Carteret

Barneville-Carteret

Ste-Marie-du-Mont

Crosville

Dou

Carteret

ISLANDS

Portbail

D 903

Carentan

D 913

D 1

Color

la Haye-du-Puits

D 900

Mont Castr

Manoir de Cantepie

N 174

Ce

la-

Jersey

St-Helier

Lessay

D 2

DES MA

ET DU BESSIN

St-Lô

Îles Chausey

Pirou

M A N C

Gratot

D 972

D 972

Saint-

Vallée de la Vire

Roches de Ham

Portsmouth, Weymouth

Château de

Coutances

Agon-Coutainville

Regnéville

Mont F

D 13

Abbaye de Ha

Channel Islands

Îles Chausey

Abbaye de l'Abbaye

Granville

Villedieu-les-Poêles

St-Sever-C

Abbaye de la Lucerne

la Lucerne

D 81

St-P

St-Pair

Carolles

D 580

Villedieu-les-Poêles

Mont-

BAIE DU MONT-ST-MICHEL

Sartilly

Sée

St-F

St-Malo

Genêts

D 911

Avranches

Bec d'Andaine

D 911

2

Dinard

le Mont-St-Michel

MICHEL

Courtils

Ducey

Ducey

N 176

St-James

N 176

N 175

St-Hilaire-du-

N 176

A 84

Mortai

D 97

Pontorson

Pontorson

CÔTES-D'ARMOR

Dinan

N 176

ILLE-ET-VILAINE

Fougères

N 137

D 155

Rance

A 84

D 177

Chai

Roman ruins

Museum, art gallery

RENNES

Vilaine

Aquarium

Viewpoint

Battle site

Wildlife park, zoo

Religious building

Bird sanctuary, aviary

Château, castle or historic house

Industrial site

Tourist train

Boat trips

Outstanding natural site

Seaside resort

Regional specialities

Outstanding man-made sight

Fortifications

Spa

Garden, park

Old town

Historic site

Picturesque village

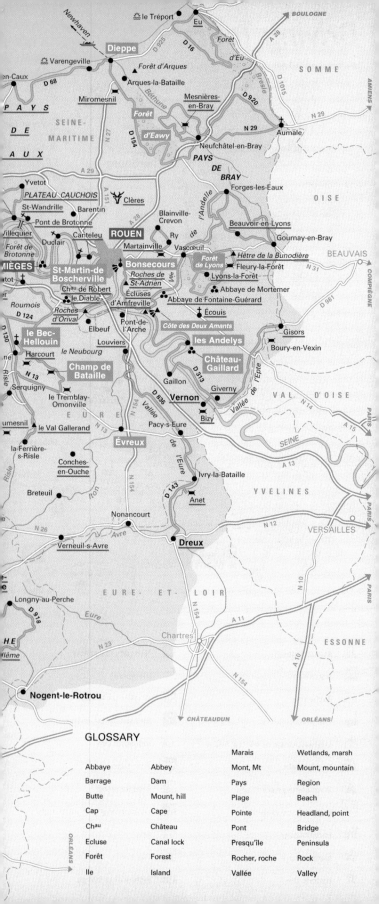

GLOSSARY

		Marais	Wetlands, marsh
Abbaye	Abbey	Mont, Mt	Mount, mountain
Barrage	Dam	Pays	Region
Butte	Mount, hill	Plage	Beach
Cap	Cape	Pointe	Headland, point
Ch^{au}	Château	Pont	Bridge
Ecluse	Canal lock	Presqu'île	Peninsula
Forêt	Forest	Rocher, roche	Rock
Ile	Island	Vallée	Valley

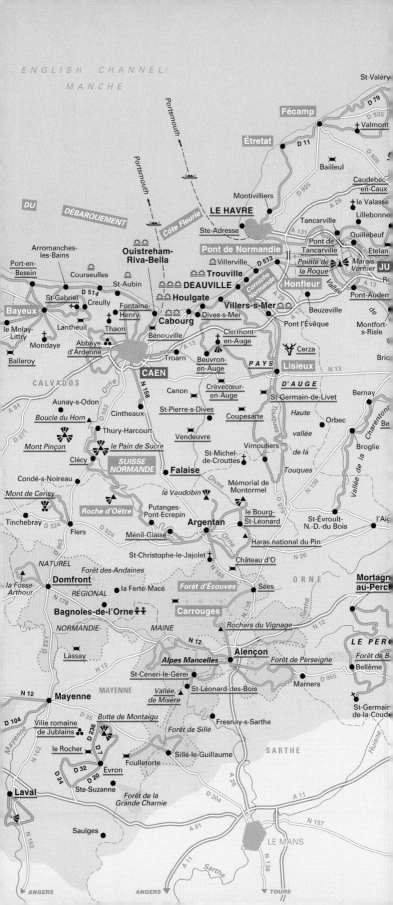

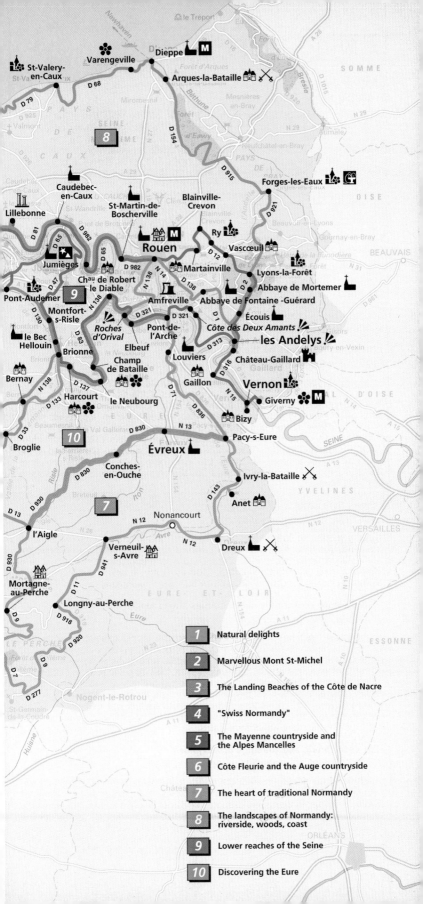

le Tréport

Newhaven

Dieppe

Varengeville

St-Valery-
en-Caux

Arques-la-Bataille

SOMME

PAYS
DE
CAUX

SEINE

8

Forges-les-Eaux

OISE

Caudebec-
en-Caux

St-Martin-de-
Boscherville

Blainville-
Crevon

Lillebonne

Ry

Vascœuil

BEAUVAIS

Jumièges

Rouen

Martainville

Lyons-la-Forêt

Pont-Audemer

Ch^au de Robert
le Diable

Amfreville

Abbaye de Mortemer

Montfort-
s-Risle

Roches
d'Orival

Abbaye de Fontaine -Guérard

Écouis

le Bec
Hellouin

9

Pont-de-
l'Arche

Côte des Deux Amants

les Andelys

Brionne

Elbeuf

Champ
de Bataille

Louviers

Château-Gaillard

Bernay

Harcourt

le Neubourg

Gaillon

Vernon

Giverny

D'OISE

Broglie

10

Bizy

Conches-
en-Ouche

Évreux

Pacy-s-Eure

Ivry-la-Bataille

YVELINES

7

Nonancourt

Anet

VERSAILLES

l'Aigle

Verneuil-
s-Avre

Dreux

Mortagne-
au-Perche

EURE - ET - LOIR

Longny-au-Perche

LE PERCHE

ESSONNE

Nogent-le-Rotrou

St-Germain-
de-la-Coudre

ORLÉANS

Driving tours

1 Natural delights
290km/180mi from Saint-Lô and back

At the western edge of the continent of Europe, off the main tourist routes, the Cotentin Peninsula (also known as the Cherbourg Peninsula) is a lovely place for a holiday. Surrounded by the sea on three sides, it is separated from the rest of the region by a swathe of wetlands. Where the countryside is lush and green, cows graze placidly. In the regional nature park, canals, rivers and ponds provide a cool resting place for tourists and migratory birds alike. On the coast, the sandy beaches are protected by cliffs and promontories. The towns and villages have a peaceful atmosphere, too, and the cities have been built (or rebuilt, after the war) in sturdy local granite. To get the most out of your tour, be sure to pack good walking shoes and a bathing suit.

2 Marvelous Mont St-Michel
210km/130mi from Granville and back

The tour starts in Granville, a town proud of its maritime heritage and the many sailors who went to sea from here. The route takes you through quiet hamlets and lively small towns, mostly rebuilt after the Second World War, using the typical regional granite blocks. The most unforgettable place on this tour is of course the Mont St-Michel, a pinnacle of art, architecture, spirituality and European culture. If you decide to walk across the Bay from Genêts or Courtils, check the tide tables first.

3 The Landing Beaches on the Côte de Nacre
180km/112mi from Caen and back

This tour takes you along the lovely coast known by the name "mother-of-pearl", and also inland through a landscape steeped in memories of the momentous events of the D-Day landings. Caen is well worth a visit, for its art collections, abbeys, lively town centre, and the moving Museum for Peace just outside the town, which was at the centre of the Battle of Normandy. Bayeux is known for its precious tapestry and also as the only town in the region to survive the war relatively unscathed. Arromanches-sur-Mer was the site chosen for the famous artificial or "mulberry" ports towed across from Great Britain to assist the Allied Landing. The coast is not only resonant of historical significance but also a fine place for sunbathing and swimming in the many family-style resorts.

4 "Swiss Normandy"
210km/130mi from Alençon and back

Perhaps you have to live in Normandy to appreciate why this area is likened to Switzerland. The hills here rise no higher than 360m/1181ft but that is enough for them to stand out clearly on the horizon, and to form a landscape of steep cliffs, deep valleys with rivers winding through them, hair-pin bends; meadows and woods alternate on the slopes. This drive is designed especially for nature-lovers.

5 The Mayenne countryside and the Alpes Mancelles
210km/130mi from Laval and back

The Mayenne Valley is quite different from the popular tourist areas of the coast. The charm of this hidden corner of Normandy lies in its many ponds, lakes and streams, and the hills of the Sarthe Valley. While the pasturelands provide the typically rural image of Normandy, the granite houses with slate roofs echo the neighbouring region of Brittany, and the mild climate and gracious lifestyle are reminiscent of the Loire. An especially enjoyable section of this drive is through the Nomandie-Maine regional nature park, where traditional agriculture and crafts are still practised, and there are many opportunities to engage in outdoor sports, including cycling, climbing, or rambling on one of the many way-marked paths.

6 The Côte Fleurie and the Auge countryside
200km/124mi from the Pont de Normandie and back

After admiring the graceful span of the bridge, take this drive to the charming town of Honfleur, on the Seine estuary, and continue to the popular beach resorts of Trouville, Deauville, Houlgate and Cabourg. When you leave the coast, you enter the Auge country, a land of green pastures and half-timbered houses, famous for its fine aged calvados and savoury cheeses. The route goes through Lisieux, birthplace of Saint Theresa, then on to Camembert, Vimoutiers and the Vie Valley. The Valley de la Risle leads back to the Seine estuary by way of the Bec-Hellouin Abbey, Pont-Audemer and the Vernier wetlands.

⑦ The heart of traditional Normandy
300km/180mi

This tour carries you through the heartland of historic, rural and culinary Normandy. Visit the site of the Battle of Ivry, the château d'Anet, the Perch nature park; keep an eye out for sturdy Percheron horses grazing in the fields; enjoy blood sausage in Mortagne, rillettes in Mamers. The gentle hills are wooded and serene, the perfect landscape for travellers seeking a spot for a bit of solitude and natural beauty.

⑧ The landscapes of Normandy: riverside, woods, coast
400km/249mi from Les Andelys and back

This drive follows the north bank of the River Seine, winding along past many spectacular sights: les Andelys and Château-Gaillard, the Fontaine-Guérard Abbey, the old town of Rouen, Duclair, the monasteries of St-Martin-de-Boscherville, Jumièges and St-Wandrille, Caudebec-en-Caux, Villequier, Ételan castle, the Roman amphitheatre at Lillebonne. Across the Pont de Normandie lies the major port of Le Havre, which is well worth a visit, as is the town itself, for its many museums and modern architecture (the city was almost obliterated during the war). The suggested tour next follows the shore known as the "Alabaster Coast", with its striking chalk cliffs and shingle beaches. The "arch and needle", two unique rock formations off the coast of Étratat, are emblematic of this area; Fécamp and Dieppe are typical fishing ports with many interesting things to see and do. The route turns inland, crossing the Eawy forest, and passing through the picturesque town of Forges-les-Eaux, continues along the Andelle Valley and into the lovely forest of Lyons. The tour finishes in the delightful village of Lyons-la-Forêt.

⑨ Lower reaches of the River Seine
300km/186mi from Vernon and back

Vernon is the starting point for a trip to Bizy castle and Monet's famous house and garden in Giverny. Follow the north bank of the Seine through the gentle meanders of the Gaillon Valley to Les Andelys; the remains of the formidable Château-Gaillard rise above the river. On the road to Rouen, you can stop and admire the statues at Notre-Dame d'Écouis, the regional art centre in Vascoeuil, the château-museum in Martainville. After enjoying a tour of the historic city of Rouen and its famous cathedral, carry on as far as the estuary and the Pont de Normandie. Here you can cross the estuary to enjoy the beaches at Trouville and Deauville before discovering the delights of the south bank. The first stop is Pont-l'Evèque, home of the eponymous cheese. After the pretty village of Pont-Audemer, the road leads into the Brotonne regional nature park, with its traditional crafts museums and recreational facilities. The Champ de Bataille château illustrates a more refined way of life with its elegant rooms and formal French gardens. From here, the route offers splendid views from the castle of Robert le Diable, the rocks at Orival and the Amfreville canal locks.

⑩ Discovering the Eure
200km/124mi

After a tour of the city of Rouen, take a trip into the département of the Eure. You can visit the châteaux of Robert le Diable and Champ de Bataille along the way. Drive along the Charentonne Valley as far as St-Évroult, then head northeast towards Évreux. The tour meets up with the River Eure at Pacy-sur-Eure, and follows the valley back north. Between Elbeuf and Rouen, the Roches d'Orival rise up on the horizon in silhouette.

Cliffs at Étretat

M. Maes/PIX

Introduction

Landscapes

Normandy is not a homogeneous geographical unit but an old province, formerly a dukedom, embracing two large areas with different geological structures, which become progressively younger from west to east. The sandstone, granite and primary schists of the Armorican Massif in the west give way to the Secondary and Tertiary Era strata of clay, limestone and chalk which belong to the geological formation of the Paris basin. Normandy can therefore be conveniently divided into two quite distinct regions, Haute-Normandie, which lies northwest of the Paris basin, and Basse-Normandie, which resembles its neighbour Brittany and consists of an eroded foundation of ancient rocks.

The administrative Region of Haute-Normandie is made up of the *départements* of Eure (27) and Seine-Maritime (76); Basse-Normandie includes the *départements* of Calvados (14), Manche (50) and Orne (61).

REGIONS OF NORMANDY

The inland areas can be divided into two types of regions, **open country** and **woodland**. In the strictest sense, the open country *(campagne)* consists of dry, windswept plains and cultivated fields. The woodland *(bocage)* is typical of the Armorican Massif, although to the east it spills over into the Maine, the Perche and the Auge regions. Typical of the countryside, and sometimes confusing for casual ramblers, a network of dense hedges grows on earthen banks, enclosing fields and meadows and forming a sort of labyrinth. The people living on the farms and hamlets scattered along the sunken roads have for a long time lived in relative isolation. Lastly, the different parts of the **coast** of Normandy also have distinctive characteristics.

Quaternary Era		Alluvial deposits
Tertiary Era		Sedimentary deposits
Secondary Era	{	Cretaceous limestone
		Jurassic limestone
Primary Era	{	Granite
		Metamorphic rocks

Open country

The **Pays de Caux** *(see p 126)* is a vast limestone plateau covered with fertile silt, ending along the coast in cliffs famous for their "hanging' valleys" *(valleuses)* and bordered to the south by the Seine Valley. The area produces wheat and industrial crops such as flax, sugar beet and rape. Most of the cattle grazing here are raised for meat rather than milk.

Trees grow in occasional clumps on the plateau itself and on the hillsides of the surrounding valleys, sustained by the moisture retained by deposits of silex clay.

Bordered by the valleys of the Epte and the Andelle, the **Vexin normand** *(see p 340)* is covered by a particularly thick layer of alluvial soil which favours the intensive cultivation of wheat and sugar beet.

The **Plaine du Neubourg** and the **Évreux-St-André** district present a flat landscape, of open fields, similar to the area known as **Caen-Falaise**. The fertility of the soil favours large-scale arable farming coupled with cattle-breeding for the production of meat. Vegetables are grown in the region of Caen.

The **Argentan-Sées-Alençon** country, north of the Sarthe Valley and the Alpes Mancelles, are composed of small chalk regions where horses and cattle graze in the open orchards.

Transitional regions

The **Roumois** and **Lieuvin** plains are separated by the Risle Valley; hedges and apple orchards create the texture of the landscape. The **Pays d'Ouche** *(see p 143)* is more densely forested, while the rolling hills of the **Perche normand** *(see p 98)*, a famous horse-breeding district, form a transition between the Paris basin and the Armorican Massif.

Woodlands

The Norman part of the **Pays de Bray** is a vast clay depression, known as the "button-hole", bordered by two limestone heights. It is stock-raising country and has increased its production of meat; it also specialises in fresh dairy produce such as yoghurts and *petits-suisses*.

The **Pays d'Auge** *(see p 72)*, which contains the river valleys of the Touques and the Dives, is different from the other regions in that the chalk strata have been deeply fissured by a network of streams, exposing many impervious soils. High local humidity promotes the growth of grassland and hedges. Apples are turned into cider and Calvados. Milk is used to make Camembert. Horse-breeding is also a tradition near the coast and the Perche region.

South of the Bessin is the **Bocage normand**, where meadows, sometimes planted with apple or pear trees, are enclosed by hedges. Raising dairy cattle is still the main activity. Local farmers have adapted their production to suit modern needs and in addition to the traditional Normandy cream and butter, they produce sterilised milk with a long shelf life and which needs no refrigeration (*UHT* milk) and a great variety of low-fat dairy products.

The **Bessin** lies on the edge of the Armorican Massif northwest of the open country. The high quality of the local dairy produce is represented by the name Isigny, famous not only in France but also abroad. Bayeux is the capital of this region where apple orchards are rare but where the breeding of saddle-horses and trotters has been a long-standing tradition.

The remote peninsula of **Cotentin** *(see p 144)*, which lies between the Vire estuary and Mont-St-Michel bay, is part of the Armorican Massif. The peninsula itself is divided from the Bocage Normand by a sedimentary depression, which is flooded at certain times of the year; there are three distinct areas within the peninsula: the Cotentin Pass, the Val de Saire and Cap de la Hague. The region is still largely devoted to stock raising except along the coast where vegetables are grown, as they are in nearby Brittany.

The Coast

The coast of Normandy from the River Bresle west to the River Couesnon is as varied as its hinterland. Erosion by the sea has transferred material from rocky projections and deposited it in sheltered coves; the sea has brought shingle to the bays and ports of the Pays de Caux, mud to the Seine estuary and to more than one port (Lillebonne was a sea port in Gallo-Roman times) and it has raised the level of several of the Calvados beaches.

The Pays de Caux meets the sea in what is known as the **Côte d'Albâtre** (Alabaster Coast – *see p 126*), a line of high limestone cliffs, like the White Cliffs of Dover, penetrated by shingle-bottomed inlets. The sea beating at the foot of the cliffs causes rock falls thus eroding the cliff face and forming hanging valleys.

The **Côte Fleurie** *(see p 162)* offers miles of fine sand beaches where the sea may withdraw more than a mile at low water; it also enjoys a high level of sunshine. The Calvados coast is composed of the low Bessin cliffs, interspersed with sand dunes and salt marshes (Caen area).

Limestone cliffs near Fécamp

To the west are the sand or sand and shingle beaches of the bracing **Côte de Nacre** (Mother-of-Pearl Coast). The Cotentin peninsula resembles Cornwall and Brittany with its rocky inlets, although there are also long stretches of sand dunes and beaches along the coast where the continental rock base does not reach the shore. Mont-St-Michel Bay is known for its vast sands and mud flats from which the sea seems to withdraw completely at times.

The **lighthouses** along the Normandy coast, which guide navigators in the Channel, also make good vantage points. The operating machinery, which may sometimes be visited, is interesting. The Norman engineer **Augustin Fresnel** (1788-1827) replaced the conventional parabolic reflector with compound lenses, which led to great progress in the length of beam projected out to sea. The nature of light sources has changed and their candlepower has considerably increased but the Fresnel system is still in use. At night, in the more difficult sectors, several lighthouses can be seen simultaneously; each has its own peculiarities: fixed, revolving or intermittent beam.

HORSES – THE PRIDE OF NORMANDY

Traditionally associated with travel, work and war, horses are now increasingly appreciated as companions in leisure activities such as games, competitions and pleasure rides. There are many economic advantages; the various trades connected with horses are particularly thriving in Normandy: breeding, insemination, dressage, veterinary care, blacksmith's work, saddlery, harness-making, managing riding centres, organising riding trips, horse-drawn carriages tours, fairs, shows, competitions...

For more than 600 years, the *départements* of the Orne, Calvados, Manche and Mayenne, have bred and trained horses ranking among the finest in the world for competitions.

More than 70% of all French thoroughbreds and trotters are bred in Basse-Normandie; the most powerful draught horses (Percherons) and some of the best carriage-horses (Cobs) are bred and raised in national or private studs.

Thoroughbreds: Thoroughbreds are the fastest, the most elegant and the most refined horses, with an outstanding physical and athletic potential. Full of spirit, they can sometimes be touchy and irritable. Their racing career does not exceed three years. The sale of yearlings takes place each year at the end of August in Deauville; it attracts international racing stable owners. The sale of brood-mares and foals is held in late November.

French Trotters: This mixed breed was developed from Normandy mares and Norfolk-roadster trotters. Their racing career (whether they are harnessed or mounted) lasts longer than that of thoroughbreds. Everyone still remembers Gelinotte, Ourasi, Une de Mai...

Cobs: Either chestnut or bay, cobs are ideal carriage-horses; they are strong, compact, likeable, full of energy and have a pleasant way of trotting. They can work in the fields or be harnessed to a carriage. In former days they used to be paraded harnessed to elegant carriages.

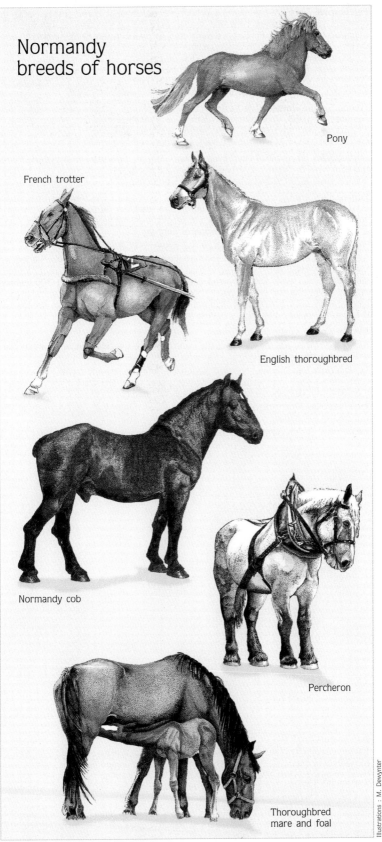

Normandy breeds of horses

Pony

French trotter

English thoroughbred

Normandy cob

Percheron

Thoroughbred mare and foal

Illustrations : M. Dewynter

23

Percherons: They are the most sought-after heavy draught horses in the world; the race was developed from cobs and Arabs, some say as far back as the Crusades. Dappled grey or black, Percherons were used for work in the fields, deliveries, army duties... and even drawing Paris's omnibuses! Nowadays they are still appreciated for heavy duties in forests and in town. One of the most famous Percherons was the stallion *Jean le Blanc*. Since then selection has been strict and the Société Hippique Percheronne keeps a stud book which spans the Perche, Mayenne and Auge regions where many fine breeding specimens can be found.

French Saddle-Horses: The name "French saddle-horse" is quite recent since it first appeared in 1958. It encompasses almost all French competition horses. Excellent jumpers as well as trotters, these horses are ideal all-rounders for show-jumping competitions either in jumping, dressage or cross-country events.

Other breeds are gradually becoming known, such as the **quarter-horse** imported from the US in 1978. Small but strong, versatile and docile, it can be used as a carriage-horse as well as for riding trips or western-type riding.

Ponies: they are becoming increasingly popular, particularly the New Forest type; the pottock, strong, hard-working and suitable as a pack or saddle-horse; and the half-linger, first bred in the Tyrol, a docile and adaptable animal perfectly suitable for forest or field work but also for pony-trekking or jumping.

National Studs: They form one of the oldest French institutions since one was founded by Colbert in 1665 and still has the same mission: to supervise all matters concerning horse-breeding and equestrian activities. In France there are 23 national studs concerned with 33 recognised breeds. In 1993 for instance, 1 300 stallions, including 691 draught horses, were lent to breeders. National studs work in close collaboration with the Institut National de la Recherche Agronomique to improve breeding techniques; they also supervise horse-racing and betting.

Horses' Coats: There are four kinds:

Plain coats: In this case the hair is of the same colour as the coat: white, chestnut, black or creamy coffee.

Two-tone coats: Bay (chestnut coat and black hair), light-bay (creamy coffee coat and black hair), mouse-grey (grey coat and black hair), grey (grey and black hair), strawberry roan (chestnut coat and white hair), dun (wolf-coloured coat).

Three-tone coats: Roan (black, white, red or chestnut mixed coat), red roan (roan coat with red as a dominant colour).

Piebald coats: mainly white coats with patches of another colour, for instance bay or black.

*This year's edition of **The Red Guide France** offers a selection of pleasant and quiet hotels in convenient locations. Their amenities are included (swimming pools, tennis courts, private beaches and gardens, etc.) as well as their dates of annual closure. The selection also includes establishments which offer excellent cuisine: carefully prepared meals at reasonable prices, **Michelin stars** for good cooking.*

*The current annual Michelin **Camping Caravaning France** lists the facilities offered by many campsites (shops, bars, restaurants, laundries, games rooms, tennis courts, miniature golf courses, playgrounds, swimming pools...).*

Historical table and notes

Roman Period

58-51BC	Roman conquest. New towns appear: Rotomagus (Rouen), Caracotinum (Harfleur), Noviomagus (Lisieux), Juliobona (Lillebonne), Mediolanum (Évreux).
56BC	The Unelli crushed by Sabinius in the Mont Castre area.
1C	Growth of main settlements (Coutances, Rouen, Évreux etc).
2C	Nordic (Saxon and Germanic) invasions of the Bessin region. Conversion to Christianity.
260	Bishopric of Rouen founded by St Nicaise.
284 and 364	Nordic invasions.

Frankish Domination

497	Rouen and Évreux occupied by Clovis.
511	Neustria or the Western Kingdom inherited by Clothaire, Clovis' son.
6C	The first monasteries founded (Castles of God).
7C	Monasteries flourish: St-Wandrille, Jumièges.
709	Mont Tombe consecrated to the cult of St Michael by Aubert, Bishop of Avranches.

Viking Invasions

	The Vikings or Northmen who sailed from Scandinavia harassed Western Europe, parts of Africa and even headed into the Mediterranean.
800	Channel coast invaded by Vikings.
820	Seine Valley laid waste by Vikings.
836	Christians persecuted in the Cotentin region.
858	Bayeux devastated by Vikings.
875	Further persecution in the West.
885	Paris besieged by Vikings.
911	Treaty of St-Clair-sur-Epte: Rollo becomes the first Duke of Normandy.

The Independent Dukedom

	Under William Longsword the dukedom takes on its final form with the unification of the Avranchin and the Cotentin.
10-11C	Consolidation of ducal powers. Restoration of the abbeys.
1027	Birth of William, the future conqueror of England, at Falaise.
1066	Invasion of England by William. King of France threatened by his vassal, the Duke of Normandy, now also King of England.
1087	Death of William the Conqueror in Rouen.
1087-1135	William's heirs in dispute; ducal authority restored by Henry Beauclerc who becomes King of England as Henry I (1100-35) after his brother William Rufus.
1120	The wreck of the *White Ship* off Barfleur Point with the loss of Henry I's heir, William Atheling and 300 members of the Anglo-Norman nobility.
1152	Marriage of Henry II Plantagenet, to Eleanor of Aquitaine, whose dowry included all southwest France.
1154-89	Henry II of England.
1195	Château-Gaillard built by Richard Lionheart.
1202	Loss of Norman possessions by John Lackland, King of England.
1204	Normandy united to the French crown.

From the French Dukedom to the Province of Normandy

1315	Granting of the Norman Charter, symbol of provincial status, which remained in being until the French Revolution.
1346	Normandy invaded by Edward III of England.
1364-84	The Battle of Cocherel marks the start of Du Guesclin's campaigns.
1417	Normandy invaded by Henry V of England.

1424	English repulsed by Louis d'Estouteville, defender of Mont-St-Michel.
1431	Trial and torture of Joan of Arc at Rouen.
1437	Founding of Caen University.
1450	Normandy recovered by the French crown after the victory at Formigny and the recapture of Cherbourg.
1469	Charles of France, last Duke of Normandy, is dispossessed of his dukedom.
1514	The Rouen Exchequer becomes the Parliament of Normandy.
1517	Founding of Le Havre.
1542	Rouen created as a self-governing city for treasury purposes.
1589	Henri of Navarre victorious at Arques and the following year at Ivry-la-Bataille.
1625	Alençon also created as a treasury district.
1639-40	Revolt of the Barefoot Peasants provoked by the introduction of the salt tax *(gabelle)*.
1692	Naval battle of La Hougue.
1771-75	Suppression of the Parliament at Rouen.

Contemporary Normandy

1789	The Caen Revolt.
1793	The Girondins' attempted uprising; siege of Granville.
1795-1800	Insurrection of the Norman royalists, the Chouans.
1843	Inauguration of the Paris-Caen railway.
1870-71	Franco-Prussian War; occupation of Haute-Normandie and Le Mans.
June 1940	Bresle Front breached.
August 1942	Dieppe Commando raid by Canadian and British troops.

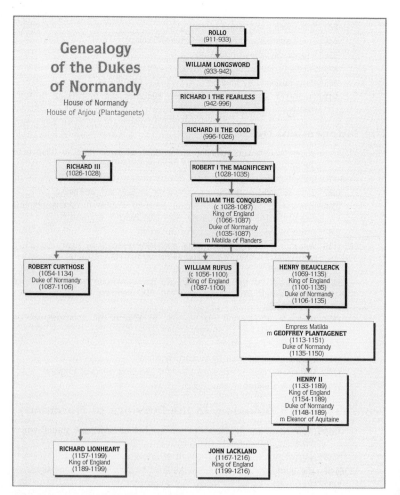

June 1944	Allied landing on the Calvados coast. Battle of Normandy.
1954	René Coty, born in Le Havre, is elected President of the Republic.
1959	Inauguration of the Tancarville Bridge.
1967	Commissioning of the Atomic Centre at La Hague.
1971	Launch of the *Redoutable*, the first French nuclear submarine, at Cherbourg.
1974	Creation of the Brotonne Regional Nature Park.
1975	Creation of the Normandie-Maine Regional Nature Park.
1977	Completion of the Normandy motorway (A 3).
1983-84	Start-up of Paluel Nuclear Power Station. Start-up of Flamanville Nuclear Power Station.
1987	Commemoration of the 900th anniversary of William the Conqueror's death.
1991	Inauguration of France's 27th regional nature park in the Cotentin and Bessin area.
6 June 1994	50th Anniversary of the Battle of Normandy.
January 1995	Inauguration of the Pont de Normandie.
1997	A violent controversy breaks out between Greenpeace environmentalists and COGEMA over nuclear waste dumped near La Hague.
1999	Tall Ships Armada of the Century on the Seine, from Rouen to Le Havre.
1999	Violent windstorms in December uproot innumerable trees and damage buildings.

NORMANS THROUGHOUT HISTORY

The story of the Norsemen, or Vikings, who settled in the Frankish kingdom and from there set out on expeditions of conquest to southern Italy and Sicily and to England, Wales, Scotland and Ireland is a fascinating one, which has inspired many tall tales and cinematic extravaganzas. Their influence on Medieval Europe was so significant that it has lingered throughout the centuries.

In the 8C, pagan barbarian parties from Denmark, Norway and Iceland began their plunder of coastal settlements in Europe and by the 9C they had established a permanent foothold in the region that is now Normandy. In the year 911, **Charles III (The Simple)** signed the treaty of **St-Clair-sur-Epte** with the Viking chief **Rollo**. According to Dudon de St-Quentin, the first historian of Normandy, the Viking placed his hands between those of the French king to ratify the agreement creating the dukedom of Normandy. This "businessman's handshake" was worth a solemn exchange of seals and signatures for no written treaty was ever drafted. The Norsemen continued to expand their holdings until well into the 11C, and region was ruled by a succession of ruthless, self-appointed dukes and counts who sought to establish their authority over the indigenous Franks.

Eventually, these wild folk from the north converted to Christianity and adopted the French language, but certain traits – call it piracy or call it bravery – continued to mark the character of this roving clan. The Normans had a reputation for recklessness, love of combat, craftiness and cunning, and outrageous treachery. At the same time, wherever they went, they showed a remarkable capacity for adapting to the local customs and environment. The most ambitious of their expansionary campaigns was led by William, duke of Normandy, who became king of England in a coup known as the **Norman Conquest** (1066). At the same time, the Norman kingdom of Sicily was founded by the descendants of Tancrède de Hauteville. Many of the early Norman rulers who came to power through these campaigns were among the most powerful and successful of their time, and even established enduring political institutions.

In Normandy, the Normans quickly adopted the precepts of feudalism, and became masters of cavalry warfare and fostered the cult of knighthood, although they were imitators rather than innovators in these fields. Eventually, their reputation for fierceness and brutality was softened by championship of religious causes, marked by pilgrimages to Rome and the Holy Land. In England, they not only brought their own interpretations of strong government to bear, but also integrated many existing customs and institutions, increasing efficiency, making the kingdom safer from foreign invasion and bringing discipline to church organisations.

Later still, explorers continued to embark from Normandy in search of new lands:

1402	Jean de Béthencourt, of the Caux region, in search of adventure, became King of the Canary Islands, but later ceded the islands to the King of Castile.
1503	Paulmier de Gonneville, gentleman of Honfleur, reached Brazil in the *Espoir*.
1506	Jean Denis, a sailor from Honfleur, explored the mouth of the St Lawrence, preparing the way for Jacques Cartier.

1524	Leaving Dieppe, in the caravel *La Dauphine*, the French Florentine Verrazano, Navigator to François I, reconnoitred New France and discovered the site of New York city, which he named Land of Angoulême.
1555	Admiral of Villegaignon set up a colony of Huguenots from Le Havre on an island in the bay of Rio de Janeiro but they were driven away by the Portuguese.
1563	Led by René de la Laudonnière, colonies of Protestants from Le Havre and Dieppe settled in Florida and founded Fort Caroline but were massacred by the Spaniards.
1608	Samuel de Champlain, Dieppe shipbuilder, left Honfleur to found Quebec.
1635	Pierre Belain of Esnambuc took possession of Martinique in the name of the King of France; the colonisation of Guadeloupe followed soon after.
1682	Cavelier de La Salle of Rouen, after reconnoitring the site of Chicago, sailed down the Mississippi river and took possession of Louisiana.

William the Conqueror

The story of William is the stuff of legend, with roots in Viking mythology and its crowning glory the very crown of England.

Born from a union *more danico*, or "in the Danish way", William was the son of Robert the Magnificent and his concubine Herleva, from the town of Falaise. A descendent of the great chief Rollo, he was first known as "William the Bastard". In 1035, when his father died on his way back from a trip to the Holy Land, William, then eight years old, became the seventh duke of Normandy. His tutors instructed him in the rudiments of Latin, the fine points of military strategy, and also instilled a deep religious faith in the young boy. Later, three of his guardians and his tutor were assassinated by parties who objected to the "Bastard's" succession. He survived the years of intrigue and treachery and forged a strong character. In 1046, barely 20 years old, he confounded yet another plot to undo him, and wisely sought out the support of the king of France, Henri I.

For the love of Matilda – With the king's soldiers at hand to support his own faithful warriors, William defended his territory and firmly established his authority. He built castles (Falaise – his birthplace – and Cherbourg), towns (Saint-James), expanded Saint-Lô and Carentan, created the city of Caen as a second capital for his dukedom, and executed a peace treaty with his enemies.

Between 1054 and 1060, William held fast against the allied forces of the king of France, Guillaume d'Arques and the Geoffrey Martell of Anjou. He consolidated his power by marrying Matilda, daughter of Baldwin V, count of Flanders. Mindful of all he had suffered as an illegitimate son, William was a faithful and trusting husband. When called away from Normandy, he left the realm in his wife's able hands. A tradition assigned the Bayeux tapestry to Matilda (it is also referred to as Queen Matilda's tapestry), but it is not likely that she busied herself with embroidery when William was abroad.

The conquest – William was the ruler of a well-run, peaceful territory when his cousin, Edward the Confessor, king of England, recognised him as his heir. When news of **Harold**'s accession to the English throne reached him, in January 1066 the duke of Normandy appealed to the Pope and Harold was subsequently excommunicated.

In less than seven months, William, henceforth "the Conqueror", realised all his political and military plans. On 12 September 1066, protected by the Pope's ensign, about 12 000 knights and soldiers embarked upon 696 ships followed by smaller boats and skiffs bringing the total number of vessels to 3 000. On 28 September, at low tide, the Normans landed at Pevensey, Sussex. William was last to disembark and he stumbled and fell full length. The superstitious Normans were alarmed, but William laughed and, according to the records, retorted: "My Lords, by the glory of God have I seized this land with my own two hands. As long as it exists it is ours alone".

The Normans occupied Hastings. Harold, who had been busy fighting other attackers, rushed to the scene and pitched camp on a hill. On 14 October William launched an assault, and after a terrible struggle the Normans were victorious; Harold died in combat. The history of the invasion is recounted in the Bayeux Tapestry, which shows fascinating details of combat dress and equipment and the gory consequences of the momentous Battle of Hastings.

With Norman assent, William was crowned on Christmas Day, 1066 at Westminster Abbey. For the first time in history, and for the century that followed, England was united with continental Europe. Suppressing revolts, bringing a new order to the corrupt aristocracy, encouraging noble Norman families to settle in England, the duke of Normandy and king of England also overcame the opposition of the Pope to keep control over church affairs, and transformed English society. William encouraged the spreading influence of Norman art, as the cathedrals at Canterbury, Winchester and Durham show.

Ruling 52 years in Normandy and 21 years in England, William the Conqueror maintained a large measure of peace and justice in his realm. He died on 9 September 1087 near Rouen. He was buried at St-Étienne church in Caen, as he had requested.

THE BATTLE OF NORMANDY

The Vikings landed on the beaches of Normandy in the 9C. William set out from Dives to conquer England. On 6 June, 1944, the coast of Normandy was the setting for yet another crucial invasion which would, in its own turn, change the course of history.

From the autumn of 1941 the British authorities had envisaged a landing on the continent of Europe but it was only after the entry of the United States that offensive action on such a scale could be seriously considered. The COSSAC plan, approved at the Churchill-Roosevelt meetings in Washington and Quebec in May and August 1943, foresaw the landing of invasion troops along the Calvados coast, which was defended by the German 7th Army. This sector was preferred to the Pas-de-Calais because it meant that the defenders had to make use of much more vulnerable lines of communication. Lower Normandy would be isolated if the bridges over the Seine and Loire were destroyed. It was known that the enemy was preoccupied by the defence of the Pas-de-Calais (15th German Army).

Preparation – The building of artificial ports – a lesson learnt as a result of the costly Dieppe commando raid of 1942 – and the construction of landing craft was carried out with other training in the winter of 1943-44. On 24 December 1943 General Eisenhower was named Chief of the Allied Expeditionary Force and General Montgomery made responsible for tactical coordination of all land forces (21st Army Group) for Operation Overlord.

Air raids to paralyse the French railway system began on 6 March 1944 and added to the destruction caused by the French resistance. During the spring of 1944 Marshal Rommel had the beaches and their approaches covered with obstacles. It became urgent to find a means of destroying these obstacles by using tanks as bulldozers or sending frogmen to dispose of them.

① – **The First Week of the Landing** – Originally D-Day had been planned for the 5 June but it was postponed for 24hr owing to bad weather.

At dawn on D-Day, 6 June 1944, British and Commonwealth ground forces established beachheads at **Sword**, **Juno** and **Gold** and rapidly linked up with the airborne troops dropped to their east. The Americans, landing on **Omaha** beach, joined up with their airborne flank only after the capture of Carentan on 12 June.

Layout of the Bridgehead – Advances were substantial but of unequal depth: the Americans threatened Caumont on 13 June; the British and Canadians were held up by very fierce fighting 6km/4mi north of Caen in the Tilly-sur-Seulles sector on 7 June and broke through only on the 20th – the village changed hands some 20 times. The Caen sector, as Montgomery had foreseen, became the principal hinge of the whole front.

② – **The Isolation of the Cotentin Peninsula and the Capture of Cherbourg** – The Americans launched their attack across the Cotentin Peninsula on 13 June and secured it, with the capture of Barneville, on 18 June. Turning north they attacked Cherbourg which fell on 26 June – a victory in the battle to ensure supply lines.

Commanders during the Battle of Normandy

General Dwight Eisenhower (1890-1969) was the Supreme Allied Commander for Overlord. He was present when the German capitulation was signed in Berlin on 8 May 1945. Eisenhower was then to become US president from 1953 to 1961.

General George Patton (1885-1945) commanded the 3rd American Army. After the Avranches breakthrough his units swept across Brittany, the Paris basin, participated in the defence of Bastogne in the Battle of the Bulge then went as far as Bohemia.

General Omar Bradley (1893-1981) commanded the American assault forces during the landing operation. He then led his troops from Brittany across Europe in the Advance to the Elbe.

General Bernard Montgomery (1887-1976) commanded the land forces for the Allied landing operation. Montgomery then led the northern wing of 21 Army Group through the Netherlands and Denmark in the Drive to the Baltic.

General Philippe de Hauteclocque (1902-47) known as **Leclerc**, commanded the 2nd Armoured Division of Free French Forces. He landed at Utah Beach on 1 August and took the 2nd Armoured Division from Cotentin to Colmar, liberating Paris on the way.

Field Marshal Erwin Rommel (1891-1944) was overall commander of German forces along the North Sea and Atlantic coasts and chief of the armies of the B group. Wounded on 17 June, suspected of having taken part in a plot against Hitler, he committed suicide on 14 October 1944.

③ – **The Battle of the Odon and Capture of Caen** – On 26 June a hard battle, which was to last a month, began for a crossing over the Odon upstream from Caen and the taking of Hill 112. Montgomery decided to outflank Caen to the southwest. The city of Caen on the left bank was attacked in force from the west and northeast and fell on 9 July.

Breakthrough Preparation – "Keep the greatest possible number of the enemy divisions on our eastern flank, between Caen and Villers-Bocage, and pivot the western flank of the Army Group towards the southeast in a vast sweeping movement in order to threaten the line of retreat of the German division." – ran a Montgomery directive of early July.

War of the Hedgerows – For the American soldiers of 1944 the Cotentin campaign – the advance to Cherbourg and the Battle of St-Lô – is summed up in the description "the war of the hedgerows".

Leafy hedges and sunken lanes such as those that divide the Normandy countryside are unknown in America and came as an unpleasant surprise for the troops but as a place for defensive warfare or guerilla tactics the terrain was ideal, offering unending opportunities.

Modern arms were not much help: 4-inch shells scarcely shook the tree-covered embankments which constituted natural anti-tank barriers; armoured vehicles moved with difficulty along the roads; only the foot soldier could fight successfully in this "hell of hedges".

The effort of fighting against an invisible enemy was exhausting; every field and orchard crossed was a victory in itself; progress was slow and was often estimated by the number of hedges passed. The terrain had to be declared clear before the tanks moved into action. So that the tanks could operate with a maximum of efficiency an American sergeant devised a system whereby a sharp steel device, not unlike a ploughshare, was attached to the front of each tank.

④ – **The Battle for St-Lô** – On 3 July the American 8th Corps launched its offensive, in the face of fierce German resistance, towards the road centre of St-Lô, thus assuring more favourable positions for the large-scale operations to come. Fighting was fierce

Eisenhower Patton Bradley

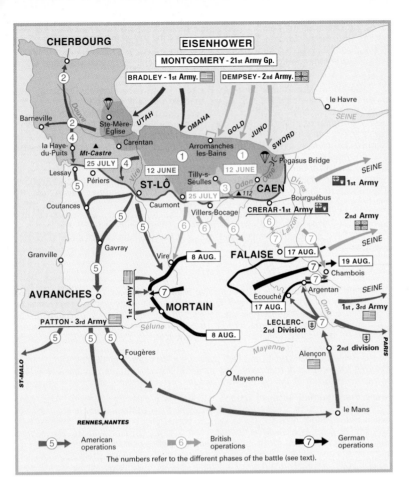

for La Haye-du-Puits and Mount Castre and in this area the troops had to adapt to hedgerow warfare. St-Lô fell on 19 July and the Americans entrenched their position behind the Lessay-Périers-St-Lô stretch of road. Progress at this time was slow in the Caen sector. A breakthrough was attempted towards the southwest of the town but was halted in the Bourguébus sector on 19 July. For one interminable week, from 19 to 25 July, bad weather suspended operations on all fronts.

⑤ – **The Breakthrough (Operation Cobra)** – At midday on 25 July, following intense aerial bombardment, the 7th corps attacked west of St-Lô, the 8th between Périers and Lessay. By the 28th, Allied armour was driving down the main roads, carrying out vast encircling movements. Coutances fell on 28 July, Granville and Avranches on 31 July. On 1 August General Patton, taking command of the 3rd Army, hurled it into the lightning war. The 8th Corps burst west into Brittany (Rennes fell on 4 August and Nantes on 12 August), while the 15th Corps and the French 2nd Armoured Division under General Leclerc moved east towards Laval and Le Mans (9 August).

Montgomery   Leclerc   Rommel

⑥ – **The Thrust south of Caen** – Backing up these operations, Montgomery, with the 1st Canadian Army (General Crerar) was brought up to the Caen-Falaise road at the eastern end of the front and the British divisions, pushing southeast from Caumont and Villers-Bocage (5 August), overwhelmed the last defences on the west bank of the Orne.

⑦ – **Battle of the Falaise-Mortain Pocket** – When the German 7th Army was threatened by the American 15th Corps to their rear and the British to the north, Hitler himself organised a counter offensive to cut off the 3rd Army from its supply bases by taking control of the Avranches bottle-neck. The German 7th Army began its westerly counter attack on 6-7 August in the Mortain region. The Allied air forces crushed the move at daybreak. After a week of bitter fighting the Germans retreated east (12 August).

During this time the French 2nd Division moved northwards from Le Mans, took Alençon on 12 August and on 13 August breached the Paris-Granville road at Écouché. The Canadians, halted between the 9 and 14 August at the River Laison, entered Falaise on 17 August thus forming the northern arm of the pincer movement, which when they met with the Americans at Chambois (19 August) was to corner the German 7th Army and force its surrender at Tournai-sur-Dive. By the night of 21 August the Battle of Normandy was over – it had cost the Germans 640 000 men, killed, wounded or taken prisoner.

RECONSTRUCTION

The Scale of Devastation – Normandy, like Britain and unlike many other French and European territories, is not on any European invasion route and so had remained unscathed since the Wars of Religion; towns had scarcely altered since the 16C. The German invasion of 1940 and the air raids and army operations of 1944 caused widespread devastation and nearly all the great towns suffered – Rouen, Le Havre, Caen, Lisieux.

Of the 3 400 Norman *communes*, new plans were elaborated for 586 of them to meet the requirements and constraints of modern life: growth of car ownership and increasing presence of the car in towns and improved standards of public housing.

Town Planning and Reconstruction – Modern town planning has altered what were narrow winding main streets into wide straight thoroughfares suitable for cars and other traffic. Public gardens, parks and car parks have been provided. Houses, flats and offices have been built and towns and villages have once more acquired an individual character; limestone is seen again in buildings on the Norman sedimentary plain and plateaux, sandstone, granite and brick in the woodland regions, combining with modern materials. Many historic monuments were damaged but most have been restored and are enhanced by improved setting.

Monasticism in Normandy

Normandy, like Champagne and Burgundy, was one of the main centres of monasticism during the religious revival that swept the 11C. Today a great many Norman abbeys still testify to the strong fervour that characterised the period. The greatest legislator of Latin monasticism was undoubtedly St Benedict of Nursia (c 480-547), who laid down a series of precepts for his monks at Monte Cassino in Italy. According to the famous "Benedictine Rule", which gradually spread to supplant other religious rules, nuns and monks were requested to make three vows on entering the monastery: obedience, poverty and chastity. They were placed under the absolute authority of the abbots, who were elected for life, and were expected to exercise fasting, silence and abstinence.

The monks' working day was taken up by divine office, holy reading and, to a greater extent, manual labour.

Divine office consisted of prayers and hymns scheduled throughout the day (matins, lauds and vespers) and night, during which the monks worshipped and praised the Lord.

Holy reading, which involved studying the Bible and other sacred texts, allowed monks to commune with God and meditate alone in their cell.

As for manual labour, it consisted of the daily chores and tasks that punctuated the life of the monastery: baking bread, weaving cloth for the monks' tunics, carrying firewood, sweeping floors, serving meals, preparing the sacristy, growing vegetables, helping in the fields etc.

It is interesting to note that throughout the Middle Ages monasticism played a vital role in society, securing the propagation of Christianity, promoting the authority of the Roman bishop and contributing to the conservation and transmission of learning. In its most prosperous years monasticism was also seen as a powerful economic and cultural force.

Layout of a Medieval Monastery

The monastic buildings were arranged around the cloisters as in the plan below.

Cloisters – Generally consisting of four galleries surrounding a central courtyard, often laid out as a garden; some monasteries made this their herb garden. The east gallery opened onto the sacristy, the chapter-house and the calefactory. The south gallery featured a lavabo, a large stone basin with water flowing from a fountain where the monks washed their hands before eating or praying. The west gallery bordered the lay brothers' range or the cellars. The north gallery adjoined the church, providing access through the monks' doorway, at the east end, and the lay brothers' doorway, at the west end.

Abbey Church – The monks spent a large part of the day and sometimes the night in church for Mass and other religious offices. The abbey church was characterised by an extremely long nave. In Cistercian churches, a rood screen placed near the high altar separated the monks' choir from that of the lay brothers.

Sacristy – Room in which ecclesiastical garments and altar vessels were stored and in which the priest would don his robes before leading the service.

Chapter-house – Used for daily monastic activities, including prayers before the day's work and the reading of a chapter taken from the monastic rule. It was here that the abbot imposed penance on those who had transgressed the rule.

Calefactory – The only heated room in the monastery. It was accessible to all monks under carefully regulated conditions.

Scriptorium – Room set aside for the copying out of manuscripts, often adjoining the calefactory.

Refectory – A large bare room where the monks took their meals, endowed with surprisingly good acoustics. During meals, the reader would recite passages from the Bible in the elevated pulpit.

1 Monks' choir
2 Sacristy
3 Chapter house
4 Calefactory (warming room)
5 Scriptorium (writing room)
6 Lavabo
7 Monk's doorway
8 Lay-brother's doorway
9 Refectory
10 Reader's pulpit
11 Kitchen
12 Lay-brothers' range or cellars
13 Guesthouse or hostel
14 Monks' dormitory
15 Lay-brothers' dormitory

Dormitories – There were generally two – one for the monks above the chapter-house and one for the lay brothers above the cellars. In the Cistercian order 7hr were allowed for rest. The monks slept fully dressed in a communal dormitory.

Outbuildings – Other conventual buildings included the barns and the porter's lodge or gatehouse, often a grand building with a huge gateway to allow the passage of both carriages and people on foot. The porter's lodge had living quarters on the first floor, where alms were distributed and justice was dispensed to the population.

ABC of architecture

Religious Architecture

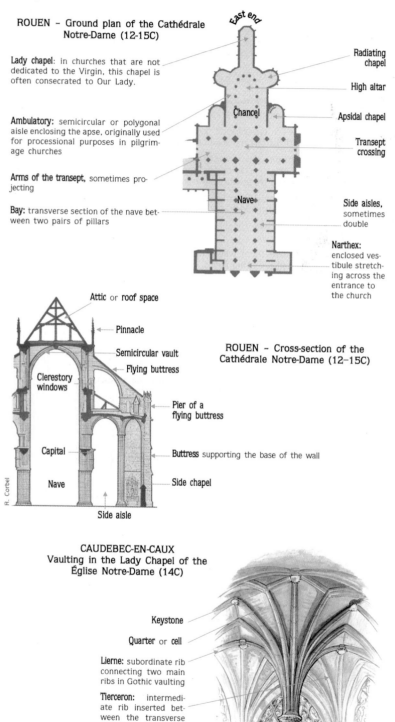

ROUEN – Ground plan of the Cathédrale Notre-Dame (12-15C)

East end

Lady chapel: in churches that are not dedicated to the Virgin, this chapel is often consecrated to Our Lady.

Ambulatory: semicircular or polygonal aisle enclosing the apse, originally used for processional purposes in pilgrimage churches

Arms of the transept, sometimes projecting

Bay: transverse section of the nave between two pairs of pillars

Radiating chapel

High altar

Apsidal chapel

Transept crossing

Side aisles, sometimes double

Narthex: enclosed vestibule stretching across the entrance to the church

Chancel

Nave

ROUEN – Cross-section of the Cathédrale Notre-Dame (12–15C)

Attic or **roof space**

Pinnacle

Semicircular vault

Flying buttress

Clerestory windows

Pier of a flying buttress

Capital

Buttress supporting the base of the wall

Nave

Side chapel

Side aisle

R. Corbel

CAUDEBEC-EN-CAUX Vaulting in the Lady Chapel of the Église Notre-Dame (14C)

Keystone

Quarter or **cell**

Lierne: subordinate rib connecting two main ribs in Gothic vaulting

Tierceron: intermediate rib inserted between the transverse and diagonal ribs

Pendant: characteristic of Late Gothic

CAUDEBEC-EN-CAUX - Église Notre-Dame (14C)

Tiered octogonal spire ornamented with 3 *fleurs-de-lis* crowns known as the "*Caudebec tiara*"

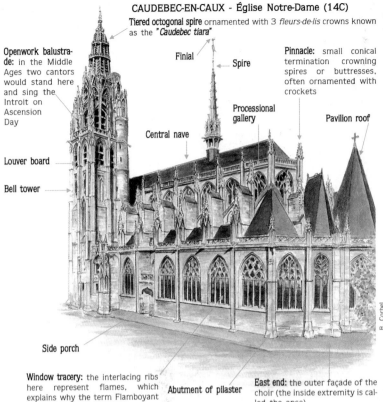

Openwork balustrade: in the Middle Ages two cantors would stand here and sing the Introit on Ascension Day

Finial

Spire

Pinnacle: small conical termination crowning spires or buttresses, often ornamented with crockets

Processional gallery

Central nave

Pavilion roof

Louver board

Bell tower

Side porch

Window tracery: the interlacing ribs here represent flames, which explains why the term Flamboyant was applied to Late Gothic architecture in France

Abutment of pilaster

East end: the outer façade of the choir (the inside extremity is called the apse)

R. Corbel

ROUEN - Portail des Librairies, Cathédrale Notre-Dame (1482)

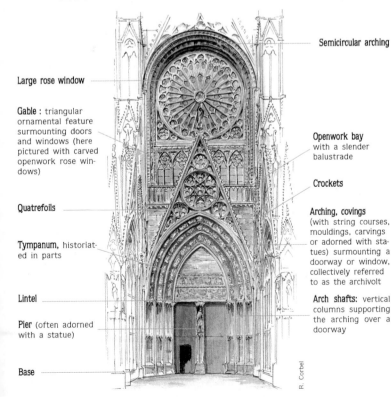

Semicircular arching

Large rose window

Gable : triangular ornamental feature surmounting doors and windows (here pictured with carved openwork rose windows)

Openwork bay with a slender balustrade

Crockets

Quatrefoils

Arching, covings (with string courses, mouldings, carvings or adorned with statues) surmounting a doorway or window, collectively referred to as the archivolt

Tympanum, historiated in parts

Arch shafts: vertical columns supporting the arching over a doorway

Lintel

Pier (often adorned with a statue)

Base

R. Corbel

ROUEN – Chancel and Transept Crossing in the Abbatiale St-Ouen (14C)

Main arcade

Clerestory windows

Arcature with mouldings

Tracery: ornamental stone ribwork in the upper part of a window

Sculpted spandrel: triangular area comprised between an arch and its framing

Equilateral arch

Mullion: vertical shaft dividing a window into two or several lights

Triforium

Diagonal rib

Compound pier

R. Corbel

CAUDEBEC-EN-CAUX – Grand Organ in the Église Notre-Dame (1541-1542)

Towers: they can be polygonal or circular

Great organ case containing the pipes

Façade: large pipes forming the organ front

Stop: a set of pipes

Flat: vertical row of pipes

Choir organ: small organ with one keyboard located behind the organist

Foundation supporting the weight of the pipes

Organ loft

Small organ case containing the choir organ (the organ case here is waisted with the upper part protruding)

R. Corbel

ÉVREUX - Stained glass (early 14C) in the Cathédrale Notre-Dame

The main function of stained glass is to provide a translucent framing for church windows and to regulate the intensity of the light inside the building. "The stained-glass windows in the chancel of Évreux Cathedral are the finest examples of 14C work. They are pure in the extreme, artfully combining light yellows and limpid blues with transparent reds and silvery whites... They are in perfect harmony with the radiant chancel, suffused with dazzling daylight", remarked Emile Mâle

Glass edging surrounding the finished panes

French T-bar armature: iron band used between panels to fix them onto the saddle-bar

Ferramenta: iron framework that provides a fixing for the panels within the window

Internal lead: strip of lead used to fit together the pieces of glass in the panel

Silver stain: pigment made of silver nitrate mixed with ochre that produces a lovely yellow after firing in the kiln

Grisaille: pigment made with iron oxide producing a variety of greys and blacks after firing in the kiln

Saddle-bars: iron shafts embedded in the masonry of windows to support the panels

R. Corbel

ÉCOUIS - Stalls in the chancel of the Collégiale Notre-Dame (14C)

High back

Elbow rest

Cheek: narrow upright face forming the end of a row of stalls

Separation between two stalls

Misericord: ledge projecting from the underside of a hinged seat which, when the seat is raised, provides support to worshippers or choir singers out of mercy (*per misericordiam*). 15C and 16C stalls were often sculpted with amusing grotesques or bizarre creatures called **"drolleries"**

R. Corbel

Rural Architecture

Thatched Cottage at LYONS-LA-FORÊT

Chimney: its weight is essential for the foundations and overall stability of the house

Chimney stack: piece of masonry enclosing the flue

Roofing: first the roof is covered with straw or reed thatching. Then a firmly-packed layer of clay is placed along the rooftop and planted with iris bulbs whose roots maintain the thatching in place, cultivating a certain dampness

Thatching: formely made with straw, it now tends to be made with reed

Angle post

Lintel

R. Corbel

Small post   **Dwarf stud**

Stone foundations

Cob: building material consisting of sand, clay and chopped straw, sometimes mixed with horsehair and cows' hair.

Foundation sill: long horizontal timber placed nearest the ground and used to distribute concentrated loads

Military Architecture

Château d'HARCOURT (13C)

Although it has suffered from the ravages of time and history, the **Château d'Harcourt** remains a perfect example of medieval defensive architecture.

Battered wall: a wall or rampart is said to be battered when it recedes as it rises, forming a slant

Inner bailey: unlike the outer bailey, this was contained within the lord's residence.

Counterscarp: outer side of a ditch

Pepperpot turret

Inner moat

Escarp: inner side of a ditch

Gatehouse with its **twin towers**

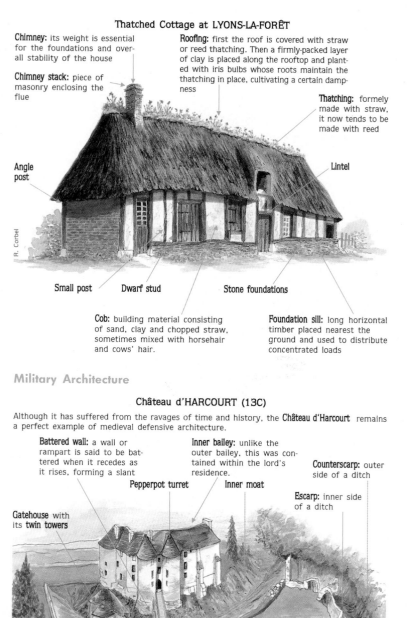

R. Corbel

Bridge

Outer moat

Garrison quaters

Arrow slit: loophole through which archers shot their arrows, converted here to receive artillery cannons in the 14C

Flanking Towers: they facilitated the firing of weapons along the outer face of the walls

Curtain wall: enclosing rampart connecting two bastions or towers

Outer bailey: courtyard lying outside the castle perimeter but protected by its ramparts; it was used to accommodate the quartermasters' lodgings and to receive the population in the event of a siege

DEAUVILLE - Villa Strassburger (early 20C)

This villa is a pastiche of the half-timbered mansions typical of the area. Its genuine Norman characteristics are combined with those from Alsace and some other French regions, complemented by a few eccentric touches prompted by the imagination of architect G. Pichereau: asymmetrical rooftops, profusion of skylights and dormer windows, projecting eaves.

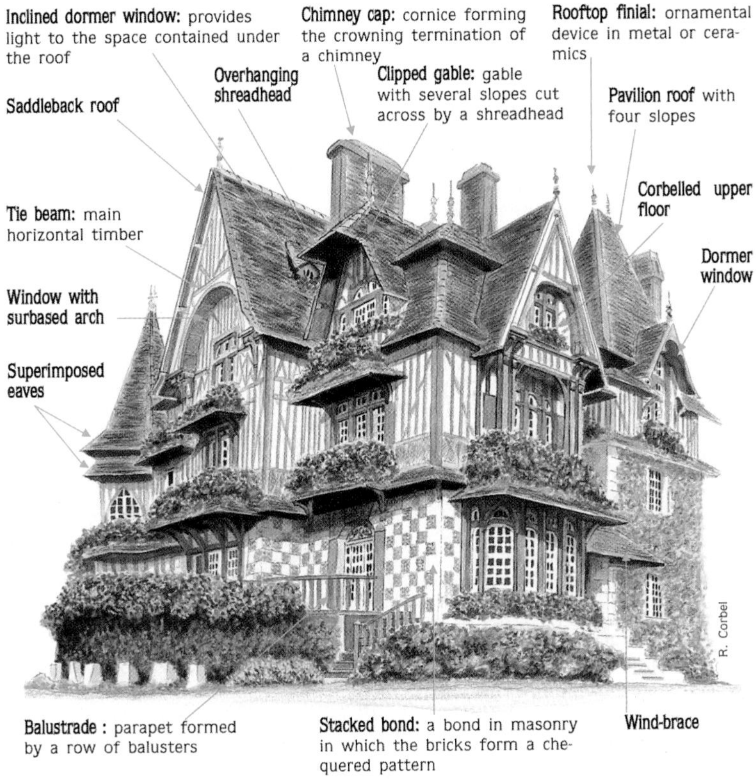

Inclined dormer window: provides light to the space contained under the roof

Chimney cap: cornice forming the crowning termination of a chimney

Rooftop finial: ornamental device in metal or ceramics

Overhanging shreadhead

Saddleback roof

Clipped gable: gable with several slopes cut across by a shreadhead

Pavilion roof with four slopes

Tie beam: main horizontal timber

Corbelled upper floor

Dormer window

Window with surbased arch

Superimposed eaves

Balustrade : parapet formed by a row of balusters

Stacked bond: a bond in masonry in which the bricks form a chequered pattern

Wind-brace

R. Corbel

The Pont de NORMANDIE (1988-1994)

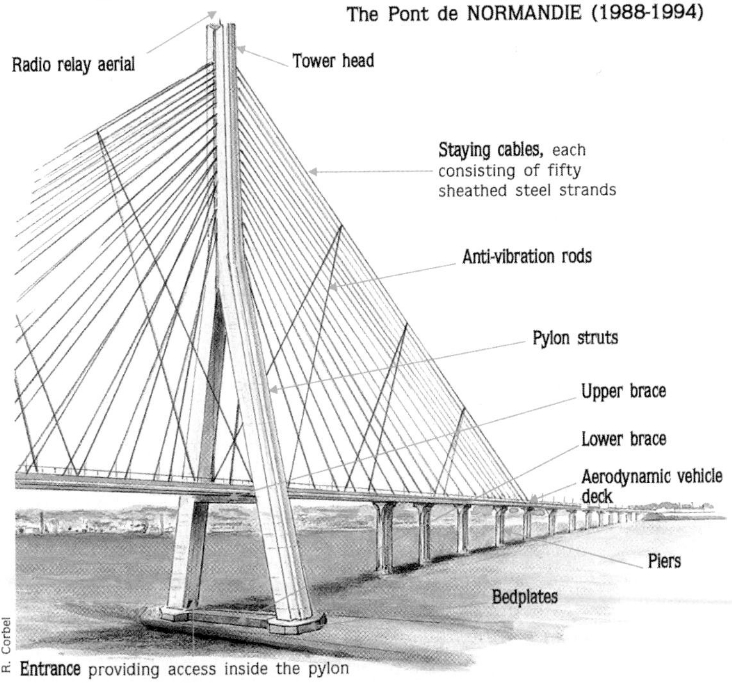

Radio relay aerial

Tower head

Staying cables, each consisting of fifty sheathed steel strands

Anti-vibration rods

Pylon struts

Upper brace

Lower brace

Aerodynamic vehicle deck

Piers

Bedplates

R. Corbel

Entrance providing access inside the pylon

Architecture and art in Normandy

Norman building materials – Rouen and the towns of the Seine are built with chalky limestone from the valley sides. A similar affinity exists between the local materials and the buildings in the Caux region, where pebbles are set in flowing mortar. Clay, in cheap and plentiful local supply, was used for the cob of the timber-framed thatched cottages and for making bricks, which were often ingeniously set to make decorative patterns.

Romanesque Art (11C-early 12C)

The Benedictines and Romanesque design – In the 11C, immediately after the period of the invasion, the Benedictines returned to their task of clearing the land and constructing churches and other monastic buildings. These architect monks retained the robust building methods employed by the Carolingians and then they embellished their constructions with the Oriental dome or the barrel vault used by the Romans for bridges and commemorative arches. This new architectural style, created by the Benedictines, was named "Romanesque" by Arcisse de Caumont, an archeologist from Normandy, who in 1840 outlined the theory of regional schools of architecture. Despite its apparent simplicity Romanesque architecture is wonderfully diverse. In England the style is known as "Norman".

Norman School and its abbey churches – The Benedictines, supported by the dukes of Normandy, played an immensely important part in the whole life of the province; only their work as architects and creators of the Norman School is described below.

The first religious buildings of importance in Normandy were the churches of the rich abbeys. Early monastic buildings may have disappeared or been altered, particularly after the Reform of St Maur, but examples of "Benedictine flowering" have survived – the ruins of Jumièges Abbey and the churches on Mont-St-Michel, in Cerisy-la-Forêt, St-Martin-de-Boscherville as well as Église St-Étienne and Église de la Trinité in Caen.

The Norman School is characterised by pure lines, bold proportions, sober decoration and beautiful ashlared stonework. The style spread to England after the Norman conquest. Durham Cathedral provides the first official example of quadripartite vaulting, erected at the beginning of the 12C. The Norman style is to be seen in Westminster Abbey, which was rebuilt by Edward the Confessor, in the two west towers and the square crossing tower of Canterbury Cathedral and in the cathedrals of Southwell, Winchester and Ely.

Norman architecture also appeared in Sicily in the 11C in the wake of noble Norman adventurers; in France it paved the way for the Gothic style.

The abbey churches are characterised by two towers on either side of the west front, giving the west face an H-like appearance, and a square lantern tower above the transept crossing which also served to increase the light inside.

The towers, bare or decorated only with blind arcades below, get lighter with multiple pierced bays the higher they rise (in the 13C many were crowned by spires quartered by pinnacles). Charming country churches are often surmounted by Romanesque belfries, which are crowned with a saddleback roof or a four-sided squat wood or stone pyramid, the forerunner of the Gothic spire.

The interior light and size of Norman abbeys is very striking. The naves are wide with an elevation consisting of two series of openings above great semicircular arches – an amazingly bold concept for a Romanesque construction. The Norman monks eschewed the heavy barrel vault in favour of a beamed roof spanning the nave and galleries, reserving groined stone vaulting (the crossing of two semicircular arches) for the aisles. The vast galleries on the first level open onto the wide bays of the nave and repeat the design of the aisles. At clerestory level a gallery or passage in the thickness of the wall circles the church. A dome over the transept crossing supports a magnificent lantern tower which lets in the daylight through tall windows.

Norman decoration – The abbey churches, like all others of Romanesque design, were illuminated on a considerable scale with gilding and bright colours as were the manuscripts of the time. The main themes were those of Byzantine iconography.

Norman sculptural decoration is essentially geometric: different motifs stand out, of which the most common is the key or fret pattern (straight lines meeting at right angles to form crenellated or rectangular designs). The decorative motifs are sometimes accompanied by mouldings, human heads or animal masks emphasising recessed arches, archivolts, cornices and mouldings. Sometimes the monks executed in low-relief motifs copied from cloth, ivories or metalwork brought back from the Orient; this is the origin of the cornerstones in the great arcade in Bayeux.

Capitals are rare and, where they exist, they are carved with gadroons or stylised foliage.

Gothic Art (12C-15C)

The style, conceived in Île-de-France, apart from quadripartite or rib vaulting which originated in Norman England, was known as "French work" or "French style" until the 16C when the Italians of the Renaissance, who were resistant to the Parisian trend, scornfully dubbed it "Gothic". The name survived. The French copied the H-shaped façades and great galleries of the Norman abbeys (the west front of Notre-Dame in Paris is based on that of the Église de la Trinité in Caen and its galleries on those of the Église St-Étienne).

The Cathedrals – Gothic is an ideal artistic style for cathedrals, as it symbolises the religious fervour of the people and the growing prosperity of the towns. In an all-embracing enthusiasm, a whole city would participate in the construction of the house of God. Under the enlightened guidance of bishops and master builders, all the guilds contributed to the cathedral's embellishment: stained-glass makers, painters, wood and stone carvers went to work. The doors became the illustrated pages of history.

Gothic Architecture in Normandy – Gradually the national Gothic style percolated into Normandy before the province was seized by Philippe Auguste in 1204.

In the 13C the Gothic and traditional Norman styles merged. The best example of this fusion is Coutances Cathedral, where the pure proportions and the lofty austerity of the Norman style combine with Gothic sophistication as in the lantern tower.

This was also the period of the superb belfries of the Caen and Bessin plains, typified by their tall stone spires, often pierced

Lantern tower, Cathédrale de Coutances

J.P. Clapham/MICHELIN

to offer less resistance to the wind, and quartered with pinnacles.

The magnificent Merveille buildings of Mont-St-Michel give an idea of total Norman Gothic ornamentation. Sobriety provides the foundation over which foliated sculpture reigns supreme: plants of every variety decorate the round capitals, cover the cornerstones, garland the friezes. The three and four leafed clover in relief or hollowed out is a frequent motif but statuary is rare. Lisieux Cathedral and the Tour St-Romain of Rouen Cathedral show the degree of French Gothic influence in Normandy by the end of the 12C.

The Flamboyant Style – By the 14C, the period of great cathedral building had come to an end. The Hundred Years War killed architectural inspiration: bits were added, buildings were touched up, but little created. When the war was over a taste for virtuosity alone remained – and the Flamboyant style was born. Rouen is the true capital of the Flamboyant, which was particularly widespread in Haute-Normandie.

In this new style, the tracery of bays and rose windows resembles wavering flames – the derivation of the term "Flamboyant". The Flamboyant style produced such single masterpieces as the Église St-Maclou in Rouen, the Tour de Beurre of Rouen Cathedral, the belfries of Notre-Dame in Caudebec and La Madeleine in Verneuil-sur-Avre. Civil architecture developed in importance and passed from Flamboyant to Renaissance – a change symbolised in the gables, pinnacles and balustrades of the Palais de Justice in Rouen.

Feudal Architecture – In medieval Normandy permission to build a castle was granted to the barons by the ruling duke, who, prudent as well as powerful, reserved the right to billet his own garrison inside and forbade all private wars. Over the years the building of castles along the duchy's frontiers was encouraged – Richard Lionheart secured the Seine with the most formidable fortress of the period, Château-Gaillard.

Originally only the austere keeps were inhabited, but from the 14C a courtyard and more pleasing quarters were constructed within the fortifications. This evolution can be seen in the castles at Alençon, and Dieppe and some of the Perche manor houses.

A taste for comfort and adornment appeared in civil architecture: wealthy merchants and burgesses built tall houses where wide eaves protected half-timbered upper storeys which overhung stone walled ground floors. The results were as capricious as they were picturesque: corner posts, corbels and beams were decorated with lively and fantastic carvings.

The Renaissance (16C)

Georges I d'Amboise, Archbishop of Rouen and patron of the arts, introduced Italian taste and usage to Normandy. The new motifs – arabesques, foliated scrollwork, medallions, shells, urns etc – were combined with Flamboyant art. Among the outstanding works of this period is the chevet of the Église St-Pierre in Caen, a masterpiece of exuberance.

Château d'O

Castles, Manor Houses and Old Mansions – The Renaissance style reached its fullest grace in domestic architecture. At first older buildings were ornamented in the current taste or a new and delicately decorated wing was added (Château d'O and the château at Fontaine-Henry); fortifications were replaced by parks and gardens.

The Classicism rediscovered by humanists took hold so that architects aimed for correct proportion and the imposition of the three Classical Orders of Antiquity.

Imperceptibly the search for symmetry and correctness produced aridity; fantasy was stifled by pomposity.

In Normandy, the Gothic spirit survived, appearing most successfully in small manor houses and innumerable country houses with sham feudal moats, turrets and battlements incorporated in either half-timbering or stone and brick.

Norman towns contain many large stone Renaissance mansions. The outer façade is always plain and one must enter the courtyard to see the architectural design and the rich decoration (Hôtel d'Escoville, Caen; Hôtel de Bourgtheroulde, Rouen).

In the 16C decoration became richer and less impulsive but the half-timbered construction technique remained the same. Many of these old houses have been carefully restored and there are good examples in Alençon, Bayeux, Bernay, Caen, Domfront, Honfleur, Pont-Audemer, Verneuil-sur-Avre and Rouen.

Classical Art (17C-18C)

In this period, French architectural style, now a single concept and no longer an amalgam of individual techniques, imposed its rationalism on many countries beyond its borders.

Louis XIII and the so-called Jesuit Style – The reign of Henri IV marked an artistic rebirth. An economical method of construction was adopted in which bricks played an important part: it was a time of beautiful châteaux with plain rose and white façades and steep grey-blue slate roofs.

The first decades of the 17C coincided with the Counter-Reformation. The Jesuits built many colleges and chapels – cold and formal edifices, their façades characterised by superimposed columns, a pediment and upturned consoles or small pavilions joining the front of the main building to the sides.

The "Grand Siècle" in Normandy – The symmetrical façades of the Classical style demanded space for their appreciation as in the châteaux at Cany, Beaumesnil, Balleroy and elsewhere. The Benedictine abbeys, which had adopted the **Maurist Reform** (the Benedictine Congregation of St Maur was founded in 1621), rediscovered their former inspiration. At the beginning of the 18C, the monastery buildings of the Abbaye-aux-Hommes in Caen and at Le Bec-Hellouin were remodelled by a brother architect and sculptor, **Guillaume de la Tremblaye**. The original plan was conserved but the design and decoration were given an austere nobility.

The urban scene was transformed by the construction of magnificent episcopal palaces, town halls with wide façades and large private houses.

Contemporary styles (19C-20C)

Following the extensive destruction caused by the Second World War many towns and villages in Normandy were rebuilt in the mid 20C in accordance with the precepts of modern town planning. A good example of successful reconstruction is Aunay-sur-Odon, with its large and imposing church.

Auguste Perret (1874-1954), the architect who pioneered the use of reinforced concrete construction, was appointed Chief Architect for the reconstruction of Le Havre; his works include the modern district of Le Havre and the Église St-Joseph. His work makes use of textured concrete and is designed to take the best advantage of natural light.

Normandy is a region of innovation as well: in Le Havre, note the **Espace Oscar-Niemeyer**, named after the Brazilian architect as an example. Two surprising white structures evoke a volcano, and stand out in contrast to the buildings designed by Perret. The Musée des Beaux-Arts André-Malraux, also in Le Havre, ressembles a glass ship at anchor. In Rouen, the renovation of the place du Vieux-Marché in the 1970s included the construction of the Église Ste-Jeanne-d'Arc, based on a design by Louis Arretche. The roof of the church is in the shape of a boat hull (upside down).

Three of Normandy's bridges are also noteworthy examples of modern architecture: the **Tancarville bridge** was inaugurated in 1959, the **Brotonne bridge** in 1977, and the colossal **Pont de Normandie**, spanning the Seine estuary, opened in 1995. The most recent bridge is not only a boon to travellers, it is also a work of art and a technological feat, a milestone of civil engineering. It is a cable-stayed bridge, more elegant and cheaper to build than a suspension bridge, made of steel and concrete, able to withstand winds of 440kph/274mph.

Popular architecture

Normandy is often associated with **half-timbered** houses. The basic box frame is essentially composed of horizontal and vertical beams, but there are very often different local methods of construction. Footings or a base of some solid material is laid to prevent damp from rising. A wooden sill or horizontal beam is laid along this base, and it ensures the correct spacing of the upright posts or studs. It is divided in as many sections as there are intervals between the vertical posts. The upper horizontal beam, sometimes known as a summer or bressumer, consists of a single beam. Along the gable ends it is known as a tie-beam. Bricks are often ingeniously used to make attractive patterns between the timbers.

Roofing materials, such as thatch, which is so vulnerable to fire, and shingles of sweet chestnut, are becoming increasingly rare. The schist slabs of the Cotentin are a typical part of the landscape. The slate which has been used since the 18C for houses and outbuildings alike has a silver tinge. A watertight roof depends on the correct hanging of the slates. The appearance of the villages is conditioned by the local materials used and the trades of the various villagers. One well-known building material, **Caen stone**, is quarried from the Jurassic deposits. It can be either friable or durable and varies in colour through grey and off-white to its more characteristic light creamy colour. The ashlar blocks are divided into two groups, one with the grain running vertically for façades, corner stones and gables and the second with a horizontal grain for courses and cornices.

Farms – In the open landscape of the **Caen plain** the typical courtyard farms are surrounded by high walls. A gateway gives access to the courtyard with the one or two storeyed farmhouse at the far end. The smaller crofts usually consist of two buildings, one long house for the living quarters and cowshed or barn and another for the stable or byre.

The farm buildings of the **Bessin** stand round a large courtyard which has two entrances, side by side, one for wheeled vehicles and a second for people. The house stands at the far end with the service and outbuildings to the right and left. There is usually a well in the middle. The house has a pristine appearance being built of limestone or Jurassic marls. The windows are tall and wide while the roofing can be made with tiles or slates.

The small flat-tiled houses in the **Argentan** area have symmetrical façades. The buildings are usually a harmonious mixture of schist, brick (chimneys and window surrounds) and limestone (the walls). Some are surrounded by walls or a screen of vegetation. Large barns are adjoined by sheds and lean-to buildings.

Brick and small laminated schist tiles predominate in the **Sées** countryside. Sometimes the buildings fit snugly one against the other, creating a jumble of roofs of varying pitch.

The farms in the region of **Alençon** are built around an open courtyard. The infinitely varied architecture reflects the wide range of rocks: granite, schist, flint, clay and kaolin.

The most common house type in the **Falaise** countryside is akin to those found in the Caen region. The walled courtyard predominates. The brick chimney replaces the rubblework one and tiles are used for roofs in the area bordering the Auge region.

The houses in the **Suisse Normande** are built of schist known as Pont-de-la-Mousse slate quarried near Thury-Harcourt and the settlements often have the rugged appearance of mountain villages. In the Orne Valley the houses huddle closely together on the floor while those on the slopes are scattered, even isolated.

The farm courtyard in the **Vire** *bocage* is often planted with apple and pear trees. On either side of the farmhouse are the barns, cattle sheds and outbuildings for the cider press. Brown or red schist is the main building stone.

Seaside architecture – In the 19C, the coast became a popular destination and bathing in the sea a novel pastime. Wealthy patrons ordered quirky houses for their holiday pleasures. Sometimes they were built around existing fishing villages, and in other places whole resort communities sprang up. Many of these villas are still standing along the coast at Cabourg, Houlgate, Villers, Deauville, Trouville, Villerville, Ste-Adresse, Étretat, Dieppe, Le Tréport, Mers-les-Bains etc. Generally, they are remarkable for their multi-coloured façades, busy with balconies, bow windows, railings, gables and other decorative elements. A profusion of skylights, projecting eaves and rooftop finials adds to the exuberance. Other models are more reserved and even stately, recalling the Renaissance style. Some are more modestly termed "chalets", and are said to be in the Swiss, Spanish or Persian style, depending on their features.

Norman Dovecots

The practice of keeping pigeons, formerly known as doves, dates back to the earliest civilizations. Although domestication is believed to have originated in 4500 BC, the practice became widespread some 2 000 years later, in ancient Egypt, where pigeon was appreciated for its succulent flesh, a fact evidenced by the many frescoes of feasts and banquets. Moreover, doves were thought to possess medicinal virtues and parts of the bird were prescribed to cure certain ailments. Egyptian dovecots, remarkable on account of both their size and their number, were chronicled and described in detail by Roman agronomists.

The Carrier Pigeon – Subsequently, the pigeon was used by man as a carrier, while remaining a gastronomic delicacy in many countries. In Arab civilizations, for instance, this has been confirmed by the discovery of special sheets of paper, far smaller and lighter than ordinary writing paper. In ancient Greece, the pigeon was dedicated to the goddess Aphrodite and was used as a messenger by lovers. It also heralded the results of sporting events during the Olympic Games.

However, the carrier pigeon is mostly known for its military role in times of war. News of the conquest of Gaul by Julius Caesar was relayed to the capital by means of pigeons, as was Napoleon's defeat at Waterloo. Likewise, during the Siege of Paris in 1870, 400 birds played an active role in defending the city by carrying tiny strips of film attached to their claws.

More recently, during the First World War, English troops entrusted some 10 000 messages to their feathered friends, who were thus instrumental in the victory of the allied forces. Carrier pigeons were also used in the Japanese invasion of southeast Asia during the Second World War. Several of these birds were to become legendary figures and some were even awarded a military decoration: *The Mocker*, *Lord Adelaide*, *Burma Queen* etc. The cities of Brussels and Lille decided to pay tribute to these worthy messengers by erecting a memorial in honour of the "winged soldier".

The Homing Pigeon – In the early 19C, a new sport saw the light of day in Belgium – pigeon racing, in which birds are trained to return to their home loft after being released in the wild. The first long-distance race (160km/100mi) was held in 1818 and the sport gradually gained prominence in Great Britain, France and the United States. The very first races organised in Great Britain – from Exeter, Plymouth and Penzance to London – date back to 1881. Today, many French villages have their own Pigeon-Fanciers Club *(Société Colombophile)* and organise races regularly every year.

For the birds – A familiar sight in Normandy, especially in the Pays de Caux, is the dovecot *(colombier)*. Norman dovecots are square, polygonal or round; the last type is the most common. The door is at ground level, usually rectangular but sometimes rounded at the top and often surmounted by the arms of the owner. The projecting ledge half-way up *(larmier)* is designed to prevent the entry of rodents. There are openings for the pigeons all round. The roofs, conical on circular dovecots and faceted on square or polygonal dovecots, are often covered with slates. The lead finial may be in the shape of a pigeon or a weathervane.

The interior is lined with pigeon-holes *(boulins)* – one hole for each pair of pigeons – and the number varies according to the wealth of the owner. They are reached by a ladder fixed to an arm attached to a central post which pivots on a hard stone. In some dovecots only the upper part is intended for pigeons; the lower part may be used as a hen house or a sheep pen. When the two parts are separated by a wooden floor, the door to the upper part is above the stone rat ledge and reached by an external detachable ladder.

There exist two ranges of dovecot. The standard type is built of ashlar stone (not common), in an attractive contrast to black flint and white stone (north and northeast of Le Havre), in brick, black flint and ashlar stone (brick tended to replace black flint after the 17C), or in brick and stone (fairly common). The secondary type includes buildings in light coloured flint (a similar shade to ashlar stone), in flint and stone, or in flint, brick and stone.

The first known laws on pigeon-breeding were instituted in the Middle Ages. In Normandy, the owners of fiefs were the only ones entitled to build dovecots. This right, known as the *droit de colombier*, was abolished on 4 August 1789 and very few new dovecots were built after the French Revolution. A total of 535 were officially registered in the Seine-Maritime in the early 20C. However, many have been abandoned and are now in a state of neglect. The French government and local authorities have recently taken measures to finance the restoration of these charming buildings, which are an essential part of Normandy's rural heritage.

Dovecotes of Normandy

Manoir de Caudemonde

Château de Crèvecœur-en-Auge

Abbaye de Mortemer

Manoir d'Auffray, Oherville

Dovecote in the hamlet of Petit Veauville, Héricourt-en-Caux

Château de Betteville

Illustrations : M. Dewynter

45

Decorative arts

Ceramics and pottery – The glazed pavement in the chapter-house of St Pierre-sur-Dives (13C) demonstrates the long tradition of ceramic art in Normandy. In the mid 16C Masséot Abaquesne was making decorated tiles, which were greatly prized, in Rouen, while potteries in Le Pré-d'Auge and Manerbe (near Lisieux) were producing "earthenware more beautiful than is made elsewhere". In 1644 **Rouen faience** made its name with blue decoration on a white ground and white on blue. By the end of the century production had increased so that when the royal plate was melted down to replenish the Treasury, "the Court changed to chinaware in a week" (Saint-Simon). The so-called "radiant" style is reminiscent of the wrought-iron work and embroidery for which the town was well known. The desire for novelty brought in the vogue for *chinoiserie*. In the middle of the 18C came the Rococo style with its "quiver" decoration and the famous "Rouen cornucopia", a horn of plenty overflowing with flowers, birds and insects. This industry was ruined by the 1786 trade treaty, which allowed the import of English chinaware into France.

Rouen faience

Norman furniture – Sideboards, longcase clocks and wardrobes – the three most characteristic and traditional pieces of furniture in Normandy – are valued for their elegance, solidity and generous proportions.

The wardrobe, which gradually replaced the medieval chest, first appeared in the 13C; by the beginning of the 17C the sideboard was already in existence and it was in the 18C that longcase clocks became widespread. The golden age of furniture-making in Normandy produced: well proportioned and delicately carved sideboards or kitchen dressers; "coffin" clocks (broader at the top than at the bottom); longcase clocks characterised by carved baskets of fruit and flowers round the clockface; tall pendulum clocks, with delicately chased dials in gilt bronze, copper, pewter or enamel; majestic oak wardrobes, ornamented with finely worked fittings, in brass or other metals, or with medallions, surmounted with carved cornices of doves, birds' nests, ears of corn, flowers and fruit or Cupid's quiver etc. The wardrobe was often part of a young woman's dowry and contained her trousseau; its transfer from her parents' house to her new home was the occasion for traditional celebrations.

Painting

Painting took first place among the arts in 19C France. Landscape totally eclipsed historical and stylised painting and Normandy, was to become the cradle of Impressionism.

The Open Air – While the Romantics were discovering inland Normandy, Eugène Isabey, a lover of seascapes, began to work on the still deserted coast. **Richard Bonington**, 1801-28, an English painter who went to France as a boy, trained there, and, in his watercolours, captured the wetness of sea beaches.

In the second half of the 19C artistic activity was concentrated on **Eugène Boudin** (1824-98) round the Côte de Grâce. This painter from Honfleur, named "King of the Skies" by Corot, encouraged a young fifteen-year-old from Le Havre, **Claude Monet**, to drop caricature for the joys of real painting and urged his Parisian friends to come and stay in his St-Siméon farmstead.

Impressionism – The younger painters, nevertheless, were to outstrip their elders in their search for pictorial light. They wanted to portray the vibration of light, hazes, the trembling of reflections and shadows, the depth and tenderness of the sky, the fading of colours in full sunlight. They – Monet, Sisley, Bazille and their Paris friends, Renoir, Pissarro, Cézanne and Guillaumin especially – were about to form the Impressionist School which gave France a front rank in the history of painting.

Box bed
(Pays d'Auge - 18C)

Longcase clock
(St-Lô - 19C)

Furniture from Basse-Normandie

Marriage wardrobe
(Bayeux - 18C)

Dairy cupboard *(Avranchin - 18C)*

Kitchen dresser
(Cotentin - 19C)

Sideboard *(Vire - 19C)*

STUDIO 3 BIS / MICHELIN / Collection Musée du Meuble Normand, Villedieu-les-Poêles

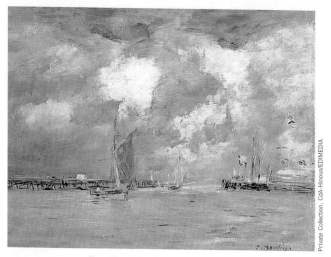

Private Collection. CdA-Hinous/EDIMEDIA

Trouville at High Tide by Eugène Boudin

From 1862 to 1869 the Impressionists remained faithful to the Normandy coast and the Seine estuary. After the Franco-Prussian War they returned only occasionally – although it was in Normandy, at Giverny, that Claude Monet set up house in 1881 and remained until he died in 1926.

Impressionism, in its turn, gave birth to a new school, **Pointillism**, which divided the tints with little touches of colour, applying the principle of the division of white light into seven basic colours, to get ever closer to a luminous effect. Seurat and Signac, the pioneers of this method, also came to Normandy to study its landscapes.

In the early 20C **Fauvism** was born as a reaction against Impressionism and neo-Impressionism. These brightly coloured linear compositions exploded on the canvas. For half a century, therefore, the Côte de Grâce, the Pays de Caux, Deauville, Trouville and Rouen were the sources of inspiration of a multitude of paintings.

Artists' Impressions of Normandy

Le Havre: Sunset in the Port (1832) Turner
Impression: Sunrise (1872) Claude Monet – Le Havre
Wild Poppies (1873) Claude Monet – Vétheuil
Rouen Cathedral (series 1891-5) Claude Monet
Water Lilies Claude Monet – Giverny
The Beach at Trouville Eugène Boudin
La Plage de Trouville (1825) Bonington
Fête Nautique au Havre (1925) Raoul Dufy
Three Boats (1929) Georges Braque – Varengeville-sur-Mer

A Pleiade of Painters – Numerous artists still came to Normandy in the first half of the 20C, notably Valloton and Gernez, the latter died in Honfleur; Marquet who had worked in Gustave Moreau's studio in Paris; Othon Friesz who particularly enjoyed Honfleur which he portrayed in its many aspects; and Van Dongen, painter of the worldly and the elegant and a frequent guest at Deauville.

Marquet, Friesz and Van Dongen were strongly influenced by Fauvism, whereas Raoul Dufy, a native of Le Havre, soon overthrew accepted convention to associate line drawing and richness of colour in compositions which were full of movement.

Literature

Literature and architecture both sprang from the monasteries. It is therefore hardly surprising that Normandy and its abbeys became rich in literary activity from the 13C. Monks and clergymen with a sound knowledge of history and legend, together with travellers and pilgrims, provided the poets with the inspiration needed to create the Christian epics known as the *chansons de geste*. Such verse appeared chronologically after the early hagiographic literature (lives of saints) but remains one of the first examples of the use of French as a literary mode of expression. In the 12C the Anglo-Norman **Robert Wace**, who was born in Jersey but brought up in Caen, wrote two notable verse chronicles. *Le Roman du Rou* (1160-74) was commissioned by Henry II of England and is a history of the dukes of Normandy.

17C – **Pierre Corneille** (1606-84) is often called the father of French classical tragedy. His main works are known together as the "classical tetralogy": *Le Cid* (1637), *Horace* (1640), *Cinna* (1641) and *Polyeucte* (1643). The dramatist enjoyed a happy life with his extended family in Rouen (he married and had seven children, his brother married his wife's sister and their households were very close), and despite occasional brushes with the authorities, his plays were generally well received. Balzac praised him, Molière acknowledged him as his master and the foremost of dramatists, Racine lauded his talent for versification. From the 20C viewpoint, it is clear that Corneille also had a great impact on the rise of comedy, and in the development of drama in general, in particular in regard to his ability to depict personal and moral forces in conflict.

Bibliothèque Municipale, Avranches

Manuscript from Mont-St-Michel

18C – Born in Le Havre, **Bernardin de St-Pierre** (1737-1814) travelled the world to fulfil his dreams, and spent part of his life on the Indian Ocean island of Mauritius. In Paris, he became the disciple of the Romantic philosopher Jean-Jacques Rousseau. His best-known works are *Paul and Virginie* (1787) and *Studies of Nature* (1784).

19C – The founder of Norman regionalism is **Barbey d'Aurevilly** (1808-99), a nobleman from Cotentin, who was born in St-Sauveur-le-Vicomte. In a warm and bright style, illuminated with brilliant imagery and original phrases, he sought, like the Impressionists, to convey the atmosphere, the quality, the uniqueness of his region. Valognes, the town where he spent most of his adolescence is mentioned in several of his works *(Ce qui ne meurt pas; Chevalier des Touches* and *Les Diaboliques)*.

Although born in Paris, **Charles Alexis de Tocqueville** (1805-59), was from an old Norman family. It was during stays at the ancestral home, the Château de Tocqueville, not far from Cherbourg, that he wrote many of the works which were to bring him fame. This political scientist, politician and historian is best-known for his timeless classic *Democracy in America*.

Gustave Flaubert (1821-80), a prime mover of the realist school of French literature, considered art as a means to knowledge. His masterful *Madame Bovary* (1857), a portrait of bourgeois life in the provinces, took him five years to complete. The French government sought to block its publication and have the author condemned for "immorality" – he narrowly escaped conviction.

Flaubert greatly influenced **Guy de Maupassant** (1850-93), a family friend born in Dieppe who regarded himself as the older author's apprentice. Maupassant's work is thoroughly realistic, the language lucidly pure and the imagery sharp and precise. The author wrote best-selling novels (*Une Vie, Bel-Ami, Pierre et Jean*), but his greatest achievement lies in his short stories; he perfected the form and many of these works are considered among the finest in French literature. Today, he is one of the most widely read French authors in English-speaking countries.

Octave Mirbeau (1848-1917) from Trévières near Bayeux was an active participant in the literary and political quarrels of his time, speaking out in defence of anarchist ideas. As a novelist, he was fiercely critical of the social conditions of the time and his work *Journal of a Lady's Maid* (*Le Journal d'une femme de chambre*, 1900) is typical of this attitude.

20C – Alain (1868-1951), his real name being Émile Chartier, made a name for himself by his columns in a Rouen newspaper. A professor of philosophy and author of many essays, he revolted against all forms of tyranny. His works Remarks on Happiness (1928) and on Education (1932) are noteworthy.

André Maurois (1865-1967) is known for his war memories, novels, biographies (*The Life of Disraeli*, 1927) and historical works (*History of England*, 1937).

ROGER-VIOLLET

Gustave Flaubert

Jean de la Varende (1887-1959) from the Ouche region evokes in his novels the Normandy of yesteryear. His work *Par Monts et Merveilles de Normandie* is a description of all he saw and admired in the region.

Armand Salacrou, born in 1899 in Rouen, called his dramatic works a "meditation on the human condition". He experimented with different dramatic styles. Two of his popular successes were *Un homme comme les autres* (1926) and *Boulevard Durand* (1961).

Raymond Queneau (1903-1976) was born in Le Havre and achieved distinction as a reader for and eventually the director of the prestigious Encyclopédie de la Pléiade, a scholarly edition of past and present authors. As the author of many poems, novels and plays, Queneau stands out for his quirky style and verbal juggling, revealing the absurdity that underlies our everyday world. One of his best-loved works, *Zazie dans le métro* (1959), was made into a char-

ming film. He created a surprising book called *100 000 Billion Poems* on the following principle: he took a sonnet (14 lines) and printed each line on 10 strips of paper, then arranged them in a spiral binding so that by flipping the strips one way and another, a reader can construct 10^{14} (10 to the 14th power) poems. Although the book is small, if you were to read a different poem every 10 seconds, it would take you millions of years to read them all!

Music

François-Adrien Boieldieu (1775-1834) – Born in Rouen, he composed operas and comic operas. His work, *The Caliph of Baghdad* (1800), earned him a glowing reputation throughout Europe. From 1803 to 1810 he was Director of Music at the Imperial Opera of Saint Petersburg at the request of Czar Alexander I. His talent was universally recognised with his masterpiece *La Dame Blanche* in 1825.

Camille Saint-Saëns (1835-1921) – He was born in Paris, but his father was from Normandy. A brilliant pianist, he composed symphonies, operas, concertos and religious works. His most famous works include the *Danse Macabre* (1875) and *Samson and Dalila* (1877).

Arthur Honegger (1892-1955) – Born in Le Havre, of Swiss origin. At first he composed melodies to poems by Cocteau, Apollinaire and Paul Fort, then *Pacific 231* (1923) and *King David* (1924). *Joan at the Stake* (1935) and *The Dance of the Dead* (1938) have texts by Paul Claudel.

Erik Satie (1866-1925) – Born in Honfleur, he began as a pianist in the cabarets of Montmartre (The Black Cat) where he met Debussy. Sarcasm and irony are dissimulated in his works, his greatest being the symphonic drama *Socrates* (1918) for voice and orchestra based on texts by Plato.

Satie exerted an undeniable influence both on his time and on musicians such as Ravel, Debussy and Stravinsky.

Food and drink

The people of Normandy have a reputation for being hearty eaters who appreciate good cooking. Most family celebrations and reunions are marked by leisurely meals for which the French are so famous. Normandy is known for its traditional recipes and specialities based on the wonderful flavour of local produce.

LOCAL SPECIALITIES

According to Normandy tradition one should eat duck in Rouen, tripe in Caen and La Ferté-Macé, leg of lamb from the salt meadows of Mont-St-Michel Bay and an omelette in Mont-St-Michel; one should also taste Dieppe sole, Duclair duckling, Auge Valley chicken garnished with tiny onions, Vire chitterlings *(andouillette)*, black pudding from Mortagne-au-Perche and white pudding from Avranches. Among the tasty meat dishes, try the *côtes de veau vallée d'Auge*, which are veal cutlets fried in butter and flambéed in Calvados then braised in cider and fresh cream.

The range of seafood is impressive: shrimps and cockles from Honfleur, mussels from Villerville and Isigny, lobsters from La Hague and Barfleur and oysters, Atlantic crabs, spider crabs, winkles and whelks from Courseulles and St-Vaast. Any selection of seafood may be accompanied by rye bread, slightly salted butter and a glass of dry cider.

The many different varieties of fish – sole, turbot and mackerel to mention only a few – are often served with a delicious sauce.

Local pastries, which are all made with butter, include apple turnovers *(chaussons aux pommes)*, flat cakes baked in the oven *(falues* or *fouaces)*, biscuits *(galettes)*, shortbread *(sablés)* and buns *(brioches)*. Those who have a sweet tooth will enjoy the Calvados-flavoured cream chocolates from Caen and Putanges, the caramels *(chiques and balivernes)* from Isigny and the boiled sweets *(berlingots)* from Bayeux, Caen and Falaise, not to mention the scrumptious Rouen sugar apples. *Douillons* are pears hollowed out and filled with butter, wrapped in pastry and baked.

Veal cutlets *"à la normande"*

P. Libert/VISA

Cream and Normandy Sauce – Cream is the mainstay of the Normandy kitchen: ivory in colour, velvety in texture and mellow in taste, it goes as well with eggs and fish as with chicken, white meat, vegetables and even game. This delicious cream is at its best in the so-called Normandy Sauce *(sauce normande)*, which elsewhere is nothing but a plain white sauce, but in Normandy both looks and tastes quite different.

Cheese – If cream is the queen of Normandy cooking, cheese is the king of all fare. Pont-l'Évêque has reigned since the 13C; Livarot is quoted in texts of the same period; the world renowned Camembert first appeared early in the 19C *(see p 345)*.

To be really creamy and soft, a **Pont-l'évêque** should be made on a farm in the Pays d'Auge when the milk is still warm from the cow. **Livarot**, whose strong odour may alarm the uninitiated, is made from milk which has been left to stand. Although cheeses claiming to be **Camembert** are now made in factories all over France, only Normandy Camembert is authentic.

The Normandy cheeseboard also includes fresh cheeses from the Pays de Bray – the **bondons**, demi-sel or double cream – whose repute is more recent but nonetheless firmly established.

The **petit-suisse** was originally a local product, like the **Neufchâtel**, in its various forms, which is also a much appreciated farmhouse cheese. Neufchâtel cheese can be eaten within only 12 days of being made, although a mature Neufchâtel takes up to three months.

How Camembert is made – There are 10 operations in all.

Camembert cheese

Selection and Preparation – The raw material is milk which only comes from one of the five Normandy regions. It must be rich in fat, protein and vitamins and is slowly heated at a maximum temperature of 30-37°C/86-99°F (its natural temperature when it leaves the cow's udder).

Coagulation – The milk must coagulate in 100l/22gal containers, helped by the curdling agent rennet. This operation (1hr 30min) is both difficult and delicate, as the temperature (30-32°C/86-90°F) and acidity of the milk must be strictly controlled. The acidification rate depends on the prevailing atmospheric conditions and on the animals yielding the milk.

Slicing – The curd is cut into rough wedges, making it easier for the whey to drain away.

Moulding – A temperature of 20-30°C/68-86°F is needed. Each mould receives 200cl poured with ladles. The average is 1500l/330gal of milk in 8hr.

Spreading – The coagulated milk tends to settle towards the middle. In order to even out the surface this operation is repeated three times.

Turning – After settling the cheese is turned over. By this time it occupies 1/3 of the mould. The operation takes place between 6.30pm and 9.30pm.

These five operations take up the whole of the first day.

Withdrawing – The soft cheese is withdrawn from the moulds and placed on planks which are then wheeled to the drying room to finish the draining process at a temperature of 18-20°C/64-68°F.

Salting – The first stage is to salt one side of the cheese and its circumference. The aim of this operation is to obtain the characteristic Camembert flavour by developing the ferment *penicillium candidum*. The temperature is 14-15°C/7-8°F. Around 6.30pm the cheeses are turned over. The following morning the other side is salted. We are now in day three.

Drying – On the fourth day the cheese is placed on a trellis and taken to the drying rooms where a system of ventilation ensures a temperature of 10-14°C/5-8°F. Mould begins to form after the fifth day. On the 14th day of the manufacturing process (10 days in the drying room), some of the cheese is put aside to mature whereas the rest is sold as fresh Camembert. The latter needs one to two day's extra drying after leaving the drying room proper. This is achieved by leaving the cheese in a draught.

In the maturing process the cheese is left to rest on planks located in cellars where the humidity rate is constant. It is turned over every day.

The cheese is dispatched half-mature after 20 days (the most common case), mature after 25 days and very mature after 30 days.

Packing – When it is dry, the cheese is sorted according to quality; it is then cooled for four days at a temperature of 9°C/48°F before being packed for dispatch.

Le Trou Normand

It is a known fact that, in the middle of a generous repast, the people of Normandy are prone to take a small break, often accompanied by a glass of Calvados: this is the famous *"trou normand"* (Norman hole) that revives the appetite of the most satiated guests.

The famous gastronome Curnonsky reflected on this curious feature of Normandy cuisine: "Was it Calvados that led to the *trou normand*? Or rather was it the *trou normand* that led to the creation of Calvados? We shall never really know the truth of it. In any case, the fact remains that this phenomenon has become a well-established custom, to the delight of all gourmets. It also has undeniable advantages in that it accelerates the digestive process and helps diners tuck into the second part of the meal in style."

The most common explanation is that alcohol tends to dissolve fat. Nutritionists, for their part, claim that alcohol dilates the abdominal wall, resulting in a new lease of appetite. Nowadays, in restaurants, an apple sorbet doused with Calvados has replaced the traditional *"trou normand"*. This said, at the end of the meal, coffee can still be liberally spiked with the brandy!

DRINK

Cider – Apple orchards have always been a characteristic feature of the Normandy landscape and cider has been made locally since the Middle Ages when it took second place to barley beer. Although most of the cider, which is now made in Normandy, is manufactured in huge factories, it is however still possible to find a farmhouse brew distilled in the traditional way.

The apples are gathered in huge baskets then stored for a short while before being emptied into a circular granite trough, where they are crushed by a round wooden mill-stone pulled by a horse. The crushed apples *(marc)* are transferred to the press, where they are laid between layers of rye straw and then pressed; the juice runs out at the bottom on to a flat surface from which it is drained into the surrounding gutter and is then drawn off through a spout. After pressing, the rye straw is extracted and the apple pulp is put to soak in a vat before being pressed a second time. The first pressing produces pure cider juice; subsequent pressings produce a weaker brew which is kept for use on the farm.

Apple crusher

J. Verroust/VLOO, Paris

Whether it is *brut* (dry, strongly flavoured with apple with an alcohol content of 4-5°), *demi-sec* or *doux* (made artificially sweet by stalling the fermentation process when the alcohol content reaches 2.5-3°), cider is the perfect accompaniment for both gastronomic dinners and lighter meals such as pancakes or desserts made with apples. It should always be served chilled .

When it matures, cider loses its sweetness and takes on a distinctive, earthy flavour. The fruity quality of cider is best preserved when it is stored in a cool cellar, where the temperature does not exceed 15°C/59°F, and it should be drunk in the months following its purchase. Bottles that have travelled or remained lying horizontally should be left to rest for a while before being opened. The most famous *appellation* is the "Cidre de la Vallée d'Auge", which is subject to strict controls and tastings. It covers five different crus: Blangy-le-Château-Pont-l'Évêque, Cambremer, Lisieux-Orbec, Livarot and Vimoutiers.

Calvados – Calvados, or *calva* as it is better known, is a cider brandy made from a mash of apples fermented with yeast; it is distilled twice and matured in oak for from six to ten years. The use of the name Calvados, from one of the regions which produces this brandy, probably dates from the early 19C, although cider brandy was first mentioned in the 16C; it was made by Gilles de Gouverville in a little village in the Cotentin. The tradition of the *trou normand* ("Norman hole" – *see inset*) is still observed; during a heavy meal a small glass of Calvados is swallowed at one go to help the digestion. Restaurants often serve an apple and calvados sorbet instead. Calvados is usually drunk after coffee, one or two glasses; for just a taste, eat a sugar lump dipped in Calvados. The AOC label for Calvados dates from 1942 and applies to two *appellations*: "Calvados" and "Calvados du Pays d'Auge". A great many distilleries and storehouses are open to the public.

Perry – Perry *(poiré)*, is similar to cider but is made from pears and usually comes from the areas around Mortain and Domfront.

Pommeau – This alcoholic beverage is made by mixing two thirds of apple juice with one third of Calvados and features an alcohol content of 16-18°. The ageing process is carried out in oak casks for a period of 18 months. In 1991 it was officially awarded an AOC label *(appellation d'origine contrôlée)* on account of its excellent taste and outstanding qualities. It can be drunk chilled as an apéritif (without ice) and served with dried apples. It can also be drunk at room temperature to accompany oysters (warm oysters with Normandy Pommeau), foie gras, melon or dessert (especially apple pie). When it is used in cooking, its full flavour matures and delicately enhances the flavour of the dish.

The Old Dock in Honfleur

Sights

L'AIGLE

Population 9 466
Michelin map 60 fold 5 or 231 fold 45

L'Aigle, between the Ouche and the Perche regions, is at its best on market day, Tuesday. It is the third largest market in France. One of the main towns in the Upper Risle Valley, the town is a centre for traditional metalwork industries: steel drawing mills produce pins, needles, staples etc. The historic centre of the town is place St-Martin, whose centrepiece is the church of the same name.

SIGHTS

Église St-Martin – St Martin's Church is an attractive building. An elaborate late-15C square tower contrasts with a small 12C one built of red iron agglomerate (*grison*) and surmounted by a more recent spire. Beautiful modern statues stand in niches between the windows of the south nave, added in the 16C. Inside, two 16C stained-glass windows (right of the chancel and first window, south aisle) complement a fine contemporary series; the Renaissance aisle is decorated with graceful hanging keystones.
Above the high altar (1656) is a beautiful carved wooden altarpiece, consisting of four twisted columns capped by Corinthian capitals and decorated with vine leaves, bunches of grapes and cherubs. The central composition, attributed to Lebrun, shows the Descent from the Cross.

Château – The château, which houses the town hall and two museums, was built in 1690 on the site of an 11C fortress, by Fulbert de Beina, Lord of L'Aigle, and vassal of the dukes of Normandy. He is said to have discovered an eagle's nest on the site, hence the name of the town. The plans were the work of Mansart.

Musée Marcel-Angot ⊙ – A double spiral staircase leads to the first floor of the museum. The Council Rooms give access to another room containing a collection of musical instruments, the gift of a former bandmaster: string and wind instruments, including an archaic bass wind instrument known as a "serpent" used in military music and other unusual instruments.

Musée "Juin 44 : bataille de Normandie" ⊙ – Located beside the castle, the "Battle of Normandy" Museum contains wax figures of leading personalities (De Gaulle, Churchill, Leclerc, Roosevelt, Stalin etc). Their voices may also be heard on recordings. The Battle of Normandy is represented on a relief map; dioramas retrace the outstanding events of this crucial period of the Second World War.

STROLLING ALONG THE BANKS OF THE RISLE

▶ *The tourist office has a very practical brochure available, which describes a walking tour through town (1hr 30min) and a longer walk around the 15 neighbouring cantons.*

St-Sulpice-sur-Risle – *3km/2mi northeast by D 930.* The **church** adjoins the 13C priory, which was partially rebuilt in the 16C. Among the works of art it contains are a 16C tapestry, a 17C painting of St Cecilia, a statue of St Anne and two stained-glass windows from the 13C and 14C.

Aube – *7km/4mi southwest of L'Aigle by N 26.* The **Château des Nouettes**, situated at the entrance to the town and now a medico-pedagogical institute, was once the residence of Countess Eugène de Ségur.
In the former presbytery at the foot of the church stands the **Musée de la Comtesse de Ségur** ⊙ which contains various mementoes, portraits and documents evoking the life and literary career of the celebrated countess and her family. The characters featuring in the writer's novels are represented by a collection of dolls and miscellaneous exhibits (toys, games, books, furniture etc).

Chevojon/Musée de la Comtesse de Ségur

La Comtesse de Ségur

On the River Risle, leaving Aube towards L'Aigle, stands the **Musée de la Grosse Forge d'Aube** ⊙, which retraces five centuries of metallurgy. This museum, which has changed very little since the 17C, is one of the best preserved workshops in the area. Note the furnace for refining metals, the massive camshaft hammer and the wooden bellows (a 1995 replica) operated by a paddle wheel.

Eating out

MODERATE

Auberge St-Michel – *61300 St-Michel-Thubeuf – 3.5km/2.2mi east of L'Aigle via N 26 –* ☎ *02 33 24 20 12 – closed 3-18 Jan, 7-30 Sept, Wed evening and Thur except holidays – 13.72/28.20€.* This Norman inn, situated on the roadside, is ideal for something to eat whilst travelling. A series of small old-fashioned rooms furnished in bistro style, beamed ceiling, dark woodwork and traditional cooking.

ALENÇON★

Population 29 988
Michelin map 60 fold 3 or 231 fold 43
Local map ALPES MANCELLES

The reputation of this former ducal city on the border of Maine has grown around the fine quality of the lace made here. A royal manufactory under Louis XIV, Alençon has a rich architectural heritage, a fine arts museum with a collection of lace work and paintings from the 15-19C, and pleasant waterways and gardens surrounding the pedestrian town centre.

Alençon was liberated on 12 August 1944 as a result of the decisive part played by the French 2nd armoured division in the battle of the 'Falaise-Mortain Pocket'.

★**Musée des Beaux-Arts et de la Dentelle** ⊙ – Located in the former Jesuit college (17C), the Museum of Fine Arts and Lace houses paintings from the 15C to the 19C as well as collections of lace. The French and Nordic schools of the 17C are well represented with canvases by Philippe de Champaigne (*Assumption* and *The Trinity*), Jean Jouvenet (*Marriage of the Virgin*), Allegrain (*Landscape*), Voet (*Portraits*), Ryckaert (*Judith and Holopherne*), Wyck (*Man Studying*)... There is also a fine selection of 19C French painting with works by Boudin, Courbet, Fantin-Latour, Lacombe, Laurens, Legros, Veyrassat etc...

The presentation of the **lace collection**★★ offers a broad review of the principal lacemaking centres in Italy (Venice, Milan), Flanders (Brussels, Malines) and France (Chantilly, Le Puy, Argentan, Bayeux). It is mostly interesting, however, for its display of Alençon lace, which uses a needlepoint technique unique in France and is represented by the elegant creations of the Alençon lacemakers from the 17C to the present day.

Alençon Lace

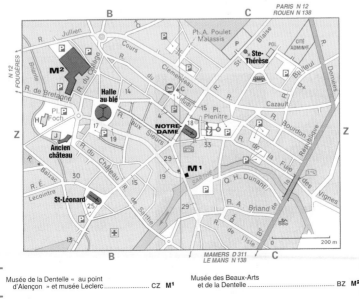

From the Venice Point to the Alençon Point

Around 1650, Madame de la Perrière perfected the Venice Point, very fashionable at the time in all the European courts, and taught her skill to the young women of Alençon. As a result, lacemaking developed and soon 8 000 people were involved in the manufacture of point lace. In order to keep up with fashion, men and women were tempted to spend large sums of money and to buy lace abroad, which prompted Colbert in 1665 to ban imported lace and to establish a royal factory in Alençon to produce French point lace. The needlewomen of Alençon subsequently developed their own style based on a specific technique and a new pattern consisting of delicate motifs arranged in close symmetry on a plain background. This was the origin of Alençon lace which, by the end of the 17C, was the only one in fashion. The Atelier National du Point d'Alençon (National Workshop of Alençon Lace, *not open to the public*) has preserved this ancient tradition of needlepoint lace, acknowledged in the 19C as the best lace.

In addition there is a collection of Cambodian exhibits (gold objects, weapons, sculptures, ritual objects, musical instruments) brought back by **Adhémard Leclères** (1853-1917), a native of Alençon and last governor of Cambodia.

Musée de la Dentelle "au Point d'Alençon" and Musée Leclerc ⊙ – This Museum of Alençon Lace serves a dual purpose since it was General Leclerc's temporary HQ on 12 August 1944. The visit explains the history and technique of Alençon needlepoint lace. Originally each lacemaker specialised in one particular stage of lacemaking. Sixteen hours of work were necessary to produce 3cm/1in and around 10 years to complete a whole piece. Three galleries contain a remarkable **lace collection**★★ of incredibly delicate masterpieces.

On the first floor, various documents and photographs are devoted to the **2ᵉ DB**, General Leclerc's 2nd armoured division, from the moment it landed on Utah Beach to its triumphant arrival in Strasbourg.

Opposite the museum stands a statue of General Leclerc behind which there is a monument representing an open book evoking the advance of the general's division; the cover is a Croix de Lorraine (Lorraine cross), the emblem of the Free French forces during the Second World War.

★ÉGLISE NOTRE-DAME ⊙ *15min*

The beautiful 14C-15C Flamboyant Gothic Church of Our Lady was begun during the Hundred Years War under the period of English domination, on the site of a Romanesque church which belonged to Lonlay Abbey. The tower, transept and chancel were rebuilt in the 18C. The elegant three-sided **porch**, built by Jean Lemoine from 1490 to 1506, is an example of the purest Flamboyant style. The refinement, elegance and splendour of the sculptures were such that they gave rise to a popular saying: *The church is built in such a way that, in order to give God the best spot, you'd have to place him out of doors...* All the decoration is concentrated on the upper parts of the church. The Transfiguration in the central gable shows Christ with the Prophets Moses and Elijah; below are the Apostles, Peter, James and John, who uncharacteristically, may be seen with his back to the street.

Descent from the cross, Église Notre-Dame

Inside, the sweeping lines of the nave rise to the lierne and tierceron **vaulting** which is highly decorated. The lines of the triforium merge successfully with those of the clerestory to form a unified whole. Note the admirable **stained glass**★ by the master-glaziers of Alençon and the Maine region. The glass in the clerestory windows dates from 1530: *(north side going towards the chancel)* Creation; Original Sin; The Sacrifice of Abraham; Crossing the Red Sea; Moses and the Bronze Serpent; *(south side)* the Presentation in the Temple; Marriage of the Virgin; Descent from the Cross; Annunciation and Visitation; Dormition and Assumption.

Eating out

MID-RANGE

L'Escargot Doré – *183 av. du Gén.-Leclerc – 2km/1.2mi south of Alençon via N 138 – ☎ 02 33 28 67 67 – closed 2-10 Jan, 24 Apr to 1 May, 17 July to 7 Aug, Sun evening and Mon – 16.46/33.54€*. If you enjoy barbecues, this place is for you. Fish and meat are grilled over embers in the fireplace of this old farm turned into a restaurant with an authentic rustic setting. There is a dining area on the mezzanine and a veranda.

Where to stay

MODERATE

La Garencière Bed and Breakfast – *72610 Champfleur – 6.5km/4mi SE from Alençon on the road to Mamers and Champfleur via D 19, continue towards Bourg-le-Roi – ☎ 02 33 31 75 84 – closed 25-31 Dec – ⌂ – 5 rooms: 33/42€ – meal 18€*.
During the crusades, this site was a stop-over for pilgrims on their way to Compostela. The modern inn has quiet rooms which have been decorated with care by the owner. The covered pool opens out onto a view of the countryside.

Le Grand Cerf Hotel – *21 r. St-Blaise – ☎ 02 33 26 00 51 – closed 1-16 Jan, Sun from Oct to Mar and holidays – 20 rooms: 41.16/54.88€ – ⌂ 6.10€ – restaurant 19.82/38.11€*. This 19C house will prompt you to dream of barouches passing beneath your bedroom-window. The façade has retained its original charm. When you feel like eating, you will be able to choose between a standard restaurant meal and a brasserie-type meal served only for lunch.

MID-RANGE

Le Moulin de Linthe Bed and Breakfast – *72130 St-Léonard-des-Bois – 0.5km/0.3mi south of St-Léonard-des-Bois on D 112 towards Sougé – ☎ 02 43 33 79 22 – 5 rooms: 44/58€*. The bedrooms have character in this old mill which looks quite picturesque even if its paddle wheel no longer turns...Amateur anglers will be able to fish for trout or pike in the River Sarthe and those with a keen interest for the unusual will make a point of visiting the ostrich farm nearby.

On the town

La Cave aux Bœufs – *10 bis r. de la Cave-aux-Bœufs – ☎ 02 33 82 99 45 – daily*. Situated above a smart brasserie with wide French windows, this pub furnished with rush mats and low wicker tables offers a warm atmosphere. The turret decorating the façade may be recent but the holly bushes standing on the terrace are over a hundred years old. Jazz concerts twice a month and exhibitions of regional art.

La Harpe d'Or – *24 r. du Pont-Neuf – ☎ 02 33 32 98 98 – Mon-Sat from 12.30pm*. When the weather is fine, the waterside terrace is in great demand. The interior is decorated with an assortment of objects (fishing nets, skis...). Warm welcome.

Showtime

La Luciole – *171 rte de Bretagne – ☎ 02 33 32 83 33 – opening times follow the calendar of performances – closed July-Aug*. This is no doubt the locals' favourite haunt. More than 70 concerts of current popular music, mainly pop-rock and varied folk music, are staged here every year.

Scène Nationale d'Alençon-Flers – *2 av. de Basingstoke – ☎ 02 33 29 02 29 – opening times follow the calendar of performances – box office open Mon-Fri 5-7pm – closed July-Sept*. Ballet, music, theatre for every taste on this national stage full of resources. Artists from all over the world meet here to share their experiences with the locals during the "Causeries au coin du bar" (Informal chats round the bar) and other themed gatherings. Public rehearsals.

Shopping

Les Caves de la Rotonde – *5 r. des Filles-Notre-Dame* – ☎ *02 33 26 20 76* – *Tues-Sat 9am-12.30pm, 2-7.30pm, Sun 10.30am-12.30pm.* Next to the wheat market. This is the place to look for local spirits: pommeau (apple brandy), poiré (pear brandy), cider, Bagnolèse, a local speciality, and a few old vintages of the famous calvados which will delight connaisseurs.

Market – *Pl. Magdelaine* – *Sat and Thur.* A fine market where farmers, breeders and craftsmen of the Orne region sell their products and a few regional specialities.

The first chapel off the north aisle, with its attractive wrought-iron screen adorned with symbolic roses, is where Marie-Françoise-Thérèse Martin was baptised. She is better known as St Teresa of Lisieux. The stained glass portrays her baptism and above the font is her white embroidered christening robe.

In place Lamagdelaine, to the left of the church, is the attractive 15C **Maison d'Ozé** (Ozé House), now the Tourist Information Centre, where the future king Henri IV is said to have stayed.

ADDITIONAL SIGHTS

Maison d'Ozé – This 15C house currently serves as the Tourist office. According to legend, the future Henri IV stayed here in 1576.

Ancien Château – From place Foch, one can see the 14C and 15C towers of the old castle, built by Jean le Beau, first Duke of Alençon and one of Joan of Arc's companions in arms.

The central tower, known as the "crowned" tower, has an unexpected outline: the main tower with machicolations is itself crowned by a slimmer round tower. The other two towers, which defend the main gate, can be seen from rue du Château. The fortress is used as a prison.

Halle au Blé – Built at the beginning of the 19C, this circular grain market was covered towards the end of the century with a glass dome which appealed so much to the ladies of the town that they nicknamed it the hoopskirt of Alençon.

Église St-Léonard ⊙ – The rebuilding of the present church was begun in 1489 by René, second Duke of Alençon, and was completed in 1505 by his widow, Marguerite de Lorraine.

Nearby *(no 10 rue Porte-de-la-Barre)* is a 15C house (Maison à l'Étal) with a slate-hung façade.

Chapelle Ste-Thérèse ⊙ – Opposite the Préfecture, a fine 17C building and former military headquarters, a double staircase leads to the chapel which adjoins the house where St Teresa of Lisieux was born on 2 January 1873.

The marked itinerary, known as "L'Encerclement" (The Encircling Movement), one of several in the Historical Area of the Battle of Normandy, starts from Alençon and continues on to L'Aigle. It traces the progress of the 2nd Armoured Division (see p 29).

EXCURSIONS

*Forêt de Perseigne

Round tour – 53km/33mi – about 3hr

From Alençon take D 311 southeast in the direction of Chartres. Beyond Le Buisson turn left onto D 236. After 4km/2mi turn sharp right onto a forest road towards Aillières-Beauvoir and right again towards Ancinnes; at the Rond de Croix-Pergeline turn left by a milestone to Gros Houx.

The road descends into a valley past fine stands of oak, beech and fir.

At the Carrefour des Trois-Ponts turn left uphill.

The road enters the picturesque **Vallée d'Enfer** (Hell Valley) in which there runs a stream. The tower-belvedere (30m/90ft high) crowns the highest point (349m/1 145ft) in the Sarthe district.

🔳 *There are 8km/5mi of waymarked paths round the belvedere and in Hell Valley, and a number of picnic areas.*

Take D 234 southeast to the twin villages Aillières-Beauvoir and take D 116 south via Villaines-la-Carelle. At the crossroads with D 311 continue southwest on D 310.

The road skirts the southern edge of the forest, providing a fine view of the trees.

Chapelle Notre-Dame-de-Toutes-Aides – The doorway of this graceful pilgrim-age chapel is surmounted by a Virgin and Child. Above the 17C altarpiece is an Assumption; below is a painting of the Annunciation.

In St-Rémy-du-Val turn right in front of the church onto the road to Neufchâtel-en-Saosnois (D 117). Turn left onto D 165.

West of Neufchâtel the road skirts the Vaubezon Pool.

From Ancinnes take D 19 to Alençon.

From the road there are glimpses of Écouves Forest, Multonne Forest and the conical silhouette of La Butte Chaumont.

The Alpes Mancelles

82km/51mi – about 3hr from Alençon and back (excluding the Misère Valley).

The designation Alps may seem a little exaggerated for this region; nevertheless the Sarthe Valley has a certain rugged charm with its steep, heather- and broom-clad slopes.

The Alpes Mancelles are part of the Normandie-Maine Regional Park and there is a wide variety of leisure activities (hiking, fishing, canoeing and cycling) available to the visitor.

On leaving Alençon take N 12 west via St-Denis-sur-Sarthe; in Lentillère turn left towards Champfrémont; then bear right to Mont des Avaloirs.

Mont des Avaloirs – A belvedere marks the summit (417m/1 368ft), which together with the Signal d'Écouves, are the highest points in western France.

The fine panorama is now screened by vegetation but it is nonetheless possible to make out the bare rounded summit of Mont Souprat (east) and the Alpes Mancelles (southeast);

A parc naturel régional *is an area whose ecological harmony is fragile, whose natural and cultural heritage is rich but threatened and whose development must be based on conservation and improvement.*

Therefore, the objectives of a parc naturel régional *are as follows:*

● *to protect the area by ensuring harmonious cohabitation between the various ecosystems and by preserving the landscapes;*

● *to contribute to the development of the area;*

● *to welcome, instruct and inform the public;*

● *to conduct experiments in accordance with the objectives mentioned above and to support research projects.*

At the second crossroads turn left onto D 204 and then fork right onto D 255. In St-Julien-des-Églantiers turn right onto D 245, then right onto D 218 and right again onto D 20.

Corniche du Pail – On a clear day, when the leaves are not too thick, the road, which climbs slowly provides a view over the Mayenne basin to the conical silhouette of Mont Margantin (northwest), to the squat belfry of Domfront Church (northwest) and to Andaines Forest (north).

In Pré-en-Pail take N 12 east and D 144 south via St-Pierre-des-Nids.

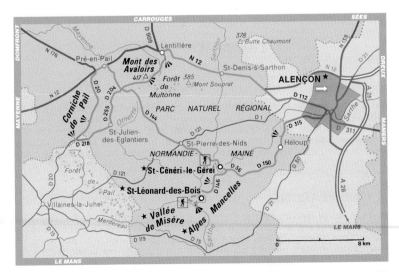

Eating out

MODERATE

Le Saint-Léo – *Pl. de l'Église* – *72130 St-Léonard-des-Bois* – ☎ *02 43 33 81 34* – *closed Dec, Jan, Mon evening, Tues evening and Wed except July-Aug* – *5.79/13.72€*. The owner, an ex-musician turned chef, prepares his dishes in front of you. Simple family cooking served in a room offering a view of the meandering river skirting the foothills of the Alpes Mancelles.

★**St-Céneri-le-Gérei** – Many an artist has been inspired by this quaint little village and its well-preserved charming setting: hilltop church, bridge spanning the Sarthe and stone houses.

The chancel of the Romanesque **church** is decorated with frescoes of Christ in Majesty, the Virgin gathering the Elect under her mantle and the crowning of St Céneri. From the chevet there is a view down to the bridge over the Sarthe and the houses lining the river banks.

From St-Céneri-le-Gérei take D 56 south; turn right onto D 146.

As the road climbs a fine view opens out northwards to the Sarthe Valley and the forested ridges of Multonne Forest.

On the descent into St-Léonard-des-Bois the bare steep slopes of the valley contrast with the lush pasturelands of the river banks.

🚶 *6km/3.6mi by car, 8km/5mi on foot – for a change of pace!*

★**St-Léonard-des-Bois** – This small town makes an ideal excursion centre for the Alpes Mancelles *(many marked trails)* as it is set in the heart of the Normandy-Maine Regional Park.

The **church**, built on the site of an oratory dedicated to St Léonard, contains a 17C group of 14 terracotta figures portraying the Entombment of the Virgin.

★**Vallée de Misère** – *1hr 30min on foot there and back.*

🚶 *On the church square take the path from the corner by the Hôtel Bon Laboureur. At the crossroads marked by a stone cross take a steep rocky path uphill. Beyond the hamlet of Le Champ-des-Pasfore turn left. At the next crossroads turn left onto a path marked in red and white.*

From a bench there is an attractive **view**★ of the wild Misère Valley, St-Léonard and the Manoir de Linthe further downstream. The heights of Multonne Forest are also visible to the left.

Return along the red-and-white marked path past a fenced field and take a downhill path, through the hamlet of La Barre, which returns to the crossroads with the stone cross, then back track to St-Léonard-des-Bois.

From St-Léonard-des-Bois take D 146 north. Turn right onto D 56; in Moulins-le-Carbonnel turn left onto D 150 which becomes D 315.

South of the small village of **Héloup**, sitting on top of a long crest, overlooking the Sarthe Valley, the view embraces (left to right) Mont Avaloirs, Multonne Forest, Mont Souprat (west of the Sarthe), La Butte Chaumont and Écouves Forest (east of the Sarthe) and, as the road turns downhill, Perseigne Forest (east).

D 315 will take you back to Alençon.

Les ANDELYS ★★

Population 8 455
Michelin map 55 fold 17 or 231 fold 24
Local map see Vallée de la SEINE

Les Andelys, dominated by the impressive ruins of Château-Gaillard, lies in one of the loveliest settings along the Seine. It once consisted of two distinct areas, Le Petit-Andely to the west and Le Grand-Andely to the east. The latter was the site of a monastery founded by Clotilde, wife of Clovis, in the 6C. The name of St Clotilde remains closely associated with the town. The street bearing her name has a fountain (29 rue Ste-Clotilde) where she is said to have turned water into wine for the workmen building the monastery chapel.

A FINE YEARLING

In 1196 **Richard Lionheart**, King of England and Duke of Normandy, decided to bar the King of France's way to Rouen along the Seine Valley by building a massive fortress on the cliff commanding the river at Andely. Work progressed rapidly so that within the year Château-Gaillard was erected and Richard was able to cry aloud "See my fine yearling!".

Despite his boldness, **Philippe Auguste** did not at first dare attack so formidable a redoubt but when Richard I was succeeded by King John he decided to try and starve the occupants into surrender. By the end of 1203 the castle had been isolated by a double moat reinforced by wooden watchtowers. In February, however, the French King learned that the defenders had enough food to withstand another year's siege, and he decided to take the castle by storm.

The only possible access was a narrow isthmus connecting the promontory, on which the fortress was built, to the hills where the King of France had pitched camp. This was where the attack took place.

The first obstacle was the triangular redoubt guarding the vulnerable approach across the isthmus. The moat (15m/45ft deep) was partially filled in and a corner tower mined by the attackers to force the outer strongpoint to fall. On 6 March the French entered the main defences through the latrines and let down the drawbridge to the outer ward. The assailants swarmed in. Repeated ramming soon breached the next line, forcing the garrison to surrender, before they had the time to seek refuge in the keep.

Three months later Rouen, too, had fallen to the French king.

★★CHÂTEAU-GAILLARD ⏱ 45min

Follow the signs from rue Louis-Pasteur.

From the car park there is an outstanding **view** of the castle, the Seine and Les Andelys.

Barbican – The redoubt, separated from the main castle by a deep moat, possessed five towers of which only one, the barbican, remains. It was the one attacked by Philippe Auguste and is encircled by a narrow slippery path.

Castle – The outer ward, the esplanade, is situated between the redoubt and the castle. By following the wall round to the left one sees the foundations of the keep which rises from the natural rock. At the far end of the wall there is a fine viewpoint.

By returning along the bottom of the moat, one passes in front of casemates *(right)* hollowed out of the rock to provide storage for the garrison's food supplies. A footbridge has replaced the drawbridge at the main entrance to the castle. The keep is round (8m/26ft in internal diameter) and has thick walls (5m/16ft). Formerly it had three floors linked by mobile wooden ladders. Adjoining *(right)* are the ruins of the Governor's residence.

Outside the perimeter wall a path leads to the edge of the rocky escarpment which provides an extended view of the Seine Valley.

Take the one-way descent to rue Richard-Cœur-de-Lion to return to the town.

ADDITIONAL SIGHTS

★**Église Notre-Dame** – A well-balanced façade of twin towers flanked by a square staircase tower fronts Notre-Dame Church in which the 16C south side is a good example of the Flamboyant style and the 16C and 17C north side is Renaissance with round arches, Ionic pilasters, balustraded roofs, caryatids and Antique-style statues.

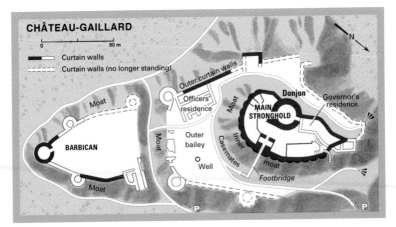

CHÂTEAU-GAILLARD

Curtain walls
Curtain walls (no longer standing)

Moat — Moat — Moat — Moat

BARBICAN

Officers' residence

Outer bailey

Well

Outer curtain walls

Donjon
MAIN STRONGHOLD

Governor's residence

Inner — moat

Casemates

Footbridge

N

Eating out

MID-RANGE

La Chaîne d'Or – *27 r. Grande* – ☎ *02 32 54 00 31* – *closed 24 Dec to 1 Feb, Tues lunch out of season, Sun evening and Mon* – *22.87/50.31€*. This fine house on the banks of the Seine will make a pleasant stopover during your tour of the region. Ask for one of the tables by the windows overlooking the river... But don't worry, wherever you are seated, you will appreciate the well-prepared renowned cuisine. A few rooms for those who wish to prolong their enjoyment...

Where to stay

MODERATE

Hameau de Surcy Bed and Breakfast – *29 r. de l'Huis* – *27510 Mézières-en-Vexin* – *13km/8.1mi southeast of Les Andelys via D 1* – ☎ *02 32 52 30 04* – *closed Nov to Mar* – *⊟* – *4 rooms: 32.01/41.16€*. Fresh air, peace and quiet and the charm of a fully operating farm. The front of the house looks undeniably gloomy but the old furniture, the fine timber-framed stairway and the rustic bedrooms add authenticity to the place. Farm products for sale.

Inside, the well-proportioned nave is 13C; the delicately ornamented triforium was remodelled in the 16C and the windows enlarged; the **organ★** and loft are Renaissance. The fine **stained glass★** in the south aisle and the tall windows in the south side of the nave date from the 16C. In the north transept and a nearby chapel are two lovely paintings by Quentin Varin. The Entombment in the south aisle beneath the tower is 16C, the Christ in the Tomb is 14C.

Église St-Sauveur – St Saviour's is Greek cross in ground plan and Gothic in style; the chancel is late 12C, the nave early 13C. The wooden porch stands on an early-15C stone foundation. Inside there is an organ dating from 1674.

Musée Normandie-Niémen ⊙ – "The 'Normandy Regiment', my companion in arms, upholds, confirms and increases the glory of France on Russian soil as on French soil for they have both suffered at the hand of a common enemy!" Those were the words written by General de Gaulle in Moscow on 9 December 1944 to pay homage to the **Normandie-Niémen squadron**. Today the museum perpetuates the memory of this illustrious regiment. Two galleries are devoted to Marcel Lefèvre, a native of Les Andelys whose career as a pilot was exceptional.

ARGENTAN

Population 16 413
Michelin map 60 folds 2 and 3 or 231 fold 43

From its hillside site, the small town of Argentan overlooks the confluence of the River Orne and River Ure.

Once part of the English possessions in France, Argentan returned to French rule during the reign of the Valois kings. It was in this small town in the 12C that the papal legates assembled to settle the disagreement between the English King, Henry II Plantagenet and his once trusted chancellor, Thomas Becket. It was from Argentan that the assassins of the Archbishop of Canterbury set out to accomplish their dire deed.

Although Colbert set up a lace factory in Alençon he did not neglect the lacemakers of Argentan. It was the rediscovery of 18C lace patterns for the "Point d'Argentan" in 1874 that enabled the characteristic Argentan pattern to regain its popularity.

The marked itinerary, known as "L'Encerclement" (The Encircling Movement), one of several in the Historical Area of the Battle of Normandy, goes through this town.

Battle of Normandy – In 1944 the closing stages of the Battle of Normandy were concentrated in the neighbourhood of Argentan. Following the success of the American breakthrough at Avranches and the failure of the German counter-attack of 7 August, the enemy forces began to realise the very real danger that was threatening their rear guard *(see map p 31)*. On 13 August the French 2nd Armoured Division

ARGENTAN

Ancienne chapelle
   St-Nicolas......................... **B**
Château (Palais
   de Justice)......................... **J**

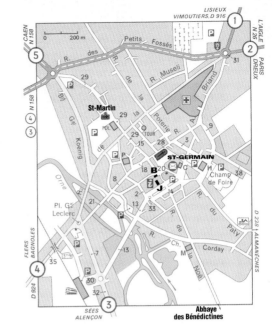

at Écouché (1) together with the American 5th Armoured Division in the Argentan sector formed the southern arm of the "pincer" action. When the Canadians took Falaise on 17 August the only course open to the German 7th Army was to retreat via the Dives Valley. A chaotic rush ensued. On the 19 August the allied troops met at Chambois and by nightfall *(6.30pm)* on the 21 August the fall of Tournai-sur-Dive marked the final stage in the Battle of Normandy.

★ÉGLISE ST-GERMAIN ⊙ *30min*

St Germanus' Church, badly damaged by shelling in 1944, was built in the Flamboyant style from the 15C to the 17C. The best view of the church is from place St-Germain. The belfry *(left)* was given its dome and lantern in 1631. The lantern tower over the transept crossing is Renaissance.

Walk round the church clockwise to view the unusual pentagonal east end (16C) and the unusual circular chapels terminating the transepts. At the base of the belfry a fine Flamboyant **porch** opens on to rue St-Germain.

The interior is characteristic of Flamboyant Gothic (ornate triforium and elaborate rib vaulting) but begins to show the influence of the Renaissance (width of the clerestory windows, ambulatory with its profusion of ribs and hanging keystones).

ADDITIONAL SIGHTS

Château – *Not open to visitors – unless you've broken the law!* The castle now serves as the Law Courts. This imposing rectangular castle, flanked by two square towers, was built in 1370 by Pierre II, Count of Alençon. The smaller central tower has some small openings and a doorway with a tympanum resting on sculpted capitals and slender columns.

Ancienne Chapelle St-Nicolas *30min* – The chapel, which was built in 1773, belonged to the castle. It was here that Marguerite de Lorraine, founder of the monastery of Ste-Claire, took her vows.

The Tourist Information Centre occupies the ground floor and the first floor houses a lovely carved 17C altarpiece *(displayed on request)*.

Église St-Martin ⊙ – The church, which was damaged in 1944, is dominated by an octagonal tower surmounted by a decapitated spire. The overall style is Flamboyant Gothic but, as the church was built early in the Renaissance, it presents several innovations, particularly in the clerestories of the nave and chancel.

(1) It was from his headquarters at the junction of D 2 and D 219 (commemorative monument) that General Leclerc made the historic decision on the 21 August to send a detachment to participate in the Liberation of Paris.

Eating out

MID-RANGE

Arnaud Viel Restaurant and La Renaissance Hotel – *20 av. de la 2e-Division-Blindée – ☏ 02 33 36 14 20 – closed 1-15 Aug, Feb school holidays, Sun evening and Mon – 18.29/39.64€.* Once you're comfortably sitting at one of the tables of the lovely and cosy dining room, Arnaud will share with you his passion for cooking. After the meal, you could play billiards or rest in the drawing room before retiring in your colourful soundproof bedroom.

Where to stay

MODERATE

Ferme de la Gravelle Bed and Breakfast – *In Sarceaux – 2.5km/1.5mi west of Argentan on the way to Flers – ☏ 02 33 67 04 47 – ⊭ – P – 4 rooms: 27.44/36.59€.* Peace and quiet are guaranteed in this country place close to Argentan. The owners will invite you to relax by the fireplace in the living room before showing you to one of their country-style bedrooms. Choose the attic room with its fine timberwork. An independent cottage is also available.

MID-RANGE

Pavillon de Gouffern – *61310 Silly-en-Gouffern – 11km/6.8mi west of Argentan via N 26 and D 729 – ☏ 02 33 36 64 26 – closed Feb, Sun evening and Mon lunch from mid-Nov to mid-Mar except holidays – P – 21 rooms: 53.36/106.71€ – ☕ 7.17€ – restaurant 14/36€.* When staying at this former 19C hunting lodge, you are likely to be woken up by birds singing in the hundred-year-old trees. Peaceful wooded surroundings and rustic setting enhanced by typical Norman half-timbering.

Sport

Hippodrome d'Argentan – *Rte de Crennes (D 113) – ☏ 02 33 67 08 02 – open for training on Tues, Thur and Fri mornings – closed July-Aug.* Vast racecourse where some twenty meetings take place every year. The timetable is available at the Tourist Office.

The "Point d'Argentan" (Argentan Lace Stitch) ⓥ – *Take boulevard du Général-de-Gaulle and rue de la Noë southeast, following signs to Abbaye des Bénédictines.*

The enclosed order of nuns has exclusive rights to this stitch. The Argentan stitch is a needlepoint lace and comprises a variety of motifs on a background which resembles the pattern of a honeycomb and looks more like tulle.

There are no workshops but one can ask to see specimens illustrating steps in the working of Argentan lace and samples of old and modern needlepoint lace.

EXCURSIONS

The Pays d'Argentan

The region around Argentan is a plain circled by woods: Écouves to the south, Gouffern to the north. The Orne Valley, which separates this region from the Pays d'Auge, entered into military history annals in August, 1944.

1 Meanders of the River Orne

32km/19.2mi – 1hr from Argentan and back. Leave Argentan travelling southwest, D 924.

Écouché – A tank from the French 2nd Armoured Division stands at the crossroads at the entrance to the town in commemoration of the fighting which took place from 13 to 20 August 1944.

The 15C-16C **church** ⓥ was never completed and the ruined 13C nave never rebuilt. The Renaissance triforium in the transepts and the chancel is worthy of note.

Take D 29 north towards Falaise; turn left.

★**Ménil-Glaise** – The **view**★ from the bridge takes in the rock escarpment crowned by a castle on the south bank of the Orne; there is another good view of the winding Orne from a terrace *(at the top of a steep and narrow climb turn sharp right and leave the car beyond the overgrown tennis courts on the left).*

Turn round; continue straight ahead passing (left) the path from the bridge and (right) the Batilly road; turn left onto D 924 to Argentan.

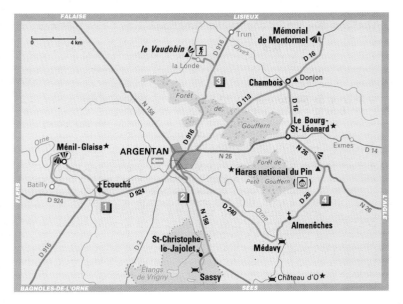

2 A church for travellers

9km/4.4mi south. Take N 158 from Argentan.

St-Christophe-le-Jajolet – The village church is a place of pilgrimage to St Christopher, the patron saint of travellers. On either side of the entrance are rather naive depictions of St Christopher watching over a car and plane and their passengers. On the day of pilgrimage (last Sunday in July and first Sunday of October) a procession of cars usually files past the monumental statue of St Christopher beside the church. Inside, in the chapel located in the right arm of the transept, there is a remarkable Flemish painting of the Virgin Mary.

Château de Sassy – The 18C château overlooks three terraces and an intricate formal garden with box hedges. The courtyard fountain and the balustrades came from the Château de Vrigny, destroyed during the Revolution.
Building began in 1760, was interrupted by the Revolution and continued in 1817 by the Marquis d'Ommy. In 1850 the château became the property of Étienne-Denis Pasquier (1767-1862), once Chancellor of France and an important figure during the Empire and the reign of Louis-Philippe. Early in the 20C a long wing was added at right angles, separating the main courtyard from the stable block.
The small salon is furnished with a tapestry after Le Brun, which belongs to the Month or the Royal Mansion series and shows Louis XVI and his queen surrounded by courtiers; the main salon presents several 17C tapestries, mementoes of Pasquier and a lock of Louis XVI's hair which was given by the king himself, while in the Bastille Prison, to Pasquier's father, who was counsel for the defence at the king's trial. The library displays a letter and telegram from Elizabeth II after her visit in 1967. The **chapel**, partly hidden by trees, contains a 15C Flemish oak altarpiece carved with scenes from the Passion, formerly in St Bavon Abbey in Ghent.

3 Le Vaudobin

12km/7mi – plus 15min walk there and back on slippery paths. From Argentan take D 916 northeast; after 7km/4mi (beyond Gouffern Forest) turn left; north of La Londe Park near the quarry; take the path left of the quarry entrance.

The path crosses the Meillon stream by stepping stones near an open-air wash-house, bears left round a large rock and climbs uphill past a rock bearing fossil imprints said locally to belong to oxen. From the top of the grassy mound there is a view of the Meillon Gorge and the Dives Valley.

4 Gouffern forests

About 3hr 30min. Leave Argentan to the northeast vie N 26, then take D 113 to the right.

As you leave Argentan, the road leads up into the Gouffern forest, crosses through it, then winds back down into the Dives Valley.

Chambois – A stele near a central crossroads recalls the joining up of Polish (1st Canadian Army) and American 3rd Army troops on 19 August 1944 to cut off the retreat of the German 7th Army.

The huge rectangular **keep** *(donjon)* buttressed by four towers is a good example of 12C military architecture. The church has an 11C stone spire and a fine *Descent from the Cross.*

Take D 16 uphill to Montormel.

Mémorial de Montormel ⊘ – The **battle** of the **Chambois** pocket, which raged from 18 to 22 August 1944, causing the death of 10 000 to 12 000 people, had a decisive impact on the outcome of the Battle of Normandy. Marshall Montgomery declared that it marked the true "beginning of the end of the war".

As you approach from the car park, the monument appears like a wrought-iron sculpture standing against a long stone wall; it commemorates the fierce fighting in this sector during the Battle of Normandy. From the American tank there is a wide **view★** over the plain, offering visitors a spectacle rendered even more moving by the use of the latest technological devices. Two galleries are particularly interesting: in one of them, a large relief map with a computer-controlled lighting system shows the different stages of the battle; the other gallery is more specifically devoted to the memory of the soldiers of the Polish 1st Armoured Division. A video on the subject is shown in a separate showroom.

★**Le Bourg-St-Léonard** – *11km/8mi east by N 26.* The Louis XV château was built by Jules David Cromot while he was chief civil servant at the Treasury. The elegance of its lines and the harmony of its design make it a most attractive building. The interior is embellished with Louis XV panelling, tapestries and splendid 18C furniture.

★**Haras national du Pin** – *See Hara national du PIN.*

From the stud farm, to the south, you can see the outline of the Écouves Forest.

Almenêches – The Renaissance church used to belong to a Benedictine **abbey**. The altars are decorated with statues or terracotta low-relief sculptures representing, on the left, the canonisation of St Opportune, a well-known local abbess.

Médavy – In the 11C a fortified house was built to defend the Orne crossing. In the 16C it was replaced by a stronghold with four corner towers. The site is now occupied by a sombre 18C **château** ⊘ consisting of a central block with two wings. The two isolated towers topped by lantern domes are relics of the former defensive ramparts.

Return to Argentan via D 240.

Château de Médavy

ARQUES-LA-BATAILLE ★

Population 2 546
Michelin map 52 fold 4 or 231 fold 11 – 8.5km/5mi southeast of Dieppe

Arques, which lies at the confluence of the River Varenne and River Béthune, was the site of a famous historical battle.

Battle of Arques – When **Henri IV** was still a king without a kingdom, he possessed the fortress of Arques, said to be "capable of withstanding cannon". He gathered within the ramparts every piece of artillery he could find and dug in, with 7 000 men, at the confluence of the River Eaulne and River Béthune, to await the 30 000 soldiers of the League under the Duke of Mayenne.

The battle took place on 21 September 1589. One of the fogs, so frequent in the region, delayed the artillery action and Henri's troops were in a very bad position indeed. Fortunately the fog lifted and the cannon thundered into the ranks of the Leaguers. Mayenne, who had promised to bring back his enemy "tied and bound", beat a hasty retreat.

A monument on the edge of Arques Forest commemorates this passage of arms.

★CHÂTEAU ⊘ 30min

From place Desceliers, where the town hall (Mairie) is located, take the second road to the right, uphill to the castle entrance; the road is very narrow and winding.

The castle is an interesting feudal ruin standing on a rocky promontory; the 12C keep occupies the highest point. The earliest part was built between 1038 and 1043. In 1053 it was attacked by William the Conqueror; it was reconstructed by Henri I in 1123. In the 14C it was strengthened by the addition of new towers and equipped to receive artillery at the beginning of the 16C. In 1584 it was taken back from the Leaguers, who had become its masters.

A triple door leads into the castle. On the back of the last one a carved low relief depicts Henri IV at the battle of Arques. At the other end of the courtyard, on the right, stands the mighty square keep with its solid buttresses. Its floors were well separated as a defensive measure.

To walk round, follow the old sentry walk on the side of the moat and enjoy the charming view of the Arques Valley.

Église Notre-Dame-de-l'Assomption – Rebuilt around 1515, the Church of Our Lady of the Assomption was given a belfry in the 17C. The façade is flanked by its twin turrets and a pierced buttress; a gallery encircles the nave.

Inside, the nave was roofed in the 16C with wood cradle vaulting on pendentives; the chancel and transept, a fine Flamboyant group, are separated from the nave by a Renaissance rood screen. The apse windows are 16C (restored). A chapel to the right of the chancel with 16C woodwork contains a small bust of Henri IV and an inscription commemorating the battle; the woodwork is 16C. Note a 15C Pietà in the south chapel.

Château d'Arques ruins

The Lady Chapel, to the left of the chancel, has 17C woodwork signed (on the right): *"Raudin, ton amy"*. (Raudin, your friend).
In the centre are the coats of arms of the donors.

EXCURSIONS

★**Château de Miromesnil** ⊘ – *12km/7mi – allow 1hr. Leave Dieppe by D 925.*
Magnificent beech trees line the road to Offranville.
The château was built after the Battle of Arques (1589). The Marquis de Miromesnil, Louis XVI's Chancellor, died there in 1796. Facing the main courtyard is the monumental Louis XIII central façade, capped by a great slate roof and articulated by pilasters surmounted by sculpted vases; it is framed by slender turrets and lower wings.
In the hall there is a display case containing documents connected with the birth of Guy de Maupassant in the château on 5 August in 1850; also souvenirs of Albert de Mun (1841-1914), politician and Catholic orator.
The **Montebello Salon** is devoted to Maréchal Lannes, Duc de Montebello; the furniture is in the Empire style; the clock on the mantlepiece was presented by Napoleon. The **bedroom** of the Marquis de Miromesnil contains a collection of books stamped with his coat of arms. In the **study** is the only copy of the land register of the marquisate.

The **south front**, in the Henri IV style, is flanked by two cylindrical pepper-pot towers; brick predominates with stone used as trims round the windows and for the coins.

Beyond a magnificent stand of beech trees is a 16C **chapel**, part of an earlier château. The sober flint and limestone walls contrast with the rich interior decoration dating from 1780: stained glass, carved woodwork, painted stone statues.

Jardins et potager fleuri – Flowers border the well-ordered vegetable plots. Brick walls enclose the garden and serve as a support for espaliered fruit trees. Here "business" and pleasure mix in lovely harmony!

Forêt d'Arques

30km/19mi – about 1hr from Arques and back. The forest roads are sometimes narrow; drive carefully. From Arques-la-Bataille take D 56 east.

This forest of beech trees is the crown atop a spur surrounded by the River Eaulne and the River Béthune; the two join forces to become the Arques. D 56 crosses the river, then the southern part of the forest, alongside traces of an ancient Roman road.

St-Nicolas-d'Aliermont – Like other villages on the narrow Aliermont plateau and along D 56, St-Nicolas is a "street-village", a type which historians associate with 12C and 13C colonisation based around the existing roads. Today, St-Nicolas is an electronic and precision goods centre manufacturing alarm and electric clocks, meters and components for telephones.

East of St-Nicolas, turn left onto D 149.

Envermeu – The Gothic church, enhanced with Renaissance motifs, is incomplete. It nevertheless has a remarkable **chancel**★ with hanging keystones and an apse in which the ribbing is charmingly light and elegant. The spiral columns are the work of a skilled craftsman. Note the beautifully carved wooden pulpit with canopy above.

From Envermeu take D 920 west; turn left onto D 54 to Martin-Église.

Martin-Église – The village, lying on the edge of the forest, is famous for its waters teeming with trout.

Take D 1 towards Arques; pass by the bridge over the Eaulne and turn left onto a narrow road. After 600m/660yd turn right by a house onto the forest road.

The road runs beside the forest providing attractive glimpses of the Arques Valley.

Monument commémoratif de la bataille d'Arques – *15min on foot there and back. Leave the car on the grass on the right of a sharp left bend.*

A path leads to the obelisk erected as a tribute to the victory achieved by Henri IV on this site. Arques-la-Bataille can be seen on the far side of the valley, dominated by its castle.

After the Rond Henri-IV at the end of a straight stretch of road, turn right onto the forest road.

The road crosses another part of the forest with fine beech trees and picnic areas and then winds its way downhill to a crossroads.

At the crossroads turn right onto D 56 to return to Arques.

ARROMANCHES-LES-BAINS

Population 409
Michelin map 54 fold 15 or 231 fold 17
Local map see Plages du DÉBARQUEMENT

Arromanches is a modest seaside resort which owes its fame to the gigantic landing operation which took place in June 1944. In the roadstead of the little port are the remains of a Mulberry harbour, the most extraordinary industrial and maritime achievement of the war.

The marked itinerary "Overlord-L'Assaut" (Overlord-The Onslaught), one of several described in the Historical Area of the Battle of Normandy, goes through this town.

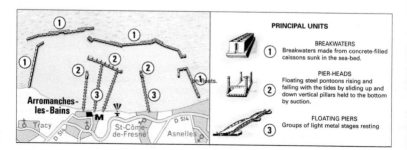

Artificial port – "If we want to land, we must take our harbours with us" was the conclusion of a British officer even before it had been decided to use the Calvados Coast as a beachhead.

The first plans for an artificial port go back to 1942. The lessons learned from the Dieppe raid confirmed the impossibility of counting on the Channel ports: if they were captured after severe fighting, their installations would have been unusable by the Allies.

The Calvados Coast, which was chosen as the beachhead for strategic reasons, offered no natural protection: bad weather could have catastrophic effects on the minutely planned landing operations. Thus from September 1943 a prefabricated port appeared to be the only solution.

Mulberries – Arromanches harbour was chosen as the landing point for Mulberry B for British troops, while Mulberry A for the Americans was taken to Omaha Beach. The establishment of these artificial ports meant the laying of 146 Phoenix caissons, representing 500 000t of concrete (each one was 70m/230ft long, 20m/66ft high and 15m/49ft wide); 33 jetties and 16km/10mi of floating "roads". All this was towed across the Channel at just over 6.5kph/4mph.

Mulberry B at Arromanches, later known as Port Winston, enabled 9 000t of material to be landed each day. This figure was equivalent to the tonnage handled by the port of Le Havre prior to the war. More than 500 000t had been landed by the end of August when the return to service of Cherbourg and Antwerp and the rapid sanding up of the artificial port ended its part in the war.

Several Phoenix caissons are still there today. The best place to spot them from (preferably at low tide) is the belvedere situated on D 514 leading to Asnelles (*See Plages du DÉBARQUEMENT*).

Musée du Débarquement ⊙ – This Invasion Museum contains a collection of models, photographs, dioramas, arms and equipment of the Allied forces. A plan, facing the anchorage, makes it easier to understand the landing operations. Royal Navy films of the landing are shown.

The new cinema **Arromanches 360** ⊙ is situated a little further on; this circular screen cinema shows the film *The Price of Freedom* in which archive footage is mixed with scenes re-enacted on the various landing sites. The 360 degree viewing makes the dramatic effect more intense and involves the spectator in the action.

Eating out

MODERATE

Le Bistro d'Arromanches – *23 r. du Mar.-Joffre* – ☎ *02 31 22 31 32 – closed 15 Dec to 25 Jan, Mon and Tues except July-Aug and holidays – 11.43/18.29€.* The owner drew her inspiration from English pubs when choosing the decoration of her bistro. The warm and comfortable setting is ideal for enjoying the carefully prepared local specialities. The mezzanine above has a selection of toys and you can watch cartoons on request.

Where to stay

MODERATE

L'Ancienne École Bed and Breakfast – *Rte d'Arromanches – 14960 Meuvaines – 8km/5mi southeast of Arromanches via D 65 – ☎ 02 31 22 39 59 – 3 rooms: 29/39€ – meal 12.96€.* There are no longer any noisy schoolchildren in the playground where tables have been set near the lawn for you to enjoy the tasty local cuisine, before retiring to one of the attic bedrooms. Past discipline has long been replaced by a convivial welcome...

MID-RANGE

Hôtel de la Marine – *Quai du Canada.* ☎ *02 31 22 34 19 – closed 12 Nov to 4 Feb –* **P** *– 30 rooms: 45.73/59.46€ –* ☳ *6.86€ – restaurant 15/30€.* The name of this hotel is very appropriate since you can see the blue horizon in the distance and, closer, the waves breaking on the beach. Ask for a room overlooking the sea. Dining-room with wooden ceiling and panoramic view. Well-prepared food.

Victoria Hotel – *Chemin de l'Église – 14117 Tracy-sur-Mer – 2.5km/1.5mi SW of Arromanches via D 516 and minor road – ☎ 02 31 22 35 37 – closed Oct to Mar –* **P** *– 14 rooms: 54.88/82.32€ –* ☳ *6.56€.* Situated in the heart of the countryside, this pleasant 19C stone-built house hides a shaded flower garden behind its outer wall. If you are looking for peace and quiet, you will find it in the spacious bedrooms with their sloping ceilings on the second floor.

Pays d'AUGE ★

Michelin map 54 folds 17 and 18 or 231 folds 19, 20, 31 and 32

The Pays d'Auge provides a wonderful hinterland to the beaches of the **Côte Fleurie** *(see p 162)*, with its pasturelands, thatched cottages, manor houses and local products including cider and cheeses.

The Auge Region is fortunate to have retained its charming rural landscapes, partially covered in original woodland, and a chalk escarpment (30m/98ft high) overlooking the Dives Valley and the Caen area. The escarpment is known to geographers as the Côte d'Auge.

Fame has come through its legendary *teurgoule*, a rice dish cooked in milk and seasoned with cinnamon, as well as its cider, calvados and tasty cheeses: Camembert, Pont-l'évêque, Pavé d'Auge and Livarot.

Manor houses – The farmhouses of the Pays d'Auge are as isolated within their orchards *(clos)* as those of the Pays de Caux in their farmsteads *(see p 126)*. The farm buildings, set around the living quarters, contain the oven, the cider press, the apple stores, the barn, the dovecot and the stables. The dairy is usually in a choice spot.

One of the main appeals of this country lies in the diversity of its many rural-style, pleasant to look at, and always perfectly adapted to the country setting.

In apple-blossom time

1 Côte d'Auge: from Lisieux to Cabourg

26km/16mi – allow 1hr.

★★**Lisieux** – See LISIEUX.

From Lisieux take N 13 ⑥ west. In La Boissière turn right onto D 59.

Ancienne Abbaye du Val Richer – Following the destruction of the Cistercian abbey, only the 17C hospice remained. The minister François Guizot (1787-1874), leader of the conservative constitutional monarchists during the July monarchy, historian and briefly Ambassador to England, retired here after the 1848 revolution until his death in 1874.

The Schlumberger brothers *(see p 157)* spent time here working on their inventions.

Further north the château of Roque-Baignard appears in a pleasant setting.

At the crossroads turn left onto D 101 and bear right onto D 117. At the next crossroads turn left onto D 16 and right onto D 85.

★**Clermont-en-Auge** – *Follow the signs "Chapelle de Clermont – Panorama".*
Leave the car at the start of the beech-lined avenue leading to the **chapel** ⊙ *(15min there and back)*. From the east end there is an extensive **panorama**★ of the Dives and Vie valleys; in the distance stretches the Caen countryside, bounded by the dark line of the Bocage hills. The church contains a number of statues. St Marcouf and St Thibeault in polychrome stone stand in the chancel and on either side of the altar St John the Baptist and St Michael.

★Beuvron-en-Auge – This charming village has kept around 40 lovely old timber-framed houses set around the central square, testifying to the history of half-timbering throughout the centuries. The former covered market, twice pulled down and now converted into a shopping centre, adds an extra picturesque note. A pleasant time can be had strolling along the winding alleys and pausing to sample a *teurgoule* served with **falues** and to purchase the delicious *produits du terroir* on sale from nearby stalls. There is a very pretty manor at the south exit from the village, decorated with wood carvings.

Teurgoule

This traditional recipe from the Pays d'Auge dates back to the prosperous days in which the commerce of spices and condiments thrived in Honfleur. Back then, the wives of local sailors hit upon an interesting idea: they began adding cinnamon to the bowls of rice that they would leave to simmer for several hours in a baker's oven.

To make *teurgoule*, carefully mix 3.5 pints of unskimmed milk with 4oz of rice and 3oz of caster sugar. Add one teaspoon of cinnamon and a pinch of salt. Pour the ingredients into a pie-dish and cook at a low temperature for at least 5hr. This dessert can be served hot or cold.

Traditionally, *teurgoule* was often accompanied by *falues*, flat brioches made with syrup and yeast.

Take D 49 north through Putot-en-Auge; cross N 175 and pass under the motorway. Fork right to Cricqueville.

Criqueville-en-Auge – The **château**, completed in 1584, and its three main buildings with vast roofs, remain typically medieval while its chequered stone and brick decoration makes it characteristically Norman.

From Sarlabot to Dives there is a beautiful panorama over the Calvados coast on either side of the mouth of the Orne.

★Dives-sur-Mer – *See DIVES-SUR-MER.*

Continue to Cabourg via D 45.

② Traditional Normandy: from Villers-sur-Mer to Lisieux

36km/22mi – about 1hr.

On this drive there are extensive views over the Lower Touques Valley. *From Villers take D 118 southeast.*

Beaumont-en-Auge – This small town, remarkably situated on a spur commanding the Touques Valley, was the birthplace of the mathematician and physicist **Simon Laplace** (1749-1827). His house and statue can be seen on place de Verdun.

Take D 58 south; turn left onto N 175; at the crossroads turn right onto D 280 and pass under the motorway.

Eating out

MODERATE

Auberge de la Route du Cidre – *14340 Montreuil-en-Auge – 14km/8.7mi northwest of Lisieux via N 13 then D 59 – ☎ 02 31 63 12 27 – closed 15 Dec to 13 Feb, Wed and Thur except July-Aug – reservation essential – 14.94/23.48€.*

If you like cider, this place is for you! In this country inn you can select a particular cider and, to go with it, you can choose one of the regional specialities suggested on the menu. Don't worry if you don't like apple juice, wine is also available!

Where to stay

MID-RANGE

Au Repos des Chineurs – *Chemin de l'Église – 14340 Notre-Dame-d'Estrées – 15km/9.3mi west of Lisieux via N 13 then D 50 – ☎ 02 31 63 72 51 – closed 1 Jan to 10 Mar, Tues and Wed out of season. – 🅿 – reservation advisable Sat-Sun – 10 rooms: 50.31/103.67€ – ☕ 9.15€ – tearoom.* Close to the station and the old town with its busy shopping area, this comfortable modern hotel is perfectly soundproof. Buffet for breakfast to start the day well.

St-Hymer – Pleasantly set in a valley, the village has a 14C **church** with traces of Romanesque in its style. It belonged to the priory and was one of the last Jansenist centres of activity in the 18C. Its belfry is a replica of that of Port-Royal-des-Champs, the famous abbey southwest of Paris.

Inside there is some fine 17C and 18C woodwork, 14C stained-glass windows and canvases by the Rouen painter Jean Restout.

The sometimes winding road from St-Hymer to Quilly-le-Vicomte is particularly pleasant in the spring when the tall hedges are in flower and the orchards in blossom. Several attractive half-timbered farms are visible from the road.

Pierrefitte-en-Auge – In the 13C **church** ⊙ the panelled arches of the nave are decorated with cameo paintings of landscapes. There is a fine 16C rood beam.

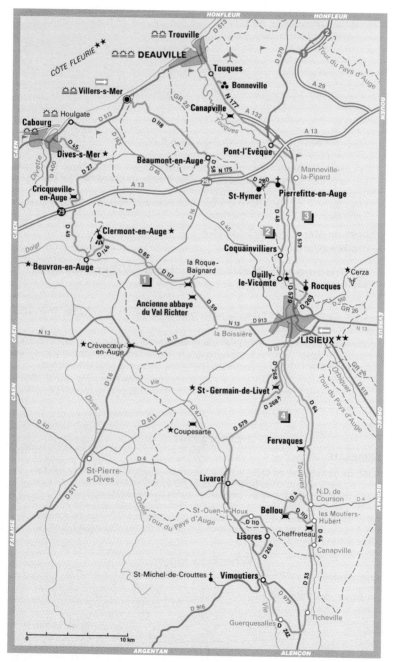

Coquainvilliers – The small village is set in the very heart of the attractive Pays d'Auge. It houses the **Distillerie du Moulin de la Foulonnerie** ⊘, where a guided tour enlightens visitors on the making of apple brandy (Calvados) and traditional distillation techniques involving the use of "continuous stills". The storehouses in which the cider distillates slowly age in oak barrels, can also be seen. The tour ends with a tasting session accompanied by comments.

Ouilly-le-Vicomte – The **church** ⊘ standing beside the road which spans the Touques, is one of the oldest in Normandy, dating from the 10C and 11C. It has a Renaissance altar in carved wood, a lectern from the same period, modern stained-glass windows by Grüber and a 17C Crucifixion (3 statues).

Continue east; at the crossroads turn right onto D 579 to Lisieux.

Few people know that the region called Pays d'Auge has given birth to no less than six AOC labels of quality (appellation d'origine contrôlée). *Three have been granted to local cheeses and three to beverages made with regional produce: Camembert de Normandie, Pont-l'évêque, Livarot, Cidre du Pays d'Auge, Pommeau de Normandie and Calvados du Pays d'Auge.*

③ Vallée de la Touques from Lisieux to Trouville

28km/17mi – about 1hr.

Although there is heavy traffic in the holiday season on the roads north along the Touques Valley (D 579 and N 177), they offer glimpses of the Touques and the alternating orchards and pasture on the fertile east bank.

Most of the place names date back to the time of the Viking invasion.

Leave Lisieux via boulevard Herbert-Fournet, D 579 north; turn right onto D 263.

Rocques – The village **church** in the centre of its old burial ground has two wooden porches. The chancel and the tower date from the 13C. Inside note the torches and painting of the Brothers of Charity and several polychrome wooden statues.

Take D 262 northwest back to D 579.

North of Manneville-la-Pipard there is a good view from the hilltop.

Pont-l'Évêque – Since the 13C Pont-l'Évêque has been famous for its cheese. As it was badly damaged during the Second World War, only a few old houses remain, mostly in rue St-Michel and rue de Vaucelles. The Aigle d'Or Inn (68 rue de Vaucelles) was a post house in the 16C and has retained the Norman courtyard of the period.

The **Église St-Michel** is a fine church in Flamboyant style flanked by a square tower. The modern stained-glass windows (1963-64) are by François Chapuis. An interesting wooden balcony decorates the old **Dominican Convent**, a 16C half-timbered building beside the Law Courts (Tribunal). Exhibitions are held in the **Hôtel Montpensier**, a building in the Louis XIII style with two corner pavilions. The 18C **Hôtel Brilly** (restored) was the birthplace of the dramatist, Robert de Flers (1872-1927); it now houses the town hall and the Tourist Information Centre. The **Leisure Centre** (Centre de Loisirs), south of the town, consists of woodland and a lake (59ha/146 acres) with windsurfing, boating and camping facilities.

★**La Belle Époque de l'Automobile** ⊘ – *South of the town along D 48, follow the marked itinerary.* Set up in the outbuildings of the Château de Betteville, this automobile collection features around 600 exhibits. Among the most remarkable are a Marne Renault AG taxi cab (1911), a Clément-Bayard fruit and vegetable van (1910), a 1910 Vinot et Deguingand, a 22 horse-power Delaunay-Belleville (1911, with new bodywork dating from 1922) which once belonged to Marshall Joffre, a model 30 Cadillac (1912) and a Ford T, reflecting the United States' economic prosperity during the 1920s. Note the collection of motorcycles (Triumph, Alcyon, Terrot, Magnat-Debon...) and the horse-drawn vehicles such as the 1865 perambulator and the late 19C omnibus. Reed organs (Mortier or Decap) provide an unexpected musical touch.

Canapville – The 13C-15C **Manoir des Évêques de Lisieux** ⊘ is one of the most charming country houses in the Pays d'Auge. It consists of the large manor, decorated with three monumental stone chimneys grouped round the stairway tower, and the small manor with a bishop's head carved on the entrance post. The furnished 18C ground floor rooms inside display collections of Chine porcelain. Visitors may also be shown the cider press.

Bonneville-sur-Touques – William the Conqueror's **castle**, of which only the moat and fortified enclosure remain, stands in a beautiful setting. From the top of the John Lackland tower there is a fine **panorama** of the sea and Deauville to the north, the Touques Valley and surrounding countryside to the south. From beneath the tower an underground passage led to the port of Touques. The origin of the castle goes back to the 11C, its position enabling the occupiers to watch over the port. Between 1203 and 1449 it belonged in turn to the English and the French. Only in 1451 did it become French for good.

Manoir des Évêques de Lisieux, Canapville

Touques – William the Conqueror's port stands at the mouth of the river, from which it takes its name. Old houses line the Ouies stream. The Église St-Thomas (12C) owes its name to a visit by Thomas Becket; the **Église St-Pierre** ⊙ (11C), now deconsecrated, is used for exhibitions.

Take N 177 to Deauville then Trouville.

⌂⌂⌂**Deauville** – *See DEAUVILLE.*

⌂⌂**Trouville** – *See TROUVILLE.*

4 HAUTE VALLÉE DE LA TOUQUES

75km/47mi – about 3hr from Lisieux and back – see LISIEUX

AVRANCHES ★

Population 8 638
Michelin map 59 fold 8 or 231 fold 38
Local map see Baie du MONT-ST-MICHEL

The pretty and lively city of Avranches is one of the oldest towns in Normandy and its origins date back to early antiquity. **St Aubert**, Bishop of Avranches in the 8C, instigated the foundation of Mont-St-Michel and the two centres are therefore closely linked not only geographically but also historically. The surrounding area is known for the Avranchin breed of sheep.

The marked itineraries "La Contre-attaque" (the Counter-Attack) and "Cobra-La Percée" (the Breakthrough) described in the Historical Area of the Battle of Normandy both go through Avranches; the former starts from here, whereas the latter ends here.

HISTORICAL NOTES

The Vision of Bishop Aubert (8C) – Legend has it that a dense forest covered Mont-St-Michel Bay when St Michael appeared twice before **Aubert** and commanded him to raise a chapel in his honour on the rock then called Mount Tombe. Although sanctuaries to St Michael were built by tradition upon high rocks, the Bishop of Avranches remained sceptical and vacillated. St Michael settled the matter by reappearing and digging an imperious finger into the doubting man's skull. Aubert could delay no longer. A skull with a hole in it is displayed in the treasury of St Gervase Basilica, recalling this legend.

Henry II Repents – Relations between the King of England **Henry Plantagenet**, who was also Duke of Normandy, and his Archbishop of Canterbury, **Thomas Becket**, became very bitter; one day the King cried out "Will no one rid me of this insolent priest?" Four knights took the words as a command and, on 29 December 1170, Thomas Becket was murdered in Canterbury Cathedral. The Pope excommunicated Henry II, who pleaded innocence of the crime and begged absolution. Robert of Torigni, Abbot of Mont-St-Michel, obtained permission to hold a council attended by the king at Avranches and so it was that at the door of the cathedral (collapsed in 1794) that Henry II, barefoot and dressed only in a shirt, made public penance on his knees on 22 May 1172 for the death of his archbishop.

Barefoot Peasants' War – The imposition of the Salt Tax in western France in 1639 brought about a revolt by the Avranches saltworkers which broke out on 7 July of the same year. Insurrection spread rapidly and armed bands led by Jean Quétil, known as John Barefoot, pillaged town and countryside. Mortain and Pontorson were held to ransom. It took all the energy of Marshal Gassion to suppress the revolt.

The "Avranches Breakthrough" – It was from Avranches on 31 July 1944 that General Patton began the swift advance which smashed the German Panzer counter-offensive launched from Mortain *(see map p 31)*. The Avranches breakthrough marked the beginning of the attack which was to take the American 3rd Army through to Bastogne in Belgium.

SIGHTS

Jardin des plantes – The botanical gardens, once the property of a Capuchin monastery that was destroyed during the French Revolution, are well situated on a gentle slope below the town. Up to 1882, the grounds were a famous botanical park used for medicinal purposes. The pleasant fragrance of the purple or white sprays of the garden heliotrope, a shrubby perennial, pervades the garden. Of particular interest among the trees are, on the left going downhill, a monkey puzzle or *araucaria* and in the centre a magnificent copper beech. From the terrace *(viewing table)* at the far end of the garden, there is a **panorama★** of the bay. On a clear day, the sweeping view extends from the Champeaux cliffs to the valleys of the River Sée and River Sélune, with the slender silhouette of Mont-St-Michel rising from the sands, whose shimmering hues with the light and time of day. The sight is particularly beautiful by moonlight. The doorway from the 11C chapel of St-Georges-de-Bouillet, which was set up in the garden in 1843, stands facing the huge, restful bay.

La Plate-forme – From place Daniel-Huet, walk along the garden of the Sous-préfecture to reach the site of the old cathedral. This little square, known locally as the Platform, contains the paving stone (chained off) on which Henry II made public penance in 1172.

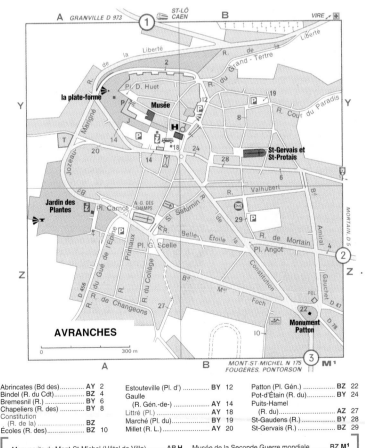

AVRANCHES

Eating out

MODERATE

Le Littré – *8 r. du Dr-Gilbert* – ☎ *02 33 58 01 66* – *nivard.littre@wanadoo.fr* – *closed 24 June to 9 July, Sun and Mon (except Mon in July and Aug)* – *15.24/19.51€*. Regular customers prefer to sit in the low armchairs at the bar and it is often difficult to find room there. However, have no fear, there is bound to be a table waiting for you in one of the other two rooms, where you can enjoy the establishment's traditional cooking.

Where to stay

MODERATE

La Croix d'Or Hotel – *83 r. de la Constitution* – ☎ *02 33 58 04 88* – *closed Jan and Sun evening from 15 Oct to 25 Mar* – 🅿 – *27 rooms: 35.06/60.22€* – ☕ *6.10€* – *restaurant 17.99/48.78€*. This low, half-timbered house, extends into the middle of an attractive garden adorned with numerous blooms in season. The rustic decor is enhanced by copper objects hanging on the stone walls. The bedrooms are elegantly decorated. The best overlook the garden.

MID-RANGE

Manoir de la Croix Bed and Breakfast – *50530 Montviron* – *8km/5mi northwest of Avranches via D 973 towards Granville then D 41* (1km/0.6mi beyond Montviron) – ☎ *02 33 60 68 30* – ☒ – *4 rooms: 42.69/65.55€*. This 19C Anglo-Norman-style house stands proudly in the middle of a fine garden planted with trees, including a few palm trees. Guests who are keen on antique furniture will love the two vast suites, one in Empire style the other in Louis-Philippe style. There are two additional cosy rooms. Smoking is banned altogether.

From the terrace there is a wide **view**★ embracing Mont-St-Michel and the surrounding countryside *(bocage)*.

Monument Patton – Erected on the site of a strategic crossroads located south of the town and destroyed during the air raids, this imposing memorial commemorates the deployment of General Patton's troops towards Brittany and the areas surrounding the Basse-Normandie (in July 1944 with the American 3rd Army). The square on which it stands is now American territory: the soil and trees were brought over from the United States.

Museum ⊙ – Housed in the outbuildings of the former episcopal palace restored in the late 15C by Bishop Louis de Bourbon, whose family coat of arms appears over the doorway, the museum contains rich and varied collections illustrating the history of the town.

Abraham sacrifice (detail),
Missal from the Mont-St-Michel monastery

Bibliothèque Municipale d'Avranches

The archeological gallery displays a number of works including several impressive granite sarcophagi and alabaster statues from 15C England, along with vestiges of the former cathedral which no longer stands. The museum's main collections consist of costumes, furniture and early exhibits that enlighten visitors on everyday life in Avranches during the 19C. Note the fine displays of sacred objects.

Lastly, as an introduction to the historical archives of the local library, an exhibition recreates the atmosphere of a scriptorium such as it would have existed in the Mont-St-Michel area during the Middle Ages.

Manuscrits du Mont-St-Michel ⊙ – Inside the town hall, an old library houses a collection of 8C to 15C **manuscripts**★★, largely from Mont-St-Michel Abbey. Avranches was known in the Middle Ages as a city of learning and its schools were reputed. A thematic exhibition, renewed every month, enables visitors to admire the best pieces of the collection: famous texts from ancient Greece and Rome (Aristotle, Cicero) and from the Middle Ages (Abélard, Chronicle of Robert of Torigni on the foundation of Mont-St-Michel), Romanesque illuminated manuscripts (patristics, history, cartulary, astronomy), Gothic books (Bibles, missals and books of hours).

Basilique St-Gervais-et-St-Protais ⊙ – This vast basilica dating from the late 19C is interesting for its treasury of St Gervase. In addition to major exhibits such as St Aubert's head reliquary, the collection includes some liturgical garments. There is also a collection of sculptures from the 14C to the 18C.

Musée de la Seconde Guerre mondiale ⊙ – *5km/3mi south by* ③ *on N 175.* This museum set up on the roadside is devoted to the Avranches breakthrough during the Second World War. Dummies all highly equipped (arms, motorcycles and transmitting equipment) recreate this historic campaign. The German exhibits are to be found on the ground floor (note the bell that sounded the alarm on the morning of 6 June 1944 on Pointe du Hoc) whereas the various Allied exhibits are upstairs.

Excursion

Barrages de la Sélune – *13km/8mi southeast.* Where the River Sélune cuts a narrow pass through the great granite cliffs of the Armorican Massif, dams have been built to control the river's flow. There are attractive reservoirs sought out by anglers and water sports enthusiasts alike.

BAGNOLES-DE-L'ORNE ✦✦

Population 875
Michelin map 60 fold 1 or 231 fold 42

Bagnoles-de-l'Orne with Tessé-la-Madeleine is the largest spa in western France. In addition to the healing waters, the countryside itself inspires well-being, and the lovely lakeside **setting★** invites calm. The lake is formed by the Vée, a tributary of the Mayenne, before it enters a deep gorge cut through the massif of the Andaines Forest. The site can be seen best by walking from Tessé-la-Madeleine to the Roc au Chien.

BAGNOLES AND ITS REJUVENATING SPA WATERS

Horse Medicine – Rather than kill his horse Rapide, when it grew old, Hugues de Tessé abandoned it in the forest. Some time later he was surprised to see Rapide return to the stables in fine fettle. He tracked the hoof marks to a spring, where the horse had bathed, and bathed in it himself, with similar rejuvenating effects.

The local peasants flocked to see and a Capuchin, cured of his ills, fulfilled a vow by making a gigantic leap (4m/13ft) between the rock spikes high above the spring. Since then the spot has been known as Capuchin's Leap.

SIGHTS

★Parc de l'établissement thermal – The undulating parkland surrounding the spa building is planted with pines, oaks and chestnut trees. The Allée du Dante on the east bank of the Vée, which is often crowded with bathers, leads from the lake to the spa building. Other alleys in the park wind towards Capuchin's Leap and to the site known as the "Abri Janolin". Shops line the lakefront rue des Casions.

Treatment

The establishment in the Vée Gorge is supplied exclusively by the Great Spring (Grande Source) where water at a temperature of 25°C/77°F gushes forth at the rate of 50 000l/11 000gal an hour. It is the only hot spring in western France and its acidic, mildly radioactive waters have a low mineral content. Bathing, the essential part of any treatment, can be accompanied by showers or localised showers, and pulverisations. The water may also be drunk and there is a pump room in the entrance hall.

The waters are usually taken for circulatory disorders, in particular after phlebitis and as a preventive treatment against varicose veins. The treatment is also recommended for glandular disorders and the after-effects of bone fractures.

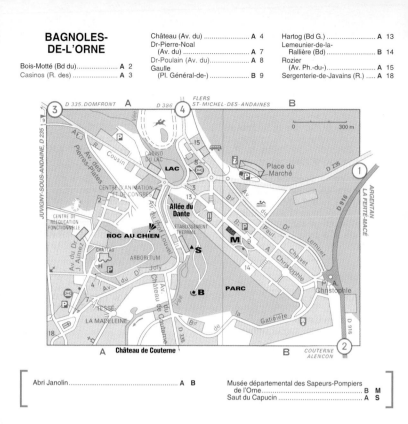

A   Château de Couterne

B   COUTERNE
ALENCON

★**The Roc au Chien** – *45min on foot there and back or in the afternoon only, 30min there and back by the small train* ⊙.

▣ Start from the church and walk up the fine avenue du Château; go through the main gateway which opens on to the avenue and enter the public park of Tessé *(arboretum containing 150 different tree species, bird-watching trail, children's playground and other amusements).*

Go to the château. It was built in the second half of the 19C in the "neo-medieval" style which appealed so strongly to Viollet-le-Duc; it presently houses the town hall. Take the avenue on the right which overlooks the Bagnoles Gorge. After passing some fine trees, notably some sequoias well over 100 years old, the path arrives at the rocky promontory, the Roc au Chien. From here there is a lovely **view**★ of Bagnoles beside the lake (left) and the spa building and its park (right).

Musée départemental des Sapeurs-Pompiers de l'Orne ⊙ (**B M**) – The Church of the Sacred Heart (deconsecrated) is home to the Fire Brigade Museum with its important collection of horse-drawn hand pumps, the oldest being *La Distinguée* which is pre-1790. The history of local fire fighting services is illustrated by badges, medals, helmets, uniforms, fire-fighting appliances, breathing apparatus and radios.

EXCURSIONS

Château de Couterne – *1.5km/1mi south of Bagnoles by D 335. Park the car by the bridge. The interior is not open to the public.* The massive brick and granite château (16C and 18C) is reflected in the waters of the Vée.

La Ferté-Macé – *6km/3.6mi north via D 916.* This small town has retained a number of 18C and 19C buildings and houses as a reminder of its past activity in the textile industry. Today, its commercial and industrial role at regional level in the fields of printing, high tech electronics and ready-made clothes is still important; gourmets acknowledge its gastronomic reputation essentially founded on *tripes en brochettes*; these are made from the stomachs and feet of cattle and skewered on to small hazel wood sticks.

The recently developed 60ha/148-acre tourist complex, which includes a leisure park (pedalos, windsurfing, fishing, climbing, swin-golf etc) and a dozen holiday houses, provides added entertainment for the guests and patients of the nearby spa, Bagnoles-de-l'Orne.

Abig, lively market is held on Thursday mornings.

Eating out

MODERATE

La Terrasse – r. des Casinos – ☎ 02 33 37 81 44 – closed 20 Nov to 27 Dec, Tue evening 1 Apr-15 Oct, Sun evening and Mon 15 Oct-1 Apr – 11.43/25.92€. This restaurant may escape your notice, for there is nothing special about the outside. But you'll be glad you walked in when you taste the good regional cuisine and the fish specialities. The atmosphere is warm and inviting and there is also a sheltered terrace.

Normandie – 2 av. Dr Lemuet - ☎ 02 33 30 71 30 – closed 13 Nov-28 Feb, Sun and Mon in Mar - 13.72/29.73€. The dining rooms are located in several adjoining buildings, including a former postal relay. The decor is country-style, in harmony with the view of the forest. Traditional cuisine.

Chez Marraine – 6 r. du Square – ☎ 02 33 37 82 91 – closed 24 Dec to 22 Jan, 27 Oct to 11 Nov and Wed from Apr to Oct – 12.20/28.20€. "In order to lead a happy life, let's hide!". This must surely be the motto of this restaurant nestling in a narrow street on the edge of the lake. Meals are served on the covered terrace, a good opportunity for you to try calf's head, a speciality of the house...

MID-RANGE

Auberge de Clouet – Le Clouet – 61600 La Ferté-Macé – 7km/4.3mi northeast of Bagnoles along D 916 – ☎ 02 33 37 18 22 – closed 13-27 Nov, Mon from Oct to Easter and Sun evening except July-Aug and holidays – 14.48/53.36€. In spring, the terrace of this peaceful inn overlooks a small vale and a true mosaic of flowers. The chef uses local produce, chickens from the farm and vegetables from the garden in season. A few rooms decorated in 1970 style are available.

Where to stay

MODERATE

Albert 1er – 7 av. du Dr-Poulain - ☎ 02 33 37 80 97 – closed Nov-Mar – booking advised on weekends – 20 rooms: 35/45€ – ☱ 6€ - meal 13/28€. This old-fashioned inn is just on the edge of the forest and a short walk from the lake. The rooms are spacious and unpretentious. There is a Belle Époque fresco in the dining room. Traditional cuisine and regional specialities.

Nouvel Hôtel – Av. A.-Christophle – 61140 Tessé-la-Madeleine – 0.5km/0.3mi south of Bagnoles centre – ☎ 02 33 30 75 00 – closed Nov to Mar – 🅿 – 30 rooms: 38.11/55.19€ – ☱ 5.95€ – restaurant 14.03/27.44€. You can't miss this turn-of-the-century villa close to the thermal establishment. The entirely renovated façade shows off the very attractive stone work. The warm bright decor of the bedrooms is more modern. Covered terrace.

An 11C Romanesque tower is all that remains of the old church demolished in 1861 because it was too small; it stands next to the modern church (which has a chime of 16 bells, the heaviest weighing 3 917kg) and is used for temporary exhibitions.

The **hôtel de ville** (town hall), houses works by the local artist, **Charles Léandre** from the village of Champsecret, near Domfront, as well as a large painting called *The Post Office Through the Ages* by Marcel Pierre and a huge group painting by Krug, dating from 1898, showing the 80-strong staff of La Pomme Company during the *Banquet of La Pomme.*

Musée du Jouet ⊙ – Set up in the municipal baths which were used from 1932 to 1981, this museum contains the collection donated by G Bonvalot and shows the evolution of games and toys during the 19C and 20C, through different themes such as drawing-room games, scientific toys, technical toys, musical instruments etc).

Rânes – 13km/8mi from La Ferté-Macé via D 916. Rebuilt in the 18C, the castle, which now houses the local *gendarmerie*, has nevertheless retained its 15C two-storeyed keep, fortified with crenels and machicolations. The staircase walls are decorated with fleur-de-lis *(panoramic view from the top).*

Vallée de la Cour – 5km/3mi southeast.
A forest road leads to a pool, a popular beauty spot known for its good fishing.

Forêt des Andaines – This forest of oak, beech, spruce, birch and Scots pine belongs to the Normandie-Maine Regional Nature Park. It offers pleasant walks and the opportunity to catch a glimpse of stags, does and the smaller roedeer roaming through the woods. Sports enthusiasts will appreciate the maze of footpaths, several specially designed courses as well as rock-climbing facilities. Of particular interest are: **Tour de Bonvouloir** – slender observation tower with bell-shaped roof; **Chapelle Ste-Geneviève** – wooden altar and statues of St Roch, St Genevieve and St Elizabeth visible through the grille of the doorway *(picnic site)*; Juvigny-sous-Andaine – picturesque village where the **Ferme du Cheval de Trait** is home to about 20 dray-horses which take part in a 1hr show which is sure to please youngsters. Rides in horse-drawn carriages and country-style meals are also offered and there is a collection of agricultural implements for use with horses.

Château de BALLEROY ★

Michelin map 54 fold 14 or 231 fold 28
Local map see BAYEUX

Balleroy Castle was built between 1626 and 1636 by François Mansart for Jean de Choisy, Chancellor to Gaston d'Orléans. De Choisy's descendants, the Marquis de Balleroy, have owned the château for three centuries. It is now owned by the family of Malcolm Forbes, the American publisher and aeronaut, who bought it in 1970.

The plain but majestic brick and stone building provides the focal point for the village's main street. Symmetrical outbuildings behind formal flower beds designed by Le Nôtre, and a terrace flanked by twin pavilions complete the picture.

TOUR

★**Interior** ⊙ – The château's exterior gives no hint of its lavish interior decoration. On the ground floor two of the salons have portraits of Count Albert de Balleroy, the Louis XIII salon is hung with hunting scenes and the smoking room displays various portraits. The portrait on the easel by Paul Baudry is another of the count. The dining room panelling is painted with scenes from the Fables of La Fontaine.

On the first floor the first bedroom is that of Émilie de Caumartin, the first Marquise de Balleroy, and is furnished in the Louis XIII style. The next room, known as the bishop's room, was reserved for the priest. Most appropriately, the Waterloo room has portraits of Napoleon and the Duke of Wellington, facing each other across the fireplace. The silk wall hangings are identical to those in the Grand Trianon at Versailles. In the drawing room note the French-style ceiling portraying the Four Seasons and the signs of the zodiac as well as a remarkable series of portraits by Juste d'Egmont depicting Louis XIII, the Great Condé, Louis XIII's niece, the Grande Mademoiselle, Anne of Austria with the future Louis XIV and Philippe d'Orléans, and Marguerite de Lorraine, the second wife of Gaston d'Orléans, with her four children.

Salon d'Honneur, château de Balleroy

Musée des Ballons ☉ – A museum of hot-air balloons is housed in the stables. Dioramas tell the story of the first passenger flight in 1783, of Gambetta's flight on 7 October 1870 from Montmartre during the Siege of Paris and the maiden flight of the balloon *Château de Balleroy* on 5 September 1973. Balloons, pilot's licences, baskets and equipment, trophies and medals record the tale of these aerostats, usually used for recreation but also as military equipment (anchored observation balloons and aerial barrages during the Second World War).

Église paroissiale – This small church stands at the entrance to the castle. It is attributed to Mansart and was built of local brown schist in 1651. The church can be pinpointed from afar by its octagonal belfry over the transept crossing. Inside, above the altar, is an Annunciation from the 18C Italian School.

BARFLEUR

Population 599
Michelin map 54 fold 3 or 231 fold 3
Local map see Presqu'île du COTENTIN

This charming fishing port, with its granite houses and its quays littered with lobster pots, has earned the status of one of the most beautiful villages of France. Tradition has it that the boat that carried William, Duke of Normandy on his invasion of England was built in the shipyards of Barfleur. A bronze plaque placed in 1966 on a rock at the foot of the jetty commemorates his departure (1066) for England and the fact that a local man was at the helm. In 1194 Richard Lionheart also embarked from Barfleur on his way to be crowned King of England. The houses around the harbour (*Cour Sainte-Catherine*) are especially pretty.

Église – This sombre and squat 17C church has the appearance of a fortified building. Inside there are some interesting wood statues. In the south transept is a remarkable 16C Pietà while in the north transept above the font is a stained-glass window of St Mary-Magdalene Postel. A rood beam hangs above the entrance to the chancel; from the timber ceiling hangs an ex-voto model of a boat.

Maison de Julie Postel ☉ – *The house is situated in La Bretonne hamlet.*
Julie Postel, the daughter of a ropemaker, was born in Barfleur in 1756. As Sister Mary Magdalen she founded the Sisters of the Christian Schools of Mercy (La Congrégation des Sœurs de la Miséricorde) and died at their headquarters in Saint-Sauveur-le-Vicomte in 1846. This house, where she lived for 30 years, contains the place under the stairs where she hid the Sacrament; the kitchen where she taught domestic science to her pupils; the dormitory where the boarders used to sleep. Scenes from her life are depicted in the stained-glass windows of the adjoining chapel.

★★POINTE DE BARFLEUR

4km/2mi north by D 116 and D 10.

Gatteville-le-Phare – The church, rebuilt in the 18C, still has its original 12C belfry. Inside, in a chapel to the right of the chancel, a 15C medallioned ciborium is surmounted by a 16C Trinity. The Mariners' Chapel (Chapelle des Marins), in the square, is built over a Merovingian necropolis. The east end is Romanesque.

Eating out

MODERATE

Le Moderne – *1 place du Gén-de-Gaulle* – ☎ *02 33 23 12 44* – *closed 3 Jan to 17 Mar, Tues and Wed from 10 Sept to 14 July* – *14/38€*. Located in a quiet street of the town centre, this restaurant, with its quaint painted bricks, offers copious and well-prepared dishes based on fresh produce. Some very reasonably priced, simple rooms are available upstairs. The owner is also an artist, and some of his paintings hang on the dining room walls.

Where to stay

MID-RANGE

Manoir de la Fèvrerie Bed and Breakfast – *In Arville* – *50760 Ste-Geneviève* – *3km/1.9mi west of Barfleur via D 25* – ☎ *02 33 54 33 53* – ⊠ – *3 rooms: 41.16/58€.*
This comfortable 16-17C manor house offers a warm welcome to its guests. Carefully prepared breakfast served on the large wooden table near the fireplace. Settee and deep armchairs in the drawing room. Refined furnishings and elegant furniture in the bedrooms. In addition, two self-catering cottages are available.

Port de Barfleur

Beyond Gatteville the scenery is wilder and rough seas pound the low rocky coast.

★★ Phare ⊙ – The lighthouse, which stands on the northeastern extremity of the Cotentin peninsula, is one of the tallest in France (71m/233ft). The light, which has a range of 56km/35mi, and the radio beacon, installed in a small 18C tower, guide ships into Le Havre.

From the top (365 steps) there is a **panorama**★★ stretching over the east coast of the Cotentin peninsula, St-Marcouf Islands, Veys Bay and, in clear weather, the cliffs at Grandcamp. The most astonishing sight is the granite tableland of the Saire as it gradually dips towards the sea and disappears in the foreground. The shallow waters and swift currents have caused many a ship to founder, including the historic *White Ship* in 1120, with Henry I's heir, William Atheling, one of his daughters and 300 members of the Anglo-Norman nobility on board.

MONTFARVILLE *2km/1mi south by D 155*

This 18C granite church has a chapel and belfry dating from the 13C and a highly colourful **interior**★. The bare granite walls lend it special character. The paintings on the vaulting are by a local artist, Guillaume Fouace and they represent scenes from the Life of Christ. The colours are very rich. Note the 18C rood beam and a 14C polychrome Virgin.

BARNEVILLE-CARTERET ≗≗

Population 2 229
Michelin map 54 fold 1 or 231 fold 13
Local map see Presqu'île du COTENTIN

Carteret, Barneville and Barneville-Plage have joined to form a continuous settlement and are now a popular seaside resort. The little port is lively, the dunes windswept, and the long beach is of fine sand. The port is the closest on the continent to the Channel Islands.

★CARTERET

A magnificent rocky headland to the north protects the Gerfleur estuary and the delightful small beach *(beware of coastal currents)*, which makes Carteret one of the most pleasant seaside resorts on the Cotentin peninsula. The harbour provides a ferry service to the Channel Islands.

★★Walk round Cap de Carteret – *45min on foot there and back.*

Follow the signs "La Corniche, le Phare"; park near the roundabout with a tree at the centre by Carteret beach. Take Sentier des Douaniers (left) which is very narrow and requires care. The view changes continually on the way to Carteret's second beach, the extensive Plage de la Vieille-Église.

CARTERET

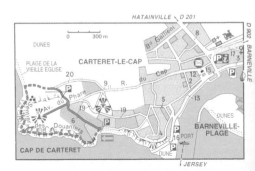

🚶 Take the road leading down to this beach to return inland. At the crossroads either turn right up to the **lighthouse** *(phare)* for an overall view or turn left (avenue de la Roche-Biard) to a viewing table: **views**★ of the coast, the Channel Islands and inland. *Allow a total of 2hr for these two walks.*

Alternatively continue straight ahead at the crossroads to return to the car.

BARNEVILLE

Église – The 11C church was given a fortified tower in the 15C. Although the late-19C restoration disfigured the chancel which lost its original ceiling, the Romanesque nave is of interest with the delightful **decoration**★ of the Romanesque arches and of the capitals carved with animals or oriental motifs. On one of these capitals, note the figure portraying the Prophet Daniel confronting a fierce lion: the features are most striking and the fixed expression on his face resembles a mask.

The monument on the way out of Barneville commemorates the cutting-off of the Cotentin peninsula on 18 June 1944 during the Battle of Normandy.

Barneville-Plage – The sea front boulevard bordered by villas leads to the beach which is usually very busy in summer. The sea between Barneville beach and Carteret harbour is a favourite spot for water sports at high tide.

EXCURSION TO MONT CASTRE

29km/18mi – about 2hr 15min. From Barneville-Carteret take the Coutances road. At La Picauderie, bear right onto D 50.

Portbail – This is one of Cotentin's most highly rated seaside resorts with its two beaches of fine sand, its sailing school and its marina, formerly a tidal dock. A 13-arch bridge links the town to the harbour and the beaches.

The **Église Notre-Dame** ⏱, now deconsecrated, was built in the 11C on the site of a 6C abbey founded in the reign of Childebert, and dates from the earliest Romanesque period; the tower was added in the 15C. The columns and capitals of the interior are decorated with carved interlacing and animals; beside the altar is a 16C polychrome statue of St James.

Excavations, begun in 1956, have unearthed the footings of the outer walls of a hexagonal **baptistère** (baptistery – *behind the town hall*) ⏱; fragments of blue schist paving and the piscina with its inflow and outflow pipes were also discovered.

Take D 15 and D 903 inland via La Haye-du-Puits towards Carentan. 1 500m/1 550yd from the first level crossing east of La Haye-du-Puits turn right onto a narrow uphill road. Leave the car on the grass before reaching the houses at the end of the road.

★ **Mont Castre** – Beyond the houses, take the path leading to the church ruins and an old cemetery, then go round a field before reaching the ruins of a Roman watch post – still a strategic point in July 1944 during the Battle of Normandy – from which the **view** extends right across the Cotentin peninsula from Carteret to St-Côme-du-Mont.

🚶 Committed hikers can climb up to the ruins of the Roman watch post by following the signposted route. There are one or two rocky areas to climb over.

Where to stay

MODERATE

La Tourelle Bed and Breakfast – *5 r. du Pic-Mallet at Barneville-Bourg –* ☎ *02 33 04 90 22 –* 🗋 *– 3 rooms: 33.54/36.59€.* A true family house with its old-world atmosphere, its antique furniture, parquet flooring and, in the morning, the lovely smell of jam made with fruit from the garden... This 16C house opposite the church is very attractive indeed.

Eating out

Le Gohan – *r. au Lait –* ☎ *02 33 04 95 33 – closed Mon and Thu out of season – 14,48/35,83€.* What a pleasure to discover this little place tucked away in an old barn, halfway between the town centre and the beach. The country-style decor, beams and stones, is the right setting for enjoying the regional fare prepared with care.

BAYEUX★★

Population 14 704
Michelin map 54 folds 14 and 15 or 231 fold 17
Local maps see below and Plages du DÉBARQUEMENT

Bayeux, the former capital of the Bessin, was the first French town to be liberated (7 June 1944) and was fortunate not to have been damaged during the war. The cathedral still keeps watch over this charming, old-fashioned town and the Bayeux Tapestry presents its unique record of the events of 1066 to the visitor.

The old houses which have been tastefully restored and the pedestrian precinct are an added attraction to the locality.

The marked itineraries "D-Day-Le Choc" (D-Day-The Impact) and "Overlord-L'Assaut" (Overlord-the Onslaught) described in the Historical Area of the Battle of Normandy pass by Bayeux; the former starts here while the latter ends here.

INTRODUCING THE GREAT NORMAN ENTERPRISE

Cradle of the Dukes of Normandy – Bayeux, the Gaulish capital of the Bajocasses people, became a large Roman town and an important episcopal city; it was successively captured by the Bretons, the Saxons and the Vikings.

Rollo, the famous Viking, married Popa, the daughter of Count Béranger who was Governor of the town. In 905, their son, the future William Longsword, was born in the town thus making it the cradle of the dynasty of the dukes of Normandy. When Rouen became French, Bayeux remained a Scandinavian town where people continued to speak Norse.

Oath of Bayeux – Edward the Confessor ruled over England. As he had lived in Normandy for many years, it was assumed that he had chosen his cousin, William of Normandy, to be his successor. He sent **Harold**, who was a favourite with the Saxon nobles, to break the news to the Duke of Normandy.

Harold set sail but was shipwrecked on the coast of Picardy in the territory of Count Guy of Ponthieu who detained him at his pleasure. He was set free by **William** and received with due solemnity at the Norman court where the Duke's daughter, Edwige, was presented to him as his wife to be. Eager to display his power, William took Harold with him to campaign in Brittany.

Harold was obliged to grant official recognition to the Duke's right of accession to the English throne; against his will he swore on saintly relics that only death would prevent him from keeping his word. When, however, Edward died on 5 January 1066, Harold accepted the English crown.

The Conquest of England – This provoked the great Norman enterprise, which earned William his nickname "The Conqueror" – the conquest of England. William set sail with the Norman fleet on 27 September 1066 from Dives-sur-Mer. On 28 the Normans set foot on English soil at Pevensey in Sussex and occupied Hastings. Harold dug in on a hill. On 14 October William advanced; in the evening, by means of a stratagem, the Normans emerged victorious. Harold fell in the fighting with an arrow in his eye.

The whole story is embroidered in detail on the Bayeux Tapestry.

★★★BAYEUX TAPESTRY *1hr*

The **Bayeux Tapestry** *(Tapisserie dite de la Reine Mathilde)* is displayed in the **Centre Guillaume le Conquérant** ⊙ in an impressive 18C building which was a seminary until 1970.

Visitors are introduced to this jewel of Romanesque art as they pass through a series of rooms. First an audio-visual film relates the exploits of the Vikings (the screens are shaped like the sails of a long Viking ship) in the William Room. Then there is a strip cartoon explaining the Viking invasions and the contents of the tapestry. Another audio-visual film describing the **Battle of Hastings** is followed by a diorama on the Conquest of England in the Odo Room. The tapestry itself is displayed under glass round the walls of the specially designed Harold Room.

The origin of the tapestry is not known. It was probably commissioned in England soon after the conquest from a group of Saxon embroiderers by Odo of Conteville, Count of Kent and Bishop of Bayeux, to adorn the cathedral he had just had built. The tapestry appears in the cathedral Treasury inventory for 1476. In the 18C it was wrongly attributed to Queen Matilda. The embroidery is in coloured wool on a piece of linen, 50cm/19in high by 70m/203ft long.

The work is the most accurate and lively document to survive from the Middle Ages and provides detailed information on the clothes, ships, arms and general lifestyle of the period.

Eating out

MODERATE

Le Petit Bistrot – *2 r. du Bienvenu* – ☎ *02 31 51 85 40 – closed Jan, Sun and Mon – reservation advisable – 15.24/27.44€*. An inventive cuisine prepared by a keen chef is the main attraction of this small establishment facing the cathedral. Original dishes inspired by Mediterranean cuisine are served in a Provençal-style decor with its ochre colour scheme, water colours and drawings.

La Table du Terroir Louis Bisson – *42 r. St-Jean* – ☎ *02 31 92 05 53 – closed 15 Oct to 15 Nov, Sun evening and Mon – 10€ lunch - 15/25€*. Praised by several gourmet brotherhoods such as the Fins Goustiers du Pré-Bocage and the Chevaliers du Goûte-Boudin, and winner in 1999 of the award of the Confrérie du plat de Tripes, the owner is a professional butcher. No wonder then that only fine cuts of meat are served at the tables laid out at the back of his shop.

La Cassonade – *35 r. du Bienvenu* – ☎ *02 31 92 47 32 – closed Dec to mid-Jan and Tues – 10.21/14.03€*. Located in the heart of Old Bayeux, this place is a must. Buckwheat and wheat pancakes, salads and omelettes will satisfy the hungry and not-so hungry... Colourful dining room and low prices.

Hostellerie St-Martin – *14480 Creully* – ☎ *02 31 80 10 11 – 10.67/35.06€*. The high vaulted ceilings of this restaurant, dating from the 16C, once sheltered the town market. Stone walls, a fireplace, sculptures and a view of the wine cellar contribute to the unique ambience. Traditional cuisine. A few rooms available.

Where to stay

MODERATE

Reine Mathilde Hotel – *23 r. Larcher* – ☎ *02 31 92 08 13 – closed 20 Dec to 1 Feb and Sun from 15 Nov to 15 Mar – 16 rooms: 38.87/44.97€ – ☐ 5.79€*. If you wish to stay in the old town, this small family hotel is conveniently situated a stone's throw from the cathedral and the famous tapestry. Exposed beams and light-wood furniture. Plain rooms, some of them with sloping ceilings.

Le Grand Fumichon Bed and Breakfast – *14400 Vaux-sur-Aure – 3km/1.9mi north of Bayeux via D 104* – ☎ *02 31 21 78 51 –✄ – 3 rooms: 30.49/33.54€*. Once part of Longues-sur-Mer Abbey, this fortified 17C farm, with its square courtyard and characteristic porch, is today a dairy and cider-making farm. The attic rooms are plain but pleasant.

La Ferme des Châtaigniers Bed and Breakfast – *14400 Vienne-en-Bessin – 7.5km/4.6mi east of Bayeux via D 126* – ☎ *02 31 92 54 70 –✄ – 3 rooms: 28.97/ 35.06€*. Set apart from the farmhouse, this converted farm building contains simple yet pleasant and comfortable rooms. Guests have the use of a fitted kitchen. Peace and quiet is guaranteed in this country house.

MID-RANGE

Le Manoir de Crépon Bed and Breakfast – *14480 Crépon – 13km/8.1mi east of Bayeux via D 12 and D 112* – ☎ *02 31 22 21 27 – reservation required in winter – 5 rooms: 53.36/68.60€*. This 17-18C house is typical of the area, with its bright-red roughcast. You will like the stone floors and fireplaces, the vast, tastefully furnished bedrooms and the authentic atmosphere of the former kitchen converted into a breakfast room.

On the town

Le Guillaume – *Allée des Tanneurs* – ☎ *02 31 92 08 13 – Tues-Sun 8am-7pm, until 10pm in summer – closed mid-Nov to mid-Mar*. Neat and peaceful waterside tearoom and ice-cream parlour. The attractive decoration of the bar draws its inspiration from the famous tapestry.

Shopping

Naphtaline – *16 parvis de la Cathédrale* – ☎ *02 31 21 50 03 – Mon-Sat 11am-7pm – closed Nov-Feb*. Two boutiques housed in a fine 18C building. Old and modern lace, 19C Bayeux porcelain, tapestries woven in Roubaix and reproductions of antique works. The charming owner is always ready to impart her considerable knowledge on the subject.

The Battle of Hastings

On 27 September 1066, William crossed to England with an army of somewhere between 4,000 and 7,000 cavalry and infantry. Harold hurried to meet him with his own army, which was probably larger but was poorly armed and trained. At dawn on 14 October, Harold's Englishmen were defending a ridge and William lined up his archers in the front lines, backed by infantrymen and three groups of knights to the rear. The closely ranged Englishmen were easy prey for William's archers, but they also swung a mean battleaxe, badly mauling the Norman cavalry, who fled. To cinch the battle, William began alternating cavalry charges and flights of arrows, and through two feigned retreats was able to draw the English from their positions and annihilate them. Two of Harold's brothers fell, then Harold himself was killed in the late afternoon. The leaderless English fought on until dusk, then scattered. William was crowned in London on Christmas day.

The illustrations give a very realistic account of the events of 1066. From the initial rivalry between Harold and William to the conquest and final Norman victory the story is told in 58 detailed scenes. In the first section a stylised tree marks the beginning and end of each sequence; in the second section the scenes follow one another in unbroken succession.

The English are distinguished by their moustaches and long hair, the Normans by their short hairstyles, the clergy by their tonsures and the women (three in all) by their flowing garments and veiled heads. Latin captions written in the Saxon manner run above the pictures while the upper and lower edges are embroidered with fantastic animals or motifs relating to the principal events.

The outstanding sections are Harold's embarkation and crossing (4-6), his audience with William (14), crossing the River Couesnon near Mont-St-Michel (17), Harold's Oath (23), the death and burial of Edward the Confessor (26-28), the appearance of Halley's comet, an ill omen for Harold (32), the building of the fleet (36), the Channel crossing and the march to Hastings (38-40), cooking and messing (41-43), the battle and Harold's death (51-58).

★★CATHÉDRALE NOTRE-DAME *30min*

The cathedral is a fine Norman Gothic building. Only the towers and crypt remain from the original church which was completed in 1077 by Odo of Conteville, William's turbulent companion in arms whom he eventually had to restrain.

Exterior – The east end is a graceful composition; flying buttresses support the chancel which is flanked by two bell turrets. The central tower dates from the 15C but it was recapped in the 19C with what is known as the "bonnet" in a most unfortunate style. The south transept is pure in style; the tympanum over the door shows the story of Thomas Becket, Archbishop of Canterbury, who was assassinated in his cathedral on the orders of Henry II. The Radiant tracery over the doorway is surmounted by a highly ornate gable.

The small porch further west on the south side is late 12C.

The two Romanesque towers on the west front must have been redesigned in the 13C with massive buttresses to take the weight of the Gothic spires. The only points of interest are on the tympana over the two side doors; the Passion (left – reading from bottom to top); the Last Judgement (right – reading from top to bottom).

The recessed arches are decorated with angels and old men.

Interior – The well-lit nave is a harmonious blend of Romanesque and Gothic. The clerestory and the vaulting date from the 13C but the wide arches are in the best 12C style. Their justly famous decoration is typical of Norman Romanesque sculp-

Duke William and Harold crossing the river Couesnon near Mont-St-Michel;
horses and men are caught in the quicksands

ture. Against an interlaced or knotted ground the spandrels are decorated with low-relief sculptures which show oriental influence transmitted by the illuminators of manuscripts. A row of four-leaf clovers and a band of foliage, running the length of the nave, mark the transition to the clerestory.

The transept crossing is supported by four huge pillars. The south transept contains two interesting pictures low on the right: the Life of St Nicholas and the Crucifixion (15C).

The three-storey chancel, with its ambulatory and radiating chapels, is a magnificent example of Norman Gothic architecture. The great arches are separated by pierced rose windows. Above the highly ornate triforium the clerestory lets in plenty of light.

The stalls are the work of a late-16C artist from Caen.

The high altar is a majestic 18C piece: the six candelabras in chased bronze, the tabernacle and the cross are by Caffieri the Elder.

The paintings (restored) on the chancel vault represent the first bishops of Bayeux. The ambulatory, like the transepts, is lower than the chancel and separated from it by handsome wrought-iron screens. The third and fourth chapels on the south side contain 15C frescoes.

Crypt ⊙ – Beneath the chancel is the crypt (11C) which is divided into three small chambers, each of which contains six bays of groined vaulting.

Above the decorative foliage of the capitals are 15C frescoes (restored) of angel musicians. A recess (left) contains the recumbent figure of a canon (15C).

Chapter-house – This is a beautiful late-12C Gothic construction. The vaulting, which was renewed in the 14C, is supported by consoles decorated with monsters or grotesque figures. A graceful blind arcade adorns the lower walls. The floor of 15C glazed bricks includes a labyrinthine design in the centre. There are several pictures and a crucifix which may have belonged to the Princesse de Lamballe. The tiles on the risers at the back of the room depict hunting scenes. The beatification of St Teresa of Lisieux was signed at the desk.

OLD BAYEUX

It is pleasant to wander in the streets of old Bayeux among the old stone or timber-framed houses which have been splendidly restored.

Rue St-Martin – No 6 is a 17C house known as the Maison du Cadran because of the sundial on the façade. On the corner of rue des Cuisiniers stands a very elegant half-timbered house★ with two overhanging upper storeys and a slate roof.

Rue St-Malo – No 4 is the Hôtel d'Argouges, a 15C-16C timber-framed house.

Rue Franche – Several private houses: no 5, Hôtel de Rubercy, is a 15C-16C turreted manor house. No 7, Hôtel de la Crespellière, is set back behind a courtyard and dates from the mid 18C. No 13, Hôtel St-Manvieu, is 16C.

Rue du Général-de-Dais – No 10, Hôtel de Castilly (18C), is in the Louis XV style. No 14, Hôtel de la Tour du Pin (18C), has an imposing façade in the Louis XVI style.

Rue du Bienvenu – No 6 is decorated with wooden carvings inspired by religion or legend.

Rue St-Jean – East of rue St-Martin, part of this street is within the pedestrian precinct which has been attractively restored. The Tourist Information Centre is housed in the old fish market. No 53 is the Hôtel du Croissant (15C-16C).

Rue des Teinturiers – Two handsome half-timbered houses face a row of stone houses.

Quai de l'Aure – On turning into this street from rue des Teinturiers, one has a fine view of the river, the water mill in what was once the tanning district, the arched bridge, the old fish market and the towers of the cathedral in the background.

The Norman army advances on Dol   The Siege of Rennes

ADDITIONAL SIGHTS

Hôtel du Doyen ⊘ – A huge 17C porch leads into the 18C mansion which houses the Bayeux lace workshop and the Diocesan Museum of Religious Art.

Conservatoire de la dentelle de Bayeux ⊘ – Bayeux lace, of the type known as bobbin lace, is characterised by floral motifs. The workshop, where the lacemakers are reviving the Bayeux pattern, has displays of lace specimens.

Musée diocésain d'Art sacré ⊘ – The Museum of Religious Art displays liturgical articles, gold and silver ware (ciboria, chalices, candlesticks) and old manuscripts. There is a reconstruction of the room where Teresa Martin (St Teresa of Lisieux), accompanied by her father, asked the Bishop of Bayeux for permission to enter the Carmelite Convent. A large gallery is hung with portraits of the bishops of Bayeux.

Bayeux porcelain

Musée Baron-Gérard ⊘ – A superb plane tree stands in place de la Liberté.

Bayeux was once an important manufacturing centre for porcelain. Founded in 1812 by J Langlois, the workshop began producing the famous glazing (red, gold and blue) which made the reputation of the town. Besides utilitarian objects and some laboratory implements, the factory also turned out luxury articles intended for the wealthy bourgeois of the town. Lavishly decorated with flowers, exotic birds and polychrome scenes involving exuberant compositions (some were enhanced with relief motifs), most of these pieces stood out for their abundant ornamentation. The Morlent family ran the business from 1878 to 1951, when it was definitively closed down. It was they who introduced the "daisy motif", a blue flower on a white background baked at a very high temperature. The museum displays several of these porcelain pieces, some of which are extremely rare.

Exhibited on the ground floor of the museum is the archeological collection, displayed in a 16C vaulted room, along with a fine collection of Bayeux porcelain, including the famous **fontaine à parfum** (perfume fountain) and an interesting collection of lace (needlepoint and bobbin lace) made in Bayeux, one of the main lacemaking centres in Europe during the 19C.

The upstairs rooms are devoted to furniture and painting, mainly 15C and 16C Italian and Flemish primitive works and 17C to 19C French works including *St Pierre et St Paul* by Philippe de Champaigne, *La Cage* by David, *Hylas and the Nymph* by Baron François Gérard, *La Rue de Fervaques* by Boudin, *Portraits à la Campagne* by Caillebotte.

The museum also houses 19C prints and drawings, including some by Septime Le Pippre, a local artist.

Conan capitulates and surrenders the keys of the city on the end of his lance to Duke William

The Siege of Dinan   Duke William gives arms to Harold

BAYEUX

Musée-Mémorial de la Bataille de Normandie ⊘ – "In our mutilated but glorious Normandy, Bayeux and the surrounding areas witnessed one of the greatest confrontations in history…" These were General de Gaulle's words in Bayeux in 1946.

Situated on the line separating the British and American sectors in 1944, the Memorial Museum recalls the tragic but later more favourable events of summer 1944. Two large galleries, named Overlord and Eisenhower, explain the chronology of the Battle of Normandy and give a detailed account of the equipment and uniforms of the various nations involved in the conflict; the displays are arranged according to nine different themes and four sections (artillery, armoured cars, air force and engineering corps).

Among the themes dealt with, the closing of the Falaise Pocket is illustrated by means of a diorama recreating with poignant realism the village of Chambois where, on 19 August, part of the 90th US Infantry Division joined forces with lancers and dragoons of the 1st Polish Armoured Division.

There is a great choice of heavy equipment exhibited. Note in particular the Churchill MK VII tank (GB) – the anti-tank armoured vehicle called Destroyer M 10 (US), the anti-tank Jagdpanzer (Germany) – a "quadruple" 20mm German Flak gun as well as a Caterpillar D 7 Bulldozer with an exceptional career to its credit since, after landing in France on 7 June 1944 with the 1st American Army, it was used to build one of the first US airfields at Colleville, then to haul fighter planes, later to clear the ruins of Caen under the banner of the Royal Engineers of the 1st Canadian Army and finally to extract stone from quarries around Calvados during its last 40 years of service!

Personal mementoes of British Tommies and American GIs, dummies in glass cases representing bomber crews, RAF and Luftwaffe pilots, or the allied armies' medical corps, as well as a film shot at the time depicting various operations, all these vividly illustrate this memorial dedicated to the fight of the Allied nations against Nazism.

Harold swears allegiance to William on two reliquaries

They set out together for Bayeux   Harold sets sail again for England

Mémorial Charles-de-Gaulle ⊘ – The Governor's mansion (15C-17C) at no 10 is the setting for a museum which retraces the life and career of the General through events associated with Bayeux (liberation of the town and speech of 1946). Some personal belongings, newspaper articles and manuscripts are also on display.

Jardin botanique – The pleasant sloping botanical gardens include a huge weeping willow.

EXCURSIONS

① Southwest of Bayeux

Round trip of 46km/29mi – about 3hr 30min. From Bayeux take D 572.

St-Loup-Hors – The 12C-13C church has retained its Romanesque tower; there are many old tombs.

Noron-la-Poterie – This is a well-known centre producing salt glaze ware; it has six workshops at present and several exhibition galleries; some of the workshops are open to the public.

In La Tuilerie turn left onto D 73 which leads to Balleroy via Castillon.

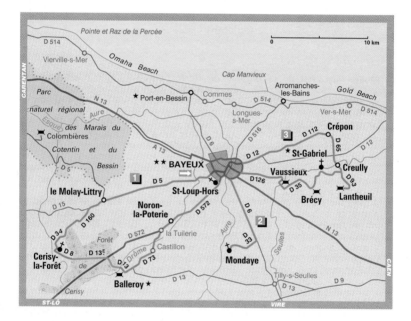

★**Château de Balleroy** – *See Château de BALLEROY.*

On leaving turn left onto D 13. At the Embranchement crossroads take D 13 and D 8 west through Cerisy Forest.

Cerisy-la-Forêt – *See CERISY-LA-FORÊT.*

From Cerisy take D 34, D 160 and D 15 northeast to Le Molay-Littry.

Le Molay-Littry – The village was once a busy coal mining centre. The first mine was opened in 1743 following the discovery in November 1741 of an outcrop of coal near Littry by a worker from the Marquis de Balleroy's ironworks. In 1744 Louis XV granted the marquis a life concession but poor financial results forced him to sell to a group of Parisian financiers, who founded the Littry Mining Company in 1747. The mine flourished until the late 19C when flooding and the import of coal from England forced it to close down. During the Second World War it was reopened and produced coal until 1950.

The **Musée de la Mine** ⊘ presents the history of mining and the life of the miners through an audio-visual presentation, a reconstruction of a mining gallery, a scale model of a pithead, made by pupils at the Douai Mining School in 1890, and a range of tools: sledgehammers, pickaxes, shovels, oil lamps, helmets of boiled leather, a combustion pump (1795), 18C coins minted by the mining company for use within the concession.

Take D 5 east to return to Bayeux.

2 Abbaye de Mondaye ⊙

11km/7mi – about 45min. From Bayeux take D 6 south. After 8km/5mi turn right onto D 33; follow the signs.

St Martin's Abbey was founded in 1215 but rebuilt in the 18C and 19C.
The abbey church, which also serves the parish, is in the Classical style (early 18C). Its uniformity of design is due to its architect and decorator, Eustache Restout, a canon in the Premonstratensian Order. The west front has pleasing proportions. The interior contains some fine pieces: high altar, woodwork in the chancel including a beautiful Crucifixion, the Assumption (a terracotta group in the Lady Chapel) and the Parizot organ (restored).
The 18C **conventual buildings** round the cloister – refectory, sacristy (18C woodwork) and library – are open to the public.

3 East of Bayeux

Round tour of 34km/20mi – allow 2hr. From Bayeux take D 12 and D 112 towards Ver-sur-Mer.

Crépon – The Romanesque church with its 15C tower and the smart farms attract attention.

Turn right onto D 65.

Creully – The **château** ⊙ is built on the foundations of an 11C castle. The main 12C building is flanked by a 16C round tower adjoining a square keep. A room with nine bays is supported by diagonal rib vaulting. During the Second World War, the BBC used the château as a relay station to broadcast news of the Battle of Normandy.
One room houses a small Museum of Radio Communications.
From the terrace there is a view of **Château de Creullet** standing in a loop of the Arromanches road. On 12 June 1944 King George VI and Sir Winston Churchill were received in the castle by General Montgomery who had set up his famous caravan headquarters camouflaged as hay stacks in the park.

Grange aux Dîmes – *On the Bayeux road, level with no 82.* The Tithe Barn is a powerfully buttressed building where wheat was stored and where the taxes and the octroi were collected.

Take D 93 south to Lantheuil.

Château de Lantheuil ⊙ – This imposing castle was built for Turgot in the reign of Louis XIII and has remained in the same family ever since. The rooms have retained their original decor: woodwork, furniture, sculptures and paintings including a remarkable collection of family portraits. Souvenirs and objets d'art concerning the Turgots and Marshal Mouton who was elevated to this rank by Louis-Philippe.

Return to Creully; turn left onto D 35. On entering St-Gabriel-Brécy turn right to the priory.

The Old Priory of St-Gabriel

A. de Valroger/MICHELIN

★**Ancien Prieuré de St-Gabriel** ⊙ – The old priory of St-Gabriel was founded in the 11C as a daughter house of Fécamp Abbey. The attractive buildings, now occupied by a horticultural school, are set round a courtyard with a monumental entrance gate. The arms of Fécamp Abbey, including a mitre and a crosier, surmount the pointed porch of the main building. A spiral stairway leads to the **prior's room** (1615): wooden ceiling beams and a Louis XIII-style stone fireplace.

The church is reduced to the magnificently designed and decorated east end and chancel (11C-12C). The great window in the chancel dates from the 14C. The altar is a Merovingian funerary slab found in the Pierrepont cemetery in Lantheuil. There are traces of a 16C fresco on the apse vault; the aisles end in oven-vaulted recesses. Beyond the church is a garden, planted with fruit trees and banks of flowers and decorated with a pool.

As St Gabriel's was the seat of a priory court, the 15C **Justice Tower**, buttressed at the corners, contained a prison on the lower floor and a lookout place at the top.

Return to D 35; continue west towards Bayeux; then follow the signs south.

Château de Brécy ⊙ – The castle is approached through a magnificent great **gateway★** (17C). Within the entrance (right) stands an old press. The terraced **gardens★** – one is laid out with box hedges forming arabesque designs – offer a beautiful perspective which terminates in a high wrought-iron grill ornately decorated. An old bread oven stands (right) beside the path down from the gardens. Near the château stands an attractive 13C church.

Take D 158; just before the church turn right onto a narrow road; after 2km/1mi turn left onto D 35; after 2km/1mi turn right towards Esquay-sur-Seulles.

Château de Vaussieux – *Not open to the public.* In 1778 this beautiful 18C mansion played a part in the Franco-American alliance. Its American owner gave it to Marshal Broglie as his headquarters. Rochambeau took part in the grand manoeuvres designed to intimidate England. The château is an elegant building with two small wings at right angles, set in its own park; the outbuildings are half-timbered or of stone.

Continue onto Esquay-sur-Seulles; take D 126 to return to Bayeux.

Le BEC-HELLOUIN★★

Population 434
Michelin map 54 fold 19 or 231 fold 21

The importance of Le Bec-Hellouin Abbey as a medieval religious and cultural centre can still be seen, in spite of damage to the building. It gave us two great archbishops of Canterbury.

A CENTURY-OLD TRADITION

In 1034 the knight **Herluin** abandoned his charger for a donkey and vowed to devote himself to God. Others, inspired by a similar calling, followed his example and by 1041 there were 32 monks in the "Bec" community.

One day in 1042 as Herluin was mending the bread oven a stranger appeared. It was the Italian clerk, **Lanfranc**, who had been teaching at Avranches, and, tired of his success, had left and come to Bec, drawn by the monastery's obscurity. He stayed for three years before Herluin persuaded him to take up his teaching once more.

It was during his siege of Brionne from 1047 to 1050 that the young Duke William got to know Lanfranc, who subsequently became his most trusted adviser – Lanfranc was the monk sent as emissary to Rome to get the interdict raised which had weighed on Normandy since William's marriage to Matilda.

In about 1060 Herluin moved the community further up the valley. Some years later William asked Lanfranc to be responsible for the building of the Abbey for Men in Caen.

Then Pope Alexander II, who had been one of Lanfranc's students at Bec, appointed his former teacher Archbishop of Canterbury, a position which made him virtual Regent of England whenever William returned to Normandy. On Lanfranc's death in 1093, Anselm, the philosopher and theologian who had come from Aosta and was by now Abbot of Bec, was transferred to Canterbury. Bec Abbey long continued as a major intellectual centre.

In the 17C Bec accepted the reform of St Maur and rose to new eminence under Guillaume de la Tremblaye (1644-1715), who was professed at Bec in 1699. The great master builder of the congregation was one of the greatest sculptors and architects of his period.

The monks were driven out during the Revolution and the abbey church, one of the largest in Christendom, demolished under the Empire. In 1948 the site was restored to the Benedictine Order. The tradition had thus been renewed and on 29 September of that year Mass was celebrated once more.

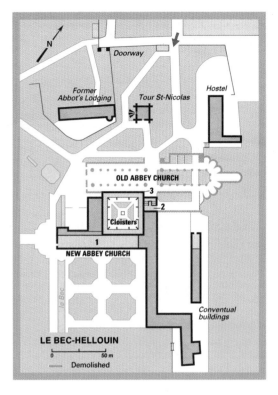

★★ABBAYE ⊘ *45min*

New Abbey Church – The New Abbey is in what was the former Maurist refectory. At the entrance is a 14C statue of the Virgin, the Fathers of the Church are 15C; the altar was presented in 1959 by Aosta, birthplace of Bishop Anselm; before the high altar lies the 11C sarcophagus of Herluin, founder of Bec (1).

Turn left on leaving. The conventual buildings are characteristic of the Maurist style and enhanced by the lush setting.

Old Abbey Church – Only the column foundations and fragments of the south transept of the old abbey church remain.

Cloisters – A monumental 18C grand staircase (2) (modern banister) leads to the cloisters. Built between 1640 and 1660, the cloisters were modelled after the cloisters of Monte Cassino (Italy), the work of Bramante. A good 14C Gothic doorway in the northeast corner (3) features a tympanum with a Virgin in Majesty.

Eating out

MODERATE

Le Canterbury – *R. de Canterbury* – ☎ *02 32 44 14 59* – *closed Feb, evenings from 15 Oct to 15 Mar except Sat, Tues evening and Wed* – *reservation advisable* – *12.96/28.97€*. There is no fuss in this place: the aim is not to impress you but to satisfy you. The result: a very well-prepared cuisine served in this fine timber-framed 18C house. More than 60 calvados to choose from...and a few rooms furnished with old Norman wardrobes.

Where to stay

MODERATE

Château de Boscherville Bed and Breakfast – *27520 Bourgtheroulde* – *10km/6.2mi northeast of Le Bec-Hellouin via N 138, D 80 and D 38* – ☎ *02 35 87 62 12* – *5 rooms: 33.54/41.16€*. The rooms of this small family castle are comfortable and bright, the small drawing room is elegant and the welcome very pleasant indeed. A must, if only to have the pleasure of strolling in the park, under the hundred-year-old oak trees like Jean de La Fontaine in his time...

Tour St-Nicolas – The 15C tower is the most important remainder of the old abbey church, although it stood apart from it. A plaque recalls the abbey's ties with England in the 11C and 12C. The **view**★ from the tower summit *(201 steps)* includes the Bec Valley and the former abbot's lodging.

TOURING SUGGESTIONS

Neubourg and Roumois reminiscent of the Caux plateau. An area dotted with small country churches guarded by yew trees:

Bouquetot (11C-12C) – Statues, 18C paintings and a 700-year old hawthorn;

Bourg-Achard – Beautiful 16C glass, outstanding 15C and 16C woodwork, 15C stone polychrome Virgin;

Bourgtheroulde – Renaissance stained-glass windows;

Cesseville – 16C west front;

Écaquelon ⊘ – Lovely 16C woodwork;

Infreville – Large Rococo altarpiece;

Le Neubourg (main town of the region) – The church houses a 17C **high altar** prettily adorned with statues. Important open-air market.

Routot – Romanesque belfry with interlacing arcatures. The **Maison du Lin**, devoted to the linen industry, enlightens visitors on the making of this noble material: growing and spinning of flax, old-fashioned traditions and recent manufacturing techniques.

St-Aubin d'Écrosville – West front.

Château de Tilly (1500) – Lozenge-patterned stone and glazed-brick front, perimeter wall quartered by pointed turrets;

Le Tremblay-Omonville – Curious mid-18C façade, terraces and outbuildings.

BELLÊME

Population 1 788
Michelin map 60 north of folds 14 and 15 or 231 south of fold 45
Local map see MORTAGNE-AU-PERCHE

Bellême, capital of the Perche, a title long disputed with neighbouring Mortagne, sits on a small spur (225m/738ft) overlooking the forest (2 400ha/5 930 acres) and the beautiful Perche countryside. The town had a particularly turbulent history in the Middle Ages and when Blanche of Castile and the future St Louis took the fortress by assault in 1229.

Ville close – The **gate**, flanked by two reconstructed towers, together with towers now incorporated into domestic buildings, are the only remains of the 15C ramparts which once enclosed the walled town and were built upon 11C fortress foundations; the portcullis grooves are visible. Rue Ville-Close, on the site of the former citadel, is lined with fine 17C and 18C Classical style houses most of which

BELLÊME

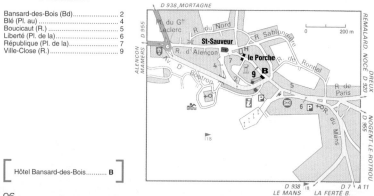

Hôtel Bansard-des-Bois............ **B**

Where to stay and eat

LUXURY

Hôtel du Golf – *Rte du Mans* – *2km/1.2mi southwest of Bellême via D 938* – ☎ *02 33 85 13 13* – **P** – *31 rooms: from 89.94€* – ☞ *9.91€* – *restaurant 15.55/39.33€.*
Located in the grounds of an 18-hole golf course, this large 16C house with exposed stone walls has been renovated to welcome golf players and in general those who love spending their holidays in the country. Ask for one of the rooms in the more recent building, they are more spacious and better fitted out. Peace and quiet guaranteed.

have retained their exterior decoration; well-proportioned balconies, wrought-iron railings and a huge gate. Outstanding are no 24, the Governor's house, and especially no 26, the **Hôtel de Bansard des Bois**. Its elegant façade can be seen from beside a stretch of water, once the castle moat.

Église St-Sauveur – The late-17C St Saviour's Church has a richly decorated interior. Note in particular the imposing high altar and canopy (1712) made of stone and marble, the chancel woodwork from the old abbey of Valdieu and the windows, each composed of six scenes from the life of Jesus. The font, decorated with garlands, stands against a three-panelled altarpiece.

EXCURSIONS

★**Forêt de Bellême** – *27km/17mi – about 1hr 30min.* This forest (2 400ha/5 930 acres) is one of the most beautiful in the Perche region with its majestic oaks and its beautiful and varied site.

From Bellême take D 938 northwest.

From the road there is a very pretty view of the town. It then crosses some remarkable woodland before reaching the Herse Pool.

Étang et Fontaine de la Herse – *A path circles the pool – 15min on foot.* The calm waters of the pool reflect the surrounding greenery and offer freshness much appreciated by tourists.
On the other side of the road, opposite the forester's lodge, is a Roman fountain. Near the fountain are two blocks of stone bearing Latin inscriptions.

Turn round and continue straight ahead; turn right at the Colbert crossroads.

The forest road (surfaced) affords lovely views.

At the Creux Valley crossroads, turn left. Follow the road along to the edge of the forest. Turn first right and enter the forest once again.
Before reaching the Montimer crossroads the road crosses a thicket. Descend on the left for 400m/0.3mi.

Chêne de l'École – This oak tree stands 40m/130ft tall and has a circumference of 22m/66ft. Even after 300 years it is still perfectly straight.

Return to the Montimer crossroads and continue to La Perrière.

La Perrière – The name comes from the Latin *petraria*, meaning "stone quarry". Indeed the village is built on a chalk promontory covered by sand. Here and there are outcrops of dark red ferruginous sandstone *(grison)*. Many of the houses have been built with this stone.
The village offers one of the best **panoramas**★ of the Perche countryside, including Perseigne Forest (west) and Écouves Forest (northwest) which can be seen from the cemetery path near the church.

🚶 To admire the old dwellings (15C-17C) and streets of the town, follow the "discovery path" *(sentier de la découverte: plan available locally)*. From La Perrière cycle tours and country walks are organised.

Return to the forest road which crosses Bellême Forest from west to east and passes through the delightful Creux Valley. At the Rendez-vous crossroads turn right onto D 310.

St-Martin-du-Vieux-Bellême – The houses of this picturesque village are clustered round the 14C-15C church.

Continue on the road which joins D 955 and turn left to Bellême.

Percheron

M.Dewynter/MICHELIN

TOUR OF THE PERCHE NORMAND

The Perche is a transitional region of complex structure between the Paris basin and the Armorican Massif. A predominance of impermeable soils and a humid climate favour the growth of dense vegetation: oak and beech woods on the schist and primary limestone, pasture and good arable land on the secondary marls and clay. Owing to its rich meadows the Perche is devoted to stock raising, particularly to the breeding of the draught horses known as **Percherons**. The region is subdivided into two areas, the Norman Perche, and the southern sector, the Perche-Gouet or Lower Perche. If you arrive from the Paris region, after crossing the flat, monotonous fields of the Beauce, you will be delighted to arrive in the Norman Perche, a rugged, yet picturesque region of wooded hillsides and hedgerows, broad green valleys and pastures, and charming villages.

While manors in the Pays d'Auge *(see p 72)* appear as welcoming country houses, those in the Norman Perche resemble small castles, standing a short distance from the road, built of stone and more or less fortified. Although most of these late-15C or early-16C lordly houses have long since been converted to farmhouses, they have retained certain defensive features; but these towers, elegant turrets and the delicate carved ornaments decorating many façades have nothing to do with military architecture.

1 From Bellême to Longny-au-Perche

68km/43mi – about 2hr

From Bellême take D 7 south.

Château des Feugerets – *Not open to the public.* A cluster of buildings – two square pavilions with a fine balustrade and moat and an elegant 16C central block – form a harmonious, well-balanced ensemble. The imposing silhouette of the château stands out against a verdant setting: the luxuriant vegetation features the fern *(fougère)*, which gave its name to the castle.

In La Chapelle-Souëf turn left onto D 277.

St-Cyr-la-Rosière – The church in this small village has a beautiful Romanesque doorway with a triple archivolt. Inside there is a remarkable 17C polychrome terracotta **Entombment★**, and a 17C painting of the martyrdom of St Sebastian.

Take the road south towards Theil.

Manoir de l'Angenardière – *Not open to the public.* This manor house built in the 15C and 16C, although restored, retains a feudal air and its still circled by well-preserved ramparts. Note the massive towers crowned with machicolations.

Continue south.

La Pierre Procureuse – According to legend, this stone serving as a roof covering to a dolmen from the late Neolithic Age (2500BC) is believed to bring luck on those who touch it.

At the T-junction turn right; go through Gémages.

St-Germain-de-la-Coudre – The church has an 11C crypt containing a beautiful *Virgin and Child* in stone.

Return to Gémages and take the road to Ste-Gauburge.

Hamlet of Ste-Gauburge – The church has been transformed to house a local arts and crafts collection, the **Musée départemental des Arts et Traditions populaires du Perche** ⊙. Crafts of the past – blacksmith, saddler, cartwright, woodcutter, cooper – are brought to life again. The short slide show on the Perche region is a good introduction to those unfamiliar with the area.

Adjoining the church are a group of buildings; they were once part of the former priory which was accountable to the Royal Abbey of St-Denis. This imposing ensemble (13C-18C) laid out around the courtyard illustrates the various aspects of monastic life: church for prayers, sleeping quarters for the monks, agricultural outbuildings and the prior's residence, in which the firepieces depict scenes taken from the Old and New Testaments.

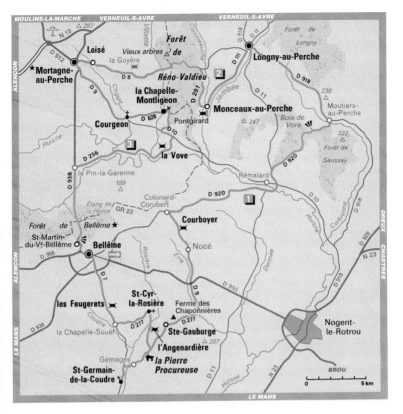

On the eastern edge of the village is **La Chaponnière Farm**. A round tower links the living area and a late-16C square pavilion.

Continue along D 277. Turn left at the crossroads onto D 9.

Manoir de Courboyer – This delightful manor house built of white stone at the end of the 15C, stands out on a hillside, and is one of the finest in the Perche. Four graceful watchtowers on machicolations quarter the main wing. The massive round tower, which greets the visitor below the level of the road, is linked by a heavy ridge pole to the slender octagonal staircase turret which adds considerable elegance to the west front.

In Colonard-Corubert turn right onto D 920.

East of Rémalard the countryside is greener and hillier; the road is picturesque.

In Moutiers turn left onto D 918 to Longny-au-Perche.

② From Mortagne-au-Perche to Longny

25km/16mi – about 30min – see MORTAGNE-AU-PERCHE

③ From Mortagne-au-Perche to Bellême

35km/22mi – about 1hr – see MORTAGNE-AU-PERCHE
From Mortagne-au-Perche take D 9 south.

BERNAY

Population 10 582
Michelin map 54 fold 19 or 231 fold 33

Bernay developed rapidly round an abbey founded early in the 11C by Judith of Brittany, wife of Duke Richard II. It was at Bernay in the 12C that the trouvère Alexandre of Bernay wrote the long poem, the *Romance of Alexander*, in 12-syllable lines known subsequently as alexandrines. The town, which nestles in the Charentonne Valley, possesses a number of renovated half-timbered houses.

SIGHTS

* **Boulevard des Monts** – This lovely hillside road commands good views of the town and the Charentonne Valley.

* **Hôtel de ville** – The 17C town hall buildings, which were formerly Bernay Abbey, are in the Maurist style.

Ancienne église abbatiale ⊙ – The abbey church was begun in 1013 by **Guglielmo da Volpiano** *(see p 202)*, summoned from Fécamp by Judith of Brittany. At the time the role of such an establishment was religious and intellectual but also political and economic. In the 15C the semicircular apse was replaced by a polygonal one. Note the carved capitals above the nave and the twin bays in the galleries. The north aisle, rebuilt in the 15C, has diagonal vaulting.

Musée municipal ⊙ – The museum is housed in the former abbot's lodge, a chequered stone and brick construction dating from the late 16C. Exhibits include a fine collection of Rouen, Nevers and Moustiers faience and old Norman furniture.

Old Dwellings – Some streets are lined with houses typical of old Bernay.

Rue Gaston-Folloppe – This is the antique dealers' street.

Rue Thiers and rue du Général-de-Gaulle – Busy shopping streets.

Rue Gabriel-Vallée – Access is through the passage du Grand Bourg, rue du Général-de-Gaulle. Note the corbelled half-timbered house at no 17.

Église Ste-Croix – The church of the Holy Cross, started in the 14C, has been heavily restored and contains fine works of art from Bec-Hellouin. Behind the portal is a 16C low relief in gilded wood: the Bearing of the Cross. There are tombstones of abbots near the organ gallery and in the south transept. The remarkable **tombstone** of Guillaume d'Auvillars, Abbot of Bec (1418) stands at the entrance to the sacristy. Sixteen great statues of apostles and evangelists from the end of the 14C are to be found on the pillars of the nave and choir decorated with the terracotta statues of St Maur and St Benoît (17C). On the high altar stands a sculpture in marble representing the Nativity scene (1683), based on a work by the Anguier brothers for the Val-de-Grâce in Paris (1662).

Basilique Notre-Dame-de-la-Couture ⊙ – *Access by rue Kléber-Mercier, south.* The interior of this 15C church, established as a basilica in 1950, has wooden vaulting; the statue Notre-Dame-de-la-Couture (16C), highly venerated by pilgrims *(see Calendar of events)* is placed on a modern altar in the north transept. The church has some fine windows, skilfully restored, representing the Ascension and Resurrection.

Eating out

MODERATE

Hostellerie du Moulin Fouret – *3.5km/2.2mi south of Bernay via rte de St-Quentin-des-Îles* – ☏ *02 32 43 19 95 – closed Feb school holidays, Sun evening and Mon from Sept to Apr except holidays – 15.24/50.31€.* Situated right out in the country, in the middle of a park on the banks of the River Charentonne, this old mill is a delightful place for a meal break on the flower-decked terrace in summer or in the convivial Norman dining room in winter. A few rooms are available for a peaceful night with no other sound than the gentle lapping of the water.

MID-RANGE

L'Étape Louis XIII – *27410 Beaumesnil – 13km/8.1mi southeast of Bernay via D 140* – ☏ *02 32 44 44 72 – closed 26-30 June, Feb school holidays, Wed except July-Aug and Tues – reservation essential – 19.82/48.78€.* This fine 17C timber-framed Norman house, located in the village, is very pleasant with its large fireplace and period wood panelling... Some might think it a pity that it is so close to the road, but those who enjoy their food will appreciate the refined cuisine and the very reasonable first-price menu.

BERNAY

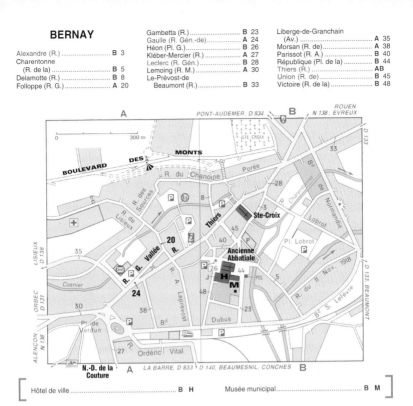

EXCURSION

★**Château de Beaumesnil** ⊙ – *13km/8mi southeast by D 140*. The château, a masterpiece of the Louis XIII style, is built of brick and stone and decorated in Baroque style; its impressive façade is mirrored in the moat.

The furnished interior boasts an extensive collection of 17C and 18C bound books as well as some fine examples of contemporary binding.

The formal gardens and the 60ha/149-acre **park** echo the sumptuous lines of the château, whose appearance has hardly altered since it was designed in the 17C. Note the intricate box tree maze of Baroque inspiration set up on an islet in the moat.

Château de Beaumesnil

BLAINVILLE-CREVON

Population 1 096
Michelin map 55 fold 7 or 231 fold 23 – 20km/12mi northeast of Rouen

This small village located in the Crevon Valley is the birthplace of the artist **Marcel Duchamp** (1887-1968), forerunner of the New York School of painting *(see The Green Guide New York City)*. Many artists from the School of Rouen stayed in the town.

Église ⊙ – The church, which was founded in 1488 by Jean d'Estouteville, is an attractive building with a chequered sandstone and silex facing. Originally a collegiate church, it became the parish church in the 19C. The interior is in the Flamboyant style.
In the left transept there is a monumental late-15C statue in painted wood of St Michael slaying the dragon; the chapel features a 15C group *(Education of the Virgin)*.

Château ⊙ – Excavations begun in 1968 on the ruins of a medieval castle have exposed a number of features belonging to 14C and 15C buildings: a staircase buried by an 11C motte, a stretch of curtain wall (100m/110yd long; 5-8m/15-24ft high), ditches and two towers of which the lower storeys are in good condition.

EXCURSIONS

South of Blainville – *Tour of 10km/6mi by D 12.*
The road winds its way down the charming Crevon Valley.

Ry – The village of half-timbered and brick houses is said to be Yonville-l'Abbaye where **Gustave Flaubert** (1821-80) set the action of his novel *Madame Bovary*.
A monument to Flaubert stands in front of the post office. The character of Emma Bovary is said to have been inspired by Delphine Couturier, wife of Doctor Delamare; the "house of the doctor" where she died in 1848 is now occupied by the chemist's shop; the pharmacy where M Homais used to pontificate has become Lagarde's dry cleaners and trinkets shop.
The 18C cider factory (restored) now houses the **Musée d'Automates** ⊙. Three hundred of the automata represent scenes from Madame Bovary; the exhibition also includes a reconstruction of Homais' pharmacy.
The 12C **church** is surmounted by a lantern tower with a corbelled cornice and entered through a charming Renaissance wooden **porch★** carved with human figures including God the Father wearing a tiara. The interior shows off the wooden roof and a wooden altar front carved in the Renaissance style. The beam ends in the south chapel are carved with angry faces.

Take D 13 southwest.

Half-timbered cart shed, Château de Martainville

★Château de Martainville ⊙ – The elegant brick and stone château dates from the end of the 15C. The great brick chimney stacks bear remarkable Gothic decoration. Near the outbuildings stand a massive dovecot (16C) and a half-timbered cart shed (18C). The interior of the château, which has been little altered, houses the Musée Départemental des Traditions et Arts Normands (Museum of Arts and Traditions of Normandy). The rooms, often embellished with beautiful chimney-pieces, display exhibits from the 15C to the 19C: furniture from Rouen and the Pays de Caux, chests, 17C buffets, 18C cupboards, earthenware and pottery, glass, pewter and copper, regional ceramics and costumes.

Eating out

MODERATE

L'Hirondelle – *40 Grand'Rue – 76116 Ry –* ☎ *02 35 02 01 46 – closed Sun evening and Mon – 12.96/23.63€.* This restaurant derives its originality from various sources: an ancient timber-framed Norman farm with a lovely brick-built fireplace and an old well, authentic cuisine from southwest France and a name which suggests the stagecoach used by Madame Bovary in Flaubert's novel of the same name.

Where to stay

MID-RANGE

Le Château Bed and Breakfast – *Pl. de l'Église – 76750 Bosc-Roger-sur-Buchy – 2.5km/1.5mi west of Bosc-Bordel, towards Buchy –* ☎ *02 35 34 29 70 – closed end of Nov to 1 Mar –* – *4 rooms: 39.64/56.41€.* This 19C castle with its Napoleon III look offers guests the use of a comfortable drawing room, a billiard table and 4 rooms, including two in the turrets, with simple but varied furniture. Cloth-covered walls and a variety of curios contribute to the impression of opulence.

BRIONNE

Population 4 408
Michelin map 54 fold 19 or 231 fold 33

In medieval times Brionne was a stronghold commanding the Risle Valley and in the 11C had close ties with the monastery in the neighbouring Bec Valley. It was in fact when William of Normandy was besieging the Duke of Burgundy in Brionne from 1047 to 1050 that he was first introduced to the cultural centre of Bec-Hellouin Abbey, which was to have such a strong influence on the organisation of religious life in England. Brionne is not only an industrial and commercial centre but also a tourist attraction because of its old keep and its park on the banks of the Risle.

SIGHTS

Donjon – *15min on foot there and back. Park in place du Chevalier-Herluin or by the church. Take rue des Canadiens and 45m/50yd further on turn right onto sente du Vieux-Château.*
The steep path leads up to the ruins of one of the best examples of a square Norman keep (11C), once supported by solid buttresses. From the base of the keep *(viewing table)* there is a pleasant view over the town and the Risle Valley.

Église St-Martin – The nave is 15C and the Gothic wood vaulting in the chancel 14C. The marble altar and altarpiece (17C) come from Bec-Hellouin Abbey. The modern windows are by Gabriel Loire.

Jardin de Shaftesbury – The small garden beside the Risle bears the name of Brionne's twin town in England.

Ancien pressoir – This former 18C press has recently been restored and now houses the Tourist Information Centre.

TOUR OF THE LIEUVEN REGION *28km/17mi – about 1hr*

The Lieuvin is a plateau covered with silex clay and alluvial mud. It is also a region of pastures and cereal crops. Together with the Roumois from which it is separated by the Risle Valley, it forms the transition between the Caux and the Auge regions.
From Brionne take D 46 north. In Authun turn left onto D 38.
The road ascends into the pleasant Livet Valley.

Livet-sur-Authou – Charming black and white half-timbered houses line the entrance. The castle and church on the other side of the road complete the picturesque scene.

St-Benoît-des-Ombres – Beyond the miniature town hall the chapel (right) is hidden in the greenery. Its 15C wooden porch is crowned by a great statue of St Benedict carved in wood. Inside, notice the fine vault and 16C font.
Bear right towards St-Georges-du-Vièvre.
The roof of the Château de Launay appears at the bottom of a steep hill.

Château de Launay ⊘ – *Turn right and walk along the castle approach.* From the main gate there is a good view of this attractive Regency building with 16C half-timbered outbuildings. There is also a remarkable **dovecot**★ with beams carved to depict monsters and generally grotesque characters and attractive formal gardens.
Return by D 137 and D 130.
The road offers a pretty view of the Risle Valley.

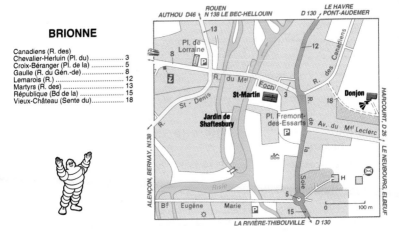

BRIONNE

EXCURSIONS

★★Le Bec-Hellouin – *6km/3.6mi north via N 138 and D 39. See Le BEC-HELLOUIN.*

★Château d'Harcourt – *7km/4.2mi southeast via D 26 or D 137. See Château du CHAMP DE BATAILLE: Excursions.*

★★Château du Champ de Bataille – *14km/8.4mi southeast via D 26 then D 39 towards Neubourg. See Château du CHAMP DE BATAILLE.*

Forêt de BROTONNE

Michelin map 55 fold 5 or 231 fold 21

The large massif, enclosed in a bend of the Seine, contributes to the rustic and sometimes lonely appearance of the south bank of the river. The breaks through the trees made by forest roads afford some fine vistas of the leafy glades of beeches, oaks or pines.

The creation of the **Parc naturel régional de Brotonne** in 1974 and the construction of the Brotonne Bridge *(see below)* have made the forest readily accessible.

A village on the southern edge of Brotonne Forest, La Haye-de-Routot *(see below)*, where traditions survive, comes under the aegis of the Écomusée de la Basse-Seine (regional open-air museum), which strives to preserve and revive ancient crafts. The road (D 65) which skirts the forest on the south bank of the Seine, known as "thatched house road", provides views of several thatched cottages surrounded by apple trees.

FROM ROUTOT TO CAUDEBEC-EN-CAUX 33km/20mi – hr

La Haye-de-Routot – The cemetery surrounding the little **church** ⊙ is shaded by two **yew trees★**, over a thousand years old (16m/52ft and 14m/46ft in circumference). The bonfire of St Clair, on the night of 16-17 July always draws a huge crowd to the village.

In an 18C building the **bread oven** ⊙ revives ancient baking methods in an old-fashioned wooden oven. Baker's tools are exhibited.

The **Musée du Sabot** ⊙ set up in a traditional 17C Roumois house presents tools and techniques used in the past by sabot-makers as well as a large collection of sabots.

Take D 40 for 4.5km/3mi; turn left onto the narrow forest road which crosses D 131.

This very pleasant road (Mare de la Chèvre) passes through several beautiful copses as it crosses the plateau and descends into the Seine Valley. As it approaches the river *(3km/2mi from D 131)* there is a beautiful **view** (left) of the Seine Valley west as far as Tancarville Bridge.

Turn right onto D 65; at Le Quesney bear right onto the road to La Mailleraye and right again onto the forest road to St-Maur Chapel.

The road passes through one of the thickest parts of the forest.

Eating out

MODERATE

Risle-Seine – *In the village centre – 27500 Bourneville – 9km/5.6mi west of Routot via D 90 –* ☎ *02 32 42 30 22 – closed Wed evening and Mon – reservation essential – 13.72/24.39€.* Tasty cuisine prepared with fresh produce is served in this town house with its light-ochre façade and simple decoration. You will find something to satisfy your appetite, whether you like to eat a lot or very little. A detail not to be overlooked… in summer, meals are served on the terrace in the garden.

Where to stay

MODERATE

Les Sources Bleues Bed and Breakfast – *Rte du Vieux-Port – 27500 Aizier – 5km/3.1mi north of Bourneville via D 139 –* ☎ *02 32 57 26 68 –* ⊨ *– 4 rooms: 36.59/41.16€ – meal 13.72€.* Situated along the estuary, this splendid Norman house dating from 1854 is surrounded by a lovely if untidy park stretching along the Seine. From there, one can see ships heading for Le Havre. Woodwork, parquet flooring and tiles make up the cosy decor. Pleasant rooms.

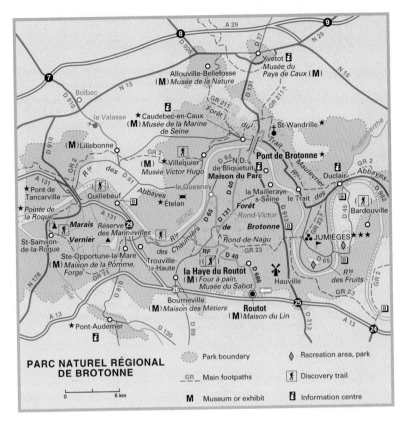

PARC NATUREL RÉGIONAL DE BROTONNE

0 ____ 6 km

- Park boundary
- ◆ Recreation area, park
- GR Main footpaths
- Discovery trail
- **M** Museum or exhibit
- Information centre

Rond-de-Nagu – A large clearing in the shape of a star.

Turn left onto D 131; continue north via Rond-Victor to St-Nicolas-de-Bliquetuit. Turn left onto D 65.

From St-Nicolas-de-Bliquetuit (where the nature park has an information centre, the **maison du Parc** ⊙), pretty gardens and half-timbered houses are strung like jewels along the silver waters of the River Seine.

★**Pont de Brotonne** – *Toll bridge.* The bridge, which spans the Seine above Caudebec-en-Caux, was opened to traffic in 1977; its measurements are: length 1 280m/4 200ft, height above water 50m/164ft, height of the pylons 125m/410ft.

Return to Caudebec via D 928.

CABOURG ⸝⸜⸝⸜

Population 3 365
Michelin map 54 folds 16 and 17 or 231 fold 19
Local map see Pays d'AUGE

The large seaside resort of Cabourg, created at the time of the Second Empire (1852-70), has always kept its elegant clientele. A huge stretch of water has been created to provide sailing facilities at the mouth of the Dives.

Famous guest – **Marcel Proust** went to Cabourg for the first time in 1881, when he was 10. As he suffered from asthma the coastal climate was beneficial to his health. Attracted by the charm of the place, he would often visit the town and stay at the Grand Hôtel. Cabourg gave him the opportunity to rediscover his childhood. French literature is indebted to him for *Within a Budding Grove* (*À l'Ombre des Jeunes Filles en Fleurs*), a vivid portrayal of life in a seaside resort at the turn of the 19-20C and of the customs of Cabourg.

THE RESORT

The town has a geometrical symmetry. The Casino and Grand Hôtel stand together on the seafront and form the focal point from which streets radiate inland, intersecting with two intermediary concentric semicircular avenues. The avenues and streets are, in many cases, lined by attractive houses set in shaded gardens.

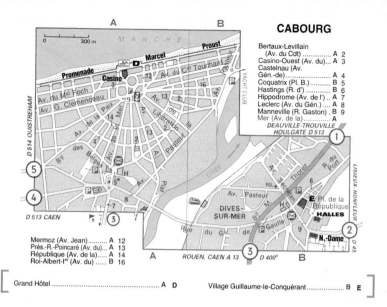

CABOURG

Bertaux-Levillain
(Av. du Cdt) .... A 2
Casino-Ouest (Av. du)... A 3
Castelnau (Av.
Gén.-de) .... A 4
Coquatrix (Pl. B.) .... B 5
Hastings (R. d') .... B 6
Hippodrome (Av. de l') .. A 7
Leclerc (Av. du Gén.) .... A 8
Manneville (R. Gaston) . B 9
Mer (Av. de la) .... A

Mermoz (Av. Jean).......... A 12
Prés.-R.-Poincaré (Av. du)... A 13
République (Av. de la)..... A 14
Roi-Albert-Iᵉʳ (Av. du) ...... B 16

Grand Hôtel .... A **D**   Village Guillaume-le-Conquérant.................... B **E**

Boulevard Marcel-Proust, a terrace running the full length of the immense fine sand beach, makes a magnificent promenade with a view extending from Riva-Bella to Houlgate with Trouville as background and Cap de la Hève on the horizon.
On the right bank of the River Dives lies the locality of Dives-sur-Mer *(see DIVES-SUR-MER)*.

EXCURSIONS

Merville-Franceville-Plage – *6km/4mi west of Cabourg by D 514*. At the time of the Allied landings in June 1944 the strongest point in the defences was the Merville Battery, composed of four concrete casemates armed with a 150mm gun with a range of 20km. It was captured by the 6th British Airborne Division. One of the casemates has been converted into a museum, the **Musée des Batteries de Merville-Franceville** ⊙.

Ranville – *8km/5mi south of Merville-Franceville-Plage on D 223*. In the Second World War Ranville was captured at 2.30am on 6 June by paratroopers of the 13th Battalion of the Lancashire Fuseliers of the 6th British Airborne Division; it was the first village to be liberated on French territory.
The town has built a War Cemetery to commemorate the events.

Eating out

MODERATE

Chez Marion – *10 pl. de la Plage – 14810 Merville-Franceville-Plage – 5km/3.1mi west of Cabourg via D 514 –* ☎ *02 31 24 23 39 – www.chez-marion.com – closed 2 Jan to 2 Feb, Mon evening and Tues except school holidays – reservation advisable – 14.94/38.11€*. People come a long way to enjoy this restaurant's fish and seafood! No fewer than 18 different kinds of shellfish and a superb selection of calvados contribute to the success of the place... If you wish to spend the night here, ask for a room with a view of the sea.

Auberge des Viviers – *81 av. Charles-de-Gaulle –* ☎ *02 31 91 05 10 – closed Oct to Mar – reservation essential in summer – 11.43/22.11€*. Do not turn back when you see the slightly gloomy decor of this inn housed in a former fishmonger's: you would make a mistake for you will find happiness on your plate here... The menu, which reflects the catch brought back by fishermen, consists of regional dishes.

Where to stay

MODERATE

Camping municipal Le Point du Jour – *14810 Merville-Franceville-Plage – 5km/3.1mi west of Cabourg via D 514 –* ☎ *02 31 24 23 34 – closed end of Nov to early Feb –* ⊟ *– reservation advisable in season – 142 places: 12.20€*. This campsite will be appreciated by those who like maritime air since it is situated on the edge of the beach! Places are cleverly defined by lovely hedges. Games and television room... But nothing can equal the sight of the sea.

MID-RANGE

Le Manoir des Tourpes Bed and Breakfast – *3 r. de l'Église* – *14670 Bures-sur-Dives* – *12km/7.5mi south of Cabourg via D 400, N 175 (towards Caen) then a minor road* – ☏ *02 31 23 63 47* – *www.cpod.com/monoweb/ mantourpes* – *closed 12 Nov to 15 Mar* – ⌿ – *3 rooms: 41.16/60.98€.* This opulent 17C manor house, surrounded by meadows through which meanders the Dives, offers a charming view of the river from every room. Ask for the "Angling" room with its stone walls and fireplace or the cosier "Red" room with its exposed beams.

Hôtel Le Cottage – *24 av. du Gén.-Leclerc* – ☏ *02 31 91 65 61* – *14 rooms: 45.73/83.85€* – ⌸ *6.10€.* This timber-framed house surrounded by its own small garden is rather stylish: all the rooms are different and the decor is old-fashioned but neat. Breakfast is sometimes served outside weather permitting...

LUXURY

Grand Hôtel – *Prom. M.-Proust* – ☏ *02 31 91 01 79* – **P** – *70 rooms: from 1 057.02€* – ⌸ *13.72€* – *restaurant 35.06/44.21€.* This early-20C palace has retained the souvenir of Marcel Proust who loved to stay here. With the sea on one side and the garden on the other, you will enjoy the luxury of a discreet service in beautifully renovated bedrooms... and why not ask for the room used by the writer, which has been redecorated as it was during his lifetime.

On the town

Bar of the Grand Hôtel – *Prom. Marcel-Proust* – ☏ *02 31 91 01 79* – *daily 11.30am-1am.* The reputation of this hotel, a model of Belle Epoque style, is well established... It is so striking and conducive to nostalgia with its huge chandeliers and full draperies. Those who are not lucky enough to spend a few days here can always have tea in the bar or, even better, enjoy a drink of 40-year-old calvados, whilst looking at the sea.

Cabourg Casino – *Prom. Marcel-Proust* – ☏ *02 31 28 19 19* – *fruit machines: Mon-Thur 10am-3am, Fri-Sat 10am-4am, Sun 10am-3am* – *boule: Mon-Thur 9pm-3am, Fri 9pm-4am, Sat 4pm-4am, Sun 4pm-3am* – *traditional games: Wed-Thur 9pm-3am, Fri-Sat 8pm-4am, Sun 3pm-3am* – *discotheque: Fri-Sun 11pm-5am.* When the original town plan was designed, the main avenues were drawn round the casino in the shape of a fan. The pedestrianised Promenade Marcel-Proust, on the waterfront, leads directly to this gaming den... How could one resist? In addition to the fruit machines and traditional games, the casino houses a discotheque (500 places), a hall (250 seats), an Italian-style theatre (up to 500 seats), and a panoramic restaurant facing the sea.

Chez Guillou – *4 av. de la Mer* – ☏ *02 31 91 31 31* – *Fri-Sun 6.30pm-1am (school holidays daily 6.30pm-2am)* – *closed Jan.* This is the most sought-after bar along the coast; the interior is delightfully old-fashioned: short curtains with red and white squares, wall-covering and old parquet flooring. Comfortable leather seats, some original cocktails based on fresh cream or champagne and fruit juice.

Sport

Miniature golf – *13 av. du Cdt-Touchard* – ☏ *02 31 24 14 44* – *July-Aug daily 10am-10.30pm; Apr, June, Sept-Oct daily 2.30pm-7pm* – *closed mid-Nov-Mar.* Created in 1952, this lovely 18-track mini-golf has reconstructions of several famous monuments in the world (such as Tancarville bridge, Big Ben, the Cheops pyramid, the Tower of Pisa, the Eiffel Tower...). At the end of the game, you will be able to have a drink on the terrace of the bar which overlooks the sea.

La Sablonnière – *Av. Guillaume-le-Conquérant* – ☏ *02 31 78 01 88* – *daily 7am-8pm.* Housed in a Norman-style building, this club organises walks along the beach (before 10am and after 7pm in summer) as well as in the hinterland. Whether you are a beginner or an experienced rider, you will find a horse to your liking among the 15 available. Children can choose one of the 10 resident ponies. Beginners' courses are provided by a teacher with a state diploma.

CAEN ★★★

Population 189 000
Michelin map 54 fold 16 or 231 fold 30
Local map see Plages du DÉBARQUEMENT

Caen is the cultural capital of the Basse-Normandie, a lively city with a distinctive identity. The bombs which fell here in 1944 could have left Caen lifeless for all their violence. But the city proved resilient and was able to draw on the strength of its history to rebuild and recreate. Today it is modern in spirit, benefits from the presence of a university (founded in the 15C, it now has more than 30 000 students), and is also, quite simply, a charming place to visit!

The marked itinerary "L'Affrontement" (The Attack), one of several described in the Historical Area of the Battle of Normandy, starts from here (see p 29).

PROUD AND FAITHFUL MATILDA

William and Matilda – Recent excavation work would seem to indicate that the site was occupied by a *vicus* (hamlet) as early as the 1C. The name Caen is thought to have originated from *Catomagos*, the name of the very first settlement. The city achieved importance only in the 11C when it became Duke William's favourite place of residence.

After defeating the rebel barons of the Cotentin and Bessin regions and thus confirming his possession of the Duchy of Normandy, William asked for the hand of Matilda of Flanders who was a distant cousin. She did not welcome his proposal and replied that she would rather take the veil than be given in marriage to the bastard son of the Beautiful Arlette. The duke swallowed the insult but one fine day, mad with love and anger, he rode headlong to Lille and burst into the palace of the Count of Flanders. According to the Chronicler of Tours, he seized Matilda by her plaits and dragged her round the room kicking her. Then he left her gasping for breath and galloped off. Proud Matilda was vanquished and consented to the marriage, which was celebrated in spite of the opposition of the Pope who objected to the cousins' distant kinship. In 1059 the excommunication, which weighed heavily on William, was lifted through the efforts of **Lanfranc**. As an act of penitence the Duke and his wife founded two abbeys. These two convents – the Abbey for Men and the Abbey for Women – made Caen a thoroughly Benedictine town; Bayeux remained the episcopal see.

When William departed to conquer England, faithful Matilda became regent of the duchy; in 1068 she was crowned Queen of England. She was buried in the Abbey for Women in 1083. William died in 1087 and, according to his wish, was buried in the church of the Abbey for Men.

BATTLE OF CAEN

Two Agonizing Months – The battle lasted for over two months. On 6 June 1944 there was a heavy bombing raid; fire raged for 11 days and the central area was burnt out. On 9 July the Canadians, who had taken Carpiquet Airfield, entered Caen from the west but the Germans, who had fallen back to the east bank of the Orne in Vaucelles, began to shell the town. The official liberation ceremony took place in Vaucelles on 20 July but another month went by before the last German shell was fired.

Abbaye-aux-Hommes

Under the Conqueror's Protection – On 6 June many of the people of Caen sought shelter in St-Étienne Church. During the battle over 1 500 refugees camped out in the abbey church. An operating theatre was contrived in the refectory of the Lycée Malherbe, which was housed in the monastery buildings of the Abbey for Men, and the dead were buried in the courtyard. Some 4 000 people found accommodation in the Hospice of the Good Saviour (Bon Sauveur) nearby. The Allies were warned by the Préfet and the Resistance and these buildings were spared.

The quarries at Fleury, 2km/1mi south of Caen, provided the largest refuge. Despite the cold and damp, whole families lived like troglodytes until the end of July.

Port of Caen – Although the River Orne has always enabled Caen to serve as a port, no major development took place until the middle of the 19C when Baron Cachin dug a canal parallel to the river. The canal (12km/7mi long) was regulated by several locks and served by an outer basin at Ouistreham. Since then the increased output of the Caen steel works has required the deepening and widening of the canal and the creation of five more docks: St Peter's Dock (St-Pierre) for pleasure boats, the New Dock, the Calix Dock, the Hérouville Dock and the Blainville Dock which came into use in 1974.

Today the transportation of cereals is the chief function of Caen harbour, the largest one in the Basse-Normandie, which can receive ships of up to 19 000t fully laden and up to 30 000t partially laden. Because of its broad range of activities, this port is ranked 11th in France.

The opening of a cross-Channel car ferry service on 6 June 1986 has established daily links between Caen-Ouistreham and Portsmouth, catering to an estimated one million passengers every year.

A WALK AROUND CAEN

★**Hôtel d'Escoville** – This mansion now houses the tourist office and the Artothèque. This beautiful residence was built between 1533 and 1538 by Nicolas Le Valois d'Escoville, a wealthy merchant. The bomb damage incurred in 1944 has been repaired. The building is one of the most typical of the Early Renaissance in Caen, where Italian influence was strongly felt in ornamentation.

Behind the plain street façade there is a **courtyard** flanked by two wings at right angles; the harmonious proportions, the arrangement of the various elements and the majestic sculptures make an elegant composition. The main block facing the entrance is surmounted by a particularly unusual ornament, a large two-storey dormer window supported by flying buttresses projecting from a steep pavilion roof. Seated at the base of each flying buttress support is a figure in high relief of Tubal Cain (a biblical character said to have invented the forge).

The niches on the ground floor contain statues of Judith with the head of Holofernes and David with the head of Goliath. Beneath the Escoville arms and supported by nymphs and spirits, are low-relief sculptures representing Perseus releasing Andromeda (left) and the Abduction of Europa (right).

Climb up to the loggia for a view of the whole courtyard.

★**Église St-Pierre** – Although only a parish church, St Peter's has frequently received liberal endowments from the wealthy citizens of Caen and is richly decorated. Construction started in the 13C, was continued during the 14C and 15C and completed in the 16C in the Renaissance style. The impressive tower (78m/256ft), which dated from 1308, was destroyed during the Battle of Caen in 1944. "The king of Norman belfries" has, however, been rebuilt as well as the nave into which it fell (all the vaulting has been redone). The west front has been restored to its 14C appearance; the Flamboyant porch is surmounted by a rose window.

The **east end**★★, built between 1518 and 1545, is remarkable for the richness of its Renaissance decor, in which the shapely and graceful furnishings (ornate pinnacles, urns, richly scrolled balustrades, carved pilasters), have replaced the Gothic motifs.

The interior is heterogeneous. The first five bays (14C) of the nave feature simple pointed vaulting. Some of the **capitals**★ (second and third pillars on the left) are interesting for their carvings which are taken from the bestiaries of the period and chivalrous exploits. The third pillar shows (from left to right) Aristotle on horseback threatened with a whip by Campaspe, Alexander's mistress; the Phoenix rising from the flames (Resurrection); Samson breaking the lion's jaw (Redemption); the Pelican in her Piety (Divine Love); Lancelot crossing the Sword Bridge to rescue his Queen; Virgil suspended in his basket by the daughter of the Roman emperor; the unicorn (Incarnation), pursued by hunters, taking refuge with a young maiden; Gawain on his deathbed with an arrow wound (damaged).

The Renaissance vaulting in the second part of the nave, near the chancel, contrasts with the vaulting in the first part: each arch is embellished with a hanging keystone, finely carved. The most remarkable keystone, in the fifth arch over the high altar, is 3m/10ft high and weighs 3t; it is a life-size figure of St Peter.

Eating out

MODERATE

Maître Corbeau – *8 r. Buquet* – ☎ *02 31 93 93 00* – *closed Aug, Sat lunch, Mon lunch and Sun* – *13.72/19.06€*. This place is entirely dedicated to cheese: boxes, adverts, tools etc… and, of course, in this unusual setting, you can only choose between cheese or cheese… or cheese, hot, cold or warm, and the establishment's generous helpings draw local connoisseurs!

Le Bouchon du Vaugueux – *12 r. Graindorge* – ☎ *02 31 44 26 26* – *closed 1-20 Aug, 22 Dec to 10 Jan, Sun and Mon* – *reservation essential* – *15€ lunch* – *17/20€*. Situated close to one of the old districts of Caen, this tavern (bouchon) is appropriately named with its sombre decor in black and red, its tables set out close together and its warm atmosphere. Menu handwritten on the traditional slate.

Dolly's English Shop – *16/18 av. de la Libération* – ☎ *02 31 94 03 29* – *closed Mon* – *7.93€ lunch* – *5.79/10.37€*. Having created a typically English atmosphere, Colette and Steve will delight you with their breakfasts, brunches, pastries and "afternoon teas" served all day. To delight you even more, the shop next door sells most of the products served at Dolly's.

La Muscade – *21 pl. St-Martin* – ☎ *02 31 85 61 84* – *closed 22 July to 12 Aug and Sun* – *10.98 lunch* – *12.96/20.58€*. Halfway between the palace of Justice and the Abbaye-aux-Hommes, this establishment has two dining rooms: one of them is reminiscent of a Parisian "brasserie" with actors' photographs on the walls, whereas the other is more simply decorated with warm yellows. Traditional cuisine with a contemporary slant.

L'Insolite – *16 r. du Vaugueux* – ☎ *02 31 43 83 87* – *closed Sun and Mon except Jul and Aug* – *reservations recommended* – *15/38€*. This 16C half-timbered house is well worth a look. The name means "unexpected", and that describes the decor: a pleasant pastiche of rustic and retro with frescoes, mirrors and dried flowers. Fish and seafood specialities.

Alcide – *1 pl. Courtonne* – ☎ *02 31 44 18 06* – *closed 21-31 Dec and Sat* – *13.26/21.19€*. This restaurant by the canal offers good fare at moderate prices. You can choose between the bar and the dining room with its bistro-style furniture and lighting reflected by mirrors.

MID-RANGE

Auberge de l'Île Enchantée – *On the banks of the River Orne* – *14123 Fleury-sur-Orne* – *4km/2.5mi south of Caen via D 562* – ☎ *02 31 52 15 52* – *closed 23 July to 11 Aug, Feb school holidays, Sun evening, Wed evening and Mon* – *16.46/30.18€*. You will no doubt be delighted by the sight of the panoramic dining room of this riverside inn. The atmosphere is warm and the owners' menus are in line with current tastes.

Where to stay

MODERATE

Bernières Hotel – *50 r. de Bernières* – ☎ *02 31 86 01 26* – *www.hotelbernieres.com* – *17 rooms: 32.01/39.64€* – ☖ *5.34€*. Do not miss the discreet entrance of this hotel for you would regret its convivial welcome, the charming breakfast room and drawing room and the delightful bedrooms. The owner's dried-flower bouquets add a personal touch to the pleasant surroundings.

St-Étienne Hotel – *2 r. de l'Académie* – ☎ *02 31 86 35 82* – *11 rooms: 24.39/35.06€* – ☖ *4.27€*. This house, going back to the 1789 Revolution, is located in a quiet district, close to the Abbaye-aux-Hommes. Note the fine wooden staircase with its beautiful sheen and the stylish bedrooms, some of them with fireplaces. Breakfast served in the dining room.

Central Hotel – *23 pl. J.-Letellier* – ☎ *02 31 86 18 52* – *25 rooms: 25.92/39.64€* – ☖ *4.88€*. As its name suggests, this hotel is located in the town centre, which makes it convenient for visiting the castle or browsing round this busy shopping area. Basic comfort at very reasonable prices.

Hôtel de France – *10 r. de la Gare* – ☎ *02 31 52 16 99* – **P** – *47 rooms: 38.11/45.73€* – ☖ *5.34€*. Situated in the town centre, close to the railway station, this 1950s hotel offers a very warm welcome. Veneered furniture in the spacious soundproofed bedrooms.

Le Fuchsia – *98 r. St-Jean* – ☎ *02 31 86 14 50* – *12 rooms.: 28.97/32€* – ☖ *4.12€*. You will recognize this hotel by the bright awnings out front. It is a convenient and comfortable place to stay if you would like to explore the cultural capital of Lower Normandy. The owners are renovating the rooms one at a time. Light meals available at the brasserie.

Le Bristol – *31 r. du 11-novembre* – ☎ *02 31 84 59 76* – *24 rooms: 41.16/50.31€* - ☖ *5.34€*. If you prefer to stay away from the centre of town, this hotel is located near the River Orne and the racetrack. The rooms have been redecorated recently in yellow tones, with modern furnishings, comfortable beds and double-glazed windows.

Hôtel du Havre – *11 r. du Havre* – ☎ *02 31 86 19 80* – 🅿 – *15 rooms: 28.97/ 39.64€* – ⊡ . Located near "La Prairie" and its racecourse, this post-war hotel offers modern, colourful and soundproofed rooms at very attractive prices.

MID-RANGE

Manoir des Tourpes Bed and Breakfast – *3 r. de l'Église* – *14670 Bures-sur-Dives* – *15km/9.3mi east of Caen via N 175 to Troarn then D 95* – ☎ *02 31 23 63 47* – *www.cpod.com/monoweb/mantourpes* – *closed 11 Nov to 15 Mar* – ⊡ – *3 rooms: 41.16/60.98€*. This opulent 17C manor house, surrounded by meadows through which meanders the Dives, offers a charming view of the river from every room. Ask for the "Angling" room with its stone walls and fireplace or the cosier "Red" room with its exposed beams.

On the town

Caen is a highly convivial and lively town. Don't hesitate to take a stroll in the pedestrianised district, you will be pleasantly greeted by all the shopkeepers. In the evening a tour of the small Vaugueux district is recommended: several pubs and restaurants have opened in fine houses spared by the war. If all this does not make you want to come back to Caen, it must surely be because you're becoming a resident!

Café Latin – *135 r. St-Pierre* – ☎ *02 31 85 26 36* – *Mon-Sat 10am-1am* – *closed 25 Dec*. Street paintings, piled-up car wheels instead of seats, corrugated iron and rusty electric fans on the ceiling give this colourful café an authentic Latino-American look and atmosphere.

La Garsouille – *11-13 r. Arcisse-de-Caumont* – ☎ *02 31 86 80 27* – *Mon-Sat 3pm-1am* – *closed holidays*. With its white-stone façade, arched windows, wall paintings and trompe-l'œil reproduction of the real bar with false customers, this café is, as it name indicates, an unusual and attractive place where reality and fantasy mingle happily. Short concerts on Friday evenings in time for drinks, between 7.30 and 9.30pm.

Le Loup Blanc – *38 r. Écuyère* – ☎ *02 31 85 72 67* – *Mon-Sat 6pm-2am*.
The thick red-satin curtain is always open onto the tiny bar of this cosy wine shop. Don't hesitate to go into this "theatre" to taste some very fine vintages under the watchful eye of the owner and his... vampires (part of the decor).

Showtime

Centre dramatique national de Normandie (Comédie de Caen) – *32 r. des Cordes* – ☎ *02 31 46 27 29* – *opening times follow the calendar of performances* – *closed July-Aug*. The programming explores all the possibilities of the theatre. Classical plays alternate with contemporary ones in an attempt to show the public how drama is continually changing. Two halls, one of 300 seats and one of 700 seats.

Caen Theatre – *135 bd du Mar.-Leclerc* – ☎ *02 31 30 48 00* – *www.ville-caen.fr* – *opening times follow the calendar of performances* – *closed June-Sept*. Inaugurated in 1963, this vast theatre with over 1 000 seats was entirely renovated in 1991. Operas, ballets and performances of contemporary dance alternate with theatre performances, classical concerts, jazz sessions and traditional music programmes. Concerts are free on Saturday at 5pm from October to May.

Shopping

Librairie Guillaume – *98 r. St-Pierre* – ☎ *02 31 85 43 13* – *Tues-Sun 9.30am-12.30pm, 2-7pm, and Mon afternoon*. The carved-wood façade of this splendid bookshop dates from 1902. There is a choice of books about the region and, on the first floor, a fine display of old books.

Sport and recreation

Hippodrome de Caen – *La Prairie* – ☎ *02 31 85 42 61* – *Mar-Nov: racing season*. A 2km/1.2mi-long racecourse in the centre of Caen. The brasserie on the first floor offers a lovely panoramic view of the town. Visits are organised on racing days (30 every year) in the morning. Not to be missed.

L'Hastings Boat – *Quai Vendeuvre* – ☎ *02 31 34 00 00* – *bateaulhastings@yahoo.fr* – *4 departures daily in season: 9am; 12.15pm; 3.15pm; 7 or 7.30pm* – *closed Dec-Feb*. Take a 2hr 30min boat trip on the canal linking Caen with the sea (Ouistreham). One way or there and back. A pleasant trip starting from St Pierre marina in the town centre.

Festyland – 🖾 – *On D 9 6km/3.6mi W of Caen* – *14650 Carpiquet* – ☎ *02 31 75 04 04* – *festyland.com* – *out of season: Wed, Sat, Sun and holidays 11am-7pm, daily during school holidays* – *circus show at 4pm for children aged 3 to 10* – *closed late Sept-late Mar*. This leisure park offers some thirty attractions: giant loop the loop, bumper boats, nautic trail, old bangers, babyland, clockwork horses, 1900-style merry-go-round as well as a new attraction, "Le Pirat'Ak"... Three daily shows (including a circus show) for young children. Food service available in the park.

CAEN

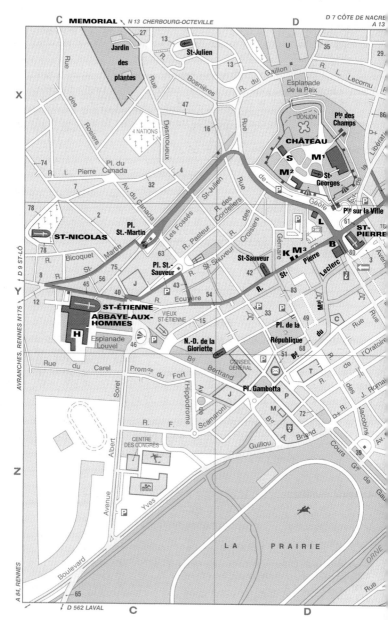

The chancel is enclosed by four arches (late 15C-early 16C) surmounted by a **frieze**★★ in the Flamboyant Gothic style with a delicate decoration of flowers and foliage.

The ambulatory leads to five chapels which were begun in 1518 and completed in the Renaissance style. The Gothic style prevails up to 2.75m/9ft from the ground but above that level the Renaissance influence increases to predominate in the **vaulting**★★ by Hector Sohier. The vaulting in each chapel is highly ornate; the pendants look like stalactites.

Rue St-Pierre – This is a lively shopping street. Nos 52 (Postal Museum) and 54, beautiful **half-timbered houses**★ (**K**) with steep gables, date from the early 16C; very few have survived in Caen. The profusion of carved decoration and the numerous small statues of saints belong to the Gothic style but there are a few Renaissance elements (balustrades and medallions).

Église St-Sauveur – St Saviour's Church, which is also known by its old name of Notre-Dame-de-Froide-Rue, is oriented north-south, its twin chevets facing rue St-Pierre: Gothic (15C) on the left and Renaissance (1546) on the right.

113

The bell-tower is in the Norman Gothic style. Enter by the west door in rue Froide, a pedestrian street, lined with old houses. The church consists of two naves side by side covered by pitched roofs: the western nave is 14C and the eastern nave 15C.

Place de la République – The pedestrian precinct, between place St-Pierre and place de la République and bounded by rue St-Pierre and boulevard du Maréchal-Leclerc, is lively both day and night. A turning off the west side of boulevard du Maréchal-Leclerc and rue Pierre-Aimé-Lair, leads into place de la République, which is laid out as a public garden; it is bordered by beautiful Louis XIII houses (Hôtel Daumesnil at nos 23-25) and the modern offices of the Préfecture. **Notre-Dame-de-la-Gloriette**, a former Jesuit church, was built between 1684 and 1689.

Place St-Sauveur – A fine collection of 18C houses borders the square, where the pillory stood until the 19C. At the centre is a statue of Louis XIV as a Roman emperor. The northeast side of the square is the site of the old St Saviour's which was destroyed in 1944.

Continue along rue Guillaume-le-Conquérant.

On your way, note the row of attractive houses in rue Jean-Marot; they date from the early 20C.

Turn right on rue St-Martin, which will take you to the Abbaye-aux-Hommes and the Église St-Étienne (described below).

Place St-Martin – The dominant feature is the statue of Constable Bertrand du Guesclin. Interesting view of the two towers of St-Étienne.

Continue northeast along the Fossés St-Julien and turn right onto rue de Géôle.

The 15C half-timbered house (no 31) is called **Maison des Quatrans**.

Rue du Vaugueux – Rue Montoir-Poissonnerie leads to this lovely pedestrian street which has kept its quaint charm: cobblestones, stone and timber houses, old-fashioned street lights.

Return to place St-Pierre.

★★THE ABBEYS *2hr*

★★Abbaye-aux-Hommes

Despite their different styles, St-Étienne Church and the monastery buildings of the Abbey for Men constitute a historical and architectural unit.

★★**Église St-Étienne** – This is the church belonging to the abbey founded by William the Conqueror; Lanfranc was the first abbot before being appointed Archbishop of Canterbury and it was probably he who drew up the plans. The church was started in 1066 in the Romanesque style, consecrated in 1077 by the Archbishop of Avranches, in the presence of the King-Duke and Queen Matilda, and was completed in the 13C in the Gothic style (east end, chancel, spires). The building was damaged during the Wars of Religion in the 16C and painstakingly restored in the early 17C by Dom Jehan de Baillehache, the Prior (chancel vaulting, lantern tower). Following the Maurist reforms (1663) the abbey enjoyed a period of prosperity until the French Revolution: the church was richly furnished (stalls, clock, organ) and the monastery was rebuilt. In the 19C St-Étienne became a parish church and the monastery was converted for use as a school. Fortunately the buildings were some of the few to survive the Battle of Caen unscathed.

Romanesque art has produced few more striking compositions than this plain **west** front; there are no ornate porches, no rose windows, only a gable end resting on four sturdy buttresses and pierced by two rows of round headed windows and three Romanesque doors. Lanfranc seems to have exercised the artistic severity of Ravenna and Lombardy in his native country. The austerity of the west front is, however, tempered by the magnificent soaring towers (11C) which rise, slim and tall, into the sky. The first storey is decorated with fluting, the second with single pierced bays and the third with paired bays. The octagonal spires with their turrets and lancets in the Norman Gothic style were added to the two towers in the 13C; the north tower is finer and more delicate in style.

The vast nave is almost bare of ornament except for the great round-headed arches. The construction of the sexpartite vaulting in the 12C altered the arrangement of the clerestory which is decorated with fretwork typical of the Norman style. At the west end of the church is the organ (1747) flanked by two telamones.

The Halbout Chapel near the north door contains an Adoration of the Magi by Claude Vignon.

The lantern tower above the transept crossing was constructed in the 11C but rebuilt early in the 17C. The gallery in the north transept houses a large 18C clock in a carved wooden surround. In the 13C the Romanesque chancel was replaced by a Gothic construction, including an ambulatory and radiating chapels; it was the first of the Norman Gothic chancels and subsequently served as a model. With the Gothic style new decorative motifs were introduced: chevrons on the archivolts, rose windows in the spandrels of the lateral arches, trefoils piercing the tympana of the bays in the galleries, capitals ornamented with crochets and foliage. Note the spacious galleries above the ambulatory and the elegant central arches. The handsome stalls and pulpit are 17C.

In front of the altar is a stone inscribed with an epitaph. The sarcophagus containing the body of William the Conqueror was originally placed beneath the lantern but it was desecrated when the church was sacked by the Huguenots in the 16C and the Conqueror's remains were scattered on the wind; all that remains is a femur which is interred beneath the stone. A monumental 18C paschal candlestick stands on the north side of the altar. The chancel is enclosed by a beautiful 19C wrought-iron screen; the cartouches bear the names and arms of the former abbots, priors and other dignitaries of the abbey.

In the sacristy there hangs an unusual portrait of William the Conqueror, painted in 1708, in which he is made to resemble Henry VIII. In the south ambulatory there are two fine paintings, *Caesar's Tribute*, a reproduction made after Rubens, and *The Stoning of Stephen*, attributed to Pierre Mellin (second chapel).

Leave the church by the chancel door and skirt the handsome **east end★★** of St-Étienne (13C-14C) to reach the continental style gardens in Esplanade Louvel which have been restored in accordance with the 18C plans.

★Monastery Buildings ⊙ – *Entrance through the town hall.* Since 1965 the town hall has been housed in these fine buildings which were designed early in the 18C by Brother Guillaume de la Tremblaye, the great master builder of the Congregation of St Maur; the **woodwork★★** is particularly beautiful.

The east wing comprises the monks' **warming room**, now a municipal exhibition hall; the **chapter-house**, formerly a collegiate chapel and now a registry office, panelled in light oak and hung with 17C paintings (Sebastian Bourdon, Mignard); the chapel **sacristy**, panelled in oak, containing a painting (17C) by Lebrun *(Moses Confronting an Egyptian Shepherd)* and a collection of Norman headdresses. The hall, which features the 18C night stairs with a wrought-iron banister, leads to the **cloisters** (18C) where the groined vaulting centres on octagonal coffers. From the southeast corner of the cloisters there is a very fine **view★★** of the towers of St-Étienne and the south side of the church. Fixed to the door into the church is a dark oak timetable of the offices said by the monks (1744). A doorway leads into the **parlour**, a large oval room with an unusual elliptical vault and beautiful Louis XV wooden doors. Beyond is the hall leading back into the cloisters for a view of the lantern tower of St-Étienne. The **refectory**, now used for meetings, is sumptuously decorated with late-18C oak panelling and broken barrel vaulting. Some of the paintings above the door and the blind apertures are by Lépicié, Restout and Ruysdael. The wrought-iron banister of the **grand staircase** is decorated with floral motifs. The bold design has no central support. The remarkable Gothic hall in the courtyard, known as the **guard-room★**, was built on the remains of a Gallo-Roman structure and is now used for meetings. The panelled ceiling is shaped like an upturned hull. Originally there were two rooms as the two chimneys suggest.

★★View of the Abbey – Walk through the gardens in Esplanade Louvel to reach the east side of place Louis-Guillouard near Old St-Étienne Church (Vieux St-Étienne), a charming ruin, with the Jesuit church of Notre-Dame-de-la-Gloriette *(see below)* in the background. This is the best view of the 18C monastery buildings flanking the impressive east end of St-Étienne with its bristling bell turrets, flying buttresses, clustering chapels and steep roofs, topped by the lantern tower and the two soaring spires.

Abbaye-aux-Dames

Founded in 1062 by **Queen Matilda**, the Abbey for Women is the sister house to the Abbey for Men; the towers of St-Étienne Church can be seen at the end of rue des Chanoines from place de la Reine-Mathilde.

★★Église de la Trinité – The old abbey church, which dates from the 11C, is a building in the Romanesque style. Its original plan was inspired by that of Benedictine abbeys, characterised by sturdy tiered apsidioles. The spires were replaced early in the 18C by heavy balustrades.

The vast nave of nine bays is a fine example of Romanesque art; the archivolts of the round-headed arches are decorated with fretwork and the false triforium with blind arcades. The upper storey was altered in the 12C when the nave was re-roofed with vaulting in a most original manner, characteristic of the early transitional phase that preceded ribbed vaulting. Broken barrel vaulting marks the transition from the nave into the spacious transept. Adjoining the south transept is an attractive chapel, which is now used as the chapter-house. It was built in the 13C replacing two Romanesque chapels similar to the two in the north transept. The late-11C groined vaulting in the chancel covers a magnificent span. In the centre of the chancel is Queen Matilda's tomb, a simple monument consisting of a single slab of black marble, which has survived unscathed despite the Wars of Religion and the Revolution.

The two-storey apse, which is later than the chancel, is separated from it by a broad transverse arch. The historiated capitals are high quality craftsmanship. In the early 18C a fresco was painted on the oven vaulting.

The crypt *(access by steps in the chapel in the south transept)* is well preserved. The groined vaulting rests on 16 columns, standing close together, which define five bays. An attempt at historiated decoration can be seen on one of the capitals, illustrating the Last Judgement, in which St Michael is portrayed gathering up the dead as they rise from their graves.

Conventual Buildings ⊙ – The buildings house the Regional Council (Conseil Régional). Extensive restoration work has enhanced the buildings' appearance in which the Caen stone plays a dominant role.

From the French-style garden in the main **courtyard** one can admire the luminous golden façades. The cloister (only three sides were completed) is a replica of the one in the Abbey for Men. Leading off it is a small oval room, the washroom **(lavabo)**, decorated with stone pilasters and a carved frieze like those in Greek temples; it is furnished with four black marble basins set in recesses ornamented with a shell. In the **refectory** (use as a reception room or as a gallery for temporary exhibitions), pilasters with Ionic capitals and two columns which flanked the abbess' chair have survived whereas the oak panelling which covered the lower walls has been removed.

The **Great Hall**, which is the focal point of the whole abbey and leads into the church, is graced by two **flights of stairs** decorated at first floor level with a cartouche bearing a plant motif; the walls are adorned with portraits of the two last abbesses, Anne de Montmorency and Marie-Aimée de Pontécoulant.

★ **CHÂTEAU** *1hr 30min including museums*

The imposing citadel dominating the mount was begun by William the Conqueror in 1060 and fortified in 1123 by his son, Henry Beauclerk who added a mighty keep (demolished in 1793 by the Convention). During the 13C, 14C and 15C it was repeatedly enlarged and reinforced.

Throughout the 19C it was used as soldiers' barracks and was severely damaged in the bombardment of Caen in 1944. Since then its massive walls have been restored to their early grandeur.

The line of the ramparts has changed little since the days of William the Conqueror. In some places the walls date from the 12C but most of them were built in the 15C. The two main gateways are protected by barbicans.

Enter the castle by the ramp which approaches the south gate opposite St Peter's Church.

After passing a round tower, a defensive outwork, one enters the citadel by the "town gate" **(porte sur la ville)**.

From the terrace (east) and the rampart sentry walk there are fine **views**★ of St Peter's Church and western Caen as far as the Abbey for Men. On the west side of the gate, behind the Normandy Museum, two canon from the fort on Gorée Island in Senegal are mounted on a platform which provides an interesting **view**★ over the southwest sector of the town and the belfries of the many churches.

The castle precinct encloses the modern **Musée des Beaux-Arts** (east) near the **Porte des Champs** (Field Gate), an interesting example of 14C military architecture; the **Chapelle St-George**, a 12C chapel which was altered in the 15C; the **Musée de Normandie** (west) in a building which was the residence of the Bailiff in the 14C and of the Governor of Caen in the 17C and 18C; a rectangular building, incorrectly called the **Salle de l'Échiquier** (Exchequer Hall) (**E**), which is a rare example of Norman civil architecture in the reign of Henry Beauclerk and was the great hall of the adjoining ducal palace (foundations only visible); adjoining it was the Normandy Exchequer (the Ducal Law Court). Further north lie the foundations of the keep which was built by Henry Beauclerk and altered in the 13C and 14C; it was a huge square structure, a round tower at each corner, surrounded by a moat which was joined to the castle moat.

★ **Musée des Beaux-Arts** ⊙ – *There is a pleasant café inside the musuem where you can enjoy a meal or a drink.* Situated within the precinct of William the Conqueror's castle, the Fine Arts Museum offers its collections from a chronological, thematic and geographical point of view. Large religious paintings and imposing historical and allegorical scenes hang in vast halls, bathed in light, while works of religious fervour and smaller paintings are essentially displayed in the small *cabinets*. The large galleries display landscapes, battle scenes and portraits.

The first three rooms on the ground floor are devoted to 15C, 16C and 17C Italian painting: the *Marriage of the Virgin* by Perugino, with a remarkable new frame, a triptych representing the *Virgin and Child between St George and St James* by Cima da Conegliano; in a room entirely devoted to Veronese, two paintings are of particular interest: the *Temptation of St Anthony* and *Judith and Holofernes*; also worth noting are *Coriolanus Implored by His Mother* by II Guercino and *Glaucus and Scylla* by Rosa Salvatore.

The next room deals with 17C French painting with outstanding works by Philippe de Champaigne (*Louis XIII's Vow*) and also religious or mythological paintings by Vouet, Vignon, La Hyre and Le Brun.

The Marriage of the Virgin by Perugino

Three intimate rooms are devoted to Dutch and Flemish 17C painting with works such as *A Seascape* by Solomon van Ruysdael, *Virgin and Child* by Roger van der Weyden and *Abraham and Melchizedek* by Rubens.

In the gallery devoted to the 18C are displayed works by French and Italian portrait and landscape painters: Hyacinthe Rigaud *(Portrait of Marie Cadenne)*, François Boucher *(Young Shepherd in a Landscape)*, Locatelli, Lalemand, Tournières...

On the lower level, the various aspects and the evolution of painting during the 19C and the early 20C are depicted through works by Romantic painters (Géricault, Delacroix, Isabey), Realists (Courbet: *The Lady with the Jewels*, Ribot), landscape painters (Corot, Dupré), Impressionists (Vuillard: *Portrait of Suzanne Desprez*, Bonnard, Dufy, Van Dongen: *Portrait of Madame T Raulet*), Cubist painters (Gleizes, Villon, Meitzinger).

Local artists are also represented: Cals, Fouace, Gernez, Lemaître, Lépine, Lebourg, Rame.

Innovations by contemporary painters such as Tobey *(Appearances)*, Mitchell (*Fields*, 1990), Soulages, Dubuffet *(Migration)*, Vieira da Silva, Szenez, Asse and Deschamps illustrate the different post-war trends: Conceptual art, Abstract landscape, Abstract art, Environmental art. From one end to the other, the museum thus presents an impressive chronology of the history of painting.

★**Musée de Normandie** ⊘ – The history and traditions of Normandy are illustrated by the presentation of the many archeological and ethnographical exhibits.

The first section is devoted to the prehistoric period up to the arrival of the Vikings in 911 and concentrates on the culture and technology of the era: excavated artefacts, miniature replica of the burial mound at Fontenay-le-Marmion, statue of a mother goddess found at St-Aubin-sur-Mer, weapons and jewellery found in medieval cemeteries (tomb of a metalworker buried with his tools).

The second section follows the evolution of agriculture: land use (models comparing different types of cultivation and farms), agricultural techniques (display of ploughs, scythes and millstones).

The third section is devoted to crafts and industrial activities: stock breeding, ceramics (jugs, funerary ornaments and decorative ridge tiles), wood (beautifully carved marriage chests), metallurgy (iron and copper work: craftsman's tools, copper ware from Villedieu-les-Poêles), textiles (costumes, headdresses and bridal ware in silk lace); the last room concentrates on the work of the candlemaker: interesting collection of candles for Easter, funerals and as votive offerings; it also contains ceremonial articles belonging to the different brotherhoods: gold thread embroidery and *tintenelles*, the tiny hand-bells used in processions by the Brothers of Charity.

Musée de la Poste et des Techniques de Communication (M³) – This Postal and Telecommunications Museum illustrates the history of the postal service through documents and equipment. The present and the old-fashioned claim equal attention: Minitels, demonstration of telematic services.

★★ LE MÉMORIAL ⊘ 3hr

Signposted from the town centre and the north ring road.

The memorial erected by the city, which in 1944 was at the centre of the Battle of Normandy, takes the form of a "Museum for Peace"; it is primarily a place of commemoration and of permanent meditation on the links between human rights and the maintenance of peace.

The façade of the sober building of Caen stone, facing Dwight-Eisenhower Esplanade, is marked by a fissure which evokes the destruction of the city and the break through of the Allies in the Liberation of France and Europe from the Nazi yoke. It stands on the site of the bunker of W Richter, the German general, who on 6 June faced the British-Canadian forces.

Le Mémorial

At the centre of the vast entrance hall a telex machine linked to a press agency prints contemporary news from all over the world. Visitors then embark on an unusual five-stage journey into the collective memory of events from 1918 to the present day. The main events of the Second World War, the causes and the issues at stake, are presented in the light of the latest historical analysis. A particularly imaginative display, centred on a spiral ramp, on such themes as the inter-war years and the advance of Fascism; the use of extensive archive material, including a gripping panoramic projection of D-Day, seen simultaneously from the Allied and the German standpoint, as well as moving testimonies by witnesses of and participants in the drama, confers on this presentation of our recent past the authenticity of living experience.

After reviewing the massive conflict which, until the dropping of the atomic bombs on Hiroshima and Nagasaki, mobilised enormous human and economic potential, the film *Hope* uses strong images and original music by Jacques Loussier to trace the alternating outbreaks of war and peace which have followed. It invites serious reflection on the precarious stability of the world.

A walk to the Vallée du Mémorial will enable visitors to see the Parc de la Colline aux Oiseaux, in which the Floralies de la Paix has been created. The Mur de la Liberté (Wall of Freedom) pays tribute to the hundreds of thousands of American soldiers who fought for freedom in Europe. Wide use is made of audio-visual and computer techniques (video-disc, Minitel linked to the Archive and Research Centre). The Caen Memorial provides a fascinating insight into contemporary history for young and old alike.

Return to place St-Pierre.

Recent Recipients of the Nobel Peace Prize

1999 – Doctors Without Borders
1998 – David Trimble (Protestant) and John Hume (Catholic) in Northern Ireland
1997 – International Campaign to Ban Landmines (ICBL, founded in 1992)
1996 – His Eminence Carlos Belo and José Ramos-Horta (East Timor)
1995 – Joseph Rotblat and the Anti-Nuclear Pugwash Campaign (Great Britain)
1994 – Yasser Arafat (Palestine), Yitzhak Rabin and Shimon Peres (Israel)
1993 – Nelson Mandela and Frederik De Klerk (South Africa)
1992 – Rigoberta Menchu (Guatemala)
1991 – Aung San Suu Kyi (Burma)
1990 – Mikhaïl Gorbatchev (Soviet Union)
1989 – The Dalaï-Lama (Tibet)
1988 – The United Nations' Peacekeeping Forces

ADDITIONAL SIGHTS

Église St-Nicolas ⊙ – St Nicholas' Church, which is now deconsecrated, was built late in the 11C by the monks of the Abbey for Men and has not been altered since. The west door is protected by a beautiful triple-arched Romanesque porch, an exceptional feature in Normandy.

The church is surrounded by an old **graveyard** *(entrance left of the west front)*; one may stroll among the mossy tombstones under the shade of the trees and admire the magnificent apse at the east end beneath its steep stone roof.

Église St-Jean – The surrounding district was badly bombed during the war; most of St John's had to be rebuilt but, fortunately, it was possible to restore it.

The fine Flamboyant Gothic building was begun in the 14C, and repaired in the 15C. The bell-tower, of which the base and first storey are 14C, was inspired by the tower of St Peter's but, owing to the instability of the marshy ground which had already caused some subsidence, the spire and the belfry were never built, nor was the central tower; the lower courses of its second storey were capped with a dome.

In the interior the same subsidence is visible in the pillars. The vast nave has a remarkable Flamboyant triforium and a highly ornate cylindrical **lantern tower** ★ over the transept crossing. The highly venerated statue of Our Lady of Protection dates from the 17C. In the south transept there is an old retable (17C) from the Carmes Convent depicting the Annunciation and bearing statues of St Joseph and St Teresa of Avila. In 1964 a statue of Joan of Arc was transferred from Oran to a site near the east end of the church in place de la Résistance.

Église St-Julien ⊙ – The old church which was destroyed in 1944 was replaced in 1958 by this modern building. The sanctuary wall, elliptical in shape, forms a huge piece of latticework in which the openings resemble the coloured sections in a huge dark stained-glass window.

Jardin des plantes – Shaded by beautiful trees, the Botanical Gardens are a pleasant place in which to relax. This pretty park features several heated greenhouses with many plant species from countries all over the world.

EXCURSIONS TO THE CAEN COUNTRYSIDE

② Cintheaux *15km/9mi.*

From Caen take N 158 south. The village, renowned for its late-12C church, stands on the southern edge of the Caen countryside, in an old mining area marked by solitary slag heaps.

The road from Caen to Falaise passes through the country which was laboriously recaptured during the Battle of Normandy between 8 and 17 August 1944 by the Canadian 1st Army (Gaumesnil cemetery) and its Polish units (Langannerie cemetery).

② Troarn *14km/8mi.*

Leave Caen going east and then take N 175. In Troarn take rue de l'Abbaye (second turning on the right after the church).

This little town, which was founded in 1048 by Roger de Montgomery, contains the remains of a 13C abbey.

③ North of Caen *Round tour of 31km/19mi – allow half a day*

From Caen take D 7 and at the top of the hill, turn right on D 401, then D 60 to the left. The road bends to the right and there is a panoramic view of Caen and its bell-towers.

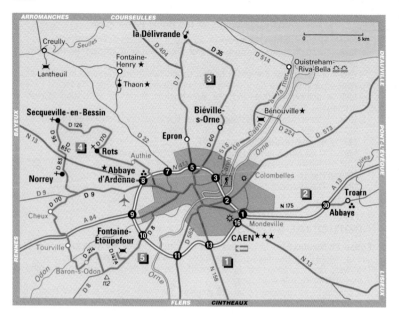

Biéville-sur-Orne – The blind arcades and oculi which decorate the west front of the church recall the architecture of Tuscany.

Take the road west to Épron.

Épron – This small locality, which was razed in 1944, has been called the "Village of the Radio" since 1948. The origin of the nickname was a radio programme which sought to determine which of France's départements had been most severely damaged. Calvados was named, and a lottery draw among 10 communes fell to Épron. The village was rebuilt thanks to a collection of small change taken up on its behalf.

② Churches and Abbeys *35km/21mi – about 2h*

From Caen take D 9 west towards Bayeux on rue de Bayeux and then rue du Général-Moulin. Half way up a hill on the outskirts of the town turn right onto the road to the abbey.

★**Abbaye d'Ardenne** – *Leave the car at the main gate.* The abbey, which was founded in the 12C by the Premonstratensians, fell into ruins during the 19C. The gatehouses and the main gate (12C) have been restored and the remaining buildings belong to two distinct agricultural enterprises. In the first courtyard stands a huge 13C tithe barn (back left) with aisles which is covered by a single asymmetrical wooden roof (restored). The 13C **abbey church** has been damaged on the outside but the nave is a very pure example of the Norman Gothic style.

Drive west to Rots via Authie.

Rots – The **church** has an attractive Romanesque west front; the nave dates from the same period; the chancel is 15C.

Take D 170 north; in Rosel turn left onto D 126.

Secqueville-en-Bessin – The 11C **church** has a fine three-storey tower and a 13C spire. The nave and transept are decorated with blind arcading.

Take D 93 and D 83 south.

Norrey-en-Bessin – The little Gothic **church** ⊘ boasts a great square lantern tower but no spire; the interior is richly carved; the **chancel** was built in the 13C.

Return to Caen by D 9.

② The Battle of Odon *37km/23mi – about 1hr.*

The name of this river recalls the hard-fought battles which took place between 26 June and 4 August 1944 southwest of Caen.

Leave Caen by D 9.

The road skirts the airfield which the 12th SS Panzers held for three days, from 4 to 7 July, against the Canadian 3rd Division.

After another 3km/2mi bear left on D 170; in Cheux turn left behind the church onto D 89; after crossing N 175, at the top of a slight rise, follow D 89 round to the right and straight through Tourville.

This is the line of the British advance, which began on 26 June in pouring rain at Tilly-sur-Seulles (northwest); the objective was the River Orne to the southeast. A memorial has been erected (right) to pay tribute to the men of the 15th Scottish Division who died in the battle.

Just when it seems that the road has reached the floor of the Odon Valley it drops into a rocky ravine, hitherto hidden by thickets; the river has created a second valley within the main valley. It is easy to see what a valuable line of defence this natural obstacle would have been and to appreciate the difficulties of the British troops exposed to heavy fire from the Germans on the far side of the valley. In fact the British lost more men crossing the Odon than crossing the Rhine.

The road climbs the opposite slope to a crossroads. The road on the left (D 214) passes straight through Baron-sur-Odon and continues to a T-junction marked by a stone monument surmounted by an iron cross (right). The raised roadway to the right, an old Roman road also known as Duke William's Way, leads to another T-junction where a stele has been set up to commemorate the battles fought by the 43rd Wessex Division. To the south stands **Hill 112** later known as "Cornwall Hill".

Take D 8 to the left towards Caen.

A monument at the junction with D 36 recalls the operations which took place in July and were marked by some fierce duels between armoured vehicles. A night attack on 15 June took place by the light of an artificial moon created by the reflection of searchlights on low cloud.

Turn left onto D 147A.

Near a farm on the right the Château de Fontaine-Étoupefour comes into view.

Château de Fontaine-Étoupefour ⊙ – *Access by a track on the right beyond the farm.* Nicolas d'Escoville, who built the Hôtel d'Escoville in Caen, was the owner of this castle. It is surrounded by a moat spanned by a drawbridge which leads to an elegant 15C gatehouse bristling with turrets and pinnacles. A sculpture of angels and warriors fighting separates the mullion windows which light the two storeys. The dining room is hung with three interesting paintings of hunting scenes. There are huge oak beams in the great chamber on the first floor. On the far side of the paved courtyard stand the ruins of one of the two main blocks (late 16C), currently undergoing restoration.

Return to D 8 to reach Caen.

Château de CARROUGES ★★

Population 760
Michelin map 60 fold 2 or 231 fold 42

For almost five centuries this immense **château★★**, set in its park (10ha/25 acres), belonged to a famous Norman family, Le Veneur de Tillières; in 1936 it was bought by the nation. From the 12C to the 15C the château was the seat of the Blosset and Carrouges families. During the Hundred Years War the lords of Carrouges remained loyal vassals of the King of France.

TOUR ⊙

Park – From the park with its fine trees and elegant flower beds there are good views of the château.

Exterior – The 16C **gatehouse★** is an elegant brick building with decorative geometric patterns. Four slender towers, with pepper-pot roofs and narrow dormer windows, flank the gatehouse. The château itself is austere but more imposing. Surrounded by a moat the buildings are arranged around an inner courtyard. The château was constructed largely during the reigns of Henri IV and Louis XIII to replace a fortress built on the hilltop above the village. The stables and domestic quarters occupy the ground floor; the apartments and state rooms are on the first floor.

Interior ⊙ – The **kitchen** presents an imposing array of copper pans. The Renaissance and Classical interior decoration of the apartments provides a gracious setting for the fine furniture. The **Louis XI Bedroom** was named after the King's visit on 11 August 1473 and retains a bed with recent hangings reproducing Bargelos work. The panelling is adorned with delicate and decorative panels of foliage highlighted in a different colour.

In the principal **antechamber** the chimney breast is decorated with a hunting scene. The main or tie-beams are adorned with carved motifs. The remarkable fireplace in the **dining room** is flanked by two polished granite piers with Corinthian capitals. The sideboards are Louis XIV; note the Restoration chairs The **portrait gallery** with its

121

Gatehouse

Louis XIII chairs assembles past lords and owners. The **drawing room** occupies part of one of the corner towers. The straw-coloured panelling dates from the late 17C or early 18C. The visit ends with the monumental great **staircase★** and its brickwork vaulting and round headed arches as they wind up and round the square stair well.

The village – Located to the northwest of Écouves Forest, Carrouges stands within the boundary of the **Parc naturel régional Normandie-Maine**. The **Maison du Parc** ⊘ (park's visitor centre) occupies the restored buildings of a former chapter of canons, an outbuilding of the château.

The **Maison des Métiers** ⊘ (Craft Centre ⊘) has several workshops as well as displays of work for sale.

NORMANDIE-MAINE REGIONAL NATURE PARK

Created in 1975 and spread over two regions (Basse-Normandie and the Pays de Loire), the **Parc naturel régional Normandie-Maine** covers 235 000ha/907sq mi and includes 150 *communes* from the Orne, Manche, Mayenne and Sarthe *départements*.

The land forming the park, lying on the boundaries of both Normandy and Maine, can be divided into an "upper stretch" *(haut pays)* featuring crests and wooded escarpments in the Alpes Mancelles, and a "lower stretch" *(bas pays)*, characterised

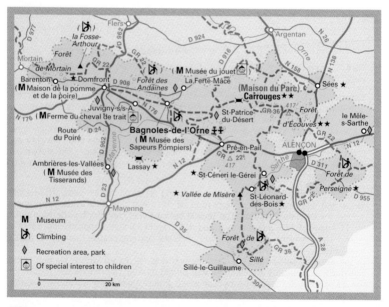

by a *bocage* landscape, the rolling hills of Saosnois and open fields around Sées and Alençon. The principal aim of this park is to conserve the traditional agricultural activities and rural way of life and at the same time encourage crafts, ancillary agricultural activities as well as sporting activities and tourism. The park can be explored by car or on a bicycle via four itineraries: the **Route des Trois Forêts** (three forests); the **Route Historique des Haras et Châteaux de l'Orne** (historic châteaux and stud farms); the **Circuit au Pays de Lancelot du Lac**; the **Route du Poiré** which reveals the different techniques involved in making cider, calvados and perry.

Every year the Maison du Parc organises demonstrations and events on a variety of themes (pottery, mycology, pomology) for which it publishes its own programme. Between April and October it hosts "nature expeditions" in conjunction with local organisations in charge of protecting the environment and with the Office National des Forêts (ONF): these outings are an opportunity to discover the forest, the banks of the river and the small creatures that inhabit the area. The forests of Andaines, Écouves, Perseigne and Sillé are particularly suitable for relaxation and the discovery of nature.

⚡ There are 2 500km/1 553mi of signposted paths, including 250km/155mi associated with different themes.

CAUDEBEC-EN-CAUX ★

Michelin map 54 fold 9 or 231 fold 21

Caudebec settles around the Seine where the Ste-Gertrude Valley runs into the river. The Brotonne bridge leads directly to the forest of the same name. It lies at the place where the **tidal bore**, a phenomenon known as the *mascaret*, driven further upstream by the Seine embankment, was highly spectacular at times. The estuary has since been made safer for navigation, and tourists can no longer stand on the river banks and hope to sprayed with foam from a fast-rising wave, but you can see photographs in the local museum.

A fire in 1940 destroyed most of the old buildings, but the fine Church of Our Lady was virtually undamaged and three old houses to the left of the church also survived and give some idea of what Caudebec must once have looked like.

A short-lived prestigious past – The name Caudebec was mentioned for the first time in the 11C on a charter granted to the monks of St-Wandrille Abbey. In the 12C the town was surrounded with fortifications in order to withstand the English who were nevertheless victorious in 1419.

Charles VII visited the town in 1449 after its liberation. Caudebec had a difficult time during the Wars of Religion but after submitting to Henri IV in 1592 it became a flourishing glove and hat making centre. The Revocation of the Edict of Nantes in 1685 put an end to this period of prosperity.

★★ÉGLISE NOTRE-DAME *30min*

Park in place du Marché, except on Saturdays when the market, which has been held on the same spot since 1390, is in full swing.

This fine Flamboyant edifice *(see illustration in Introduction: Religious architecture)* which Henri IV described as "the most beautiful chapel in the kingdom" was built between 1425 and 1539.

Exterior – The belfry (53m/174ft high) adjoining the south wall, has a delicately worked upper part surmounted by a stone crown spire.

The west face is pierced by three beautiful Flamboyant **doorways** – the larger of the two is said to portray 333 different characters – and by a remarkable rose window surrounded by small statues.

Interior ⊙ – The proportions of the building are pleasing although there is no transept. The triforium and tracery are the most characteristically Flamboyant features.

The 17C **font** (left) is decorated with intricately carved panels. The **great organ** (early 16C – *see illustration in Introduction: Religious architecture*) was restored in 1972; its 3 345 pipes of repoussé pewter produce a sound that is distinguished for its fine quality; the oak organ case is finely carved.

The stained-glass windows are 16C, the most outstanding being those above the high altar of St Peter beside Christ Crucified (left) and the Coronation of the Virgin and St Paul (right).

Some attractive old statues have been cleaned and now appear in all their original colouring and character; they may be seen in the side chapels.

Chapelle du Saint-Sépulcre – The Chapel of the Holy Sepulchre inspired Fragonard, who make a sketch of it. Beneath the 16C baldaquin a recumbent Christ, carved in incredible detail, faces some very large stone statues – all from Jumièges Abbey. The Pietà between the windows is 15C.

Chapelle de la Vierge – The Lady Chapel is famous for its **keystone★**, a 7t monolith supported only by the dependent arching and forming a 4.30m/13ft pendentive *(see illustration in Introduction: Religious architecture)*. The architect of this feat, Guillaume Le Tellier, lies buried in the chapel and is commemorated in a plaque beneath the right window.

The right window is composed of 16 lights, 12 of which recount the life of St Nicholas. The uppermost tells of the martyrdom of St Catherine.

A WALK AROUND CAUDEBEC

There are car parks on place du Marché (except Saturday morning), place Henri-IV and place d'Armes. The walk takes about 1hr (2km/1mi), starting from the Tourist office. From place du Général-de-Gaulle, take rue de la Vicomté.

On the right, the **old prison** is set in the 14C ramparts.

Continue along rue Thomas-Basin. The statue of Thomas Basin recalls a native son (b 1412) who campaigned for the rehabilitation of Joan of Arc.

Maison des Templiers ⊘ – The Templars' House is a precious specimen of 13C civil architecture which has retained its two original gable walls intact. It is now the Local History Museum.

Follow cours de la Sainte-Gertrude.

You walk by two towers: **tour des Fascines** and **tour d'Harfleur**.

Take rue du Havre, on the left, and then turn left again on rue Planquette.

Église Notre-Dame – *See description above.*

Town Hall Terrace – This terrace, on the banks of the Seine, affords a pleasant view over the river.

Musée de la Marine de Seine ⊘ (**M**) – The museum is wholly devoted to the history of navigation along the River Seine: ports, commercial exchanges, shipbuilding, crossings. Mention is also made of the long-standing traditions and customs associated with river traffic. Visitors can learn about a bygone phenomenon, the **tidal bore**.

The visit starts with a display of wooden vessels, notably a *gribane* of 1886, used for transporting building materials in the Seine-Maritime region.

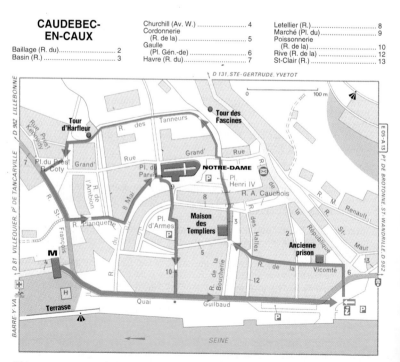

Eating out

MID-RANGE

Auberge du Val-au-Cesne – *Le Val-au-Cesne* – *76190 Yvetot* – *3km/1.9mi south of Yvetot via D 5* – ☎ *02 35 56 63 06* – *www.pageszoom.com/val-au-cesne* – *closed 8-28 Jan, 20 Aug to 2 Sept, Mon and Tues* – *24.39/50.31€*. Nestling in a remote vale, this Norman inn is delightful with its timber-framed walls, the dense vegetation of its garden and its aviary. The cuisine is in perfect harmony with the decor: carefully prepared, it has an authentic taste. Cosy rooms.

Where to stay

MODERATE

La Normandie – *Quai Guilbaud* – ☎ *02 35 96 25 11* – *closed 13 Feb to 6 Mar and Sun except holidays* – **P** – *15 rooms: 35.06/57.93€* – ☕ *5.34€* – *restaurant 59/220F.* Located along the road which skirts the Seine, this small unpretentious hotel offers simple, well-kept, functional rooms with a view of the river in the front. The cuisine served in the brightened-up restaurant is reasonably good.

THREE ROUND TOURS

Around St-Wandrille

Round tour of 8km/5mi. Leave Caudebec by rue St-Clair and follow chemin de Rétival keeping to the right.

The road runs along the top of a small escarpment with tantalising glimpses of the bend in the river.

At the bottom of a steep descent take D 37 on the left.

The road goes up a delightful little **valley**★ with thatched farmhouses scattered here and there, some of which have been converted into holiday homes.

Before Rançon, turn right on D 33 to St-Wandrille.

★**Abbaye de St-Wandrille** – *See Abbaye de ST-WANDRILLE.*

Take D 22 and D 982 back to Caudebec.

Latham-47 Monument – This stands as a commemoration of the expedition by the polar explorer Roald Amundsen and his companions, who disappeared in the Arctic in 1928 while trying the rescue the crew of the dirigible *Italia*.

Take D 22, than D 982 to return to Caudebec.

Around Barre-y-Va

Round tour of 21km/13mi. Leave Caudebec to the north on the Yvetot road and turn left onto D 40.

Ste-Gertrude – The small **church** stands in attractive surroundings. It was consecrated in 1519 and is Flamboyant in style. Inside, to the right of the high altar there are some interesting statues, including a Christ in stone, and a rare 15C stone tabernacle.

Head west on D 40, then D 30. Turn south on D 440 towards Anquetierville. At the junction with D 982 turn left, then at St-Arnoult right onto D 440. Turn right onto D 281 and almost immediately left down a steep hill to Villequier.

★**Villequier** – Villequier occupies a beautiful **site**★ on the banks of the Seine at the foot of a wooded height crowned by a castle. In the past this was the point where the river pilots handed over to or took over from the estuary pilots who navigated through the shallows.

In 1843, six months after their marriage, Charles Vacquerie and his wife, Léopoldine Hugo, the daughter of Victor Hugo, were drowned in the Seine at Villequier.

A house once owned by the Vacquerie family, rich boat-builders from Le Havre, has been converted into the **Musée Victor-Hugo**★ ☉, which recalls the life of Léopoldine: letters, portraits, family, furniture, views of old Normandy, the poems, *Contemplations*, in which Victor Hugo expressed his grief, his autograph.

The churchyard contains the tombs of Adèle, Victor Hugo's wife and of Charles and Léopoldine who were buried in the same coffin. The **church** (15C and 16C but much altered) has a timber roof and beautiful 16C stained-glass windows: one depicts a naval battle.

Take D 81 back to Caudebec.

Barre-y-Va – This tiny hamlet is named after the tidal wave or bore *(barre)* which used to swell upstream along the Seine. An oratory and a small **chapel** ⊙ perpetuate the memory of former pilgrimages and present tokens of gratitude made by sailors who worked along the Seine (ex-votos).

Return to Caudebec via D 81.

Around Yvetot

22km/14mi – 1hr 30min. Leave Caudebec and go north on D 131. After 4km/2mi, turn right on D 33 then left on D 37 towards Yvetot.

Beyond Touffreville-la-Corbeline, typical farmhouses are set in the midst of shady trees.

Yvetot – The town, made famous in song by Béranger as the legendary capital of an imaginary kingdom, is in fact a large market town on the Caux plateau. The **Église St-Pierre** (1956) contains remarkably large **stained-glass windows★★** by Max Ingrand, which produce a dazzling effect; the colours gradually become more brilliant towards the centre of the church where the Crucified Christ is surrounded by the Virgin and the Apostles; other windows show founders of religious orders, saints of the Rouen diocese and the saints of France. The Lady Chapel (behind the altar) is illuminated by stained-glass windows depicting episodes in the life of the Virgin.

Take D 131 south; turn right on the by-pass; turn left on D 34.

Allouville-Bellefosse – The village is known for the **oak tree** *(chêne)* which grows in front of the church; it is believed to the more than 1 300 years old, one of the oldest in France and the most famous tree in Normandy. The trunk and larger branches have had to be supported. A small sanctuary dedicated to Our Lady of the Peace and a superimposed hermit's cell have been built into its hollow trunk *(access by stairs and galleries).*

Follow the signs to Musée de la Nature (1.5km/1mi).

Musée de la Nature ⊙ – The Nature Museum is located in an old Caux farmhouse. Two diorama displays show local bird families and a reconstitution of the Normandy countryside (coastline, marsh, plain, forest and farmyard). The coastline is shown before and after the effects of pollution.

Return to Allouville, take D 34 then turn left on D 40; take D 131 back to Caudebec.

Pays de CAUX

Michelin map 52 folds 2-5, 11-15 or 231 folds 7-10

The Caux is a massive chalk plateau covered by an impermeable layer of silex clay and alluvial mud, monotonous but prosperous, good arable land; it is bordered by the Channel, the Lower Seine and the Bresle Valley. The region is mainly known for its impressive coastline, where holidaymakers delighting in the natural beauty return each year to the beaches below the chalk cliffs.

CHALK, WAVES AND GREENERY

Côte d'Albâtre – Along the Alabaster Coast, the chalk cliffs with alternate strata of flint and yellow marl are worn away ceaselessly by the combined action of the tides and the weather. The Étretat needle rocks and underwater shelves 1mi from the present shore indicate the former coastline. At the particularly exposed point of **Cap de la Hève** erosion is 2m/6ft a year; the water is milky with chalk, and flints are pounded endlessly upon the beaches. The cliffs lose annually 3 million m³/106 million cu ft.

The hollows **(valleuses)** cut into every cliff top as far as the eye can see are dry valleys, truncated by the retreating coastline; now isolated they seem to be suspended in mid-air; only abundant water courses actually reach the sea. Ports and harbours have been constructed in the natural inlets; the hanging valleys provide the seaside resorts with access to the beaches and the sea.

Caux Farmsteads – Seen from a distance, the farms appear as green oases but on closer inspection the plan becomes evident: 2m/6ft high embankments topped by a double row of oaks, beeches or elms act as a wind-break. The **farmstead** comprises a meadow (2-3ha/5-7 acres) planted with apple trees in which stand the half-timbered farmhouse and other buildings. The entrance is often through a monumental gateway. Farms have their own ponds, wells and cisterns although the provision of mains water has led to the construction of water towers.

Caux cattle raising is unusual; in spring cattle and horses pasture tethered to a post **(tière)** and each animal marks out his territory in the form of a perfect circle. Milk – the chief source of income – is sent to the towns of the Lower Seine or the butter and cheese factories in the valleys.

Eating out

MODERATE

L'Assiette – 13 r. du Dr-Girard – 76980 Veules-les-Roses – ☎ 02 35 57 85 30 – closed 15-30 Nov, 5-30 Jan and Tues except from 15 June to 15 Sept – reservation advisable – 14.48/42.69€. This 17C coaching inn represents all the charm of Normandy! You will be able to enjoy well-prepared traditional cuisine in its pretty courtyard or in its dining room with exposed stone walls, and if you feel like staying a little longer, ask for one of the comfortable suites.

Restaurant du Lac de Caniel – 76450 Cany-Barville – ☎ 02 35 97 40 55 – www.lacdecaniel.fr – closed evenings – 9.15/23.63€. This leisure park centres round a lake: water skiing, pedalos and small sailing boats. If you need bucking up, you have the choice between a brasserie with a terrace facing the lake, offering a buffet and simple dishes, and a more traditional and also more comfortable restaurant.

MID-RANGE

Le Belvédère – 76280 St-Jouin-Bruneval – 10km/6.2mi south of Étretat via D 940 then D 111 – ☎ 02 35 20 13 76 – closed 23 Dec to end of Jan, Sun evening and Mon – reservation essential in summer and Sat-Sun – 22.11/28.20€. Unusual blue building standing on top of the Pays de Caux cliffs. The interior is simple but who cares...the view of the sea is exceptional! Enjoy fish, mussels and shellfish whilst admiring the view is a pleasure you must not deny yourself.

Les Hêtres – 76460 St-Valery-en-Caux – 3km/1.9mi from St-Valery along the road to Fécamp towards Le Bourg-Ingouville via D 925 and D 68 – ☎ 02 35 57 09 30 – closed 8 Jan to 12 Feb, Mon and Tues out of season – 25.15/35.83€. Charming 17C farm in a colourful park... Take a rewarding break by the fireside in winter or outside in summer. In this cosy decor, you will enjoy traditional cooking adapted to today's taste and based on regional products. A few lovely rooms.

Where to stay

MODERATE

Camping municipal – 76450 Cany-Barville – south of Cany-Barville via D 268 – ☎ 02 35 97 70 37 – ✉ – reservation advisable – 100 places: 9.30€. Situated a few miles inland, in the Durdent Valley, this campsite, originally set up for the personnel of the Paluel nuclear plant, is now open to tourists in season. Places are well marked and most of them are concreted.

Camping municipal de la Plage – 100m/110yd from the sea – 76860 Quiberville-sur-Mer – 7km/4.3mi east of Veules-les-Roses via D 68 then D 75 – ☎ 02 35 83 01 04 – closed Nov to Mar – reservation advisable in July and Aug – 202 places: 14.18€. Situated on the road running along the sea, between Dieppe and St-Valery-en-Caux, this campsite has well-kept basic facilities. Places are separated by bushes and there is a play area for children.

MID-RANGE

Le Clos du Vivier Bed and Breakfast – 4 chemin du Vivier – 76540 Valmont – 2km/1.2mi east of Valmont via D 150 towards Ourville – ☎ 02 35 29 90 95 – ✉ – 3 rooms: 73.18/80.80€. Through the years, the outbuildings of Valmont Castle have been converted into a lovely thatched cottage. How pleasant it is to sit by the fire in the drawing room before going up to your room, comfortably furnished in country style. Hens, peacocks, ducks and black swans roam around the garden.

Les Vergers Bed and Breakfast – R. des Vergers – 76860 Quiberville-sur-Mer – 7km/4.3mi east of Veules-les-Roses via D 68 then D 75 – ☎ 02 35 83 16 10 – chauclert@aol.com – 5 rooms: 39.64/53.36€. The rooms of this elegant house, close to the sea, are pleasant, comfortable and decorated in a traditional way. The vast park, where it is possible to take a stroll, invites rest and relaxation. Ideal base for a tour of the area.

LUXURY

Château de Sassetot – 76540 Sassetot-le-Mauconduit – 13km/8.1mi east of Fécamp via D 925 then D79 – ☎ 02 35 28 00 11 – www.chateau-de-sassetot.com – 🅿 – reservation essential Sat-Sun – 28 rooms: from 79.27€ – ☕ 9.15€ – restaurant 24.39/53.36€. This delightful castle is the ideal stopover to get a glimpse of the region's history and discover its charm. Unforgettable memories of Sissi, who was a guest here one summer, linger on. You can take a stroll in the park, have a meal in the lovely dining room and sleep in a comfortable bedroom.

Leisure time

"Eau et Nature" Leisure park – 🖾 – Société du Lac de Caniel – 76450 Cany-Barville – ☎ 02 35 97 40 55 – www.lacdecaniel.fr – beginning of Apr to end of Oct. For those who haven't the inclination to go to the seaside, this leisure park is an excellent substitute for all water sports and leisure activities: water skiing, rowing, kayaking, windsurfing, etc.

Pebbles, the Precious Stones of Normandy's Coast

Originally pieces of flint that broke off from the points of rocky cliffs and were eroded by the sea, pebbles are a common feature along the Alabaster Coast. In the early 20C, builders and craftsmen alike began showing an interest in this unusual mineral, which, with diamonds, ranks among the hardest in the world. Pebbles have been used as a material for crushing, for building houses and for making sandpaper. As they feature pure silicium, they were also included in the composition of pottery and ceramics after being finely ground.

Today pebbles are used to make the resistant paint intended for road markings. This prolonged exploitation over the past few decades has contributed to depleting France's natural resources and the gravel beds lining Normandy beaches no longer play their natural role of protecting the cliffs. Consequently, since 1985, it has been officially forbidden to collect pebbles off the Normandy coast.

★CÔTE D'ALBÂTRE

① From Dieppe to Étretat

104km/65mi – about 5hr – see local map p 128

By many twists and turns, the road serves a whole string of beaches set at the mouth of a short coastal river or a deep dry valley. Glimpses of the sea and the cliffs and pleasant views of the setting of some resorts are the main features of the drive, which is at its best in the morning. The monotony of the Caux plateau is fortunately broken by the islands of green formed by the farms and villages.

★★**Dieppe** – *See DIEPPE.*

Leave Dieppe by D 75.

Pourville-sur-Mer – This seaside resort, pleasantly situated near jagged cliffs, has risen from the ruins resulting from the Dieppe raid made by Commandos on 19 August 1942; the Cameron Highlanders and a Canadian Regiment, the South Saskatchewan, landed to the sound of the pipes, inflicted severe damage on the enemy and, under cover of the Navy and by sacrificing their rearguard, re-embarked early in the afternoon. A commemorative stele of pink marble stands on the seafront.

Continue west on D 75.

⌂**Varengeville-sur-Mer** – *See VARENGEVILLE-SUR-MER.*

Ste-Marguerite-sur-Mer – The 12C church, which has no transept, was considerably remodelled in the 16C. Inside, four of the original **arches**★ remain on the north side; those on the south date from 1528. The second column on the right is twisted and scattered with shells; the high altar dates from 1160 and is one of the very few of this date still extant. Notice on the front and at each end the colonnettes with Romanesque capitals.

At St-Aubin bear left onto D 237.

Le Bourg-Dun – Notre-Dame-du-Salut is a vast composite church, outwardly remarkable for its **tower**★ built on a massive square 13C base. The hatchet-shaped roof is 17C. A Renaissance door opens into the south aisle.

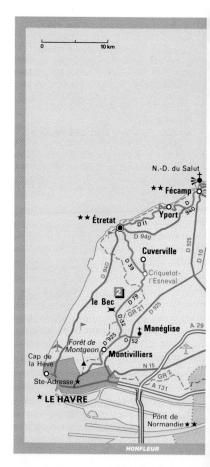

Most of the rood screen is missing; extant are the pedestals supporting statues of St Anthony and St Sebastian. Beneath Flamboyant vaulting in the south transept are a Renaissance bay and piscina; three arches in the chancel open into the beautiful south aisle which was added in the 14C. The font in the north aisle is Renaissance.

Return to St-Aubin.

Veules-les-Roses – The seaside resort is sheltered in a small valley which is particularly attractive higher up. **St-Martin**, in the town itself, is a 16C-17C church with a 13C lantern. A timber framed roof covers the nave and aisles. Inside are five 16C twisted, carved limestone columns and ancient statues together with two fine paintings.

Turn left onto D 37.

Église de Blosseville – The church, surmounted by a 12C belfry, possesses beautiful Renaissance stained-glass windows and some old statues.

Continue towards Ermenouville on D 37.

Château du Mesnil-Geoffroy ⊘ – Surrounded by a 9ha/22.3-acre formal French park (maze with trees whose branches meet to form a leafy gallery overhead), this 17C and 18C château is a interesting testimony to the sweet art of living under Louis XV.

After leaving the château, turn onto D 70.

Le Mesnil-Durdent – Do not fail to visit this charming village and its carefully signposted "wild garden", an irregular plot of land with many paths and embankments, planted with all manner of herbs carrying quaint, old-fashioned names typical of the Caux region: the Virgin's blouse, the stag's antlers, the doe's weed etc.

St-Valery-en-Caux – St-Valery is both a popular seaside resort, with a promenade overlooking the long shingle beach, and a fishing and coastal trading port; the harbour is connected to the sea by a channel and can accommodate a large number of pleasure boats.

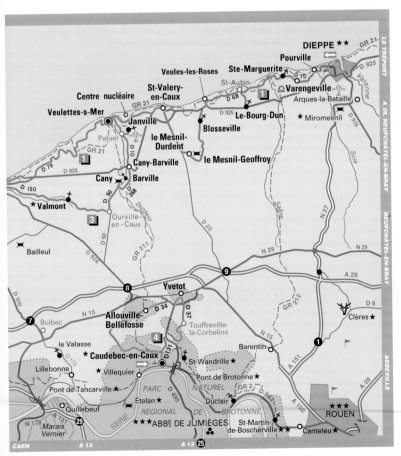

Port of St-Valery-en-Caux

The **Falaise d'Aval★** (West Headland) *(access on foot via sentier des Douaniers and steps)* is crowned by a monument commemorating the battles of June 1940 (51st Highland Division and the French 2nd Cavalry Division). The view embraces the Ailly lighthouse and, on a clear day, Dieppe.

The **Maison d'Henri IV** *(quai du Havre)* is a beautiful Renaissance house with carved beams.

On the **Falaise d'Amont** (East Headland) *(access by steps)* stands the 51st Highland Division Monument overlooking the town, harbour and beach. The more modern monument nearby was erected in memory of Coste and Bellonte who in 1930 made the first flight from Paris to New York in their aeroplane, *Point d'Interrogation*; its name means Question Mark.

Centre nucléaire de production d'électricité de Paluel ⊙ – The nuclear power station consists of 45 autonomous units each with a capacity of 1300 MW. Enriched uranium is used to fuel the station and cooling ensured by sea water pumped from the ocean. The thermal energy generated by the fuel is transformed into mechanical, then electrical energy. The visitor centre has an exhibition on the range of energy sources, the choice of nuclear energy, and the history and operation of the power station. A cartoon show tells the story of energy throughout the ages.

Veulettes-sur-Mer – The 11C and 13C church stands half way up a hill overlooking the seaside resort in the wide green valley below.

The finest **panorama★★** is to be seen between Senneville *(narrow road)* and Fécamp, near the **Chapelle Notre-Dame-du-Salut** (sailors' pilgrimage), from the belvedere with viewing table.

The road quickly loses height. The cliffs to the west of Fécamp stretch as far as Étretat. Fécamp and its harbour appear after a sharp bend to the left.

★★Fécamp – See FÉCAMP.

Yport – Yport is a seaside resort tucked away in a valley. Despite the lack of harbour facilities, there was a sizeable fishing fleet until 1970; the fishermen used boats designed to be drawn up on the shingle *(caïques)*.

★★Étretat – See ÉTRETAT.

"Between Dieppe and Le Havre, the coast runs along an uninterrupted stretch of cliff face, 100yd high, and straight as a wall. In places, this massive expanse of white rock unexpectedly dips and a narrow valley, framed by steep slopes covered in grass and bulrushes, wends its way from the cultivated plateau to a pebble beach onto which it opens out through a gulley reminiscent of that of a mountain stream. Over the years, nature has produced valleys and the relentless action of rainstorms has caused them to turn into these ravines, digging trenches into what remained of the cliff, extending the river bed down to the sea, mapping out the waterways so essential for human activity. Visitors to the area may sometimes discover a small village tucked away between these valleys, where the coastal winds can be heard swirling above the rooftops."

Guy de Maupassant – Le Saut du Berger

VALLÉE DE LA LÉZARDE

② From Étretat to Le Havre

33km/21mi – about 1hr – see local map p 128

★★Étretat – See ÉTRETAT. *Leave Étretat by D 39.*

The road passes through a small valley as it heads inland.

At Criquetot-l'Esneval turn left onto D 239.

Cuverville – The writer **André Gide** (1859-1951) is buried beneath a plain concrete slab in the small church cemetery.

The road descends into the pleasant Lézarde Valley.

Château du Bec – The 12C-16C castle has an enchanting setting of trees and still waters.

In Épouville turn left onto D 925 and then right onto D 52.

Manéglise – The small church is one of the most graceful examples of Romanesque architecture in Normandy. In spite of its minuteness, the 12C nave is flanked by aisles. Notice the geometrical patterns on the portal.

Return to Épouville; continue south.

Montivilliers – *See Le HAVRE.*
The road leaves the Vallée de la Lézarde via Rouelles, just outside Le Havre. There is a pleasant recreation area here, and an interesting slate dovecote. The road then goes along the edge of the Montgeon forest, and leads to the Jenner tunnel, which provides access to the centre of town.

★★ **Le Havre** – *See Le HAVRE.*

VALLÉE DE LA DURDENT

③ From Veulettes-sur-Mer to Fécamp

36km/23mi – about 3hr – see local map p 128

The Durdent, which flows idly into the sea at Veulettes-sur-Mer, has cut a wide valley across the Caux plateau.

Veulettes-sur-Mer – *See above.*
From Veulettes take D 10 south. In Paluel turn left onto D 68. After a sharp right hand bend, turn left at the top of a rise to the chapel.

Chapelle de Janville – The old pilgrimage church on the edge of the plateau contains an attractive wrought-iron grille in the chancel.

Return to Paluel. Turn left onto D 10.

Cany-Barville – The church ⊙ on the west bank, rebuilt in the 16C in its original pointed arch style, has a 13C belfry. Notice on entering the two 16C **carved panels**★: Our Lady of the Seven Afflictions (represented by the seven swords piercing the heart of the Virgin) and St Martin (details include the beggar with a wooden leg and the snail provoking the horse). Dominating the high altar (18C) stands a Christ in Majesty consisting of more than 80 angels in relief work: they form a huge monstrance, with the central stained-glass pane symbolising the host.

The **moulin St-Martin** is the setting for a folk museum, the **écomusée des Arts et Traditions populaires** ⊙. The exhibits show tools and other everyday obejcts from times past.

Barville – The small church has a delightful **setting**★ between two arms of the River Durdent.

Take D 131.

Château de Cany ⊙ – Beyond a large courtyard lined with two symmetrical outbuildings, extended by two pavilions, stands an imposing stone and brick château built at the end of the Louis XIII era. It is surrounded by moats fed by the River Durdent.

Château de Cany

The main building has two projecting wings and is approached by a double stairway in the form of a horseshoe. The apartments have retained fine 17C and 18C furnishings. On the second floor the bedrooms are decorated with beautiful Flanders tapestries. The Green Room contains Regency woodwork.

In the basement the former pantry and kitchen contain utensils, ovens, crockery and costumed figures.

Take D 50 to Ourville, then turn right onto D 150 which descends into the Valmont Valley.

Valmont – *See VALMONT.*

Return to D 150 towards Fécamp.

★★**Fécamp** – *See FÉCAMP.*

★PLATEAU DE CAUX

④ Round tour starting from Yvetot

See the description on p 126.

Ancienne Abbaye de CERISY-LA-FORÊT

Population 784
Michelin map 54 fold 14 or 231 fold 16 – 8.5km/5mi west of Balleroy
Local map see BAYEUX

The abbey at Cerisy is a remarkable example of Norman Romanesque architecture.
The earliest mention of this abbey dates back to the 6C when Christianity was beginning to spread throughout Gaul. Around 510 Vigor, a missionary from Bessin had a monastery built at Cerisy and dedicated it to St Peter and St Paul. In 1032 Robert I of Normandy, the father of William the Conqueror, founded a new monastery which he dedicated to Vigor, former bishop of Bayeux.

★ÉGLISE ABBATIALE ⊙ 15min

The nave, now reduced to only three bays of the original seven, is remarkable for its height. The great arches are topped by a gallery; semicircular arches frame the clerestory windows.

The monks' choir and the apse reproduce the three storey elevation of the nave and give a fine overall effect. The choir vaulting with its slim ribs is very graceful; the stalls date from 1400. The choir and especially the apse are a striking example of Romanesque architecture characterised by their delicacy and abundance of light, when most 11C buildings were often massive and sombre.

Outside, near the entrance are parts of the 13C nave (left) giving some idea of its original length. Walk round the church to the east end to admire the **chevet★** with its tiered effect formed by the apse, the choir and the belfry.

BÂTIMENTS CONVENTUELS ⊙ 30min

These 13C buildings were bought by the nation during the French Revolution. They were then quarried for building purposes or to pave the streets.

Musée lapidaire – A low chamber with pointed vaulting houses the Archeological Museum containing pieces of statues as well as 14C and 15C decorative floor tiles. At the far end of the chamber, on the left, are the remains of a dungeon with 15C and 16C graffiti.

Chapelle de l'Abbé – The Abbot's Chapel built in the 13C with a gift from St Louis is a good example of Norman Gothic architecture. Note the double piscina beneath twin rounded arches (right) and the 15C frescoes above the altar. There is a good collection of vestments including stoles, chasubles and copes.

Salle de justice – The Judgement Room contains furniture, documents and manuscripts.

Château du CHAMP DE BATAILLE★★

Michelin map 54 fold 20 or 231 fold 34 – 4km/2.5mi northwest of Le Neubourg

This splendid stone and brick 17C residence, surrounded by woodland, comprises two identical relatively low buildings standing on either side of a vast courtyard and linked by porticoes.

TOUR ⊙ *about 1hr*

In the 17C, the forecourt stretching in front of the castle's entrance became a bowling green. Notice the busts of several Roman emperors which were beheaded during the Revolution.

Main courtyard – This quadrangle is entered through a gate pierced in a wall adorned with pilasters and closed off by a monumental gate, its twin lying in the same axis, surmounted by four goddesses embodying the four elements, earth, water, air and fire.

Interior – *Entrance through the main courtyard on the left.* The Palladian entrance (inspired by the 16C Italian architect Andrea Palladio) gives access to the grand staircase embellished with wrought-iron banisters bearing the monogram of the Duke of Beuvron, who owned the castle in the 18C. On the first floor, in the north wing, you can admire the Louis XVI dining hall, the large drawing room with lavish ornamentation and a billiards room decorated with a display of 16C **tapestries** from Brussels showing the signs of the zodiac.

Large Beuvron salon

The tour continues through the south wing with its **marble lounge** and outstanding collection of antiques, the drawing room (large Beuvron salon) and the library with its sumptuous neo-Egyptian furniture which a dedicated art lover could have brought back from his travels to the land of the Pharaohs. The small gallery featuring Chinese and Japanese porcelain (17C-18C) opens onto the ceremonial bedroom reminiscent of the 17C style. Note the huge Louis XIV four-poster bed; and the superb furnishings: the fine **embroidery** reproducing Chinese motifs on a background of silk fabric enhanced by gold threads, the sculpted panels executed by master cabinetmaker Verberck, and the wall clock in gilded bronze inlaid with Boulle marquetry. The visit ends with the chapel (17C-18C), which has recently been restored.

Park – When work on the formal French gardens is completed, they will take on the appearance they had in the 17C, evoking the brilliant compositions of André Le Nôtre. It will be possible to stroll along the park's alleyways and see the 18C follies *(fabriques)*, the ice house, a pyramid-shaped structure where ice collected in ponds during the winter could be stored, and the Actéon aviary of neo-Classical inspiration. The Bassin des Masques is decorated with vases and grotesque figures based on those adorning the waterfall in St-Cloud.

EXCURSION

★Harcourt – *7km/4mi southeast of Brionne by D 26 and D 137*. This small town is on the road to Le Neubourg – which gives it name to the well-farmed plain – and is located at the intersection of roads leading to the banks of the River Risle and River Charentonne and Beaumont Forest.

Not far from the 13C **church**, the old wooden market place stands intact. Legend has it that the Viking king Rollo handed the lands of Harcourt over to his faithful ally, Bernard the Dane, after a successful raid.

★Château d'Harcourt ⓒ – Since 1827 the ancestral home *(see illustration in Introduction: Military architecture)* of the Harcourt family and its park (100ha/247 acres) have belonged to the French Agricultural College.

The castle was built in the late 12C by Robert II of Harcourt, companion to Richard Lionheart. It was subsequently reinforced and modernised in the 14C by John IV of Harcourt. In the 17C, on the orders of Françoise de Brancas, Princess of Lorraine and Countess of Harcourt, it was converted into a comfortable residence.

At the end of the drive stands the imposing mass of the castle, sheltered by its curtain wall. On the left a path circles the 20m/66ft wide moat surrounding the ramparts flanked by dilapidated towers. The small castle at the south entrance gives access to the outer bailey, separated from the keep by an inner ditch. The medieval entrance and its bridge have been restored. Near the façade dating from the 17C stands a 12C well 70m/30ft deep: it was probably fitted with a wheel for drawing water in the 14C. The rim was carved out of a single block of stone.

★Arboretum ⓒ – Adjoining the main courtyard, a 10ha/25-acre arboretum presents over 400 tree species coming from the five continents, mainly conifers and pine trees. A marked itinerary takes visitors round the "orchard" *(clos)*, planted with the rarer and more exotic varieties; here a great many essences can be seen, represented by few individual plants only. To the west lies the charmingly laid-out "shrubland" *(arboretum de peuplement)*, offering a small number of essences, cultivated together in bunches of 25 plants over a 1ha/2.5-acre plot. Among the most striking trees, the two 30m/99ft high Lebanon cedars near the entrance, planted around 1820, as well as the profusion of spruce (east Himalayan spruce), thuyas and venerable oak trees will undoubtedly catch the attention. In the **forest** (84h/230 acres) there are superb rare trees from all parts of the world (larches from Poland, beech trees from Chile, firs from the Caucasus, sequoias, thuyas) as well as exotic and decorative species of interest to foresters.

Îles CHAUSEY ★

Michelin map 59 folds 6 and 7 or 231 fold 25
Access: see The Red Guide France

The Chausey Islands, a day excursion popular with those staying in Granville *(1hr by boat)*, make up a small archipelago of granite islands, islets and reefs, which according to legend were once part of the ancient Scissy Forest submerged by the sea in 709.

Quarries which once supplied the brown granite for such edifices as Mont-St-Michel are no longer worked. Today, the islands are uninhabited with the exception of Grande Île where the winter population of six rises to 100 during the summer. The major part of the Chausey Archipelago is private property, the State owning just 7ha/17 acres around the lighthouse and fort.

★La Grande Île – The Island (2km/1mi long by 700m/2 300ft at its widest point)

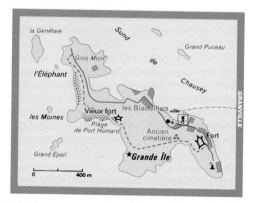

is the largest and the only one accessible to visitors. The **lighthouse** stands 37m/121ft above the sea. The beam carries 45km/38mi.

Fort – The fort was built between 1860 and 1866 against British attack but was never involved in a conflict. It now serves as a shelter for local fishermen.

Go round the fort anticlockwise.

The path goes past an old cemetery with four tombs.

MID-RANGE

Hôtel Fort et des Îles – *50400 Chausey (Îles) –* ☎ *02 33 50 25 02 – closed 17 Oct to 14 Apr – 8 rooms, half board: 48.48€ –* ⌷ *5.34€ – restaurant 16/21€.* The sound of the wind and that of the waves are the only ones you are likely to hear at night in this white house standing in the middle of a flower garden and facing the islands. A few simple rooms. Seafood gathered or bred on the island can be enjoyed in the dining room while admiring the view.

Vieux fort – The so-called Old Fort was rebuilt in 1923 by Louis Renault on the remains of another fort built in 1558. Its proud silhouette dominates all the coastline and especially the beach, Plage de Port Homard, where the tide goes far out at low tide. The tidal range is 14m/46ft.

The Moines and the Éléphant – These granite rocks, which can be reached at low tide, owe their names (the monks and the elephant) to their highly evocative shapes and colour.

Local tradition has it that there are 52 or 53 islands above the water at high tide (which number corresponds to the number of weeks in the year); 365 are visible at low tide (the number of days in a year). In fact, there are more than 200 rocks, known locally as *grunes*, which are revealed when the tide is out. It is hard going without a good local navigator, and sailors looking for the perfect secluded beach would be well-advised to get some advice and double-check charts before setting out on an adventure.

Incoming tide, Îles Chausey

Saint-Ange/EXPLORER

CHERBOURG

Population 92 045
Michelin map 54 fold 2 or 231 fold 2
Local map see Presqu'île du COTENTIN

Cherbourg, on the northern shore of the Cotentin Peninsula, is a seafaring town with the largest artificial harbour in the world. Different vessels stop in the yacht marina, the military harbour, the commercial port or the fishing port. Despite some hard luck over the centuries, the city boast some beautiful monuments, and is known for its remarkable breakwater.

The marked itineraries "Cobra-La Percée" (The Breakthrough) and "Objectif-Un Port" (Objective-A Harbour), described in the Historical Area of the Battle of Normandy, both go by Cherbourg; the former starts from here, while the latter ends here.

CONSTRUCTION AND DESTRUCTION

Titanic Undertakings – Vauban, in the 17C, was the first person to see the possibilities of Cherbourg as an Atlantic port. Work on the initial breakwater, proposed by a certain La Bretonnière, began in 1776. This offshore barrier was to run between Querqueville Point and the island, Île Pelée. La Bretonnière planned to submerge 90 huge timber cones filled with rubble and mortar at a depth of 20m/66ft. Louis XVI was present at the installation of one of these cones. For 75 years the sea gradually washed away all the underwater constructions placed on its bed.

Slowly all the material accumulated over the years on the sea bed began to form an artificial island. The sea gave it its curve. Following this line a fortified breakwater was eventually built which withstood the force of the sea. Work was completed in 1853. The naval base planned by Napoleon I was officially opened by Napoleon III in 1858. The first transatlantic passenger ship – belonging to the Hamburg America Line – berthed there in 1869.

Today, the breakwater is carefully maintained. Although it no longer has any significant military role, it is essential for maintaining a safe harbour in an area where storms can be especially violent.

Frogmen at Work – When the American 7th Corps took Cherbourg they found the harbour completely devastated and mined. In record time repairs were made and the mines and wrecks were cleared with the aid of Royal Navy frogmen, so that the Mulberry Harbour at Arromanches could be taken out of service, and Cherbourg could supply the Allied armies. This role of single supply port was stepped up during the Ardennes offensive when Cherbourg was handling, twice the tonnage every month, that New York had handled in 1939.

A second invention also alleviated the logistic burdens. The undersea pipeline **PLUTO** (**P**ipe **L**ine **U**nder **T**he **O**cean) from the Isle of Wight also emerged at Cherbourg, bringing petrol to the Allies from 12 August 1944.

The capture of Cherbourg on 26 and 27 June 1944 marked a decisive stage in the Battle of Normandy since it allowed for the landing of heavy equipment on a large scale.

Dreamboats – The *Queen Mary*, launched in 1934, the *Queen Elizabeth* launched in 1949 and the *Queen Elizabeth II*, as of 1967, all flying the colours of the Cunard Line, called at Cherbourg on their way to New York.

SIGHTS

🔼 Have a stroll and get to know Cherbourg: there are six historic trails set up throughout the city, with explanatory markers in French and English to guide you. Starting points are across from the SNCF train station, across from Saint-Trinité and across from the former Transatlantique station.

Parc Emmanuel-Liais – The park, created by the naturalist and astronomer Emmanuel Liais (1826-1900), is famous for its tropical plants which flourish under the influence of the Gulf Stream.

Place Napoléon – A bronze statue of the emperor by Armand Le Veel dominates this square with its attractive flowerbeds.

Nearby is the **Église de la Trinité** a Flamboyant Gothic church.

Musée Thomas-Henry ⊘ – This Fine Arts Museum is now housed in a custom-built cultural centre. The first floor is set aside for temporary exhibitions. The first gallery, on the second floor, is devoted to paintings with Cherbourg and the sea as themes. The 15C to 19C paintings are on display in the other galleries: Fra Angelico's altarpiece panel, *The Conversion of St Augustine*, Filippo Lippi's *Entombment*. The 17C to 19C collection has works by Murillo *(Christ on Calvary)*, Vernet *(An Italian Scene)* and Chardin *(Still Life)* as well as canvases by Poussin, Largillère and Rigaud, a *Nude* by David and numerous neo-Classical works from the early 19C. The local artist Jean-François Millet (1814-75) is represented by a fine collection comprising numerous portraits, especially canvases of his two wives Pauline Orno and Catherine Lemarre. The last gallery has several works by another local artist from Réville, Guillaume Fouace (b 1837): still-life paintings, portraits *(Self-Portrait Holding a Palette)* and *The Hopeful Fisherman*.

Bronzes by the sculptor Armand Le Veel (1821-1905), another Cotentin artist, are displayed throughout the various galleries; note his medallion self-portrait and a bust of Camille Claudel.

Muséum d'Ethnographie, d'Histoire naturelle et d'Archéologie ⊘ – The ethnographic, natural history and archeological sections of the museum include, on the ground floor, shells, mammals and birds collected since 1830. Upstairs Egypt, Asia, Africa, Oceania and the Americas are represented by collections of mineral specimens, statuettes, musical instruments as well as arms. One showcase has exhibits illustrating the life of the Inuit (Eskimos).

Port militaire ⊘ **(arsenal)** – Only French nationals are allowed to visit the Naval Base and the Arsenal. The Arsenal is the headquarters for shipbuilding and naval armament and specialises in the building of traditional and nuclear submarines.

Most of the naval vessels are berthed in the Charles X and Napoléon III docks.

Cherbourg's logo represents a blue gull perched on the lines of a musical score. The drawing symbolises the city's close relationship with the sea and with music – who can forget *Les Parapluies de Cherbourg*? The iconic musical comedy starring Catherine Deneuve was filmed in Cherbourg in 1964. Local firemen provided the downpours required in order to raise the umbrellas of the title.

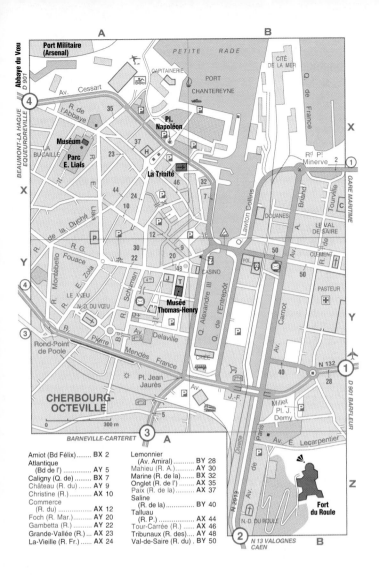

Boat trip round the roadstead ⊙ – Board at L'Épi, a former fish-auction dock. Visitors sail past the central fort of the seawall, which Napoléon called his "pyramid", and the military port.

Station Voile Nautisme et Tourisme – This recreational facility offers lots of choice for nautical fun: sea kayak, windsurfing, sailing, boat trips, schooner trips, diving, sand sailing, off-road biking, hang-gliding, delta planing and even more!

Fort du Roule – A road winds up to the fort with its mid-19C buildings; it stands on top of Roule Hill (112m/367ft), which owes its name to its main geological feature, *grès* (sandstone), formerly called *roule*. In June 1944, the Germans entrenched in the fort offered fierce resistance before surrendering. The terrace on the ramparts, commands a good **panorama★** *(viewing table)* of the town, the harbour buildings, the arsenal and the vast expanse of water (1 500ha/6sq mi) of the roadstead sheltered from the sea by breakwaters.

Musée de la Libération ⊙ – Entirely renovated with the help of modern scenery, the museum is a historical centre and a memorial retracing the dark years of French history from 1940 to 1944, without showing any arms or uniforms. In order to gain access to this memorial situated where the action took place, visitors have to walk alongside a grill standing in a pool whose water ripples like the sea on a beach.

In the basement there are sound and audio-visual recordings as well as maps and historical documents showing the laborious way which led from darkness (the Exodus, the Occupation, the propaganda which permeated the whole

Eating out

MID-RANGE

Café de Paris – *40 quai Caligny – ☎ 02 33 43 12 36 – closed 1-15 Mar, 1-15 Nov, Sun evening and Mon from Oct to Apr except holidays – 16.01/32.01€.* Enjoy a selection of seafood whilst admiring the view of the harbour in one of the two dining rooms. This bistro-style restaurant is bright and warm with its pastel-shade decor reflected in mirrors.

Le Faitout – *25 r. Tour-Carrée – ☎ 02 33 04 25 04 – reservation required –16.77/27.44€.* This little restaurant in the centre of town has many faithful customers. The old-fashioned façade and the panelled walls have a nautical feel about them. The cuisine is traditional and features specialities of Normandy.

Where to stay

MODERATE

La Croix de Malte – *5 r. des Halles – ☎ 02 33 43 19 16 – hotel.croix.malte@wanadoo.fr – closed 15 days at Christmas – reservation recommended – 24 rooms 27.44/45.73€ – ☕ 4.57€.* This hotel is near the theatre and the casino. The rooms, furnished in pine, are well lit and soundproofed, but most of them are not very spacious.

Hôtel Angleterre – *8 r. P.-Talluau – ☎ 02 33 53 70 06 – 23 rooms: 28.97/44.21€ – ☕ 5.34€.* Situated in a quiet part of the town centre, this simple hotel with its white-roughcast façade offers functional rooms brightened up by light-wood furniture. Good value for money.

Manoir St-Jean Bed and Breakfast – *At St-Jean – 50110 Tourlaville – 1km/0.6mi beyond the castle – ☎ 02 33 22 00 86 – ⊭ – 3 rooms: 33.54/44.21€.* Located on the edge of Ravalets Castle, this converted 18C farmhouse, overlooking the green Trotebec Valley, has retained its authentic aspect. You will be spoilt by the owner who willingly shares with her guests her considerable knowledge of the natural and cultural wealth of the region.

On the town

Cherbourg is a sailors' town and, just like their beloved sea, under its peaceful daytime atmosphere runs an unsuspected agitation which seems to come to the surface after midnight, in the late-night bars where storms sometimes gather.

Art's Café – *69 r. au Blé – ☎ 02 33 53 55 11 – Mon-Sat 11am-1am.* Creased wallpaper enhanced by a frieze of bright suns, wrought-iron wall lights representing huge crickets...this original and convivial café was entirely redecorated by an artist. Add to all this a warm welcome, a chess table and a small madeleine served automatically when you order coffee.

Café du Théâtre – *Pl. du Gén.-de-Gaulle – ☎ 02 33 43 01 49 – daily except Sun evening 9am-11.30pm.* With its large covered terrace, this café is ideal for relaxation after an evening at the theatre. In the back-room, the deep armchairs, covered with red velvet, are a reminder that this place once belonged to the theatre.

Cherbourg Casino – *2-4 r. des Tribunaux – ☎ 02 33 20 53 35 – daily 10.30am-4am.* Built in 1827, this casino is the oldest in France. Gamblers will have a choice between trying their luck with fruit machines or playing boule. Some might prefer the leather armchairs of the elegant bar, others the discotheque and its old-fashioned music. Activities include concerts and popular dancing to accordion music...

Le Commerce – *42 r. François-La-Vieille – ☎ 02 33 53 18 20 – Mon-Sat 8am-1am – concerts on Thur in summer.* This family-style café-brasserie is decorated with paintings and greenery. Philosophical debates and blues/rock concerts.

Le Solier – *52 Grande-Rue – ☎ 02 33 94 76 63 – June-Sept: Mon-Sat 4pm-2am; Oct-May: 4pm-1am – closed 15 days in summer, usually in Aug.* This former covered passage owes its name to the fine cross-beam which, in the 16C, used to shore up the adjacent buildings. It became a cider shop in the 19C and a pub after the Second World War. Poems hanging on the blue-schist walls, black wood, panelling, a fireplace, an old darts board... all this contributes to create a charming atmosphere enhanced by the owner's conviviality. Concerts take place at the end of every month.

Yalta Conférence – *46 quai Caligny – ☎ 02 33 43 02 81 – daily 4pm-3am.* Very attractive late-19C style pub. Fitted carpets, wall covering and seat covering in velvet make up the muffled decor of the many jazz and world-music concerts programmed by the owner who wants her establishment to remain a model of its kind.

Showtime

Cherbourg Theatre – *Pl. du Gén.-de Gaulle* – ☎ *02 33 88 55 50* – *box office open Tues-Sat 1.30-7pm* – *visits on set dates, apply to the tourist office* – *closed June-Aug.* Designed in 1882 by Charles de Lalande, a student of Garnier, this Italian-style theatre is now a historic monument. The ceiling of the auditorium, from which hangs a huge chandelier in baccarat crystal weighing a tonne, was decorated by Clairin with allegorical figures representing Comedy, Drama, Music and Dance. Visits are scheduled, but the Théâtre de Cherbourg is above all a national theatre with a 600-seat capacity and very eclectic programmes.

Shopping

La Cave au Roy – *47 r. Tour-Carrée* – ☎ *02 33 53 01 21* – *Tues-Sat 9am-12.30pm, 2.30-7.30pm, Sun 10am-12.30pm* – *closed during Apr school holidays.* This well-stocked wine store in the town centre has various local specialities.

Les Tonnelles du Val – *102 r. Médéric* – *50110 Tourlaville* – ☎ *02 33 22 44 40* – *Tues-Sat 9am-noon, 2-7pm.* This huge warehouse, decorated with beams and casks, was once a foundry, then a dairy before it became the favourite haunt of connoisseurs of good wine and old Calvados. Charming.

Philippe-Lelanchon Bookseller-Publisher – *13-15 r. des Portes* – ☎ *02 33 01 21 10* – *daily 9.30am-noon, 2-7pm except Sun and Mon morning.* Located in a charming pedestrianised shopping street, this shop contains a great many books about the region and a few rare items.

Sport

Station Voile Nautisme et Tourisme de Cherbourg Hague – *R. du Diablotin* – ☎ *02 33 78 19 29* – *station-voile-cherbourg-hague@wanadoo.fr* – *summer: daily 10am-6pm; winter: Mon-Fri 9am-12.30pm, 1.30-6pm.* This watersports club offers numerous activities, depending on the season: sea-canoeing, kayaking, wind-surfing, sailing, sea trips aboard old sailing ships, sports catamarans and sailing dinghies, diving, sand yachting, speed sailing, beach sports, mountain biking, paragliding, hang-gliding... Tuition and hiring of equipment

country, the defence policies) towards light (the D-Day landing, the liberation of Cherbourg and the rebuilding of the port which became a major step towards the liberation of Europe).

EXCURSIONS

Abbaye du Vœu – *On the outskirts of town, exit 4 along rue de l'Abbaye.*
Founded in 1145 by Empress Matilda, the abbey has suffered a lot of misfortune; however, during the past few years, several projects have aimed at restoring its beautiful ruins.

The Fort Central, Cherbourg

Tourlaville – *5km/3mi east. From Cherbourg take avenue de l'Amiral-Lemonnier southeast. In Tourlaville, at the crossroads before the Hôtel Terminus, turn right onto rue des Alliés. 800m/875yd further on at the junction with D 63 turn right again onto D 32. Park the car and continue on foot.*
The **Parc du château** ⊘★ of the lovely Renaissance Tourlaville Château with its crenellated windows flanked by Corinthian pilasters, is quite surprising for its tropical plants, lovely stretches of water and fine beech trees.

Musée maritime Chantereyne ⊘ – This museum is devoted to the four main aspects relating to maritime matters: the navy, the merchant navy, fishing and sailing. More than 100 miniature models and a few early boats, such as the rescue boat *Raz Blanchard* are carefully maintained. A display of prints, paintings and miscellaneous objects evoke the memory of those who stopped by or visited Cherbourg. A reference library may be consulted by researchers and scientists.

Discover the suggested Driving tours at the beginning of the guide
Plan a trip with the help of the Map of Principal Sights.

CLÉCY★

Population 1 182
Michelin map 55 fold 11 or 231 fold 29 – Local map see La SUISSE NORMANDE

This township, tourist centre of the Suisse Normande, is close to some of the most picturesque beauty spots of the Orne Valley. The river sweeps round in a majestic curve, at the foot of steep wooded slopes topped by fine rocky escarpments which overshadow the river banks emphasising the bend. Clécy is, above all, an excellent starting point for outings. fishing, canoeing, climbing, walking, hang-gliding and riding enthusiasts will likewise find facilities here.

SIGHTS

Musée du Chemin de fer miniature ⊘ – ▣ In this Model Railway Museum, locomotives and wagons speed round a vast layout with landscapes from the Suisse Normande or Flanders. The layout becomes a fairyland in the dark when the châteaux, houses, factories and trains are lit up. A little train can take visitors for a ride around the domain.

EXCURSIONS

Croix de la Faverie – *Either from the car park between the post office and the church drive towards La Faverie Cross. At the stop sign turn right; then turn left and continue to climb. At a junction turn left; at the next junction bear left again and continue to the crossroads where the cross stands.*
Or drive to the cross by following the sign posts; at a corner on the surfaced road by a grassy area, turn off onto a rough track which leads to the cross.
At the end of two fields turn sharp left. 45min there and back on foot.

▣ From the group of pine trees *(picnic site)* there is a very pretty **view**, one of the most characteristic of the Suisse Normande: the Rochers des Parcs, seen from the side, overlook the river passing under the Lande Viaduct.

★**Le Pain de Sucre** – *2hr on foot there and back. From Clécy take the route de La Serverie. Cross the bridge over the Orne and the level crossing; after 100m/110yd turn right. A sign (left) shows the start of the path to the Sugar Loaf.*

Eating out

MODERATE

Auberge du Chalet de Cantepie – *14570 Cantepie – 1km/0.6mi north of Clécy –* ☎ *02 31 69 88 88 – closed 10-30 Jan, Sun evening and Mon out of season – 14.94/28.81€.* This is a typical Norman inn, with its half-timbered façade. The waitresses are dressed in regional costume and the cuisine is truly traditional. In the dining room, draperies and paintings contribute to the cosy atmosphere.

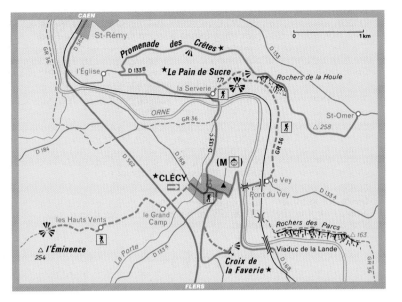

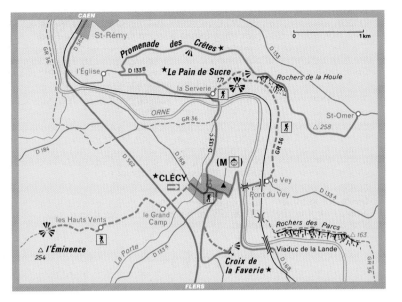 This path *(blazed with red and white markers)* climbs up the side of a valley on the right bank of a stream. Cross the stream. Entering the copse, keep to the right of a trail that rises quickly and obliquely to the right, and leads to the foot of a hillock; climb up. From the top of the Sugar Loaf, the sweep of the Orne is the outstanding feature in the **panorama**. On the way down, on reaching the foot of the hillock, keep to the right along the slope opposite that by which you came, and follow a winding path *(blazed with red and white markers of the Long Distance Footpaths)* which, passing below the Rochers de la Houle, comes out at the little rustic church of Vey.

The Éminence – *2hr on foot there and back. From Clécy take D 168. After 300m/328yd turn left towards the valley, pass in front of the police station and cross D 562 towards Grand Camp. Bear right into this hamlet and turn left to Les Hauts Vents.*

 The road rises along the north slope of the Éminence. The top of the hill (254m/833ft) is covered with thorny bushes but it is pleasant to stroll across the fields looking out over a wide panorama of the Normandy countryside and the Orne Valley.

César Dumont d'Urville

The famous navigator César Dumont d'Urville was born at Condé-sur-Noireau in 1790. In 1820 he commanded two voyages of exploration in the Black Sea and the Aegean Sea. During his stay on the Island of Milos, he was struck by the beauty of some fragments of a statue unearthed by a local farmer. He informed the French authorities of his findings and helped them to gain possession of the precious marble artefacts: they were to become one of the best-known Greek sculptures, the Venus de Milo, which is now displayed in the Louvre Museum.

In February 1828 Dumont d'Urville was sent on a charting expedition of the wreckage of the *Astrolabe*, the boat of La Pérouse which ran aground off Vanikoro in the Santa Cruz Islands. The voyage resulted in the revision of charts of South Sea waters and the redesignation of island groups into Melanesia, Micronesia, Polynesia and Malaysia.

In 1837 he headed towards the Antarctic and sighted the Adélie Coast south of Australia, which he named after his wife. Each of his expeditions proved extremely fruitful in the field of scientific research since he conducted many experiments relating to hydrography, mineralogy and botanics.

D'Urville and his family died in a railway accident between Paris and Versailles, the first in the history of France, which caused the deaths of 150 passengers. In 1844, his home town erected a statue on place de l'Hôtel-de-Ville to honour his memory. Three rocks taken from the Adélie Coast were placed at the foot of the statue by the 20C explorer Paul-Émile Victor.

*Promenade des Crêtes – *8km/5mi – about 45min. From Clécy Church take D 133C towards La Serverie. Cross the bridge over the Orne, turn left to St-Rémy; after 1.5km/0.9mi turn right into a hairpin bend and follow the Ridge Road.*

The road overlooks the valley and all along the drive offers beautiful viewpoints of the lazy wanderings of the Orne and its surroundings especially by the Pain de Sucre and the Rochers de la Houle. Follow the wooded banks and bear left on the road *(sharp bend)* which returns to St-Omer by the south.

To the southwest – *18km/11mi. Take D 133A southwest from Clécy, then D 36 south and a minor road west to Pontécoulant Château.*

Château de Pontécoulant ⊙ – This majestic château (16C-18C) with two domed turrets is set in a wooded valley between two stretches of water. It was given by the Pontécoulant family to the Calvados *département* and converted into a museum. The ground floor and first floor rooms display a fine collection of old furniture and family portraits. The pretty landscape garden rounds off the visit nicely.

Follow the River Durance south along D 298.

Condé-sur-Noireau – This small village in the Suisse Normande is the birthplace of **Admiral César Dumont d'Urville**, famous for his voyages of exploration to New Guinea, New Zealand and the Antarctic.

CLÈRES ★

Population 1 302
Michelin map 52 fold 14 or 231 fold 23

One of Normandy's greatest attractions is the zoo, which has occupied part of Clères Park since 1920. The château lying at the heart of the park consists of two main sandstone buildings: the western wing was built in the neo-Gothic style whereas the eastern wing dates from the 15C but was subsequently remodelled towards 1505. Both are decorated with motifs in brick and flint.
In the market square stands a covered market, a wooden structure with slate roof.

Flamingos, Parc zoologique
de Clères-Jean-Delacour

*Parc zoologique de Clères-Jean-Delacour ⊙

The exceptional natural setting of the park in Clères provides a wonderful opportunity to discover the birds and mammals which were brought here by the famous botanist and ornithologist **Jean Delacour** (1890-1985): 200 in all representing seven different species which inhabit the rivers, lawns, groves, and trees.
The garden is populated by flamingos, ducks and exotic geese. Beyond is the park proper where antelopes, kangaroos, gibbons, different types of deer, cranes and peacocks roam in partial liberty. More than 300 couples of palmipeds of 120 different species live and nest around the lake. Higher up indoor and outdoor aviaries are reserved for lesser-known birds, some on the endangered species list (around 2 000 birds belonging to 250 different species). In the former main room of the château, a gallery houses rare exotic birds.

To observe the animals under the best possible conditions (nesting, communal life in herds or colonies, ritualised mating displays), it is advisable to visit the park before 30 June.

Where to stay and eat

MID-RANGE

Au Souper Fin – *76690 Frichemesnil – 4km/2.5mi northeast of Clères via D 6 and D 100 – ☎ 02 35 33 33 88 – closed 16-31 Aug, Sun evening from Oct to Mar, Wed evening and Thur – 25.15/35.06€.* This restaurant is housed in a small brick-built house, once the café-cum-grocery shop of Frichemesnil hamlet. The owner-chef prepares an imaginative cuisine. The dining room is attractive and there are three delightful bedrooms.

EXCURSIONS

Parc du Bocasse ⊙ – *2km/1mi west by D 6.* Children's amusement park and picnic area.

Montville – *6km/3.7mi south on D 155.*

Musée des Sapeurs-Pompiers de France ⊙ – In a modern building, a fine collection of red fire engines, banners and uniforms, tall ladders and gleaming helmets retrace the glorious history of the French fire brigade, whose motto has always been *"Courage and dedication"* (for those in the French provinces) or *"To rescue or to perish"* (for those in Paris).
The 60 or so large exhibits belong to three successive periods in the history of fire prevention: hand pumps manned by a special fire-fighting force *(gardes-pompes)* from 1722 to around 1910; horse-drawn vehicles operational between 1880 and 1920; finally, the motorised fire engines that made their first appearance just before World War I. Note an extremely rare 1721 **hand pump** *(pompe à bras des échevins de Rouen)*, a horse-drawn steam pump (1886); a 1937 Somua pump truck and a 30m/99ft long manually raised ladder mounted on a 1939 Delahaye chassis.
The tour ends with a collection of old prints and some rescue equipment.

Château de Bosmelet – *Leave Clères to the north on D 2, then take D 3 towards St-Victor-l'Abbaye; after crossing N 29, go on until you reach the locality called "Le Bocage" and turn right onto D 96. After 1km/0.5mi, turn onto the wide concrete driveway on the left.* This château recently restored in the Louis XIII style nestles in a sumptuous setting. Some of the ground floor rooms are open to the public. The double avenue lined with 300-year-old lime trees rising to a height of over 40m/132ft and the lawns stretching for more than a mile will surely enchant visitors, as will the amazing "rainbow" **vegetable garden**: during the summer season it offers a remarkable combination of flowers, vegetables and aromatic plants which compose a dazzling kaleidoscope of colours. Beside it an Asian vegetable garden has also been planted.

CONCHES-EN-OUCHE ★

Population 4 009
Michelin map 55 fold 16 or 231 fold 34

The town of Conches, on the edge of the woodlands which mark the northern limits of the Pays d'Ouche, is remarkably situated on a spur encircled by the River Rouloir. There is particularly good view of the town if it is approached along the Rouloir Valley (from Évreux). The keep of the ruined castle is illuminated from April to September.

From Rouergue to the Pays d'Ouche – On his return from a campaign against the Spanish Moors with Don Sanche of Aragon (1034), Roger de Tosny made a pilgrimage to Conques, in Rouergue (southwest France) and brought back relics of **St Foy**. He may have given the name of the famous sanctuary to the growing town. Roger dedicated a church to St Foy; at the end of the 15C it was replaced by the present building.

SIGHTS

Jardin de l'hôtel de ville – The Gothic doorway of the town hall – entrance to the former castle – leads to the garden in which stands the ruined keep of the lords of Tosny, surrounded by 12C towers.
From the terrace, with its wild boar in stone, there is a fine view of the Rouloir Valley and the elegant Flamboyant apse of St Foy's Church. Below there is another terrace with a Flamboyant balustrade and offering a similar view.

Rue du Val – There are two interesting buildings on this street. One is the 16C half-timbered **maison Corneille**, home to the famous dramatist's family. At the end of the street, the **hospital** was built on the site of the former abbey; the vaulted cellars are open to visitors.

The Communauté des communes de Conches publishes a walking guide to the area, which also shows trails for bike and horseback riding, on sale at the Tourist office. There are four suggested tours though town.

★**Église Ste-Foy** – The south tower of this church is crowned by a tall spire of wood and lead, a copy of the one blown down in a storm in 1842. The fine carved panels of the façade doors are early 16C. Notice the many gargoyles.
Inside there are some beautiful statues: St Roch (17C) in the south aisle and near the great organ; St Suzanne (13C) at the entrance to St Michael's Chapel; a polychrome Pietà (16C) in the north aisle; a statue of St Peter wearing a tiara (16C) at the entrance to the Lady Chapel; Christ resurrected in stone (16C) in the east end.

★**Stained-Glass windows** – The Renaissance windows, dating from the first half of the 16C, have retained their unity in spite of restoration. Those in the north aisle depict the life of the Virgin. The second window (1510), showing the Virgin between St Adrian (left) and St Romanus (right) is, like its pair which evokes the life of John the Baptist, of an earlier date than those that follow, and probably adorned the original church.

The seven windows (10.5m/34ft) in the chancel are divided into two by a trilobed transom, the upper part being given to the illustration of the Life of Christ, the lower to that of St Foy and portraits of the donors. The whole series, inspired by German master engravers such as Dürer and Aldegrever, is said to be by Romain Buron, called the master of Gisors, who was a pupil of Engrand Le Prince from Beauvais.

The windows in the south aisle were made in either Île-de-France or at Fontainebleau. The Mystical Wine Press (fifth window) is the best known.

The houses facing the church are 15C and 16C. The vaulted cellars (11C-12C) are open to visitors.

Musée du Livre, du Verre et de la Pierre ⊘ – This museum has a collection of objects made of molten glass by the man known as the "sorceror of Conche", François Décorchement (1880-1971). There are also minerals and fossils on display.

EXCURSION

Breteuil-sur-Iton – *14km/9mi south by D 840.* The town stands on the eastern edge of Breteuil Forest in a loop of the River Iton which forms a small lake in the public gardens laid out on the site of the old castle.

The **church**, where in 1081 William the Conqueror's daughter, Adèle the Beautiful, married Stephen, Count of Blois, dates from the 11C; the local reddish stone *(grison)* gives it a rustic appearance. The belfry is a large square tower above the transept crossing. The interior is dominated by the great nave arches supported on 12 massive stone pillars. The pillars in the transept crossing date back to the days of William the Conqueror. The five arches in the apse rest on columns with foliated capitals. The balustrade of the organ loft is decorated with Italian Renaissance motifs and 12 angelic musicians.

Presqu'île du COTENTIN★★

Michelin map 54 folds 1-3, 11-13 or 231 folds 1-3

The pronounced thrust of the Cotentin peninsula into the Atlantic corresponds with an equally uncharacteristic landscape: the austere landscape around La Hague is less a reminder of Normandy than a foretaste of Brittany.

The wooded hinterland deserves to be better known; it was the cradle of a race who for a time assumed control of the central Mediterranean area.

Geographically, it can be divided into three areas. The **Cotentin Pass** is the lower plain. The **Val de Saire** includes the river valley and the whole northeast part of the peninsula. **Cap de la Hague** is the granite spine jutting out into the sea.

Cotentin *vaquelotte*

J. Blonde/Musée Maritime, Tatihou

Norman Kings of Sicily (11C-12C) – Early in the 11C many of the inhabitants of the Cotentin, who were dissatisfied with the harsh authority of the Duke of Normandy, set out for the Holy Land; their devotion to St Michael led them to southern Italy where the feudal barons were in a perpetual state of war.

A lord in Apulia, in revolt against Byzantium, asked the wandering Normans to return home and raise troops for him; they had no difficulty in finding recruits in the Cotentin which was poor and overpopulated.

The exploits of three sons of **Tancrède de Hauteville**, a minor baron from the Coutances area, aroused great enthusiasm. The eldest William, known as Iron Arm, profited from the Italian imbroglio to drive out those who had employed him and became William of Apulia in 1102. His two brothers, however, were the true founders of Norman power in the Mediterranean: Robert Guiscard de Hauteville and, even more, his younger brother Roger, who became one of the most powerful Christian monarchs. The reign of Roger II from 1101 to 1154 surpassed that of all others in brilliance and display. The last Norman King of Sicily was Manfred, who was killed at Benevento in 1265 by Charles of Anjou, brother of St Louis, and whose tragic fate was celebrated by Dante, Byron and Schumann.

THE MARAIS DU CONTENTIN ET DU BESSIN REGIONAL NATURE PARK

The marked itineraries "D-Day-Le Choc" (The Impact), "Objectif-Un Port" (Objective-A Harbour) and "Cobra-La Percée" (The Breakthrough) described in the Historical Area of the Battle of Normandy, go through the Parc des Marais. This nature park, formerly known as the Marais de Carentan, was inaugurated in June 1991 and embraces 117 communes. With a total area of 120 000ha/465 sq mi these wetlands stretch from the Bay of Veys on the east coast of the Cotentin peninsula to Lessay haven on the west coast. This area of marshland (25 000ha/97sq mi) and *bocage* with its many canals is rich in plant and animal life. The relatively tall vegetation of these treeless wetlands provides good nesting and wintering grounds for migratory species.

Several museums, nature reserves and study centres offer invaluable information on the various aspects of wildlife in the park. *For further information apply to Maison du Parc, BP 282, 50500 Les Veys Cantepie.*

"**Les Ponts d'Ouve**" is a visitor centre for the Marais du Cotentin et du Bessin Park. In addition to the exhibits indoors on flora and fauna, there is a **discovery trail** through the park with informative panels. There are observation areas set up for bird watchers.

★EAST COAST

① From Carentan to Barfleur

75km/47mi – about 2hr 45min

Carentan – Carentan is situated at the head of an estuary – a marina was opened in 1982 – in the low-lying area of the Cotentin peninsula; it is an important cattle market town and one of the largest centres of the regional dairy industry. The octagonal spire of the belfry of the **Église Notre-Dame** dominates the whole region.The church (12C-15C) has elegant Flamboyant Gothic decoration on its southern side. A Renaissance screen encloses the chancel. The fine stone house at the corner of rue de l'Église and place Guillaume-de-Cerisay was described by Balzac under the name Hôtel de Dey in his work *Le Réquisitionnaire*.

The arcades of the old covered market in **place de la République** date from the late 14C. The **hôtel de ville** (town hall) occupies the elegant 17C-19C buildings of an old convent.

From Carentan take N 13 towards Ste-Mère-Église. Shortly before St-Côme-du-Mont, turn right onto D 913.

Ste-Marie-du-Mont – The impressive **church** is identified by its square 14C tower of which the top storey is a Renaissance addition (restored in 1843 after a storm). The nave is early 12C; the transept and chancel date from 14C as do the nave's windows and vaulting. Inside, is a late-16C figured pulpit; in the chancel, on the left, is a funerary statue of Henri Robert aux Espaulles carved in the early 17C.

A roadside monument commemorates the 800 Danish sailors who took part in the D-Day landings.

Utah Beach – This beach entered history on the day following the landings of Allied forces at the other beaches involved in the D-Day landings. Despite murderous fire from the German coastal batteries, the troops of the American 4th

Eating out

MODERATE

L'Estaminet – *Pl. de l'Église – 50480 Ste-Marie-du-Mont-Village –* ☎ *02 33 71 57 01 – closed Jan, Tues evening and Wed from late Sept to late June – 14.48/25.61€.*
Stop on the tiny charming square next to the church, which, on a certain day in 1944, was stormed by thousands of allied vehicles on their way from Utah Beach. This lovely Norman inn is the right place to appease your appetite, with its tantalizing meals where sea flavours dominate.

Ferme-auberge La Huberdière – *Le Pommier – 50480 Liesville-sur-Douve – 8km/5mi NW of Carentan via D 913 (as far as St-Côme-du-Mont) then D 270 –* ☎ *02 33 71 01 60 – closed Sun evening and Mon –* ✉ *– reservation essential – 11.43/19.82€.* After visiting this farm which breeds milk cows and young she-goats, you will know all about milking and cheese-making...and you might be eager to sit down to a meal in order to enjoy the specialities of the house.

Le Moulin à Vent – *50440 St-Germain-des-Vaux – 9km/5.6mi N of Nez de Jobourg via D 202, D 901 then D 45 –* ☎ *02 33 52 75 20 – closed evenings and Sat from 1 Nov to 14 Mar, Sun evening and Mon from 15 Mar to 30 Oct – 15.24.25.92€.* This charming flower-decked granite house stands on top of a cliff, at the end of the Cotentin peninsula. In the dining room with its exposed beams, you will enjoy the fresh-produce cooking and the view of the sea.

MID-RANGE

Le Manoir de Cantepie – *Aire de Cantepie – 50500 Les Veys –* ☎ *02 33 71 19 55 – group reservation essential – 16.31/35.37€.* This huge 16C farm/manor house in a green setting houses a museum and a shop displaying the region's specialities. Try them at their best, prepared by the competent chef of the imposing restaurant.

Where to stay

MODERATE

La Dannevillerie Bed and Breakfast – *Rte de Quettehou – 50630 Le Vast – 6km/3.6mi NW of Quettehou via D 902 then D 26, take the path on the right before Le Vast –* ☎ *02 33 44 50 45 –* ✉ *– 3 rooms: 29/40€.* Nestling in the Val de Saire, among the greenery lining the river, which abounds in fish, this lovely small farm is a pleasant restful place. At breakfast time, gourmets will enjoy delicious brioches and bread, baked in a wood-fired oven by the village baker.

Le Fort du Cap Lévi Bed and Breakfast – *7 le Cap Lévi – 50840 Fermanville – 5km/3mi NW od St-Pierre-Église via D 210 –* ☎ *02 33 23 68 68 – closed 1-15 Jan – 6 rooms: 28/42€ –* ☕ *21€.* This establishment will delight visitors who like picturesque places and sea air. The comfortable rooms are housed in a former fort built on the orders of Napoleon. Breakfast is served on the veranda which offers a magnificent view of the sea.

Hôtel du Commerce et de la Gare et Rest. L'Escapade – *34 r. du Dr-Caillard, across from the train station – 50500 Carentan –* ☎ *02 33 42 02 00 – closed Christmas holiday through Jan – 15 rooms. 28.20/41.16€ –* ☕ *5.34€ – restaurant 21€.* This impressive building covered with Virginia creeper was a post-relay at the time of Napoleon III. The guest rooms are of various sizes, all recently renovated, and the dining room has a polished parquet floor that looks as if you could eat off it!

Division (7th Corps) disembarked on 6 June near La Madeleine and Les Dunes-de-Varreville *(see below)* and managed to make contact with the airborne troops of the 82nd and 101st Divisions, who had landed in the region of Ste-Mère-Église. Three weeks later the whole of the Cotentin peninsula had been liberated.
At **La Madeleine** there is a milestone – the first on the Road to Liberty – erected in 1947 to pay tribute to the soldiers killed during the landings and a memorial to the 4th Division. A German blockhouse (left) has been converted into a monument to the dead of the 1st Engineer Special Brigade; a stele and a crypt commemorate the action of the American 90th Division. On an area of dunes, presented by the commune of Ste-Marie-du-Mont as official American territory, there stands a huge stele erected on the 40th anniversary of the landings by the Americans in homage to those who died at Utah Beach. It provides a fine view of the sea; the wrecks of several "blockships" are still visible at low tide (north).

War of the Hedgerows

For the American soldiers of 1944 the Cotentin campaign – the advance to Cherbourg and the Battle of St Lô – is summed up in the description "the War of the Hedgerows".

Leafy hedges and sunken lanes such as those that divide the Normandy countryside are unknown in America and came as an unpleasant surprise for the troops but as a place for defensive warfare or guerilla tactics the terrain was ideal, offering countless opportunities.

Modern arms were not much help: 4-inch shells scarcely shook the tree-covered embankments which constituted natural anti-tank barriers; armoured vehicles moved with difficulty along the roads; only the foot soldier could fight successfully in this "hell of hedges".

The effort of fighting against an invisible enemy was exhausting; every field and orchard crossed was a victory in itself; progress was slow and was often estimated by the number of hedges passed. The terrain had to be declared clear before the tanks moved into action. So that the tanks could operate with a maximum of efficiency an American sergeant devised a system whereby a sharp steel device, not unlike a ploughshare, was attached to the front of each tank.

The **Musée du Débarquement** ⊙ provides a great deal of information connected with the exhibits: display of arms and equipment, documentary film, model and diorama with commentary reconstructing the landing operations.

A **monument to General Leclerc** was erected at Les Dunes-de-Varreville where the general landed with his famous armoured division.

Les Dunes-de-Varreville – In an opening in the dunes, 100m/110yd from the route des Alliés, a rose granite monument in the form of a ship's prow and bearing the cross of Lorraine commemorates the landing of the 2nd French Armoured Division under General Leclerc on 1 August 1944.

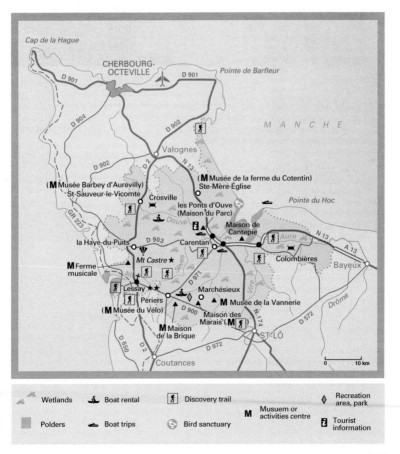

Wetlands	Boat rental	Discovery trail		Recreation area, park
Polders	Boat trips	Bird sanctuary	**M** Musuem or activities centre	Tourist information

The coastal road is separated from the sea by a line of dunes which successfully hide the water from sight; in some places however, between Les Gougins and Quinéville, the view extends along the coast from the Grandcamp cliffs to the Hougue Fort and Pointe de Saire.

The low granite houses with their slate roofs are typical of the Val de Saire.

Quinéville – Family seaside resort. Good view of St-Vaast roadstead from the square near the church.

Musée de la Liberté ⊙ – This museum is devoted to recreating the atmosphere of daily life during the dark days of the Occupation. There is a re-creation of a village street, a blockhouse, and various documentary material from the period.

Quettehou – The 13C granite **church** on a height is flanked by a tall 15C belfry. From the cemetery there is a view of Morsalines Bay, the Hougue Fort and Pointe de Saire.

Val de Saire, near Cap Lévy

★**Val de Saire** – A detour inland from Quettehou runs through a pleasantly green countryside and affords good views of the east coast of the Cotentin peninsula.

From Quettehou take D 902 north towards Barfleur; turn left onto D 26 which climbs through apple orchards. In Le Vast turn right.

The countryside with its rolling woodlands and pastures in the valleys has the appearance, in places, of a park.

In Valcanville turn right onto D 125. At the D 328 crossroads turn left into the road to La Pernelle; after 300m/300yd turn right at the sign "Église, Panorama".

Beyond the rebuilt church of **La Pernelle** is a former German blockhouse, once an observatory, which commands a **panorama**★★ *(viewing table)* extending from the Gatteville lighthouse (north) to the Grandcamp cliffs (south) by way of the Pointe de Saire, Réville Bay, Tatihou Island, Hougue Fort and the St-Marcouf Islands; in clear weather Percée Point is visible.

Take D 909 following signs to "Pernelle Bourg".

St-Vaast-la-Hougue – *See SAINT-VAAST-LA-HOUGUE.*

Continue north on D 1 along the port and the coast.

Beyond Réville the road passes La Crasvillerie, a delightful 16C manor house. This is market gardening country where they specialise in cabbages. As you approach Barfleur, the countryside begins to look a bit like Brittany, with granite houses, rocky bays and gnarled trees bent by the wind. Gatteville lighthouse stands to the north.

Barfleur and excursions – *See BARFLEUR.*

★★NORTH COAST

② From Barfleur to Cherbourg

33km/20mi – about 1hr 30min

Barfleur – *See BARFLEUR.*

Between Barfleur and St-Pierre-Église, the road crosses the Saire Valley.

Tocqueville – This was the family seat of **Alexis de Tocqueville** (1805-59) the historian and author of *Democracy in the United States* and *The Ancien Régime and the Revolution.*

St-Pierre-Église – The 17C church has a 12C Romanesque doorway. The 18C **château** was the family home of the Abbé de St-Pierre, the 17C author of a plan for peace entitled *Projet de Paix Perpétuelle.*
There are several good **viewpoints** ★ from the Fermanville-Bretteville corniche, notably those at Pointe du Brulay and Brick Bay.

Shortly after Brick Bay turn left at the Auberge Maison Rouge, to climb uphill towards Maupertus-sur-Mer. A track on the right leads to the television relay station.

★ **Belvedere** – There is a magnificent view of the coast and Cherbourg in the distance.

Return to D 116; continue west; in Bretteville take D 320 left towards Le Theil.

Allée Couverte (Gallery Grave) – This collective burial chamber, which dates back 4 000 years, consists of a double row of upright stones supporting flat slabs laid horizontally.

Return to Bretteville; take D 116 west.

On approaching Cherbourg one can see the roadstead and Pelée Island which serves as an anchor for the mole which, with the great breakwater, divides the harbour from the sea. To the left is Roule Fort.

Cherbourg – *See CHERBOURG.*

③ FROM CHERBOURG TO BEAUMONT

47km/29mi – about 2hr

Cherbourg – *See CHERBOURG.*
Leave Cherbourg by D 901.

Équeurdreville-Hainneville – The hall, stairway and first floor council room of the **hôtel de ville** ⊘, are the setting for some thirty 19C paintings by Chrétien, Campain, Jaron, Mac'Avoy, Faucon and Leroux.

Querqueville – Beside the parish church stands the 10C **Chapelle St-Germain** (left), the oldest religious building of the Cotentin area and perhaps of western France; note the trefoil plan and the fishbone motif on the walls. From the chevet *(path between the chapel and the church)* there is an interesting view over the Cherbourg Roadstead, its forts and jetties. The panorama stretches from Cap Lévy (east) to the Pointe Jardeheu (west).

From Querqueville take D 45 west in the direction of Urville-Nacqueville; turn left just before the hamlet of La Rivière.

Château de Nacqueville ⊘ – This beautiful 16C edifice, its postern and towers covered with ivy, makes a romantic sight, standing by a pool in its **park** ★ of oak trees and rhododendrons *(visit in May-June when the rhododendrons are in bloom).* Only the great hall with its beautiful Renaissance fireplace is open to the public.

Return to D 45; continue west.

At the entrance to Landemer, on the left, are the oddly grouped towers of the old **Manoir de Dur-Écu** restored in the 16C but resting on 9C foundations.
After Landemer the road rises in the Habilland Ravine, soon a beautiful perspective (right) opens up from the Cap Lévy lighthouse to the Pointe Jardeheu.

Gréville-Hague – The small squat church served as a model for the painter **Jean-François Millet** (1814-75) in his works of Norman landscapes. The artist's bust can be seen on a rock at the crossroads and the house where he was born in **Gruchy** is open to the public.

★ **Rocher du Castel-Vendon** – *1hr on foot there and back. Leave the car by a public wash-house on the left and continue straight ahead on foot by a sunken road which then becomes a footpath; certain parts of this itinerary are difficult.*
🚶 The path winds through bracken as it follows the right-hand side of the valley. From a rocky promontory, there is soon a **view** of the coast from Cap Lévy to Pointe Jardeheu. In the foreground stands the granite rock spine surrounded by deep ravines, known as the Rocher du Castel-Vendon.
The sea reappears during the long hydrangea-bordered descent to Omonville-la-Rogue. In **Omonville-la-Petite**, there lies a charming country graveyard surrounding the church. The poet **Jacques Prévert** (1900-77) is buried there alongside his close relatives *(left of the entrance).* To visit the **Maison Prévert** ⊘ (300m/987ft on foot), you will need to park the car on the church square.

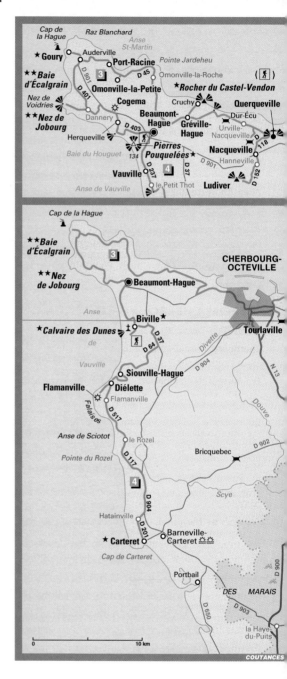

The road rising towards St-Germain-des-Vaux affords views of the tiny hamlet of **Port-Racine**, thought to be one of France's smallest ports, named after Captain Racine, who set up his naval base there under Napoleon I. The landscape is predominantly moorland broken by rocky spikes.

At the entrance to **Auderville** a road down to Goury enables you to explore the north end of Cap de la Hague. Beyond the foam lined shore at the island lighthouse of La Hague and, in the distance, the steep cliffs of Alderney.

★**Goury** – The small harbour, only refuge for fishermen caught in the Alderney Race, is an important coastguard and lifeboat station. In its octagonal station, the lifeboat swivels around a revolving turntable that enables it to be launched from two slipways: either towards the port at high tide or towards the open sea at low tide.

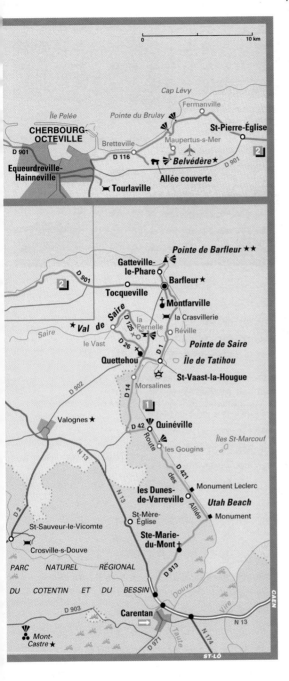

★★**Baie d'Écalgrain** – This desolate beach backed by heathland is one of the area's wild but imposing beauty spots. To the left of Alderney one can make out Guernsey and Sark and on the horizon the west coast of the Cotentin peninsula.

From Dannery take D 202 to the headland, Nez de Jobourg.

★★**Nez de Jobourg** – The long, rocky and barren promontory, surrounded by reefs, is the most impressive cape of the wild Hague coast. It is now a bird sanctuary (seagulls). Its most impressive aspects can be admired by taking a walk along the **Nez de Voidries**. From the Auberge des Grottes there is a view north of Écalgrain Bay, the lighthouse off Cap de la Hague and the Channel Islands: Alderney, the nearest, Sark, Guernsey and Jersey. Further south the Nez de Jobourg itself

151

Baie d'Écalgrain

comes into view, separated from the Nez de Voidries by Senneval Bay, a small inlet, fringed by a lonely beach, lying at the foot of a steep rocky amphitheatre. The site is particularly grandiose when the sea is rough and the waves break noisily on the rocks. In the distance Vauville Bay curves south to the cliffs at Cap de Flamanville.

Take D 403, a steep downhill road, opposite the power station.

The road is particularly difficult between Herqueville and Beaumont. Leave the car in a lay-by in a bend beyond **Herqueville** to look at the **vista★★** across Vauville Bay and over the Flamanville cliffs. The descent continues with Houguet Bay on the right.

Beaumont-Hague – This was the home town of the 17C smuggling family, the Jallot de Beaumont. Many of the staff from the atomic power station live in the town.

★★WEST COAST

④ From Beaumont-Hague to Carteret

45km/28mi – about 1hr 30min

Between Beaumont-Hague and Biville, the road goes down towards the shore and then climbs up again to the plateau.

★**Pierre-Pouquelée** – *45min walk there and back starting from D 318.*
🚶 Leave the car 200m/220yd before the first houses of Vauville and walk inland up a steep path on the right. When it reaches the plateau turn left to reach the almost totally ruined Pierre-Pouquelée gallery grave. Continue right to a small rise from which there is a magnificent **panorama** of the coast from the Nez de Jobourg to the Flamanville cliffs. In clear weather you can also see Alderney and, inland, Jobourg village and the Beaumont belfry. This is now a popular spot for hanggliding.

Vauville – The village nestles snugly on the heather-clad moors as they roll away to the horizon. The 12C church and the 17C manor make an attractive picture. The **Botanical Garden** ⊘ in the grounds of the manor specialises in evergreen plants and regroups over 450 different species, mainly from the southern hemisphere.
Beyond the village of Petit-Thot the road climbs steeply and affords a good **view★**, especially at dusk, of the moor land around the bay of Vauville.
Gliding enthusiasts have used Camp Maneyrol since 1923.

★**Biville** – The village is set on a plateau overlooking the desolate shoreline of Vauville Bay. Locals make pilgrimages to the church, where the glass coffin of the Blessed **Thomas Hélye** (1187-1257), a native of Biville, who was a priest and missionary in the diocese of Coutances, is enclosed in a marble sarcophagus in the 13C chancel, adorned with small 15C low-relief sculptures. On the right is the carved marble slab which covered the original tomb and in a chapel off the south side of the chancel is Blessed Thomas' chasuble. On the north side is a 19C bronze group showing Thomas Hélye with some of his followers.

The arrival of the Allies and the liberation of the region is commemorated in a stained-glass window by Barillet (1944) *(first on the right in the nave).*

Walk along the street beside the church; by a fence walk through a chicane and take the path which passes in front of a small chapel dedicated to the Virgin and continue to the Calvary.

★**Calvaire des Dunes** – *45min on foot there and back. At the end of the street next to the church, go through the gate and take the path which passes by a little chapel dedicated to the Virgin before leading up to the cross.*

From the foot of the cross there is a panoramic view: in the foreground the desolate landscape of Vauville Bay stretches from the Nez de Jobourg to the cliffs at Flamanville; out at sea the Channel Islands are visible in fine weather.

At **Siouville-Hague** the road runs once again beside the dunes, the hills and the sea. On the way down to Diélette there is a lovely view of this small port.

Diélette – The small port of Diélette, at the foot of the dark cliffs, is the only refuge between Goury and Carteret. As the tide goes out, a beach of fine sand appears between its two breakwaters.

Centre nucléaire de production d'électricité de Flamanville ⊘ – This nuclear power station, occupying 120ha/300 acres, stands in part on the granite bedrock, and in part on an artificial platform that juts into the ocean. Two production units are planned with an installed capacity of 1 300 million kW each. The first was completed in 1985 and the second a year later. Each unit produces 9 000 million kWh.

The plant uses enriched uranium to fuel the reactor and water as the cooling agent and for the production of steam to activate the turbines.

Between Flamanville and Le Rozel the road overlooks a small bay, the **Anse de Sciotot**; Cap de Flamanville and, to the south, the Pointe du Rozel are visible. The cliffs become lower, giving way to dunes.

Between Hatainville and Carteret the road runs along the dunes, the highest on the Norman coast. The grass covered hollows between the dunes are known locally as *mielles.*

★**Carteret** – *See BARNEVILLE-CARTERET.*

COUTANCES ★★

Population 9 715
Michelin map 54 fold 12 or 231 fold 26

Coutances, the religious and judicial centre of the Cotentin peninsula, is perched on a hillock crowned by the town's magnificent cathedral.

In the 3C the town changed its name from that of Cosedia to Constantia after the Roman Emperor Constantins-Chlorus (293-306) who had abandoned Rome in favour of Trier (Trèves in French). The name Cotentin itself is derived from the fact that this was the diocese of Constantinus.

In the 14C Coutances acquired an aqueduct *(ancien aqueduc).* Today only three arches remain standing to the northwest of the town on the Coutainville road.

The marked itinerary "Cobra-La Percée" (The Breakthrough), one of several described in the Historical Area of the Battle of Normandy, goes through this town.

★★★CATHÉDRALE *30min*

This cathedral, through the elegance of its proportions and the purity of its lines, is one of the most successful of Norman Gothic buildings.

Geoffroy de Montbray – one of those great prelate knights Duke William gathered round him before he went to England – completed the first nave in 1056. Then, thanks to the generosity of the sons of Tancrède de Hauteville whose amazing Mediterranean adventure had just begun, he built the chancel, transept, central tower and the façade with its twin octagonal towers reminiscent of those at Jumièges.

In 1218, after the town had been burnt down, a new Gothic cathedral was literally mounted on the remains of the 11C church, involving prodigious adaptations of style as can be seen from the way the Romanesque towers of the old façade were incorporated in to a new rectangular front and surmounted by spires.

Exterior – Above the great window a beautiful gallery crowns the façade while on either side rise the towers, quartered at their highest, octagonal level, by graceful elongated pierced turrets. The profusion of ascending lines, so remarkable in their detail, culminates in the flight of the spires which rise to 78m/256ft. The bold turreted lantern tower at the transept crossing is noteworthy for its slender ribbing and fine, narrow windows.

At the east end, the double series of flying buttresses are supported by the same vertical buttresses; the lower series receives the thrust from the vault and the ambulatory and the upper series the thrust from the vault of the choir at the same level as the pointed arches.

Interior – Pause at the beginning of the nave for a remarkable general view of this singular building with its upswept lines: to right and left wide arcades are lined above by galleries where the lower windows, surmounted by blind rose windows, have been blocked up; above again, along the bottom of the clerestory windows, a second balustrade of a different design, lines the walls.

In the transept, two massive pillars which formed part of the original Romanesque building were ornamented in the Gothic period with graceful upsweeping columns. Dominating the transept crossing is the octagonal **lantern tower★★★**. It is 41m/135ft high at its apex and the best example of its type in Normandy. On the first level of the lantern is a balustrade and twin arches; at mid height the columns of a second gallery support the ribs of the pointed vaulting and flank the tall windows illuminating the eight sided cupola.

At the base of the south transept pillar stands the beautiful and deeply venerated 14C statue of Our Lady of Coutances. Miraculously the statue survived the 1944 bombing of St Nicholas' Church.

The north transept contains the oldest, 13C stained-glass windows; the south, a 14C window, in sombre tones, of the Last Judgement.

The chancel, with the same architectural simplicity as the nave, is later in date and wider. As you walk round the two ambulatories, note the false triforium formed from two arches each covering twin bays. The radiating chapels are shallow and the ribs of their vaulting combine with the corresponding ambulatory bay rib to form a single arch. The central apsidal chapel, known as the Circata, was enlarged during a late-14C rebuilding by Sylvestre de la Cervelle. Above the slender painted columns small figures and animals peer out from the foliage of the capitals.

★★Upper Storeys ⊙ – In summer guided tours are organised in the upper storeys of the cathedral to discover the Romanesque parts of the original building; the walk starts at one of the west front towers, continues through the attic of the aisle then on to the third floor galleries to finish at the top of the lantern-tower. The panorama extends from Granville, over the Chausey Islands to Jersey and on a clear day even Mount Pinçon is visible.

COUTANCES

Eating out

MODERATE

Le Vieux Coutances – *55 r. Geoffroy-de-Montbray* – ☎ *02 33 47 94 78* – *closed Mon evening and Sun* – *12.96€ lunch* – *18.29/26.68€*. Situated close to the cathedral, this 17C building houses a charming small restaurant with a cosy atmosphere. Note the lovely old beams and stone staircase leading down to the ancient cellars. Imaginative cuisine which promotes the use of various spices.

MID-RANGE

La Voisinière – *R. des Hêtres – 50210 Savigny – 10km/6.2mi east of Coutances towards St-Lô* – ☎ *02 33 07 60 32* – *closed 1-15 Jan, Feb and Nov school holidays, Sun evening, Tues lunch and Mon* – *14.94/34.76€*. Convivial country atmosphere in this spacious 1805 building, once a farm and now a restaurant with its rustic decor and large fireplace, where customers enjoy a selection of regional menus. Four simple rooms. Unpretentious establishment.

La Verte Campagne – *50660 Trelly – 13km/8.1mi S of Coutances via D 7, D 49 then D 539 and a minor road* – ☎ *02 33 47 65 33* – *closed 24 Jan to 7 Feb, 4-10 Dec, Sun evening except July-Aug and Mon* – *21.34/35.06€*. This 18C farm, covered with Virginia creeper in summer, has retained its authentic charm: wide ceiling beams, stone walls and old fireplaces. This renowned restaurant has a few rooms available upstairs.

Where to stay

MODERATE

Le Quesnot Bed and Breakfast – *3 r. du Mont-César – 50660 Montchaton – 6.5km/4mi SW of Coutances via D 20 then D 72* – ☎ *02 33 45 05 88* – *closed end of Sept to Easter* – ⊡ – *3 rooms: 35/40€*. Guests have at their disposal a small 18C stone-built house with its own terrace and tiny garden with a view of the small church perched on a promontory. Modern bedrooms above the large country-style dining room.

Shopping

Market – *Pl. du Gén.-de-Gaulle* – *Thur mornings*. Lively colourful market stocked with a wide choice of country produce, including the famous Coutances cheese.

Sport

Centre équestre du Parc – *La Galaisière 50200 St-Pierre-de-Coutance* – *"km/2mi S of Coutance via D 971* – ☎ *02 33 47 91 28* – *open daily in summer* – *go to the annexe known as Le Camargue, on the road to Pointe d'Agon-Containville* (☎ *06 86 93 19 22*) – *closed first fortnight in Sept*. This small equestrian centre specialises in horses from Camargue, famous for their even temper. This is the ideal place for learning to ride through the Coutances countryside.

ADDITIONAL SIGHTS

★**Jardin des plantes** ⊙ **(YZ)** – The gardens' entrance is flanked by an old cider press on one side and the Quesnel-Morinière Museum on the other. The terraced promenade traverses the sloping gardens with its many flowerbeds and pine trees. The obelisk in the centre commemorates a former mayor, Jean-Jacques Quesnel-Morinière.

Musée Quesnel-Morinière ⊙ **(YZ M)** – The museum is in the former Hôtel Poupinel, which was bought in 1675 by the king's counsellor of the same name. The collections are mainly local: regional pottery, paintings by local artists (portrait of Marianne Delanoy by Blaisot, one of David's pupils as well as a St Luke and a St Augustine by Robert Bichue).
Outstanding, however, are Rubens' *Lions and Dogs Fighting* and the *Last Supper* by Simon Vouet. The popular arts and traditions section includes 18C-20C costumes from the Coutances area, 18C-19C regional pottery (jugs, fountains and ceramic finials used to decorate roof crestings), headdresses, furniture and kitchen utensils.

Les Unelles (Y) – A new steel frame and glass-walled building adjoins the former seminary buildings which have been transformed to house an arts centre, the tourist office and the local authority offices. The name is derived from the Unelli whose capital was Cosedia, present day Coutances.

Tour à la Fée

According to legend, one of the lords of Gratot fell hopelessly in love with a beautiful young maiden whom he had met at the fountain. In reply to his proposal of marriage the damsel avowed she was a fairy and that she could marry him only on the condition that he never pronounced the word "death". The lord promised. One day during a reception at the château, the lord grew impatient waiting for her ladyship; he went up to her room and in an ill-considered reprimand pronounced the fateful word. The fairy gave a heart-rending cry, then clambered onto the window sill and was seen no more.

Église St-Pierre (**Z**) – This fine 15C-16C church built by Bishop Geoffroy Herbert, was given a lantern tower over the transept crossing. In accordance with Renaissance custom, it was decorated ever more richly as the height increased.

FROM COUTANCES TO THE COAST *Round tour of 50km/31mi*

Leave Coutances by ④, D 44 and then turn right onto D 244.

On the way out of Coutances the road passes the overgrown remains of the aqueduct.

★**Château de Gratot** ⊙ – For five centuries, following the marriage of Jeanne de Gratot to Guillaume d'Argouges, the château belonged to the Argouges family. In 1439 Jean d'Argouges sold the port of Granville to the English, thus giving them control of Mont-St-Michel. This sale brought dishonour on the Argouges family but in the following century they redeemed the family name through appropriate marriages and proved their loyalty to the King of France.

The château has been converted into an arts centre that regularly hosts cultural events.

A small three-arched bridge over the moat leads to the entrance gatehouse and then the inner courtyard. On either side are the bare walls of the service buildings; to the west are the ruins of a square corner tower. Within the courtyard from left to right are the 18C pavilion and the 17C main building, flanked by the Round Tower, and the Fairy's Tower with the North Tower to the rear.

Maison seigneuriale – Two flights of steps lead up to the entrance of the now roofless former living quarters. The ground floor was lit by tall windows, the upper floor by dormers.

Tour ronde – This early-15C round tower is quite medieval in appearance. The narrowing of the staircase as it moved upwards was devised to hinder an attack as only one person could pass at a time.

The entrance to the basement is at the foot of this tower.

Caves – The groined vaulting of these fine cellars is supported by stout piers. The masonry is composed of stones placed edgewise.

The late-15C tower, now called the Fairy's Tower, is reinforced by a powerful buttress. It is octagonal at the base but becomes square at the top and is crowned by a saddleback roof. The wall head is decorated with gargoyles and a balustrade.

Tour d'angle – This corner tower, the only part of the medieval castle which remains, probably dates from the late 13C or the early 14C; the door has been walled up.

Communs – One of the rooms in these 16C outbuildings hosts an exhibition on the château, its construction and restoration.

In St-Malo-de-la-Lande take D 68 towards Tourville-sur-Sienne then turn right onto D 272 to Agon-Coutainville.

⌂**Agon-Coutainville** – Coutainville is one of the more popular resorts on the west coast of the Cotentin peninsula. Its long beach of fine sand is bounded by the Channel to the west and the Sienne estuary to the east. At low tide these great wet sandy stretches are popular for those looking for shrimps, cockles and clams.

Take the road leading to the Pointe d'Agon.

This stretch of countryside has an unreal look about it with its unusual vegetation associated with the sandy habitat.

Pointe d'Agon – The line of stones on the right-hand side of the road is a memorial to the author **Fernand Lechanteur** (1910-71) who wrote in the Norman dialect. From the headland there is a good view of this part of the Channel coast and especially of the port of Regnéville on the other side of the estuary.

Return to Agon-Coutainville, then follow the road to the hamlet, rue d'Agon.

D 72 soon overlooks the silted up port of Regnéville.

Where to stay

MODERATE

Village Grouchy Bed and Breakfast – *11 r. du Vieux-Lavoir – 50560 Agon-Coutainville – 2km/1.2mi north of Agon-Coutainville – ☎ 02 33 47 20 31 – closed mid-Jan to mid-Mar – ⌖ – 4 rooms: 28.97/35.06€*. This was once a mere fishing village. One of the fishermen's cottages has now been converted into a guesthouse with large wood-panelled rooms. A pleasant stop-over close to the sea. On the garden side, a summer kitchen is available for use by the guests.

Tourville-sur-Sienne – The roadside statue is of Amiral de Tourville, who lost the Battle of La Hougue. From the terraced cemetery (road from the statue) there is a good view of Regnéville harbour "closed off" by the sandy headland, Montmarin belfry, the Rocher de Granville, and in clear weather, the Chausey Islands.

Drive to Pont-de-la-Roque along D 650, then to Regnéville-sur-Mer along D 49.

Regnéville-sur-Mer – This small port located at the mouth of Sienne harbour used to be one of the most prosperous spots along the coast. Unfortunately, the site has silted up, causing the locality's influence to decline.

From the 13C **church**, follow signposts to the **Musée du Littoral et de la Chaux** ⊙ set up in the former Rey lime kilns. This splendidly restored example of mid-19C industrial architecture presents traditional activities connected with the Channel coast: sea-sand and kelp picking, ropemaking, the manufacturing of fishing craft etc. The various uses of lime as well as the techniques involved in its making are illustrated by a number of models and ancient tools.

Return to Coutances by D 44.

In the final descent there is a view of Coutances dominated by its towers.

Rey lime kilns, Regnéville-sur-Mer

Admission times and charges for the sights described are listed at the end of the guide. Every sight for which there are times and charges is identified by the symbol ⊙ in the Sights section of the guide.

CRÈVECŒUR-EN-AUGE

Population 554
Michelin map 54 fold 17 or 231 fold 31
Local map see Pays d'AUGE

Crèvecœur is a welcoming town situated in the Auge Valley. Some 500m/500yd to the north and to the right of N 13 is the Château de Crèvecœur.

★CHÂTEAU ⊙ *1hr*

Encircled by trees and moats, the timber-framed buildings of the **château** – its motte was erected in the 11C – were transformed in the 15C and restored in 1972. They now form a highly picturesque sight that perpetuates the medieval tradition: an outer bailey and feudal motte surrounded by a filled-in moat. The 16C gatehouse, which used to stand beside the former Château de Beuvilliers near Lisieux, features a ground floor with chequered brick and stone masonry and a half-timbered upper floor. The 16C barn and 15C manor are home to the collections of the **Musée Schlumberger**, named after two German brothers Conrad and Marcel: in 1928 these geophysicists and petroleum engineers invented the continuous electric logging of boreholes, a technique that was to be extended to countries all over the world. The museum is devoted to oil prospecting and presents drilling equipment, vehicles used for prospection, photographic reproductions, videotapes etc.

Dovecot and farm building at Crèvecœur-en-Auge

The **dovecot**, a remarkable construction, is square-shaped. Note the projecting eaves formed by the shingled roofing, visible on all four sides of the building. At the top two dormer windows are decorated with the cross of St Andrew. On the side facing winds, a shelf from which the pigeons are released has been set up. The interior woodwork is pierced with 1 500 pigeon holes *(boulins). For more information on dovecots, see p 44 in the Introduction.*

The 12C chapel features oak framework in the shape of an upturned hull, as well as fragments of a medieval wall painting.

The farm buildings contain the second part of the museum, devoted to **Normandy architecture**, which presents examples of traditional timber-framed architecture from the Pays d'Auge (including a 35min videotape). The History Room (Salle d'Histoire) displays miscellaneous objects retracing the history of Crèvecœur-en-Auge over the centuries.

Eating out

MODERATE

La Galetière – *Rte de Falaise* – ☎ *02 31 63 04 28* – *closed 15-22 Mar, 15-25 Oct, Sun evening from Sept to June, Mon evening and Tues* – *9.91/27.14€*. The owners of this modest restaurant on the road to Falaise do their utmost to satisfy their guests and you will get a warm welcome... whilst you enjoy your very reasonably priced meal. A pleasant break in spite of the noise from the road.

★MANOIRS OF THE PAYS D'AUGE *Round tour of 30km/19mi*

From Crèvecœur take D 16 south; then turn left onto D 101ᴬ.

Château du Mont de la Vigne – A shady drive leads uphill to the château, built on the site of a former 14C fortress. It consists of a central yard around which stand the main building, chapel and outbuildings in a pleasant rural setting. Visit the outside and discover the remains of the fortress.

In Monteille turn right onto D 101A; in Leucade turn right onto D 269.

Château de Grandchamp – The castle *(private)* is surrounded by a moat and consists of a 17C main building in brick and stone and a 15C-16C half-timbered gateway, flanked by two four-storey turrets surmounted by slate domes with skylight windows. The main building has a raised projection terminating with a pediment. An attic makes up the top floor.

Continue on D 269; in St-Julien-le-Faucon take D 47.

★**Manoir de Coupesarte** ⊘ – This charming residence *(closed to the public)* surrounded by water on three sides is the main house of a farm building. The construction goes back to the end of the 15C or beginning of the 16C. From the field on the left beyond the small lock there is a good view of the half-timbered façade with its two corner turrets reminiscent of watchtowers.

The half-timbered outbuildings contribute to the originality of the whole.

In St-Julien-le-Faucon turn left onto D 511. In Le Godet turn right onto D 154. Turn right onto D 16 to return to Crèvecœur.

D-DAY BEACHES

See Plages du DÉBARQUEMENT

DEAUVILLE ✿✿✿

Population 4 261
Michelin map 54 fold 17 or 231 fold 19
Local maps see Pays d'AUGE and ROUEN

Facing Trouville, a small resort already fashionable in the 1830s, Deauville became known in the 1860s thanks to the Duc de Morny, Napoleon III's half-brother, to Doctor Oliffe, the physician of the British embassy in Paris, and to a financier called Donon. Today the town owes its worldwide fame as much to the luxury and refinement of its various establishments as to the elegance of its entertainment with a choice of festive events held throughout the year but mainly during the summer season: racing (including the Grand Prix), polo world championship, regattas, tennis and golf tournaments, galas and the international yearling fair. Every year, in early September, the city hosts the prestigious **American Film Festival**, an international showcase for cross-Atlantic cinema, attended by independent producers and Hollywood stars alike.

THE RESORT

The season in Deauville opens in July and ends with the Deauville Grand Prix on the fourth Sunday in August and the Golden Cup of the international polo championship. Horse racing takes place alternately at La Touques (flat racing) and Clairefontaine (flat racing and steeplechasing) and the international yearling sales are held in Deauville in August. In 1995, 400 yearlings were acquired for a total sum of 100 million francs, of which 75% were paid in foreign currencies. Out of season the resort organises numerous conventions as well as seminars.

The coming and going on the **Planches** – a plank promenade running the whole length of the beach, made of *azobe*, a dark brown wood with purplish undertones coming from Equatorial Africa – is the most distinctive feature of beach life in Deauville. Several elegant buildings – the Pompeian Baths and the Soleil Bar where stars and celebrities like to be seen – form the background of a picture in which the beach tents provide the brightest colour.

Between the Casino and the Planches, the Centre International de Deauville (C.I.D.) is a remarkable ensemble of suspended gardens, fountains and transparent façades which welcomes all kinds of professional, cultural and festive events. A walk along the seafront, boulevard Eugène-Cornuché, will prove that Deauville is not called the "beach of flowers" *(plage fleurie)* for nothing.

The yacht marina on the Touques and the Yacht Club strike an elegant note.

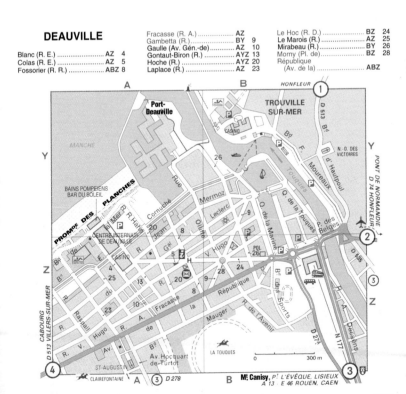

Eating out

MID-RANGE

La Table d'Auge – *Pl. du Marché* – ☎ *02 31 88 30 58* – *www.deauville-terroir.com* – *reservation advisable in summer and Sat-Sun* – *26.68/57.93€*. Shellfish served in this restaurant is guaranteed fresh since it is taken out of the tank only when needed. However, if you don't go in for shellfish, you will be able to savour tasty genuine local products. In the evening, have your meal on the terrace, weather permitting.

La Galerie de Tourgéville – *14800 Tourgéville* – *3km/1.9mi south of Deauville via D 278 and D 27* – ☎ *02 31 87 31 11* – *info@galerie-de-tourgeville.com* – *closed Feb, Tues and Wed* – *24.39€*. Don't judge this former dairy by its dull façade for it houses an art gallery and a restaurant decorated with an assortment of objects. The menu is simple but with it, the atmosphere is pleasant and Deauville Parisians simply adore it!

Chez Marthe – *1 quai de la Marine* – ☎ *02 31 88 92 51* – *closed Jan except Sat-Sun, Wed except in the evening during school holidays and Tues evening out of season* – *16.77/44.21€*. This bistro, located on the quayside, is the latest fashionable place in Deauville. People come here to enjoy good popular fare served in an amusing old-fashioned-café decor or in the veranda... and, since stars come to be seen, it is always crowded!

Yearling – *38 av. Hocquart-de-Turtot* – ☎ *02 31 88 33 37* – *closed 15-31 Jan, 12-21 Feb, 13-28 Nov, Tues and Wed except Aug* – *20.28/54.88€*. You've no doubt guessed that the owner is a horse lover: the walls of his house, situated near the racecourse, are covered with photographs of horses... and, since his popular cuisine is appetising and there is lobster on the menu, the place is very much sought after! Prices are rather reasonable for Deauville.

Where to stay

MODERATE

Le Chantilly Hotel – *120 av. de la République* – ☎ *02 31 88 79 75* – *17 rooms: 29.73€* – *⌼ 6.10€*. Located on the road to Caen, this town house looks simple with its roughcast façade, but the spacious rooms are well kept and attractive with their pastel-coloured walls and rustic furniture. There are even two single rooms at a very low price... A good address.

MID-RANGE

L'Espérance – *32 r. V.-Hugo* – ☎ *02 31 88 26 88* – *closed 25-30 June* – *10 rooms: 41.92€* – *⌼ 6.10€* – *restaurant 105/170F*. Situated in a quiet street of the town centre, these two houses, separated by a courtyard used as a terrace in summer, are simple but very well kept. Ask for one of the larger rooms overlooking the street. Cheap dishes served in a bistro decor... A good family address.

LUXURY

Normandy Hotel – *38 r. J.-Mermoz* – ☎ *02 31 98 66 22* – **P** – *265 rooms: from 242.39€* – *⌼ 19.82€* – *restaurant 43.45/49.55€*. This elegant timber-framed manor house dating from 1912 is situated in the liveliest part of town: facing the sea and a stone's throw from the casino and the shopping area. This sumptuous place will satisfy all your needs whatever they are... A real must in this town where everything glitters.

On the town

Au Petit Navire – *17 quai de la Touques* – ☎ *02 31 88 53 67* – *Mon-Sat 9am-9pm (July-Aug daily)*. Run by the same family for four generations, this bar looks from the outside like an unpretentious little shack in the harbour. Inside, however, the old-fashioned decor will come as a surprise: old postcards, old stove, hi-fi from the 1950s and the inscription "CAFÉ" on the window... in case you still have a doubt.

Brok Café – *14 av. du Gén.-de-Gaulle* – ☎ *02 31 81 30 81* – *brok-cafe@wanadoo.fr* – *daily 6.30pm-2am*. This is Deauville's fashionable Cuban café... not really surprising since it is one of the few night bars in town. The bar is decorated with mosaics, the walls are coloured and old sewing machines are used as tables... the ideal place to enjoy cocktails and cigars before or after dinner.

Les Planches – *Le Bois Lauret* – *14910 Blonville* – *about 6km/3.7mi southwest of Deauville in the hinterland, marked itinerary* – ☎ *02 31 87 58 09* – *www.lesplanches.com* – *Fri-Sat 11pm to dawn (school holidays daily)* – *closed Jan*. All the preppies come to this discotheque sought after for its Cuban bar, its loft and heated pool. During the Deauville festival, it is crowded out (never before midnight) with people hoping to see some stars...

Sport

Aéro-club de Deauville – *St-Gatien-des-Bois Airport – 14130 St-Gatien-des-Bois – on D74 between Deauville-Trouville and Saint-Gatien des Bois – ☎ 02 31 64 00 93 – open daily 9am-noon, 2-7pm.* With its six planes (TB 20s and Robins) and a team of competent... and reassuring coaches, this flying club offers first flights in excellent conditions, discovery flights and beginners' flights as well as training for basic licences and European private pilot licences.

Deauville Aventure – *Chemin de la Performance – 14800 St-Arnoult – about 4km/2.5mi south of Deauville along D27 – ☎ 02 31 81 25 25 – yduprat@club-internet.fr – daily 10am-7pm.* Paint ball, four-wheel drive rally, strategic games, rock climbing, archery, water ball... This new leisure parc should appeal to sport enthusiasts of all ages.

Driver's Club – *Rte de Caen – 14800 St-Arnoult – about 4km/2.5mi south of Deauville along D27 – ☎ 02 31 81 31 31 – yduprat@club-internet.fr – daily 10am-7pm.* Under the same ownership as Deauville Aventure, this vast leisure park specialises in motorised activities, go-carting, Formula 1 (replica of F3), Formula 500, speed boat (on special racing circuit) and jet ski...

Poney Club – *R. Reynaldo-Hahn – ☎ 02 31 98 56 24 – Sat-Sun and holidays (school holidays daily) – offices open 10am-12.30pm, 3-6pm – closed 11 Nov, Christmas and Easter school holidays.* Exciting pony and horse riding on the beach. Get there in the morning, it is less crowded and you will be able to watch racing horses being trained in sea water, which is excellent for their tendons, so the specialists say.

Leisure time

La Deauvillaise – *11 quai de la Marine – ☎ 02 31 88 56 33 – Paris schools holidays: daily 9am-6.30pm; outside school holidays: Tues-Sun 9am-6.30pm.* Cycling enthusiasts will be able to rent bikes, mountain bikes and quadricycles, the smart Deauville cycles specially designed to accommodate up to 9 persons.

Deauville Port – The port is enclosed on the west side by a breakwater extending from the beach to the mouth of the Touques and on the east by a jetty marking the port entrance to the channel. The deep access channel means that the port is accessible 80% of the time. It consists of three docks, entered though a double lock, which provide deep water moorings and ample capacity: 800 berths along 4 000m of quays. At the centre are the slate-roofed marinas, the harbour master's office, an annexe of the Marina Deauville Club (quai des Marchands, near the lock) and space for shops and hotel services.

Air Trips ⊙ – Flights over the coast and main resort, by plane or by helicopter, are available from Deauville-St-Gatien Airport.

EXCURSIONS

The mileage given is calculated from the Pont des Belges, which links Deauville to Trouville.

Turn from the endless horizon of the coast to the patchwork of the inland garden. In summer, the coast between Honfleur and Cabourg is one of the busiest in France, but is lovely despite the crowds.

★Mont Canisy

Round tour of 15km/9mi – about 45min. Leave Deauville to the southwest on N 177.

Bénerville Church stands overlooking a crossroads.

Turn left up the hill before the church; after about 200m/200yd by the town hall turn left again. At the top bear onto a local road leading to Mont Canisy. Leave the car by a gate.

A path leads to the blockhouses where the **view** extends from Cap de la Hève to the Orne estuary.

Return to the car and go right.

Once beyond the more recent housing estates of Canisy there are views over the Touques Valley as the road descends to the St-Arnoult crossroads.

Turn left onto D 278 to Deauville.

The Casino in Deauville

★★ THE CORNICHE NORMANDE: FROM DEAUVILLE-TROUVILLE TO HONFLEUR

21km/13mi – about 1hr. Leave Deauville-Trouville to the northeast by D 513.

This very pleasant tour passes through magnificent scenery and affords views over the Seine estuary between gaps in the hedges and orchards. Handsome properties are scattered along the road. Just before Villerville there is a fine view of the oil refineries on the estuary. To the left Le Havre can be recognised by its thermal power station and the belfry of St Joseph's Church.

Villerville – This lively seaside resort, with its nearby meadows and woods, has kept its rural character. Notice the Romanesque belfry on the local church. Rocks stretch beyond the beach, notably the Ratier bank which is visible at low tide. From the terrace overlooking the beach there is a view of Le Havre and Cap de la Hève. The road is thereafter narrow with hidden bends.

Cricquebœuf – The 12C **church**, with its ivy-covered walls, is a familiar feature on travel posters. The countryside around, with its apple orchards, grazing cows and tranquil ponds add to the emblematic beauty.

In Pennedepie, take D 62; after 2.5km/1.5mi turn right onto D 279.

Barneville – The church, hidden away in the greenery, is backed by the magnificent park of the 18C château.

Take D 279 north; after 4km/3mi turn left by a château to reach Honfleur via the Côte de Grâce.

★★ THE CÔTE FLEURIE FROM TROUVILLE-DEAUVILLE TO CABOURG

19km/12mi. Leave Deauville to the southwest by D 513.

Bénerville-sur-Mer and Blonville-sur-Mer – The hillsides are dotted with villas overlooking a long sandy beach which stretches to the slopes of Mont Canisy. At Blonville, there is an amusement park near the sea. The Chapelle Notre-Dame-de-l'Assomption houses some modern frescoes, the work of the artist Jean-Denis Maillart; most of the scenes come from the Old and New Testaments.

Villers-sur-Mer – This elegant seaside resort with its casino and excellent sports facilities is known for its large beach and its wooded hilly countryside crisscrossed with small paths leading down to the town centre. The beach (5km/3mi) extends from Blonville to the Vaches Noires Cliff; below Villers it is bordered by a lively promenade almost 3km/1.9mi in length. The **Musée paléontologique** ⊙ *(access through the tourist office)* has exhibits of fossils and stuffed birds from the area together with a stone armchair and seashells which belonged to Ferdinand Postel, artist and photographer who lived in Villers from 1880 to 1917. He collected fossils and created many montages printed subsequently in the form of postcards. Just before Houlgate, on a downhill hairpin bend, there is a viewing table (right): **panorama** from the mouth of the River Dives to the mouth of the River Orne.

★**Falaise des Vaches Noires** – Between Villers-sur-Mer and Houlgate, the Auberville plateau ends in a crumbling and much-eroded cliff face, which owes its name of "Black Cows Cliff" to its strange appearance and the many fossils found in the sand there. It is best to walk along the beach at low tide *(about 2hr on foot there and back)* to appreciate the site and enjoy the panorama which extends from Trouville to Luc-sur-Mer and over most of the Seine bay.

The steep cliff face is composed of clay and dark marl, divided by ravines. The sea eats away at the base of the cliff and the freshwater streams from the Auge plateau create ravines and mud slides. In places large pieces of limestone have broken away from the cliff top and piled up at the base where they have been colonised by seaweed; these are the Black Cows (Vaches Noires).

⌂⌂**Houlgate** – Houlgate is another "concentrate of Normandy" – the coast and the surrounding countryside are beautifully matched. It is set in the verdant Drochon Valley; the shady avenues and the houses and gardens add to the overall charm of this resort.

The promenade overlooks the fine sandy beach which is popular among bathers. Shell fishers prefer the east end under the Falaise des Vaches Noires.

The road runs along the coast and, before Dives-sur-Mer, passes in front of a monument commemorating the departure of **Duke William** for the conquest of England.

Return to Cabourg via D 45.

For historical background on the region see the Historical Table and Notes in the Introduction

Plages du DÉBARQUEMENT ★

Michelin map 54 folds 3, 4 and 13-17 or 231 folds 15-18

The marked itineraries, known as 'Overlord-L'Assaut' (Overlord-The Onslaught) and 'D-Day-le Choc' (D-Day-The Impact), which are two of several such itineraries in the Historical Area of the Battle of Normandy, partly follow the tour described below.

This tour includes that part of the **Calvados Coast** between the mouths of the Orne and the Vire, also known as the **Côte de Nacre** (Mother-of-Pearl Coast), where the Normandy landings took place on D-Day in June 1944; it is from this event that the beaches take their name.

The variety of the Calvados coast reflects its hinterland; the open farmlands of the Caen countryside produce a perfectly flat shoreline.

The more indented coast west of Asnelles consists of low and often crumbling cliffs, which correspond to the undulating pastures of the Bessin.

THE D-DAY LANDINGS

Dawn of D-Day – The formidable armada, which consisted of 4 266 barges and landing craft together with hundreds of warships and naval escorts, set sail from the south coast of England on the night of 5 June 1944 *(for further details see "The Battle of Normandy" on p 29)*; it was preceded by flotillas of minesweepers to clear a passage through the mine fields in the English Channel.

As the crossing proceeded airborne troops were flown out and landed in two detachments at either end of the invasion front. The British 6th Division, charged with guarding the left flank of the operation, quickly took possession of the Bénouville-Ranville bridge, since named Pegasus Bridge after the airborne insignia,

---

The name Calvados: A Source of Controversy

According to tradition, the Calvados *département* owes its name to *El Salvador*, a Spanish ship belonging to the Armada that sank onto the rocky Norman coast: on several maps dating from the 17C one can find the spelling *Salvador* or *Calvador*. However, it would seem that this legend is unfounded since no boat bearing that name and belonging to Phillip II's fleet is believed to have been shipwrecked in the area.

The other possible explanation for the origin of the word Calvados was put forward by a lecturer of Caen University, who claims that the name comes from the Latin *calva dorsa*, meaning barren hills. This expression, used as a proper noun and gallicized without ever being translated, was subsequently mentioned on many oceanographic charts. Admittedly, seen from the sea, the heights running along the Côte du Bessin are, in parts, quite bare!

and stirred up trouble in the enemy positions between the River Orne and the River Dives to prevent reinforcements arriving from the east or south. West of the River Vire the American 101st and 82nd Divisions mounted an attack on key positions such as Ste-Mère-Église or opened up the exits from Utah Beach.

British Sector – Although preliminary bombing and shelling had not destroyed Hitler's Atlantic Wall, they had had the desired effect of disorganising the German defences. The land forces, usually preceded by commandos charged with destroying the most dangerous pockets of resistance, were therefore able to reach their objectives, divided into three beachheads, each assigned to a pre-determined force.

The hastily organised attempts to counter-attack by German tanks were crushed under naval bombardment. The destruction of enemy strongpoints – Douvres held out until 17 June – was the major objective immediately following the landing.

Sword Beach – The Franco-British commandos landed at Colleville-Plage, Lion-sur-Mer and St-Aubin. They captured Riva-Bella and the other more obdurate strongpoints at Lion and Langrune (which resisted until 7 June) and then linked up with the airborne troops at Pegasus Bridge. The main strength of the British 3rd Division then landed. This area, which was completely exposed to the Germans' long range guns in Le Havre, became the crucial point in the battle. The Allies did not launch a major offensive against the east bank of the River Orne until 18 July.

Juno Beach – The Canadian 3rd Division landed at Bernières and Courseulles and reached Creully by 5pm. Almost a month later they were the first troops to enter Caen on 9 July 1944.

6 June 1944

Gold Beach – The British 50th Division landed at Ver-sur-Mer and Asnelles; by the afternoon a flanking movement had made them masters of Arromanches and the artificial Mulberry harbour could be brought into position. The 47th Commandos advanced 20km/12mi through enemy territory and captured Port-en-Bessin during the night of 7 June.

On 9 June the British sector joined up with the Americans from Omaha Beach. On 12 June, after the capture of Carentan had enabled the troops from Omaha and Utah beaches to join forces, a single beachhead was established.

American Sector – The events involved in the landing of American troops at **Omaha Beach** and **Utah Beach** are described under OMAHA Beach and Presqu'île du COTENTIN.

Eating out

MODERATE

Ferme-auberge de la Piquenotière – *14710 St-Martin-de-Blagny – 7km/4.3mi south of the Château de Colombières via D 5 and D 145 – ☎ 02 31 21 35 54 – ☞ – reservation essential – 13.72/22.87€*. A table worthy of a king in an authentic farmhouse! The owner is delighted to make you enjoy her ducks and geese: she concocts carefully prepared tasty dishes and grills her fillets of duck breast in the fireplace.

Café Gondrée – Pegasus Bridge – *12 av. du Cdt-Kieffer – 14970 Bénouville – ☎ 02 31 44 62 25 – closed 15 Nov to 8 Mar – ☞ – 7.62€*. This small authentic pre-war café, the first house on French soil to be liberated in 1944, has strong historic and emotional connotations. Arlette Gondrée, who was four at the time, still prepares the traditional family omelette any time of the day.

Au Miroir du Temps – *4 r. 8²-Armée – 14114 Ver-sur-Mer – ☎ 02 31 92 17 77 – closed Jan and Tue from Oct to Mar – reservation recommended – 11.89/21.04€*. Three small dining rooms have been set up in this 200-year-old house. The decor has been created with care – some fine old pieces share the space with objects whose value is mostly sentimental. Traditional French cooking.

La Trinquette – *7 rte du Joncal – 14450 Grandcamp-Maisy – ☎ 02 31 22 64 90 – www.restaurant-la-trinquette.com/ – closed Dec, Jan, Tues evening and Wed from Oct to Easter – 14.03/23.93€*. The sea is hidden by the fish-auction building but never mind, the fish ends up in your plate: cooked in tinfoil, with leeks slowly melted in butter, or cooked in an earthenware dish or served as a soup with a spicy rust-coloured sauce...and don't hesitate to try the local fishermen's favourite fish recipe, "marmite grandcopaise".

Le Bistrot d'à Côté – *10/12 r. Lefournier – 14520 Port-en-Bessin – ☎ 02 31 51 79 12 – closed 7 Jan to 12 Feb, Tues evening and Wed except July-Aug – 14.48/22.71€*. The originality of the decoration in this cheerful dining room, with its wide panoramic window, is the contrast between the deep blues and the bright yellows. The menu includes fish and shellfish listed on the large blackboard, next to old photographs of the harbour.

La Flambée – *2 r. Émile-Demagny – 14230 Isigny-sur-Mer – ☎ 02 31 51 70 96 – closed 1 week in Mar, 2 weeks in Oct, Sun evening and Mon – 11.89€ lunch – 14.94/24.09€*. The wood fire gives off a wonderful smell in this typical Norman restaurant. Fish and meat are grilled in the vast fireplace of the traditional dining room with its exposed beams. A cart wheel hanging on the wall is used to store the daily stock of local wine.

MID-RANGE

La Mer – *Prom. Aristide-Briand – 14830 Langrune-sur-Mer – ☎ 02 31 96 03 37 – 19.05/30.20€*. Here, you can give your order to waiters dressed as officers while looking out to sea. The "royal" plate of shellfish is worthy of its name and so are regional specialities such as tripe which melt in your mouth after being home-cooked for 15hr.

Le Vauban – *6 r. du Nord – 14520 Port-en-Bessin – ☎ 02 31 21 74 83 – closed mid-Dec to mid-Jan, Tues evening out of season and Wed – 12.80€ lunch – 21/27.45€*. One of the locals' favourite eating places. The owner/chef has his heart set on fresh produce and trusts his experience to make the best of what land and sea provide.

L'As de Trèfle – *420 r. Léopold-Hettier – 14990 Bernières-sur-Mer – ☎ 02 31 97 22 60 – closed 15 Jan to 8 Feb, Sun evening from 16 Sept to 14 June and Mon – 15.24/33.54€*. This is not a bluff in a poker game but a true success. The chef sets the stakes and his team follows. What is his aim? To prepare and ensure you enjoy all the wealth of the local produce. Do not miss your turn and think of the joker... a nice little menu for children.

Manoir d'Hastings et la Pommeraie – *14970 Bénouville – 10km/6.2mi northeast of Caen via D515 – ☎ 02 31 44 62 43 – closed 12 Nov to 4 Dec, Sun evening and Mon – 26.68/54.88€*. This former 17C priory, enclosed within its garden, has retained its old-world aspect with weathered stone walls and exposed beams. There are several dining rooms including an attic one. A few bedrooms, some with sloping ceilings.

Where to stay

MODERATE

Manoir de l'Hermerel Bed and Breakfast – *14230 Géfosse-Fontenay – 8km/5mi N of Isigny via D 514 then D 200 in Osmanville – ☎ 02 31 22 64 12 – closed 11 Nov to 31 Mar – ✉ – reservation required in winter – 4 rooms: 42/50€.* This fortified 17C farm once belonged to the local squire as the elegant dovecote facing the entrance porch testifies. Don't forget to visit the small 15C Gothic chapel before retiring in one of the attractive bedrooms. Simple but convivial welcome.

Le Logis Bed and Breakfast – *Escures village – 14520 Commes – 2.5km/1.5mi SE of Port-en-Bessin via D 6 – ☎ 02 31 21 79 56 – ✉ – 4 rooms: 30.49/38.11€.* You will be seduced by the charm of these old houses inhabited by a family who have a highly developed sense of hospitality. Breakfast is served in the former stables with black paving stones and a stone drinking trough. The rooms and the self-catering cottage are comfortable.

Le Clos Fleuri Bed and Breakfast – *At Lefèvre – 14450 St-Pierre-du-Mont – 2km/1.2mi from the Pointe du Hoc along the road to Vierville – ☎ 02 31 22 96 22 – ✉ – 3 rooms: 30.49/38.11€ – meal 90F.* In this charming 19C house, close to the sea, you will be welcomed without fuss. Meals, served at the family table, take your wishes into account, rooms are comfortable and the large garden is ideal for kids to play and grown-ups to rest after lunch.

La Ferme d'Escures Bed and Breakfast – *At Escures – 14520 Commes – 2.5km/1.5mi S of Port-en-Bessin via D 6 – ☎ 02 31 92 52 23 – ✉ – 4 rooms: 30.49/39.64€.* Located a few miles from the beaches and Bayeux, this 17C farm built with the local stone (named after the town of Caen), is the ideal starting point or a tour of the area. The decoration of the rooms is simple but pleasant and the self-catering cottage, located in the former farm bakery, has its own small garden.

Ferme le Petit Val – *24 r. du Camp Romain – 14480 Banville – ☎ 02 31 37 92 18 – closed between Nov and spring school holidays – ✉ – 5 rooms: 33,54/39,64€.* This farm is typical of the Bessin region, and probably dates from the 17C. You can really get away from it all in the countryside, and take advantage of cosy guest rooms, a family breakfast room and a pretty flower garden.

MID-RANGE

Château de Vouilly Bed and Breakfast – *14230 Vouilly-Église – 8km/5mi SE of Isigny via D 5 – ☎ 02 31 22 08 59 – closed Dec to Feb – 5 rooms: 47/62€.* The moat abounds with fish, the gardens are well looked after, there is an orangery, imposing drawing rooms and dual-coloured paving in this 18C residence which has retained its charming atmosphere. In 1945, it was the General Headquarters of the American press; today its owner offers her guests a warm welcome which contributes to make their stay a pleasant one.

Le Clos Normand – *89 r. Pasteur 14750 St-Aubin-sur-Mer – ☎ 02 31 97 30 47 – closed 2 Nov to 31 Mar – 🅿 – 27 rooms: 51.83/60.98€ – ☕ 6.10€ – restaurant 17/49€.* At high tide, the froth from the waves almost licks the base of the terrace of this 1950s hotel overlooking the beach. All the rooms offer a view of the sea and the dining room opens out to a small inner garden.

★THE BEACHES

① Sword Beach – Juno Beach – Gold Beach

71km/43mi – about 1hr 15min. From Caen take D 515 northeast.

The road to Riva-Bella runs down the lower Orne Valley west of the ship canal.

Bénouville – The town hall, which stands alone in a fork in the road near Pegasus Bridge, was occupied by the British 5th Parachute Brigade at 11.45am on 5 June. The **château** ⊘, one of the major works by the Parisian architect, **Claude-Nicolas Ledoux** (1736-1806), is a fine example of French neo-Classical architecture at the end of the 18C. The courtyard façade presents an impressive peristyle of Ionic columns surmounted by a tympanum decorated with arms and figures in round relief; the garden front presents the same Ionic order but on pilasters supporting military trophies.

The interior contains a suite of five rooms and a magnificent **staircase★★** rising through three landings to the first floor. The coffered ceiling is pierced by a large oculus revealing a painted sky. The adjoining chapel contains an exhibition on Ledoux.

Pegasus Bridge – The two Ranville-Bénouville bridges were captured after a brief engagement soon after midnight during the night of 5-6 June 1944 by the British 5th Parachute Brigade: Pegasus was their emblem. A small French enclave was liberated. Major Howard had won the Battle of **Pegasus** – a field where the Horsa and Hamilcar gliders could land, a mobile bridge made of steel, a house at the water's edge... and the Gondrée family, who waited up to 11am before reinforcements arrived: **Lord Lovat** (1911-95) and his Green Berets, marching to the strains of Bill Millin's bagpipes *(see inset below)*.

Near the bridge, between the canal and the River Orne, stands a commemorative monument. From there one can see the peristyle façade of the imposing 18C Bénouville Château.

Bill Millin and his Bagpipes

"Down the road came Lord Lovat's commandos, cocky in their green berets. Bill Millin marched at the head of the column, his pipes blaring out *Blue Bonnets over the Border*. On both sides the firing suddenly ceased, as soldiers gazed at the spectacle. But the shock didn't last long. As the commandos headed across the bridges the Germans began firing again. Bill Millin remembers that he was "just trusting to luck that I did not get hit, as I could not hear very much for the drone of the pipes."

The most famous literary work about the Battle of Normandy is undoubtedly *The Longest Day*, written by the late Irish author **Cornelius Ryan** (published by Simon & Schuster in New York).

Ouistreham-Riva-Bella – *See OUISTREHAM-RIVA-BELLA.*

From Riva-Bella to Asnelles, the road *(D 514)* follows the line of a section of the Mother-of-Pearl Coast, through summer resorts where houses and blocks of flats are proliferating.

Colleville-Montgomery – At dawn on 6 June the 4th Anglo-French commandos landed here under the command of Captain Kieffer. In gratitude, the local commune of Colleville-sur-Orne added to its name that of the Victor of El Alamein (monument) and commander of the British forces.

Lion-sur-Mer – This family seaside resort has a 16C-17C **château**, in Haut-Lion, set in a park. The **church** has retained its 11C Romanesque tower and handsome capitals.

Luc-sur-Mer – Luc is a seaside resort known for its bracing air; at low tide the rocks are covered with seaweed. The spa offers hydro sodium iodate cures; there is a marine zoology laboratory. The **municipal park ★** *(35 rue de la Mer)*, a beautiful garden with trees and flowers, provides an oasis of greenery. The local curiosity is the skeleton of a whale which was washed up on the beach in January 1885; beside it are two Gallo-Roman sarcophagi.

Langrune-sur-Mer – The name of this resort on the Mother-of-Pearl Coast is Scandinavian in origin and means "green land": it should probably be attributed to the abundant seaweed which fills the air with iodine. The 13C **church** has a very handsome bell-tower similar to the tower of St Peter's in Caen.

Take D 7 inland.

La Délivrande – The tall spires of the basilica in La Délivrande, the oldest Marian sanctuary in Normandy, are visible for miles across the Caen countryside and far out to sea. The present **basilica**, Notre-Dame de la Délivrande, is a neo-Gothic 19C building housing a highly venerated statue of the Virgin (late 16C); it replaces the earlier Romanesque chapel. There is a steady flow of pilgrims throughout the year. At the Convent of **Notre-Dame-de-Fidélité** (Our Lady of Fidelity), the last house on the Cresserons road, the chapel chancel is lit by three stained-glass windows, made of crystal and chrome, by **René Lalique** (1931) who was also responsible for the door of the tabernacle. There is more glasswork by this specialist in moulded glass at **Millbrook** in Jersey. Note the Stations of the Cross in lacquer (1946) and a Crucifix in the side chapel.

Continue on D 7 for 3km/2mi until you reach D 404 leading to Courseulles-sur-Mer. Follow the signs for the Musée-Radar up to D 83 on the right.

Douvres-la-Délivrande – The **Musée-Radar** ⊙ is, it seems, the first museum in the world to retrace the history of radar equipment. Blockhouses, situated on the site of the German radar station at Douvres, have been renovated and provide an insight into the daily lives of German soldiers stationed along the Atlantic Wall, while the role of aerial or maritime search equipment in the last war and their evolution since 1945 is explained with the help of realistic scenery. Outside there is an impressive 'Wurzburg Riese' with a strange past: three radars of this type, seized almost intact by the British army in 1944, were given to the French Navy who, in

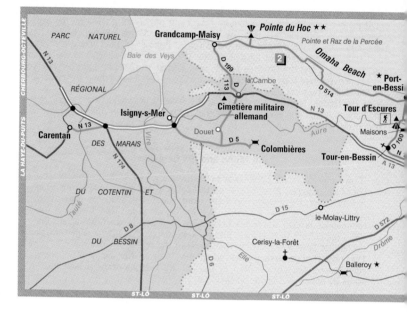

turn, handed them over to an admiral in the reserves, head of a physics laboratory; in 1957, he turned two of them into radio telescopes for the Nançay Observatory, near Orléans. After a few decades spent in the service of radio astronomy, one of these devices, one of 1 500 built from 1941 onwards, has found its way here.

St-Aubin-sur-Mer – Bracing seaside resort with an offshore reef for shrimping and crab catching.

Bernières-sur-Mer – The French Canadian "Chaudière" Regiment landed on this beach and it was here that the press and radio reporters came ashore and the first reports of the landings were dictated.
The church has a justly famous 13C **bell-tower★**; the three storeys and the stone spire together measure 67m/220ft. The nave and aisles are Romanesque; the vaulting has been remodelled. The raised chancel dates from the 14C. Note the great stone altarpiece in the Louis XIV style, which was altered during Louis XVI's reign, and in the north chapel a Crucifixion painted on wood in 1570.

Crabs and AVREs and DD Tanks

Ingenious Fighting Machines to Breach the Atlantic Wall

These bizarre fighting machines, known as "Hobart's Funnies", formed the 79th Armoured Division commanded by their foremost inventor Major-General Sir **Percy Hobart**. The tanks were designed to swim ashore (Duplex Drive: Sherman amphibious tank); to clear a path through the minefields (Crab: Sherman flail tank); to double as flame-throwers (Crocodile: Churchill VII tank); to lay matting on soft sand (Bobbin); and to double as bridges to carry other tanks over obstacles (Ark: Churchill tank).
The tanks were a complete surprise to the enemy and after the Normandy landings the 79th Armoured Division pursued its advance, crossing the Rhine and entering Germany.
Eisenhower paid a vibrant tribute to "Hobart's Funnies", pointing out that many lives had been saved thanks to the "successful utilisation of our mechanical inventions". A Duplex Drive can still be seen on Canada Beach (Plage du Canada) at Courseulles-sur-Mer.

Courseulles-sur-Mer – In 1944 several important people landed on the west beach at Courseulles, then part of Juno Beach: on 12 June Winston Churchill, on 14 June General de Gaulle on his way to Bayeux and on 16 June George VI on a visit to the British troops. The mouth of the Seulles sheltered the port used by the British and Canadian troops before the Mulberry harbour in Arromanches was in operation.
Courseulles is also a seaside resort well known for its large marina.

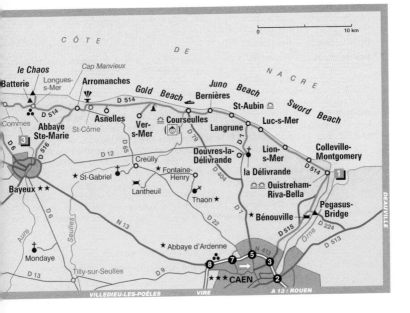

The **Maison de la Mer** ☉, at the entrance to the harbour, displays an astonishing collection of sea shells gathered over the years by Roger Degouet, the Sacristan; an aquarium (100 000l/2 200gal of sea water) containing local marine fauna, with a tunnel through the middle; a diorama on oysters and the regional cultivation of oysters.

Ver-sur-Mer – On 6 June 1944 this tiny resort was the main British bridgehead in the Gold Beach sector.

A monument commemorating the landing was erected at the junction where D 514 meets avenue du Colonel-Harper. The **tower**★ of St Martin's Church is the original robust 11C Romanesque structure of four storeys.

The **lighthouse**, equipped with a radio beacon enjoying a range of 46km/28mi, works in conjunction with the lights of Portland and St Catherine's Point in England and at Antifer, Le Havre and Gatteville in France to guide the shipping in the Channel. Extensive view from the lantern.

West of Ver-sur-Mer, the cliffs of Arromanches come into view.

Asnelles – This little resort with its sandy beach lies at the eastern end of the artificial harbour established at Arromanches. From the mole there is a good view of the cliffs and the roads of Arromanches (traces of the Mulberry harbour still exist). On the beach stands a monument raised to the memory of the British 231st Infantry Brigade.

West of Asnelles the road climbs to the eastern edge of the Bessin plateau; the Romanesque church in St-Côme comes into view. West of St-Côme, on the right-hand side of the road, a belvedere *(viewing table and parking area)* offers a beautiful **view**★ down over the harbour of Arromanches, the cliffs and the last remaining elements of the Mulberry harbour.

Arromanches-les-Bains – *See ARROMANCHES-LES-BAINS.*

After Arromanches, the road goes through the grassy fields of Bessin. You can see the bell-towers of Bayeux in the distance.

★ 2 Omaha Beach

Tour-en-Besson – The church has a 12C doorway. The spire above the transept crossing dates from the early 13C. The Romanesque nave with its pure lines has been renovated. Admire the beauty of the Gothic chancel (early 15C). Around the central stained-glass window, the apsidal chapels with their slim columns are very graceful. On the columns of the arcade to right, notice the 12 sculpted scenes which represent the months of the year.

Tour d'Escures – *Park beside D 100; take the private path (left) uphill (15min on foot there and back).* Steps on the outside of the wall lead to the top of the round tower which provides an extensive view of the rolling Bessin countryside and of Bayeux.

★Port-en-Bessin – *See itinerary D below. From Port-en-Bessin, as far as Grandcamp-Maisy, the road continues through the Bessin region, which is criss-crossed by hedgerows.*

Omaha Beach – *See OMAHA BEACH.*

★★Pointe du Hoc – *From D 514 turn right to the car park. 1hr on foot.* The Jurassic limestone plateau ends in a tall cliff (over 30m/99ft) dominating the lower rocky shoreline at Grandcamp.

The Pointe du Hoc was heavily defended by the Germans; their observation post covered all that sector of the sea where the American invasion fleet appeared on the morning of 6 June 1944. As the troops landing on **Omaha Beach** would have been particularly vulnerable to attack from this battery the American commander ordered a naval bombardment in which the **Texas** fired 600 salvoes of 14-in shells. The 2nd Battalion of specially trained Rangers captured the position by assault at dawn on 6 June scaling the cliffs with ropes and extendable ladders but not without heavy losses – 135 Rangers out of 225. It took the full force of the commandos of the 116th Regiment of the US infantry, assisted by tanks, to subdue the German defence. The gaping craters and battered blockhouses give some idea of the intensity of the fighting. A slim granite column on the edge of the cliff commemorates the battle: fine **views★** of the sea and the coast westwards to the Cotentin peninsula.

Continue west on D 514.

View of Veys Bay and the east coast of the Cotentin peninsula.

Grandcamp-Maisy – Little fishing port and marina. Extensive offshore rocks.

Take D 199 and D 113 inland.

Cimetière militaire allemand de la Cambe – This impressive German cemetery with its rectangular lawn (2ha/5 acres), is the last resting place of 21 500 German soldiers who fell in the fighting in 1944. For an overall view of the groups of five black crosses climb the central mound to the great cross flanked by two life-size figures.

Château de Colombières ⊘ – The **château** stands on the southern edge of marshlands which cover the floor of the Aure Valley and all lie within the perimeter of the Cotentin and Bessin Marshes Regional Nature Park. It was one of the most important strongholds in the Bayeux region and today it makes a most attractive picture with its massive machicolated round towers reflected in the waters of the moat. The two wings, at right angles, are quartered by three towers. Curtain walls once closed off the courtyard on the two remaining sides. The towers are interesting examples of 14C military architecture. The rest of the château was heavily restored in the 17C and 18C.

Isigny-sur-Mer – The town has been famous for the production of milk and butter since the 17C.

Carentan – *See Presqu'île du COTENTIN: East Coast.*

★ ③ La Côte du Bessin

From Bayeux to Port-en-Bessin – 34km/20mi – about 1hr 45min. Leave Bayeux on D 516.

Arromanches-les-Bains – *See ARROMANCHES-LES-BAINS.*

After visiting Arromanches, return to the road you came in on and, about 1km/0.5mi outside of town, turn right on the road to Port-en-Bessin. At Longues-sur-Mer, turn right on D 104 towards the sea.

The Norman Ancestors of Walt Disney?

As is well known, in 1066, Duke William of Normandy sailed across the Channel and conquered England. After these historic events, two Norman soldiers who had accompanied his troops, **Hugues d'Isigny** and his son **Robert**, chose to settle on British soil. They were born in Isigny-sur-Mer, a small village near the mouth of the River Vire.

Over the years, their surname "d'Isigny" underwent a series of changes, becoming "Disgny", then "Disney", which sounded decidedly more Anglo-Saxon. In the 17C, a branch of the Disney family emigrated to Ireland. In 1834, Arundel Elias Disney and his brother Robert, along with their families, embarked on a voyage to North America. Leaving from Liverpool, they arrived on Ellis Island off New York on 3 October, after travelling for one month. That was the start of their American adventures. On 5 December 1901, Elias Disney's fourth child was born in Chicago: he was to become the famous illustrator **Walt Disney**, whose legendary animated cartoon characters like Mickey Mouse and Donald Duck have delighted many a generation of children. He died on 15 December in 1966.

Batterie allemande de Longues-sur-Mer – Half a mile down this road, a tarred road (left) leads to the site of the powerful German battery. In spite of the release by 124 RAF planes of 600t of bombs during the night preceding 6 June, the four guns were still operational on the morning of 6 June and they began firing at 5.37am. The French cruiser *Georges-Leygues* was the first to return their fire, followed by the *Montcalm* and the American battleship *Arkansas*. Three guns having been put out of action, the Germans were silent for a while but resumed firing in the afternoon and the battery was only finally reduced to silence at 7pm by two direct hits from the *Georges-Leygues*. Built on a rather picturesque cliff, it was composed of four 150mm guns with a range of 20km/12.5mi which enabled it to control Omaha and Gold beaches. Situated 300m/985ft in front of the casemates, on the very edge of the cliff, the observation post and control room was the setting of one of the most famous scenes of the film *The Longest Day*.

Le Chaos – The track descends steeply and is liable to rockfalls; there is a view of the coast from Cap Manvieux in the east to the Pointe de la Percée in the west.
This part of the Bessin coast is composed of soft marl which has eroded into a chaotic jumble: entire sections have crumbled into heaps of fallen rocks, perched in the most extraordinary positions.

Take D 104 south towards Bayeux.

Abbaye Ste-Marie ☉ – All that remains of the 12C abbey church is the main door and a few footings of the chancel and transept. The tombstones of the lords of Argouges and an attractive collection of glazed tiles from Le Pré-d'Auge can be admired in the refectory.

Return north to D 514; continue west to Port-en-Bessin.

★**Port-en-Bessin** – The town, which is known locally as "Port", lies in a hollow in the marl cliffs of the Calvados Coast. It is a lively port made more picturesque by its narrow confines. The beach, which is revealed as the tide recedes, is in the southern part of the outer-harbour; the eastern harbour is used by leisure craft.
The town's main activity however is fishing (gade, whiting, skate, mullet, shellfish and molluscs): scallops from the bay of the Seine and deep-sea fishing off the coast of southwest England.
The **harbour** is protected by two granite jetties forming a semicircle. From the end of the Letourneur Quay, at low tide, one can see the resurgent springs of the River Aure in the outer harbour. From the jetties, a favourite haunt of rod fishermen, there is a view of the cliffs of the Bessin coast, from Cap Manvieux to the Pointe de la Percée. A tower erected by Vauban in the 17C dominates the eastern outer harbour. There is a good **view** of the whole harbour from the blockhouse on the clifftop.
Just outside Bayeux on D6, there is a good view of the **Château de Maisons** (15C-18C), surrounded by a moat fed by the river.

DIEPPE★★

Population 35 894
Michelin map 52 fold 4 or 231 folds 10 and 11
Local map see Pays de CAUX

Dieppe, the beach closest to Paris, is the oldest French seaside resort; the harbour is modern but many old corners and alleys remain, making it one of the most unusual towns in Normandy. The town's past is evoked in its churches, castle and museum. The seafront promenade, boulevard du Maréchal-Foch, runs the length of the shingle beach which is usually more crowded at the west end where the castle stands high on the cliff top. On the town side are gardens and sports areas and a second parallel avenue, boulevard de Verdun. Near the casino can be seen the west harbour gateway, a part of the 14C town defences now known as Les Tourelles. Below the castle and west cliff in square du Canada stands a monument commemorating the men of Dieppe who explored Canada in the 16C, 17C and 18C, a reminder of the 250 years of common history uniting the two countries. A plaque recalls the Commando Raid in 1942.

THE KEY ROLE OF THE SEA

Jean Ango and the Privateers' War (16C) – When the Portuguese decided to treat any ship adventuring off the African coast as a pirate ship, François I threatened reprisals and issued letters of marque.
The seamen of Dieppe, who had acquired fame through their voyages of exploration, took the lead. **Jean Ango**, shipbuilder and naval adviser to François I, produced a fleet of privateers "which would make a king tremble". Among his captains were the Parmentier brothers who, while crossing the equator in 1529, invented the ceremony of **Crossing the Line**, which is still practised on the ships of all nations, and **Verrazano** from Florence who was the first to discover the site of New York (1524) which he named Land of Angoulême.

Within a few years Ango's ships had captured over 300 Portuguese vessels.

Fearing the ruin of his country's maritime trade, the King of Portugal set about purchasing Ango's letter of marque; after prolonged negotiations Ango was forced to give it up (1531).

He built himself a splendid wooden mansion in Dieppe; less sumptuous but of equally good taste was his country residence in Varengeville. In 1535 he played host to the king and was appointed Governor of Dieppe. He died in 1551 and was buried in the chapel which he had prepared in St James' Church.

Dieppe Spa – According to the chronicler Pierre de l'Estoile, in 1578 Henri III, who was suffering from scabies, was advised by his doctors to bathe in the sea at Dieppe. It was thought that certain diseases, including rabies, could be cured by sea water, in particular at Dieppe.

Later Madame de Sévigné mentioned in her letters that some of the court ladies, who had been bitten by a dog, went to Dieppe. She wrote of one of them: "The sea received her bare naked and thus was made proud; I mean to say the sea was proud, for lady was greatly embarrassed."

Sea bathing really became popular early in the 19C. Although Queen Hortensia of Holland, sister-in-law of Napoleon, went to Dieppe in 1813 to improve her health, it was the Duchess of Berry who made the Norman town popular with both aristocrats and followers of fashion by regularly spending her summers in Dieppe from 1824 to 1830.

Throughout the 19C the baths and casinos of Dieppe were patronised by extravagant people anxious to show off their fine clothes and also by celebrities such as Louis-Philippe, Napoleon III, Eugène Delacroix, Camille Saint-Saëns, Alexandre Dumas and Oscar Wilde.

Canadian Commando Raid in 1942 – On 19 August 1942, Operation Jubilee, the first Allied reconnaissance in force on the coast of Europe, was launched with Dieppe as the primary objective.

Seven thousand men, mostly Canadians, were landed at eight points between Berneval and Ste-Marguerite but the only German strongpoint to be taken was the battery near the Ailly Lighthouse. The Churchill tanks floundered hopelessly on the beach under intense fire and were finally sacrificed to protect the re-embarkation. Five thousand men were killed or taken prisoner; the Allies learned from this raid that German defences were concentrated round the ports and, as naval losses were small, that amphibious operations on a larger scale might be successful; the Germans, however, concluded that future Allied attacks would be directed particularly at the ports.

DISCOVER DOWNTOWN DIEPPE AND THE BEACH

About 1hr 30min from the parking area at place Nationale, near St-Jacques. There are other car parks in the neighbourhood: quai Henri-IV and the corner of quai Duquesne and rue d'Écosse.

Place Nationale – In the centre of the circle stands a statue of **Abraham Duquesne** (1610-1688), famous for defeating the Dutch navy and for hunting down and disarming pirate ships in the Mediterranean. Captain of his first ship at merely 17 years of age, he never rose beyond the rank of lieutenant general because he refused to renounce his Protestant faith. Two of the buildings on place Nationale (nos18 and 24) date from the early 18C. On the wall of the pharmacy, there is a commemorative plaque celebrating the chemist Descroizilles, inventor of the coffee filter!

★**Église St-Jacques** – Begin by going round the outside of the church which has been considerably rebuilt over the centuries.

The 14C central doorway is surmounted by a fine rose window; the façade tower is 15C, the east end and radiating chapels are 16C; the south transept, on the other hand, has been left untouched and is a good example of early Gothic.

Interior – The well-proportioned nave, which is 13C, was ornamented in the 14C with a triforium and given tall windows a century later.

The first chapel in the south aisle, the Chapel of the Holy Sepulchre, has a fine stone screen and is 15C. The other chapels were all given by the shipbuilders of old. The transept, the oldest part of the church, supports the dome which was rebuilt in the 18C while above the chancel are star vaulting and a 16C pierced triforium. A fine 17C wooden statue of St James stands above the high altar. The Sacred Heart Chapel on the right facing the high altar has original Flamboyant vaulting; the centre chapel in known for its consoles on which are carved major events in the life of the Virgin. Left, above the sacristy door, is a frieze (from Jean Ango's Palace destroyed by British naval bombardment in 1694); the upper frieze shows a file of Brazilian Indians and recalls the voyages of Dieppe explorers.

Grand-Rue – This busy pedestrian street is located on the site of an old Gaulish road which enabled travellers to pass from one cliff to another at the time when the city was a vast tidal marsh. Many of the houses in white brick date from the reconstruction of Dieppe which took place after the British naval bombardment of 1694. The wrought iron balconies are the work of craftsmen from Arques-la-

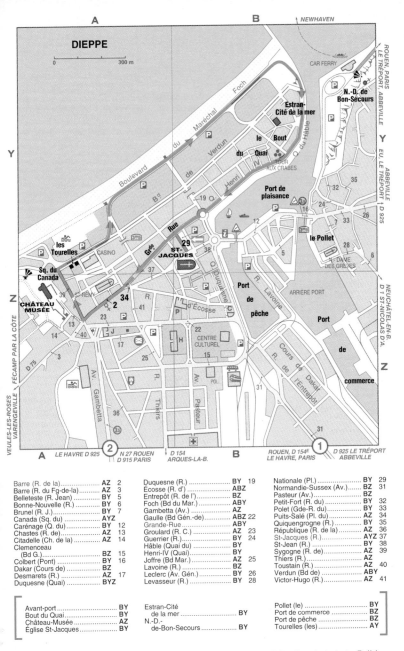

Bataille. No 21 (now the Globe café) was once the home of the dreaded pirate Balidar, terror of the English Channel. In the courtyard of no 77, there is a fountain dating from 1631. At no 186, an apothecary's old sign on the first floor illustrates three elements of nature: an obelisk (mineral), a palm (vegetable) and a sun (fire).

Place du Puits-Salé – At the junction of six roads, this is the liveliest quarter of Dieppe. The name is reminiscent of an old salt-water well, which was replaced by a fountain in the 16C (the current well is a decorative artifice). The large white façade of the Café des Tribunaux is a local landmark, with a clock dating from 1709. The early 18C building was renovated in the beginning of the 20C. The pastry shop is located it what once was the Admiralty (also early 18C). There was once an art supply shop at nos 137-139, frequented by Pissarro, Monet, Renoir, Boudin, Sisley, Van Dongen, Dufy and Braque.

Rue de la Barre – The pharmacy at no 4 was founded in 1683. Voltaire lodged here when he returned from exile in England, at the home of his friend, the apothecary Jacques Féret. The houses here are once again early 18C, with period balconies (nos 40, 42, 44). The Protestant church at no 69 was once the chapel of a Carmelite convent (1645).

Eating out

MID-RANGE

Auberge du Clos Normand – *76370 Martin-Église – 7km/4.3mi southeast of Dieppe via D 1 –* ☎ *02 35 04 40 34 – closed 15 Nov to 15 Dec, Mon evening and Tues – 25.92/41.16€.* Comfortably seated in this 15C inn with brick and timber walls covered with Virginia creeper, you will be able to watch the chef prepare the food and, if you decide to stay, you will appreciate the restful bedrooms overlooking the river from the bottom of the colourful garden planted with trees.

La Marmite Dieppoise – *8 r. St-Jean –* ☎ *02 35 84 24 26 – closed 27 June to 2 July, 21 Nov to 10 Dec, Feb school holidays, Sun evening, Thur evening and Mon – 22.87/33.54€.* This small central restaurant with a yellow-brick façade specialises in seafood. You will enjoy, in particular, the "marmite dieppoise", a speciality of the house and a favourite with the locals.

Where to stay

MID-RANGE

La Villa Florida Bed and Breakfast – *24 chemin du Golf –* ☎ *02 35 84 40 37 –* ✍ *– 3 rooms: 48.78/53.36€.* This contemporary slate house is amazing: the interior, flooded with light, is superb. All the rooms, simply yet elegantly fitted out, have their own small terrace. The lovely garden overlooks Dieppe's golf course. Peace and quiet guaranteed, warm welcome.

Hôtel de la Plage – *20 bd de Verdun –* ☎ *02 35 84 18 28 – 40 rooms: 42.69/54.88€ –* ☕ *5.95€.* This hotel, facing the beach and close to the town centre, offers a family atmosphere, cosy decor and functional rooms. Ask for one of the rooms on the waterfront.

On the town

La Clef de Sole – *11 r. Charpenterie – Île de Pollet. –* ☎ *02 32 14 08 75 – la-clef-de-sole@netclic.fr – summer: daily 7pm-2am; winter: daily 5pm-2am.* You certainly won't find many bars as stylish as this one in France... Oriental carpets on the floor, a real fireplace, exotic furniture, its ochre colour standing out against the white walls... Worthy of an Impressionist painting! In addition, the vaulted cellars have been converted into a café with live entertainment and the menu is up to the mark.

La Rotonde – *Bd de Verdun – on the waterfront –* ☎ *02 35 06 16 28 – café: daily 9am-midnight – discothèque: Fri-Sat 10.30pm-4am – café closed end of Sept to beginning of Apr.* If this most attractive café just off the beach is only open in summer, the adjacent discotheque, housed in the former building of the thalassotherapy centre, will invite you to dance all year round under the sails and sunshades of its maritime decor. Concert every week.

Le Cactus – *71 quai Henri-IV –* ☎ *02 35 82 59 38 – daily 10am-2am – closed 15 days in Feb and 15 days in Nov.* This recent West-Indian-style bar has been popular from the start. Its terrace overlooking the harbour and, above all, its large cellar, with brightly painted walls and barrels, contribute to its success.

Le Rade – *12 r. de la Rade –* ☎ *02 35 82 34 15 – Tues-Sun 5pm-2am (4am Sat-Sun) – closed during the week from Jan to Feb school holidays.* For the locals, this is the type of bar which can be found in old harbours, where sailors drop in to have a pint and talk about their day's work whilst smoking their pipe. Lively authentic place.

Le Rétro – *73 quai Henri-IV –* ☎ *02 35 84 05 79 – Sept-May: Tues-Sun afternoons; June-Aug: daily noon-2am.* Located opposite the harbour, this bistro has a fine façade, listed as a historic monument. In order to admire it properly, have a drink on the terrace. Activities and concerts every two weeks in summer.

Scottish Pub – *12 r. St-Jacques –* ☎ *02 35 84 13 16 – July-Aug: Sun-Thur 2pm-2am, 4am Fri-Sat; the rest of the year: Mon-Thur 11am-2am, Fri-Sat noon-4am.* This friendly pub will make you feel home right away. Keeping watch over the cheerful crowd, the owner has a welcoming smile for visitors. A real haven of peace, warm and convivial, with live music on occasion... Enjoy!

Leisure time

Armement Legros: Boat trips – *Jean-Ango marina – next to the tourist office –* ☎ *02 35 84 82 85 – daily from 2pm – closed Sept-June except holidays.* Mr Legros suggests pleasant 40min boat trips and fishing trips. You can rent equipment. Invigorating and convivial.

Take the rue de la Sygogne, which overlooks the château, to the right.

A monument in the **square du Canada** recalls the 350 years of history uniting Dieppe and Canada, starting with the 17C colonists who left for Québec and continuing through the raid of 19 August 1942. In the summer, you can enter the château-museum from the square.

Boulevard de Verdun leads to the beach through the monumental gate **Les Tourrelles**, the only one of the five gates (15C) in the old fortifications to have survived.

From the end of the jetty, there is a good view of the cliffs and the château.

Continue your walk along the quai du Hâble in the neighbourhood known as **le Bout du Quai**. The little streets off the place du Moulin-à-Vent have traditionally been home to local fishermen. The maritime museum *(Estran, see below)* is on the north side. Just before the corner of rue de la Rade and quai du Hâble, you can spot the vestiges of a 14C tower (the Tour aux Crabes) which once guarded the entrance to the port. Follow quai Henri-IV along the marina. The Hôtel d'Anvers takes its name from a bas-relief in the courtyard, depicting the town of Antwerp.

Return to place Nationale on the left, via Grand-Rue.

THE PORT, LE POLLET AND THE CLIFF

About 2hr, starting from the tourist office. Go up the cliff from the fishermen's neighbourhood known as Le Pollet for a great view.

Avant-Port – This marina is the most unusual part of Dieppe harbour with tall, dark stone buildings surrounding the basin where the Newhaven-Dieppe ships used to moor. The coming and going beneath the arcades and along the quays to the old shipping harbour enhance its atmosphere.

A yachting marina designed to accommodate up to 400 boats was recently built following the 1994 transfer of the car ferry terminal onto the new outer port, where a modern harbour station has been set up.

To reach the terminal on foot, cross two bridges, pont d'Ango and pont Colbert, built in 1889 from designs by Gustave Eiffel. They lead to the Pollet district. Follow along the base of the cliffs, where you can see *gobes*, former cliff dwellings, now walled up.

Go back to the Colbert bridge and take ruelle des Grèves (next to a butcher's shop). From rue Guerrier, take rue du Petit-Fort which ends in a stairway to the top of the cliffs.

Le Pollet and cliff – There is a very old picturesque street leading off rue Guerrier, rue Quiquengrogne; the strange name was a rallying cry shouted by pirates on the Channel in the 15C. Next to no 3 rue du Petit-Fort, a tiny fisher-man's cottage, its roof caved in, and uninhabitable, predates the 1694 bombard-ment. A little farther on, between two houses, there is a good view of the marina. On top of the cliff stands the **Chapelle Notre-Dame-de-Bon-Secours**, built in 1876. Inside, there are names of local sailors lost at sea. The military light signal is operational 24hr, and equipped with a radio and radar team. Step away from the mast for an extensive **view★** of the city and harbour.

Port de Pêche (bassin Duquesne) – A non-industrial fishing port 2hr away from the capital, Dieppe has a large fishing fleet which goes out to sea on shortish expeditions (one to five days), bringing back a variety of fish and seafood for auction. Those eager for a touch of local colour will doubtless enjoy the early morning fish market. Dieppe is France's leading source of scallops *(coquilles St-Jacques)*, and also provides a plenty of sole and other fine fish to tables around the country.

Port de commerce – The shipment of fruit is a major business in Dieppe harbour. Bananas, pineapples and mangoes from the Ivory Coast arrive here, as well as citrus fruits, potatoes and vegetables from Morocco. Oils, grain and wood are also handled in considerable quantity.

THE CHÂTEAU AND THE MARTIME MUSEUM

Château – From the east end of **boulevard de la Mer**, there is a magnificent **view★** of the city and the beach. Dieppe Castle, faced with alternate blocks of flint and sandstone, was built round a massive circular tower which formed part of the earlier, 14C, town fortifications. 17C curtain walls link the castle to the square St-Rémy tower. Formerly belonging to the Governors of the town, it now houses the Municipal Museum.

★Museum ⊙ – The collections in the Musée de Dieppe centre on two main themes: the navy and ivory. As soon as visitors enter, they are told the glorious past of this maritime city by viewing a display of ship models, maps and navigational tools. Note the 1:20 scale replica of the *Beaumont*, a ship belonging to the East India Company

The fishing port in Dieppe

(18C). On the first floor, several rooms are devoted to Dutch painting and furniture – many seascapes and still-life pictures of fish (Pieter Boel, 17C) – as well as to 19C and 20C French painting: Isabey, Noël, Boudin, Renoir, Pissaro, Mebourg, Sisley and Jacques-Émile Blanche. Many of these artists were inspired by the sea or by the city of Dieppe – a favourite theme of the English artist Walter Sickert, some of whose pictures are displayed in the museum. There is an important collection of Pre-Colombian Peruvian pottery and, in a niche, a sculpture by Jean-Baptiste Carpeaux, *The Winkle-Picker.*

The most original feature of the museum is its incomparable collection of **Dieppe ivories★**.

The craftsmanship is as meticulous as that of Oriental artists, whether in the case of model ships and navigational instruments, already mentioned, or the religious exhibits (crucifixes, chaplets, missal-holders, small statues etc) and secular artefacts (toilet articles, sewing requisites, fans, snuff boxes, clocks, sculptures and various models) displayed on the first floor.

A small workshop has been reconstituted to show the tools of the local ivory carvers, craftsmen who came to Dieppe to carve ivory being imported from Africa and the Orient. In the 17C there were 350 ivory carvers in the town.

An adjoining room is devoted to the work of **Pierre-Adrien Graillon** (1807-72) whose carvings, not only in ivory but in bone and wood as well, evoke his childhood.

Musée de Dieppe - B. Regent/PHOTONONSTOP

Dieppe ivory

One **gallery** is dedicated to the musician **Camille Saint-Saëns**: drawings, portraits, academic robes, objects received after his concerts, holiday souvenirs (Egyptian statuettes, sunshades...) and his first piano.

Several modern and contemporary paintings by Dufy, Lurçat, Édouard Pignon, Gilles Aillaud etc are displayed together with a collection of prints by Georges Braque, exhibited in rotation. The temporary exhibitions which are renewed on a regular basis, may sometimes impinge on the space taken up by the museum's standing collections.

E. Baret

★Estran-Cité de la Mer ⊙ **(BY M)** – Situated at the heart of an old fishermen's district, this museum is devoted to the various local maritime professions; covering such themes as shipbuilding, navigational instruments, coastal fishing and long-distance industrial fishing, the means used to slow down the erosion of the Côte d'Albâtre and the ecosystem of the eastern Channel.

EXCURSIONS

Varengeville-sur-Mer – *See VARENGEVILLE-SUR-MER. 8km/5mi southwest via D 75.*

Offranville – *12km/7mi southwest via D 54B/D54.* This village has a 16C church, and standing next to it is a thousand year old tree more than 7m/23ft around. The William-Farcy gardens are planted with roses, tulips, cyprus, magnolias, camelias, azaleas and many other lovely flowers and trees.

Arques-la-Bataille – *See ARQUES-LA-BATAILLE. 5km/3mi south via D 154 or D 154E.*

★Château de Miromesnil – *See p 69. 12km/7mi south via D 915 or D 54B.*

Forêt d'Eawy

67 km/40mi From Dieppe to Neufchâtel-en-Bray.

Eawy Forest – a name of German origin meaning wet pastureland and pronounced Ee-a-vee – covers a jagged ridge (6 600ha/16 300 acres) flanked by the Varenne and Béthune valleys.

Eawy Forest, like Lyons Forest, is one of Normandy's most beautiful beech woods. A straight ride, the allée des Limousins, bisects it, passing through deeply shaded valleys.

Leaving from Dieppe *(D 915)* the road crosses the plateau between the River Varenne and the River Scie. Going downhill *(D 107)* from Le Bois-Robert there are pretty views of the wooded crest separating the Varenne from one of its tributaries. Brick manor houses are dotted all along the Varenne Valley *(D 149, D 154)*, and the beech forest cover gets gradually thicker. A pretty detour is offered by the Road of the Long Valleys *(D 97)* between Rosay and the Carrefour de l'Épinette junction. The small town of **St-Saëns** beckons attractively from the edge of the forest to those on the road that winds back through the woods *(D 12)*. Heading up the side of the valley to the east *(D 929, N 28)*, past the last stands of Eawy Forest, eventually brings the visitor to Neufchâtel-en-Bray.

DIVES-SUR-MER ★

Population 5 344
Michelin map 54 folds 16 and 17 or 231 fold 19
Local map see Pays d'AUGE

Dives faces Cabourg from across the river bearing the same name. At the mouth of the Dives, there is a small fishing harbour and a marina. In the Middle Ages, it was a large port.

If Cabourg is known as a holiday resort, Dives tends to be associated with history, for it was from here that William the Conqueror, Duc de Normandie, and his men set out to invade England in the 11C.

SIGHTS

★Halles – 15C and 16C. The magnificent oak frame of the covered market is in very good condition and goes perfectly with the tiled roof. Wrought-iron signs characterise the different stalls of the merchants.
On the other side of place de la République stands Bois-Hibou Manor (16C).

DIVES-SUR-MER

The Halles

Église Notre-Dame de Dives – This massive church, a centre of pilgrimage until the Religious Wars, is 14C and 15C except for the transept crossing, a remnant of an older sanctuary built in the 11C. Inside, the elegant 15C nave contrasts sharply with the massive pillars and plain arches of the Romanesque transept crossing. The transepts themselves, the chancel and the Lady Chapel were built in the Rayonnant Gothic style of the 14C. Notice on the back of the west wall a list carved in 1862 of William's companions-in-arms during his expedition to England.

Village Guillaume-le-Conquérant – This pleasant enclave of art and craft shops is located within the precincts of the old inn of the same name, dating from the 16C. Famous guests included Mme de Sévigné and Alexandre Dumas. The shops border the yard of the former coaching inn.

Eating out

MODERATE

Chez le Bougnat – 27 r. G.-Manneville – ☎ 02 31 91 06 13 – closed Mon evening and Tues in season, and evenings except Fri and Sat out of season – 12.50€. Odds and ends make up the decor of this former hardware shop with old posters covering the white-tiled walls...As for the cuisine, helpings are copious and the menu includes dishes based on fresh produce and specialities of the house. Not expensive.

Guillaume le Conquérant – 2 r. Hastings – ☎ 02 31 91 07 26 – closed 22 Nov to 25 Dec, Sun evening and Mon except July-Aug and holidays – 14.94/ 48.78€. After a stroll in the village, have a meal in the courtyard of this former 16C coaching inn. This restaurant will take you back in time with its old-style furniture decorating the fine dining room... In summer, the terrace is particularly pleasant.

Where to stay

MODERATE

La Maison Normande Bed and Breakfast – In the village centre – 14510 Gonneville-sur-Mer – 7km/4.3mi east of Dives via D 45 towards Lisieux then D 142 – ☎ 02 31 28 90 33 – closed All Saints' Day to Easter – ☌ – 2 rooms: 38.11/39.64€. It's impossible to miss this beautiful timber-framed façade opposite the village church. Peace and quiet, fine furniture and rustic decor in the rooms. Self-catering cottage for five persons near an authentic wooden cider-press. Garden and orchard.

Ferme de l'Oraille Bed and Breakfast – Chemin de Deraine – 14430 Douville-en-Auge – 7km/4.3mi southeast of Dives-sur-Mer via D 45, D 27 towards Lisieux then a minor road – ☎ 02 31 79 25 49 – ☌ – 3 rooms: 30.49/ 36.59€. There is no pretentious display of luxury in this 18C timber-framed Norman farm, which is still operating. It offers you the opportunity of rediscovering the authentic taste of milk served for breakfast with a choice of home-made jams. Simple restful rooms.

178

DOMFRONT ★

Population 4 410
Michelin map 59 fold 10 or 231 fold 41

Domfront lies spread along a rocky ridge of Armorican sandstone commanding from some 70m/200ft the gorge through which the River Varenne pierces the last line of hills of Lower Normandy. The town commands a panorama of the Passais *bocage* country, a pear-growing area which produces a pear cider or perry. Domfront is capital of the Passais.

In addition to its strategic **site★** the small town features some interesting historic ruins and a well-restored town centre to offer the visitor.

DOMFRONT AND THE MONTGOMERY FAMILY

Under English Rule – In the mid 6C St Front founded a hermitage in Passais Forest. At the beginning of the 11C Guillaume Talvas, Duc de Bellême and later Comte d'Alençon built a fortress around which the town developed. In 1092 the townspeople of Domfront rose up against their overlord Roger de Montgomery and sought the protection of **Henry Beauclerk**, the son of William the Conqueror. In 1100 Henry became King of England and Domfront an English possession.

In the 12C Domfront was often visited by Henry II Plantagenet and his Queen Eleanor of Aquitaine with their brilliant court of troubadours and poets. It was here in August 1170 that the papal legates attempted to achieve a reconciliation between Henry II Plantagenet and his estranged Archbishop of Canterbury, Thomas Becket.

Domfront passed from English to French hands and it was often under siege during the Hundred Years War. In 1356 the town surrendered to the English who ruled for 10 years and only left once a ransom had been paid. The town once again passed to the English in 1418 who relinquished it for good in 1450, only three years before the English rule in Aquitaine ended with the Battle of Castillon.

Matignon's Siege – The town's most important siege took place in 1574. Gabriel, Comte de Montgomery (1530-74), a former captain in the Scottish guard, who had mortally wounded the French King Henri II in a tournament, defended Domfront against the royal or Catholic forces under the Comte de Matignon. Montgomery surrendered to Matignon on the understanding that his life would be saved but was executed on the orders of Henri's widow, Catherine dei Medici.

★OLD TOWN CENTRE *30min*

The old town is enclosed by a wall and 13 of the original 24 towers. The best preserved are those on the south side; one is still crowned with machicolations. For a good view walk along rue des Fossés-Plisson. Many of the façades have been cleaned of layers of plasterwork to reveal the timber-frame structure.

Several 16C stone houses, formerly inhabited by noble or well-to-do families, have been restored.

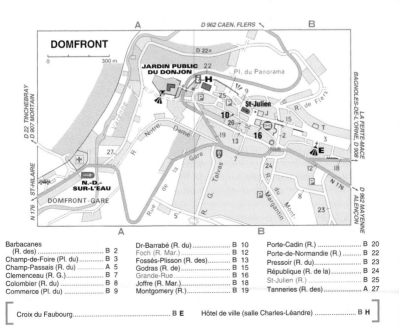

Barbacanes (R. des)	B 2	
Champ-de-Foire (Pl. du)	B 3	
Champ-Passais (R. du)	A 5	
Clemenceau (R. G.)	B 7	
Colombier (R. du)	B 8	
Commerce (Pl. du)	B 9	
Dr-Barrabé (R. du)	B 10	
Foch (R. Mar.)	B 12	
Fossés-Plisson (R. des)	B 13	
Godras (R. de)	B 15	
Grande-Rue	B 16	
Joffre (R. Mar.)	B 18	
Montgomery (R.)	B 19	
Porte-Cadin (R.)	B 20	
Porte-de-Normandie (R.)	B 22	
Pressoir (R. du)	B 23	
République (R. de la)	B 24	
St-Julien (R.)	B 25	
Tanneries (R. des)	A 27	

Croix du Faubourg .... B E   Hôtel de ville (salle Charles-Léandre) .... B H

179

Eating out

MODERATE

Auberge Le Grand Gousier – *1 pl. de la Liberté* – ☎ *02 33 38 97 17* – *closed Sept, Feb school holidays, Wed evening and Thur* – *12.96/22.87€.* Situated at the heart of the old town, near the post office, this inn is just what you need to buck you up after a pleasant walk. Get a table in the dining room with the lovely 16C fireplace. Good value for money.

Grande-Rue – This sloping street, now a pedestrian zone, has kept its original paving.

Rue du Docteur-Barrabé – There are some lovely timber-framed houses, notably at no 40 and at the corner of ruelle Porte-Cadin.

Église St-Julien – This modern church (1924) in neo-Byzantine style is dominated by a tall cement belfry. The interior plan consists of an octagonal dome resting on four great round headed arches intersecting to form a square. An immense mosaic depicts Christ in Majesty.

The area around the church, in particular rue St-Julien and place du Commerce, has been well restored, and is a pleasant area for a stroll.

Terre-plein Nord des remparts – From the north terrace of the ramparts, there is a restricted but interesting view of the deep valley of the Varenne, known locally as the Valley of the Rocks.

Hôtel de ville ⊙ – In the town hall, the **Salle Charles-Léandre** houses several paintings and drawings by the local artist Charles Léandre who had a very caustic talent.

ADDITIONAL SIGHTS

★**Jardin public du Donjon** – Cross the bridge over the old moat to the public gardens laid out on the site of the fortress which was razed in 1608 on the orders of Sully. Nothing remains of the early-11C timber fortress built by Guillaume Talvas. Of Henry Beauclerc's 1092 fortress there remain two imposing sections of the keep's walls and two towers from the flattened curtain wall. The eastern section of the fortress' wall was reinforced in 1205 by a system of blockhouses. Inside the curtain walls stand the ruins of the late-11C Chapelle St-Symphorien. Eleanor of Aquitaine's daughter was born in Domfront and christened in this very chapel. The chapel belonged to a priory which in turn was dependent on Lonlay Abbey.

Skirt the ruins of the keep to reach the terrace *(viewing table)* which affords an extensive and pleasant **panorama★** of the Passais countryside and its three rivers, the Mayenne, Varenne and Égrenne. To the southeast Mont Margantin is recognisable by its conical silhouette. In the foreground to the right is the Ste-Anne hillock.

★**Église Notre-Dame-sur-l'Eau** – This charming Romanesque Church of Our Lady on the Water (late 11C) was badly mutilated last century when five of the seven nave bays were destroyed to make way for a road. Following damage in 1944 the church was restored. The bridge over the Varenne or the side of the road climbing up to the town centre, provide the best overall views of the church with its squat belfry pierced by twin openings and its chevet with radiating chapels.

According to legend, at Christmas in 1166 Thomas Becket, Archbishop of Canterbury, celebrated Mass in this church while in exile in France.

In the middle of the chancel with its lovely arcades is the altar composed of a granite slab supported by three squat pillars.

Several 12C frescoes have been uncovered in the south transept representing the Doctors of the Church (theologians who expounded the Christian doctrine). A Gothic canopy covers a recumbent figure with a lion at its feet.

Croix du Faubourg – From the foot of the Calvary, there is a **panorama★** similar to the one from the public gardens, but it extends further east towards Andaines Forest.

EXCURSIONS

Northwest of Domfront – *Round tour of 35km/22mi – about 2hr. Leave Domfront by D 22.*

The roads recommended, particularly those from Lonlay-l'Abbaye to D 907, are narrow but beautiful, especially in spring.

Lonlay-l'Abbaye – The church, once part of an 11C abbey, enjoys a pleasant country setting. It was damaged in 1944. The 15C porch opens directly into the transept; the south arm is typical of Romanesque construction and decoration. The Gothic chancel and its granite pillars have been restored.

The **Biscuiterie de l'Abbaye** makes a kind of shortbread according to an old recipe.

5km/3mi west of the village turn left onto D 134.

La Fosse-Arthour – The most interesting part of the drive is between two bridges. From a rock height on the left there is a view of the setting in which La Fosse-Arthour lies with the River Sonce running swiftly between two steep sandstone banks and opening out into a pool before continuing on its way in a series of small cascades. Fishing and canoeing enthusiasts are able to indulge in their favourite sport on the 3ha/7-acre stretch of water.

The area has many rocky outcrops which, for the more agile, provide good viewpoints of the *bocage* countryside.

Take D 134 south towards St-Georges-de-Rouelley; at the first junction turn left onto the Rouellé road. In Rouellé turn left into D 907 to Domfront. After 1.5km/1mi turn right onto a narrow road, unsurfaced towards the end, which leads to the Saucerie Manor set amid farm buildings.

Manoir de la Saucerie – The entrance pavilion flanked by two round towers with loopholes is all that remains of this 16C manor house. The barrel-vaulted passage on the ground floor was originally approached by a double drawbridge spanning a moat. The combination of different building materials (stone, brick and timber) provides a certain charm.

Return to D 907 to return to Domfront.

DREUX ★

Population 35 230
Michelin map 60 fold 7 or 231 folds 47 and 48
Local map see Vallée de l'EURE

Dreux is set on the boundary between Normandy and Île-de-France; it is a lively regional market town earning its living from diverse industrial activities.

The name of Dreux is linked to that of **Jean Rotrou** (1609-50), poet and lieutenant of the bailiwick of his native town. His devotion to his birthplace – he returned to Dreux during an outbreak of the plague – led to his death. His memory is perpetuated by a statue standing on the square carrying his name; it was executed by the sculptor Allaseur. It is pleasant to stroll in the pedestrian zone near the belfry. The main street, formerly called Grande-Rue and renamed rue Maurice-Viollette, is usually very lively, particularly on market day. On the corner with rue Illiers are two timber-framed houses whose corbelled floors are supported by beams.

A FRENCH BORDER AND THEN A KINGDOM

Dreux rose to importance when the Normans settled west of the River Avre and Dreux Castle had to defend the French frontier against a very belligerent neighbour.

The castle, which stood on the hill now occupied by St Louis' Chapel, was besieged many times. It was dismantled on the orders of Henri IV, who in 1593 burned the town, which had sided with the League and withstood a three-year siege.

In 1556 the Paris Parliament decided that the County of Dreux should in future be the exclusive property of the French royal family, which had formerly often pledged it to certain noble families.

In 1775 Louis XVI ceded Dreux to his cousin, the Duc de Penthièvre, son of the Comte de Toulouse. Eight years later, when at the king's insistence the Duc was forced to give up his magnificent property at Rambouillet, he arranged for the family tombs in the parish church of Rambouillet (subsequently destroyed) to be transferred to the collegiate church adjoining Dreux Castle. When the Duc's daughter married Louis Philippe d'Orléans, known as Philippe Égalité, her dowry included the County of Dreux. It was thus that Dreux, which until the Revolution had been a simple family burial place, became the mausoleum of the Orléans family.

SIGHTS

★**Belfry** ⊘ (**AY B**) – At the end of rue Maurice-Viollette, formerly the Grande-Rue, rises the ornate façade of the Hôtel de Ville (town hall), which was built from 1512 to 1537. The ground and first floors are decorated in the Flamboyant style; the second floor shows the skill of a young Renaissance architect from Dreux, during the reign of François I, **Clément Métézeau** (1479-1555): window bays framed by pilasters, a frieze and lantern turrets.

Église St-Pierre ⊘ – Built in the early 13C and partly damaged during the Hundred Years War, St Peter's Church was heavily remodelled from the 15C to the 17C. The façade dates from the 16C. Of the two towers designed to flank it, only the left one was actually completed. The gate, chancel and left arm of the transept are 13C. The right arm of the transept dates from the 16C to the 17C.

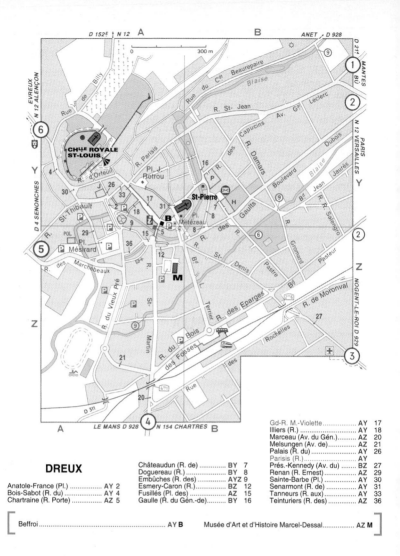

The church interior is notable for its fine 15C and 16C **stained-glass windows**, to be found especially in the side chapels (1st, 2nd and 3rd on the right; 2nd, 3rd and 4th on the left) and apsidal chapel. A curious stoup carved out of a 12C capital depicts the Holy Women at the Grave. The outstanding organ case (1614) is the work of the local cabinetmaker Toussaint Fortier.

Chapelle royale St-Louis ⊘ **(AY)** – Before the Revolution this site was occupied by the Collegiate Church of St Stephen. In 1783 it received the remains of members of the Toulouse Penthièvre families.

In 1816 the dowager Duchess of Orléans, widow of Philippe Égalité, erected a chapel designed in the form of a Greek cross in the neo-Classical style. It was enlarged by Louis-Philippe when he became king, and the exterior was embellished with bell turrets and Gothic pinnacles. The building as a whole is a monument to the 19C both for the quality of its architecture and the participation of talented artists.

The side windows added to the upper chapel under Louis-Philippe make it possible to admire the stained glass representations of the patron saints of France and the royal family: *(left)* St Philip, St Amelia, St Ferdinand (the heads are portraits). The stained glass in the apse illustrates the life of St Louis.

The main crypt contains the tombs of the Princes of Orléans; the recumbent figures form a little museum of 19C statuary by Mercié, Pradier, Dubois, Chapu, Millet, Lenoir etc. Among those interred are King Louis-Philippe and Queen Marie-Amélie, the Duc d'Orléans, the Duc d'Aumale and the Duc de Nemours, Prince de Joinville, the Duc and Duchesse d'Alençon.

The tomb of the Duc Ferdinand d'Orléans, Prince Royal, and of his wife, Princess of Mecklenburg-Schwerin, illustrates the divide between Catholic and Protestant through its design and the unity of the couple by their tender relationship.

On the lower level, five extremely rare **glass panes painted with enamels★★** catch the visitor's attention. They were made in the Sèvres workshops, as was the other glasswork. Impressive effects can be obtained in both natural and artificial light.

The crypt under the rotunda of the high chapel has twelve burial places prepared for the family of the Count of Paris. One of them has been occupied since 1960 by Prince François d'Orléans who died for his country during the Algerian War. In a nearby crypt lies Prince Thibaut d'Orléans who died in 1983.

The park contains several remains of old fortifications. A fine **view** can be had of the town.

Stained-glass window, Chapelle royale St-Louis

Musée d'Art et d'Histoire Marcel-Dessal ⓥ (**AZ M**) – Set up in a neo-Romanesque chapel, the museum displays furnishings taken from the Collégiale Saint-Etienne, a 12C collegiate church built on the same site as the King's Chapel (historiated capitals and fragments of stained glass).

Shown alongside local archeological exhibits, dating from Prehistoric, Gallo-Roman and Merovingian times, are early archives and manuscripts evoking the history of the Dreux region from the Middle Ages to the III Republic (documents relating to the Orléans family). A set of 18C furniture taken from the Château de Crécy-Couve, formerly owned by the Marquise de Pompadour, is also on show. The painting gallery displays both ancient and contemporary works. Impressionist and post-Impressionist movements are well represented with canvases by Vlaminck, Montezin and Le Sidaner, arranged around a painting by Claude Monet: *Wisteria*.

EXCURSIONS

Vallée de l'Eure

1 **From Dreux to Pacy-sur-Eure** – *42 km/25mi – about 3hr (including château visit). Leave Dreux via D 928 north and take D 16¹ to the left.*

The landscapes of the Eure river valley are a study in contrasts: the banks of the river are green, while the sharp profiles of the hilltops are stark against the horizon.

Outside Dreux, the aqueduct crosses the valley, carrying water from the Avre to Paris. Off to the right, you can see the church in the little town of Montreuil as you drive by, and the Dreux forest off to the left. In Ézy-sur-Eure, formerly known for the manufacture of horn combs, an old humpback bridge (pont St-Jean) crosses the river to Saussay. The slopes are bare, punctuated by caves.

Eating out

MODERATE

St-Pierre – *19 r. Sénarmont – ☎ 02 37 46 47 00 – closed 15-28 July, Sun evening and Mon – 12.04/20.89€.* Mouth-watering menus and reasonable prices have ensured the local renown of this small restaurant in the town centre. Bistro-style decor and warm welcome from the owners.

MID-RANGE

Auberge de la Vallée Verte – *Near the church – 28500 Vernouillet-centre – 2km/1.2mi south of Dreux via D 311 – ☎ 02 37 46 04 04 – closed 1-20 Aug, Fri evening, Sun evening and Mon – 22.11/38.11€.* Tradition is the rule in this family-run inn. You will enjoy the cuisine based on fresh market produce, served in the rustic dining room with its mezzanine. Ten simple, well-kept rooms.

Where to stay

MID-RANGE

Le Beffroi Hotel – *12 pl. Métézeau – ☎ 02 37 50 02 03 – closed 1-10 Aug – 16 rooms: 44.97/49.55€ – ☕ 4.57€.* If you intend to visit the belfry and the Église St-Pierre, you could not be closer... The hotel is not exactly luxurious, but the rooms are functional and adequate. We prefer those on the riverside, they are more restful.

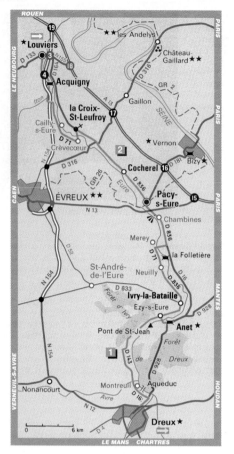

★Château d'Anet ⊘ – Of all the French Renaissance châteaux, Anet was reputedly the most ornate. The drawing below shows what remains and how much was lost, mainly owing to speculation during the Revolution.

Successive owners since 1840 have endeavoured to maintain the original appearance of the buildings which have survived.

A Queen without a crown – Shortly after her arrival at court, **Diane de Poitiers**, widow of Louis de Brézé, Seneschal of Normandy and Lord of Anet, caught the attention of Henri, second son of François I and 20 years her junior. Beautiful, intelligent and a patron of the arts, Diane captivated the young prince with no difficulty, since Henri's wife was merely the daughter of a Florentine banker, "a Medici". Diane was 32 when the dauphin met her and he was still fascinated by her when he became king. She had not disappointed him at the age of 60 when, in 1559, Henri was killed by Montgomery during a tournament.

With her constant charm she reigned for 12 years over sovereign, court, artists and royal finances. Anet, which she had rebuilt, was the symbol of her power and taste. Better still, it was she who brought up the royal children. In 1559 Catherine de' Medici took Chenonceau but left Anet to Diane who retired there and died in 1566 after completing a number of embellishments to the first Henri II style château.

Work began c 1548 under the architect **Philibert Delorme**. Until then buildings had been in the François I style: construction in the French architectural style, decoration in the Italian style. At Anet there is strong Italian influence in the design as seen in the use of pilasters and columns.

The centrepiece of the main building overlooking the courtyard was well ahead of its time; it now stands in the courtyard of the Fine Arts School (École des Beaux-Arts) in Paris.

The greatest artists of the day embellished the château: the sculptors Goujon, Pilon and the silversmith Cellini, the enameller Limosin and the Fontainebleau tapestry-makers. Contrary to legend, none of the effigies of the goddess Diana, often depicted at Anet, is a portrait of the duchess.

In the 17C alterations were made by the Duke of Vendôme, grandson of Henri IV and Gabrielle d'Estrées. The duke suppressed the covered walk around the gardens and added a break-front and main stairway to the left wing of the main courtyard, the only one surviving today, and had the court of Diane closed to the west by a hemicycle.

Entrance gate – The work of Philibert Delorme. Above the central arch, the tympanum consists of a casting of Benvenuto Cellini's bronze low relief now in the Louvre: *Diane Recumbent*. Above the door is a clock dominated by a stag held at bay by four dogs. The statues are casts. Once the animals told the time, the dogs barking, the stag stamping its foot. The main entrance is flanked by terraces; the outlying buildings are surmounted by chimneys capped with coffins as evidence of Diane's constant mourning.

Left wing of the main courtyard – The visit begins on the first floor with Diane's bedroom. The main attraction is the Renaissance bed, decorated with the three crescents of Diane. The stained-glass windows include fragments of the original greyish monochrome designs *(grisailles)*, a discreet decoration in keeping with Diane's mourning.

Entrance gate, Château d'Anet

The **main stairway**, added by the Duke of Vendôme in the 17C, affords views of the lake and park. The vestibule, dating back to the same period, leads to the Salon Rouge containing furniture from the French and Italian Renaissance.

The Faience Room, which has kept part of its original tiling, leads into the dining room where the huge fireplace is supported by two atlantes by Puget. In the centre note the medallion by Jean Goujon depicting Diane snaring the royal stag.

Chapel – It was built in 1548 by Philibert Delorme and is in the form of a Greek cross. A dome and lantern cover the circular nave, one of the first to be built in France. The skilfully executed diamond-shaped drawing on the coffers produces a surprising optical illusion, the whole cupola seeming to be drawn upwards. The design of the floor tiling recalls this geometrical subtlety. Diane de Poitiers used to attend Mass from the gallery, which communicated with her rooms in the right wing *(demolished)*.

The alcoves house statues of the 12 Apostles by Germain Pilon (mouldings). Jean Goujon is thought to be responsible for the low-relief sculptures on the corner stones and arches depicting angelots bearing symbols of the Passion and allegorical characters (Fames), announcing the Resurrection of Christ.

Chapelle funéraire de Diane de Poitiers – *Entrance from place du Château, left of the main entrance.* The chapel, built according to the design of Claude de Foucques, architect to the princes of Lorraine, was begun just before the death of Diane in 1566 and completed in 1577. The white marble **statue**★ representing Diane kneeling on a tall sarcophagus in black marble, is attributed to Pierre Bontemps; so too is the altarpiece. Since the spoiling of the tomb in 1795, Diane's remains have rested against the chevet of Anet parish church, between two buttresses.

Ivry-la-Bataille – There are a few picturesque timber-framed houses: a typical local house *(no 5 rue de Garennes)* may have been the lodging of Henri IV in 1590; the 11C doorway *(at the end of rue de l'Abbaye)*, decorated with three sculpted key stones (renovated), may have been part of Ivry Abbey which ceased to exist at the Revolution. Diane de Poitiers was the founder of the **Église St-Martin**, a late-15C to early-16C church, attributed in part to the famous architect of the period, Philibert Delorme. The Gothic pinnacles on the tower are decorated with gargoyles and dragons; the south door (bricked up) is surmounted by an elegant pediment and flanked by fluted pillars with Corinthian capitals. The nave and aisles are covered by a handsome panelled barrel vault.

Between Neuilly and the mills of Merey, the **Château de la Folletière** can be seen through the foliage. It was built in brick and stone in the late 16C, and sits in a pretty park.

From Chambine to Pacy, D 836 rises above the Eure and there are pleasant views upstream.

2 **From Louviers to Pacy-sur-Eure** – *See LOUVIERS.*

ÉCOUIS ★

Population 714
Michelin map 55 southeast of fold 7 or 231 fold 24

The village of Écouis in the Normandy Vexin region centres on the twin towers of its old collegiate church. This was built between 1310 and 1313 by Enguerrand de Marigny, Superintendant of Finances to Philip the Fair. Victim of the feudal leagues in reaction to the king's financial policies, his life ended tragically upon the gibbet in 1315. His politics have been outlived by his policy of local artistic patronage as may be seen from the remarkable works of art in the church, the result of his encouragement of sculptors from the Paris region.

★**Collégiale Notre-Dame** ⊙ – The sober building of the Collegiate Church – the roof timbers were replaced by the present brick and stone vaulting at the end of the 18C – has an immense chancel terminating in a three sided apse. The chancel is flanked by two chapels with broken barrel vaulting and contains some beautiful furnishings and remarkable **statues**★ dating from the 14C to the 17C.

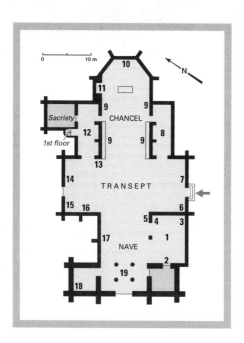

1) Chapel of the Immaculate Conception (16C) with attractive lierne and tierceron vaulting.

2) Christ on the Cross (13C).

3) St Nicaise.

4) St Ann and the Virgin (14C).

5) Our Lady of Écouis (14C).

6) Statue of St Margaret (14C).

7) Statue of Jean de Marigny, brother of Enguerrand, who was Archbishop of Rouen when he died in 1351.

8) St John Chapel – the wooden vault enables us to imagine the former vault of the nave. Statue of Alips de Mons, wife of Enguerrand de Marigny. Stained glass (14C) depicting the Crucifixion with St John and Mary at the foot of the Cross.

9) 14C choir stalls; 16C doors and woodwork.

10) Door of former rood screen.

11) Christ and his Shroud (16C).

12) North side chapel: St Martin, St Francis, St Laurent (14C), St Cecilia.

13) Madonna of the King (14C).

14) St Agnes (14C).

15) St Veronica (14).

16) *Ecce Homo* in wood (15).

17) Annunciation (15C). The statue of the Virgin is supported by a charming group of small angels reading prophecies relating to the mystery of the Incarnation. The hands and face of the Virgin, together with the face of Archangel Gabriel, are in marble encrusted in stone.

18) St John the Baptist (14C).

19) Organ case (17C).

In a **room** ⊙ on the first floor beautiful works of art are displayed including a cope chest and the chalice of Jean de Marigny (14C).

EXCURSION

★**Abbaye de Fontaine-Guérard** ⊙ – *12km/ 7mi northwest via N14. Just before Fleury-sur-Andelle, take D 321 left, then the second road on the right.*
The ruins of the 12C abbey, on the north bank of the Andelle, are both evocative and moving, owing to their isolation and the threat of flooding. In the 13C the community adopted the Cistercian rule.

Beside the approach path stands St Michael's Chapel (left), built in the 15C over vaulted cellars. There is an underground passage to the abbey storerooms. The ruins of the abbey church date from 1218; the square chevet with its elegant windows and some apsidal vaulting have survived. The **chapter-house** (right), which opened off the cloisters (demolished), is divided into three by a double row of slim columns with crocheted capitals; it is a fine example of early-13C Norman architecture. A second vaulted room, possibly the workroom, resembles the knights' room in the abbey of Mont-St-Michel. A stair leads to the upper floor where each **dormitory** cell was lit by a narrow window.

Abbaye de Fontaine-Guérard

To find the description of a town or an isolated tourist attraction, consult the index.

ELBEUF

Population 52 000
Michelin map 54 fold 20 or 231 southeast of fold 22
Local map see Vallée de la SEINE

Strategically located in a loop of the Seine, Elbeuf was once an important centre for the French drapery industry. The manufacture of cloth began in the 15C, reached its peak at the end of the 19C and became mechanised in 1870.

The subsequent decline of this textile industry, described with talent by the most famous native of Elbeuf, the novelist **André Maurois**, has been offset by the development of other industries: chemicals, electrical goods, machinery, metallurgy and automobiles.

SIGHTS

Old town – 🚶 *45min. Leave your car in the parking lot across from the town hall. Take rue Henry and when you reach St-Jean Church, turn left on rue Guymener.*

Across from the church, place St-Jean and the Puchot district (named after a river which now flows underground) are at the heart of the old town.

Go straight ahead along rue R.-Poulain and take the first right to place de la République.

On the square the old cloth manufactory (18C, attack and chimneys 19C) is being restored. More than 350 people worked here in 1889; it went out of business in 1961.

Take rue aux Bœufs then cross rue Boucher-de-Perthes. Go through the gardens to reach St-Étienne Church, then continue up rue de la République on the right.

The **Jardins de la Source** have been in place since 1994, and have opened up this former manufacturing area.

Continue straight along rue des Martyrs and take the first left back to the town hall.

Eating out

LUXURY

Le Tourville – *12 r. Danielle-Casanova* – *76410 Tourville-la-Rivière* – *11km/6.8mi northeast of Elbeuf via D 7* – ☎ *02 35 77 58 79* – *closed Aug, 25-29 Dec and Mon* – *reservation essential* – *35.06/70.13€*. Sought after by local gourmets, this opulent house, hiding behind high walls, is a bastion of good traditional cuisine, characterised by authentic, delicate flavours, served by the fireplace in winter. Really worth the detour.

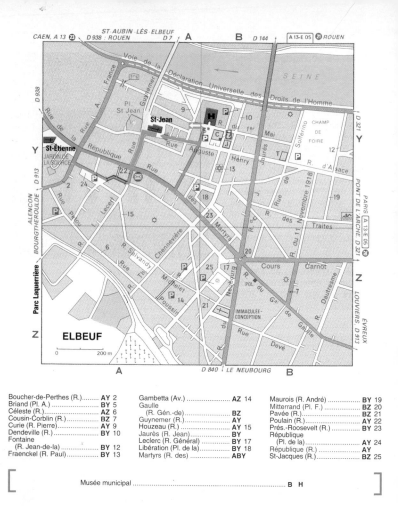

Musée municipal d'Elbeuf ⊙ – This **natural history museum** comprises nine rooms, all at ground-floor level, where large collections of zoological (stuffed animals, skeletons and shells), mineralogical and archeological (remarkable Gallo-Roman burial places) exhibits are displayed. One room is devoted to local history: paintings and sculptures treating the Elbeuf conurbation.

Église St-Jean ⊙ – A Gothic church with Classical ornament and furnishings. Notice the 16C stained-glass windows on the 1st, 3rd, 4th and 5th windows in the north aisle and the first in the south aisle. They are the oldest (1500) and best conserved. Two of the windows in the south aisle date from the same period but have been restored. There are also a number of modern windows. The new and the old form an attractive combination.

Église St-Étienne ⊙ – This Flamboyant church has retained its 16C stained-glass windows. Note the Crucifixion on the top window to the right in the apse and other windows retracing scenes from the life of the Virgin in the north aisle. Near the Lady Chapel in the north aisle there is a fine stained-glass representation of the Tree of Jesse.
St Roch is depicted in the stained glass of a chapel in the south aisle. One of the panels shows the drapers in working clothes. Woodcarving is represented by a Louis XV style rood beam, a 13C recumbent figure of Christ (lower north aisle) and on either side of the chancel statues of St Stephen and St John.

EXCURSIONS

Saint-Ouen-de-Pontcheuil – *6km/3.5mi south via D 840.* The **Moulin Amour** ⊙, the very last hydraulic windmill officially registered along the banks of the River Oison, is still operated during special demonstrations and presentations to the public. The flour obtained is then sieved at an old boulting factory. In addition to the machinery, which one can observe in good working order, the mill stages exhibitions of old-fashioned trades that contribute to reasserting the importance of Normandy's regional heritage.

Les roches d'Orival – *See HONFLEUR.*

★**Château de Robert le Diable** – The castle is one of the popular viewpoints in the Seine Valley. Robert the Devil, its legendary builder, is in fact a mythical character, vaguely based on Robert the Magnificent, the father of William the Conqueror. The fortress built by the first dukes of Normandy was destroyed by John Lackland in 1204; it was rebuilt by Philippe Auguste and was probably destroyed again in the 15C by the French to prevent it falling into the hands of the English.

The **Musée des Vikings** ⊘ *(over the drawbridge)* presents a reconstruction of a Viking longboat *(drakkar)* housed in a building derived from a Norwegian chapel. The boat (12.40m/70ft long and 5.50m/18ft wide) could carry 40 men. In the basement there is a tableau of wax figures depicting the Norman Golden Age. The Bourgtheroulde Tower contains a low relief of Rollo and a scale model of the castle as it was in 1418. The life of William the Conqueror is evoked by wax figures in the Rouen Tower; from the top there is a magnificent **panorama**★ over the bend in the river and Roumare Forest.

ÉTRETAT ★★

Population 1 565
Michelin map 54 folds 7 and 8 or 231 fold 8

Étretat, now an elegant resort, has always had a great reputation because of the originality of its setting. The grandeur of the high cliffs and crashing waves is unforgettable whatever the season. It is no wonder that the town has inspired many writers, artists and film directors. Maupassant spent his childhood here, "leading the life of a wild foal", according to his own words, and Maurice Leblanc described the Aiguille Creuse through his famous character, Arsène Lupin. Other famous personalities who helped to establish the fame of the town included Alexandre Dumas, André Gide, Victor Hugo, Gustave Courbet, Jacques Offenbach and Claude Monet.

Setting – The shingle beach, skirted by a sea wall promenade, lies between the well-known cliffs; to the east the Amont (Upstream) Cliff with its small chapel Notre-Dame-de-la-Garde and its museum; to the west the Aval (Downstream) Cliff with its monumental arch cut through the chalk, known as the Porte d'Aval (Downstream Gateway).
Offshore stands a solitary needle rock, the Aiguille (70m/200ft high). On the beach are three traditional thatched fishermen's huts which have been restored. They were used for storing fishing equipment.

CLIFF WALKS

★★★**Falaise d'Aval** – *1hr on foot there and back. From the west end of the promenade climb the steps to the path which scales the cliff face. Walk along the edge of the cliff as far as the ridge of Porte d'Aval.*
The view is magnificent: the massive Manneporte arch (left), the Aiguille opposite and the Amont Cliff on the far side of the bay. The variations in colour according to the time and natural lighting are truly enchanting.

G. Targat/MICHELIN

Falaise d'Aval

Eating out

MODERATE

Le Clos Lupin – *37 r. Alphonse-Karr* – ☎ *02 35 29 67 53* – *closed 5 Jan to 10 Feb, Mon evening and Tues except school holidays.* – *reservation essential Sat-Sun* – *14.48/38.11€*. In spite of its smart painted façade and lace trimmings, this small restaurant is simple with its pale-green walls and dark woodwork. The menu offers traditional dishes, based on fresh produce, at reasonable prices.

MID-RANGE

Le Galion – *Bd René-Coty* – ☎ *02 35 29 48 74* – *closed 15 Dec to 15 Jan, Tues evening and Wed except school holidays* – *18.75/34.76€*. Situated in the town centre, this residence was built with materials from an old house which once stood in Lisieux; note, in particular, the 14C ceiling with its carved beams. It is one of the worthwhile restaurants in the area for the quality of its cuisine and extremely competitive prices.

Where to stay

MID-RANGE

La Résidence Hotel – *4 bd René-Coty* – ☎ *02 35 27 02 87* – *15 rooms: 42.69/105.19€* – ☐ *5.34€*. This 14C manor house is located in the town centre. Pleasant rooms with amusing ill-assorted furniture. Mind the steps: the superb period staircase leading to the reception is lopsided owing to its grand age!.. Pleasant welcome. Cycle hire.

Dormy House Hotel – *Rte du Havre* – ☎ *02 35 27 07 88* – 🅿 *49 rooms: 50.31/115€* – ☐ *8€* – *restaurant 190/255F.* Ideally situated within a peaceful park, this rather cosy hotel offers a superb view of the sea and the cliffs... from the restaurant, the terrace and even some of the bedrooms. Ask to stay in the recent building, which is more comfortable.

At La Manneporte there is a view towards Cap d'Antifer. From the promontory overlooking the second arch there is a view south to the petroleum port of Le Havre-Antifer.

★★**Falaise d'Amont** – *1hr on foot there and back. From the east end of the promenade take the steps cut into the chalk cliffs (180 steps, handrail) and the path to the clifftop.*
Access by car: take D 11 "Fécamp par la Côte"; just before the sign indicating the end of the built-up area, turn sharp left onto a steep and narrow uphill road. Park near the monument.
From the seamen's chapel dedicated to **Notre-Dame-de-la-Garde** there is a magnificent **view**★ of Étretat and its surroundings. Below is the long shingle beach between the Aval arch and the Aiguille. Behind the chapel an immense spire

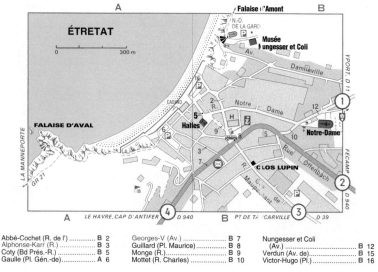

points towards the sky. The memorial was erected as a tribute to Nungesser and Coli, the two French aviators who made the first, unsuccessful attempt to fly the Atlantic on 8 May 1927. It was here that their aircraft, the *Oiseau Blanc*, was seen for the last time.

Several steps at the rear of the spire lead up to the base of the former monument which was in the shape of the aeroplane: the name in large white letters, the nose, the French tricolour markings on the wing tips, the tail.

Musée Nungesser-et-Coli ⊙ – The museum opposite the monument contains mementoes of the two aviators, "the first to dare".

The Seine-Maritime *département*, between the Channel to the north and the River Seine to the southwest, has all of the things that make Normandy such a lovely place, in abundance. Apple orchards, green fields for grazing dairy cows, fish and shellfish from the coast, and farmyards full of querulous ducks and hens all participate in the great gastronomic reputation of Normandy. The "Alabaster Coast", so-called for the white cliffs which line the shore, is the source of excellent sole, coquilles St-Jacques (scallops) and other fresh seafood. Here is a recipe (serves four) for preparing filets of lotte (a kind of monkfish):

Medaillons de lotte à la mode d'Étretat

Monkfish filets (4)
Butter
Bacon or salt pork (lardons), chopped in small pieces (about half a cup)
2 large onions
Flour
Dry white wine
Cream
Vinegar

Rinse 4 filets in cold water, pat them dry with paper towels, and then roll them in a mixture of salt, pepper and flour to coat them. Sauté 2 chopped onions in 2 tablespoons of butter with about half a cup of chopped salt pork or bacon bits. When the onions are golden, remove them and the bacon from the pan, and use the butter to brown the filets on both sides. Remove the filets and set them aside, keeping them warm. Add another tablespoon of butter to the pan and when it has melted, sprinkle with 2 tablespoons of flour, and blend it into a smooth mixture (this is called a roux blond). Stirring constantly and gently, mix in the equivalent of two glasses of dry white wine and one glass of water and keep stirring over a medium flame until the mixture thickens. At this point, add salt, pepper and a dash of vinegar to taste. For the "Normandy" touch, add a cup or more of fresh cream and blend. Place the fish, the onions and the bacon in the sauce and heat them all together (without boiling, which can ruin a cream sauce!) for about 10 minutes.

This dish can be attractively presented in the centre of a round serving dish, with a ring of boiled potatoes around it.

SIGHTS

Halles – This reconstruction of a wooden covered market gives place du Maréchal-Foch its distinctive character.

Église Notre-Dame – Once a dependency of Fécamp Abbey, it has a Romanesque doorway with a 19C tympanum. Around the church is a cornice with carved modillions.
Inside, the first six bays (11C) are characteristic of Romanesque style with geometrical decoration and gadrooned capitals. The rest of the building is 12C. Go forward to the transept crossing to admire the 13C lantern turret.

Le Clos Lupin ⊙ – Arsène Lupin is a famous character from French fiction, conjured up by Maurice Leblanc. A dandy and a gentleman burglar, Lupin is easily recognizable by his top hat, monocle and walking stick. The museum intermingles mementoes of the real-life author and his creation.

EXCURSION TO LE HAVRE-ANTIFER PORT AND TERMINAL

15km/9mi to the south. Leave Étretat by D 940; turn right onto D 111, direction "La Poterie, cap d'Antifer".

Bruneval – A German radar installation not far from the beach was the objective of an Allied raid on the night of 27-28 February 1942 when three detachments of British parachutists landed and, after destroying the enemy position, re-embarked almost without loss. The monument, up from the beach, on the left, commemorates the part played by the French Resistance and British Paratroopers.

Between Bruneval and St-Jouin, the winding road passes through picturesque countryside and vegetation of different colours.

The long downhill road leads to the oil terminal.

Le Havre-Antifer Terminal – The Le Havre-Antifer port was created in 1976 to receive oil tankers exceeding the capacity of the facilities at Le Havre. On the way back to St-Jouin, a narrow road on the right (signalled Port du Havre/Antifer/Belvédère), leads to a belvedere with a fine **view** over the beach and the port installations.

"On a sun-drenched beach, when the galloping waves toss the fine shingle, a charming sound rings out, dramatic as the tear of a canvas sail and merry as an elfin peal of laughter, a soft rumbling that echoes all along the coastline, racing against the foamy peaks, resting a while, then resuming its lively, intoxicating dance with the ebbing of the ocean waters. The very name Étretat – spirited and lively yet deep and melodious – seems to have sprung from the sound of pebbles being rolled by the receding waves. And its beach, whose beauty has been immortalised by so many painters, is the embodiment of magic, with its two formidable tears in the cliff face known as the doors."

Guy de Maupassant – Étretat

EU ★

Population 8 344
Michelin map 52 fold or 231 fold 12

Eu, a small town on the River Bresle between the sea and the forest from which it gets its name, lies peacefully grouped round its beautiful collegiate church built in the times when this was a land of princes – from Rollo in the 11C to the last of the powerful dukes of Orléans in the 19C. It was in Eu that the two **Anguier** brothers, **François** (1604-69) and **Michel** (1612-86) were born: these accomplished sculptors, who specialised in the Baroque period, made an invaluable contribution to the building of the Louvre and the Val de Grâce in Paris.

★COLLÉGIALE NOTRE-DAME-ET-ST-LAURENT *30min*

The collegiate church, dedicated to Our Lady and St Lawrence O'Toole, Primate of Ireland who died in Eu in 1180, was erected in the 12C and 13C in the Gothic style. In the 15C the apse was remodelled and in the 19C Viollet-le-Duc undertook a general restoration of the building.

The exterior is marked by the number of pinnacled and turreted buttresses supporting the aisles and east end.

The **interior** is striking for its size and harmonious proportions. The second ambulatory chapel on the right, the Chapel of the Holy Sepulchre, has, beneath a Flamboyant canopy, a 15C **Entombment★**; opposite is a magnificent head of Christ in Sorrow, also 15C. The statue of Our Lady of Eu, attributed to one of the Anguier brothers *(see Chapelle du Collège below)*, is in the apsidal chapel. The north transept chapel contains a lovely statue of the Virgin (16C). A shrine at the back of the chancel contains the remains of St Lawrence.

Crypt ⊙ – The crypt, which is beneath the chancel, was restored in 1828 by the Duke of Orléans who became King Louis-Philippe. He reigned from 1830 to 1848 when he abdicated and fled to England where he died – at Claremont in Surrey – in 1850. In the crypt he placed the effigies of the counts of Eu, House of Artois (14C and 16C), their graves having been desecrated at the time of the Revolution. The 12C-13C recumbent statue against the north wall portraying St Lawrence O'Toole is believed to be one of the oldest in France.

Eating out

MODERATE

Les Bains – *On the beach – 80350 Mers-les-Bains – 6km/3.7mi west of Eu via D 1015 – ☎ 02 35 50 23 50 – closed 15 Sept to 1 May – 15.24/33.54€.* Look around this beach restaurant and you will find souvenirs from the owners' latest journey... desirously hung on the grey wood panels of the dining room decorated like a beach hut. Grilled fish is on the menu.

Where to stay

MODERATE

Manoir de Beaumont Bed and Breakfast – *Rte de Beaumont – 2km/1.2mi east of Eu via D 49 (towards Eu Forest) – ☎ 02 35 50 91 91 – www.chez.com/demarquet – closed Jan and Feb – ⇄ – 3 rooms: 33.54/44.21€.* This former hunting lodge of Eu Castle overlooks the valley. The smart comfortable rooms offer peace and quiet within the park... the house itself is charming and the welcome gets top marks. A really worthwhile address.

M. Lucien's self-catering cottages – *15 r. Octave-Leconte – ☎ 02 35 50 68 64 – ⇄ – 2/4 people, 53.96/59.46€ per night.* Two self-catering units are housed in this splendid presbytery dating from 1726, with its red-brick walls and slate roof so typical of the region, situated at the heart of the royal city of Eu, between sea and forest. Minimal prices.

MID-RANGE

Le Maine – *20 pl. de la Gare – ☎ 02 35 86 16 64 – P – 20 rooms: 41.16/53.36€ – ☕ 6.10€ – restaurant 14.48/32.78€.* This old building was decorated in a rather pleasant old-fashioned style, no doubt to recall bygone days with more conviction. Rooms are small, restful and plainly fitted out whereas the dining room is full of curios, bunches of flowers and old portraits.

ADDITIONAL SIGHTS

Château – Nothing remains of the original castle where **William the Conqueror** married Matilda of Flanders in 1050. It was destroyed in 1475 on the orders of Louis XI. The present château, a huge brick and stone building begun by Henri of Guise and Catherine de Clèves in 1578, has been restored several times since. It passed to the Orléans family and became one of the favourite residences of Louis-Philippe, who received Queen Victoria there twice. Viollet-le-Duc was commissioned to redecorate between 1874 and 1879 for the Count of Paris, grandson of the king.
The château, which now belongs to the town of Eu, is occupied by the town hall and the communal archives, and houses the Louis-Philippe Museum.

Musée Louis-Philippe ⊙ – On the ground floor visitors are shown the grand staircase and the Duchesse d'Orléans' suite, redecorated by Viollet-le-Duc in 1875, as well as the two salons and the bedroom where Queen Victoria and Prince Albert slept in 1843 and 1845, embellished with a superb inlaid parquet floor made under Louis-Philippe.
In the newly restored portico overlooking the garden, note the dazzling **"wall of light"** conceived by Viollet-le-Duc and the master-glazier Oudinot.
On the first floor you can visit the 19C bathroom, the gold bedroom with its pretty green and gilt wainscoting bearing the monogram of the Grande Demoiselle, the Louis-Philippe **dining hall** with its lovely 17C coffered ceiling, the Black Salon, with its strange pink and black colour scheme, and the vast **Galerie des Guise** containing 10 000 volumes, including books from the library of Eu's Jesuit College and those belonging to the last Comte d'Eu.
The south wing of the first floor, which once housed the private suites of Louis-Philippe and Marie-Amélie, is currently being restored to its former glory.

The Park – Most of the trees are beeches, one of which, known as the *Guisard*, was planted in 1585, there are also rhododendrons, azaleas and conifers planted by King Louis-Philippe.

★**Chapelle du Collège** – The college, founded by Henri de Guise in 1582, now bears the name of the 17C Anguier brothers, one-time students of the Jesuit college. The chapel was commissioned in 1624 by Catherine de Clèves, the widow of Henri de Guise, to whom she brought the County of Eu as a dowry in 1570. The Louis XIII **façade**★ is quite remarkable. The beautifully restored brick and stone masonry lends both warmth and harmony to the whole ensemble that captures the visitor's attention as soon as he enters the nave. Although on a smaller scale, this chapel is built according to the same plan as the Gesù Church in Rome. The carved stone font (15C) comes from the former Église de la Trinité.

EU

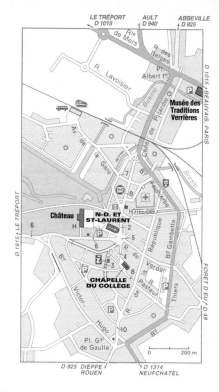

Musée des Traditions verrières ⊘ – The former stables of the Bresle cavalry have been renovated to house the collection of this interesting little museum devoted to glass-making techniques.

► ► **The Forêt d'Eu** covers three isolated massifs with beautiful beech glades: St Martin's Priory Chapel (pretty doorway); **St Catherine's Viewpoint** (over Yères Valley); **La Bonne Entente** (mutual understanding – an oak and a beech growing so close together that they seem to spring from a single bole); **St-Martin-le-Gaillard** (13C church).

ÉVREUX ★★

Population (conurbation) 57 968
Michelin map 55 folds 16 and 17 or 231 fold 35

Évreux, the religious and administrative capital of the Eure, standing on the River Iton which here divides into several arms, is the main agricultural market for the surrounding regions. Industry centres primarily on the manufacturing of electrical equipment and automobile accessories.

When the city centre was rebuilt after 1945, opportunity was taken to provide attractive settings for the last of the town ramparts, the old bishop's palace, the cathedral and the 15C belfry, all of which remained undamaged. Flower gardens have been planted along the banks of the Iton, offering pedestrians a pleasant, serene place to stroll in the heart of the city.

A French City throughout the Wars of History – Évreux's story, like that of many towns in France, is a lengthy chronicle of fire and destruction:

5C – The Vandals sacked Old Évreux, a prosperous market town on the plateau going back to the time of the Gauls.

9C – The Vikings destroyed the fortified town established by the Romans on the present site beside the Iton.

1119 – Henry I, King of England, set fire to the town when fighting the Count of Évreux who was supported by Louis VII.

1193 – King Philippe Auguste, betrayed here by King John of England, fired the city in reprisal.

1356 – Jean the Good, King of France, laid siege to Évreux in his struggle against the House of Navarre, and set fire to the town.

1379 – Charles V besieged the town which suffered cruelly.

June 1940 – Following German air raids the centre of the city burned for nearly a week.

June 1944 – Allied air raids razed the quarter round the station.

A STROLL THROUGH THE STREETS OF EVREUX

3km/2mi – about 1hr 30min (not including the cathedral and the museum). Park at place Clemenceau. The tour begins at place du Général-de-Gaulle.

Place du Général-de-Gaulle – A castle once stood on this square. Today, there is a fountain which represents the River Eure as a woman holding an oar and the city's coat of arms. The children symbolise the two tributaries, the Iton and the Rouloir.

Promenade des remparts – The walk runs beside the River Iton. The section up to rue de Grenoble Bridge is named after Robert de Floques, who liberated the town in 1441; from the bridge to the clock tower it is named after Charles II (King of Navarre and Count of Évreux, 1332-87).

Tour de l'Horloge – The elegant 15C clock tower stands on the site of one of the two towers which flanked the town's main gateway. It is crowned by a spire decorated with lead-covered wooden pinnacles.

Ancien évêché – The former bishop's palace was built in the 15C by the architect Pierre Smoteau on the orders of Bishop Raoul du Fou; its façade looks out onto the cathedral and has a fine Flamboyant air with dormer windows, ornamented window pediments and a staircase tower. The Municipal Museum is inside.

Ancien cloître des Capucins – These old Capuchin cloisters comprise four galleries with timber roofs and monolithic columns; moral texts are inscribed on the walls. In the garth is a flower garden with a central well.

Église St-Taurin – This former abbey church established in 660 and dedicated to the first Bishop of Évreux dates back to the 14C and 15C. A beautiful Romanesque blind arcade runs along the foot of the north aisle to the Renaissance font. The well-proportioned 14C chancel is lit by superb 15C windows. Three windows in the apse trace the life of St Taurinus.

Eating out

MID-RANGE

La Gazette – *7 r. St-Sauveur* – ☎ *02 32 33 43 40* – *closed 8-15 Jan, 31 July to 20 Aug, Sat lunch and Sun* – *16.01/35.83€.* The locals often come here to have a meal in the rather dark yet cosy dining room of this restaurant. One must admit that the young owner does his utmost to prepare dishes adapted to today's taste at very reasonable prices, and it works...

Where to stay

MID-RANGE

Hôtel de l'Orme – *13 r. des Lombards* – ☎ *02 32 39 34 12* – *closed Sat-Sun from 1 Nov to 1 Mar* – *40 rooms: 47.26/59.46€* – ☐ *6.25€.* Situated in the town centre, this convenient and functional hotel is an ideal stopover. Like the façade, the rooms are plain with wicker or veneered furniture...

On the town

Le Grand Café – *11 r. de la Harpe* – ☎ *02 32 33 14 01* – *Mon-Thur 7.30am-9pm, Fri-Sun 7.30am-1am.* Located in a pedestrianised street, on the banks of the canal, the two terraces of this traditional café offer a pleasant view of the cathedral. One concert (rock and pop) per month, on Saturdays.

Le Hasting's – *17 r. de la Harpe* – ☎ *02 32 39 06 22* – *Mon-Sat 11am-1am.* The family atmosphere and discreet music of this bar with its walls covered with coasters attract a great number of locals. The service is rather original too: 150 beers are available in large refrigerators, it's up to you to choose the one(s) you fancy.

Le Matahari – *15 r. de la Petite-Cité* – ☎ *02 32 38 49 88* – *Mon-Sat 11am-1am, Sun 4-9pm.* Decorated with a mixture of objects from Indonesia, works of art and brightly coloured, ill-assorted seats, this café is the most popular in town owing to its original style and festive atmosphere. Large terrace.

Shopping

Chocolatier Auzou – *34 r. Chartraine* – ☎ *02 32 33 28 05* – *Tues-Thur 9am-12.45pm, 1.45-7.30pm, Fri 7.30pm, Sat 8am-7.30pm, Sun and holidays 8.30am-1pm.* Among the delicious regional specialities made in this confectioner's, choose the small almond flavoured cakes known as "Caprices des Ursulines" (the recipe was invented in 1748 by young girls from the Ursuline convent). The "Pavé d'Évreux", a sugared almond, coated with nougatine and chocolate, is another fine speciality of the house.

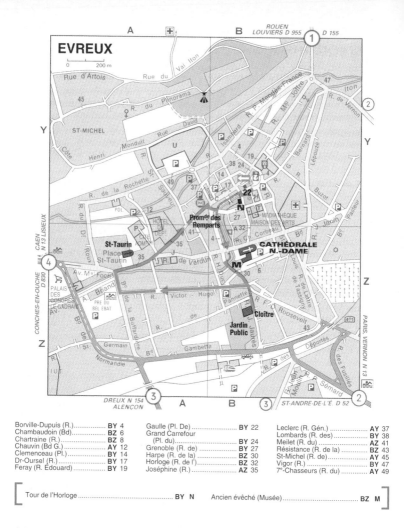

★★**Châsse de St-Taurin** – This masterpiece of 13C French craftsmanship in the north
transept was given to the abbey by St Louis to contain St Taurinus' relics and was
probably made in the abbey workshops. The silver gilt reliquary enriched with
enamel (the best are on the lower
level) is in the form of a miniature
chapel and even shows St Taurinus
with his crosier.

The Châsse de St-Taurin

SIGHTS

★**Cathédrale Notre-Dame** – The
great arches of the nave are the only
extant part of the original church,
which was rebuilt between 1119
and 1193, before being damaged a
second time by fire. The chancel was
built in 1260 and the chapels added
later in the 14C.
Following the fire of 1356 the
church was not repaired for two
centuries; then the lantern tower
and the Lady Chapel were added.
At the beginning of the 16C the
master builder Jean Cossart devised
the magnificent north transept
façade and doorway. The reconstruction was completed by remod-
elling the south tower in the Henri II
style and the termination, in the 17C
only, of the north tower.

It was the upper parts of the cathedral that suffered in the 1940 conflagration: the silver belfry, a lead spire above the transept lantern tower, melted and the west façade towers lost their crowns.

Exterior – *Walk along the north side.* The aisle windows were redesigned in the 16C in the Flamboyant style. The north door is a perfect entity in which all the richness of the Flamboyant, then at its height, can be seen.

Interior – To view the **stained glass★** *(see illustration in the Introduction: Religious architecture)* and the **carved wood screens★** of the ambulatory chapels stand in the transept, between the pillars supporting the graceful lantern tower. The lower part of the lantern tower is ornamented with Flamboyant decoration. The nave – completely restored – still features the original massive Romanesque arches surmounted by an elegant triforium of Gothic bays.

The light chancel is closed by a superb 18C wrought-iron grille and is very beautiful. The apse windows have been declared the most beautiful and the most limpid of the 14C.

Fine wood screens dating from the Renaissance mark the ambulatory entrance in which the first chapel on the right, the **Treasury Chapel** (15C) is quite unique: it is closed off by sturdy wrought-iron bars ending in spikes and hooks, onto which an iron frame has been attached, level with the window. The window hinges have been carefully chiselled. The **screen★** to the fourth chapel is a masterpiece of imagination and craftsmanship, particularly the lower figures; the chapel glass is early 14C.

The central or Lady Chapel, given by Louis XI, has 15C windows of considerable documentary interest. The upper parts, including fleurs-de-lis, depict the peers of France at the king's coronation; the central window has a Tree of Jesse in which the Virgin is surrounded by a crowd of people. Two windows further on is Louis XI himself. On the altar is the venerated statue of Our Lady, said to be late 15C.

The chapels off the ambulatory are also enclosed by screens; the second, of Gothic design, has Renaissance motifs in its lower part.

The third, fourth and sixth chapel screens are the oldest and purely Gothic – note the fantastic animals at the base of the sixth screen.

★★**Museum** ⊙ – On the ground floor of the museum, the first two rooms are devoted to the history and geography of the Eure region and of the town itself (engravings, paintings). Costumes, banners and *torchères* of the Brothers of Charity illustrate popular traditions.

The former chapter-house (Room 3) has a monumental fireplace and contains medieval and Renaissance collections, such as 16C stalls and wooden polychrome statues. Notice the series of 17C Aubusson tapestries on the theme of the Prodigal Son. Room 4 contains medieval exhibits: tomb inscriptions in engraved stone, capitals... The 15C hearth bears the arms of Bishop Pottier de Novion.

In the basement the **Archeological Room★** uses the former Gallo-Roman rampart enhanced by an appropriate lighting arrangement. The collections include domestic and religious objects, statuettes, jewels etc from the Paleolithic (3 000 000-9 000 BC) Age to the Gallo-Roman era (1C-4C AD). Among the finest exhibits are bronzes of Jupiter Stator and Apollo and a late-3C glass goblet.

The first floor contains 17C and 18C paintings as well as various decorative items: furniture, crockery, including apothecary jars in Nevers and Rouen faience from Évreux Hospital. Contemporary art exhibitions and a collection of 19C paintings and objects (Lebourg, Jongkind) take up the second floor; the third floor, with its diagonal vaulting at the top of the stairway, has an exhibition room with a panelled ceiling devoted to 20C art, in particular Abstract painting (Hartung, Soulages).

ÉVRON ★

Population 6 904
Michelin map 60 fold 11 or 232 fold 8

Évron, a small town at the foot of the Coëvrons, possesses one of the finest churches in the Mayenne *département*, visible from a good 10km/6.7mi away. In the 19C the town prospered with its linen mills; today it is classified as a *station verte de vacances* – recognised for the beauty and preservation of the natural surroundings.

★BASILIQUE NOTRE-DAME *30min*

A massive square 11C tower, embellished with corner buttresses and turrets, links the Romanesque part of the nave to the 18C abbey buildings which are a reminder that Évron was the seat of an abbey a very long time ago.

The nave's four original bays are Romanesque, contrasting with the remainder of the basilica which was rebuilt to an enlarged plan in the 14C in the Flamboyant Gothic style. Note the very fine 16C organ case and in the trefoil the fragments of a fresco depicting the Nursing Virgin.

The bare Romanesque nave enhances the sense of space, soaring height, luminosity and contrasts with the Gothic decoration elsewhere (restored 1979). At the transept crossing the pointed arches rest on attractively carved corbels.

Note two polychrome stone statues – a 14C Pietà at the end of the north transept and a Virgin and Child, at the entrance to the ambulatory.

Chancel – Slender columns, pure lines and subtle decoration give the chancel considerable elegance. The overall effect is embellished by five windows with 14C stained glass, which was restored in 1901. During repair work to the chancel paving, a crypt and several sarcophagi were discovered. One of the sarcophagi dates from the 10C.

Bust reliquary of St Leon

★★Chapelle Notre-Dame-de-l'Épine – The 12C Chapel of Our Lady of the Thorn opens off the north side of the ambulatory. Above is plain broken barrel vaulting supported by transverse arches. Christ is shown in a mandorla surrounded by the symbols of the Evangelists. The chapel contains many works of art. Four lovely Aubusson tapestries represent Abraham's Sacrifice of Isaac, Hagar and Ishmael in the desert, Lot and his daughters leaving Sodom and Jacob's Dream. Three 17C terracotta statues depict St Benedict, St Placide and St Maur.

At the altar is a large 13C statue of Our Lady of the Thorn in wood plated with silver and two bust reliquaries of St Hadouin and St Leon. Beneath a remarkable 13C crucifix, a **cabinet** contains two outstanding pieces of metalwork: a delightful 15C silver Virgin and a 16C reliquary.

EXCURSIONS

Le Bois de Mirebeau

35km/22mi – about 1hr 45min. From Évron take D 20 north.

As the road starts to climb there are views to the west over woods and lakes.

Beyond Ste-Gemmes-le-Robert turn right onto the Mont Rochard road which is sometimes in poor repair.

Le Gros Roc – From this rocky escarpment surrounded by vegetation there is an extensive view over the *bocage* countryside.

After skirting Mont Rochard (357m/1171ft), with its television relay station, the road passes through undergrowth, before rejoining D 20 and then begins to descend to Bais.

Turn left onto D 241 just before a bridge.

The itinerary passes the **Château de Montesson**: the entrance pavilion is crowned by an unusual roof. The adjoining round tower has a highly original onion-domed roof. The château and its grounds are encircled by a moat.

In Hambers, opposite the church, turn left onto D 236. After 2.5km/1.3mi turn left again onto the narrow road leading to the Butte de Montaigu.

★Butte de Montaigu – *15min on foot there and back from the car park.* The mound, crowned by an old chapel, is only 290m/925ft high but, because of its isolation, makes an excellent **viewpoint** from which to see the Coëvrons rising to the southeast, Évron, Ste-Suzanne on its rock spike, to the south, Mayenne and its forest, to the northwest and the forests of Andaines and Pail to the north and northeast.

Return to D 236 and continue south through Chellé. At the T-junction turn left onto D 7 at the entrance to Mézangers village; turn right to the Château du Rocher.

★Château du Rocher ⊘ – *30min on foot there and back.* A gallery of five low rounded arches runs the length of the Renaissance façade. From the courtyard entrance one can admire the delicate sculptures adorning the buildings. The more austere 15C façade faces the lake in the park. Its tall windows lighten the granite structure and the three towers capped with pointed roofs make a pleasant ensemble.

Return to D 7 and continue south to return to Évron.

Les Bois des Vallons

36km/22mi – about 1hr. From Évron take D 32 west. On the west side of Brée turn right onto D 557. On approaching St-Ouen-des-Vallons turn right to the Château de la Roche-Pichemer.

Château de la Roche-Pichemer ⊙ – *Enter the park but do not cross the moat.* The château consists of two main Renaissance wings built at right angles and covered with tall slate roofs. Massive square pavilions project from each corner, adding considerable dignity to the building which is preceded by formal gardens.

From St-Ouen-des-Vallons take D 129 and D 24 south via Montsûrs to La Chapelle-Rainsouin.

La Chapelle-Rainsouin – A room off the church chancel contains a beautiful 16C polychrome stone **Entombment★**. The church itself has an unusual rood beam and two tombstones with dogs supporting coats of arms.

Take D 20 northeast. In Châtres-la-Forêt turn right onto D 562. Further on turn right again to the Château de Monteclerc.

Château de Monteclerc – *(Not open to the public)* – *Leave the car at the beginning of the avenue.* The château, built at the very beginning of the 17C, stands in sober dignity at the far end of a vast courtyard. The remaining sides of the court are framed by plain outbuildings and an attractive turret. However, the château's most eye-catching building is the drawbridge lodge with a rounded roof crowned by a lantern turret.

Return to Châtres-la-Forêt; turn right onto D 20 to return to Évron.

FALAISE★

Population 8 119
Michelin map 55 fold 12 or 231 fold 30

The small town of Falaise is the proud birthplace of **William the Conqueror**. Falaise suffered cruelly in the war during the fighting that took place in the Falaise-Chambois pocket in August 1944 during the Battle of Normandy.

The town's setting in the Ante Valley, a ravine marked by scattered rock spurs, is quite rugged and made even more medieval by being dominated by the enormous fortress (one of Normandy's first stone castles) haunted by the memory of Arlette and her victorious son William.

It is a friendly and lively centre for excursions into Suisse Normande.

The marked itinerary "Le Dénouement" (The Outcome), one of several described in the Historical Area of the Battle of Normandy, goes through this town.

Beautiful Arlette

One evening in 1027, on returning from the hunt, Robert (later known as "The Magnificent"), younger son of King Richard II, Duke of Normandy, was struck by the beauty of a local girl, her skirts drawn high as she worked with her companions washing clothes at the stream. A lad of 17, he watched for her daily and desired her. Arlette's father, a rich tanner, let her decide for herself and she, refusing all secrecy, entered the castle over the drawbridge on horseback, finely apparelled.

Then, as the chroniclers of the time wrote, "When Nature had reached her term, Arlette bore a son who was named William."

THE STREETS OF FALAISE

A peaceful stroll through this small town provides the chance to admire its 17C-18C residences, the fountains and doorways of yesteryear.

★**Église de la Trinité** – The west front of the church features a triangular Gothic porch. On the south side note the gargoyles and small carved figures. At the east end the Renaissance flying buttresses are highly ornate.

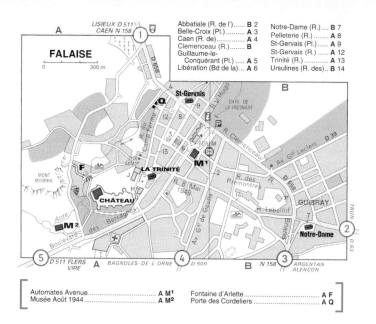

Fontaine d'Arlette – The fountain in the Ante Valley stands quite close to a public swimming pool. A high relief (1957) recalls the meeting of Robert and Arlette. From this spot there is an impressive view of the castle towering above.

Église St-Gervais – The building of the church went on from the 11C to the 16C; the lantern tower is 12C. Inside, the contrast between the two architectural styles is striking: the south side is Romanesque, the north Gothic. The capitals are carved with military subjects, monstrous animals and hunting scenes. The modern stained-glass windows are by Le Chevallier.

Porte des Cordeliers – This lovely stone gateway was part of the town wall. It is flanked by a round tower and has a pointed arched 14C-15C porch.

★CHÂTEAU GUILLAUME-LE-CONQUÉRANT ⊙

This medieval ensemble (12C-13C) characteristic of defensive Anglo-Norman archi-tecture, has been heavily restored: the two keeps now feature their original size and roofing, whereas the stronghold has been preceded by an amazing concrete gatehouse. It was within the castle walls that William the Bastard, Duke of Normandy, was born in 1027. It was also in this castle on 8 July 1199 that John Lackland, King of England, and Duke of Aquitaine signed a charter founding the Jurade de St-Émilion, a body responsible for controlling the quality of the famous St-Émilion wines.

Inner courtyard – Visitors walking through the Porte St-Nicolas enter a large area of about 1ha/2.5 acres, defined by 15 towers. Plans have been made to liven up this part of the castle, which was once bustling with activity.

Main keep – This rectangular structure built as late as the 12C is surprisingly large; the great flat buttresses, which mark the line of the walls, still convey an impression of impregnability. The huge *aula* on the second floor was the main reception room. Its ambitious restoration involved the latest and most sophisticated techniques: the flooring is made of alternating squares of glass and lead, while the ceiling consists of a Teflon covering stretched over an iron frame. Note the Chapelle St-Prix, a small oratory attended by the lords of the castle.

Small keep – This luminous, well-balanced construction commissioned by Henri I Plantagenet in the late 12C was designed for a special purpose: to guard the main keep from attack from the rock platform and provide more comfort for the Duke. The loopholes under the elegant windows have been adapted for gun fire.

Tour "Talbot" – This impressive round tower, 35m/115ft tall with walls 4m/12ft thick, was allegedly named after John Talbot, governor of the castle in 1449, who undertook to restore it. It is linked to the smaller keep by means of a curtain wall. An incredibly deep well (65m/197ft) carved out of the wall ensures that water is distributed to all floors of the castle.
The rock platform commands a lovely **view** of the surrounding countryside.

Eating out

MODERATE

L'Attache – *Rte de Caen – 1.5Km/0.9mi north of Falaise –* ☎ *02 31 90 05 38 – closed 20-30 Apr, 1-15 Sept and Wed – reservation advisable – 14.48/ 50.31€.* You'll find this restaurant quite interesting: the owner is very keen on wild herbs and he will impart his enthusiasm to you through his carefully prepared recipes based on local produce. Discretion is the keynote in the dining room of this former coaching inn.

Where to stay

MODERATE

Le Chêne Sec Bed and Breakfast – *14700 Pertheville-Ners – 9km/5.6mi east of Falaise via D 63 towards Trun then a minor road –* ☎ *02 31 90 17 55 – closed in winter –* ✏ *– 3 rooms: 30.49/44.21€.* Peace and character are the main features of this 15C manor house situated in a hamlet. Ask for the two upstairs rooms reached by a spiral staircase; exposed beams, stone walls and country furniture. Don't forget to look at the small 11C house in the grounds.

Showtime

Théâtre du Forum – *Bd de la Libération –* ☎ *02 31 41 61 51 – opening times follow the calendar of performances – closed June-Sept.* Spacious hall, adaptable according to the different performances and the size of the audience. The eclectic programming includes well-known artists and local theatre companies.

Musée Août-1944 (Battle of the Falaise Pocket) ⊙ – Housed in a former cheese factory, this private collection displays heavy English, American and German war equipment. Several realistic scenes, enhanced by thoroughly kitted out dummies, depict the various spots where the fierce fighting of the Falaise pocket took place.

Automates Avenue ⊙ – Manufacturers of automatons for more than 100 years, the Decamps company traditionally decorated the windows of Parisian department stores with animated scenes during the Christmas festive period; this went on until the 1950s to the delight of the population. The museum presents a collection of more than 300 of these automatons still in working order. Some of the shop window displays can be seen functioning just as they did in the past.

Église Notre-Dame-de-Guibray – The church, which was already under construction in the days of William the Conqueror, has survived better than the horse fair of the same name *(see inset)*. Although the interior has been remodelled, the apse and the apsidal chapels are still pure Romanesque. The magnificent organ is by Parizot (1746).

EXCURSIONS

Versainville – *2.5km/1mi north of Falaise by rue Victor-Hugo. After crossing the bridge over the Ante turn right onto the path to Versainville.*
The château *(not open to the public)* was completed in the 18C; it features a central wing with a peristyle, linked by a gallery to a huge pavilion forming the left wing.

Noron-l'Abbaye – *4km/2.5mi west of Falaise by* ⑤ *along D 511. Then turn right onto D 243.*
This village has a 13C church with a charming two-storey Romanesque belfry.

Guibray Fair

For nine centuries the suburb of Guibray to the southeast of Falaise was famous for its fair. Already in the 11C the horse fair was attended by thousands from all over Europe, and was the occasion for much popular merry-making. The streets, vennels and alleys of Falaise with their many inns and taverns, were alive with minstrels and dancers. Since the 19C increasing mechanisation has reduced the horse to a minor role and caused the decline of the fair which is now little more than a memory.

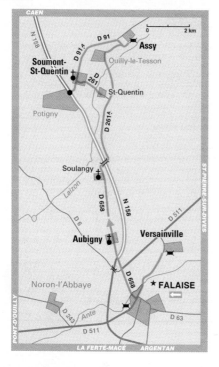

Vallée du Laizon

Round tour of 26km/16mi – about 1hr. Leave Falaise on D 658, north of town.

Aubigny – At the entrance to the village, on the left, stands a late-16C château and its outbuildings.

The parish **church** contains statues of six consecutive lords of Aubigny, kneeling in the chancel, which provide interesting details of contemporary dress. As you continue, notice the tall 13C belfry of **Soulangy** to the left.

Turn right onto D 261. In Ouilly-le-Tesson turn right. At the next junction turn right again.

Assy – A magnificent avenue (left) leads to the Château d'Assy, a handsome 18C mansion, considerably enhanced by an elegant Corinthian portico; the attractive chapel dates from the 15C.

Return to the junction and turn right; turn left onto D 91.

Soumont-St-Quentin – The church dates from the 13C and 14C. The belfry is Romanesque below and Gothic above.

Return to Falaise by N 158.

FÉCAMP★★

Population 20 808
Michelin map 54 fold 8 or 231 fold 8
Local map see Pays de CAUX

Fécamp is known today as a fishing port – it is France's most important port for cod, landed from the boats which sail regularly to the Newfoundland banks. The town is also famous as the home of Benedictine liqueur – a link with its monastic past. Three interesting museums and a lovely pebble beach are other attributes which make the town well worth a visit. **Guy de Maupassant** was one frequent visitor to the town, which features in several of his works.

The "Gate of Heaven" – As early as the 7C there was a monastery in Fécamp to house the relic of the Precious Blood, miraculously directed to the town with the fig tree which Isaac, nephew of Joseph of Arimathea, had "entrusted to the sea and the grace of God".

Not content with rebuilding a fine church to the Holy Trinity, Richard II's father made his son promise to found a Benedictine abbey. While in Burgundy, Richard was greatly impressed by the Cluniac reforms which had already been instituted in several communities by **Guglielmo da Volpiano**, the Abbot of St Benignus in Dijon. In 1003 Richard asked Volpiano to establish a community in Fécamp. The new abbey acquired considerable importance and its influence extended throughout the dukedom. Before the rise of Mont-St-Michel, Fécamp was the foremost place of pilgrimage in Normandy, where the dukes traditionally celebrated Easter. During the 11C the troubadours and minstrels, who were under the protection of the local abbots, helped to spread the renown of the Precious Blood and of Holy Trinity Church. In the opinion of the Bishop of Dol the monastery was "worthy of being compared with a heavenly Jerusalem. It was called the Gate of Heaven, the Palace of Our Lord. Silver and gold and silken ornament gleamed on every hand".

Port – The Freycinet port is mostly used for commercial shipping. Quai de Verdun is a dock for ships loaded with gravel, sand for use in glass-making, salt from the Midi region and timber.

Deep-sea Fishing, an Old Tradition

As the Latin origin of its name suggests (*Fiscannum* or *Fisci campus*), Fécamp has always had strong links with the sea and fishing; as early as the Middle Ages, the herrings of "Fescan" were known throughout the kingdom and during the Renaissance the first ships fitted out in Fécamp sailed to Newfoundland to fish for cod.

For nearly 400 years, fishing techniques did not alter a great deal: the fish was caught with a ground line by two men aboard a 5-6yd long flat-bottomed boat called a *doris*; sometimes the fog was so thick that the men got lost and never got back to their schooner... The fish was then gutted, cleaned, boned, salted and stored in the hold; this was called fishing for "green" cod by contrast to fishing for "dried" cod which implied that the fishermen had to settle during the season along the coast of Newfoundland, build huts for themselves and drying racks for their catch.

At the turn of the century, more than 2 500 fishermen from Fécamp braved the cold weather, the fog and the storms from the end of February to the end of July.

During the 1970s, 15 huge trawlers with a crew of 900 men salted and froze 21 000t of cod in the icy waters of the North Atlantic.

Today, pleasure boats have replaced the trawlers, but, some while back, one could still meet a few old fishermen recalling their memories at the 'Bout Menteux' (situated between quai de la Vicomté and quai de Bérigny).

SIGHTS

🔳 *Four walking tours have been set up to guide visitors around the town and through its history. Detailed maps are available at the tourist offices.*

★**Abbatiale de la Trinité** – The abbey church built by Richard II was struck by lightning and burned down. The subsequent building (12C-13C) was modified several times between the 15C and 18C. The town hall now occupies the old monastic buildings abutting the north wall which date from the later period. Pilgrims in great numbers come to venerate the relic of the Precious Blood on the Tuesday and Thursday after Trinity.

Exterior – The cathedral is one of the longest (127m/416ft) in France. The Classical façade does not accord with the rest of the building and the nave walls are austere. Skirt the south porch: the tympanum above the door is a good example of Norman Gothic decoration.

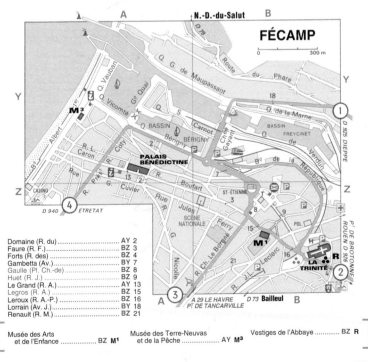

Domaine (R. du)	AY 2
Faure (R. F.)	BZ 3
Forts (R. des)	BZ 4
Gambetta (Av.)	BY 7
Gaulle (Pl. Ch.-de)	BZ 8
Huet (R. J.)	BZ 9
Le Grand (R. A.)	AY 13
Legros (R. A.)	BZ 15
Leroux (R. A.-P.)	BZ 16
Lorrain (Av. J.)	BY 18
Renault (R. M.)	BZ 21

Musée des Arts et de l'Enfance	BZ **M¹**	
Musée des Terre-Neuvas et de la Pêche	AY **M³**	
Vestiges de l'Abbaye	BZ **R**	

Above the transept crossing rises the square lantern tower (65m/210ft high), designed in the typical Norman style.

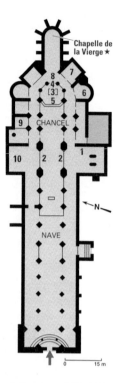

Chapelle de la Vierge ★

CHANCEL

NAVE

0   15 m

Interior – The majestically proportioned nave with scarce ornamentation ends at the transept where the lantern tower rises in a sweep to 40m/125ft.

The south transept contains a beautiful late-15C **Dormition of the Virgin★** (**1**). Two groups of figures, taken from the former rood screen, frame the altar. On the right of the altar is the Angel's Footprint. In 943, when the reconstructed church was being consecrated before William Longsword, an angel pilgrim appeared before the bishops deliberating on the church's patronage and commanded them to dedicate the sanctuary to the Holy and Undivided Trinity. Before disappearing in a blaze of light, the angel left his footprint on the stone for all to see for ever.

The chancel's dimensions make it magnificent. The stalls (**2**), baldaquin and high altar (**3**) are all good 18C works by the Rouen artist, De France. A Renaissance altar (**4**), commissioned by Abbot Antoine Bohier from Girolamo Viscardo, stands behind the high altar. In the centre of the sanctuary is an ancient shrine (**5**) adorned with low-relief sculptures dating from the 12C.

The chapels off the chancel aisles and radiating chapels were embellished with wonderful **carved screens★** in the 16C. In the fourth chapel, on the right, is the **tomb★** (**6**) of Abbot Thomas of St-Benoît who died in 1307; the tomb is decorated with scenes from the abbey's history on its base. The radiating chapel (**7**) contains abbots' tombs.

The **Lady Chapel★**, rebuilt in the 15C on a crypt of the same dimensions, forms a separate group in the Flamboyant style. The wood medallions are 18C; the windows are 13C, 14C and 16C. Facing the chapel is the white marble **tabernacle★** of the Precious Blood (**8**) by Viscardo.

The following two radiating chapels are the only remains of the earlier Romanesque church destroyed by lightning.

The 17C tomb (**9**) in the chapel of the Sacred Heart belongs to **Guglielmo da Volpiano**, first abbot of Fécamp, who returned to die in 1031 in the abbey he had founded.

The north transept contains fragments of the former rood screen (**10**).

Abbey Ruins – *23 rue des Forts.* From the courtyard of the old choir school there is a view of the chevet of Holy Trinity Church.

Musée des Arts et de l'Enfance ⊙ – The museum is in an 18C residence. On the ground floor, to the right, there is a display of faience from Rouen, Delft, Quimper and Nevers . A portrait of Dr. Léon Dufour (1856-1928) is a homage to the founder of an association *(la Goutte de lait)* organised to reduce infant mortality rates. The collection of baby bottles, from ancient times to the present, is another reminder of the museum's theme. Other rooms on the ground floor are devoted to Chinese and Japanese porcelain, a collection of 18C watch cocks and a late-17C Neapolitan terracotta **nativity scene**. At the foot of the stairs stands a beautiful 16C painted stone statue of St Barbe. Upstairs, displays include religious items, furniture, ivories, and 19C landscape paintings. Most of the artists spent time on the coast of Normandy and chose subjects there (Courant, Colin, Gabriel, Dubourg). On the second floor, there is a collection of arms from the 18-19C. On the attic floor, there is a reconstitution of a home in the Caux countryside illustrating daily life in the past (regional furnishings from the 16C-19C).

In the wooded park, there is a monument to the memory of sailors lost at sea.

★★Palais Bénédictine ⊙ – In 1510 a Venitian monk, Bernardo Vincelli, conceived the idea of distilling a mixture of regional plants, and spices. From the resulting elixir, a merchant in Fécamp, Alexandre le Grand, made the famous liqueur *Bénédictine* in 1863. The building, designed by Camille Albert in the late 19C, is a mixture of neo-Gothic and neo-Renaissance styles.

The **museum** displays a large collection of objets d'art: silver and gold work, ivories, Nottingham alabasters (late 15C), wrought-iron work, statues and many manuscripts. The Gothic Room is covered by a fine pitched roof made of oak and chestnut, shaped as the upturned hull of a ship; it houses the library, where most of the exhibits were taken from the former abbey church in Fécamp: 15C Books of the Hours with fine **illuminations**, numerous **ivories**, a collection of **oil lamps** dating from the early days of Christianity and a Dormition of the Virgin, a painted low-relief wooden carving of the German School. The Dome Room displays a set of four 15C painted wooden panels depicting the martyrdom of St Margaret. The Renaissance Room contains an important collection of locks and keys as well as wooden coffers, of which the oldest is from Nuremberg and dates from the late 16C. One room is more specifically devoted to painting (14C-18C) from many different countries: Germany, Flanders, Italy... The Cardinals Room houses a four-poster bed dating from 1587 and, as its name suggests, mementoes of the various cardinals and abbots of Fécamp.

The Alexander the Great Room displays objects and documents relating to the history of the liqueur and the chief ideas which guided its creator: advertising posters by Mucha, Cappiello, Sem and Lopes Silva. A pyramid of more than 500 bottles shows the numerous counterfeits and imitations inspired by the famous Bénédictine bottle.

In the Plant Room some of the 27 plants and spices used in the distillation of Bénédictine are on show in bundles or growing in pots.

The tour continues in the laboratory, where the alcohol and plants are converted in copper stills, and in the cellars where the spirit ages in oak vats.

The visit ends with the Gallery of Contemporary Art (Espace Contemporain) which holds annual exhibitions promoting the work of gifted artists.

★**Musée des Terre-Neuvas et de la Pêche** ⊘ – The Newfoundland and Fishing Museum, which is devoted to the conservation of a proud maritime past, recalls the days when Fécamp was great and evokes memories of fishing and its associated activities in the Caux country, inland from Fécamp.

It consists of two superimposed galleries overlooking a pebble bank supporting a wrecked fishing smack, *Notre-Dame-de-Bon-Secours*, built in Fécamp in 1948 in the Viking manner known as clinker-built. Deep-sea fishing which began early in the 16C is illustrated by reproductions of graffiti and drawings of prow and poop. The lower gallery explores the development of the great adventure of the cod fishermen on the Newfoundland banks in the days of the sailing ship and the dory, a flat-bottomed craft rising at bow and stern. The showcases display models of three-masted ships, the implements used by the fishermen and various objects recalling the hard life on board. Fine collection of votive offerings and seascapes. One room is devoted to ship-building with an authentic model of the construction of the *Belle Poule*, the naval training ship built in Fécamp in 1931 and a reconstruction of a sail loft. There is a section on Yport.

The first floor is devoted to drift netting for herring. There is a section on gathering shellfish at low tide (surprising pair of galoshes with huge nails in the soles). The exhibits trace the development of fishing methods and types of craft from fishing and salting equipment to navigation equipment, from herring boats to the large modern trawlers with stern ramps such as the *Marie de Grâce*. One room is entirely devoted to the history of Fécamp port (interesting relief plan of the port in 1830).

The outdoor terrace provides a magnificent **view★** of the sea and the long pebble beach backed by cliffs. The last section of the museum is devoted to sea rescue.

Eating out

MODERATE

Le Maritime – *2 pl. Nicolas-Selle* – ☎ *02 35 28 21 71 – reservation advisable – 14.48/32.01€.* You get a strong whiff of the sea air when you enter this restaurant situated in the marina: navigational instruments and wood panelling create the maritime atmosphere. Seafood, of course, is on the menu, but also meat dishes for hungry pirates!

La Plaisance – *33 quai de la Vicomté* – ☎ *02 35 29 38 14 – closed Feb school holidays, evenings during the week from Dec to Apr, Tues evening and Wed from May to Nov – 12.96/31.25€.* This harbour restaurant is rather pleasant with its maritime decor and terrace set well off the road. The menu tries to match the setting by favouring fish and seafood.

Where to stay

MID-RANGE

Hôtel de la Plage – *87 r. de la Plage* – ☎ *02 35 29 76 51 – 24 rooms: 47.26/60.98€* – ☕ *5.34€.* Situated not far from the waterfront, this simple family hotel is an unpretentious stopover. The rooms are neat and the breakfast room rather picturesque with its bar shaped like a ship's hull and its maritime decor...

EXCURSIONS

Château de Bailleul – *10km/6mi southeast by D 73*. This elegant château *(not open to the public)* was built in the mid 16C by Bertrand de Bailleul. It consists of a central square building flanked by four pavilions. The figures on the latter represent the four cardinal virtues: Justice, Prudence, Fortitude and Temperance. The main façade is articulated by the three Greek orders: Doric on the ground floor, Ionic on the first floor, Corinthian on the second floor. The medieval side façades are almost blind. A chapel stands in the well-established wooded park.

Valmont – *11km/7mi east via D 150*. Located in the very heart of the Pays de Caux and dominated by a castle built on a rocky spur, the village of Valmont possesses the ruins of a Benedictine abbey.
The town grew in importance with the arrival of the Estouteville family, probably of Viking origin and very successful in the 12C. Robert I d'Estouteville took part in the Battle of Hastings in 1066 beside William the Conqueror.

★**Abbey** ⊘ – Founded in the 12C, the Benedictine abbey of Valmont was rebuilt in the 14C following a fire and was radically altered in the 16C. The conventual buildings (1680) were rebuilt by the Maurists (a congregation of Benedictine monks). After the Revolution the abbey became a private residence and in the 19C it belonged to cousins of Delacroix – the artist visited here several times. Of the old abbey church, only the Renaissance choir remains and its roof has fallen in. The Flamboyant influence dominates in the aisles and the remains of the transept.
The **Chapelle de la Vierge★**, or Six o'Clock Chapel (the monks celebrated mass every day at this time), which has remained intact among the ruins, has an overall effect of great grace. The highly decorated arches are very delicate. The five 15C windows are devoted to the life of the Virgin Mary. Above the altar is a tiny room which has exquisite decorations and also a picture of the Annunciation attributed to Germain Pilon.
Notice on the right the tomb and recumbent figure of Nicolas d'Estouteville, founder of the abbey, and a low relief depicting the Baptism of Christ.
The altar is made of one large stone resting on columns from the triforium which was partly destroyed. The 12C altar cross dominated the former monks' cemetery. To the right, a high relief over a fountain portrays the Baptism of Christ in Jordan. Recently restored, the Renaissance sacristy has windows of the period and 18C panelling.

Château ⊘ – Property of the Estoutevilles, lords of Valmont, this former military fortress preserves a Romanesque keep flanked by a Louis XI wing, crowned by a covered watch-path, and a Renaissance wing. *The château and its grounds are closed to the public.*

Dormition of the Virgin

E. Baret/MICHELIN

FLERS

Population 17 888
Michelin map 60 fold 1 or 231 fold 41

Flers has managed both to modernise itself and remain true to the Normandy *bocage* industrial tradition.

Linen and hemp-making flourished until the Revolution and were finally superseded by cotton manufacturing in the 19C. The clothing industry then grew up alongside the cotton mills. The industrial sector of Flers has been diversified and bolstered by the introduction of two new industries: mechanical engineering and electrical appliances. The original fortress was the seat of the barons of Aunou, the lords of Flers. Foulque d'Aunou was one of William the Conqueror's companions and he equipped 40 ships to take part in the conquest of England. During the Revolution, the castle was a rallying point for the Chouans, the Republicans recaptured it in January 1800.

CASTLE

Musée du Château ⓥ – The present castle, with a moat on three sides, has a 16C main building by the alchemist, **Nicolas Grosparmy**, lord of Flers from 1527 to 1541, with an 18C Classical main front. The building now houses the museum and the town hall.

In the basement lies the former castle kitchen. Two adjoining rooms assemble exhibits relating to weaving: looms, spinning wheels and hemp combs.

On the ground floor, the Countess' salon still features its original panelling. The registry office (Salle des Mariages) and the council chamber are hung with several fine canvases including the works of the artist **Charles Léandre**. The first floor rooms contain the painting and decorative art sections. In the gallery devoted to the regional schools of the 19C there are works from the Barbizon School by Corot and Daubigny, pre-Impressionists such as Boudin and Lépine and Impressionists (Caillebotte). The modern art gallery contains ceramics by Jean Cocteau: some are originals while others are copies after cartoons.

Musée de la Blanchardière ⓥ – This museum is devoted to around 40 crafts of bygone days (baker, sabot-maker, cartwright, weaver...) with the help of thousands of everyday tools and objects.

Eating out

MID-RANGE

Au Bout de la Rue – *60 r. de la Gare – ☎ 02 33 65 31 53 – closed Sun and holidays – 16.46/20.58€.* This place is a genuine local bistro with its red walls, decorated with old posters and black-and-white photographs, which contribute to the charming and convivial atmosphere. You can enjoy more privacy in the separate cubicles. Several menus including one for children.

MODERATE

Auberge Le Relais Fleuri – *115 r. Schnetz – ☎ 02 33 65 23 89 – closed 7-17 Jan, 31 July to 14 Aug, Sun evening and Mon – 14.94/29.73€.* The rustic decor (exposed beams and stonework) creates a cosy atmosphere appreciated by regular guests. If you wish to have peace and quiet during your meal, ask for a table in one of the small rooms.

Auberge de la Mine – *Le Gué-Plat along the road to Dompierre: 2km/1.2mi – 61450 La Ferrière-aux-Étangs – 10km/6.2mi from Flers via D 18 – ☎ 02 33 66 91 10 – closed 2-15 Jan, 16-31 Aug, Tues except lunch from May to Aug and Wed – 16.01/38.11€.* This entirely renovated restaurant was once the canteen of an old iron mine. A place to remember for its warm welcome and its carefully prepared cuisine based on fresh produce. Very good value for money.

Where to stay

MODERATE

Galion Hotel – *5 r. Victor-Hugo – ☎ 02 33 64 47 47 – P – 30 rooms: 36.59/42.69€ – ☕ 5.34€.* Situated in a peaceful district, close to the town centre, this small hotel is a recent construction. From here you can walk to the foot of the castle for a visit or a stroll in the park. Rooms are traditional. There is a buffet breakfast.

A TOUR AROUND MONT DE CERISY

Round tour of 24km/15mi – 3hr. Take D 924 west.

La Lande-Patry – Two giant yews grow in the old cemetery.

Continue west on D 924.

Tinchebray – On 28 September 1106 a battle took place in the vicinity of this market town in the heart of the Norman *bocage* between two of William the Conqueror's sons. As a result the elder son, Robert Curthose, Duke of Normandy, was forced to cede the Duchy of Normandy to Henry Beuclerk, then Henry I of England.

Tinchebray specialises in ironmongery, wrought iron and chocolate manufacture. The fortified belfry of the old 12C church of St-Rémy and the royal prison recall the town's past.

The **Prison royale** *(rue de la Prison)* houses an Ethnographic Museum. Shoemaker's and other tools are displayed in two of the ground floor cells. A Norman interior has been reconstructed and furnished as a kitchen. The exhibits of headdresses, bonnets and shirt fronts demonstrates detailed and patient work. The revolutionary tribunal was set up on the first floor. Two cells have fireplaces as some prisoners could pay for coal. The thick walls and wooden doors with impressive locks bear many graffiti, the oldest of which dates from 1793. The chapel contains religious objects and statues from Montiers Church, which was built in the 17C on the site of a leper house.

From Tinchebray take D 911 northeast. In St-Pierre-d'Entremont turn right onto D 18. Before crossing the River Noireau turn right onto a narrow road along the river bank.

Les Vaux – After passing between Mont de Cerisy *(left)* and St-Pierre Rocks *(right)*, the road ends in the old hamlet of St-Pierre where a small Roman bridge spans the river.

Continue southeast on D 18 to Cerisy-Belle-Étoile.

★**Mont de Cerisy** ⊙ – A road *(public right of entry)* bordered by rhododendrons *(in flower May to June)*, climbs up the slope to the ruined castle which commands extensive **views**★ over the countryside *(bocage)* even to the foothills of the Suisse Normande. The plateau and its immediate surroundings is the venue for the Rhododendron Festival *(last Sunday in May)*.

Continue on D 18 to return to Flers.

The most important sights in this guide can be found on the Principal Sights map, and are described in the text. Use the map and plans, the Calendar of events, the index, and read the Introduction to get the most out of this guide.

Château de FONTAINE-HENRY ★★

Michelin map 54 fold 15 or 231 folds 17 and 18

TOUR ⊙

This beautiful building is a fine example of Renaissance architecture. A member of the Harcourt family built it in the 15C and 16C over the dungeons, cellars and foundations of the original 11C-12C fortress.

An immense steeply sloping slate roof, taller than the building itself, covers the 16C pavilion on the left. It is quartered by a polygonal tower with a slender conical roof and a smaller attractively decorated turret. The main building to the right of the pavilion stands on the site of the earlier fortress. This part is a wonder of delicately worked stonework: lace-like balustrades; finely patterned friezes, triple mouldings and ogee arches to the windows, and crocketed finials in abundance. Inside there is a similar richness of stonework and the François I **staircase** catches the attention.

Furnished throughout, the château has some fine paintings by Correggio, Mignard, Rigaud and Hubert Robert and displays many mementoes of former owners. The chapel was built by Henry de Tilly. The nave was altered in the 16C.

The small village is pleasantly situated in the Mue Valley not far from the Côte de Nacre and the D-Day beaches. In the 14C the village took the name of its former overlord, Henry de Tilly, who died in 1305.

Église – The church has a 13C chancel with some fine arcading.

The château

EXCURSION

▸ *The lane (15min on foot there and back) branches off D 170 on a corner, about 500m/550yd from Thaon Parish Church. This downhill path will take you to the bottom of the valley; ask at the house for permission to visit the church.*

★**Ancienne église de Thaon** – This small 12C Romanesque church *(deconsecrated – closed to the public)* is enhanced by its attractive setting in an isolated valley. Blind arcades decorated the flat east end and a modillioned cornice runs right round the building. The belfry, one of the most original in Normandy, is capped by a pyramid roof and deeply recessed twin bays. The interior has great purity of style. Although the arcades dividing the nave from the aisles have been bricked up, the decoration on the capitals is visible; the chancel is decorated with blind arcades.

FORGES-LES-EAUX

Population 3 600
Michelin map 52 fold 16 or 231 fold 24

Located in the green heart of the Pays de Bray, Forges-les-Eaux is a spa resort and source of iron-rich waters reputed to be clear, refreshing and stimulating. An amusing legend has it that, during a gathering of fairies, a certain Uger (a handsome local lad) was given the gift of a magical bottle of cider in exchange for a turn on the dance floor. The bottle, his enchanted partner told him, would never be empty so long as he kept the fairies' secret safe. Uger couldn't resist sharing with his friends, and the secret got out, whereupon the bottle dried up. Now in Forges, they drink the water.

SIGHTS

Musée de la Faïence de Forges ⊙ – Until the 19C, Forges manufactured good quality earthenware and it is possible to see the collection of a hundred or so plates and dishes displayed in the main reception hall at the town hall. The typically green and blue motifs were inspired by the army of the First Empire, or used naive representations of quaint cottages, flowers, animals and peasantry.

The spa – Rue de la République boasts some half-timbered façades (17C-18C), and leads into avenue des Sources, where it passes under the old railway line (now a footpath).

The resort grounds and Casino are to the left, just after the bridge. The façade of the building facing the park comes from a Louis XV hunting lodge which once stood near Versailles.

The park and spa are managed by the Club Med, in a modern and elegant setting with all the typical resort attractions. Louis XIII, his queen and Cardinal Richelieu took the waters here.

Parc Montalent and Épinay forest – On the other side of avenue des Sources, four pleasant and well-marked **nature trails** wind among the ponds and into the woods.

EXCURSIONS

Ferme de Bray

Leave Forges via D 915 northwest, after 8km/5mi, turn left before Sommery and follow the signs.

On the banks of the Sorson, this charming, restored site shows what a prosperous farm establishment in the 17C-18C was like. Visitors may see the bread oven, the cider press and the mill in use. There are regular exhibits in the main house, a spacious 16C building whose façade was redone in the 17C.

Southern Pays de Bray

52km/31mi. Leave Forges-les-Eaux via D 921 south.

The Pays de Bray is a lush strip at the centre of the vast bare stretches of the Caux plateau. It owes its chief characteristic, known as the Bray "Buttonhole", to a geological accident, which created a hollow in the surrounding chalk. The landscape is more clearly defined than anywhere else in Normandy. Running parallel to the valley of the River Seine, the region is a sparsely inhabited patchwork of vales, limestone bluffs, hills, meadows and forests.

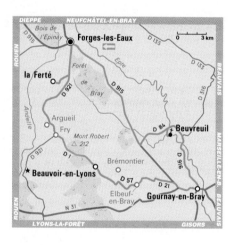

La Ferté – The village is perched just before the main edge of the Bray "Buttonhole" *(see above)* which the Andelle and its affluents have cut up into regularly shaped mounds. From the approach to the church there is an extended view of the Pays de Bray depression with its clearly defined rim. In the main square is the gracious 16C **Henri IV's house** (Maison d'Henri IV) transported in 1968 from the region of Dieppe and rebuilt.

In Fry, before the church, turn left onto D 1.

The road runs along the southwest Bray escarpment of massive bare mounds crowned with beech trees (Mont Robert).

★Beauvoir-en-Lyons – *Park beyond the town hall; walk up the street on the left to the church.*

From the east end there is a **view★** of the green Bray Valley cutting away in a straight line southeast. In clear weather Beauvais Cathedral is visible.

Return to the car and continue southeast on D 1. At a crossroads, turn left downhill onto D 57. Then follow D 21.

★Gournay-en-Bray – Gournay and Ferrières are the busiest towns in the Pays de Bray. The local dairy industry supplies most of the fresh cheese consumed in France. In 1850 a local farmer's wife, helped by a Swiss cowherd, had the idea of mixing fresh cream with curds before these had been broken. The *petit-suisse* met with instant success.

Église St-Hildevert – The church, which is largely 12C, has withstood several wars but the late-12C doors have suffered from excessive restoration.

Inside, the massive columns are surmounted by capitals interestingly carved with animal and plant motifs. The oldest and most worn, at the end of the south aisle, are among the earliest examples of attempts at human portrayal and date from the Romanesque period. In the side aisles the polychrome wooden statues of the Virgin and St Hildevert are 15C.

Take D 916 north.

Beuvreuil – The wooden porch of the small 11C country **church** is decorated with enamelled bricks. Inside the church note the 11C font stoup, a 15C holy-water stoup, the Gothic statues, the 15C altarpiece and a 16C lectern.

Take D 84 west; turn right onto D 915 to Forges.

Vallée de l'Andelle

56km/34mi – about 2hr 30min. From Forges take D 919 and D 13 southwest.

Sigy-en-Bray – The village on the banks of the Andelle boasts a good example of medieval architecture. The **abbey church** is all that remains of Sigy Abbey, founded in the 11C by Hugh I. It has kept its 12C chancel and seven-sided apse, a 13C portal and the nave vaulting, restored in the 18C. The 15C bell-tower overlooks a cemetery with a late-15C sandstone calvary.

Take D 41 east towards Argueil, then D 921 south.

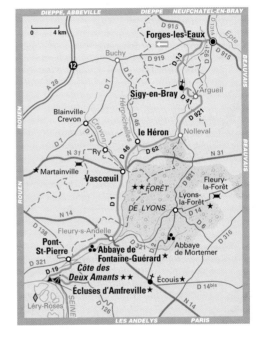

Le Héron – This small village enjoys a pleasant site alongside the park – designed by Le Nôtre – of the château which once belonged to the Marquis de Pomereu. It is said that Gustave Flaubert, then 16 years old, discovered the worldly life within its walls, an inspiration for the descriptions found in *Madame Bovary*.

Vascœuil – *See p 257.* The valley beyond Vascœuil is industrialised but smart houses standing in their well-tended grounds help to maintain the rural atmosphere.

★**Abbaye de Fontaine-Guérard** – *See p 186.* The road continues past a surprising sight, the ruins of a spinning mill built at the turn of the century in Troubadour style – a superficial imitation of the Medieval and Gothic styles.

Pont-St-Pierre – The town which stretches across the Andelle Valley owes much to the nearby 12C-18C château and surrounding park which can be glimpsed through a gap in the main street.

The 11C and 12C church is decorated with **woodwork★**, complemented by Henri II stalls and a 17C altarpiece from Fontaine-Guérard. A 14C Virgin in the chancel wears a dress inlaid with cabochon stones. In the porch (right) stands a great Crucifix (15C) between the Virgin and St John.

After Romilly station turn right; follow D 19 which crosses D 20. After the Sabla factory, turn left along the Seine.

★**Écluses d'Amfreville** – The locks together with the Poses Dam constitute the main control of the water flow in the Lower Seine and divide the stretch below Paris from the tidal section which flows into the Channel. The locks are operated by a central control station fitted with a television circuit. Take the footbridge overlooking the locks to see the water pouring over the Poses Dam; go over to the left bank where the 8 000kW power station stand. Along the bank, a spillway specially designed for fish with an observation room shows how the different species make their way upstream. Follow the towpath which skirts the village of Poses to see the *Fauvette*, a tug built in 1928, and the barge called the *Midway*, which have been converted into a museum.

To return to the coast, continue on D 19 as far as Amfreville-sous-les-Monts and take D 20 up a steep hillside.

FRESNAY-SUR-SARTHE

Population 2 452
Michelin map 60 folds 12 and 13 or 232 fold 9

Fresnay occupies a picturesque site perched high above a meander in the River Sarthe: good view from the bridge on the road to Sillé-le-Guillaume (southwest). It is a good centre for excursions into the Alpes Mancelles or Sillé Forest and is a favourite place with anglers.

In 1063 the town was occupied by the troops of William, Duke of Normandy; subsequent revolts in 1068 and 1078 were put down by William himself. In 1100, following incessant local fighting, Henry I of England evacuated the region of Maine which allied itself with Anjou. Fresnay enjoyed a period of peace until the end of the 14C when the Hundred Years War renewed the strife. This was when the young Ambroise de Loré rose to fame as an ardent opponent of the English; he was recognised as a local hero in 1418.

Fresnay has preserved its network of narrow streets and alleys bordered by old houses from the time when the town was on the Maine frontier.

SIGHTS

Église Notre-Dame ⊙ – The Church of Our Lady is built in the transitional Romanesque style with the local stone which is rust coloured owing to its high iron content. It is dominated by a remarkable octagonal belfry pierced with twin windows and adorned with openwork pinnacles. The round-headed doorway frames the oak door (1528); its carved panels depict (left) the Tree of Jesse and (right) Christ Crucified, flanked by the two thieves and the Twelve Apostles.

Roussard or Grison

The building material known as *roussard* or *grison* is a type of sandstone made with flint stones held together by a thick paste featuring a high iron content. When it comes into contact with damp air, the iron becomes oxidised and the stone takes on russet hues. This stone can be seen in the façades of many buildings, both religious and secular, in the Eure, Sarthe and Orne *départements*.

Musée des Coiffes ⊙ – This Headdress Museum is installed in the fortified gatehouse of the former castle. The gatehouse is flanked by two round towers, while the central part houses the portcullis and machinery for the drawbridge. The right-hand tower has a selection of French headdresses from various regions (Normandy, Poitou, Brittany...) but particularly from the Sarthe. Some are full size while others are miniature versions. Note the lovely English lace christening shawl. The walls of the dungeons still carry inscriptions made by the Chouan prisoners.

The left-hand tower is devoted to natural history. Beyond the oubliettes a spiral staircase leads up to the rooms containing stuffed animals, mineral specimens and tribal arms from Africa. Other interesting items include the letters of patent signed by Louis XIV and the bistoury or surgical instrument used for embalming Victor Hugo.

Terrasse de l'hôtel de ville – A public garden has been laid out in the castle's former precincts. From the terrace there is a pleasant view down over the Sarthe with its attractive bridge and old houses.

Cave du Lion ⊙ – This underground cellar opens off ruelle du Lion, on the far side of the stone-built covered market. The chamber has an octagonal central pillar supporting ribbed vaulting. The capitals are sculpted with leaf shapes and crockets. The cellar is now used for exhibitions of works by local artists.

Gisors, a one time frontier town in the possession of the dukes of Normandy, is the capital of the **Norman Vexin**. Although badly battered in 1940, the town has retained considerable historical character.

The town owes its origins to the castle, greatly coveted for its strategic location. The fortress formed part of a line of defence running from Forges-les-Eaux to Vernon and included the castles of Neaufles-St-Martin and Château-sur-Epte.

★★**Château fort** ⊘ – The castle was built as early as 1097 by William II, King of England and son of William the Conqueror. It was fortified in the 12C by Henry II. In 1193 it was taken by Philippe Auguste of France. During the Hundred Years War the castle changed hands several times before returning to the French crown in 1449.

This magnificent group of 11C and 12C Norman military architecture dominates the town and commands a view of it, including the church of St Gervase and St Protase, built, as can clearly be seen, throughout many different architectural periods.

The 11C **keep**, on its 20m/65ft artificial mound in the centre of the fortified perimeter and surrounded now by a public garden where once there was a moat, is flanked by a watchtower. This, and a solid surrounding wall, were added by Philippe Auguste at the end of the 12C.

A staircase leads to the top from where there is a fine **view** over the surrounding woodland.

★**Église St-Gervais-et-St-Protais** – The oldest parts of the church, dedicated to St Gervase and St Protase, date back to the 12C but construction continued to the end of the 16C, as is evident both outside and inside. The Gothic chancel was completed in 1249; the side chapels adjoining the ambulatory were added in 1498 and 1507 and are immediately noticeable outside by their pointed gables well separated from the main east end which they nevertheless surround. The transept doors are 16C and Gothic, as is the very tall nave. The monumental west front is Renaissance: the doorway is delicately carved and flanked by two towers, that on the north being built in 1536 in the François I style and crowned by a cupola, that on the south in the Henri II style and left unfinished in 1591.

In spite of the mixture of architectural styles the church as a whole appears perfectly harmonious, particularly inside.

The bare, light walls add to the architectural lines and richness of the carved decoration. The large monochrome window in the chapel on the right of the choir dates from the 16C. The chapel below the South Tower contains a charming spiral staircase by Jean Grappin and a huge late-16C Tree of Jesse.

Tree of Jesse (details)

EXCURSIONS

Château de Boury-en-Vexin ☉

6km/4mi south by D 157 and D 6

This castle, located on the boundaries of the Oise *département*, was built in 1685 after the plans and drawings of Jules Hardouin-Mansart. It is a fine example of late-17C Classical architecture.

Surmounted by a pediment bearing a coat of arms, the central part of the castle is split into two levels, lit by high-arched windows decorated with *mascarons*, symbolic representations attributed to the sculptor Poissant, who worked on the decoration at Versailles. The upper section of the front façade is punctuated with twin pilasters embellished with Ionic capitals.

Interior – The entrance gallery displays 18C faience vases from Nevers. The semicircular private chapel, added in 1718, is embellished with stained glass bearing the coat of arms of the Aubourg, Marquis of Boury. On the high altar, note a large painting from the workshop of Charles Le Brun depicting St Charles Borromée.

The tour continues with the suite of salons: 17C and 18C furniture, family portraits and a low relief above each door in the Blue Salon, illustrating country pleasures – fishing, hunting, harvesting, grape picking, music and games. Visitors are then shown the dining hall (18C Delft vases and two big pastels executed by C Coypel portraying the third Marquis of Boury and his young wife) and the former kitchen with its 18C decor (large hood with three fireplaces, copper pans, blue Caen glassware).

Tour of the Epte Valley

41km/25mi – allow 2hr

The road from Gisors to Vernon follows the west bank of the Epte. Long appreciated by painters and tourists, the area has also played a significant role in the history of Normandy, as the ruined strongholds at Neaufles-St-Martin and Château-sur-Epte testify. The riverside is shadey, in contrast with the bareness of the slopes hewn out of the chalk bed of the Vexin plateaux.

From Gisors take D 10 west.

Neaufles-St-Martin – The village is dominated by a keep standing upon a perfectly preserved artificial mound. The only remaining walls are those facing France.

At the junction turn left onto D 181.

Dangu – The main features of the Gothic **church** ☉ are the 18C woodwork and painted panelling in the chancel, the 16C Montmorency Chapel in which a *grisaille* window above the altar shows St Denis, St Lawrence and, on his knees, William, fifth son of Anne of Montmorency, High Constable of France. Near the pulpit is an 18C Beauvais tapestry of the Crucifixion and at the end of the church a fine wood carving of the Annunciation.

Take D 146 south into the valley.

The History of the Dukedom of Normandy

It was at St-Clair-sur-Epte in the year 911 that Charles the Simple – the nickname, meaning honest and straightforward, is in no way disparaging – met with **Rollo**, the ruler of the Vikings. Dudon de St-Quentin, Normandy's first historian, recounts that, to ratify the agreement creating the Dukedom of Normandy, the Viking placed his hands between those of the French king. This informal deal concluded in the manner of tradesmen carried the same legal weight as a formal exchange of seals and signatures for a written treaty was never signed. The dukedom is bordered by the River Epte north of the River Seine and by the River Avre to the south. The boundaries of Normandy were often fought over throughout history by the kings of France and the dukes of Normandy, who became the kings of England in the late 11C.

Château-sur-Epte – Standing on an artificial mound surrounded by a moat are the remains of a massive keep built by William Rufus, second son of William the Conqueror and King of England from 1087 to 1100, to protect the Norman frontier against possible attack from the King of France.

Return to Vernon via D 313. Continue southwest by D 5.

GIVERNY ★

Population 548

Michelin map 55 middle of fold 18 or 231 fold 36 – 2km/1mi southeast of Vernon

Claude Monet lived in this village from 1883 until his death in 1926, and attracted many other artists to the area. It was here that he painted the huge canvases of the water lilies which can be seen in Paris at the Orangerie Museum and the Marmottan Museum.

Claude Monet's pink and green house

E. Baret

★**Maison de Claude Monet** ⊙ – Claude Monet's garden slopes gently to the banks of the River Epte. The house has been converted into an exhibition area that pays tribute to the artist by displaying reproductions of his greatest paintings.

His large studio *(grand atelier)* is now a visitor centre where reproductions of the water lily paintings are on display.

The house stands at the top of the garden; it contains reproductions of his works and his collection of Japanese prints (18C-19C). The tour includes the blue salon, the bedroom with the bed and roll-top desk, the old studio, the yellow dining room with its painted wooden furniture and the tiled kitchen.

Eating out

MODERATE

Restaurant-Musée Baudy – *81 r. Claude-Monet* – ☎ *02 32 21 10 03* – *closed Nov to Mar and Mon except holidays* – *14.64/20.73€*. This hotel once welcomed Impressionist painters. You can admire their paintings while you enjoy the dish of the day and a choice of salads before going through the delightful rose garden preceding a studio... A must!

MID-RANGE

Les Jardins de Giverny – *Along D 5* – ☎ *02 32 21 60 80* – *closed 1-15 Nov, Feb and Mon* – *19.82/35.06€*. Like so many famous people, you will appreciate the refinement of this Norman house in the middle of a park with wonderful flower beds. Quality produce is served in fine porcelain tableware and crystal glasses... and, in addition, the owner is very convivial.

Where to stay

MODERATE

Le Bon Maréchal Bed and Breakfast – *1 r. du Colombier* – ☎ *02 32 51 39 70* – ☞ – *3 rooms: 33.54/54.88€*. This house originally served refreshments to Monet and his artist friends. Ideally situated between the famous gardens and the American Art Museum, it now offers board in cosy comfortable rooms, with prices to match!

The garden comprises the walled garden *(clos normand)*, planted according to Monet's own design, and *(via a tunnel to the other side of the road)* the Japanese-inspired water garden, fed by the River Epte: Japanese style bridges over the water lily pond, the great weeping willow, bamboo and rhododendrons at the waterside.

★**Musée d'Art américain Giverny** ⊙ – This museum, which stands within a few hundred yards of the house of Claude Monet, was founded by Daniel and Judith Terra and commemorates the fruitful inter-relationship of French and American art. The collection of about 100 works of art by 40 American artists has come largely from the Terra Museum of American Art in Chicago. It is housed in three adjoining galleries; the first two galleries contain the core collection and the third presents collections on different themes.

The exhibition opens with two pictures of major historical interest: *Gallery of the Louvre* by Samuel FB More, which reflects the great attraction held by the Louvre for American artists, and *The Wedding March* by Theodore Robinson, which has been described as a graphic representation of the "marriage of French Impression-ism with American Art".

The first two galleries present views of Giverny by the first wave of American artists to visit the area in the 1880s (Louis Ritter, Theodore Wendel, Willard Metcalf...) and by the second wave of 1895-1920 (Lilla Cabot Perry, Richard Miller, Theodore Butler...). Many of the paintings were executed out-of-doors and show the spontaneity of open-air painting methods.

The third gallery houses works of art from the period 1840 to 1920; American artists' impressions of other parts of France, in particular of Brittany and Paris. There are canvases by artists such as Mary Cassatt, Henry O Tanner and John Singer Sargent.

GRANVILLE ★

Population 12 413
Michelin map 59 fold 7 or 231 fold 26

Granville, set on its rocky promontory, is often called the "Monaco of the north". This lively seaside resort, known for its carnival, is also a busy port with an active fishing fleet and a marina. The invigorating climate makes it an ideal choice for a sea-water therapy centre. The upper town, still encircled by its ramparts, retains the rather severe appearance and all the atmosphere of a fortified town. The lower town, partly built on reclaimed land, is the business and bustling resort area.

Granville is the departure point for ferries to the Chausey and Channel islands.

FISHERMEN, PRIVATEERS AND BATHERS

The town developed in the 15C when the English fortified the rocky promontory as a base from which to attack Mont-St-Michel, then occupied by the Normans. The town was recaptured by the knights of Mont-St-Michel in 1442 and remained French from then on. Prosperity came with deep-sea fishing for cod in the 18C and it was during the same century that several Granville sailors were known for their heroic priva-teering: Beaubriand-Lévéque and Pléville-Lepelley who was to become Minister for the Navy during the Directory.

The 1793 siege of the town resulted in the defeat of the Chouan army led by Henri de la Rochejaquelein. With the growing popularity of sea bathing in the 19C Granville became a famous seaside resort. Distinguished regular visitors included Stendhal, Michelet and Victor Hugo.

HAUTE-VILLE *2hr*

The Main Gate (Grand'Porte) with its drawbridge was and remains the principal entrance to the fortified, upper part of town. A plaque commemorates the 1793 siege *(see above)*. The fortified town with its old houses, built of granite from the Chausey Islands, concentrates all Granville's military and religious past within its ramparts.

The Carnival at Granville

This long-standing tradition was originated by local fishermen. Before leav-ing for long fishing expeditions out in Newfoundland, cod fishermen would go out to spend their money in the streets of the city, dressing up in various costumes for the occasion. Today the carnival takes place during Shrove Tuesday celebrations; it lasts for four days and includes a funfair with a procession of floats, an orchestra and majorettes. On the last day the residents, dressed up and masked, pay a visit to their friends; a Carnival effigy is burned on the beach, marking the end of festivities.

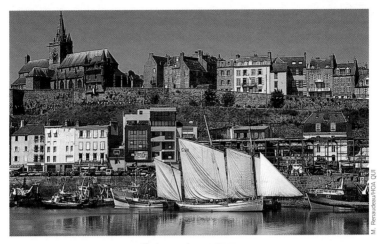

Harbour and upper town

Église Notre-Dame – The oldest parts of this austere granite church with a fine tower over the transept crossing go back to the 15C. The nave itself and the west front, adorned with monolithic columns, were erected in the 17C and 18C. Inside, there are a few carved capitals round the chancel which has interesting modern stained-glass windows by Le Chevallier. On the north side note David, Isaac and Ezekiel and, on the south, Jacob and Eli. The 14C statue, in the north chapel, of Our Lady of Cape Lihou – the traditional name for the tip of the Pointe du Roc – is greatly venerated locally. The statue is particularly honoured in the Great Pardon of the Corporations and of the sea *(see Calendar of events)*.

From the promenade beside the church there is a plunging view of the harbour area, where the boats stand high and dry at low tide.

Pointe du Roc – This is an exceptional site★. The point which marks the northern limit of Mont-St-Michel Bay is linked to the mainland only by a narrow rocky isthmus. In the 15C the English dug a trench, known as Tranchée aux Anglais, as part of their fortifications. Shortly afterwards the Governor of Mont-St-Michel, Louis d'Estouteville, recaptured Granville.

◪ The walk (the path starts from the harbour) to the lighthouse offers a fine view of the sea and the rocks. The granite monument shortly before the lighthouse commemorates those lost at sea.

★**Rampart Walk** – *Park on the parvis of Notre-Dame Church and go through the Grand'Porte and over the drawbridge. Turn right onto rue Lecarpentier to follow the south rampart to place de l'Isthme.*

◪ The **view**★ from the enormous square extends, on a clear day, to the coast of Brittany *(viewing table)*. Below the square, is the trench dug by the English which separated Le Roc from the mainland.

Continue along the inside of the ramparts by rue du Nord.

At this point the town and the landscape are at their most severe but the view is spectacular in stormy weather. The Chausey Islands lie to the northwest.

Turn left onto rue des Plâtriers to reach rue St-Jean, then turn right.

Note at no 7 rue St-Jean, an old house with a ground floor shop and then at no 3, a house dating from 1612, with carved figures of Adam and Eve.

The street opposite, montée du Parvis, leads back to the starting point.

Do not miss the large half-timbered house with a two-storey turret.

BASSE-VILLE

The lower part of town is where most of the shops, cafés and attractions are. The old neighbourhoods have been linked by a central crossroads commonly known as *le Pont*.

La Plage – The narrow beach at the foot of shale cliffs backing the bay is overlooked by the Plat-Gousset Breakwater promenade.

Jardin public Christian-Dior ⊘ – This public garden formerly belonged to the couturier's family. Its setting of greenery makes it a most secluded and restful spot. From the upper terrace you look down on the Granville promontory, north towards Regnéville and directly opposite, out to the Chausey Islands.

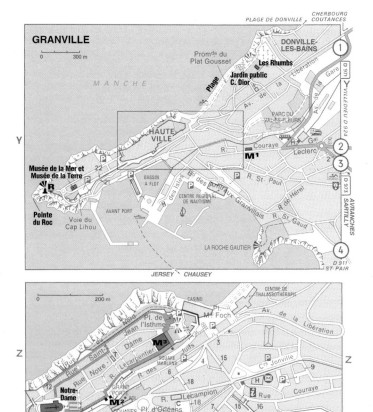 The cliff path passes the cemetery to reach the great expanse of Donville beach, the complement to Granville's. Low tide reveals the numerous stakes used for mussel growing.

Musée de la Mer and Musée de la Terre ⊙ – *Enter from boulevard Vaufleury.*

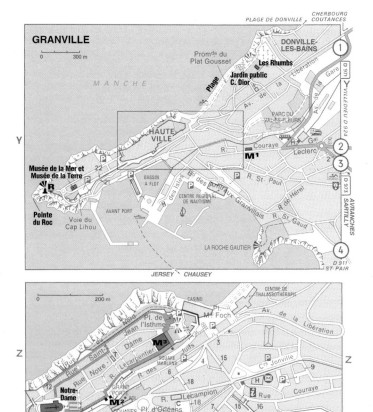 Granville's maritime past is evoked by tableaux and models of sailing ships, as well as one of the transatlantic liner *France*. The tanks contain fish from local waters – note the sea perch with its powerful jaw and specially adapted conical teeth for feeding off shellfish – as well as exotic and freshwater species. Nounours, the sea lion, amuses all with his antics.

Féerie des Coquillages – In this Shell Wonderland, spotlights highlight the many delightful shell compositions: Egyptian minarets, the Angkor Temple, a dream gown for a princess and a coral cave.

Just as surprising, is the **Musée de la Terre**, where brightly coloured minerals are used to compose attractive mosaics: flowers, butterflies, Egyptian frescoes and fabulous trees.

A collection of mounted insects (exotic-coloured butterflies, trapdoor spiders, beetles, blue or pink grasshoppers) evoke the atmosphere of the tropical forests.

Musée du Vieux Granville ⊙ – *In the fortified gatehouse, Grand'Porte.*
Various documents recount the history of Granville and its seafaring past. A collection of local furniture and other domestic items help to recreate household interiors of the past: cupboards, chests, dressers and copperware.

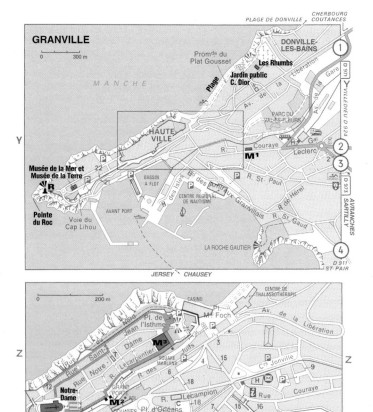

Eating out

MODERATE

L'Horizon – *Pl. du Mar.-Foch* – ☎ *02 33 50 00 79* – *closed Mon and Tues from Oct to Mar* – *12.04/24.39€*. This restaurant belongs to the elegant Casino situated on the waterfront. Do not hesitate to enter in order to reach the dining room which offers a panoramic view of the sea and the coast. The decor is in 1930 style but the cuisine caters for today's taste.

Crêperie Grill l'Échauguette – *22/24 r. St-Jean* – ☎ *02 33 50 51 87* – *closed 1 week in Mar, 12 Nov to 10 Dec, Wed (except during school holidays) and Tues* – *7.62/22.41€*. Nestling in one of the narrow streets of Old Granville, this unassuming *crêperie* is sought after by the locals. In addition to buckwheat *crêpes*, you will be able to enjoy grills cooked in the fireplace of the restaurant...

La Citadelle – *34 r. du Port* – ☎ *02 33 50 34 10* – *closed 15 Feb to 15 Mar, Tues lunch from Nov to Mar, Tues evening and Wed from Sept to June* – *12.96/28.97€*. Before setting off for the islands, you will be able to have a meal in the dining room with its blue wood panelling or sit on the small raised terrace. Specialities: seafood including lobster caught in the chef''s fish pool.

Where to stay

MID-RANGE

Hôtel des Bains – *19 r. G.-Clemenceau* – ☎ *02 33 50 17 31* – *47 rooms: 45.73/135.68€* – ☐ *5.95€*. Waves break just beneath the terrace. Ask for a room with a view and enjoy the sun setting over the sea, or ask for one of those equipped with a jacuzzi.

Beaumonderie Hotel – *50290 Bréville-sur-Mer* – *4.5km/2.8mi NE of Granville along D 971^E towards Coutances* – ☎ *02 33 50 36 36* – **P** – *13 rooms: 53.36/132.63€* – ☐ *8.38€* – *restaurant 20/59€*. This charming 1920s villa, just 1km/0.6mi from the sea, faces the Chausey Islands. Cosy atmosphere in the bedrooms, which all have their personal touch, and in the English-style lounge/bar. The restaurant, known as the Orangerie, is housed in a veranda with timberwork. Covered swimming pool and tennis.

On the staircase are lovely examples of illustrated glazed earthenware known as Jersey ware. On the first floor, there is a particularly attractive collection of Norman costumes and headdresses as well as a section on Hambye cloth, which was commonly used to decorate box beds. Hambye cloth was made by using canvas or grain sacks, covered with a layer of paint which served as background for a stylised decoration. On the second floor exhibitions devoted to the sea are presented in rotation: they either illustrate trade and fishing activities, as well as the function of the Royal Navy, or else evoke the popular seaside resort that Granville used to be towards the turn of the century. Each year a new exhibition on a different subject, usually related to the sea, is held in the Halle du Blé *(near the panorama at Pointe du Roc)*.

Musée Richard-Anacréon ⊙ – This museum of modern art presents a standing collection of works by 20C artists, displayed alternately in a series of temporary exhibitions.

Historial granvillais ⊙ – This waxwork museum relates Granville's history through tableaux representing important events: scenes of privateering, rue Notre-Dame in the 19C, the 1793 siege of Granville, the old harbour and quai d'Angoulême in the 18C. Every tableau has an accompanying recorded commentary.

EXCURSIONS

Îles Chausey – *See Îles CHAUSEY.*

St-Pair-sur-Mer – St-Pair has a breakwater promenade protecting a beach of golden sand which is perfect for children.

The origins of the **church** are said to be a monastery founded in the 6C by two local evangelists, St Pair and St Scubilien. The building consists of the Romanesque belfry and the bay beneath, the 14C chancel and a neo-Gothic nave and transepts which were added in the 19C. The points of interest in the interior are a large 14C Christ in wood (south transept chapel); an old stone font with a wooden cover (baptistery on the north side of the nave); a canopied tabernacle flanked by two gilded wood statues (18C) of St Lô and St Senier (nearby chapel); 6C sarcophagi and the 15C recumbent figures of St Pair and St Scubilien (old chancel behind the high altar); a 16C Virgin and the reliquary of St Gaud, Bishop of Évreux (early 7C) in all his finery (north chapel).

Le Havre, a great seaport and the final milestone along the beautiful Seine Valley, spreads its modern installations to the edge of the furthest Caux promontory. In 1945 Le Havre bore the least enviable title of Europe's worst damaged port; today it is France's leading commercial port.

Car ferries also operate to England and the Republic of Ireland. Le Havre-Octeville airport handles regular traffic both within France and abroad (London, Brussels, Rotterdam).

Le Havre town, including the residential area of Ste-Adresse and the old port of Harfleur, is a remarkable example of large-scale reconstruction and successful town planning. A university opened its doors to students in 1986.

A LONG AND EVENTFUL HISTORY

A Judicious Choice – In 1517, to replace Harfleur which was silted up, **François I** ordered the construction of a new port, called Havre-de-Grâce. The marshy site chosen by Bonnivet, Grand Admiral of France, was not impressive to view but the fact that high tide lasted for over 2hr was crucial.

In 1518 the first warship, *Hermine*, together with the admiral's flagship, entered the King's Dock (Bassin du Roi), the forerunner of the modern port. Very provisionally the king granted the town his name – Françoise-de-Grâce – and his arms – a salamander argent on a field gules.

An Ocean Port – The career of Le Havre as a trading and transatlantic port began during the American War of Independence when supplies for the "rebels" were shipped from Le Havre; the harbour became a forest of masts. St-François district, known to sailors the world over, was stacked with goods; every sort of colonial import – cotton, coffee, tobacco, timber – was distributed throughout Europe.

The voyage to New York became shorter. In 1850 the *Franklin*, using sails and paddles, made the crossing in two weeks. In 1864 the steamship *Washington* was put into service by the Compagnie Générale Transatlantique.

In succession came some of the great liners nicknamed "The Ambassadors of the Sea" such as the *Normandie*, the *Île-de-France*, the *Liberté* (a German boat) and the *France*. The people of Le Havre repeat such names with a certain nostalgia for the glorious era, now gone, of the great transatlantic liners, which hooted three times as they cleared the quayside escorted by tug boats (known in French as *abeilles* which means bees).

People spoke of "La Place du Havre" when referring to the powerful commercial and banking organisation which developed in this great international market.

Le Havre during the War – Le Havre suffered 146 raids, more than 4 000 killed, 9 935 dwellings totally destroyed and 9 710 partially destroyed. The siege of the town began on 2 September 1944 – the Battle of Normandy was over and Paris liberated, but Le Havre was still occupied.

Allied air raids went on ceaselessly for eight days from 5 September; the Germans were determined to blow up any port installations still in existence. On 13 September 1944 Le Havre was liberated. It took two years, even with the aid of the Allies, to clear the destruction and reconstruction was, therefore, able to begin only in 1946.

★★THE PORT

Traffic – Le Havre is a deep-water port situated in the Seine estuary; it ranks first among French ports for exports and fifth in

Poster of the *Normandie* by Cassandre (1935)

Eating out

MID-RANGE

La Petite Auberge – *32 r. Ste-Adresse* – ☎ *02 35 46 27 32 – closed 1-21 Aug, Feb school holidays, Sun evening and Mon except holidays – 18.29/35.06€.* Situated near Ste-Adresse, this small restaurant with its elegant façade serves tasty dishes based on regional recipes and fresh market produce... Cosy, muffled atmosphere to satisfy current tastes, white tablecloths and white-leaded furniture.

Auberge des Falaises – *Le Hode – 76340 St-Vigor-d'Ymonville – 14km/8.7mi east of Le Havre via the motorway and D 982* – ☎ *02 35 20 06 97 – closed 24 July to 7 Aug, Sun evening, Mon evening, Tues evening and Sat lunch – 17.53/31.25€.* Located at the foot of the cliffs, this inn occupies a modern pavilion with rustic decor and wood-panelled ceiling, roughcast walls and a beautiful carved-wood fireplace. Well-prepared cuisine.

Where to stay

MODERATE

Ferme de Beaucamp Bed and Breakfast – *Rte d'Oudalle – 76430 St-Aubin-Routot – 15km/9.3mi east of Le Havre via N 15 and a minor road* – ☎ *02 35 20 52 01 – closed 10-20 Sept – ⌷ – 5 rooms: 33.54/39.64€ – meal 16.77€.* Far away from the hustle and bustle of Le Havre, this lovely 17C farm is enhanced by a colourful garden. The food is renowned, particularly during the hunting season. Three small attic rooms and two more spacious ones. Charming welcome.

Le Petit Vatel Hotel – *86 r. L.-Brindeau* – ☎ *02 35 41 72 07 – 27 rooms: 30.49/42.69€ – ⌷ 4.57€.* The rooms are small and simple, prices reasonable... three good reasons to choose this hotel in the town centre.

MID-RANGE

Marly Hotel – *121 r. de Paris* – ☎ *02 35 41 72 48 – 37 rooms: 57.93/73.18€ – ⌷ 7.62€.* Located along the avenue leading to the harbour, this rather austere-looking hotel is convenient. The rooms are large enough, facilities are adequate and functional... The right place to combine business with tourism.

On the town

L'Abri-Côtier – *24 bd Albert-1er* – ☎ *02 35 42 51 20 – summer: daily noon-2am; winter: Mon-Sat 2.30pm-2am, Sun 2.30-8pm.* This lively bar overlooking the sea is the refuge of wild animals, toucan, boa, iguana and elephant... An eccentric colourful setting popular with the locals, whatever their age!

La Petite Rade – *3 pl. Clemenceau – 76310 Ste-Adresse* – ☎ *02 35 54 68 80 – planete-b.fr/hotel-des-bains – daily noon-2pm, 7.30-10pm.* Dark interior with maritime decor lit by fake oil lamps, bright open terrace overlooking the sea... this is the style of this "harbour" (rade) where it is pleasant to find a mooring, particularly when there's a rock or pop concert on.

Le Camp Gourou – *163 r. Victor-Hugo* – ☎ *02 35 22 00 92 – Wed-Mon 6pm-2am.* Behind the drawn blinds is the interior of a log cabin with mezzanine and wooden seats. Beneath the straw ceiling, the novel decor of this lively Australian café appeals essentially to the student population.

Le Mac Daid's – *97 r. Paul-Doumer* – ☎ *02 35 41 30 40 – daily 2pm-2am – closed Sun in Aug.* This large Irish pub on three levels stages two concerts a week. Ask for the programme! Billiards upstairs.

Les Trois Pics – *Prom. des Régates – 76310 Ste-Adresse* – ☎ *02 35 48 20 60 – daily 9am-2am – closed in Jan.* This establishment overlooks the sea. Whether you sit on the terrace in summer or behind the wide windows in winter, you can enjoy fish and seafood or choose something on the menu of the café-cum-tearoom, whilst admiring the exceptional panorama of the Seine estuary.

Sport

Abeille Parachutisme – *6 pl. St-Martin – Aéroport du Havre-Octeville* – ☎ *06 11 62 40 06 or 02 32 30 27 46 – abeille-parachutisme.com – open daily 9am-8pm.* You feel the urge to try parachuting? Well this is the time to go for the big jump... You will be dropped from a minimum height of 3 000m/9 842ft and for 35 seconds you will experience free falling at a speed of 200kph/124mph before your parachute opens and you glide through the air admiring the extraordinary panorama of the coast. All this under the guidance of a very nice instructor. It is possible to film or photograph the drop. The only snag: high prices.

Aéro-Club du Havre – Jean Maridor – *R. Louis-Blériot – Aéroport du Havre-Octeville* – ☎ *02 35 48 35 91 – aeroclub@club-internet.fr – daily 9am-7pm.* First flights and beginners' flights lasting 30min! Short but packed with sensations...You will fly along the coast to Étretat aboard a two- or four-seater Cessna and fly back over the countryside and the Pont de Normandie before going round Le Havre via the estuary.

Europe. Le Havre is also France's main container port, accounting for 56% of the total market. An important proportion of the traffic is energy supplies: import of crude oil, refined oil products, gaseous hydrocarbons and coal; other goods which transit through Le Havre include cereals, chemical and petrochemical products, liquids and gases in bulk, which are stored and handled within the vast harbour industrial zone. To these should be added the Channel traffic as well as a considerable quantity of trailers and new cars.

In passenger traffic Le Havre holds a high place owing to its frequent car-ferry links with Great Britain (Le Havre-Portsmouth) and Ireland (Le Havre-Rosslare, Le Havre-Cork).

Each year 7 000 merchant ships dock in Le Havre, including 2 250 container ships; 250 different maritime companies organise regular links with more than 500 ports throughout the world.

Port Tour – Information about the port and shipping movements can be obtained from the receptionist at the Centre Administratif, Port Autonome, Terre-plein de la Barre. Audio-guides can be hired for unaccompanied visits of the port.
Boat trips from quai de la Marine take their passengers round the port facilities (1hr 15min – information from the tourist office).

Looking towards the future – The plans adopted by the port authorities for the expansion of the harbour are geared to the development of its favourable geographical conditions and its strategic location as a European crossroads, ensuring rapid and effective service. Faced with the growth of containerisation, Le Havre has installed quays fitted with specialised equipment for handling containers on land (gantries and warehouses) and for rail traffic.

The Port Authority of the Le Havre has launched an ambitious project, **Port 2000**, which is in the first phases of implementation and should be completed by 2003. The improved facilities should help Le Havre keep its rank as the world's fifth busiest port, and France's first. The main thrust of the programme is the improvement of container transfer from shipboard to rail and road links. To enable more and speedier transfers, the docks are being extended, motorways will be laid down and other roads improved, the national rail company is to carry out works, and additional engineering projects will improve connections with inland waterways as well.

Le Havre is among the two or three only harbours able to accommodate the huge container ships reaching 6 000 EVP (representing 6m/20ft). With Port 2000, even more big ships (300-350m/985-1 159ft long, 45m/148ft wide, drawing 14.5m/48ft of water) can be accommodated, whatever the tidal conditions, without having to wait.

The **René-Coty Dock** leads to the François-1er Lock, which is one of the largest of its type in the world (length: 400m/1 321ft, width: 67m/220ft, depth: 24m/79ft) and can accommodate ships of 250 000t fully laden. It links the tidal docks with the docks and canals where the water level is constant, including the **Grand Canal du Havre** which serves the industrial zone where unloading can take place irrespective of the tides.

★A WALK THROUGH THE MODERN TOWN

The old town which had been planned on a chessboard principle by the Italian architect Belarmato in 1541 was virtually wiped out in 1944. A new town was planned by **Auguste Perret** (1875-1954), the pioneer of reinforced concrete construction (he also designed the Théâtre des Champs-Élysées). Remarkable architectural unity has been achieved; a perfect balance between volume and space. The centre offers wide perspectives, the horizontal lines of the vast living units contrast with tall tower blocks. The impressive town hall and St Joseph's Church, both by Perret, pierce the sky.

The impressive perspective which avenue Foch offers towards the Porte Océane symbolises the important part the sea has always played for the town.

Bassin du Commerce and Espace Niemeyer – The commercial dock has been made the focal point of the new quarter accessible by an elegant footbridge, designed by the architects, Gillet and Du Pasquier, which won a prize in 1972 for the most beautiful metal structures.

At the west end, facing the war memorial, the urban landscape has had a facelift with the new Espace Oscar-Niemeyer complex on place Gambetta. The concrete curves contrast with the rectangular buildings nearby. The work of Brazilian architect **Oscar Niemeyer**, the ultra-modern centre's vocation is cultural. The main pavilion (Grand Volcan) is fitted with a large theatre, a cinema and several exhibition rooms.

★**Place de l'Hôtel-de-Ville** – The square, which was designed by Auguste Perret, is one of the largest in Europe. It is bordered by three-storey buildings with flat roofs, punctuated by taller 10-storey blocks. The open space is laid out with pools and fountains, lawns, arbours and yew hedges. At the centre stands a Memorial to

Le Volcan by Oscar Niemeyer, Bassin du Commerce

A. Février/DIAF

the Deportation and the Resistance, symbolised by "two wounded birds" by the sculptor Adam. The **hôtel de ville**, an austere building, is distinguished by a great tower (72m/236ft high) in concrete.

Leading off the square opposite the town hall is **rue de Paris**, the finest street in Le Havre in the 18C, now fronted by arcades.

★**Avenue Foch** – This street is laid out as a promenade, the finest urban composition in Le Havre. The central roadway is bordered by lawns shaded by trees, the modern buildings are unified by the horizontal lines of their architecture, and the Porte Océane marks the west end of the street on the seafront. Modern sculptures in the neo-Figurative style decorate the imposts and corners of some of the buildings.

The Ocean Gate, which is interposed between two buildings flanked by towers, implies a welcome on shore and an invitation to set sail.

North dike and the beach – The north breakwater, supplemented by a jetty, encloses the marina (Anse des Régates and Anse de Joinville). From the far end there is a fine view of the outer harbour. The Le Havre and Ste-Adresse beach (shingle at high tide and sand at low tide), which is favoured by windsurfers, stretches from the North Breakwater to the Hève Cape *(2km/1mi)*. The promenade, the local seafront walk, provides views of the Seine estuary. In summer the shore is lined with white-painted wooden beach huts.

★**Église St-Joseph** – This sober **church** typical of Auguste Perret's style was built of concrete between 1951 and 1957. It is surmounted by an octagonal lantern-belfry (109m/358ft high). The **interior**★★ is monumental and impressive: the square plan contains four clusters of four square pillars supporting the lantern (84m/275ft high). Stained-glass windows in the lantern and in the walls cast a kaleidoscope of coloured lights that vary throughout the day.

Sémaphore – The signal station tower (52.40m/172ft) uses available means (radar, radio, telegraph) to communicate between land and sea. The tugs, known as bees (*abeilles* in French) moor alongside, fitted with the most sophisticated fire-fighting equipment. The view from the end of the pier embraces the harbour entrance and the long southern breakwater protecting the outer harbour; in the foreground are the berths of the methane tankers and the liquid methane storage tanks. From this vantage point all the shipping movements are in view.

SIGHTS TO VISIT IN TOWN

Cathédrale Notre-Dame – Built between 1575 and 1630, the cathedral is a combination of Gothic and Renaissance styles and bristles with buttresses decorated with gargoyles in the shape of salamanders. Ionic columns flank the north door, which is called the Ave Maria door because of the inscription above the Flamboyant rose window. The west front is articulated by three pairs of ringed Ionic columns surmounted by urns. The upper level, decorated with the Corinthian order, is pierced by a large window bay.

The interior consists of a nave and two aisles culminating in a chapel. The organ (1637) was presented by Richelieu and bears his arms.

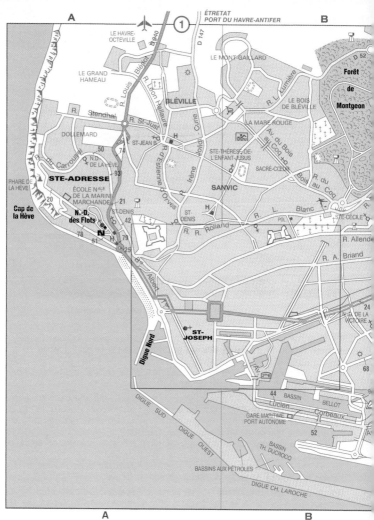

Index of streets and sights in Le Havre

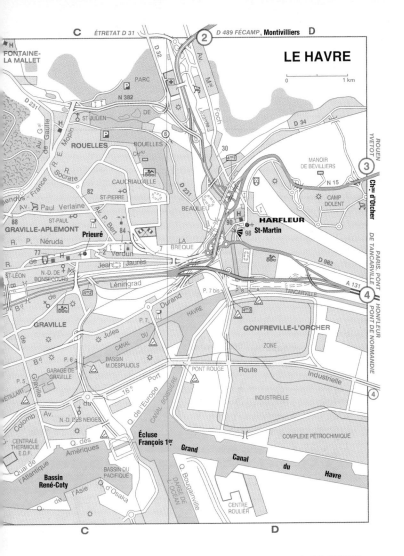

★**Musée des Beaux-Arts André-Malraux** ⊙ – *The museum is located at the
entrance to the port.* The glass and metal building, which houses the Fine Arts
Museum, looks out to the sea through a monumental concrete sculpture known
locally as Le Signal. The roof, designed to provide the best possible light to the
galleries inside, is highly original. It consists of six sheets of glass covered by a
horizontal slatted aluminium sun blind through which natural light passes, together
with electric light which is subsequently filtered through clear or opaque ceiling
lights. The galleries are linked on different levels by gangways similar to those on
the outside of the building and reminiscent of those on board ship.

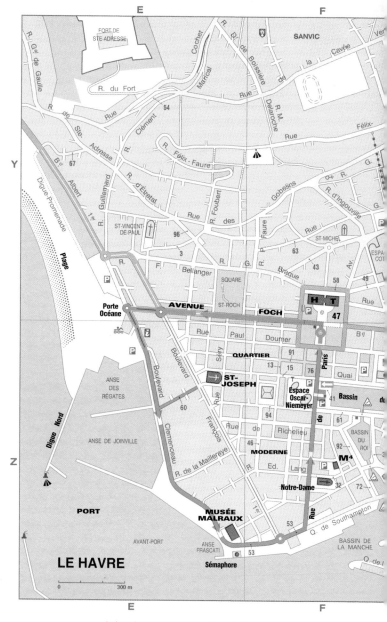

Index of streets and sights on preceding page

The museum presents a fine **collection**★ of works of art (paintings, watercolours, sketches) by **Raoul Dufy** (1877-1953). Dufy, who was born in Le Havre, was one of the main representatives of **Fauvism**, characterised by expressive bursts of colours. He also underwent the influence of Paul Cézanne and, subsequently, that of Cubism. His subject matter is essentially drawn from life: concerts, regattas, racecourses, esplanades, Normandy beaches, village festivities, streets and allegorical themes. Light, airy brushwork, a bright palette, a sense of movement conveyed by the disassociation of shapes and colour and a lurid imagination are the hallmarks of his work. The museum also displays works by **Eugène Boudin** (1824-98), a native of Honfleur who spent many years in Le Havre. Boudin, whom the poet Charles Baudelaire had dubbed "the King of the Heavens", was a forerunner of **Impressionism**. The pictures on show illustrate the development of his technique, ranging from his painstaking portrayal of reality in the style of the Dutch masters *(The Pardon of Ste-Anne-de-la-Palud)* to his very last paintings, in which imagination and freedom of expression border on Abstraction *(Yellow Boats in Étretat, Church Interior in Brittany)*. He excelled at portraying the Normandy countryside as well as beach scenes in Deauville and Trouville.

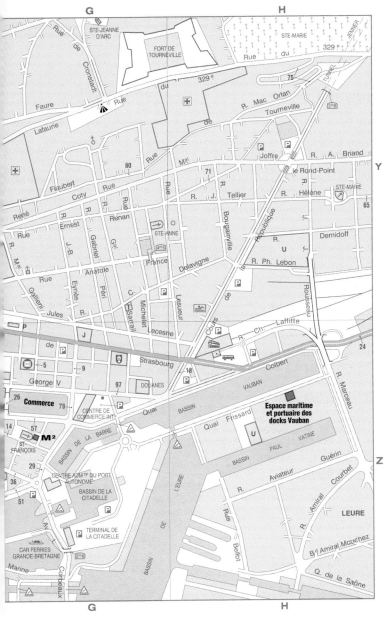

Muséum d'Histoire naturelle ⊙ – The Natural History Museum is housed in the old 18C law courts. The ornithological collection is illustrated by a model of Tilleul Cliff, north of Le Havre, showing the different species of birds which nest there. One room displays works by the naturalist painter **Charles-Alexandre Lesueur** (1778-1846).

Musée de l'Ancien Havre ⊙ – The museum is to be found in the old St-François District in a 17C house (restored), which belonged to the navigator Dubocage de Bléville.

A display of miniature models, photographs, posters, engravings, tools and archive documents enlightens visitors on the eventful history of the city between 1517 and the present day. Many exhibits are devoted to the development of shipbuilding, ranging from early galleys to contemporary liners. Other collections evoke port and maritime trade, nautical activities (swimming, regattas) and town planning (from the Renaissance to Auguste Perret).

Espace maritime et portuaire des Docks Vauban ⊙ – Set up in 19C dockland, this new exhibition area displays collections from the former Musée Maritime et Portuaire (now closed) and the Association French Lines, which perpetuates the memory of the prestigious cross-Atlantic liner. Special emphasis has been placed on maritime life in Le Havre at the turn of the century: whalers, the exodus towards the New Continent, the drawing room of the *France* in 1912, the luxury lifestyle on board some of these sumptuous ships. Other exhibits are devoted to the expansion of the merchant navy, navigational aids and the handling of portuary equipment.

SIGHTS NEARBY

★★Ste-Adresse – *1hr*. In the 14C a tidal wave laid waste the port of Ste-Adresse, then a lively maritime community, known as St-Denis-de-Caus. Today it is a pleasant district extending from the edge of Le Havre towards the Hève Cape and consisting of a seaside resort and the old town of Ste-Adresse which is situated on the slope overlooking the Ignauval. The resort developed early in the 20C under the impetus of Dufayel, a Parisian businessman. The steep slopes of the Hève Cape are covered with handsome villas, each with its own garden, built on terraces overlooking Le Havre and the Seine estuary.

During the First World War (1914-18), when the Germans invaded Belgium, the Belgian government moved to Ste-Adresse, where it enjoyed the privilege of extraterritoriality.

★Round Tour of Ste-Adresse – Boulevard Albert-1er alongside the beach to place Clemenceau and the statue of Albert I, King of the Belgians from 1909 to 1934.

Follow the signs for Pain de Sucre and Notre-Dame-des-Flots.

After a few bends in the road you arrive at the **Pain de Sucre**, erected by the widow of General Lefèbvre-Desnouettes who perished in a shipwreck off the Icelandic coast in 1822. A little higher up on the right the **Chapelle Notre-Dame-des-Flots** contains sailors' votive offerings.

Turn left onto the route du Cap.

The road passes in front of the École Nationale de la Marine Marchande (Merchant Navy College), one of the most modern in Europe.

Cap de la Hève – *The lighthouse (15min on foot there and back)*. This rocky site overlooks the mouth of the Seine and the entrance into the harbour. View of Second World War casemates.

Boulevard du Président-Félix-Faure to the right and facing the ocean offers an extensive **view★** of the beach, city, port and Seine estuary.

Return to place Clemenceau.

Forêt de Montgeon – *Access via the Jenner Tunnel, the continuation to the north of cours de la République*. The woodland (280ha/691 acres) consists of oaks, beeches and birches and is organised as a leisure park: walks, canoeing on the lake, a camp site, games and sports fields.

Prieuré de Graville – *Access by rue Aristide-Briand, then rue de Verdun (follow directions Rouen-Paris), then left to rue de l'Abbaye (signposted). Enter by the cemetery.*

A sanctuary was erected in the 6C on this spot to shelter the relics of St Honorine. These, however, were later removed to Conflans near Pontoise to preserve them from the "fury of the Vikings".

On the left of the entrance to the priory, stands a **Black Madonna**, so called because of the colour of the metal it is composed of, placed here after the Franco-Prussian War of 1870. **St Honorin's Church**, the former abbey church dating from the 11C and the 13C, has beautifully embellished capitals.

The terraced gardens (left of the church) bordered by conventual buildings (13C but rearranged in the 17C), offer pleasant views of the city and the Seine Bay. From rue du Prieuré stairs descend to the museum located in the conventual buildings.

Musée du Prieuré de Graville ⊙ – The museum features an impressive collection of religious art from the 16C up to the present day. Exhibits include tombstones, capitals, 12C-15C stone statues, low-relief sculptures and polychrome wooden statues. A "retrospective of human habitat", consisting of 100 or so 19C models of houses, illustrates the history of French regional architecture.

Harfleur – *Access by rue Aristide-Briand and rue de Verdun following the direction of Rouen*. Harfleur, once a port in its own right at the mouth of the Lézarde, has retained a certain character, in spite of now being at the centre of Le Havre's industrial zone.

The bell-tower (83m/272ft) of the **Église St-Martin** ⊙ has been famous in the Caux region since the 15C. There are beautiful keystones; the pillars on the north side have foliated capitals, those in all other parts of the church rise straight up to the vaulting. The first chapel on the south aisle contains an 18C altarpiece and a 14C tombstone of a local lord and lady. The organ case which dates from the 17C is ornamented with delicately carved sculptures.

Take rue des 104 and rue Gambetta, right, to the **bridge** over the Lézarde from which there is a good view of the church belfry.

Château d'Orcher ⊘ – *10km/6mi east of Le Havre by* ③, *N 15, on the plan and a minor road (right) to Gonfreville.* The castle stands on a cliff overlooking the Seine. In the 11C it was part of a defence line protecting the estuary. So as not to fall into English hands it was dismantled in the 14C.

It was purchased in the 18C by a Rouen dealer who had three sides demolished and the fourth redone in the Louis XV style.

The visit takes in the library, the dining room (fine collection of plates from the East India Company) and the salons containing an attractive collection of rocaille woodwork. Note the octagonal buttressed **dovecot** in stone and blue flint.

Montivilliers – *8km/5mi from the centre of town. Leave Le Havre on D 489.* The town, now a suburb of Le Havre, took its name from a monastery founded by St Philibert in the 6C. An 11C lantern tower above the transept crossing and a Romanesque belfry surmounted by a spire (restored in the 19C) identify the **Église St-Sauveur**★. The Romanesque nave was doubled by a 16C Gothic nave when the church passed to the parish: solid oak 17C pulpit; Flamboyant gallery in three sections.

In the **Aitre de Brisegaret** *(access from the road to Fécamp; turn left in front of a stonemason's)* stand the remains of a charnel house – 16C gallery beneath a timber roof with carvings on the pillars.

Château de Filières ⊘ – *20km/12mi northeast via N15; take D 31 left after St-Romain, then D 80 to the right.* The château stands in a fine park, at the end of an avenue which opens into the moated courtyard. The building, built in white Caen stone after designs by Victor Louis, is in two parts: a late-16C wing (left) and a plain 18C central pavilion with a Classical façade; on the pediment are the arms of the Mirvilles who built the château and ancestors of the present owners.

The prime pieces on display are Oriental porcelain and wall hangings, souvenirs of the kings of France (Sèvres biscuit medallions), furniture and mementoes belonging to the Maréchal de Lauriston.

In the park, west of the château, are seven rows of magnificent beech trees, known as the "**Cathedral**★" because their branches meet overhead in a living vault.

HONFLEUR ★★

Population 8 272
Michelin map 54 fold 8 or 231 fold 20

The lovely town of Honfleur, located on the Siene estuary, has a holiday feeling all year round. The impressive Pont de Normandie has made it easier to get to and from the town, and to visit the Pays d'Auge and the Côte de Grâce. Visitors delight in walking around the old dock (Vieux Bassin), Ste-Catherine Church, the narrow winding streets and port, where the fishing fleet unloads fresh fish and shellfish every day. Today, Honfleur can rightly claim to be both a river port and a seaport, as evidenced by the many large liners that choose the welcoming city as a stopover: it is becoming more and more frequent to see 220m/722ft long ships, able to accommodate up to 1 200 passengers in optimal conditions, glide along the quays, where the waters are 7.5-9.5m/24-31ft deep.

CANADA, A NORMAN COLONY

Ever since the early 16C navigators had been anchoring briefly along the coast of a land named Gallia Nova by Verrazano, the discoverer of the site of New York; in 1534, however, **Jacques Cartier** stepped ashore and claimed the territory in the name of France. He named it Canada, the Huron word for village. François I, however, was disillusioned as the explorer brought back no spices, no gold, no diamonds. Canada was left unexplored until the 17C when the experienced navigator, **Samuel de Champlain**, received orders to colonise this vast territory. He set sail from Honfleur, and in 1608 founded Quebec.

On Colbert's advice Louis XIV took an interest in Canada and the country rapidly became a Norman and Percheron colony settled by over 4 000 peasants who made their living by agriculture, fishing, hunting and fur trading.

The Iroquois Indians, however, bitterly opposed the French colonists who by 1665 had to appeal to France for aid against mounting attacks. A thousand soldiers arrived; simultaneously a decree was issued compelling each man to marry, within a fortnight upon her arrival, one of the women, known as the king's daughters *(filles du roy)*,

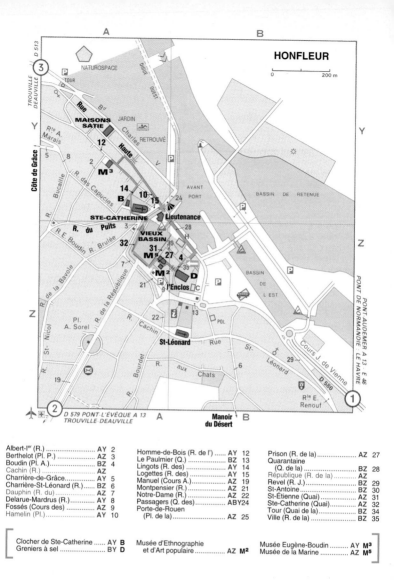

HONFLEUR

who were sent out from France to help increase the sparse population. The queen took an interest in the selection of the young women who were to be "not ugly... not repulsive... healthy and strong enough for working on the land".

From Canada, **Cavelier de La Salle** journeyed south to explore and colonise Louisiana in 1682. He established the communication route along the Ohio Valley which was to lead to war with the British and finally the loss by the French of Canada in 1760.

HONFLEUR, AN ARTIST'S PARADISE

The character and the atmosphere of Honfleur have inspired painters, writers and musicians.

At a time when the coast of Normandy was fashionable with the Romantics, Musset came to stay in St-Gatien and Honfleur began to fill with painters – not only those who were Norman-born such as Boudin, Hamelin and Lebourg but also Paul Huet, Daubigny, Corot and others from Paris and foreigners such as Bonington and Jongkind.

It was in the small St-Siméon Inn, at Mère Toutain's that the Impressionists first met. Artists have continued ever since to visit Honfleur.

Baudelaire, who stayed in the town with his mother in her old age, declared "settling in Honfleur has always been the dearest of my dreams" and while there wrote his *Invitation au Voyage*.

Other Honfleur citizens include the composer Erik Satie (1866-1925), the poet and novelist Henri de Régnier (1864-1936), the author Lucie Delarue-Mardrus, the economist Frédéric Le Play and the historian Albert Sorel.

★★A TOUR OF THE OLD TOWN

⏱ *About 1hr 30min, not including visits to museums. Leave from place Arthur-Boudin to the east of the old dock. You can park your car on quai de la Tour.*

Walking along the streets and alleys of the old town, stopping to admire an old house or a painter at work, sipping a bowl of cider on a café terrace on a fine sunny day are unforgettable experiences.

Place Arthur-Boudin – Old slate-shingled houses stand around the square: no 6 is a Louis XIII house with stone and flint chequered decoration. The Saturday morning flower market brings colour and life to the area.

Greniers à sel ⏱ – *Rue de la Ville*. These tile-covered stone buildings were constructed in the 17C in order to store the salt required by the cod fishing fleet. The fine oak beams are visible only during temporary exhibitions.

Rue de la Prison is very picturesque, with its line of old timber-framed houses. At the end of the street, on the right, is the former church of St-Étienne, its bell-tower rising up above the old port. The building now houses the **Musée de la Marine** (naval museum).

★★**Vieux Bassin** – The quaysides of the old dock – designed by Duquesne on the orders of Colbert – are picturesque, enhanced by the pleasure boats alongside. The contrast is striking between **St-Étienne Quay** with its splendid two-storey stone dwellings, and **Ste-Catherine Quay** where the tall – rising up to seven storeys high – slender houses are faced with slate and timber. The Governor's House (La Lieutenance), next to the swivel bridge completes the scene. St-Étienne Quay affords a pretty **view** of the façades of Ste-Catherine Quay reflected in the water.

La Lieutenance – Only a relic now remains of the 16C house in which the king's lieutenant, Governor of Honfleur, once lived. The façade facing the square now incorporates, between two bartizans, Caen Gate, one of the two main entrances to the city in the Middle Ages. The façade facing the harbour bears a plaque commemorating the departures of Samuel Champlain for Canada. From the corner of the passenger quay you get a good view of the house, the old dock and, on the other side, the outer harbour.

Rue de Logettes, a reference to the numerous wooden stalls that once lined the street, leads to place **Ste-Catherine**, in the heart of the neighbourhood of the same name. Once a suburb of the town, it was incorporated into the Enclos neighbourhood in the 19C when the moat separating it from the other districts was filled in. In addition to the pretty street and half-timbered houses, the neighbourhood is famous for its unique church and bell-tower.

★**Église Ste-Catherine** – This church is a rare example in Western Europe of a building constructed, apart from the foundations, entirely of wood. After the Hundred Years War all masons and architects were employed on the inevitable post-war reconstruction, but the Honfleur "axe masters" from the local shipyards determined to thank God immediately for the departure of the English and built a church with their own skills. The interior has twin naves and side aisles, the timber roof over each nave being supported by wooden pillars. The carved panels ornamenting the gallery are 16C, the organ 18C. There are also many wooden statues.

★**Clocher de Ste-Catherine** ⏱ – The massive oak belfry, a building covered in chestnut wood, stands apart from the church on a large foundation which contained the bell-ringer's dwelling. Today it is used

Église Ste-Catherine

Eating out

MID-RANGE

Thé et Tradition – *20 pl. Hamelin* – ☎ *02 31 89 17 42* – *closed Dec, Jan, Wed except in Apr and July to Aug and Tues* – *18.29€*. Somewhere between a tearoom and a restaurant, this smart house is one of the most charming meeting places in town. Close to the old dock, it appealed to us for the elegant simplicity of its decor, its first-class welcome, its tasty dishes and reasonable prices.

Au P'tit Mareyeur – *4 r. Haute* – ☎ *02 31 98 84 23* – *closed 4-31 Jan, Mon evening and Tues* – *18.29€*. This tiny restaurant, close to the harbour, has a definite maritime slant, as much for its decor as for its cuisine. The menu changes quite often but, in any case, fish and seafood lovers will be delighted.

Au Vieux Honfleur – *13 quai St-Étienne* – ☎ *02 31 89 15 31* – *closed Jan* – *25.92/44.97€*. This restaurant by the old harbour extends its terrace along the quayside in summer, but even if you come in winter and find a table in the dining room decorated with curios, posters and paintings, you will be able to enjoy the view of the dock... while savouring Norman dishes and seafood.

L'Absinthe – *10 quai de la Quarantaine* – ☎ *02 31 89 39 00* – *closed 15 Nov to 15 Dec* – *26.68/57.93€*. Beams, fireplace, copper utensils and flowers contribute to the warm atmosphere pervading the two dining rooms of this old house... and, in summer, the terraces overlooking the fishing harbour are quite attractive. Whatever you choose, the tasty cuisine is in the hands of a talented chef!

Where to stay

MID-RANGE

Le Clos Saint-Gatien – *4 chemin des Brioleurs* – *14130 St-Gatien-des-Bois* – *9km/5.6mi south of Honfleur via D 579* – ☎ *02 31 65 16 08* – *www.clos-st-gatien.fr* – **P** – *58 rooms: 57.93/138.73€* – ☕ *10.67€* – *restaurant 22.87/56.46€*. All the charm of the Norman countryside a few miles from the coast. This delightful timber-framed house, surrounded by greenery, offers pleasant cosy rooms. Two swimming pools, including a covered one, a sauna and a fitness club will appeal to those who are keen on physical activity.

L'Écrin Hotel – *19 r. E.-Boudin* – ☎ *02 31 14 43 45* – **P** – *26 rooms: 68.60/137.20€* – ☕ *8.38€*. This old house, situated a stone's throw from the old dock, is very restful. The mouldings, gilt decorations, chandeliers with pendants, canopies, draperies and wood panelling may appeal to some... Others will no doubt prefer the simplicity of the veranda and garden.

Otelinn Hotel – *62 cour A.-Manuel* – ☎ *02 31 89 41 77* – **P** – *50 rooms: 48.02€* – ☕ *5.79€* – *restaurant 13.57/17.53€*. Located away from the town centre, this hotel offers reasonable prices. The small functional rooms are good value for money. In addition, the garden and terrace will give you the opportunity of experiencing the gentle Norman sun.

LUXURY

Le Manoir du Butin – *R. A.-Marais* – ☎ *02 31 81 63 00* – **P** – *9 rooms: from 97.57€* – ☕ *9.91€* – *restaurant 28.20/43.45€*. This is without a doubt one of the loveliest stopovers along the Côte Fleurie. In the fine manor house overlooking the estuary there is no extravagant display of luxury, but refined, discreet comfort instead. The spacious well-kept rooms are all different and decorated with antique rustic furniture... Delightful!

On the town

L'Albatros – *32 quai Ste-Catherine* – ☎ *02 31 89 25 30* – *Oct to Mar: daily 8am-1am; Apr to Sept: daily 8am-2am*. Baudelaire loved Honfleur and this café, named after one of his most famous poems, would no doubt have appealed to him: the terrace offers a fine view of the harbour and allows you to enjoy the changing light at different times of the day. Inside, you will be warmly welcomed by the owner and his staff.

La Petite Chine – *14 r. du Dauphin* – ☎ *02 31 89 36 52* – *Tues-Fri 11am-7pm, Sat-Sun 10am-7pm*. Small blue and yellow tearoom (Monet's favourite colours) with a view of the harbour. Here you will enjoy regional specialities: gingerbread, countrystyle tart and apples in calvados. CDs and a library are at the disposal of the customers.

Le Perroquet Vert – *52 quai Ste-Catherine* – ☎ *02 31 89 14 19* – *Fri-Wed 8.30am-2am – Easter to Sept: daily 8.30am-2am – closed mid-Nov to mid-Dec*. Housed in a 17C building, this former sail-loft has been converted into a convivial café-cum-tearoom with a fine terrace overlooking the harbour. Occasional concerts.

Sport

Centre équestre du Ramier – *Ferme du Ramier – 14600 Équemauville – drive southwards from Honfleur to Équemauville – very well signposted from Équemauville – ☎ 02 31 89 04 20 – open: Wed, Sat-Sun and holidays 9am-5pm, other days by appointment.* Located in a remote part of the Norman countryside, this lovely equestrian centre has 15 training horses available. Rides lasts between 1hr and 1hr 30min.

Leisure time

Jolie France – *Quai de la Quarantaine – ☎ 02 31 89 58 01 – closed early Oct to end of Mar.* The longest cruise available in Honfleur follows in the tracks of Proust and Baudelaire... In the space of 1hr 30min, you will be able to discover the Pont de Normandie, a view of Le Havre, Vasouy and the Côte de Grâce. If the sun shows through, this boat trip will delight you....

Station Total – *Cours Jean-de-Vienne – ☎ 02 31 89 91 73 – daily 6am-10pm – cycle hire 9am-6.30pm.* Be original, rent a bike from the only cycle hire business in Honfleur, right here in this petrol station!

as an extension of the Musée Eugène-Boudin and contains religious works. Inside there are fine wooden beams and displays of sacred art (wood polychrome monk, 16C, a glass statue of Christ from the liner *Île-de-France*), ornaments and torchères used by the Brothers of Charity and medallions.

Rue des Lingots, narrow and winding, goes around the tower; the old cobblestones lead to **rue de l'Homme-de-Bois**, named after a covered wooden head on the house at no 23.

Turn left rue de l'Homme-de-Bois; 400m further on, across from the Hôtel-Dieu chapel, take rue du Trou-Miard to the right, then turn right again on rue Haute.

The hospital's old lighthouse, on place Jean-de-Vienne, is now mostly used by seagulls. **Rue Haute**, formerly a pathway outside the fortifications, was home to many local shipbuilders. Erik Satie was born at no 88, where the timbers are painted red; inside there is an unusual museum devoted to the composer. Continue on to **place Hamelin**, birthplace of Alphonse Allais (no 6), a French humorist of the late 19C.

You may finish your tour of Honfleur by going straight on (quai de la Lieutenance and quai de la Quarantaine) to return to place Arthur-Boudin on the right. Or enjoy yourself a little longer by taking a turn through the public garden and walking as far as the Seine along the digue de l'Ouest, where a pleasant pedestrian path has been created on the jetty.

SIGHTS

Musée Eugène-Boudin ⊙ – An old Augustinian chapel and a more recent building house this museum, which was laid out in 1973-74 according to the new ideas in museum presentation; it is chiefly devoted to the painters of Honfleur and those of the estuary.

On the first floor one room presents a rich collection of coffers, cupboards, costumes, headdresses, dolls, engravings and paintings, the majority of which concern daily life in Normandy in the 18C and 19C. The second and third floors display works by 20C artists who, for the most part, worked in the region: Dufy, Marquet, Friesz, Villon, Lagar, Grau-Sala, Saint-Delis, Gernez, Driès, Herbo, Vallotton, Bigot etc.

In 1988 three new galleries adjoining the chapel were opened:

– 19C paintings by Eugène Boudin (the museum possesses 87 of his paintings and drawings) and by painters influenced by St Siméon: Monet, Jongkind, Dubourg, Isabey, Pécrus, Courbet, Cals;

– the Hambourg-Rachet bequest of some 300 canvases (19C-20C) by Derain, Foujita, Garbell, Marie Laurencin, Van Dongen and Hambourg;

– a drawings room in which about 100 works are rotated each year.

The museum puts on regular temporary exhibitions.

Musée du Vieux Honfleur – The museum presents three sections – one on the navy, one on popular art and finally the Manoir du Désert *(see Nearby sights, below)*.

Musée de la Marine ⊙ – The museum, which is housed in St Stephen's Church (deconsecrated), traces the history of the port of Honfleur and contains a large number of scale models and topographical information on the town. Maritime activities include: fishing, shipbuilding etc.

Musée d'Ethnographie et d'Art populaire ⊙ – Ten Normandy interiors have been reconstructed in this museum located in 16C residences. Note particularly the timbered manor house, the bourgeois dining room, the weaver's and printer's workshop, the bedroom and a shop on the ground floor.

A large variety of objects are displayed: pewter, furniture, paintings, costumes and jewellery pieces.

★Maison Satie ⊙ – The museum is innovative in its use of sound, light, images and objects in juxtapositions which are at once fantastic and humorous, just like the works of the famous modern composer (1866-1925).

Wearing headphones, the visitor is guided from one surprise to another through a series of stage-like settings recalling the many aspects of the career of Erik Satie – "born young in an old world". Dreamy and surrealist, the museum offers the opportunity to hear the music and understand more about the life of the man who came out with such conversational pearls as: "Give me a minute to get my skirt on, and I'll be right with you!"; "Although our information is false, we cannot guarantee it."; "What do you prefer, music or cold-cuts?"; "The piano is like money, it's only agreeable when you've got your hands on it."

Église St-Léonard – The façade of this church is a bizarre combination of an ornate Flamboyant doorway and a 17C belfry tower.

Inside are two immense shells which have been converted into fonts. The narthex is roofed with restored quadripartite vaulting. At the entrance to the chancel stand statues of Our Lady of Victory and St Leonard with two prisoners kneeling; note in the chancel the wooden statues of St Peter, St Paul and the four Evangelists. The narthex is furnished with an 18C copper lectern from Villedieu-les-Poêles.

NEARBY SIGHTS

Pont de Normandie – The bridge *(see illustration p 39)* was started in 1988 and officially opened in January 1995; it is the third largest bridge to span the Lower Seine after the Pont de Tancarville and the Pont de Brotonne.

Its impact on the economy is three-fold: it brings Le Havre and Honfleur closer together by removing the detour via Tancarville Bridge (24km/15mi instead of 60km/37mi); it is one of the major motorway links between the Channel Tunnel and the west and southwest of France; it represents one of the many connections in the so-called **Estuaries Route**, which will tie up the north and south of Europe without going through Paris by the year 2000.

The Pont de Normandie, a truly remarkable work of art and a technological feat, was seen as a milestone in the history of civil engineering, since it established the record of the longest cable-stayed bridge (more elegant and cheaper to build than a suspension bridge). Although Lisbon's Vaso de Gama Bridge (1998) is now the longest in Europe, the Pont de Normandie is higher. This steel and concrete mass, which defies the laws of gravity, is surprisingly light and extremely stable. Careful attention was devoted to the subject of safety: the bridge is designed to withstand winds of up 440kph/274mph; it can resist shocks caused by the largest cargo boats, which could only collide with the north tower, protected by 9m/30ft of concrete; the road surfacing has in-built sensors triggered off by the presence of black ice; tollbooth operators can monitor traffic continually thanks to surveillance cameras.

Besides the standard lighting for road traffic, the Breton architect **Yann Kersalé** conceived a sophisticated lighting system called *Rhapsody in Blue and White* – a bi-coloured display of static lights outline the two towers (blue on the underside, white on the outside), while a row of blue twinkling lights run underneath the deck.

Manoir du Désert – *2km/&mi southeast – take rue Charrière-St-Léonard, la côte Vassal and Chemin du Buquet.* This elegant half-timbered builging (15C) was once the home of maritime traders, the Le Danois brothers.

Pont de Normandie

E. Baret/MICHELIN

★★Côte de Grâce

The peaceful beauty of this famous hillside, appreciated by all Honfleur enthusiasts, is also appealing to passing tourists.

★★**Calvaire** – *Telescope*. From the cross there is a good **panorama** of the Seine estuary, the Le Havre roadstead, to the right, the Pont de Normandie and, in the distance, Tancarville Bridge.

Chapelle Notre-Dame-de-Grâce – In the centre of the esplanade beneath tall trees, stands the small chapel of Our Lady of Grace and within it the statue after which it is named. This graceful 17C building which has replaced a sanctuary said to have been founded by Richard II, 4th Duke of Normandy, is visited by pilgrims throughout the year. It was here that navigators and explorers came to pray before leaving on journeys of discovery or colonisation to the North American continent. The north transept chapel is dedicated to all Canadians of Norman origin. There are numerous small, ex-voto vessels.

Mont-Joli Viewpoint – The view complements the one from the Calvary: in the foreground are the town, the port and the coast; to the east is the semicircle of hills. Tancarville Bridge can be seen in the distance.

★★② SOUTH BANK OF THE SEINE – HONFLEUR TO ROUEN *130km/81mi – about 5hr – see map p 306*

This charming drive takes you through forests and along roads overlooking the river below.

Leave Honfleur via cours Jean-de-Vienne and take D 312 towards Berneville and Pont-Audemer.

The road follows the lower Risle Valley. Beyond Berville, they are many fine views of the esturay. In the spring, the blooming apple orchards turn the landscape into a wonderland.

★**Pont-Audemer** – *See PONT-AUDEMER.*

Take D 810.

Ste-Opportune-la-Mare – *See QUILLEBEUF.*

Take D 95.

After a section on a crest road, between Val-Anger and Vieux-Port, the Seine Valley comes into view again.

Vieux-Port – The thatched cottages are half hidden by their orchards.

Aizier – The stone bell-tower of the 12C church looks very old. Near the church there is a manhole slab – the remains of a covered way dating from around 2000 BC.

Take D 139 which leads to the Roumois plateau.

Bourneville – The **Maison des Métiers** ⊘ includes the Musée des Métiers presenting the traditional crafts of Upper Normandy (metalwork, woodwork, textiles, farming) as well as an exhibition area on patchwork and counterpanes where a number of early blankets and hangings are displayed.

Return to Aizier. From here to Quesney, D 95 and D 65 follow the edge of the Brotonne Forest.

Vatteville-la-Rue – The nave of the church dates from the Renaissance; it bears a black mourning band which was painted on the wall for the funeral of the lord of the manor. The Flamboyant chancel is lit by 16C stained-glass windows.

Turn left onto D 65 which leads to La Mailleraye (ferry).

Running alongside the Seine to the right, the road offers views of typical Norman thatched cottages half-hidden by trees. After Notre-Dame-de-Bliquetuit, you can see the two ferries which cross at Yainville and Jumièges. D 65 then rises in hairpin turns.

★**Viewpoint** – *Picnic area. Viewing table.* To the right can be seen the towers of Jumièges Abbey, particularly impressive at sunset, and to the left the Seine Valley.

300m/330yd further on stop on the right in La Mailleraye lay-by.

Chêne à la Cuve – *100m/110yd from D 913, opposite the 11km post.* Four oak trunks growing from a single bole form a kind of natural vat, 7m/23ft in circumference.

Take D 313 towards Bourg-Achard and turn right on D 101.

Moulin d'Hauville ⊘ – This 13C mill is one of the few surviving stone mills in Upper Normandy and once belonged to the monks of Jumièges Abbey. Its cap can be oriented according to the direction of the wind and is supported by oak beams. The stone tower and large sails are most impressive. If the weather allows one can see the mill in operation.

Take D 101 in the other direction and turn left on D 712. Going down the hill, turn onto D 45 (nice views on the forest and the river), then take D 265 which crosses the Mauny Forest, then D 64 towards La Bouille.

Between La Ronce and La Bouille, the road goes along the river's edge.

La Bouille – La Bouille, which enjoys a handsome setting at the foot of the wooded slopes of the Roumois plateau, has always attracted artists and over the years a great many writers, poets and painters have succumbed to the irresistible charm of its landscapes. In the old days, people from Rouen would come here to sample local gastronomic delights: eels stewed in cider, La Bouille cheese and *douillons aux pommes* (apples hollowed out, filled with butter, wrapped in pastry and baked).

Today the village still offers a charming combination of terraces, inns and avenues. The town has remained popular among painters, who set up their easel and draw sketches of the quaint streets and surrounding countryside.

On the quayside, a plaque on one of the houses reminds visitors that the author **Hector Malot** was born in the locality.

Moulineaux – The **church** ⊙ with its slender spire dates from the 13C. Inside there is an attractive woodwork group formed by the pulpit and rood screen (one side of the latter is Gothic and the other Renaissance). In the apse is the 13C **stained-glass window**★ that was the gift of Blanche de Castille. Note also the 16C tableau of the Flemish School depicting the Crucifixion and a monk in prayer. There is a far-reaching view of the Seine Valley from the cemetery.

Take D 3, a steep hill.

Monument "Qui Vive"– *At the crossroads of D 64 and D 67*[A]*.* There is a remarkable view *(viewing table)* of the Seine as it curves round to encircle Roumare Forest. Road D 64 goes down to the Seine so that one gets a view of the river bend commanded by Robert the Devil's castle and the Rouen industrial suburbs.

★**Château de Robert le Diable** – *See ELBEUF: Excursions.*

Go back to D 64 up a steep climb. Take D 64 right through the Londe Forest. At the crossroads known as "Le Nouveau Monde", follow D 938 to Orival, to the south.

★**Orival** – From Oissel to Orival the road is overhung by curious rocks which are part of the chalk escarpment. They dominate the peaceful riverine landscape. Orival Church is an unusual semi-troglodytic 15C building.

Return to "Le Nouveau Monde".

★**Roches d'Orival** – *Park on D 18 by a sign "Sentier des Roches"; 1hr on foot there and back by a steep path which is slippery when wet. At the top turn right onto a path which passes in front of some caves hollowed out of the rocks.*
🚶 The path follows the cliff. By a grassy knoll (300m/330yd) there is a **view** of the Seine and of the rock escarpment, broken by a grassy corniche on which the path continues.

Follow D 18 along the Seine.

Oissel – Pleasant public garden.

To return to Rouen, take D 13, then N 138 to the right.

The pine forest of Rouvray is an oasis of calm, reminiscent of the Landes of southwest France.

Ville Romaine de JUBLAINS ★

Michelin map 60 fold 11 or 232 fold 8 – 14km/9mi northwest of Evron

There was originally an important Gaulish sanctuary on the archeological site of Jublains.

Following the conquest of Gaul by Julius Caesar, the Romans divided the country into districts and built towns which correspond to the present administrative centres. The district of Aulerques Diablintes was named after the local Gaulish people and the town of Noviodunum was built at an ancient crossroads. The predominant role of the Roman town as a sanctuary is made evident by the alignment of the public buildings along the axis of the temple.

The main buildings have already been uncovered and can be visited: the baths which were discovered during the restoration of the church, the ruins of Jublains Roman fort, the temple and the theatre are the best local remains of the Gallo-Roman period in the region. Further excavations are being carried out to uncover the forum.

On the outskirts of the town, the fortress (3C) seems to have been not only an entrenched camp but also one of the staging posts to be found on the roads of the Roman Empire. The number of roads which have been found in the vicinity, in particular those linking the Channel to Lyon and Tours, suggests the importance of the town as an overnight stop for travellers and messengers but also as a centre with shops, government offices and police.

Where to stay

MODERATE

Ferme du Maupoirier Self-catering cottage – *53160 Jublains – 2.5km/1.5mi south of Jublains towards Montsûrs along D 129* – ☎ *02 43 04 52 75 – closed Feb and Mon* – 🛏 *– 7 rooms, per night/per person: 10.67€.* This farm, situated right out in the country at the bottom of a dead end, specialises in deer breeding and lets a few rooms as well... rather austere but well kept. No food service except for groups.

Musée départemental d'Archéologie ⊙ – *At the entrance of the fortress.* This museum offers an introduction to the different sites and main archeological themes of the Mayenne region, in particular the paleolithic site at Saulges with its decorated cave, the Gaulish and Gallo-Roman sanctuaries, the development of the Roman town of Jublains and medieval pottery in the Laval region. The site of Jublains is dealt with in more detail with the help of an audio-visual presentation and a large model which gives a good idea of what it looked like in ancient times.

Forteresse gallo-romaine ⊙ – It consists of three concentric parts.
The central building, the oldest part of the fortress dating from the early 3C, is a massive rectangular storehouse with four angle towers. It is lit by means of a central courtyard and is equipped with several wells and water tanks. The gates and the external wall coverings are made of squared blocks. The two small buildings in the north and south angles were bathhouses.
During the crisis which shook the Roman Empire at the end of the 3C (invasions, military anarchy, peasant rebellions...), the storehouse was surrounded by a rampart of raised earth and a moat. This moat was later filled in to enable the construction of fortified walls around AD 290, just before the whole site was abandoned.

Public baths ⊙ – *Below the church, entrance through the Syndicat d'Initiative.* The building, which dates from the late 1C, was altered in the 3C and transformed into a Christian church at the end of the Gallo-Roman period. The baths, which have a peristyle entrance, are situated in the middle of a courtyard *(palestra)* which is bordered on the north side by shops and libraries. The west side, facing the church, was occupied by the furnace which supplied hot air to the hypocausts (a system of underfloor heating) in the warm and hot rooms.
An audio-visual presentation illustrates life in Jublains in the Gaulish and Gallo-Roman period. The layout of the baths is shown on a plan; one can see the main rooms: the cold bath *(frigidarium)* paved in blue schist, the warm room *(tepidarium)*, the sweating room *(laconicum)*. The hot bath *(cella soliaris)* is situated beyond the excavated part. Against the right wall are sarcophagi (skeletons of a man and a child) found in a Merovingian burial ground uncovered on the site.

Theatre ⊙ – Situated at the southern end of the town, the theatre was offered to the town by a rich Diablinte, Orgetorix, who lived during the reign of Domitian (c 81-83). Part of it was made of wood.

Temple ⊙ – *It can be visited freely with the help of information leaflets to be found in the museum or at the Syndicat d'Initiative.* The temple is situated at the other end of the Roman town, 800m/0.5mi from the theatre. A number of weapons offered as gifts were found on the site of the Gaulish sanctuary which was rebuilt under Nero in AD 65; its proportions were vast (each side being about 80m/262ft long) and limestone was brought especially from the Loire region. A covered canal carried rain water to a heated pool situated on the outside of the temple.

Gallo-Roman stag and wild boar from Jublains

Abbaye de JUMIÈGES★★★

Michelin map 54 fold 10 or 231 fold 22

Jumièges is one of the most impressive ruins in France and it occupies a splendid site on the Lower Seine.

The galleries, the south aisle, the nave roof, the transept crossing, the chancel apse and the roofless cloisters are much more interesting when a well-informed imagination can bring them to life.

Jumièges Almshouse – In the 10C Duke William Longsword rebuilt Jumièges on the ruins of the former abbey founded in the 7C by St Philibert and destroyed by the Vikings. The new Benedictine abbey soon became popularly known through its benefactions as the Jumièges Almshouse. Charity did not however preclude learning and Jumièges also became widely recognised as a centre of scholarship and wisdom.

The large abbey church was consecrated in 1067 in the presence of William the Conqueror.

The last monks dispersed at the Revolution and in 1793 the abbey was bought at a public auction by a timber merchant from Canteleu who intended to turn Jumièges into a stone quarry and used explosives to bring down the lantern in the church. A new proprietor in 1852 set about saving the ruins which now belong to the nation.

★★★ABBAYE ⊘ *30min*

Église Notre-Dame – The projecting porch is flanked by twin towers (43m/141ft high), which are square at the base and octagonal above; their spires were visible until 1830.

The entire nave (27m/89ft high) still stands, together with part of the transept and the chancel. At the west end there is a deep gallery overlooking the nave, which is articulated by strong square pillars, quartered by columns, alternating with more slender clusters of columns; the aisles are covered with rib vaulting. Most of the transept was demolished in the 19C. Only the west side of the lantern has survived, resting on an arch which is impressive for its height and reach. A slim pepper-pot turret is attached to the northwest corner.

The original chancel was enlarged in the 13C and 14C; traces of an ambulatory have been discovered but only a vaulted chapel has survived.

Passage Charles-VII – The passage leading to a small church, dedicated to St Peter, was named in memory of King Charles VII's visit to Jumièges.

Église St-Pierre – The porch and first bays of the nave are Norman Carolingian (oculi and twinned arcades), the remaining ruins date from the 13C and 14C. The arched entrance porch is flanked by two small doors behind which are stairs to the gallery towers; it is surmounted by an arched gallery. The first two bays of the nave are a rare example of 10C Norman architecture. Above the round-headed arches are the medallions once decorated with frescoes. Above them is a nave gallery of twinned round-headed arches.

Abbaye de Jumièges

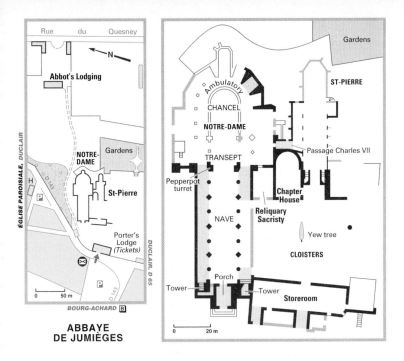

ABBAYE DE JUMIÈGES

Chapter-house – *Between the abbey church and St Peter's Church.* The chapter-house opens off the cloisters, in accordance with the monastic rule, and dates from the early 12C. The square body and the apse were covered with some of the earliest ogival vaulting known to have existed.

Sacristy – The sacristy for relics was covered by barrel vaulting and supported by buttresses.

Cloisters – In the middle of the cloisters grows an ancient yew tree. The four galleries once consisted of 26 bays. The refectory was on the south side.

Storeroom – The great cellar dates from the end of the 12C. The exterior face of the west wall is divided into bays framed by arcading or trilobed pediments.

Gardens – Beyond a fence, a 17C set of steps leads to a broad terrace and the gardens.

Abbot's Lodging – Beyond the lawn rises the former abbot's lodging, a majestic 17C rectangular building, which has a pedimented break-front and a mansard roof.

Église paroissiale St-Valentin ⊙ – The parish church has an 11C-12C nave and a 16C chancel and ambulatory; inside, altarpieces and 15C-16C stained-glass windows in ambulatory chapels.

LASSAY-LES-CHÂTEAUX

Population 2 459
Michelin map 60 fold 1 or 232 fold 41

This ancient market town (the emblem of commerce is on the town's coat of arms) owes its name to a Roman town called Lacciacium or Laceio because it used to be surrounded by lakes. A few remarkable buildings have been restored, revealing some splendid red granite façades (Maison du Bailly, a half-timbered inn). On the edge of this small town stands an imposing fortress.

Where to stay

MODERATE

La Prémoudière Bed and Breakfast – *61330 St-Denis-la-Villenette – 11.5km/7.1mi N of Lassay-les-Châteaux via D 117 towards Domfront and Sept Forge, then take D 52 – ☎ 02 33 37 23 27 – ⚲ – 4 rooms: 27.44/35.06€ – meal 12.20€.* Apple and pear cider is made in this Norman farm where the former cellars have been converted into guestrooms. Peace and quiet is guaranteed in this rural environment. Delicious home-made red-berry jam is served for breakfast.

★CHÂTEAU ⊘ 30min

The castle, which dominates the village with its eight pepper-pot towers linked by a strong curtain wall, was built in 1458 in place of an older building which had been dismantled in 1417 during the Hundred Years War. The castle is a prime example of military architecture under the reign of Charles VII. Its history evokes three famous people – King Henri IV, the writer and poet Victor Hugo and the chemist Lavoisier who was a prisoner in the castle during the Revolution and used a curious "Chinese oven" situated in one of the towers not only to carry out his experiments but also to produce the first porcelain objects made from hard paste. The bridge spanning the moat leads to the barbican, a fortified structure defending the entrance to the castle. The two towers guarding the drawbridge are linked by living quarters, in which 16C and 17C weapons and furniture are displayed. The casemates can be seen at the foot of the barbican. The tour ends with a stroll in the park.

For a good overall view of the castle, walk down the path which passes under the stone bridge and skirts the foot of the towers and the pool on the right-hand side. ◰ The nearby landscape crisscrossed by hedges and trees offers some pretty signposted footpaths.

LAVAL ★

Population (conurbation) 57 000
Michelin map 63 fold 10 or 232 fold 7

The first thing that strikes any visitor to Laval is the River Mayenne, which flows gently through town, providing its central focus, as it has since the year 1000. It must also provide something special to the people that are born here, for a number of them have made names for themselves in various fields *(see below)*. Laval has been awarded the prestigious status of *Ville d'Art et d'Histoire*, affirming its cultural significance.

FAMOUS CITIZENS OF LAVAL

Laval is the birthplace of many exceptional men.

Ambroise Paré (1517-90) aroused the anger of the traditionalists by the boldness of his methods in the treatment of wounds: he was the first to practise the ligature of arteries during amputations. He developed the first instruments used in trepanning and deserves to be known as the father of surgery. He was modest about his success: "I dress their wounds, God cures them".

Henri Rousseau (1844-1910), whose nickname was "Le Douanier" (the Customs Officer), was a tax collector in Paris. He was the archetype of the modern naive artist, and was known for the meticulous approach which he brought to his paintings of lush jungles, wild beasts and exotic figures. Before painting a portrait he measured his sitter with a tape like a tailor. Marie Laurencin and Jarry were among the long-suffering subjects of this meticulous artist. He wrote to the mayor of Laval asking him to purchase his magically enchanting painting, "The Sleeping Gypsy", but the mayor was merely amused. He must have regretted his refusal, for within a few years, Rousseau was receiving praise and recognition from the likes of Matisse, Derain and De Vlaminck, and Vollard, the most exclusive dealer in Paris, was handling his work. He was fêted by the great artists of the day at an extravagant banquet organised in Picasso's studio.

Alfred Jarry (1873-1907) was the inventor of "pataphysics", the science of imaginary solutions, and the forerunner of the Surrealists. He created the grotesque satirical character of Père Ubu, King of Poland, when he was still in his teens. In his play, Jarry denounced the crass stupidity and avarice of the bourgeoisie, and acts of cruelty committed in the name of questionable principles. A brilliant youth when he came to Paris, Jarry soon ran through his family funds and died destitute and largely unappreciated. Today, however, he is honoured as one of the creators of the Theatre of the Absurd, and his most famous character has entered the French language in adjective form: "ubuesque".

Alain Gerbault (1893-1941) was not only the favourite tennis partner of King Gustave V of Sweden and Jean Borotra (1898-1994), who was the Wimbledon Men's Singles Champion in 1924 and 1926, but also sailed singled-handed in his cutter (in 1923 he made the transatlantic crossing); he died in the Polynesian islands. His second boat, the *Fire-Crest II*, is exhibited in the Jardin de la Perrine.

"Chouans" – In 1793 the Royalists *(Les Blancs)* occupied the town and beneath its very walls on the low ground at La Croix-Bastille defeated the Republican army of General Lechelle whose sole military precept was to march majestically and in large numbers. The Vendéan (Royalist) cavalry was commanded by La Trémoille, Prince de Talmont. Some time later, however, La Rochejaquelein had to evacuate Laval and the Republicans *(Les Bleus)* captured the Prince de Talmont whom they guillotined at the gate of his own castle. It was in the Laval countryside that the name **Chouans** was first applied to the royalist troops; they were led by Jean Cottereau, called Jean Chouan, who gave his name to the movement; their rallying cry was the hoot of the tawny owl *(chat-huant)*.

★THE OLD TOWN *1hr*

Place de la Trémoille – The square is named after the last of the local lords. On the east side stands the Renaissance façade of the **Nouveau Château** (**J**); the "new castle" was built in the 16C as the residence of the Count of Laval; it was enlarged in the 19C and now houses the law courts.

Rue des Orfèvres – The narrow street which runs south into Grande-Rue is lined with beautiful 16C overhanging houses and 18C mansions.
At the T-junction stands the Renaissance house (1550) of the Master of the Royal Hunt (Grand Veneur); the façade and the windows in carved tufa are similar to those at the castle.

Grande-Rue – This was the main street of the medieval city; it descends to the River Mayenne between rows of old houses, some half-timbered with projecting upper storeys, others in stone with Renaissance decoration.
Turn right onto rue de Chapelle.
The street climbs between medieval and Renaissance houses to a charming statue of St René in a niche (right) at the top.
Go straight ahead onto rue des Serruriers.
Just south of the Beucheresse Gate are two slightly askew half-timbered houses.

Porte Beucheresse – In former days this gate, then called Porte des Bûcherons, opened directly into the forest. It was built in the 14C with a pointed entrance arch and is flanked by two round towers, topped with machicolations, which were once part of the town walls of Laval. Henri Rousseau was born in the south tower where his father exercised his trade as a tinsmith.

Cathédrale – The building has been altered many times but the nave and the transept crossing are covered with Angevin vaulting: the Angevin or Plantagenet style is characterised by curved rib vaulting in which the keystones are at different heights.
The walls are hung with Aubusson tapestries (early 17C) depicting the story of Judith and Holophernes in six panels. On the left pillar near the chancel is a very beautiful triptych painted by the Antwerp Mannerist School in the 16C; it presents the Martyrdom of St John the Apostle when closed and three scenes from the life of John the Baptist when open. In the north transept there is an imposing revolving door carved in the 18C.
On leaving the cathedral, walk round the east end to admire the northeast door (facing the law courts) which is decorated with 17C terracotta statues.

Rue de la Trinité – This is a street of old houses, one of which dates from the 16C and is adorned with statues of the Virgin and the Saints.
Turn left onto rue du Pin-Doré which ends in place de la Trémoille.

★**Quays** – The quays on the east bank provide the best overall **views**★ of Laval across the still waters of the River Mayenne which was canalized in the 19C. From Aristide-Briand Bridge the eye travels from the old bridge to the old town and then step by step up to the dark bulk of the old castle and the lighter mass of the new one. From the **Pont Vieux**, a 13C humpback bridge, which was originally fortified, there is a more detailed view of the old town: the slate roofs, the narrow streets of half-timbered houses and the keep of the old castle with its hoarding.
The **bateaux-lavoirs**, the last public washing stages in Laval, are moored along quai Paul-Boudet. They first appeared in 1880 and the last of them were in use until 1960; they resembled landing-stages surrounded by washboards where the housewives came to beat their linen and rinse it in the running water; in the centre were enormous vats for boiling and drying the laundry. One of these, the **St-Julien** ⊙, has been restored; it also incorporated a lodging for the owner.

★**Jardin de la Perrine** – The terraces of these public gardens command attractive views of the River Mayenne, the lower town and the castle keep.
As well as a rose garden there are many tall trees: palms, limes, chestnuts, larches and cedars of Lebanon. Ponds and waterfalls alternate with lawns and flower beds.

★VIEUX CHÂTEAU ⊙ *1hr*

To the right of the railings in front of the law courts stands a noble 17C porch decorated with pilasters and simulated masonry joints, next to an early-16C half-timbered house. Through the porch is the courtyard of the old castle enclosed by ramparts (from the top of the walls there is a picturesque **view**★ of the roofs of the old town). On the terrace to the left of the castle, overlooking the Mayenne, stands a statue of Béatrix de Gavre, Baroness of Laval in the 14C, who promoted the development of weaving in Laval. In its present state the bulk of the castle dates from the 13C and 15C; the windows and dormers in white tufa, carved with scrolls in the Italian style, were added in the 16C. The crypt and the keep are the oldest parts (12C-13C). The rooms are decorated with French and foreign paintings as well as handsome fire backs.

Eating out

MID-RANGE

La Bonne Auberge – *170 r. de Bretagne* – ☎ *02 43 69 07 81* – *closed 28 July to 27 Aug, 23-31 Dec, Feb school holidays, Fri evening from 15 Nov to 28 Feb, Sun evening and Sat* – *13.72/39.64€*. The pastel-coloured decoration of the dining room contributes to the general cosy atmosphere of this inn. The veranda adds light and an impression of spaciousness. Reasonable prices.

Gerbe de Blé – *83 r. V.-Boissel* – ☎ *02 43 53 14 10* – *closed 2-8 Jan, 30 July to 21 Aug, Mon lunch and Sun lunch except holidays* – *20.58/38.11€*. This renowned family run establishment is worth a detour. The warm decor of wood panelling in shades of golden wheat is conducive to relaxation. The traditional cuisine is well prepared and attractive. A few spacious rooms.

La Table Ronde – *Pl. de la Mairie* – *53810 Changé* – *4km/2.5mi north of Laval via D 104* – ☎ *02 43 53 43 33* – *closed Sun evening and Mon* – *12.96/ 36.28€*. Before taking a stroll along the banks of the River Mayenne, stop in at this restaurant housed in the former stables of the castle. You can choose between the downstairs bistro with its Art Nouveau decor or the upstairs dining room where the work of a local artist is exhibited and the cuisine is more refined.

Where to stay

MODERATE

Camping Village Vacances – *53170 Villiers-Charlemagne* – *20km/12.4mi south of Laval via N 162* – ☎ *02 43 07 71 68* – *open Apr to Sept* – ⌿ – *reservation advisable* – *20 places: 13.72€*. Keen anglers will be able to indulge in their hobby at leisure. The lake abounds in pike, pikeperch and carp. Campers have their own bathroom installations and fishing-equipment premises. It is possible to rent small chalets with individual terraces raised on piles.

MID-RANGE

Grand Hôtel de Paris – *22 r. de la Paix* – ☎ *02 43 53 76 20* – **P** – *39 rooms: 42.69/73.18€* – ⌸ *6.10€*. Situated in the town centre, close to the shopping area, this hotel has been entirely renovated. The rooms, which are plain with whitewashed walls and coloured furniture, are completely sound-proof.

LUXURY !

Le Bas du Gast Bed and Breakfast – *6 r. de la Halle-aux-Toiles* – ☎ *02 43 49 22 79* – *closed Dec and Jan* – *4 rooms: from 90/185€* – ⌸ *15€*. Built in the centre of the old town of Laval, this 17C-18C castle is surrounded by a beautiful garden adorned with trimmed box trees. As you go in, note the lovely smell of wax on the oak parquet flooring and period furniture. The spacious bedrooms are carefully decorated.

On the town

Café des Arts – *69 r. du Val-de-Mayenne* – ☎ *02 43 56 86 33* – *Tues-Sat open Mon in summer*. Beautiful reconstruction in late-19C style. Marble, tiles and wrought iron add to the appeal of this café which is as pleasant during the day as in the evening. Exhibitions, concerts and themed evenings make it a convivial place; in addition, it is has one of the few terraces overlooking the Mayenne.

Le Johannesburg – *5 r. de la Trinité* – ☎ *02 43 53 21 21* – *Thur-Sat 10pm-2am*. Behind the superb 17C façade lies what remains of a former Cistercian abbey. The establishment includes a tavern on the ground floor and a pub in one of the cellars with a cosy atmosphere. Undoubtedly the most pleasant place for a night out in Laval.

Showtime

La Coulée Douce – *177 r. du Vieux-St-Louis* – *53000 Changé 4km/2.4mi N of Laval via D 104* – ☎ *02 43 56 73 37* – *daily from 5pm*. A true cabaret-style café: tables are lined up in front of a wide stage where customers can watch local and international artists (musicians, humorists, poets...) in a convivial atmosphere. A three-monthly programme is available at the tourist office.

Shopping

Boucherie – Charcuterie du Pont Vieux – *28 r. du Pont-de-Mayenne –* ☎ *02 43 53 67 80 – Mon-Sat 7.30am-1pm, 3.30-7.30pm – closed Mon during school holidays, 1 week in Feb and 3 weeks in Aug.* A fine old fashioned butcher's and delicatessen. Typical local produce: meat, prepared dishes and *charcuterie* made from local suckling pig fattened on cereals. Selected farm beef from the Maine region is also a speciality of the house.

Épicerie Fine Papin – Launay – *27 pl. Jean-Moulin –* ☎ *02 43 53 63 55 – Mon 10am-12.30pm, Tues-Sat 9.30am-12.30pm, 2.30-7.30pm.* Founded in 1909, this fine Hédiard delicatessen offers a wide choice of spirits from Normandy, prepared dishes from the Mayenne such as chicken cooked with apples and honey and delicious confectionery: chocolates, crunchy biscuits flavoured with aniseed or apple and cinnamon…

Les Ruchers du Maine – *433 rte de Tours –* ☎ *02 43 67 04 85.* Small honey making concern on the way out of town. In the shop you will find honey, royal jelly and other products derived from bees such as wax, pollen or mead (fizzy drink made from water and honey), the drink of the gods according to Celtic mythology.

Sport

Laval-Changé Golf course – *La Chabossière – 53810 Changé 4km/2.4mi N of Laval –* ☎ *02 43 53 16 03 – golf53.laval@wanadoo.fr – daily 9am-7pm, until 5.30pm in winter – closed 23 Dec to 2 Jan.* Laid out on undulating ground covering 82ha/203 acres, this splendid golf course offers two rounds of 9 and 18 holes by the River Mayenne, suitable for beginners as well as for players with a handicap. From the bar/restaurant, there is a superb view of the course. Beginners' courses and rental of equipment. Covered practice area and approach green.

Halte Fluviale – *100 r. du Vieux-St-Louis / Square de Boston –* ☎ *02 43 53 31 01 – opening times vary: on average 10am-9pm (Sat-Sun and holidays).* Situated in the town centre, the marina offers a choice of activities on the River Mayenne: rental of rowing boats, pedalos, canoes, speed boats…

Donjon – Originally separated from the courtyard by a moat, the keep was later incorporated between the two wings of the castle. It has retained its original roof and hoarding, a projecting wooden gallery, clearly visible from the river, from which the castle troops could defend the bridge and the base of the walls. Within the keep is a display of the old tools used by the journeymen carpenters and their ribbons which varied in shape and colour according to the status, guild and craft of the journeyman; another room contains the trepanning instruments attributed to Ambroise Paré and some paintings and watercolours of Laval by Jean-Baptiste

View on the old town and castle

LAVAL

Église de Pritz

N.-D. d'Avesnières

Messager, a local artist. The most interesting feature is the extraordinary **timber roof★★** which was built c 1100 to an ingenious circular design. Great beams, radiating from the centre like the spokes of a wheel, project beyond the walls (which are over 2m/6ft thick) to support the hoarding.

SIGHTS IN TOWN

★**Musée d'Art naïf** ⊘ – The Museum of Naive Painting, which can be visited separately from the castle and the keep, displays a number of canvases by painters from France, Croatia, Germany, Brazil etc. A reconstruction of Rousseau's (the tax collector) studio contains mementos of the artist.

Musée des Sciences ⊘ – The Science Museum is housed in an imposing building; flanking the stone steps are two bronze animal groups by the sculptor Gardet. The bust in the square is of Alain Gerbault, the navigator.

The archeological exhibits are the result of excavations carried out in the Laval region. There are also temporary exhibitions on a particular theme: botany, geology, zoology etc. The 19C astronomical clock in its carved wooden case is a fine exhibit.

Notre-Dame-d'Avesnières – *1.5km/1mi south*. This ancient sanctuary dedicated to the Virgin Mary was made into a basilica in 1898. The Romanesque **east end★** is best seen from Avesnières Bridge: the chancel, the ambulatory and the five radiating chapels. The attractive Gothic-Renaissance spire is an identical copy, made in 1871, of the original which was erected in 1538.

The 19C restoration, which is quite visible on the west front, has not spoiled the uniformity of the Romanesque basilica nor the atmosphere of meditation with which this place of pilgrimage is imbued.

Inside, flanking the entrance, are two colossal painted wooden statues. One (16C) is of St Christopher carrying the infant Jesus; the other (15C) represents the Holy Saviour: Christ, dressed in a long stiff robe and crowned with a tiara, is standing on tip toe about to ascend into heaven. The fine Romanesque chancel consists of three storeys of arches and bays; among the capitals note a 15C painted wooden figure of Christ and, at the level of the triforium, a miraculous statue of Our Lady. The modern stained-glass is by Max Ingrand. In the axial chapel there is a 16C Breton Pietà in terracotta. The south chapel is hung with a 17C Aubusson tapestry.

Église St-Vénérand – The nave of the church is flanked by double aisles. The north front, facing the street, has a Flamboyant door decorated with an attractive 17C terracotta figure of the Virgin and carved canopies and is surmounted by a pediment supported on an arch with Renaissance motifs.

Tour Renaise – This 15C round machicolated tower belongs to the old walls.

★**Église Notre-Dame-des-Cordeliers** – Built between 1397 and 1407, this former chapel of a Franciscan monastery contains a remarkable set of seven **altarpieces★★** from the 17C. Six of them can be seen in the north aisle (lighting is essential; token available from the Tourist Information Centre); they were carved out of tufa and marble by the local architect Pierre Corbineau (1600-78). The large altarpiece over the main altar is also believed to be by Corbineau. The chapels situated in the south aisle date from the 19C.

Ancienne église du Pritz ⊙ – *2km/1mi north. Leave Laval by allée de la Résistance, rue du Vieux-St-Louis and D 104.* This simple church stands on the right of the road in the hamlet called Pritz and is surrounded by a garden. It dates from about the year 1000 and was altered and enlarged in the Romanesque period. In the nave there is a large stone statue (left) of St Christopher and a 17C terracotta of Christ bearing the cross. The wooden convent screen, which was restored in 1776, dates from the Renaissance. The altarpiece (1677) is signed by Lemesle. The most interesting feature of the church is the series of **mural paintings.** The very beautiful 11C frescoes above the chancel show scenes from the life of the Virgin: the Visitation, Mary mothering the Infant Jesus (the only one from the Romanesque period), her Son's triumph over evil and the Nativity. The 13C frescoes on the chancel arch show the calendar of the months. The frescoes in the chancel show the old men of the Apocalypse and those on the double arch three signs of the zodiac. The nave was painted in the 14C with the Virgin and Child and the Good News being delivered to the shepherds; in the 15C a huge figure of St Christopher was painted (8m/26ft high) which was partially covered by another one in the 16C.

EXCURSIONS

Abbaye de Clermont ⊙ – *15km/9mi west by rue du Général-de-Gaulle and N 157.* The ruins stand in open country watered by many streams. The abbey was founded in 1152, as a daughter house of Clairvaux, by St Bernard with the support of Guy V, Count of Laval; it was a thriving monastic community until the Revolution. At the entrance is a 17C residential building.

The square east end of the **church** comes into view before the dilapidated west front and the austere Romanesque porch with its three round-headed openings. Little remains of the aisles, but the size of the church is still impressive owing to the extreme simplicity of the architecture and the vast window bays in the broad transept. Three rectangular chapels open off each transept in the usual Cistercian manner. The chancel is lit by six windows arranged in three rows.

South of the church is the **cloister garth** originally bordered by the choir monks quarters (east) and the refectory, library, kitchen and warming house (south). The wooden cloister galleries have not survived but the **lay brothers' range** (west) contains the cellar, where the rib-vaulting is supported by four central pillars, and the refectory, which has three pillars supporting the schist vault and is lit by five windows with double embrasures.

Return to Laval and then take by quai d'Avesnières and D 1 south out of town.

The road goes down to the banks of the Mayenne the rises again, providing a nice view over the former Porte de l'Huisserie.

Bear left onto D 112 towards Entrammes; after 1km/0.6mi fork left onto a narrow road to L'Enclos et Bonne (Lock).

The road descends to the bank of the River Mayenne: very attractive **view★** of the river, the lock, a mill and a castle.

Return to D 112 and continue south; bear left onto D 103.

Trappe du Port-du-Salut – Until 1959 the famous Port-Salut cheese was made here by the Trappist monks. They still make cheese today but under a different name and the electricity which they produce from a dam on the Mayenne supplies the national grid.

The **large and small chapels** are open to the public.

Craftwork is sold in the gatehouse.

Continue east on D 103.

Entrammes – This small town, which developed next to a ford at the confluence of several rivers, gets its name from the Latin *inter amnes* meaning between rivers; during recent restoration work inside the church, remains of the town's **ancient baths** ⊙ were discovered (including an 8m/26ft high wall); this find tends to confirm the importance of Gallo-Roman houses in the Mayenne region *(see Ville romaine de JUBLAINS).* An audio-visual presentation on the site clearly explains the role played by public baths in Gallo-Roman times.

Parné-sur-Roc – The church belonging to the village on the rock was built in the 11C and contains some interesting **mural paintings** (late 15C to early 16C). On the left one sees the silhouette of the resurrected Christ against a background of red stars and a Madonna Dolorosa; on the right, Cosmas and Damian, two brothers who practised medicine and were popular in the Middle Ages.

Take D 21 to return to Laval.

Population 1 719
Michelin map 54 fold 12 or 231 fold 14

Barbey d'Aurevilly, a native of St-Sauveur-le-Vicomte, described the austere beauty of the moorlands surrounding Lessay. The town is particularly lively in September during the Holy Cross Fair which originated in the 13C. Lessay grew up round a Benedictine abbey founded in 1056 by a Norman lord, Turstin Haldup, Baron of La Haye-au-Puits, his wife Emma and their son Eudes au Capel. The first monks under the leadership of Abbot Roger came from Le Bec-Hellouin. The abbey buildings date from the end of the 18C.

★★ABBEY CHURCH *30min*

Although the magnificent Romanesque abbey church was reconstructed between 1945 and 1957, the original building materials were used wherever possible and the result is one of the most perfect examples of Romanesque architecture in Normandy. The original church was built in two stages. The death of Eudes au Capel in 1098 was followed by the construction of the apse, chancel transept and two bays of the nave with their vaulting; the remaining bays of the nave were completed several years later.

Abbatiale, Lessay

Exterior – The full beauty of the lines of the apse, abutting on a flat gable, can best be seen from the War Memorial Square. The rather squat square belfry with its Hague schist slates is also worth noting.

Interior – From the south doorway one is impressed by the plan, the blending of the stonework and the simple lines of the nave and chancel.

The seven broad bays of the nave and the transepts are roofed with pointed vaulting; there is rib-vaulting in the aisles. The gallery in front of the clerestory windows passes round the entire building in the thickness of the walls.

The chancel terminates in an oven-vaulted apse lit by two rose windows.

The furnishings are very plain. The high altar consists of a large monolithic slab resting on two huge supports. A 15C chapel with a cobbled floor (right of the chancel) contains the baptistery and the font, a white monolith with an incised bronze cover.

When Barbey d'Aurevilly visited Lessay in 1864 he deplored the abbey's plain glass. The new glass is subtly coloured and the design is inspired by Irish manuscripts as are some of the capitals in the nave.

La Foire de Sainte-Croix

Lessay is extraordinarily lively during the days of the Holy Cross Fair (second weekend in September). The origins of the fair are lost in the 11C – it is supposed that the Benedictines were the first sponsors.

Friday is fair day for horses, donkeys, dogs, ferrets and fowl; Saturday welcomes cattle, sheep and goats. For three days, more than 1 500 exhibitors spread out over 7km/4mi of alleyways and dozens of carnival rides are set up alongside.

To feed the 400 000 visitors, about 2 800 local lambs are grilled up in the traditional manner along an alleyway reserved for this purpose.

LILLEBONNE

The small industrial town of Lillebonne was once a Celtic capital city. After the conquest of Gaul by Julius Caesar, the military camp of Juliobona, named in honour of the Proconsul, became a major port on Bolbec Bay which is now silted up.

Lillebonne flourished towards the end of the 19C with the arrival of several textile factories in the region. From Bolbec to Lillebonne the valley came to be known as the "Golden Valley".

SIGHTS

Théâtre-Amphithéâtre romain ⊙ – From place de l'Hôtel-de-Ville it is possible to see the general layout of this Roman amphitheatre. Built in the 1C, it was transformed and enlarged in the 2C. The central arena is characteristically shaped, reflecting the usual plan of amphitheatres in northwest Gaul, where all kinds of spectacles were held (mythological scenes, fights opposing Gallic gladiators, exhibitions of performing animals, hunts with small game). The arena was enclosed by a **podium**, consisting of two parallel walls, and surrounded by a ditch to drain away the surface water. The crowd watched on from the **cavea**, a series of stands probably made of wood. There terraces were split into a first (lower level) and a second (upper level) **maenianum** resting on brickwork. The main access was on the west side: the spectators came first through the **corona**, a circular gallery, then along a secondary tunnel, known as the **vomitorium**, before reaching the stands. Beneath the main road, recent archeological excavations have uncovered elements of infrastructure that once supported the walls of the arena.

Château – *Access by 46 rue Césarine.* Little remains of the fortress (rebuilt in the 12C and 13C), where William the Conqueror assembled his barons before invading England: one wall of an octagonal tower and, on the left, a round three-storey keep surmounted by a platform.

Église Notre-Dame – This 16C church has a double entrance with central pillar. The sweeping spire (55m/181ft) rises above a square tower. Inside there is a stained-glass window devoted to the story of John the Baptist. The stalls were originally from the Abbaye du Valasse.

Musée municipal ⊙ – *Jardin Jean-Rostand.* The museum, which is devoted to popular art and traditions, exhibits craftsmen's tools, objets d'art, furniture and documents relating to the history of Lillebonne and Normandy. The basement houses archeological finds from local excavations (cremation tombs, pottery and ironwork from the 1C to the 3C). From the garden there is a view of the medieval castle and its enclosure.

EXCURSIONS

Le Mesnil-sous-Lillebonne – *2km/1mi south.* The extremely ancient parish **church** ⊙ has recently been restored. It presents a display of religious art and a collection of fossils and minerals.

Abbaye du Valasse ⊙ – *6km/4mi northwest by D 173.* The foundation of the abbey resulted from two vows, one made by Waleran de Meulan for escaping safe and sound from a shipwreck, and one made by Empress Matilda, William the Conqueror's granddaughter, for escaping from her enemies during the struggle for the throne of England against her cousin Stephen of Blois.

The abbey was consecrated in 1181 in the presence of Henry II Plantagenet, and a host of bishops and great lords.

The abbey prospered and acquired many possessions in over 100 parishes until the 14C when the Hundred Years War and the Wars of Religion brought ruin.

In the 18C under the aegis of Dom Orillard, the abbey was transformed. It was sold as national property at the Revolution, was converted into a château, then sold to a dairy; in 1984 it was bought by the municipality of Gruchet-le-Valasse.

The main façade is an elegant 18C pedimented composition with two return wings. The central pediment bears the arms of Empress Matilda: three Normandy leopards (from William the Conqueror) and an eagle (from her husband, the German emperor, Henry V).

The capitals in the 13C chapter-house are decorated with gadroons and palmettes.

LISIEUX ★★

Population 23 703
Michelin map 54 fold 18 or 231 fold 32
Local map see Pays d'AUGE

Lisieux on the east bank of the Touques has become the most important commercial and industrial town in the prosperous Pays d'Auge.
The town's renown centres today on the "Lisieux of St Teresa".

ST TERESA OF LISIEUX

Thérèse Martin was born on 2 January 1873, to a well-to-do and very religious family in Alençon; she was an eager and sensitive child, who soon showed intelligence and will-power. On the death of his wife, Mr Martin brought the family to Lisieux where they lived at Les Buissonnets. Thérèse grew up in an atmosphere of kindness and piety and at nine years felt the call of the Church. Notwithstanding her father's permission given on Whit Sunday 1887 that she might join her sister at the Carmelite Convent, the authorities felt she was too young and it was only in April 1888, after a pilgrimage to Rome and a request to the Holy Father, that she entered the Order at the age of 15 years and three months.

A soul of such quality should not be treated as a child; "dispensations were not intended for her", said the Prioress of the new postulant who undertook the severe life of a Carmelite.

Leading a solitary life in the cloisters where she had come "to save souls and, above all, to pray for the priests", Sister Teresa of the Child Jesus, with humility and courage, mounted the difficult path to perfection. Her gaiety and simplicity cloaked a consuming energy. She wrote the story of her life, *History of a Soul*, finishing the last pages only a few days before entering the Carmelite hospital in which, after an agonising illness, she died in 1897. She was beatified in 1923 (her remains were transferred from the municipal cemetery to the Carmelite Chapel) and canonised in 1925. On 19 October 1997 Pope Jean-Paul II officially proclaimed her a Doctor of the Church, an exceptional honour bestowed on saints of great spiritual influence.

THE PILGRIMAGE

J. Sierpinski/PHOTONONSTOP

St Teresa of Lisieux

Les Buissonnets ⊘ – This is where Thérèse Martin lived from the age of four to 15. The tour of the house includes the dining room, Thérèse's bedroom, where she was miraculously cured at the age of 10, her father's bedroom and a display of mementoes from her childhood days – Communion dress, toys and games.
In the garden a group of statues represents Thérèse asking her father permission to enter the Carmelite Convent.

Chapelle du Carmel – The saint's shrine, a recumbent figure in marble and precious wood, is in the chapel on the right and contains her relics. Above the shrine in a marble niche is a statue of the Smiling Virgin which belonged to the Martin family.

Salle des Souvenirs – A series of display windows with recorded commentary shows mementoes relating to the saint's convent life (bowl, footwear, white gown and veil).

Basilique Ste-Thérèse – This impressive basilica was consecrated on 11 July 1954 and is one of the biggest 20C churches. Its total surface area measures 4 500 m²/150 000sq feet and its dome is 95m/311ft high. The **dome** is open to visitors.

The construction of the bell-tower (45m/147ft high) was interrupted in 1975; it ends in a flat roof and contains the great bell, three other bells and a carillon of 44 bells. Notice on the tympanum of the door the carvings by Robert Coin depicting Jesus teaching the Apostles and the Virgin of Mount Carmel. On either side of the central doorway stand statues of the Virgin and St Joseph, protectors of the Carmelite order. The single and immense nave is brightly coloured and decorated with marble, stained glass and mosaics by Pierre Gaudin, a pupil of Maurice Denis. In the south transept stands a reliquary offered by Pope Pius XI containing the bones of the saint's right arm. The **crypt** *(entrance outside, beneath the galleries)* is decorated with mosaics (scenes in the life of St Teresa). Behind the chevet are the tombs of St Teresa's parents and the Way of the Cross.

"Le Carmel de Ste-Thérèse" ⊘– *Beneath the north cloister*. This permanent exhibition retraces the history and life of the Carmelites with the reconstruction of a cell and the papal enclosure behind which the sisters lived and which could be crossed only with the permission of the Pope.

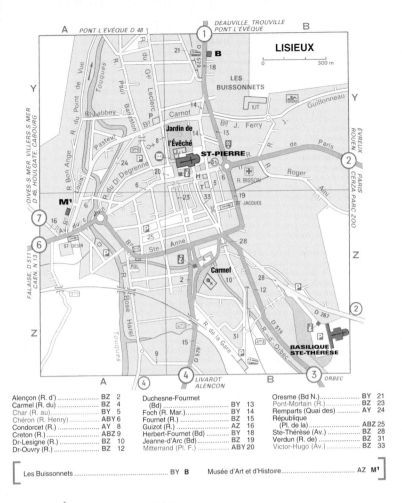

LISIEUX

0   300 m

★CATHÉDRALE ST-PIERRE *15min*

The cathedral was begun in 1170 and completed only in the middle of the 13C.

Exterior – The façade, raised above the ground on stone steps, is pierced by three doors and flanked by towers. The one on the left, though incomplete, is beautiful with bays and quartering columns.
Walk round the church by the right to the south transept's Paradise Door. The massive buttresses linked by an arch surmounted by a gallery were added in the 15C.

Interior – The transept is extremely simple with the lantern rising in a single sweep at the crossing. The nave has great unity with blind bays topped by relieving arches and robust round pillars surmounted by circular capitals supporting the wide arches. Walk round the 13C chancel, to the huge central chapel which was remodelled in the pure Flamboyant style on the orders of Pierre Cauchon, Bishop of Lisieux, after the trial of Joan of Arc. His tomb lies to the left of the altar. It was in this very chapel that Thérèse Martin attended mass. Note the series of 15C carved low-relief sculptures.

NEARBY SIGHTS

Musée vivant de la Basse-cour ⏱ – *5km/3.5mi north. Leave Lisieux by ①, D 579, then follow directions for the museum and turn left.* At the heart of the Pays d'Auge, in **Norolles**, this unusual reserve peopled with farmyard animals (poultry and rabbits) has been laid out as a 2km/1.2mi itinerary winding its way among the wooded hillsides. Visitors will discover around 900 types of farmyard animals living in hen houses, dovecots and hutches. The impressive, extensively restored 15C mansion used to belong to the bishops of Lisieux: it contains a huge cider press. The stables present an exhibition devoted to the history of farmyard animals and their various breeds.
At the end of the tour, a park where animals roam in semi-liberty will delight children, who can approach sheep, rabbits and miniature goats.

Eating out

MODERATE

Auberge de la Levrette – *R. de Lisieux – 14140 St-Julien-le-Faucon – 14km/8.7mi southwest of Lisieux via D 511 – ☎ 02 31 63 81 20 – closed Oct, 3-12 Jan, Sun evening and Mon – 14.94/32.01€.* Take a break in this authentic 16C coaching inn located right in the village centre. The owners themselves will show you to a cosy comfortable dining room with a fine period fireplace. Traditional cooking. Children's menu.

Aux Acacias – *13 r. de la Résistance – ☎ 02 31 62 10 95 – closed Sun evening and Mon except holidays – 14.94/44.21€.* You will be pleased to spot this restaurant on a small central square: tasty regional dishes are served in fine tableware and glassware, the soft colours of the decor are pleasant and prices are affordable. Very inexpensive children's menu.

Where to stay

MODERATE

Manoir de Cantepie Bed and Breakfast – *Le Cadran – 14340 Cambremer – 11km/6.8mi west of Lisieux via N 13 then D 50 – ☎ 02 31 62 87 27 – closed 24 Dec to 1 Jan – ⊭ – 3 rooms: 33.54/53.36€.* As you enter this splendid 17C manor house, you will be instantly won over by the refinement and elegance of the house, the simple yet warm welcome and the extremely reasonable prices. One of the best addresses in the Pays d'Auge.

Le Colombier Campsite – *14590 Moyaux – 16km/9.9mi northeast of Lisieux via D 510 then D 143 – ☎ 02 31 63 63 08 – open May to 15 Sept – reservation advisable in July and Aug – 180 places: 21.34€ – food service.* This camp site has character with its manor house, old buildings and French-style gardens. The interior decoration has been carefully thought out to convey a sense of authenticity and add warmth... rather successful on the whole! Swimming pool and friendly welcome.

MID-RANGE

Grand Hôtel de l'Espérance – *16 bd Ste-Anne – ☎ 02 31 62 17 53 – closed 16 Oct to 14 Apr – P – 100 rooms: 48.78/68.60€ – ☕ 5.95€ – restaurant 13.57/22.71€.*
Large hotel indeed... this imposing building located in the town centre is a good example of Norman style with its traditional timber-framed structure and balconies! The rooms are simply furnished yet well kept and soundproof.

On the town

Le Rétro – *100 r. Henry-Chéron – ☎ 02 31 31 28 27 – Mon 2pm-1am, Tues-Sat 7.30am-1am, Sun 3-9pm.* In addition to techno-music evenings and themed evenings hosted by a DJ, this bar stages a blues concert every month and a jam session every other month (on the second Tuesday). Convivial and eclectic: something for everyone...

Shopping

Chez Billoudet – *44 r. Henry-Chéron – ☎ 02 31 62 17 91 – Tues-Sun 7.30am-7.30pm – closed 15 days during the Feb-Mar school holidays and 15 days in July.* This confectioner is a master craftsman who will tempt you with his delicious specialities such as the calvador (chocolate with calvados and milk caramel) and the traditional apples in calvados. Tearoom on the premises.

Le Père Jules – *Rte de Dives-sur-Mer – 14100 St-Désir-de-Lisieux – northwest of Lisieux along D 45. – ☎ 02 31 61 14 57 – daily 8am-12.30pm, 1.30-8pm.* Housed in a delightful 19C Norman building, this family concern, created in 1919, owes its name to the grand father who founded it. You will be invited to visit the cellars stocked with home-made calvados and, of course, taste a drop of the famous brandy.

Leisure time

Grand Hôtel de l'Espérance – *16 bd Ste-Anne – ☎ 02 31 62 17 53 – www.lisieux-hotel.com – open daily.* In addition to hiring mountain bikes and children's bikes, the establishment organises outings on request.

★**CERZA** ⊙ – *12km/7.5mi northeast. Leave Lisieux by D 510, ② on the plan;
3km/2mi after Hermival-les-Vaux turn right onto D 143.* The Centre d'Élevage et de
Reproduction Zoologique Augeron is much more than a zoo; while providing a
pleasant, natural setting for a great many endangered animal species, it undertakes
to ensure both their protection and reproduction in the best possible conditions.
The 52ha/129 acres of the domain offer interesting topographical contrasts –
valleys and plains, meadows and forests, barren stretches and lush pockets of
vegetation, charmingly dotted with small ponds and burbling streams. Signposted
routes will take you through the **African Reserve** (a vast area set aside for rhinoce-
roses, zebras, watussi, ostriches and giraffes) or on a tour of the valley. Note the
delightful country path – not suitable for pushchairs – and the large enclosures for
the Sumatra tigers. A great many primates (gelada baboons, macaques, capuchins,
gibbons) as well as lemurs live in semi-liberty, in a biotope specially designed to
meet their needs.
*Small trains run across the open fields peopled with herbivores and
through the forests that are home to Asian deer, offering a pleasant and
instructive opportunity to discover these rare animal species.*

④ HAUTE VALLÉE DE LA TOUQUES

*75km/47mi – about 3hr – from Lisieux and back. From Lisieux take D 579 south. After
4km:2mi turn left onto D 64. See local map p 74.*

Fervaques – The **château** ⊙, which, like the manor and the postern gate overlooks
the Touques, dates from the 16C and 17C. It is a vast building of brick and stone.
For 22 years Fervaques was the retreat of Delphine de Custine, a friend of
Chateaubriand who also stayed there.
In Notre-Dame-de-Courson turn right onto D 4; after 3km/2mi turn left.

Bellou – In the village centre stands Manoir de Bellou, a pleasant 16C timber-
framed manor house.
The road (D 110) runs southeast through the Moutiers-Hubert Forest and passes
the Manoir de Cheffreteau.
*In Les Moutiers-Hubert turn right onto D 64 towards Gacé. At the crossroads turn left
onto D 16 and immediately right. Cross the river in Canapville; turn right onto D 33
and continue south. South of Ticheville station cross the railway line. At the next
junction turn right onto D 242; after 1km/0.5mi turn right to Vimoutiers.*

Vimoutiers – See VIMOUTIERS.
*Take D 579 north; turn right onto D 268 which climbs steeply.
Continue north and west through St-Ouen-le-Houx. From D 110 turn right onto
D 579.*

Livarot – The village, which is the home of the cheese of the same name, has
some beautiful old houses.
Continue north on D 579; bear right onto D 268.

Château de St-Germain-de-Livet

★**St-Germain-de-Livet** ⏱ – This delightful **château** consists of a 16C wing, decorated in a highly original stone and brick check pattern, adjoining a 15C half-timbered structure. The south and southwest wings were demolished in the 19C. The inner courtyard contains an Italian-style gallery with four basket-handle arches. The 15C wing contains the guard-room, decorated with 16C **frescoes** (battle scene; Judith bearing the head of Holofernes), and a dining room, both with ornamental fireplaces and Empire-style furniture. The hall contains a display of lithographs of Norman architecture; two rooms are furnished in the styles of Louis XV and XVI. On the first floor of the 16C wing are two rooms, beautifully tiled in terracotta from the Pays d'Auge, the so-called bedroom of Eugène Delacroix (photo of the painter by Pierre Petit), the gallery decorated with paintings by the Riesener family (19C) and a small round Louis XVI salon located in the south turret, with a Louis XIV cupboard inlaid with ebony and copper.

Take D 268 and D 579 north to Lisieux.

Normandy's Literary Ghosts

Many of Normandy's towns, villages, manor houses, coastal and rural scenes were described often under a fictional name by one of the region's celebrated writers.
Cabourg – the Balbec in Marcel Proust's *À la recherche du temps perdu.*
Ry – the Yonville-l'Abbaye of Gustave Flaubert's *Madame Bovary* (1857).
Le Havre – Guy de Maupassant's *Pierre et Jean* (1888).
Inland from Yport – Maupassant's *Une Vie* (1883).
The Cotentin – Barbey d'Aurevilly was to become the Walter Scott of the region; *Le Chevalier des Touches, Une vieille maîtresse* and *L'Ensorcelée.*

LOUVIERS★

Population 18 658
Michelin map 55 folds 16 and 17 or 231 fold 35

Located in the middle of the Seine, Eure and Iton valleys, Louviers is an interesting town to visit with its modern commercial area and an old town north of Notre-Dame Church with its pretty half-timbered houses, such as in rue Tatin, rue du Quai and rue Pierre Mendès-France. Those who like fishing have three rivers to choose from. The woollen textile industry, particularly the making of cloth traditionally associated with the town since the 13C, has progressively disappeared but, in the industrial estate to the north, new plants manufacture batteries, television aerials, records and plastic foam.

SIGHTS

Ancien couvent des Pénitents – All that remains of this Franciscan convent, built in 1646, on a tributary of the Eure, is the inhabited main building together with three small arcaded galleries belonging to the cloister. The western gallery is in a ruinous state and overlooks a square with lawn and trees.

Eating out

MID-RANGE

Les Saisons – *27400 Vironvay – 5km/3mi east of Louviers via N 155 then N 15 – ☎ 02 32 40 02 56 – closed Feb, Sun evening and Mon – 20.58/56.46€.* Situated right at the heart of Normandy, these former farm buildings have been converted to look somewhat like English cottages... However, in the elegant dining room, opening on to a large enclosed garden, French tradition takes over again with elaborately prepared dishes and quality products. Terrace, swimming pool and tennis.

Where to stay

MID-RANGE

La Haye le Comte – *4 rte de La Haye-le-Comte – 700m/0.4mi south of Louviers via D 113 – ☎ 02 32 40 00 40 – P – 16 rooms: 42.69/83.85€ – ☕ 8.38€* – restaurant 21.34/28.97€. An old-fashioned charm, characteristic of ancient family residences, pervades this hotel. The rooms are all different and more traditional in style than the restaurant and the drawing room. Before sitting down to a meal, take a stroll in the park or have a game of tennis or croquet.

Rue de la Trinité (on the left) leads into the former manufacturing district and to **rue Terneaux** where the buildings have large attics which were once used for drying out dyed fabrics. Take the short rue Polhomet to the right, then turn right again on rue du Quai to see the pretty half-timbered houses. Rue au Coq, on the left, leads to the museum; rue Pierre-Mendès-France takes you back to the east end of Notre Dame Church.

★**Église Notre-Dame** – The plain 13C church was redecorated in the late 15C in the Flamboyant style and it is for this that it has become famous. The **south front**★ is outstanding for its profusion of Flamboyant features. Pointed gables rival with openwork balustrades, pinnacles, festoons and gargoyles. On top of the buttresses are some interesting statues. The **south porch**★, with all its delicately carved detail, looks more like silverwork than masonry. Note the Renaissance door panels and the hanging keystones of the Gothic arcades.

The 14C west door is adorned by the lovely statue of the Virgin.

Interior – The 13C nave with double side aisles is an elegant interior which shelters several fine **works of art**★.

1) Entombment (late 15C).

2) Salome and her sons, James and John (16C).

3) Throne.

4) Above the altar are three statues: Christ, the Virgin and St John (15C). On each side are carved panels depicting the Virgin Mary and the Centurion at Calvary (14C).

5) Altar decorated with carved panels depicting the life of the Virgin (16C).

6) and **7**) Early-17C tableaux by local artist Jean Nicolle: the Nativity and Adoration of the Magi.

8) Mausoleum by Robert d'Acquigny (late 15C).

9) Restored Renaissance stained glass.

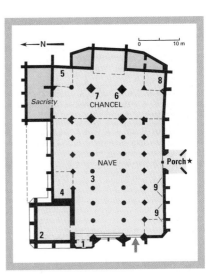

Musée municipal ⊘ – The museum hosts exhibitions of faience, furniture and painting. One of the rooms is devoted to the clothing industry. Temporary art shows are held in rotation.

Maison du Fou du Roy – The half-timbered house located in the main street is also the tourist office. It owes its name of King's Jester's House to the fact that it once belonged to Guillaume Marchand, an apothecary, who became Henri IV's jester.

EXCURSIONS

Vironvay – *5km/3mi east by N 155, then the minor road on the left which crosses A 13 and N 15.* The isolated church overlooks the Seine Valley. The view on approaching extends over the river spanned by the bridge at St-Pierre-du-Vauvray and, further east, the ruins of Château-Gaillard standing guard over Les Andelys.

Pont-de-l'Arche – *11km/7mi east by D 321 along the south bank of the Seine.* The small town is pleasantly set in a valley below the confluence of the Seine and the Eure. On the south side is Bord Forest; in summer its pine trees add a Mediterranean note to the scene. The town was named after the first bridge to be built over the lower Seine, long before Rouen had a bridge.

The **Église Notre-Dame-des-Arts** exhibits the Flamboyant Gothic style in the doorway and the ornate gable on the south side. The interior is lit by 16C and 17C windows; the second window in the south aisle depicts the watermen of the town labouring to manoeuvre a boat through an arch of the bridge. The Louis XIII altarpiece on the high altar shows the Resurrection by Le Tourneur; the font is 16C; the organ is worthy of note; the choir stalls are 18C, the Pietà against the first pillar in the north aisle is 16C, the Virgin on the north side of the nave is 14C; the polychrome St Peter on the south side is 16C. A painting of the Birth of the Virgin, a 16C popular work of art, hangs in the sacristy.

Vallée de l'Eure

2 **From Louviers to Pacy-sur-Eure** *34km/20mi – about 3hr (including Château d'Anet) – see local map p 184.*

Leave Louviers via D 71 south.

Acquigny – From the bridge spanning the river, there is a pretty view of the late-16C castle. The **formal French gardens** lying at the confluence of the River Eure and River Iton have retained their long avenues and orangery, whose brickwork features light, low-key hues. Note the fine trees and their imposing boughs (Lousiana cypresses, plane trees, Chinese pagoda trees). Waterfalls, artificial streams and a series of fords reminiscent of the Romantic period add an extra touch of charm.

The drive is lovely between Cailly-sur-Eure and Crèvecœur, where you cross the river.

La Croix-St-Leufroy – The **church** ⊘ has a carved Renaissance font and an interesting collection of pictures from the old abbey of Croix-St-Ouen.

Follow D 836.

The landscape continues to charm between Chambray and Cocherel, and all the way to Pacy-sur-Eure.

Cocherel – This town, together with Pacy-sur-Eure, are associated with the memory of **Aristide Briand**, who was very fond of the area and bought up several properties. From 1908 until his death in 1932 this statesman and "apostle of peace" spent all his leisure time in Cocherel where he owned three houses in succession. He is buried in the local cemetery beneath a massive dark granite stone. There is a statue in his honour, *Les Méditations*, located on the far side of the bridge across the Eure.

Pacy-sur-Eure – A memorial to Briand stands at the entrance to the town. The **Église St-Aubin** is a fine 13C Gothic church, remodelled in the 16C; the nave is remarkable for its symmetry and unity of style. The modern ornaments include four glass powder-paste low-relief sculptures round the altar and amber-coloured stained-glass windows by Décorchemont depicting the Ascension. There are also beautiful 16C stone statues – the Virgin and Child attributed to Germain Pilon, St Anne and a Pietà – and an early-17C statue of St Michael slaying the dragon.

Abbaye de LUCERNE

Michelin map 59 folds 7 and 8 or 231 fold 25 – 12km/8mi southeast of Granville

The sizeable ruins of Lucerne Abbey stand in an isolated spot in the pleasantly green Thar Valley. The abbey was founded in 1143 by two Premonstratensian monks following a donation by Hasculfe de Subligny, the great nephew of William the Conqueror. It was not before 1164 that construction started. The abbey is in a fine parkland setting.

Abbey Church ⊘ – The Romanesque doorway in the 12C façade is decorated with flat heads on the archivolts. The Cistercian-style nave (great square pillars and arcades without mouldings) consists of seven bays. The six arches of the north side, which collapsed in the 19C, were reconstructed using the south side as a model. The transept crossing (restored) supports a late-12C Gothic square **bell-tower★**, pierced on each side with narrow lancets.

The chancel windows are unusually tall.

The south transept houses a fine 18C organ with 33 stops. Concerts are given throughout the year.

Cloisters and Conventual Buildings – The arcades of the northwest corner and the entrance to the chapter-house are still standing. In the southwest corner, near the door to the old refectory (entirely rebuilt), is a 12C lavatorium with four beautiful little Romanesque arcades.

South in the park are the remains of an aqueduct built in 1803 to provide water for the spinning mill set up in the abbey precincts.

Overlooking a stretch of water is the fine Classical façade of the abbot's lodging *(private)*.

Temporary exhibitions are now held in the rooms above the 12C to 15C porch (Almonry Gate), which used to accommodate court hearings.

The way back to the porter's lodge passes the old tithe barn and the dovecot, a huge round tower with 1 500 pigeon holes.

LYONS-LA-FORÊT ★

Some towns have a way of imprinting themselves on your memory with an inalterable image of heart-warming beauty. Lyons is such a place. The half-timbered houses, old brick buildings, the sylvan setting create a picture book vision of Normandy.

The town is on the banks of the River Lieure, in the heart of the forest of Lyons, once the favourite hunting ground of the dukes of Normandy. The name may have a Scandinavian origin, from *Li Homs*, meaning "the villages", but there are also old texts mentioning *Leons* (1015) and *Saltus Leonis* (1050). The final "s" is pronounced, which is an exception in the French language. In any event, it would seem that the name was used to designate the surrounding area in general, as the names of the villages attest: Beauvoir-en-Lyons, Beauficel-en-Lyons, La Haye-en-Lyons.

IN THE VILLAGE

Les Halles, Lyons-la-Forêt

G. Targat/MICHELIN

Halles – The old covered market holds pride of place in the centre of place Benserade. The remarkable carpentry work was restored in the 18C. In 1932, it was used for filming scenes in Jean Renoir's *Madame Bovary*. The fountain is a souvenir of another film version of the story, made here by Claude Chabrol in 1990.

Pretty half-timbered houses surround the square, including the house where the poet Isaac de Benserade (1612-1691) was born, distinguished by its wrought-iron window fittings. The musician **Maurice Ravel** used to live in the steep street west of the square; it was there he composed *Le Tombeau de Couperin*, and completed the orchestration for Mousorgski's *Pictures at an Exhibition*.

Rue Bout-de-Bas leads to St-Denis Church, at the edge of the village, on the riverside.

Église St-Denis ⊙ – The church was built here in the 12C, perhaps on the site of an older, pagan place of worship. It was completely renovated in the 15C. The stonework and the timber belfry are admirable. Inside, the large wooden statues recall the great forest nearby. In the chancel, the statue of St. Christopher carrying the infant Jesus dates from the 16C.

★★FORÊT DE LYONS

70km/42mi – allow one day.

While the forest is not as extensive as it was when the dukes of Normandy ruled, it still covers 10 700ha/26 440 acres, and is known for its glorious beech trees, some with trunks 20m/60ft tall. While enjoying your tour through this lovely woodland, you can also stop to admire, among other things, an old abbey and two interesting châteaux.

Leave Lyons via D 6ᴱ.

Notre-Dame-de-la-Paix – From this statue there is a fine **view** of the town of Lyons.

Take D 169 left.

Chapelle St-Jean – Behind the 17C chapel a path leads to the Chêne St-Jean (St John's Oak) which has a circumference of 5m/16ft at a height of 1.30m/4ft from the ground.

Take the second road on the left (D 11) towards Rosay.

Rosay-sur-Lieure – The **church** and churchyard are in a pleasant setting.

D 11 goes on to Ménesqueville.

Ménesqueville – The small 12C country **church** which has been skilfully restored, contains some very old statues. The stained-glass windows by Décorchemont portray the *Song of Songs*. From here, D 12 goes along the pretty Fouillebroc Valley as far as Lisors.

Lisors – The **church** contains a crowned Virgin dating from the 14C, which was found buried in 1936.

Take D 175; on the right, you will see the ruins of the abbey.

Abbaye de Mortemer ⊙ – In a hollow surrounded by the forest stand the ruins of the 12C-13C Cistercian abbey which had a huge church (90m/295ft long; 42m/138ft wide). The chapter-house entrance is flanked by two pointed arch bays and surmounted by the dormitory windows. A **museum** has been installed in the area below the conventual building which was reconstructed in the 17C. The exhibits illustrate monastic life and evoke the stories and legends connected with the abbey. In the cellars sound and lighting effects and wax figures create an atmosphere of magic and mystery. A 14C stone Virgin stands at the end of one of the corridors.

In the furnished **living quarters** on the first floor are a 15C parchment antiphonary (a collection of liturgical verse), illuminated and protected by a studded leather cover and a 19C fireplace.

Across from the abbey, on the left-hand side of D 175, a short path leads to the Croix-Vaubois crossroads.

Carrefour de la Croix-Vaubois – The very simple monument erected at this crossroads commemorates the foresters who died in the Resistance.

As you continue along D 175, look for two springs (sources) off to the left.

Source de Ste-Catherine-de-Lisors – A footbridge spanning the Fouillebroc leads to an oratory, traditionally visited by young girls in search of a husband.

Source du Fouillebroc – This spring is set in pleasant forest surroundings.

After crossing D 6, the road leads into Beauficel via the hamlet of La Bouvetière.

Beauficel-en-Lyons – The **church** ⊙ is preceded by a 17C porch and contains beautiful statues, including a 14C virgin in polychrome stone inlaid with glass.

D 14 goes alongside Fleury-la-Forêt Castle (to the right) and into the village of Bosquentin.

Château de Fleury-la-Forêt ⊙ – Beyond a magnificent wrought-iron gate, a majestic avenue of ancient lime trees leads to the early-17C château built of red brick, flint and sandstone. Flanking the main building are two low symmetrical wings with mansard-style roofs, which were added in the 18C.

The ground floor rooms house an interesting collection of toys and dolls. There is also a huge kitchen abundantly decorated (copper, porcelain and pewter utensils and chimney plaque bearing the arms of Charles de Caumont, who rebuilt the château in 1647 following a fire). A series of rooms on the first floor – the Blue Room, the Empire and Directory Chamber – display 17C Italian cabinets, a wardrobe, a dressing table which can be converted into a bureau and an armchair which also serves as a prayer stool. On the top floor there is a collection of antique dolls.

Outside, on the right, activity in the old wash-house has been recreated as it was at the end of the 19C with the help of dummies, clothes, bat, wringer and various other specialised tools.

Bosquentin – Signposted from Lyons-la-Forêt, the **Musée de la Ferme et des Vieux Métiers** ⊙ illustrates rural life in the area during the past 100 years by depicting 15 or so crafts, most of which are now obsolete: saddler, butcher, cartwright, blacksmith, grocer, milkman. Thousands of objects relating to these crafts are displayed.

Turn left after Bosquentin and follow D 241.

★**Hêtre de la Bunodière** – Indicated by a signpost on the right as you leave N 31 to enter the forest, this magnificent beech which is 40m/131ft tall stands near the Câtelier Reserve where oak, ash and maple trees thrive.

Its circumference measures 3.3m/11ft.

N 31-E 46 leads back to La Feuillie.

La Feuillie – The slender church **spire**★ is a bold piece of carpentry.

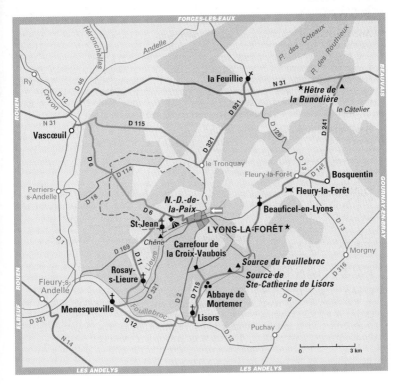

Vascœuil – This little village (pronounced Va-coy) on the edge of the forest is famous for its château (14C-16C), which has become a cultural centre. In the grounds are reconstructions of traditional Norman cottages.

Centre régional d'Art et d'Histoire ⊙ – Restored rooms of the château are used to display contemporary art.

The **Musée Michelet** holds a collection of mementoes of the historian Jules Michelet and his family (portraits, posters, manuscripts); at the top of the tower, you can visit his office.

Église St-Martial ⊙ – Inside this church is the tomb of Hugues de Saint-Jovinien, a holy man who died in the 12C. The painted stone statues represent the Virgin Mary and St Martial.

You can return to Lyons-la-Forêt via D6/D6^E.

MAYENNE

Population 13 549
Michelin map 59 fold 20 or 232 fold 7

Mayenne is a bridgehead town whose strategic importance in the past was compounded by the existence of a powerful fortress. Cardinal Mazarin had no sooner acquired the Duchy of Mayenne in 1654 than he undertook to make the River Mayenne navigable from Laval to Mayenne. After 150 000 *livres* had been spent, construction materials could be brought up as far as the town by barge but the course and installations were not maintained and the river again fell into disuse. New projects were studied and in 1852 forty-five locks were constructed. By 1874 barges were calling regularly at the recently completed quays, but with the advent of the rail transport the river traffic finally died.

Its key role was proved again during the Second World War. By 8 June 1944, the town had been nearly levelled, but the bridge remained intact. Thanks to the heroism of an American sergeant, Mack Racken, the only bridge still spanning the River Mayenne was saved to serve the Allies. The route to the region of Maine was thus kept open.

The town has been spaciously rebuilt over the hillsides running down on either side to the River Mayenne.

SIGHTS

Ancien château – Abutting on rock escarpments, the old castle stands on the hill on the west bank of the river. It was built in the 11C by Juhel I, Lord of Mayenne, and was one of the major local strong points and as such suffered frequent siege. It was only through sheer cunning that William the Conqueror took the castle.

The perimeter wall remains, giving the castle a truly feudal appearance. An attractive shady promenade runs between the curtain walls and the town gardens. The promenade commands an attractive **view★** of the town with the river flowing through it between the granite quays and under the three bridges.

Basilique Notre-Dame – This church in a composite style has been remodelled several times. The west front like the pillars and arches in the nave are 12C, the transept walls and windows are 16C. The windows throughout are modern, dating from 1962. When the church was rebuilt at the end of the 19C in the Gothic style, it was also enlarged.

Église St-Martin ⊘ – *On the hillside on the bank facing the castle.* This church is built with rust-coloured granite enhanced by a lovely glowing patina. In the 11C the church belonged to Marmoutiers Abbey in Tours, and both the apse and transept date from this period. The modern stained glass like that in the Basilica of Our Lady, is by the master glazier Maurice Rocher. The wooden statue of St Martin portrays him as a soldier sharing his cloak with a poor man.

EXCURSIONS

Ernée – *24km/15mi to the west by N 12.* Standing on the outskirts of this town, to the right of the road, is the **Chapelle de Charné** sheltered by plane trees. The chapel is all that remains of the former village of Charné, which slowly declined over the centuries to the advantage of its neighbour Ernée. The chapel comprises a Gothic chancel and transept. The transept crossing is crowned by a Romanesque tower. The polychrome wood statue of the Virgin is 15C. Ernée and the surrounding region was the setting for Balzac's novel *Les Chouans.*

▶▶ **Forêt de Mayenne** (oak, elm and coppice): **Fontaine-Daniel** (a pool overlooked by an attractive chapel), flower-decked houses and an old Cistercian abbey; **Chailland** (statue of a Virgin on top of a rocky escarpment).

Eating out

MODERATE

L'Auberge Campagnarde – ⌂ – *53640 Poulay – 13km/8.1mi northeast of Mayenne on the way to Lassay via D 34 then a minor road – ☎ 02 43 32 07 11 – closed 10 days in Dec, Sun evening and Wed – reservation advisable – 8.99€ lunch-16.01€.* Roast meat, poultry from neighbouring farms, organically grown vegetables and other local products are served in this former presbytery, on tables covered with red-and-white tablecloths... enough to give you an appetite! Rustic decor with lovely fireplace. The small zoo appeals to children.

Beau Rivage – *53100 Moulay – 4km/2.5mi south of Mayenne via N 162 – ☎ 02 43 00 49 13 – closed Feb school holidays, Sun evening from Sept to June and Mon – 10.67/26.68€.* The River Mayenne flows just below the terrace shaded by a large chestnut tree. In cool weather, you will no doubt prefer to sit in the vast dining room with exposed timberwork and watch meat and fish being grilled in the brick-built fireplace.

La Marjolaine – *At the Domaine du Bas-Mont 53100 Moulay – 6.5km/4mi south of Mayenne via N 162 – ☎ 02 43 00 48 42 – closed 1-8 Jan, 1-8 Aug, Feb school holidays and Sun evening – 13.42/48.78€.* This stone house stands in rural surroundings, in the middle of a peaceful park. There is a cosy atmosphere in the dining room with its white-leaded furniture and Louis-XVI chairs. A few comfortable rooms with bright furniture and draperies.

Where to stay

MID-RANGE

Le Vieux Presbytère Bed and Breakfast – *53640 Montreuil-Poulay – 12km/7.5mi northeast of Mayenne towards Lassay-les-Châteaux via N 12 and D 34 – ☎ 02 43 00 86 32 – closed end of Oct to beginning of Mar – ⊭ – 2 rooms: 48/52€.* Situated in the country, close to the village, this former presbytery dates from the 15C and 18C. On the ground floor there remain a bread oven and an ancient granite fireplace. Traditional bedrooms. Charming garden planted with fruit trees. Copious breakfast.

MONT-ST-MICHEL ★★★

Population 72
Michelin map 59 fold 7 or 231 fold 38

What is the reason for the world's fascination with Mont-St-Michel? No doubt it is something which goes beyond the beauty of the architecture or its long history; perhaps it is the whiff of mystery that seems linked to the movement of the tides, to the play of twilight on the water and walls, to the cry of gulls gliding above the salty grass marsh... It is impossible to take the measure of Mont-St-Michel without including its unique natural setting. The rock and the bay are truly one. Known as a "Marvel of the Western World", the monument and its site are also now classified World Heritage sites by the UNESCO.

Like its counterpart St Michael's Mount off the south coast of Cornwall, Mont-St-Michel is a granite island about 900m/984yd round and 80m/262ft high.

As the bay is already partially silted up, the mount is usually to be seen surrounded by huge sand banks which shift with the tides and often reshape the mouths of the neighbouring rivers. It is linked to the mainland by a causeway which was built in 1877.

FROM ITS FOUNDATION UP TO THE PRESENT DAY

An amazing achievement – The abbey's origin goes back to the early 8C when the Archangel Michael appeared to Aubert, Bishop of Avranches, who founded an oratory on the island, then known as Mount Tombe. In the Carolingian era the oratory was replaced by an abbey and from then until the 16C a series of increasingly splendid buildings, in the Romanesque and then the Gothic style, succeeded one another on the mount which was dedicated to the Archangel.

The abbey was remarkably well fortified and never fell to the enemy.

The construction is an amazing achievement. The blocks of granite were transported from the Chausey Islands or from Brittany and hoisted up to the foot of the building. As the crest of the hill was very narrow the foundations had to be built up from the lower slopes.

Pilgrimages – Even during the Hundred Years War pilgrims came flocking to the mount; the English, who had possession of the area, granted safe conduct to the faithful in return for payment. People of all sorts made the journey: nobles, rich citizens and beggars who lived on alms and were granted free accommodation by the monks.

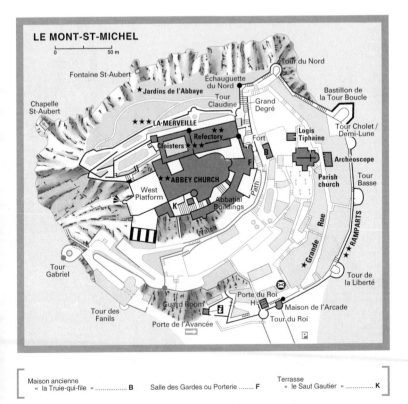

LE MONT-ST-MICHEL

Maison ancienne « la Truie-qui-file » .... **B** Salle des Gardes ou Porterie .... **F** Terrasse « le Saut Gautier » .... **K**

In periods of widespread disaster the pilgrimage incited such excess of fervour that the church authorities were obliged to intervene.

Hotels and souvenir shops flourished. The pilgrims bought medals bearing the effigy of St Michael and lead amulets which they filled with sand from the beach. Of the many thousands of people crossing the bay some drowned, others perished in the quicksands; the dedication was lengthened to St Michael in Peril from the Sea.

Decline – The abbey came to be held in commendam (by lay abbots who received the revenue without exercising the duties) and discipline among the monks grew lax. In the 17C the Maurists, monks from St Maur, were made responsible for reforming the monastery but they only made some deceptive architectural changes, tinkering with the stonework. Further dilapidation ensued when the abbey became a prison. From being the local Bastille, before the Revolution, it was converted in 1811 into a national prison for political prisoners such as Barbès, Blanqui and Raspail. In 1874 the abbey and the ramparts passed into the care of the Historic Monuments Department (Service des Monuments Historiques). Since 1966 a few monks have again been in residence conducting the services in the abbey church.

Stages in the Abbey's Construction – The buildings date from the 11C to the 16C.

Romanesque Abbey – 11C-12C. Between 1017 and 1144 a church was built on the top of the mount. The previous Carolingian building was incorporated as a crypt – Notre-Dame-sous-Terre (Our Lady Underground) – to support the platform on which the last three bays of the Romanesque nave were built. Other crypts were constructed to support the transepts and the chancel which projected beyond the natural rock.

The convent buildings were constructed on the west face and on either side of the nave. The entrance to the abbey faced west.

– the abbatial buildings (13C-15C) on the south side comprising the administrative offices, the abbot's lodging and the garrison's quarters;

– the main gatehouse and the outer defences (14C) on the east side, which protected the entrance which was moved to this side of the mount.

The chancel of the Romanesque church had collapsed and was rebuilt more magnificently in the Flamboyant Gothic style (1446-1521) above a new crypt.

Alterations – 18C-19C. In 1780 the last three bays of the nave and the Romanesque façade were demolished.

Mont-St-Michel

The present bell-tower (1897) is surmounted by a beautiful spire which rises to 157m/515ft and terminates in a statue of St Michael (1879) by Emmanuel Frémiet. The 4.5m/15ft tall archangel, in position for over 100 years, was recently removed for restoration. St Michael once again proudly wields his sword, which had been struck off by lightning.

THE VILLAGE

Outer Defences of the Village – The outer gate is the only breach in the ramparts and opens into the first fortified courtyard. On the left stands the Citizens' Guard-room (16C) occupied by the Tourist Information Centre; on the right are the "Michelettes", English mortars captured in a sortie during the Hundred Years War.

A second gate leads into a second courtyard. The third gate (15C), complete with machicolations and portcullis, is called the King's Gate because it was the lodging of the token contingent maintained on the mount by the king in assertion of his rights; it opens onto Grande-Rue where the abbot's soldiers lodged in the fine arcaded house (right).

★Grande-Rue – This picturesque narrow street climbs steeply between old (15C-16C) houses and ends in a flight of steps. In summer it is lively and crowded with the stalls of souvenir merchants even as it was in the Middle Ages at the height of the most fervent pilgrimages.

★★ Ramparts – These are 13C-15C. The sentry walk offers fine views of the bay; from the North Tower the Tombelaine Rock, which Philippe Auguste had fortified, is clearly visible.

★ Abbey Gardens ⊘ – A pleasant place for a stroll with a view of the west side of the mount and St Aubert's Chapel.

Archéoscope ⊘ – Magic and mystery accompany this journey back in time to the beginning of the history of the mount since Scissy Forest disappeared and the Archangel Michael appeared to Bishop Aubert. The different stages in the construction of the abbey and its architectural splendours are explained by means of sophisticated techniques controlled by computer; there is a model emerging from the water, a projection of slides on several screens as well as other audio-visual effects.

Église paroissiale St-Pierre – The parish church which dates from the 11C has been much altered. The apse spans a narrow street. The church contains a Crucifix and other furnishings from the abbey; the chapel in the south aisle houses a statue of St Michael covered in silver; in the chapel to the right of the altar there is a 15C statue of the Virgin and Child and another of St Anne and the Virgin as a child.

Logis Tiphaine ⊘ – When Du Guesclin was captain of the mount, he had this house built (1365) for his wife Tiphaine Raguenel, an attractive and educated woman from Dinan, while he went off to the wars in Spain. The house was heavily restored in the 19C.

★★ABBEY ⊘

The tour passes through a maze of corridors and stairs floor by floor, not from building to building or period by period.

B. Kaufmann/MICHELIN

Outer Defences of the Abbey – A flight of steps, the Grand Degré, once cut off by a swing door, leads up to the abbey. At the top on the right is the entrance to the gardens; more steps lead up to the ramparts.

Through the arch of an old door is a fortified courtyard overlooked by the fort, which consists of two tall towers shaped like mortars standing on their breeches and linked by machicolations. Even this military structure shows the builder's artistic sense: the wall is attractively constructed of alternate courses of pink and grey granite. Beneath a flattened barrel vault a steep and ill-lit staircase, known as the Escalier du Gouffre (Abyss Steps), leads down to the beautiful door which opens into the guard-room, also called the Porterie.

Eating out

MODERATE

La Sirène – ☎ 02 33 60 08 60 – closed 15 Nov to 20 Dec and Fri – 9.45/19.06€. This 14C building served as an inn until recently when it became a *crêperie* accessible by a spiral staircase. Wood-framed mullioned windows testify to the authenticity of the place.

Where to stay

MODERATE

La Bergerie Bed and Breakfast – *La Poultière* – *35610 Roz-sur-Couesnon* – *16km/9.9mi SW of Mont-St-Michel* – *D 797 coast road to St-Malo* – ☎ 02 99 80 29 68 – ⊟ – 5 rooms: 35.06/42.69€. Located in the attic of this former sheep farm, the comfortable rooms somehow lack charm but enjoy the peaceful atmosphere of the small hamlet. The kitchen set aside for guests is very much appreciated as is the garden where sheep still graze. A self-catering cottage is also available.

Mme Gillet Bed and Breakfast – *Le Val-St-Revert* – *35610 Roz-sur-Couesnon* – *15km/9.3mi SW of Mont-St-Michel, D 797 coast road to St-Malo* – ☎ 02 99 80 27 85 – ⊟ – 4 rooms: 27.44/45.73€. This family house overlooks the bay and offers a beautiful view of Mont-St-Michel and the surrounding countryside. Four rooms where an olde worlde charm lingers on: two on the sea side and a more recent and brighter one with a terrace facing the garden.

Le Bretagne Hotel – *59 r. Couesnon* – *50170 Pontorson* – *9km/5.6mi south of Mont-St-Michel via D 976* – ☎ 02 33 60 10 55 – closed 5 Jan to 5 Feb and Mon out of season – 🅿 – 15 rooms: 30.49/57.93€ – ☕ 5.95€ – restaurant 13.57/42.69€. Regional-style house. Admire the lovely 18C wood panels, the grey-marble fireplace and the plate-warming radiator (very unusual!) in the first room... Cosy, typically British bar and spacious, pleasantly furnished rooms.

MID-RANGE

Beauvoir Hotel – *50170 Pontorson* – *4km/2.5mi S of Mont-St-Michel via D976 towards Pontorson* – ☎ 02 33 60 09 39 – closed 16 Nov to 14 Feb – 🅿 – 18 rooms: 44.21/54.88€ – ☕ 6.40€ – restaurant 11.43/42.69€. Located on the roadside, this large house covered with Virginia creeper stands in the last village before Mont-St-Michel. The rooms, of various sizes, are simply furnished and well kept. Half board is compulsory. Children's menu available.

Manoir de la Roche Torin – *In Bas-Courtils* – *50220 Courtils* – *8.5km/5.3mi E of Mont-St-Michel on the way to Avranches* – ☎ 02 33 70 96 55 – closed 13 Nov to 13 Dec and 3 Jan to 12 Feb – 🅿 – 13 rooms: 73.18/129.58€ – ☕ 9.91€ – restaurant 130/320F. The place is ideal for a panoramic view of the bay with, in the forefront, salt meadows with grazing sheep and, in the distance, Mont-St-Michel. As for the manor house, it will appeal to you with its refined decor, cosy bedrooms and perfect tranquillity.

LUXURY

Auberge St-Pierre – *Grande-Rue* – ☎ 02 33 60 14 03 – closed Jan – 21 rooms: from 79.27€ – ☕ 7.62€ – restaurant 14.03/44.21€. This inn, housed in a 15C building, offers you the choice between a large brasserie-style dining room on the ground floor, where food is served any time of the day, a more rustic but convivial room upstairs or a small terrace close to the ramparts. Bedrooms are located in three separate houses.

Salle des Gardes or Porterie (B) – This gatehouse was the focal point of the abbey. Poor pilgrims passed through on their way from the Merveille Court to the Almonry. The abbot's visitors and the faithful making for the church used the abbey steps.

Abbey Steps – An impressive flight of 90 steps rises between the abbatial buildings (left) and the abbey church (right); it is spanned by a fortified bridge (15C).

The stairs stop outside the south door of the church on a terrace called the Saut Gautier (**Gautier Leap – E**), after a prisoner who is supposed to have hurled himself over the edge. The tour starts here.

West Platform – This spacious terrace, which was created by the demolition of the last three bays of the church, provides an extensive view of the bay of Mont-St-Michel.

Omelette de la Mère Poulard

Annette Boutiaut was born in Nevers in 1851. She was employed as a lady's maid by the architect Édouard Corroyer, a disciple of Viollet-le-Duc, who was commissioned by the Monuments Historiques (a State-run organisation) to restore Mont-St-Michel Abbey. Annette followed her employers there and met the son of a local baker. They married and took over the running of the St-Michel Tête d'Or Hotel. At that time (around 1875), the causeway had not been built yet so that tourists and pilgrims reached Mont-St-Michel on foot, on horseback or aboard a *maringotte* (a small two-wheeled horse-drawn cart), tide permitting. They were usually very hungry and could not bear to wait for food to be prepared. Annette knew that a good innkeeper should not be taken unawares. She therefore always had eggs in store and quickly beat up an omelette for her guests while they waited for more substantial dishes. Her welcome and the quality of the food she served gradually brought her fame. When Annette Poulard died in 1931, food critics speculated on the secret recipe of the omelette... Some talked about fresh cream, specially selected eggs and butter, others argued it was all due to fast cooking; Annette herself explained in a letter dated 1922: "I break the eggs in a bowl, I beat them up well, I put a nice knob of butter in the frying pan, I throw the eggs in and stir continuously."

Curnonsky (1872-1956), the "Prince of gourmets", said that the secret lay in the recipe of Dr Rouget, the hero of Balzac's *La Rabouilleuse*, who beat up the yolks and whites separately before mixing them in the frying pan!

★★**Church** – The exterior of the church, particularly the east end with its buttresses, flying buttresses, bell turrets and balustrades, is a masterpiece of light and graceful architecture. The interior reveals the marked contrast between the severe, sombre Romanesque nave and the elegant, luminous Gothic chancel.

The church is built on three crypts which are visited during the tour.

★★★**La Merveille** – The name, which means the Marvel, applies to the superb Gothic buildings on the north face of the mount. The eastern block, the first to be built between 1211 and 1218, comprises from top to bottom, the refectory, the Guests' Hall and the cellar.

From the outside the buildings look like a fortress although their religious connections are indicated by Almonry; the western block, built between 1218 and 1228, consists of the cloisters, the Knights' Hall and the the simple nobility of the design. The interior is a perfect example of the evolution of the Gothic style, from a simplicity, which is almost Romanesque, in the lower halls, through the elegance of the Guests' Hall, the majesty of the Knights' Hall and the mysterious luminosity of the Refectory, to the cloisters which are a masterpiece of delicacy and line. The top floor comprises the cloisters and the refectory.

★★★**Cloisters** – The cloisters seem to be suspended between the sea and the sky. The gallery arcades display heavily undercut sculpture of foliage ornamented with the occasional animal or human figure (particularly human heads); there are also a few religious symbols. The double row of arches rests on delightfully slim single columns arranged in quincunx to enhance the impression of lightness. The different colours of the various materials add to the overall charm. The lavatorium (lavabo) on the right of the entrance recalls the ceremonial "washing of the feet" which took place every Thursday.

Archangel St Michael

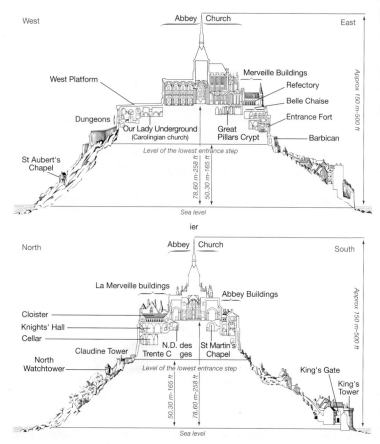

★★Refectory – The effect is mysterious; the chamber is full of light although it appears to have only two windows in the end wall. To admit so much light without weakening the solid side walls which support the wooden roof and are lined with a Row of slim niches, the architect introduced a very narrow aperture high up in each recess. The vaulted ceiling is panelled with wood and the acoustics are excellent.

Old Romanesque Abbey – The rib vaulting marks the transition from Romanesque to Gothic. The tour includes the Monks' Walk and part of the dormitory.

Great Wheel – The wheel belongs to the period when the abbey was used as a prison. It was used to haul provisions and was operated by five or six men turning the wheel from within as if on a treadmill.

Crypts – The transepts and chancel of the church are supported by three undercrofts or crypts; the most moving is **Notre-Dame-sous-Terre** (accessible only during guided tours): the Carolingian structure which stands on the very spot where St Aubert officiated, is a simple rectangle (8x9m/26x30ft), divided into two small naves by a couple of arches resting on a central pillar. The place is awe-inspiring because of the complete silence which prevails and because of the memory of the events which took place here more than 1 000 years ago! The most impressive is the **Crypte des Gros Piliers★** (Great Pillared Crypt) which has 10 pillars (5m/16ft in circumference) made of granite from the Chausey Islands.
The second floor consists of the Guests' Hall and the Knights' Hall.

★Guests' Hall – Here the abbot received royalty (Louis IX, Louis XI, François I) and other important visitors. The hall (35m/115ft long) has a Gothic ceiling supported on a central row of slim columns; the effect is graceful and elegant.
At one time it was divided down the middle by a huge curtain of tapestries; on one side was the kitchen quarters (two chimneys) and on the other the great dining hall (one chimney).

★Knights' Hall – The name of this hall may refer to the military order of St Michael which was founded in 1469 by Louis XI with the abbey as its seat.

The hall is vast and majestic (26x18m/85x58ft) and divided into four sections by three rows of stout columns.

It was the monks' workroom or *scriptorium* where they illuminated manuscripts, read and studied religious or secular texts and, for this reason, it was heated by two great fireplaces. The almonry and cellar occupy the rooms on the lower floor.

Cellar – This was the storeroom; it was divided into three by two rows of square pillars supporting the groined vaulting.

Almonry – This is a Gothic room with a Romanesque vault supported on a row of columns.

A TOUR OF THE SURROUNDINGS

★★Mont-St-Michel Bay

About 100km/60mi of coast line border the bay. The islands, cliffs, beaches and dunes form a series of ecosystems which are home to many species of flora and fauna.

Travelling along the coast, you will be rewarded by stunning views of Mont-St-Michel, and you can enjoy walks along pleasant paths rambling between the polders and grassy fields.

Tall tales and natural phenomena – Pilgrims liked to tell frightening tells of the perils of an excursion to Mont-St-Michel, but in fact the natural phenomena of the site are now well understood. What used to be thought of as "quick sand" is more precisely the effect of swathes of firm sand sitting on top of pockets of more liquid sand. The fearsome fog which occasionally envelops the whole bay with such speed can now be predicted by weather forecasters, and there is no longer a need to ring the church bell to warn of its imminence. And the tide racing in faster than a

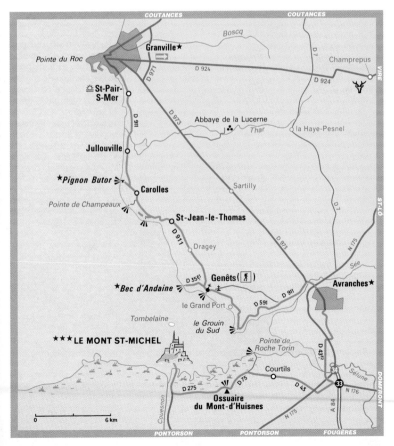

galloping horse? Although there are specific points where the action of the spring tide combines with geological features to create a movement of water at a speed of up to 25-30kph/15-18mph, the average rate of speed of the incoming tide is 3.75kph/2.25mph – about the speed of a person walking.

Shifting sands – The movement of the tides in the bay is considerable and the difference in sea level between high and low water can be over 12m/40ft, the highest in France. As the sea bed is flat the sea retreats a long way leaving 15km/9mi of sand exposed. Mont-St-Michel has been silting up for several decades. Indeed, every year the sea deposits around 1 000 000m³/35 315 000cu ft of sediment in the bay. This can partly be blamed on mankind since between the mid 19C and 1969 a number of regional initiatives were taken, resulting in constructions that accelerated the formation of polders (channels for navigation of the River Couesnon, a dike and a dam). In 1995 a joint project was commissioned by the State and local municipalities, intended to return the mount to the sea. Ideally, this would make it possible to replace the dike by a footbridge under which cross-currents would once again flow between the mainland and the island. It would also help restore the scouring action of the Couesnon and two other coastal streams.

From Granville to Mont-St-Michel

40km/25mi – about 2hr 30min

Between Granville and Carolles, there is a wide open view of the bay.

St-Pair-sur-Mer – *See page* 219.

Jullouville – The houses are scattered among pine trees.

Carolles – The beach is at the foot of the cliffs; the village is set on the last headland before the sandy expanse of Mont-St-Michel Bay. In the vicinity there are several attractive walks with fine views.

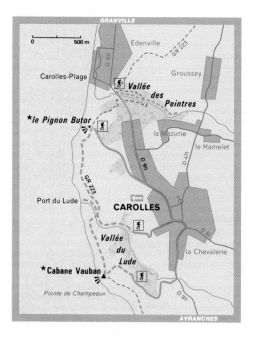

The **Vallée des Peintres** (Artists' Valley) is an attractive spot, green and rock-strewn *(car park at Carolles-Plage, north of Carolles)*.

The view from **Le Pignon Butor★** *(viewing table)* on the clifftop extends north to Granville Rock and west to Pointe du Grouin and Cancale in Brittany *(1km/0.6mi – 1hr on foot there and back, northwest of the village)*.

The path through the **Vallée du Lude** (Le Lude Valley) crosses an area of gorse and broom to reach the lonely cove, Port du Lude, on the coast *(1hr on foot there and back from the car park; signs)*.

The **view★** from the Vauban Hut, a stone building standing on a rocky mound, includes Mont-St-Michel in the middle of the bay *(south of Carolles on D 911 beyond the small bridge turn right; park at the end of the road; take the downhill path (left) which then climbs (right) towards the cliff)*.

St-Jean-le-Thomas – This seaside resort is very busy in the summer months.

On entering Genêts turn right.

★Bec d'Andaine – From this beach of fine sand backed by dunes there is a good **view** of Mont-St-Michel near at hand.

Genêts – The solid granite 12C to 14C **church** is preceded by an attractive porch with a wooden roof. Inside, the transept crossing leaves an impression of considerable strength, as it rises from four square granite piers with animal and foliage

Relais des Genêts

🚶 Guides offer visitors a chance to join in walking tours through the bay area, some with special themes, and all centred around enjoying the natural beauty, learning about the flora and the fauna. *Place de la Mairie, 50530 Genêts,* ☎ *02 33 70 86 46.*

The **Relais des Courtils** has a schedule of programmes and activities concerning the bay. *Bas-Courtils, 50220 Courtils,* ☎ *02 33 89 66 00.*

decorated capitals. The high altar is crowned by a canopy resting on gently swelling columns. Note the 13C stained-glass window at the east end and some lovely statues.

On leaving Genêts turn right before the calvary.

The coastal road goes through Le Grand Port and offers good views, at very close quarters, of Mont-St-Michel, especially from the **Pointe du Grouin du Sud** (Grouin du Sud Point). The famous salt marshes can also be seen from this stretch of the drive.

Take D 591 and D 911 to Avranches.

★ **Avranches** – *See AVRANCHES.*

At Bas-Courtils, turn left onto D 75; after 2km/1mi turn right onto D 107.

Ossuaire Allemand du Mont-d'Huisnes – This circular construction with its 68 compartments contains the remains of 11 887 German soldiers. From the belvedere there is a good view of Mont-St-Michel.

Continue along D 275.

The coastal road skirts the salt marshes where flocks of sheep are put out to graze on the special grass there. The lambs are prized for their succulent tender meat. Again there are fine views of Mont-St-Michel.

MORTAGNE-AU-PERCHE ★

Population 4 584
Michelin map 60 folds 4 and 5 or 231 fold 45

This pretty country town was once the stronghold of the Perche region, well-placed atop a knoll overlooking a lush green and undulating countryside, the home territory of the **Pecheron** horse. Although little remains to testify to its once-powerful role, the streets yet have a medieval design, and the houses are clustered together, presenting a jumble of brown tile roofs contrasted with the lighter-coloured façades. Mortagne is known for its blood sausage *(boudin noir)*, and during the annual Lenten fair, some 5km/3mi of it is consumed! If you approach from the north, on D 930, you will enjoy an excellent view of the town.

DISCOVER MORTAGNE

To visit the town and discover the quaint, old-fashioned houses and hotels, leave your car in the Montcacune car park. Several itineraries have been mapped out and signposted and explanatory brochures can be obtained from the tourist office.

Jardin public – These well-laid out gardens with attractive flower beds offer good views of the Perche countryside. Near the lime trees, note the bust of **Jules Chaplain** (1839-1909), an engraver and sculptor from Mortagne. An outstanding equestrian statue by E Frémiet, inspired by Ovid's legendary poem *Metamorphoses*, depicts Neptune as a horse, setting out to conquer Ceres.

Where to stay and eat

MID-RANGE

Le Tribunal – *4 pl. du Palais* – ☎ *02 33 25 04 77* – closed 20 Dec to 6 Jan – *14 rooms: 39.64/48.78€* – ⌚ *6.10€* – restaurant *13.72/28.97€.* Situated in the medieval district, near the church and the museum, this welcoming 13C and 18C house is an ideal stopover. The dining room has the atmosphere of an inn and the distinctive rooms are charming. Enjoy the terrace in fine weather.

Hôpital – Delightful 16C cloisters with panelled vaulting and an 18C chapel are all that remain of the former convent of St Clare.

Porte St-Denis — The St-Denis Gate is the sole remnant of the town's fortifications. In the 16C two storeys were added to the original 13C Gothic arch and they now house the **Musée Percheron** ⊘ with its local archeological and historical sections.

Maison dite des Comtes du Perche – This 17C house stands on the site of a former manor house. The ground floor houses the public library whereas the first floor contains the Musée Alain.

MORTAGNE-AU-PERCHE

Maison des comtes
du Perche :
  Musée Alain .... M¹

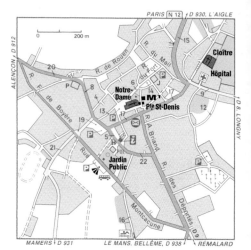

Église Notre-Dame – The church was built between 1495 and 1535 and combines elements of both Flamboyant Gothic and Early Renaissance styles on the exterior decoration.
There is a magnificent 18C **altarpiece★** in the apse. The altarpiece, choir stalls and pulpit all come from the Carthusian monastery of Valdieu which once stood in the heart of the nearby Réno Forest. The stained-glass window in the third chapel, off the north aisle, recalls the part played by local people in the colonisation of Canada in the 17C.

Musée Alain ⊘ – The French philosopher **Alain**, whose real name was **Émile Chartier**, was born in Mortagne in 1868; he died in 1951 in Le Vésinet, to the west of Paris. The museum includes photos, manuscripts, correspondence and other personal belongings. The study from his Le Vésinet home has been recreated on the second floor. The armchair and walking stick recall the difficult years when he suffered from rheumatism. The "**Journées Alain**", which are organised in early October, are devoted to the philosopher: conferences, debates and theme tours.

THE PERCHE AND TRAPPE FORESTS

Round tour of 51km/32mi – about 1hr 30min. From Mortagne take N 12 north and after 12km/7mi turn right onto D 290.

Parc naturel régional du Perche – This park is the most recently created (1998) of French "nature parks", zones where both the environment and the traditional economy are protected. It is located in the regions of Basse-Normandie and Centre, and covers 182 000ha/449 722 acres of gentle hills, deep forests, hidden ponds, hedgerows, green valleys and interesting architecture. The Percheron horse on the park's logo is a fitting emblem for this area.
The wooded heights are covered with groves of beech, oak and pine.

Autheuil – The Romanesque church (restored) has arcades in the nave, a fine chancel arch at the entrance to the transept and handsome capitals on the transept's square piers as well as a 16C statue of St Leonard.

Make a U-turn and take D 290 west in the direction of Tourouvre.

Tourouvre – The **church** contains 15C choir stalls and above the high altar a 15C painting, **The Adoration of the Magi★**, has been incorporated into a 17C altarpiece. Two stained-glass windows relate the story of local families associated with the founding of Quebec.

Beyond the church turn right onto a road which climbs steeply towards Perche Forest.

After a steep climb the road enters Perche Forest and, after 2km/1mi, reaches the beautiful Étoile du Perche crossroads. Continue straight ahead and on reaching the Avre Valley turn left to admire the various pools. The white mass of the Château des Étangs is reflected in the waters of the pool, itself encircled by pine trees.

West of Bresolettes the road enters Trappe Forest.

At the road junction turn right onto D 930 and then left onto the minor road.

The Chaumont pool can be glimpsed through the trees.

Abbaye de la Trappe ⊘ – The abbey occupies an isolated site in a forest dotted with pools. It was named after an area where hunters would catch game by means of a device known as a *trappe*. It was founded in 1140 by Benedictines from Breuil-Benoît and then passed to the abbey of Cîteaux in 1147 before being reformed in the 17C by Abbot de Rancé who introduced the Strict Observance. The name has been adopted by other Cistercian monasteries which, like La Trappe, adopted the strict rule; their members form the Order of Reformed Cistercians of the Strict Observance, which is strictly contemplative, contrary to the usual Cistercian Rule.

Make a U-turn and take D 930 south to Mortagne.

② From Mortagne-au-Perche to Longny

25km/16mi – about 30min – See map p 99.

Loisé – The 16C church is flanked by a monumental square tower.

Forêt de Réno-Valdieu – This 1 600ha/4 000-acre state forest has beautiful stands of very old trees – oaks and beeches almost 300 years old and rising to more than 40m/131ft. Visitor centres have been set up near the access roads. North of the forest a clearly signposted itinerary enlightens tourists on the massif and its treasures. A farm in a restful setting has replaced the former Abbaye de Valdieu which gave its name to the forest joined in 1789 with that of the Comte de Réno.

West of the forest the road *(D 8)* traverses a remarkable landscape of hills, passing Château de la Goyère (right) as it climbs to Mortagne.

On leaving the forest, take D 291 right.

Monceaux-au-Perche – This village standing at the confluence of two small valleys is one of the prettiest in the area. Nestling along the banks of the River **Jambée**, the **Manoir de Pontgirard** (16C), modernised in extremely good taste, features some fine terraced **gardens** tucked away behind its walls.

Longny is reached by taking D 11 which runs through the shady Jambée Valley.

Longny-au-Perche – Longny occupies a pleasant location beside the River Jambée near Longny Forest.

There is a good view of the town from the charming 16C **Chapelle de Notre-Dame-de-Pitié** *(access by rue Gaston-Gibory on the right of the town hall)*, which is approached by a flight of steps leading up to the apse.

The square belfry set at an angle to the façade and the pinnacled buttress add a touch of elegance to the building.

The west door is surmounted by a delicate Renaissance decoration framed by sculpted pilasters; unfortunately the statues were destroyed during the Revolution. Above the lintel is Our Lady of Mercy dominated by a bust of the Eternal Father. Higher still is a medallion of the Sacrifice of Isaac by Abraham.

The carved wooden doors are by a local 19C-20C artist, Abbé Vingtier. The west door shows the Visitation and the Annunciation; the north door bears a medallion of the Virgin of Sorrow and the south door a representation of the face of Christ from Veronica's veil.

The rib vaulting in the nave is embellished with pendant keystones. Two side chapels flanking the chancel form a false transept. There is an annual pilgrimage to the statue of the Our Lady of Mercy at the high altar.

The **Église St-Martin** dates from the late 15C and the early 16C. The square belfry is supported by carved buttresses and the stair tower. Three statues are set in the blind window bay. Above them, in a niche, is St Martin on horseback dividing his cloak.

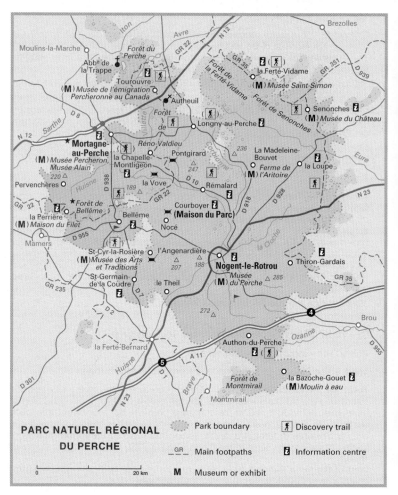

PARC NATUREL RÉGIONAL DU PERCHE

Park boundary

__GR__ Main footpaths

M Museum or exhibit

[⚐] Discovery trail

[i] Information centre

0   20 km

---

③ From Mortagne-au-Perche to Bellême

35km/22mi – about 1hr – see map p 99.

From Mortagne-au-Perche take D 9 south.

Courgeon – The late-11C Romanesque **church** was flanked in the 17C by two aisles and a four-storey tower crowned by a stone shingle dome topped by a lantern.

La Chapelle-Montligeon – This village is dominated by an immense neo-Gothic basilica (1894-1911) lit by modern, highly coloured stained-glass windows. The altars in the transepts were designed in the Art Deco style.
The basilica is visited by numerous pilgrims. The premises of the printing works (240 employees) around the central courtyard are a reminder of the original community.
There is a good view of the surrounding countryside from the basilica terrace.

At the junction of D 213, turn right, then left on D 10.

Manoir de la Vove ⊙ – This large manor house, with its military appearance guards the Huisne Valley and is one of the oldest in the Perche region. The roof of the 12C keep is supported by oak beams. The living quarters on three floors are served by a spiral staircase located in an octagonal tower flanked by a round turret. The long wing, built at right angles, with its pilasters and high windows, was added in the 17C.

Take D 256 west. In Le Pin-la-Garenne turn left onto D 938.

The road rises up to **Bellême Forest**, where you can admire Herse Lake in its sylvan setting, then continues on to provide a fine view of the town of Bellême and its surroundings.

MORTAIN ★

Population 2 416
Michelin map 59 fold 9 or 231 fold 40

This small pleasantly well-kept town is built half way up a hillside in a attractive **setting**★ where the River Cance, cutting through the last of the Basse-Normandie's southern hills, emerges on to the vast wooded Sélune Basin, leaving in its wake a rock strewn countryside.

The name of the town is derived from the word Maurus and could refer to the Moors who served in the Roman army.

During the Middle Ages Mortain was the capital of the county held by Robert, the step brother of William the Conqueror. The town has been rebuilt over the ruins left after the Battle of Normandy.

The marked itinerary "La Contre-attaque" (The Counter-Attack), one of several described in the Historical Area of the Battle of Normandy goes through Mortain.

SIGHTS

Grande Cascade

★**Grande Cascade** – ⚞ *Either park in avenue de l'Abbaye-Blanche in the parking space at a bend in the road and take the path downhill or park in rue du Bassin (signposted) and take the path which follows the river bank.*

The waterfall (25m/82ft) is created by the River Cance flowing through a wooded gorge; the foaming waters recall the mountain streams of the Pyrenees or the Alps.

★**Petite Cascade** – *45min on foot there and back. From place du Château take the downhill path south (left) along the wall of the Caisse d'Épargne (signpost).*

⚞ The path crosses the River Cance and follows the bank upstream past the Aiguille Rock. It then crosses the Cançon stream on stepping stones before reaching the waterfall (35m/121ft) in a rock amphitheatre.

★ **Petite Chapelle** – *From Mortain take the road south towards Rancoudray; in front of the Gendarmerie turn left; park in the car park at the top of the hill; walk up the avenue of fir trees.*

Just before the chapel there stands a small monument (left) in memory of the American soldiers who fell on nearby Hill 314.

To the left and beyond the chapel there is a belvedere *(viewing table)* providing a **view**★ of the wooded heights of Mortain and Lande-Pourrie. On a clear day Mont-St-Michel and the Breton coast are visible on the horizon (right).

Abbaye Blanche ⊘ – This former monastery in a landscape of rocky outcrops was founded in the 12C by Adeline and her brother Vital, chaplain to Count Robert. The abbey now serves as a retreat house.

Chapter-house – There is an audio-visual presentation on the abbey's history. The chapter-house is composed of two bays with pointed vaulting. The sisters usually sit by order of seniority on the white stone benches which run round the walls. The side opposite the cloisters was reserved for dignitaries.

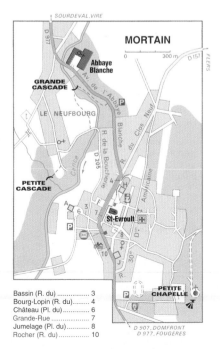

Bassin (R. du) 3
Bourg-Lopin (R. du)......... 4
Château (Pl. du) 6
Grande-Rue 7
Jumelage (Pl. du)............ 8
Rocher (R. du) 10

Cloister Gallery – Contrary to other Romanesque cloisters in the region, which have twinned columns or clusters as at Mont-St-Michel, the gallery here consists of a simple row of single columns. The vaulting is of timberwork.

Abbey Church – The church displays the usual features of the Cistercian plan: flat east end with its oculus and transept chapels. The diagonal ribs are a precursor of the Gothic style. The nave is lit by a series of six lancet windows which increase in size towards the west end.

Lay Sisters Refectory – The groined vaulting is supported by two central columns.

Storeroom – There are two barrel vaults of four bays each. The capitals are carved with foliage and scrolls.

Église St-Évroult – This old collegiate church reconstructed in the 13C is built of sandstone in a somewhat severe Gothic style. The gabled façade is lightened by three pointed windows and, below, by the main door. The 13C belfry, pierced on three sides by two single lancets, is attractively plain and simple. The fine door in the second bay shows all the decorative elements known to Norman Romanesque. The single arch relies neither on columns nor capitals.

In the chancel, the stalls have carved misericords representing satyr-like figures. The altar is of Maine marble; the font is 15C.

The **treasury** ⊘ contains the Chrismal, an exceptional 7C casket of Anglo-Irish origin. The casket or portable reliquary is made of beechwood, lined with copper and engraved with runic inscriptions and images of sacred personages.

VALLÉE DE LA SÉE

Round tour of 58km/36mi – about 3hr. From Mortain take D 977 north towards Vire.
North of La Tournerie, where the road winds downhill, there is a view of the vast Sourdeval Basin, through which runs the River Sée.
In Sourdeval turn left onto D 911.
The road follows the curves of the narrow **Sée Valley★** offering a new view at each bend.

Moulin de la Sée ⊘ – This mill, which once housed factory premises, is also know as the **Écomusée de la Vallée de Brouains.** Today it is the setting for a museum devoted to rivers and related activities: the breeding of fish belonging to the *Salmonidae* family (mention is made of the exceptional quality of the waters of the Sée, one of France's first rivers for salmon); the development

Auberge du Moulin – *Moulin de la Sée – 50150 Brouains –* ☎ *02 33 59 50 60 – www.aubergedumoulin.fr – closed Jan, Mon and Sun evening except July-Aug – 12.04/ 27.44€.* Located in the grounds of the quaint mill museum with its tall factory chimney, this inn stands on the banks of the Sée with a view of the surrounding countryside. In summer you can enjoy the terrace. The rooms are unpretentious, like the prices.

of hydraulic energy (at the turn of the 19C more than 150 paper mills operated along the 10km/6.2mi-long valley, with a difference of altitude of 100m/328ft); the riverside population and the evolution of technology, ranging from the early days of pewter ware to the manufacture of stainless steel cutlery.

Eating out

MODERATE

Auberge Paysanne – *In the "Village enchanté de Bellefontaine" – 50520 Bellefontaine – 7km/4.3mi north of Mortain via D 33 –* ☎ *02 33 59 01 93 – www.village-enchante.fr – closed Oct to Apr. – 9.91/29.73€.* Situated at the entrance of the village, this old barn converted into a restaurant is truly bewitching with its old beams, granite fireplace and original hard-packed-earth floor still partly showing to complete the rustic atmosphere. If you wish to stay, there are several possibilities: guestrooms and self-catering cottages.

Where to stay

MODERATE

Le Logis Bed and Breakfast – *50520 Juvigny-le-Tertre – 12km/7.5mi west of Mortain via D 977, D5 then D55 (towards St-Hilaire) –* ☎ *02 33 59 38 20 –* 🖃 *– 3 rooms: 30.49/36.59€ – meal 12€.* Rooms have been fitted out in two separate 17C buildings. The first two in contemporary style are located in the dovecote whereas the third, more traditional in style with its granite fireplace and its beams carved with fleur-de-lis, is located in the main building. Two cottages.

From Pewterers to Guy Degrenne

In the early 19C men would leave their native village and take to the roads to try their luck throughout France. They would buy used cutlery made of pewter from farms and would melt it to make new kitchen utensils. These men, who were born in Sourdeval, Gathemo or Fresne-Porêt, were known as *grillous*: they were the ancestors of the industrialists who gradually converted their old paper mills into small metalworking factories. Over the years the manufacture of cutlery was to become a speciality of the canton. It was originally made in pewter, then in steel-coated metal and eventually in stainless steel, as is the custom today. The firm Guy Degrenne, named after its original founder, is one of France's most prestigious manufacturers of cutlery today.

After passing the church in Chérencé-le-Roussel, turn right onto D 33.

St-Pois – Fine views south of the Sée Valley.

In St-Pois turn right and right again onto D 39 which climbs uphill.

St-Michel-de-Montjoie – At the southwest entrance to the village there is a terrace which affords an attractive view *(viewing table)* which, on a clear day, extends as far west as Mont-St-Michel. The village is known for its granite quarry *(northwest off D 282 towards Gast)* and for its mineral water, Eau de Montjoie. The **Musée du Granit** ⊘ displays a series of granite objects – capitals, pediments, sarcophagi, balusters, millstones – in a wooded park.

Photographs and panels describe the history of quarrying, of working granite, its use in craftwork, in religious art, agriculture, building and architecture. The exhibition hall displays modern works: carved and polished sculptures, animal statues, bracelets and rings.

Take D 39 east; in Gathemo turn right onto D 55. In Chérencé-le-Roussel turn left onto D 33.

Village enchanté de Bellefontaine ⊘ – This "enchanted village" recreates the world of childhood and make-believe: fairy stories, model villages from all over the world, feudal castle, clockwork theatre and leisure park (railway, games, theatre of automata).

Take D 33 north; in La Hardière turn right onto D 179. Near Bellevue turn right onto D 977 to return to Mortain.

Maison de la Pomme et de la Poire ⊘ – *9km/6mi southeast by D 907 to Barenton.* The Apple and Pear Museum comprises two buildings in which the history, the techniques, the economic development and the present problems of the production of cider, perry and calvados are presented by means of paintings, photographs, engravings, old and new material. There are also two orchards: standard trees which bear fruit after six to eight years and half-standard trees which bear after three years. There are tasting sessions at the end of the visit.

NEUFCHÂTEL-EN-BRAY

Population 5 322
Michelin map 52 folds 15 and 16 or 231 fold 12

The town was formerly the administrative capital of the Pays de Bray. Neufchâtel produces a cylindrical cheese *(Bondon)*, which was the first to earn Bray a name for cheesemaking, and also the *petit-suisse*. The famous **fromage de Neufchâtel** is one of the French cheeses which has its own name of origin *(appellation d'origine)*; this means that the milk, the cheesemaking and maturing must be produced or affected within a strictly defined geographic area. Neufchâtel is a farm cheese which is produced in several shapes *(bonde, briquette, carré, cœur, double bonde)*.

Église Notre-Dame – The church tower houses three bells beneath its slate roof. The doorway dates from the end of the 15C; the early-16C nave contains Renaissance capitals. The eight windows in the aisles depict local saints: St Radegonde, St Vincent, St Anthony. In the 13C chancel round columns support the pointed vaulting; against a pillar is a gilt wood Virgin crowned.

Musée J.-B.-Mathon-A.-Durand ⊘ – The museum is devoted to the traditions and crafts of the Pays de Bray: wrought-iron work. In the garden are a cider mill (1746) and a press (1837), both typical of the region.

THE NORTHERN PAYS DE BRAY

46km/28mi – 1hr30min – Leave Neufchâtel-en-Bray to the north on D 1314.

From the road, which runs north through a strangely barren landscape on the northeast slope of the so-called "Bray Buttonhole" formation, there are ever more extensive views of the Béthune Valley (left) and Hellet Forest (north).

The Bray Buttonhole

The movement of the earth's crust which brought about the raising of the Alps in the Tertiary Era had repercussions as far as the Paris Basin. The shocks which disturbed the ancient shelf formed ridges in the upper layers deposited in the Secondary Era. Wide and deep undulations were formed in a southeast-northwest direction and subsequently one of these swelled into a large dome with a steep northeast face.

Erosion relentlessly ate into the dome, exposing subjacent Jurassic soil in its considerable geological complexity. This narrow cut with its clearly defined rim, is known as a "buttonhole" and explains the variations in landscape resulting from the differences in the nature of the soil.

Turn left on D 56.

The road crosses through Hellet Forest. From Croixdalle, D 77 *(turn left)* goes down the Béthune Valley as far as Osmoy-St-Valery, where it rises again to climb the southwest slope, and passes through a gap. The view below is of Nappes Another pass leads out of the Mesnil-Follemprise Valley. The view unfolds over a chalky landscape. In the distance, the bell-tower of Bures-en-Bray appears.

Bures-en-Bray – The **church** ⊘, partly 12C, has a modern brick façade with porch and a bold twisted wooden spire. In the north transept is an Entombment, a 16C stone polychrome altarpiece and a 14C Virgin and Child.

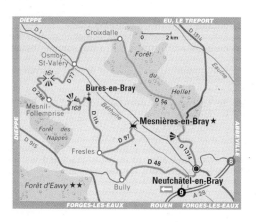

Forest.

Uphill after the church take the first road, D 114, left near the café-tobacconist.

The road follows a terrace at the foot of the southwest face on which the villages have been built.

At Fresle turn left onto D 97.

Before crossing the Béthune there is an attractive view of Mesnières Château.

★Château de Mesnières-en-Bray ⊘ – The majestic château, which houses a private institution, is a Renaissance construction; it was begun in the late 15C and is flanked by powerful, although purely ornamental, machicolated towers. The sweeping staircase in the main courtyard is 18C. The main central building, with its steep roof, arcaded gallery, superimposed orders, ornamented dormer windows and antique style busts, is decorated in the Classical style.

The tour includes the gallery, adorned with real antlers, the Map Room (Salle des Cartes) decorated with 17C paintings on wood, and the main chapel (1860). The 16C family chapel is covered by an axe-shaped roof and decorated with panelling (1670), life-size statues of Christ, John the Baptist and the Four Evangelists and windows composed of fragments of the original stained glass.

Return to Fresles; take D 114 and D 48 to return to Neufchâtel-en-Bray.

The churches of the Bray

Round tour of 63km/39mi – about 2hr
Leave Neufchâtel northwards on N 28, then N 29.

Aumale – In the 17C this town belonged to the Duke of Maine, but subsequently passed by marriage into the Orléans family. It is now an important dairy farming centre. The **Église de St-Pierre-et-St-Paul** displays both the Flamboyant and the

Château de Mesnières-en-Bray

Renaissance styles. The south portal, attributed to Jean Goujon, has been damaged. Inside, there are interesting embellished arch keystones, especially in the chancel and the Lady Chapel, and a 16C stained-glass window in St Joseph's Chapel.

Take N 29 towards Neufchâtel, but turn almost immediately right onto D 920.

Foucarmont – The somewhat squat impression given by the concrete **church** (rebuilt 1959-64) is alleviated to some extent by the wonderful irregular stained-glass windows in rich warm colours and by the precious stones inlaid in the walls. Inside there is a vast nave, a baptistery and a chancel, lit by a glass dome.

N 28 leads back to Neufchâtel.

NOGENT-LE-ROTROU

Population 11 591
Michelin map 60 fold 15 or 232 fold 12

Nogent-le-Rotrou on the banks of the River Huisne, dominated by its castle, is the capital of the Perche region. Between 925 and 1226 the Gallo-Roman town became a powerful fief of the Rotrou family, counts of Perche, who gave the town its name (Nogent derives from the Gallic word *novio-mago* meaning "new market"). Nogent was burned down in 1449 at Charles VII's command to prevent the English from capturing it and using it as a base for operations. The town was rebuilt soon afterwards, which explains why many of the buildings are in the Flamboyant or Renaissance style.

Nogent has become an important centre for the slaughtering of animals to supply meat for the Chartres area, the Paris Basin and Germany. The orchards and textiles (especially muslin) of past centuries have been succeeded by pharmaceutical laboratories, electronics engineering and food processing, and a training centre for civilian rescue operations.

The old town borders the main road *(N 23)* at the foot of St John's Hill; the new town covers the flat land beside the River Huisne.

FAMOUS NATIVE SONS

Rémi Belleau (1528-77), one of the founders of the Pléiade group, was a graceful and subtle poet who glorified the art of living by depicting banquets and other festive occasions; he was also a great nature lover and would enjoy describing rural landscapes and the beauty of natural shapes. His art was epitomized in the pastoral *La Bergerie*, published in 1565. He wrote about pastoral life and precious stones such as diamonds, agate, sapphire and amethyst. "Belleau and Ronsard are one" said Ronsard in one of his *Elegies*. As a sign of friendship and literary respect at his funeral in Notre-Dame in Paris, his coffin was carried by Ronsard, Baïf, Philippe Desportes and Amadis Jamyn, most of whom came from the region between Chartres and Angers.

Where to stay and eat

MODERATE

L'Aulnaye Bed and Breakfast – *3.5km/2.2mi west of Nogent towards Alençon – ☎ 02 37 52 02 11 – ⬛ – 3 rooms: 36.59/51.83€*. Nestling in a splendid colourful park, this opulent 19C house will delight you with its fine staircase and lovely fireplace, its antique furniture and parquet flooring in the rooms. Pretty veranda for a cosy breakfast. One apartment available.

LUXURY

Le Moulin de Villeray – *61110 Villeray – 11km/6.8mi north of Nogent via D 918 and D 10 – ☎ 02 33 73 30 22 – ⬛ – 25 rooms: from 114.34€ – ⬛ 11.43€ – restaurant 22.11/74.70€.* This charming mill is ideal for a lunch break or a romantic weekend on the banks of the River Huisne! You will be seduced by the gentle way of life here: it is so nice to laze about in this beautifully fitted out place nestling in green surroundings... In summer, enjoy the terrace along the river and beside swimming pool. Fine bedrooms.

Maximilien de Béthune, Duc de Sully (1560-1641) who also owned Rosny, Sully, La Chapelle-d'Angillon, Henrichemont and Villebon, collected the rents and, although he was a strict Protestant, the tithes (eg St-Benoît-sur-Loire). In 1624 the château and manor of Nogent were sold by Henri II de Condé, father of the conqueror of Rocroi, to the duke. He managed the income from his Nogent estate and encouraged agriculture and stockraising. The estate remained the property of the family of Henri IV's great financier until the Revolution.

SIGHTS

It is advisable to leave your car on place de la République, and to continue visiting the old quarter of Nogent on foot.

Église Notre-Dame – The building was formerly the chapel of the Hôtel-Dieu (workhouse) and dates from the 13C and 14C. At the end of the north aisle there is a 16C-17C crib; the figures are of painted terracotta. Carved keystones on the chancel vaulting and an organ dating from 1634.

Tombeau de Sully – *Access is through rue de Sully: you will come to a small courtyard containing the oratory and the tomb.* The entrance to the Hôtel-Dieu (17C) is a Classical doorway with Sully's coat of arms and emblems on the pediment. As Sully was a Protestant, his tomb is next to the church but not part of it. An attractive pedimented door opens into the domed hexagonal oratory containing his empty tomb which was sculpted by Barthélemy Boudin from Chartres. The expression of the face and the modelling of the hands of the statue (1642) of Sully are very good. The effigy of his wife, Rachel de Cochefilet, who died 18 years later, is not so well done.

NOGENT-LE-ROTROU

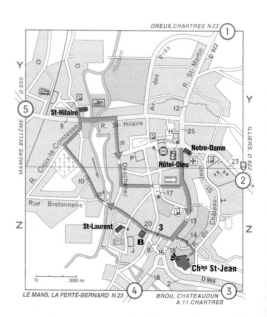

Château St-Jean – *Access on foot by rue des Marches-St-Jean, or by car along rue de Sully, then rue du Château-St-Jean which provides glimpses of Nogent and the Huisne Valley.*

This impressive castle, with its walls and massive towers, stands on a rock spur. It is enclosed within a wall and further protection from attack is provided by ditches. Within the circular enclosure are two terraces separated by a stout wall and a deep well.

The Rotrous, counts of Perche, lived in the huge rectangular keep (35m/115ft high) which is supported by unusual buttresses. The twin windows date from the 13C. The enclosing wall with its semicircular towers was built from the 12C to the 13C. The remarkable gatehouse is flanked by round towers with arrow slits and machicolations of tufa stone; its whiteness contrasts with the grey stone of the rest of the building. Above the pointed-arched entrance is a 15C terracotta medallion of the Italian School. The courtyard provides a pleasant view of the town.

Musée du Perche ⊙ – Some of the rooms in the château are devoted to regional ethnography (reconstruction of a Percheron interior with local furniture), the history of the château (engravings, documents) and handcrafted objects.

A path runs round the outside of the walls.

Rue Bourg-le-Comte – Several of the houses are of interest: a 13C turreted house (no 2) which is better seen from rue des Poupardières; 16C house (no 4); Renaissance house with mullioned windows (no 3).

Maison du Bailli – *47 rue St-Laurent.* Two turrets flank the entrance to the 16C mansion built by Pierre Durant, bailiff of St Denis' Abbey, and his wife Blanche Dévrier, as is recorded in the inscription. The dormer windows are particularly fine.

Église St-Laurent ⊙ – The square surrounding the church was once the graveyard. The building is in the Flamboyant style, surmounted by a tower with a Renaissance top; it is linked by an arch to the house of the Provost of St Denis' Abbey.

The interior contains old statues and a late-15C Entombment (right of the chancel) with very expressive figures.

Église St-Hilaire – The church (13C-16C) stands beside the River Huisne. Its square tower dates from the 16C. The unusual polygonal chancel (13C) was modelled on the Holy Sepulchre in Jerusalem; above the window bays are two attractive oculi.

OMAHA BEACH

Michelin map 54 folds 4 and 14 or 231 fold 16 – Local maps see below and Plages du DÉBARQUEMENT

The name Omaha Beach, which until 6 June 1944 existed only as an operational code name, has continued to jointly designate the beaches of St-Laurent-sur-Mer, Colleville-sur-Mer and Vierville-sur-Mer in memory of the American soldiers of the 1st (5th Corps of the 1st Army) Division who landed east and west of Colleville and suffered heavy casualties in the most costly of the D-Day battles.

Dramatic Clash – Here nature, in the form of a strong coastal current which swept landing craft off course, and shingle, which proved at first insurmountable to heavy armour, combined to strengthen an extremely well organised defence by the Germans. Companies at first baulked, later rallied and by evening certain companies of the 116th Regiment had taken the Port-en-Bessin-Grandcamp road enabling the motorised units to gain the plateau. Some parts of the road had been built during the afternoon under the fire of enemy snipers. The Mulberry A harbour installed for the American troops lasted only until a storm broke it up on 19 June. Never in 40 years had this part of the coast seen such a wild storm.

The austere and desolate appearance, at least, in its eastern part along the narrow beach backing on barren cliffs, makes the invasion scene easy to imagine even today.

FROM COLLEVILLE-SUR-MER TO VIERVILLE

9km/6mi – about 1hr – see local map below

Colleville-sur-Mer – The last Germans did not leave the area around the village church until 10am on 7 June. The church has been entirely rebuilt.

Just before the church, turn right towards the coast.

Monument to the 5th Engineer Special Brigade – The monument, built on the remains of a blockhouse, commemorates those who lost their lives while protecting all movements between the landing craft and the beach, as well as the setting up of beach installations and organising beach exits when traffic became heavy. This is the best belvedere on Omaha Beach.

Where to stay

MODERATE

Ferme du Clos Tassin Bed and Breakfast – *14710 Colleville-sur-Mer – in the village, on D 514 –* ☎ *02 31 22 41 51 – 5 rooms: 29/34€ – meal 14.50€.* The owners of this farm make their own cider, calvados and pommeau (a mixture of calvados and apple juice). Tasting on the premises, in the shop. Simple, country style bedrooms and dinner for residents in the evening.

MID-RANGE

Hôtel-restaurant du Casino – *Bd de Chauvigny – 14710 Vierville-sur-Mer –* ☎ *02 31 22 41 02 – closed 15 Nov to 1 Mar –* 🄿 *– 12 rooms: 48.78/55.64€ –* 🍽 *5.79€ – restaurant 27€.* Look forward to the sea breeze and fine sand when you stay in this seaside hotel dating from the 1950s. Small shingles set in the walls and mosaic on the floor complete the seaside atmosphere. Ask for a room overlooking the sea and enjoy seafood in the dining room while admiring the sea.

Eating out

L'Omaha – *pl. du Monument - 14710 St-Laurent-sur-Mer -* ☎ *02 31 22 41 46 - fermé 15 nov. au 15 fév. - 13,57/25,76€.* This restaurant has the advantage of a great ocean view, and is very close to the D-Day landing beach. The atmosphere is relaxed, there are two outdoor terraces and a small souvenir shop. The menu features seafood.

American Military Cemetery (St-Laurent-sur-Mer) – The 9 385 Carrara marble crosses stand aligned in an impressive site. A memorial, inscribed with a map of the operations, and preceded by a pool stands in the central alley and is surrounded by trees. The commemorative list includes 1 557 names.

There is a belvedere *(viewing table showing the landing operation)* overlooking the sea. The path down to the beach *(30min there and back)* passes a second viewing table.

A monument has also been erected just outside the cemetery to the US 1st Infantry Division.

Continue west on D 514 to St-Laurent-sur-Mer.

St-Laurent-sur-Mer – This village was not liberated until 7 June after heavy combat. This "beach exit" was therefore not available to the Allies on D-Day.

Take D 517 down to the beach: the road runs through a valley to another memorial.

Standing on the side of D 517, the **Musée Omaha 6 Juin 1944** ☉ offers a chronological presentation of the German Occupation up to the American landing in the area. Dummies in full uniform, various pieces of armament (including a long 155 gun offered by the War Ministry in Washington), posters, display boards and newspaper articles illustrate this dramatic period.

Les Moulins – This site is marked by the **Monument to the D-Day Landing.** Turn right onto the road that runs along the beach and follow it to the end; there, at the foot of the American cemetery, you can look out onto the Ruquet Valley and the road opened by the Engineers unit after the blockhouse was destroyed around 11.30am.

Operation Overlord

This was the name given to the Allied invasion of Europe on 6 June 1944. Following an initial postponement due to bad weather, the largest invasion fleet in history set out for the Normandy coast and the landing beaches, code-named Utah, Omaha, Gold, Juno and Sword.

It was by following this road – the first road opened – that heavy equipment, motorised units and the infantry were able to reach the plateau and then advance to the town of St-Laurent. A plaque on the blockhouse is a reminder that it served as the first headquarters for the movement of traffic between the beach and the interior. In front of the blockhouse stands a monument commemorating the 7 June landing of the 2nd Infantry Division, "Indian Head".

Return to the Monument to the D-Day Landing.

It was here that the first units found shelter at dawn on 6 June 1944. A platform has been erected for the Omaha Beach Monument; from the platform there is a view of the cliffs the infantry had to scale in order to reach the plateau.

Vierville-sur-Mer – Follow boulevard Maritime west several hundred metres towards Vierville to arrive at a stele which marks the spot where the first to fall in the Battle of the Beaches were temporarily buried (the first American cemetery on French soil of the Second World War).
The road leaves the coast by another beach exit. A monument has been erected on one of the most redoubtable of the German blockhouses to the American National Guard who served in France in both World Wars. The village was invested on 6 June when the church was severely damaged as the belfry fell. Today the restored church stands proudly with its new belfry.

ORBEC

Population 2 709
Michelin map 54 fold 18 or 231 fold 32

Orbec is a small and lively town with a long history as witnessed by the many old half-timbered houses in the busy shopping street rue Grande. The town stands quite close to the source of the River Orbiquet in one of the pleasantest valleys in the Auge region.
At the entrance to the town stands the famous Pierre Lanquetot factory, which has been producing its delicious **Camembert** cheeses for the past century.

Église Notre-Dame – The Church of Our lady is flanked by a massive tower with an early-15C base and a late-16C Renaissance upper part. The three 16C windows were damaged during the bomb attacks of 1944. Notice in the south aisle the small carved wood statue of St Roch. A 17C statue of the Virgin Mary, also of carved wood, and a 14C tombstone engraved with the effigy of Dame Juliane Chardonnel are to be found in the chancel.

Musée municipal ⊘ – The museum is located in a beautiful 16C timber-framed house which was built for a rich tanner and is known as the **Vieux Manoir★**. Carved figures and geometric patterns of tile fragments, flint and stone decorate the exterior. The collections cover local history, popular arts and traditions and paintings by local artists.

Eating out

MODERATE

Auberge de la Truite – *27390 Montreuil-l'Argillé – 9km/5.6mi southeast of Orbec via D 519 and D 819 –* ☎ *02 32 44 50 47 – closed 15 Jan to 15 Feb and 24 June to 3 July, Tues evening and Wed – 13.72/28.97€.* The owner, a keen collector of antique hurdy-gurdies, displays them in one of the rooms. The dining room with its fireplace, wooden chairs, old beams and blue-and-white-squared tablecloths is as conventional as the typically Norman cuisine.

Excursion to the source of the River Orbiquet

4.5km/3mi south of Orbec

There is a small road (Chemin de la Folletière-Abenon) which goes along the river. Leave the car by the bridge and take a path on the left, which leads to the river's source. The GR 26 itinerary (signposted in red and white) will take you on a charming tour of one of the most appealing valleys in the Pays d'Auge.

OUISTREHAM-RIVA-BELLA ⌂⌂

Population 6 709
Michelin map 54 fold 16 or 231 fold 18
Local map see Plages du DÉBARQUEMENT

At the mouth of the Orne and astride the canal from Caen, the combined facilities of the town of Ouistreham and the beach of Riva-Bella make an excellent seaside resort with especially good amenities for water sports.

As the seaport for Caen the harbour is a busy one providing berths for a fishing fleet, mainly trawlers, pleasure craft and the cross-Channel ferries plying between Ouistreham and Portsmouth.

The marked itinerary "Overlord-L'Assaut" (The Onslaught), one of several described in the Historical Area of the Battle of Normandy, goes through this town.

OUISTREHAM

The town is well known as an international yachting centre.

★**Église St-Samson** – This ancient 12C fortress church was built on the site of an earlier wooden church destroyed by Norsemen in the 9C. The gabled west front with its three superimposed tiers of blind arcades above the recessed doorway is particularly remarkable. Step back to get a good view of the late-12C belfry supported by buttresses. To the right of the doorway a buttress is decorated with a pinnacle crowned by a pyramid-shaped roof. In the nave note the round piers with gadrooned capitals and the lovely clerestory windows. The narrow chancel's elevation comprises three superimposed tiers of arches.

Port de Plaisance – *Leave the car in place du Général-de-Gaulle.* A large basin on the opposite bank of the canal (Canal de Caen à la Mer) has been equipped as a marina and provides berths for a considerable number of yachts. In season it is a lively and quite colourful spot.

Lighthouse ⊙ – The beam of the lighthouse (30m/98ft tall) has a radius of 36km/22mi. From the top there is a good view of the harbour and marina.

RIVA-BELLA

The seaside resort of Riva-Bella has arisen from the ruins produced by the German Occupation and evacuation at the Allied invasion. The magnificent fine sandy beach bustles with life.

Big Bunker ⊙ – *(avenue du 6-Juin near the tourist office)* This former German 17m/56ft high range-finding station overlooks the mouth of the River Orne. Its mission during the war was to give firing instructions to the artillery units in

Eating out

MODERATE

Le Métropolitain – *1 rte de Lion – 14150 Riva-Bella* – ☎ *02 31 97 18 61 – closed 19-27 Nov, Mon evening and Tues from Oct to May – 10.67/ 30.03€.* This old Parisian metro carriage takes you back to the turn-of-the-century Belle Epoque. The decor and thereby the character have been preserved: wooden seats, covered with cushions, and luggage racks. Regional cuisine with a wide choice of menus at very reasonable prices.

MID-RANGE

Le St-Georges – *51 av. Andry* – ☎ *02 31 97 18 79 – closed 2 Jan to 3 Feb – 17.53/50.31€.* The first sea-bathing enthusiasts came here towards the end of the 19C. Try the seaside specialities served in both dining rooms, the modern one with its large picture windows, offering a panoramic view of the coast, and the traditional one with its wooden ceiling and fireplace. Also has a few guest rooms.

Where to stay

MID-RANGE

Thermes Riva-Bella Normandie – *Av. du Cdt-Kieffer – 14150 Riva-Bella* – ☎ *02 31 96 40 40 – closed 1-15 Dec –* 🅿 *– 46 rooms: 99.09/120.43€ –* 🍽 *8.38€ – restaurant 17/37€.* A stay in this place is invigorating: there is a thalassotherapy centre and beauty salon in the hotel and walking along the vast beach is conducive to relaxation. Spacious, simple rooms. Health-food menus.

Landing beach

Ouistreham. The visit of the five levels of this concrete tower offers the opportunity to see various rooms furnished and rearranged as they were in 1944. Dummies, objects and weapons are displayed on each level. There is the ventilator room, the watch room, the maps room, the telephone exchange and above all, on level 5, the range-finding room from which it is still possible to study the horizon with the range-finder over a 180° angle and a distance of 45km/28mi.

Musée du Débarquement "no 4 Commando" ⊙ – *(avenue Pasteur, near the tourist office)* The 4th Anglo-French Commando under the command of Kieffer reduced the enemy strong points on the morning of 6 June. The museum displays models, documents, uniforms, badges, arms and other items belonging to the French, English and German armies. The collection of uniforms is quite good.

Haras national du PIN ★

Michelin map 60 fold 3 or 231 fold 43

Le Pin Stud Farm, one of the most famous horse breeding establishments in France, is attractively set amid woods and meadows on the southern edge of the Auge region. Its activities include racing and schooling. The National School houses the Experiment, Training and Development Department of the **Institut du Cheval** and provides training for the staff of other national and private stud farms (smithery, artificial insemination...).

Royal Approval – The stud farm dates from 1665, when Colbert, acting with the approval of Louis XIV, founded national stables to promote and improve horse breeding in France. Plans drawn by Pierre Le Mousseux, a disciple of Mansart, were executed from 1715 to 1730 and the estate was arranged according to Le Nôtre's criteria. The king's riding master, François Gédéon de Garsault, was appointed head of Le Pin. The system was abolished at the Revolution but Le Pin regained its former glory in the 19C, particularly during Napoleon III's visit in August 1863.

TOUR ⊙ 45min

⊚ *Between mid-July and mid-February, all of the stallions are at the farm. The rest of the time they are stationed in breeding farms in the area and only 20 or so stallions remain in the stables.*

Three magnificent woodland rides converge on the horseshoe-shaped courtyard known as Colbert's Court. The château contains the manager's apartments and the reception rooms. The brick and stone stable wings accommodate the 40 or more stallions grouped according to their breed (English thoroughbreds, French trotters, and saddle horses, Anglo-Arabs, Norman cobs, Percherons, French ponies, New Forest and Connemara), coat, pure-bred Arabs, and size. Other outbuildings house the collection of 19C carriages used for official events in France and abroad.

Haras national du Pin

S. Chirol

There is always plenty of activity around the stud farm with the daily exercising of the stallions and training sessions for the carriage teams.

The annual equestrian events organised by the Haras national du Pin racecourse are popular local events *(see Calendar of events)*.

EXCURSIONS

St-Germain-de-Claire-feuille – *10 km/6mi south-east (via Nonant-le-Pin)*. The **church** ⊙ is distinguished by its magnificent woodwork including 13 **painted panels** ★ of the Life of Our Lord by the early-16C Flemish School.

A little tour of the countryside
23km/14mi – 30min

Take N 26 east and turn left at Tête-au-Loup on D 26, which runs along the forest edge.

Shortly before Exmes, the road rises up the hillside, and there is a view of the Haute-Dive hollow to the left.

Exmes – This former historic capital of the Argentan region has a church with a Romanesque nave and a 15C chancel.

Heading northward, D6 follows a downward slope; the road to Omméel branches off left. In Omméel, D 305 leads south anew, to the village of Villebadin. This little tour offers a view of the hilly landscape where wooded groves meet meadows, and the branches of apple trees in orchards bend appealing over the fence to tempt horses and cows at pasture. Outside the village, a small rod to the left leads to the Argentelles manor house, which stands in the middle of a large open field.

Manoir d'Argentelles ⊙ – The 15C house with corner and watch turrets is embellished with 17C dormer windows. A dovecote, also 17C, stands on a feudal mound.

Château de PIROU

Michelin map 54 fold 12 or 231 fold 26 – 10km/6mi south of Lessay

The fortress, which once stood on the coast beside an anchorage, served as an outpost for the defence of Coutances. The original wooden structure was replaced in the 12C with a stone building by the lords of Pirou who were related to the Hauteville family, who was involved in the foundation of the Norman kingdom in Sicily. The castle passed to other noble families until the late 18C when it was used as a farm and finally a hideout for smugglers dealing in tobacco from Jersey.

Eating out

MODERATE

La Mer – *50770 Pirou-Plage – 2.5km/1.5mi west of the Château de Pirou via D 94 – ☎ 02 33 46 43 36 – closed 12 Dec to 15 Feb, Mon, Tues and Wed out of season – 13.42/37.20€*. Small restaurant located at the end of a street leading to the beach. From your table you will discover the coastline and the sea with the oyster and mussel beds... and, if the weather is good, you will even catch a glimpse of the Channel Islands! The cuisine has a definite sea flavour.

The Legendary Geese of Pirou

When the Norse invaders failed to take the fortress they decided to lay siege to it. After several days of waiting they realised that there was no longer any sign of activity within the castle but, being suspicious, they decided to delay a little longer before making the final assault. Imagine their surprise when they found that the only remaining occupant was a bedridden old man, who informed them that the lord, his wife and other occupants of the castle had transformed themselves into geese, to escape from the hands of their attackers. Indeed the Norsemen recollected having seen a skein of wild geese flying over the castle walls the previous evening. According to Norse traditions the human form could only be reassumed once the magic words had been recited backwards. The geese came back to look for their book of magic spells but alas the Norsemen had set fire to the castle. Legend has it that the geese come back every year in the hope of finding their book of spells which explains why there are so many skeins of geese in the vicinity of the castle.

TOUR ⊘ *30min*

Three fortified gatehouses – there were originally five – lead to the old sheepfold (tickets and souvenirs), the outer bailey and then to the castle itself, a massive structure encircled by a moat. The towers are built directly on top of the ramparts.

Outer Bailey – The service buildings (left) include the bake house with its great fireplace and oven, the press house and chapel. The room where justice was dispensed, displays a **tapestry** similar in style to the Bayeux tapestry, recounting the conquest of southern Italy and Sicily by the Cotentin Normans.

The original tapestry can be seen only in July and August; otherwise a copy is on display.

Castle – A stone bridge replaces the drawbridge. To the right of the entrance is the guard-room which also served as a bake house (note the two ovens). In the living area the kitchens are on the ground floor with the two dining halls above. A staircase leads up to the wall head.

From the top of the square tower there are views of the surrounding countryside.

Château de Pirou

S. Chirol

PONT-AUDEMER ★

Population 8 975
Michelin map 54 fold 19 or 231 fold 21

Visitors to Pont-Audemer will enjoy this quaint town, full of surprises and a variety of shops. Sometimes it is called "The Venice of Normandy", in reference to its canals, which once served a prosperous tanning trade. Some of the old attics used to dry out skins, set beneath slate roofs, are also reminders of leather working, which has marked the history of the town. **Charles-Émile Hermès**, founder of the luxury line of leather products and the famous silk scarves which bear his name, was born into a family who moved to Pont-Audemer in order to learn the secrets of the saddler's craft.

SIGHTS

The itinerary "Pont-Audemer au Fil de l'Eau", marked out by painted compass cards placed on the ground, is a charming opportunity for ramblers to discover the town's prettiest sights and their proximity to the River Risle. Explanatory panels provide details on each remarkable site.

PONT-AUDEMER

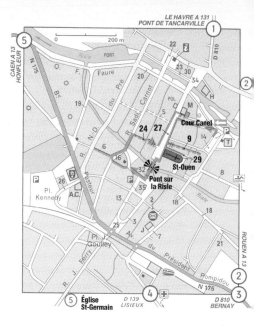

The Old Town

🅝 *About 45min, departing from place du Général-de-Gaulle (leave your car in the car park there). Take rue des Carmes and turn left on rue de la République. 100m/109yd further on, turn left again into the impasse de l'Épée. Farther down the street, also on the left is the impasse St-Ouen.*

It is worth walking down these lanes and back to view the half-timbered houses, and to see the northern side of the church.

Take rue Thiers to the left.

From the **bridge over the Risle**, there is a nice view of the river, lined with slate-roofed houses.

From place Victor-Hugo, continue to place Louis-Gillain, to the right, and enter rue des Cordeliers.

At the corner of rue des Cordeliers and rue Notre-Dame-du-Pré stands a building with a small tower, the timber beams resting on a ground floor of stone.

Return to place Louis-Gillain, cross the branch of the Risle and take rue Sadi-Carnot.

There are several residences with sculpted doorways (nos 8, 16, 18, 20, 27bis).

To the right, **rue Place-de-la-Ville**, a winding cobblestone street, leads over a little bridge and onto rue de la République, in front of St-Ouen Church.

Go up rue de la République and take the first passage to the right, just after rue des Carmes.

Cour Canal also has some lovely half-timbered buildings to admire.

Churches

Église St-Ouen – The church was begun in the 11C and enlarged in the 16C but the west front was never completed. The nave, which has a coffered vault, was given a Flamboyant veneer at the end of the 15C. The decoration of the triforium is unusually rich. The lancet arches are ribbed in Flamboyant style.

The aisles have hanging keystones and are lit through magnificent Renaissance **stained-glass windows★**: the most interesting illustrate the legend of St Ouen (second chapel of the south aisle), Redemption (first chapel at the east end of the north aisle) and the legend of St Nicholas (second chapel). Notice the 16C font in the last chapel of the north aisle.

Stained-glass window, Église St-Ouen

Eating out

MODERATE

Auberge du Cochon d'Or – *27210 Beuzeville* – *14km/8.7mi west of Pont-Audemer via N 175* – ☎ *02 32 57 70 46* – *closed 15 Dec to 15 Jan, Sun evening from Oct to Mar and Mon* – *12.50/37.35€*. Situated in a small Norman village, this inn has been run by the same family for a very long time. Comfortable, with large tables and armchairs upholstered with tapestry, it is renowned among the local population and praised for its varied menus... If you love your food, this is for you!

MID-RANGE

Le Petit Coq aux Champs – *La Pommeraie Sud* – *27500 Campigny* – *6km/3.7mi south of Pont-Audemer via D 810 and D 29* – ☎ *02 32 41 04 19* – *www.lepetitco-qauxchamps.fr* – *closed 2-26 Jan* – *reservation essential* – *29.73/59.46€*. Situated at the heart of "bocage" country, this fine thatched cottage houses a renowned restaurant. If you feel like a weekend in the country, book one of the rooms and enjoy peace and quiet as well as the chef's tasty cuisine.

LUXURY

Auberge du Vieux Puits – *6 r. N.-D.-du-Pré* – ☎ *02 32 41 01 48* – *closed 17 Dec to 26 Jan, Mon and Tues except evening in season* – *36.59/50.31€*. These 17C houses with their old timber-framed structure once housed a tannery before being converted into an inn in 1920. The restaurant looks reassuringly authentic with its antique furniture. If you wish to stay the night, ask for one of the more recent rooms.

Where to stay

MID-RANGE

Le Prieuré des Fontaines Bed and Breakfast – *Rte de Lisieux* – *27500 Les Préaux* – *5km/3.1mi southwest of Pont-Audemer via D 139* – ☎ *02 32 56 07 78* – 🖃 – *5 rooms: 48.78/68.60€* – *meal 22.87€*. Following extensive restoration work, this 17C house looks almost new. Warm welcome, spacious comfortable rooms with a mixture of antique furniture, exposed beams and floor tiles. No smoking throughout. Enjoy a stroll in the park and a dip in the pool.

Les Cloches de Corneville – *Rte de Rouen* – *27500 Corneville-sur-Risle* – *6km/3.7mi east of Pont-Audemer via N 175* – ☎ *02 32 57 01 04* – *www.cloches-de-corneville.fr* – *closed Jan* – 🅿 – *12 rooms: 48.78/64.03€* – 🖃 *6.86€* – *restaurant 25.92/39.64€*. The peal of Corneville is on the top floor of this hotel and if you wish to be acquainted with its long history, you will have to climb and see it... and, since the restaurant is convivial and the rooms delightful and soundproof, your stay will be a pleasant one.

The modern glass in the chancel and above the organ, including the striking reds and greens in a Crucifixion, is by Max Ingrand.

Église St-Germain ⊙ – *Access by rue Jules-Ferry to the south*. This very old church, parts of which date back to the 11C, was considerably remodelled in the 14C and truncated in the 19C. The arches of its squat Romanesque tower have been rebuilt in the Gothic style.

EXCURSIONS
From Pont-Audemer to La Ferrière-sur-Risle

77km/46mi – about 4hr
From Pont-Audemer take D 130 southeast.

Corneville-sur-Risle – The 12-bell **carillon** ⊙ at the Hôtel des Cloches was instituted following the runaway success of a 19C operetta, *Les Cloches de Corneville*.

Appeville-Annebault – The large church was rebuilt in the 16C, conserving the 14C chancel, when the Governor of Normandy laid plans to make the river navigable up to this point. There are keystones in the nave and the fine collection of Brothers of Charity staffs.

Montfort-sur-Risle – The village lies close to the rolling Montfort Forest.

★★**Le Bec-Hellouin** – *See Le BEC-HELLOUIN*.

Brionne – *See BRIONNE*.
The sugar refining factory of Nassandres stands by the road leading out of La Rivière-Thibouville.

Ding! Dong!

In the early 15C, the English had occupied almost the whole of Normandy and the small village of Corneville-sur-Risle, a stone's throw from Pont-Audemer, appeared to be seriously threatened. The enemy had its eye on the abbey, its riches and especially, its much sought-after bells: because of recent demands in artillery, metal had become a precious commodity. After several attempts, the English succeeded in taking down the largest bell, which they put into a boat, planning to cross the river. However, owing to the weight of their booty, the vessel eventually capsized. While they were trying to retrieve the bell from the icy waters, French soldiers arrived on the scene and the robbers were compelled to abandon their prized possession.

Rumour has it that, since that day, the bell resting on the bed of the River Risle starts to chime in unison with the other bells of the locality to celebrate good news or herald some fortunate event.

Beaumontel – The belfry on the well-sited church is 16C.

Beaumont-le-Roger – The ruins of the former 13C Trinity Priory, with its impressive buttresses visible from the road, stand on a terrace: access to this is by a ramp running beneath a porch.

The **Église St-Nicolas** ⊙ built in the 14C and 16C, has been restored following war damage. Modern stained-glass windows make a pleasant addition to those of the 15C and 16C.

Drive south towards Grosley-sur-Risle.

The road runs alongside Grosley Lake (rowing and fishing facilities). Thereafter it becomes narrow and winding.

★**Le Val Gallerand** – Superb old Norman farm buildings in a woodland setting.

Continue south and turn right at the crossroads. Turn right again onto D 35.

La Ferrière-sur-Risle – The small village has a remodelled 13C and 14C church. Inside note a large 17C oak altarpiece with gilt carvings. The centrepiece is a Descent from the Cross by a pupil of Leonardo da Vinci. There is an interesting collection of statues: a Virgin and Child (14C), St Anne in polychrome stone (16C), a St Michael (17C) and a polychrome wooden Pietà. The picturesque village square is completed by a number of old houses and a restored 14C covered market.

An Artist's Impressions of Normandy

Many of Claude Monet's attempts to capture the play of light were made as he portrayed Normandy scenes. The important *Impression: Soleil Levant* captured Le Havre emerging from the morning mist. Monet painted several versions of Rouen Cathedral's west front as well as the cliffs near Étretat, the poppy fields near Vétheuil and most famous of all the lily pond in his garden at Giverny.

PONTMAIN

Population 935
Michelin map 59 fold 19 or 231 fold 39 – 6 km/4mi southwest of Landivy

A pilgrimage dedicated to the Virgin makes its way to this village on the border of Brittany on 17 January, the anniversary of the day in 1871, during the Franco-Prussian War, when the Virgin appeared to several of the village children, including Eugène and Joseph Barbedette, with a message of prayer and hope; 11 days later an Armistice was declared.

SIGHTS

Grange Barbedette – It was from this thatched barn that the children, and then the other villagers, saw the Virgin in the sky above the house of Augustin Guidecoq on the far side of the square. The barn has been transformed into a chapel and there are documents recounting the apparition.

Basilique – The vast neo-Gothic basilica with its twin granite spires was built at the end of the 19C. It dwarfs the other buildings of this small village. The statue at the entrance is of the Virgin.

The 10 stained-glass windows in the chancel depict the Virgin's Apparition in Pontmain in Lourdes and La Salette, as well as scenes from the life of Christ. A gallery goes right round the nave which is roofed with pointed vaulting.

Église paroissiale – Standing alongside the basilica, the parish church appears quite modest. The interior is colourful. Note the statues of the church's patron saints Simon and Jude on either side of the altar. The granite font is carved with Gothic arches.

Chapelle des Pères Oblats – Behind the basilica are the park and Mission of the Oblate Fathers of Mary Immaculate. An oblate is a lay person or member of a congregation, devoted to a specific work. The 1953 chapel has a heavy appearance from outside – but is surprisingly pleasing within, illuminated by a golden light diffused by the lower stained-glass windows and an enormous stained-glass window of Christ in Majesty above the chancel.

The adjoining **Musée des Missions** ⊙ displays handicrafts from various foreign countries and describes the Missions' work throughout the world.

PONTORSON

Population 4 376
Michelin map 59 fold 7 or 231 fold 38

Pontorson, the last Norman village before Brittany, is a favourite stopping place for visitors on their way to Mont-St-Michel.

The town is named after a local baron, Orson, who in 1031 built a bridge (*pont* in French) over the Couesnon to allow his army to cross the river on its way back from an expedition in Brittany.

Église Notre-Dame – The church is said to have been founded in the 11C by **William the Conqueror** in gratitude to the Virgin for having saved his army from the Couesnon quicksands. The episode is portrayed in one of the chancel's stained-glass windows and also in scene 17 in the Bayeux tapestry.

The church was given pointed vaulting at a later date and has been remodelled several times. The massive rough granite west front has kept its original Romanesque appearance. It is decorated with a great arch, only slightly pointed, and a south doorway with a carved tympanum representing a man and a bird.

On the north side of the chancel a Gothic arch opens into a chapel dedicated to St Saviour; it has a fine white stone altarpiece known as the "Broken Saints" dating from the 15C. The Life of Christ is depicted in 24 compartments. Despite the fact that it was mutilated during the Wars of Religion and the Revolution, it is a work of great richness. Note the large 18C polychrome wood statue of Christ, opposite.

EXCURSION

St-James – *15km/9mi east by D 30*. St-James lies between the Beuvron and the Dierge valleys on the confines of Normandy and Brittany. William the Conqueror founded the settlement in 1067 making it one of western Normandy's oldest cities. The 15C ramparts and several old streets are a reminder of its historic past.

The **Cimetière américain et Mémorial de Bretagne** ⊙ is to be found on the outskirts of St-James (*D 230 in the direction of Louvigné*). This cemetery regroups the graves of over 4 400 Americans. In the chapel regimental colours, stained-glass windows, coats of arms and maps commemorate the events of 1944.

The tower opposite provides a view of the Brittany coast and Mont-St-Michel.

Where to stay and Eating out

MODERATE

Auberge du Terroir – *50170 Servon* – *10km/6.2mi northeast of Pontorson via N 175 towards Avranches then D 107* – ☎ *02 33 60 17 92* – *closed 18 Feb to 13 Mar, 17 Nov to 3 Dec, Sat lunch except 15 June to 30 Sept and Wed* – *13.72/36.59€*.

A presbytery turned into a restaurant... what a palatable conversion! The owner's cuisine is carefully prepared and helpings are generous in this large stone house. Three bedrooms upstairs and another three in the former village school.

QUILLEBEUF

Michelin map 54 folds 8 and 9 or 231 folds 20 and 21

Quillebeuf was a favourite Viking hideout, and until the 19C it continued to be a navigational hot spot. Captains waited there for high tide in order to pass through the dangerous channel known as "the cemetery of ships". Tidal bores have also been observed here – during spring tides, a flood with an abrupt high front like a wave can push upstream with great force. In 1790 *Télémaque*, which was supposed to have the crown jewels on board, sank offshore.

Today, the old port is overwhelmed by the oil refineries and petrochemical installations in Port Jérôme on the north bank. Nonetheless, the town has managed to retain its traditional character.

VISITING THE TOWN

Keep an eye out for the markings on the pavement which guide you through a tour of the town (informative panels are set up in front of the most interesting places).

Pointe de Quillebeuf – From the lighthouse at the end of the promontory separating the marsh and the old port, there is a good view up and down river, of Port Jérôme on the north bank and of Tancarville Bridge downstream.

Église Notre-Dame-de-Bon-Port – Surmounted by a fine but incomplete Romanesque tower, the church has a 12C door. The nave is purely Romanesque in style with archaic capitals; the soaring chancel is 16C.

MARAIS VERNIER
From Quillebeuf to the Roque Point

23km/14mi – allow 1hr

The Vernier Marsh, once a bend in the River Seine, cuts a vast bay of 5 000ha/20sq mi out of the Roumois plateau between Quillebeuf and Pointe de la Roque. It forms part of the **Parc naturel régional de Brotonne**.

This suggested tour goes from the valley of the River Seine to the Risle Valley. Between Quillebeuf and Ste-Opportune-la-Mare, the roads runs above the wide Seine Valley. On the other side of the river, you can see Port Jérôme.

Ste-Opportune-la-Mare – The village contains two elements of the Lower Seine Regional Open-Air Museum: the **Maison de la Pomme** in the old presbytery (exhibition on apples, their varieties and an audio-visual explanation of the cider-making process) and an old **forge** (tools used by the blacksmith in his craft; demonstrations on certain days).

Follow the signs *Panorama de la Grande Mare* to a viewpoint over the Great Marsh and beyond to the reclaimed Marshland.

The CEDENA organises outings during the summer season that give tourists an opportunity to discover the nearby woods, marshes and hillsides. The Réserve naturelle des Mannevilles can be visited on Wednesdays and Sundays in July and August. Information and reservation on place de l'Église in Ste-Opportune-la-Mare, ☎ ***02 35 56 94 87.***

Réserve naturelle des Mannevilles ⊙ – The area is protected and enables the visitor to discover the flora and fauna of the Marais area and to approach Camargue horses and highland cattle.

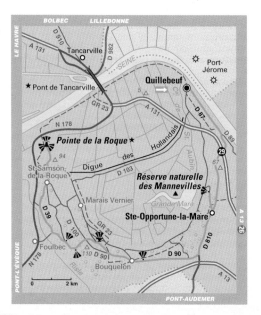

Marais Vernier, Highland cow and calf

West of Bouquelon, bear right onto D 103.

At the top of a downhill stretch (right), the road (D 103) provides an attractive view *(viewing table)* over the marsh to Tancarville Bridge.

Bear left to rejoin D 90; then take D 39 north to St Samson-de-la-Roque.

At first the corniche road overlooks the Risle Valley. North of St-Samson-de-la-Roque a narrow winding road leads to the headland.

★**Pointe de la Roque** – *Picnic area.* From the lighthouse on the cliff the **panorama** extends over the Seine estuary to Cap de la Hève and the Côte de Grâce. Tancarville cliffs and bridge can be seen to the right.

Remember these rules when enjoying a visit to a natural reserve or other protected area:

– Do not pick fruit or flowers or dig up any roots or fossils;

– Carry all litter out with you for disposal;

– Do not bring your pets (dogs can disturb young animals);

– Do not stray from marked paths and do not make short-cuts between paths or down hills - this damages plants and causes erosion.

ROUEN ★★★

Population (conurbation) 380 161
Michelin map 55 fold 6 or 231 folds 22 and 23

Rouen, capital of Upper Normandy, numbers about 400 000 inhabitants in 22 communes if the surrounding built-up areas are included. The town, particularly the old town, has been restored and attracts many visitors.

Site – The town has been developing since the Roman *Rotomagus* was established at the first point on the river at which a bridge could be built. The site is in many ways similar to that of Paris, at the start of a bend protected by encircling hills, where valleys provide access to the hinterland; it is also above the floodwater mark and provides easy access to this stretch of the river where there are a number of islands. The hills surrounding Rouen are high, and from this vantage point there are extensive views of the city.

HISTORICAL NOTES

Rollo the Forerunner – After the **Treaty of St-Clair-sur-Epte**, Rollo was baptised at Rouen, the capital of the new duchy, and took the name Robert. He proved to be a far-sighted planner: he narrowed and deepened the river bed, built up unused marshlands, linked the downstream islands to the mainland and reinforced the banks with quays. His works lasted until the 19C, unrivalled for their efficiency.

Goddons – Rouen was hard hit during the Hundred Years War: in 1418 Henry V besieged the town which was starved into capitulation after six months. Alain Blanchard, who embodied the heart and soul of the resistance, was captured and hanged. Revolts and plots followed against the Goddons – the nickname for the English derived from their common swear word "God damned". Harsh repression reigned until hope was reborn in the hearts of the Normans by the exploits of Joan of Arc and the coronation of Charles VII.

Then Joan was taken prisoner at Compiègne by the Burgundians. The English threatened the Duke of Burgundy with economic sanctions and through the mediation of Cauchon, Bishop of Beauvais, Joan was handed over against a payment of 10 000 gold ducats. On Christmas Day 1430 she was imprisoned in one of the towers – "the Tower of the Fields" – in the castle of Philippe Auguste. The Captain of Rouen, Lord Warwick, organised widespread military presence in the city in order to deter all attempts at a popular uprising.

Joan of Arc was beatified in 1909

Trial of Joan of Arc – Bishop Cauchon promised "a fair trial" and opened the first session on 21 February 1431. An amazing dialogue began between Joan and her judges: bold but without pride or concern for herself, thinking only of God, her mission and the King, the Maid replied to all the tricks and subtleties of the churchmen and lawyers.

The questioning went on for three months. The charge declared Joan to be "heretical and schismatic". On 24 May, in the cemetery of the abbey of St Ouen, tied to a scaffold, Joan was pressed to recant; she finally gave in, was granted her life but condemned to life imprisonment.

The English were furious and threatened the judges; Cauchon replied "We will get her yet". On Trinity Sunday the guards took away Joan's woman's clothes which she had promised to wear, and gave her men's clothing instead. At noon "for the necessities of the body, she was constrained to go out and indulge in the said habit". She was thus said to have broken her promise and was condemned to the stake. On 30 May she was burned alive in place du Vieux-Marché. Her heart, not consumed by the fire, was thrown into the Seine. The English murmured that they were lost as they had burned a saint.

In 1449 Charles VII entered Rouen; in 1456 Joan was rehabilitated and in 1920 she was canonised and made Patron Saint of France.

Golden Century – The period situated between the French reconquest and the Wars of Religion was a golden century for all Normandy and particularly for the city of Rouen. Cardinal d'Amboise, Archbishop and patron, introduced the Renaissance style to the city. Local dignitaries began to build sumptuous stone mansions and carved woodwork adorned the façade of burgesses' houses. The law courts built by Louis XII for the Exchequer were transformed into a Parliament by François I.

Rouen merchants in cooperation with Dieppe navigators traded all the main maritime routes: the coat of arms of the powerful merchant haberdashers' guild showed three ships built and masted of gold and the device "O sun, we will follow you to the ends of the earth".

The former linen weaving town now wove silk and cloth of silver and gold. In 1550 the first Colonial Exhibition was mounted in the town.

Industrial Upsurge – Early in the 18C a rich merchant unable to sell his stock of cotton, used up to then to make wicks for candles, spun and wove the fibre into a cloth that had an immediate success: dyed indigo blue and known as *Rouennerie*, it outstripped all others. In 1730 came the first velveteen and twill.

Dyeing made equal progress, keeping pace with textile production, transformed by mechanisation. Finishing, bleaching and textile printing were to follow.

Industrialisation called for changes in the port: in the 19C docks were constructed, the railway was built; the old city on the right bank spread to the tributary valleys and hillsides.

Modern City – Industrial expansion accelerated at the beginning of the 20C and Rouen's urban development increased considerably with the creation of industries associated with its port.

During the Second World War, the old districts close to the Seine and the industrial zone on the south bank were destroyed. The cathedral narrowly escaped total destruction. When the people of Rouen rebuilt their city, they removed damaged factories to purposely planned industrial zones and converted the south bank into a residential area with a population nearly equal to that of the north bank; it is also an administrative centre with a Préfecture (Hôtel du Département) flanked by a tower 80m/262ft high. The Préfecture will be transferred to the old Hôtel-Dieu (16C and 17C) west of the historic centre.

Lacroix Island, formerly industrial, has become residential with parks and open spaces which include sports grounds, a skating rink, a swimming pool and a pleasure boat harbour.

The north bank has remained the centre of modern Rouen and has rediscovered its business and tourist character.

The Port – Rouen is France's fifth busiest port after Marseilles, Le Havre, Dunkerque and Nantes-St-Nazaire, and the country's third most important river port. It has a considerable advantage in being located between Paris and the sea.

Owing to improved means of access – Rouen can accommodate 140 000t ships and container carriers loading 1 500-2 000 containers – the modernisation of port equipment and facilities (cranes, gantries...), and the building of silos and new terminals, the growth of the port has been constant.

Each year Rouen receives around 3 500 ships flying the flags of 60 different countries. It is the country's number one port for exports, especially agricultural produce (first French port for cereals with 8.4 million tonnes), and stands in third place for container traffic. The city is also an important stopover for luxury liners. Wood, pulp and paper are unloaded for the nearby printing presses and the industries in or near the port are the cause of traffic as diversified as phosphates, sulphur, chemical products, fertilizers, coal and by-products of refined oil.

The port stretches from Rouen to Tancarville on the north bank of the Seine and from Rouen to Honfleur on the south bank.

★★★ CATHÉDRALE NOTRE-DAME *1hr 30min*

The cathedral of Rouen is one of the most beautiful examples of French Gothic architecture. Construction began in the 12C but after a devastating fire in 1200 the building was reconstructed in the 13C. The cathedral took on its final appearance in the 15C under the master builder Guillaume Pontifs and in the 16C under Roulland le Roux. In the 19C it was crowned with the present cast iron spire. Badly damaged during the Second World War, the cathedral is open for services but the enormous restoration work started over 40 years ago continues.

Exterior – The attraction of Rouen Cathedral lies in its infinite variety including an immense façade bristling with openwork pinnacles and framed by two totally different towers: the Tour St-Romain on the left and the Tour de Beurre on the right.

West front – This imposing façade was used in a series of paintings by Monet to study the effects of lighting at different times of the day on the same subject. Dating from the 12C, the **Portail St-Jean** (left) and the **Portail St-Étienne** (right) doorways each have a delicately carved semicircular arch crowned by a small colonnade: note the workmanship of the foliage scrolls which surround the door leaves. The two tympana are 13C, that of St Stephen (badly damaged) shows Christ Enthroned and the Stoning of St Stephen; that of St John shows the Martyrdom of St John the Baptist and the Feast of Herod. The lattice-work window gallery (1370-1420) above the two portals is in the Flamboyant style; the long and narrow niches decorated with statues and topped by openwork gables are 14C and 15C.

Eating out

MODERATE

Les Maraîchers – *37 pl. du Vieux-Marché* – ☎ *02 35 71 57 73* – *13.57/ 22.11€*. This timber-framed house with its terrace is an unusual setting for a Parisian-style bistro! Nothing is missing: the bar, upholstered seats, tables arranged close to one another, old advertising plaques, collections of hats and jugs. Matching menu, of course. Norman-style second room.

Pascaline – *5 r. de la Poterne* – ☎ *02 35 89 67 44* – *www.pascaline-restaurants.fr* – *reservation advisable* – *15.09€*. Located next to the law courts, this bistro-style restaurant is very pleasant. Inside, it is rather like a brasserie with fine wooden bars, upholstered seats and yellow-painted walls. Choice of attractive menus. You would do well to book since the place is often full.

MID-RANGE

Le Beffroy – *15 r. Beffroy* – ☎ *02 35 71 55 27* – *closed Sun evening and Tues* – *reservation essential* – *30.49/41.92€*. This 16C typically Norman house with its timber-framed structure offers you the choice between three lovely dining rooms, all as attractive as one another. The cuisine is plentiful and carefully prepared from good-quality products.

La Butte – *69 rte de Paris* – *76240 Bonsecours* – *3.5km/2.2mi southeast of Rouen along N 14* – ☎ *02 35 80 43 11* – *closed 1-22 Aug, Sun and Mon* – *22.87/51.83€*. This 17C coaching inn, named after the "Butte Montmartre" in Paris, is, of course, typically Norman: timber-framed façade, paved courtyard, welcoming opulent dining rooms and drawing rooms. In such pleasant surroundings, you can but enjoy the traditional cuisine.

La Couronne – *31 pl. du Vieux-Marché* – ☎ *02 35 71 40 90* – *22.87/ 37.35€*. The decor or this 14C house, located on the market square, is superb: beams, carved woodwork, fireplace and frescoes. According to some, it is the oldest inn in France...True or false? nobody knows but one thing is certain, the Rouen-style duck is a real treat!

Dufour – *67 r. St-Nicolas* – ☎ *02 35 71 90 62* – *closed Sun evening and Mon* – *18.29/35.06€*. Seafood lovers, do not hesitate... This timber-framed inn, founded in 1906, offers traditional fare in an authentic Norman family atmosphere.

La Marine – *At the foot of the bridge (D 982)* – *76430 Tancarville (Pont routier de)* – ☎ *02 35 39 77 15* – *closed 24 July to 20 Aug, Sun evening and Mon* – *22.87/48.78€*. Fish and seafood served in pleasant surroundings with riverside gardens, ships sailing upriver and the Tancarville suspension bridge... The landscape is worth savouring as much as the food! Garden and terrace in summer.

Where to stay

MODERATE

Hôtel des Carmes – *33 pl. des Carmes* – ☎ *02 35 71 92 31* – *h.des. carmes@mcom.mcom.fr* – *12 rooms: 38.11/42.21€* – ☐ *5.18€*. Situated in the town centre, not far from the cathedral, this hotel makes an attractive stopover. The reception area is delightfully decorated with a slight touch of Bohemian style, the charming rooms are free of excessive furniture yet well fitted out. An excellent place for budget-conscious travellers.

MID-RANGE

Le Vieux Carré – *34 r. Ganterie* – ☎ *02 35 71 67 70* – *vieux-carre@mcom.fr* – *14 rooms: 50.31/54.88€* – ☐ *5.95€* – *restaurant 11.43€*. With its coloured timber-framed façade, this fine building dating from 1710 looks like a private mansion... why not your own for a night, in total peace and quiet? Pleasant library/drawing room and modern bedrooms furnished with English wardrobes. Bistro-style menu in the restaurant.

Dandy Hotel – *93 bis r. Cauchoise* – ☎ *02 35 07 32 00* – *closed Christmas to New Year's Day* – **P** – *18 rooms: 60.98/71.65€* – ☐ *7.62€*. Located in a central pedestrianised street, close to place du Vieux-Marché, this small hotel is rather charming: it is carefully decorated and, even if the rooms look a little overcrowded with furniture, they are nevertheless very cosy. Breakfast is served in a small attractive room.

Versan Hotel – *3 r. J.-Lecanuet* – ☎ *02 35 07 77 07* – **P** – *36 rooms: 44.97/63.27€* – ☐ *5.95€*. This hotel is conveniently situated along an avenue within easy reach of the town hall. The rooms are all similar, functional and well fitted out.

On the town

Bar de la Crosse – *53 r. de l'Hôpital* – ☎ *02 35 70 16 68* – *Tues-Sat 9am-9pm*. The reputation of this small unpretentious bar is due to its very convivial atmosphere. Between concerts and exhibitions, guests express a real joie de vivre and it is not unusual to see tourists happily chatting away with the locals.

Bar du Palais – *4 r. Percière* – ☎ *02 35 71 56 83* – *Oct-July: daily; Aug to early Sept: Thur-Sat 6.30pm-2am*. This elegant bar decorated with old beams was once a brothel and the list of regular customers and prostitues is still hanging on the wall. Today, it is one of the favoured dives of the student population attracted by the fine cellar.

Big Ben Pub – *95 bis r. du Gros-Horloge* – ☎ *02 35 88 44 50* – *Tues-Sat noon-2am, Sun-Mon 6pm-2am* – *karaoke from 9pm*. This pub, located beneath the Gros Horloge, is a must for its electrifying atmosphere... whether you wish to have a beer in the ground-floor bar, listen to rock music on the second floor or sing on the third!

El Guevara Café – *31 r. des Bons-Enfants* – ☎ *02 35 15 97 67* – *Tues-Sat 5pm-2am* – This is without a doubt the friendliest place in town. Don't be put off by the slightly kitsch decor of the entrance hall, the action is in the basement, orchestrated by Gerald in the vaulted cellar decorated with photos of Che Guevara and revolutionary posters. A great fan of Cuba, this West Indian gives salsa lessons, prepares cocktails and organises debates round the bar.

L'Emporium Galorium – *151 r. Beauvoisine* – ☎ *02 35 71 76 95* – *Mon-Sat 8pm-2am* – *closed Aug*. Situated in the student district, this 17C building houses a friendly pub which keeps extending. Every Thursday, the large partitioned cellar is the venue of themed evenings and rock, jazz or mixed concerts...

L'Exo 7 – *13 pl. des Chartreux* – ☎ *02 35 03 32 30* – *exo7.net* – *discotheque: Fri-Sat 11pm-5am* – *concerts follow the calendar of events* – *closed Aug*. This is the discotheque of Rouen and of the whole Seine Maritime *département*! The favourite dive of the 18-25-year-olds, this night club is used as a concert hall and regularly programmes pop, rock and reggae stars.

La Boîte à Bières – *35 r. Cauchoise* – ☎ *02 35 07 76 47* – *Tues-Sat 3pm-2am* – *closed 15 days in Aug*. To be honest, this fine two-storey timber-framed house complete with terrace in no way looks like a night club. Its a friendly authentic place where students gather for lively, often improvised, evenings. Themed evenings from October to June.

La Luna – *26 r. St-Étienne-des-Tonneliers* – ☎ *02 35 88 77 18* – *Tues-Thur 10pm-4am, Fri-Sat 10pm-5am*. Very popular Cuban night club in the town centre. This colourful discotheque, decorated with frescoes and plants, rings every night with the sound of salsa in an electrifying atmosphere.

Le Baroque – *51 r. St-Nicolas* – ☎ *02 35 89 44 43* – *Tues-Sat 7pm-2am*. Behind its discreet façade, this bar comes alive as one of the most sought after in Rouen. If you are a fan of horror films, you will probably appreciate the atmosphere created by the decor... mirrors, candles and church-style high-backed chairs... However, don't be put off! The temperature rises very fast as this is the favoured dive of students and VIPs who take part in often wild evenings. Two concerts a month.

Le Bateau Ivre – *17 r. des Sapins* – ☎ *02 35 70 09 05* – *Wed-Sat 10pm-4am (plus Tues sometimes)* – *closed in Aug*. Always looking for new talents, this bar has been livening up Rouen night life for the past twenty years: concerts on Fridays and Saturdays, songs and poetry on Thursdays, café-theatre or French songs on Tuesday evenings. A limited number of programmes are available at the tourist office.

Taverne St-Amand – *11 r. St-Amand* – ☎ *02 35 88 51 34* – *Mon-Fri 11am-2am, Sat 7pm-2am* – *closed 3 weeks in Aug*. The owner of this 17C house has, for the past 25 years, played host to painters, writers and actors, all loyal to one of the oldest establishments in Rouen. On the last Thursday in the month, go and listen to a programme of popular songs: guaranteed atmosphere in friendly company!

Traxx – *4 bis bd Ferdinand-de-Lesseps* – ☎ *02 32 10 12 02* – *Fri-Sat 11pm-5am*. This discotheque specialising in techno has become renowned in the region. On Fridays, themed evenings (holiday party, chocolate galore, baby evenings...) draw the Rouen youth for a wild experience. The car park is guarded.

Underground – *26 r. des Champs-Maillets* – ☎ *02 35 98 44 84* – *Mon-Sat 7pm-2am*. As soon as you enter, this bar strikes you as being most friendly. The list of cocktails and beers is attractive, the customers are contented, and the owners are full of drive... When, suddenly, the old piano gives the signal for the start of a wild jam session or a karaoke.

Shopping

Chocolatier Auzou – *163 r. du Gros-Horloge* – ☎ *02 35 70 59 31* – *Mon 2-7.15pm, Tues-Fri 9.30am-7.15pm, Sun 9.30am-1pm.* Housed in a timber-framed building, this renowned confectioner will tempt you with his specialities, including "Jeanne d'Arc's tears" (lightly roasted almonds coated with nougatine and chocolate) and "Rouen lamb" (a kind of sponge cake).

Faïencerie Augy – *26 r. St-Romain* – ☎ *02 35 88 77 47* – *sitedefrance.com./eure/rubrique artisanat d'art* – *Tues-Sat 9am-7pm. Tour of the workshop by appointment.* The last earthenware workshop in Rouen! Pink and white earthenware, copies of many traditional motifs in blue monochrome or polychrome style, from lambrequin to cornucopia.

The **central doorway** (early 16C) was executed by Roulland le Roux; it is flanked by two powerful pyramid buttresses reinforcing the façade; their embrasures are decorated with statues of the Prophets and Apostles and were formerly topped by a series of archbishops. The tympanum is decorated with a Tree of Jesse, destroyed by the Huguenots and restored in 1626. An immense elegant gable cut along a superb lattice-work gallery surmounts the portal.

The **Tour St-Romain**, to the left, is the oldest tower (12C), and in the Early Gothic style. The sumptuous **Tour de Beurre** (Butter Tower) was thus named in the 17C when it was believed that it had been paid for by dispensations granted to those who did not wish to fast during Lent but on the contrary drank milk and ate butter. It never received a spire but was surmounted by an octagonal crown. Inside is a carillon of 56 bells.

South side – The **central lantern tower** with its spire is the tallest in France (151m/495ft) and the glory of Rouen. It was started in the 13C and was raised in the 16C. The present spire, in cast iron, replaced in 1876 the wooden spire covered in gilded lead which dated from 1544. The **Portail de la Calende** (Calende doorway) which opens between two 13C square towers is a 14C masterpiece. The lower embrasures, its most original feature, are decorated with four leaf medallions inspired by French ivories.

North side – On skirting the **Cour d'Albane** (Albane Court) closed to the east by the cloister gallery, one can see the north side, the lantern tower and spire and the upper section of the Booksellers' transept.

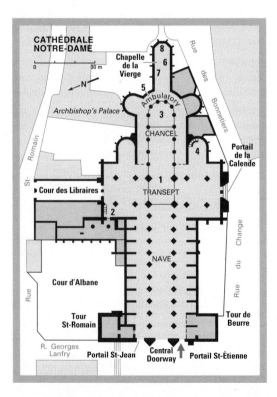

In the background, the south doorway of Rouen Cathedral

A little further on the **Cour des Libraires** (Booksellers' Court) is closed by a magnif-icent stone gateway in the Flamboyant style. At the end of the court is the **Portail des Libraires** (Booksellers' Doorway) *(see Introduction: Religious architecture)* which opens on to the north side aisle. It is topped by two tall gables framing a large rose window and a clerestory with a fine balustrade. The sculpted decoration is exquisite, the lower embrasures are ornamented with medallions representing beasts of the Middle Ages.

The tympanum (late 13C) is decorated by a Last Judgement with, in the lower register, the Resurrection of the Dead and, in the upper register, the Separation of the Saved and the Damned depicted in terrifying detail.

Return to the parvis to enter the cathedral by the main door.

Interior – An impression of simplicity and harmony reigns in this cathedral in spite of the differences of style found in the nave and chancel.

Nave – In the Early Gothic style the nave is made up of 11 bays four storeys high: tall arcades, false tribunes, triforium and clerestory, the capitals are crocketed and leaf shaped. The side aisles are very high because the tribunes were to appear at mid-height, as is shown by the curiously clustered small columns. Dominating the transept crossing is the **lantern tower** (**1**) rising with incredible boldness 51m/167ft from pavement to keystone on enormous piles which in groups of no fewer than 27 columns sweep upward in a simple thrust.

Transept – On the back of the Calende and Booksellers' doorways are attractive 14C carvings, the decoration is the same for the two gables: four large windows topped by crocketed gables frame and line the walls.

In the north arm – embellished by a large rose window restored with its 14C stained-glass windows – is the famous Escalier de la Librairie (Booksellers' Stair-way) H (**2**), the work of Guillaume Pontifs; from a charming little balcony – where there is a door elegantly topped by a gable – rise the two flights of the staircase (the first is 15C, the second 18C). In the south arm are lovely 14C and 16C stained-glass windows.

Chancel – The choir of finest 13C style is of great beauty. It is the most noble part of the cathedral on account of its simple lines and the lightness of its construction.

It presents a level of very high and pointed arcades, a triforium and a clerestory. Three of them are decorated with 15C stained glass representing the scene at Calvary. The pillars supporting the arcades have massive circular capitals (13C) with charming stylised plants which are crowned by abaci held by carved heads.

The high altar is made of a marble slab from the Valle d'Aosta, and dominated by a Christ (**3**) by Clodion in gilded lead (18C). On either side of the altar are two angels in adoration by Caffieri. The angels originally came from St Vincent's Church destroyed in 1944. Opening off the south arm is the apsidal chapel dedicated to Joan of Arc (**4**) and embellished with modern stained-glass windows by Max Ingrand.

Tomb of the Cardinals of Amboise

Crypt, Ambulatory, Lady Chapel ⊘ – The 11C ring-shaped **crypt** preserves its altar and its curb stone well (5m/16ft deep). On display are fragments of columns, and Roman capitals found during excavations. The heart of Charles V is preserved in a coffer embedded in the east end wall.

The **ambulatory** *(access south arm – exit north)* which is made up of three apsidal chapels (including the Lady Chapel) holds the recumbent figures of Rollo, Richard Lionheart (late 13C), Henry (second son of Henry II of England) the Young King (13C), and William Longsword, Duke of Normandy and son of Rollo (14C). Also shown are five 13C **stained-glass windows★**, the bottom one of which, depicting St Julian the Hospitaller, was presented by the Fishmongers' Guild and inspired Flaubert to write a tale. The fine windows representing the history of Joseph (**5**) are signed by Clément, a glassmaker from Chartres and then, finally, come those of the Passion and Good Samaritan with their remarkable colours.

The **Lady Chapel** (14C) contains two admirable 16C tombs. To the right, the **tomb of the Cardinals of Amboise★★** (**6**) of the Early Renaissance (1515-25) was carved after drawings by Roulland le Roux. The two cardinals – Georges d'Amboise (left), Minister under Louis XII and Archbishop of Rouen and his nephew, also Georges (right) – are shown kneeling. In the base are the Four Cardinal Virtues (Justice, Strength, Temperance and Prudence) and two of the Theological Virtues (Charity and Faith); the third (Hope) occupies a niche on the left upright; on the right upright is Chastity. The background of the monument is occupied by the Virgin, John the Baptist, St Romanus and various prelates; the frieze round the top is decorated by Sibyls, Prophets and Apostles. Note the head of Roulland le Roux carved in the right-hand corner. On the left, stuck on the recess of the Gothic tomb of Pierre de Brézé (15C) is the **tomb of Louis de Brézé★** (**7**), Seneschal of Normandy and husband of Diane de Poitiers. It was built between 1535 and 1544. The design of the monument and the decoration of the lower part are said to be by Jean Goujon. The mausoleum consists of two parts: below, the body of the Seneschal is treated in the pathetic style favoured in the 16C; at the foot of the recumbent figure stands the Virgin, while Diane de Poitiers is portrayed weeping at the head. The upper part of the tomb is irregular in style: the caryatids are extremely fine but the effigy of Louis de Brézé on horseback is too solemn and the rider too small in relation to the size of his mount.

In addition, the chapel possesses 14C stained-glass windows representing the Archbishop of Rouen and a fine picture by Philippe de Champaigne, *The Adoration of the Shepherds*, framed in a rich altarpiece (**8**) of 1643.

★★★OLD ROUEN

🔲 *About 30min, departure from place de la Cathédrale.*

Place de la Cathédrale – Opposite the cathedral on the corner of rue du Petit-Salut stands the former **Bureau des Finances** (House of the Exchequer – *Tourist Information Centre*), an elegant Renaissance building erected in 1510 by Roulland le Roux. North of the square, the Palais des Congrès houses in its entrance hall the vestiges of the fine **façade** which once fronted the Hôtel de Ville (town hall), in which the Cour des Comptes has been set up.

★★**Rue St-Romain** – One of Rouen's most fascinating streets with its beautiful 15C-18C half-timbered houses and at the end the spire of the Église St-Maclou. Note no 74, a Gothic house with 15C bay windows.

Archevêché – Next to the Booksellers' Court stands the 15C Archbishop's Palace (altered in the 18C) with its vigorous façade and its almost military like towers. A gable pierced by the remains of a window which frames the cathedral spire is all that remains of the chapel in which was held the solemn session of the trial of Joan of Arc on 29 May 1431, and where her rehabilitation was proclaimed in 1456. The doorway in rue Bonnetiers leads into the courtyard and a view of the interior façade of the building.

Cross rue de la République to reach **place Barthélemy** bordered with picturesque half-timbered houses where St Maclou's Church stands.

★**Rue Martainville** – The street has kept some marvellous 15C-18C half-timbered houses. On the corner northwest of St Maclou's Church is a lovely Renaissance fountain. The north door of the church has attractive panels depicting scenes from the life of the Virgin: on the left the Ark of the Covenant; on the right her death.

★★**Aître St-Maclou** – *184-186 rue Martainville*. This 16C ensemble is one of the last examples of a medieval plague cemetery. The half-timbered buildings which surround the yard were built from 1526 to 1533; the south side was built in 1640 and never served as a charnel house.

The ground floor of these buildings is made up of galleries which were once open – as in a cloister. On the column shafts (formerly door frames) are carved figures (damaged) portraying the Dance of Death; they support a double frieze decorated with macabre motifs: skulls, crossbones, grave diggers' tools etc.

Above the ground floor, the "attic" was used as a charnel house until the 18C when it was transformed into its present state.

These buildings now house the School of Fine Arts (École des Beaux-Arts).

Return to the west end of St-Maclou and turn right.

★**Rue Damiette** – The street is lined by half-timbered houses and offers a nice vista of the central tower of St Ouen's Church. Note on the right the picturesque blind alley of the Hauts-Mariages.

In place du Lieutenant-Aubert bear left onto rue d'Amiens to the 17C **Hôtel d'Étancourt** and admire its façade embellished with large statues.

Return to place du Lieutenant-Aubert; turn left onto rue des Boucheries-St-Ouen; turn right onto rue Eau-de-Robec.

Rue Eau-de-Robec – In this street, lined with old houses boasting recently restored timber framing, flows a little stream, spanned by a series of footbridges, recalling the time when the Robec waters ran alongside the dwellings of wealthy cloth merchants. Several of these tall buildings are crowned by a sort of workshop-attic, where drapers would leave their skeins of cotton and sheets of fabric out to dry after the spinning and dyeing process had taken place on the ground floor.

Half-timbered houses, Rouen

E. Baret/MICHELIN

Musée national de l'Éducation ⊘ – The National Museum of Education is housed in a handsome **residence**★ known as the **Maison des Quatre Fils Aymon**. This lofty mansion built around 1470 is a fine example of a 15C timber-framed house with corbelled upper floors. It was once an inn or a bar patronized by somewhat dubious characters: in those days it was referred to as the "House of Marriages" on account of the many casual encounters that took place there.

The museum presents mementoes, objects and early photographs evoking school life from nursery schools under the Ancien Régime to the state primary schools of the early 20C. Temporary exhibitions are regularly held on different themes: school life in France at the turn of the century, the schoolmaster figure portrayed by various artists, scenes taken from the classroom etc.

On the corner of rue du Ruissel, note the **Pavillon des Vertus**, a fine 16C mansion and its portico with stone columns, decorated with statues of women symbolising the cardinal virtues.

Return to rue des Boucheries-St-Ouen, take rue de l'Hôpital left in front of **St-Ouen Church**★★ *(described below).*

At the corner of rue des Carmes stands the attractive Gothic fountain, Crosse fountain (restored) and further on at the corner of rue Beauvoisine and rue Ganterie is a handsome half-timbered house.

ROUEN

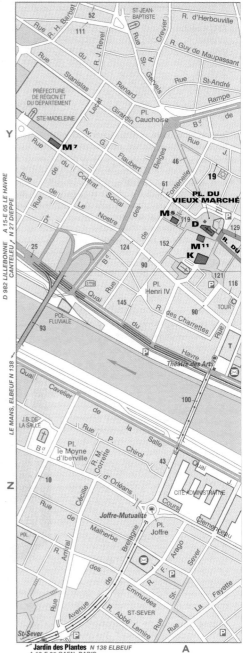

Jardin des Plantes N 138 ELBEUF
A 13-E 05 CAEN, PARIS

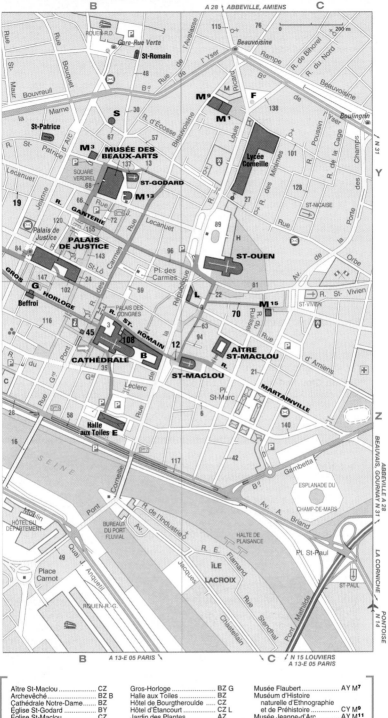

Aître St-Maclou .... CZ
Archevêché .... BZ B
Cathédrale Notre-Dame .... BZ
Église St-Godard .... BY
Église St-Maclou .... CZ
Église St-Ouen .... CY
Église St-Patrice .... BY
Église St-Romain .... BY
Église Ste-Jeanne-d'Arc ...... AY D
Fierté St-Romain .... BZ E
Fontaine Ste-Marie .... CY F

Gros-Horloge .... BZ G
Halle aux Toiles .... BZ
Hôtel de Bourgtheroulde .... CZ
Hôtel d'Étancourt .... CZ L
Jardin des Plantes .... AZ
Lycée Corneille .... CY
Musée des Antiquités
de la Seine-Maritime .... CY M1
Musée des Beaux-Arts .... BY
Musée de la Céramique ...... BY M3
Musée Corneille .... AY M5

Musée Flaubert .... AY M7
Muséum d'Histoire
naturelle d'Ethnographie
et de Préhistoire .... CY M9
Musée Jeanne-d'Arc .... AY M11
Musée Le Secq
des Tournelles .... BY M13
Musée national
de l'Éducation .... CZ M15
Palais de Justice .... BY
Tour Jeanne d'Arc .... BY S

*The **Michelin Maps scale 1:200,000** for this region are shown
in the diagram on page 6
The text refers to the maps which, owing to their scale or coverage,
are the clearest and most appropriate in each case*

Turn right onto rue Beauvoisine which crosses rue Jean-Lecanuet, one of Rouen's most commercial and lively streets.

In rue Beauvoisine note no 55, a carved half-timbered house with courtyard: no 57 is a Renaissance house. Turn left onto rue Belfroy, bordered at the beginning by 15C to 16C half-timbered houses, to reach place St-Godard *(the* **church★** *is described below).*

Across rue Thiers and square Verdrel, allée Eugène-Delacroix leads to the charming **rue Ganterie★**, lined with old half-timbered houses. In the other direction, towards place Cauchois, this street is **rue des Bons-Enfants**, where several 15C houses still stand; on no 22, notice the sculpted figures.

Take rue des Carmes to the right, then turn right again on rue des Juifs, which runs alongside the Palais de Justice.

★★Palais de Justice – Built to house the Exchequer of Normandy (law courts), this splendid 15C and early-16C Renaissance building is said to be the work of Roulland le Roux. Rebuilt in the 19C it was badly damaged in August 1944.

The **main court** ⊙ – excavations have revealed a 12C Hebrew place of worship – is flanked by two wings, the **façade★★** (1508-26) of which is exquisite.

The decoration of the façade, the most beautiful part of the building, is typical of the Renaissance, infinite care being taken to enrich the ornament at each level – the base is therefore quite plain but the ornamentation increases on each floor so that the roof line is a forest of chiselled stone with pinnacles, turrets, gables and flying buttresses above a rich balustrade. The main turret is delicately carved.

The left-wing stone staircase leads to the **Salle des Procureurs** (Prosecutors' Room). This large room has a splendid modern panelled ceiling.

★Place du Vieux-Marché – This modern architectural complex made up of a small covered market, church and national monument is the work of Louis Arretche, the architect responsible for the restoration of St-Malo. In the Middle Ages the square was the scene of public mockery and executions. There are many 16C to 18C half-timbered houses in the district.

★★Rue du Gros-Horloge – Connecting place du Vieux-Marché to the cathedral is the abbreviated "rue du Gros", one of Rouen's most evocative streets. It bristled with tradespeople during the Middle Ages and was the seat of local government from the 13C to the 18C. Once again with its large cobblestones and attractive 15C-17C half-timbered houses, rue du Gros-Horloge has recaptured its original commercial role as a bustling pedestrian street and is nowadays one of the city centre's major tourist attractions.

Gros-Horloge – This is the most popular monument in Rouen. The clock, formerly placed in the belfry *(see below)*, was moved to its present location in 1527 when the arch was specially constructed to receive it.

In addition to the single hand which gives the hours, there is the central section telling the phases of the moon and the lower inset indicating the weeks.

The underside of the arch is decorated with a carving of the Good Shepherd and his flock, a reference to the lamb of John the Baptist, which figures in the Rouen coat of arms.

Gros-Horloge

Belfry ⊙ – This small tower is topped by a dome added in the 18C to replace the one removed by Charles VI in 1382 to punish the citizens of Rouen who organised a revolt, known as La Harelle, against the taxes levied by the Duke of Anjou.

Within there is a spiral staircase (1457). Several rooms contain wrought-iron work, bronze bells, 16C and 17C clock hands and the movement of the St-Vivien Clock (15C). Note also the two bells (13C) which gave the signal for the Harelle uprising: on the right the "Rouvel" (not operated since 1903) for raising the alarm (from 1724 it rang the curfew); on the left, the Cache-Ribaud which replaced it (in 1903) and sounds the curfew every night at 9pm. The dome houses the movement of a 14C clock by Jehan de Félains, said to be one of the oldest in France.

From the top of the belfry there is a majestic **vista**★★ *(current restoration work may hinder or prevent access)* of the city, its port and the surrounding countryside, rue du Gros-Horloge, the cathedral, the church of St-Ouen, the law courts, the Joan of Arc Tower and the church of St-Godard.

Next to the belfry is the Renaissance loggia where the Great Clock keeper used to stand as well as a beautiful 18C fountain.

On the corner of rue du Gros-Horloge and rue Thouret stands the old town hall (1607).

Rue du Gros-Horloge leads back to place de la Cathédrale.

After this long walk around town, you will be pleased to see the outdoor cafés set up around the square, colourful parasols inviting you into their shade. It is a lovely place to sit and enjoy a drink.

From place de la Calende, rue de l'Épicerie leads to the Fierté St-Romain and the Halle aux Toiles.

Fierté St-Romain – An original Renaissance building. The stone lantern used to contain the relics of St Romanus.

The building adjoins the **Halle aux Toiles** (Linen Hall), a partly modern construction with exhibition, conference and banquet rooms. The façade looking out onto place de la Haute-Vieille-Tour has nicely arranged windows under a high slate roof.

St Romain and the Gargoyle

In the 7C, St Romain was the bishop of Rouen, and at the time, a terrible monster known as the Gargoyle was terrorising the city. To rid Rouen of this horrible beast, St Romain needed help. A man who had been condemned to death was the only person brave enough to come forward. Together they set out to confront the dragon. The bishop managed to wrap his stole around the dragon's neck and they led the beast back into town, where it was killed. The courageous prisoner was freed. From the 12C and until the Revolution, one prisoner was chosen by the cannons of the church every year to present the reliquary holding the holy remains of St Romain to the crowd from the top of the Haute-Vieille tower. In return, he would be freed. Nowadays, the legendary event is recalled in the annual fun fair held in the month of October.

THE CHURCHES OF ROUEN

★★**Église St-Maclou** – This beautiful church of Gothic-Flamboyant style is remarkable for its homogeneity. It was built between 1437 and 1517. It is a remarkable fact that in the heyday of the Renaissance style, the purest Gothic was preserved. Only the spire of the belfry is modern.

The west facade, the finest part of this building, is preceded by a large five panelled porch set like a fan. Two of the three doorways, the central one and that on the left, are celebrated for their Renaissance **panels**★★, some of which are attributed to Jean Goujon.

These panels are divided into two parts: the leaf of the door has charming little bronze heads of lions and other animals and designs in semi-relief of pagan inspiration, whereas the upper panel, which is a little heavy, has a carved medallion. The medallions on the central door represent the Circumcision on the left and the Baptism of Christ on the right; the upper part of the door represents on the left God the Father before the Creation; on the right, God the Father after the Creation.

The Font Door on the left has only one panel. The medallion represents the Good Shepherd entering the pasture from which he has expelled the thieves. This motif is sustained by four statues which seem to represent Samson, David, Moses and Solomon; beautiful figures of men and women outlined in the background represent Error in the triple guise of Greco-Roman paganism, Egyptian idolatry and Islam.

Inside, the **organ case**★ (1521) is remarkable for its Renaissance woodwork, supported by marble columns which are attributed to Jean Goujon. The **spiral stairs**★ (1517), magnificently carved, are from the choir screen.

The medallions on the central door,
Église St-Maclou

E. Baret/MICHELIN

The chancel, severely damaged by bombing raids on 4 June 1944, has been restored: note the chapel of Notre-Dame-de-Pitié (left) with its 18C panelling, as well as the Christ and two Angels, elements in the Glory adorning the 18C apse.

★★Église St-Ouen ⊙ – Remarkable for its proportions and the purity of its lines this former abbey church is one of the jewels of High Gothic architecture. The construction, which began in 1318 and slackened during the Hundred Years War, was completed in the 16C.

Exterior – On the south side is the beautiful door named after the wax candle merchants *(ciriers)* who held their market here. The **east end★★** is beautiful with delicate flying buttresses and pinnacles and individually roofed radiating chapels. At the transept crossing the square **central tower★** flanked by small towers rises two tiers before ending decoratively in a ducal coronet. On the façade of the south transept, above the great rose window in the Flamboyant gable, are statues of kings and queens of Judah.

The **Porche des Marmousets** (the true origin of the name Marmousets Door is not known) which occupies the lower level is gracious but somewhat unusual: its arching leans to one side and appears to end in mid-air, resting not on colonnades but on two false keystones. This doorway gives direct access to the south arm of the transept.

Interior – The **nave** *(see illustration in Introduction: Religious architecture)*, of a light construction, catches the eyes on account of its sheer elegance and its harmonious proportions. Upon entering, the visitor is struck by the overall sense of balance and unity of the 144m/473ft nave, designed in the shape of a Latin cross. Such perfection could be explained by the "golden mean", which in this particular case would be a ratio of 1 to 3: the piers are each separated by 11m/36ft and the vaults reach a height of 33m/109ft. This exceptional nave is also characterised by its three levels: a row of tall arcades, a delicately carved openwork triforium and clerestory windows.

This slender structure is further enhanced by the warm, radiant light that filters through the large **stained-glass windows★★**. The oldest ones date from before 1339 and are still embedded in the chapels surrounding the chancel. The 16C clerestory windows in the nave are devoted to the Patriarch (north) and to the Apostles (south). The two 15C rose windows in the transept arms illustrate the Celestial Court (north) and a Tree of Jesse (south). The modern Crucifixion adorning the axial bay is attributed to Max Ingrand (1960). The big rosette to the west, characterised by deep blue, red and gold hues, is the work of Guy le Chevalier (1992).

The imposing organ chest dates from 1630 but the actual instrument (4 keyboards, 64 stops and 3 914 pipes) was executed by the 19C organ maker Aristide Cavaillé-Coll. Note the reeds arranged horizontally *en chamade*, as in Spanish Baroque organs. The chancel is closed off by gilded **grilles★★** (1747) executed by Nicolas Flambart.

★Église St-Godard ⊙ – This late-15C church contains wonderful **stained-glass windows★**, in particular a 16C one on the right side showing the Tree of Jesse.

Near to it is the window of the Virgin which is made up of six 16C panels. Above the three naves is a 19C plastered wood vault pierced with clerestories.

Beside the church stand Rouen's two most fascinating museums: the Fine Arts Museum and the Secq des Tournelles Museum *(see below)*.

Église Ste-Jeanne-d'Arc – Completed in 1979, the church is shaped like an up-turned ship; the inspiration drawn from naval architecture is also evident in the roof covering, made of slate or copper scales. Inside are 13 panels of superb **Renaissance stained glass★★** (16C) from St Vincent's Church, which was destroyed in 1944. Covering an area of 500m²/600sq yd. This unique ensemble illustrates the faith of 16C Christians and depicts the Childhood of Christ, the Passion, the Crucifixion, the Resurrection, the lives of St Anne, St Peter and St Anthony of Padua in a variety of rich colours.

Église St-Patrice ⊙ – This Gothic church is remarkable for its **stained-glass windows★** made between 1538 and 1625. The windows on the north side of the chancel depict the Triumph of Christ; in the adjoining chapels are St Faron, St Fiacre, St Louis and St Eustache, and an Annunciation in Italian Renaissance style as well as a Nativity scene. In the north aisle are the stories of St Barbara and St Patrick and Job. An 18C gilt baldaquin crowns the altar.

Église St-Romain – The former 17C Carmelite chapel, restored in the 19C and again in 1969, contains interesting Renaissance **stained glass**.

MUSEUMS AND MONUMENTS

★★★ **Musée des Beaux-Arts** ⊘ – The Museum of Fine Arts – the only museum of Rouen which from the early 19C has enjoyed the privilege of having a building specially set aside for its collections – underwent heavy renovation work between 1989 and 1994. There were two main ideas behind this project: on the one hand, the desire to rehabilitate all that had suffered from the ravages of time as well as from passing trends; on the other hand, a wish to restore the perspective and harmonious proportions of the original building. This new approach to museums has resulted in the creation of a central core with rooms and inner courtyards housing the reception area, the bookshop and a space for temporary exhibitions. This "heart of the museum" is surrounded by 63 galleries devoted to works of art ranging from the 15C to the present day, laid out on two levels. The collections are presented in chronological order, enabling visitors to compare the evolution of painting and sculpture, as well as that of furniture, drawing or gold work at any given period of history.

A plan handed out at the entrance clearly explains the layout of the museum and helps you find your way around the different sections. For a chronological visit, it is advisable to start with the south wing, to the right of the reception area.

15C-17C Painting – One of the most striking canvases is an oil painting on wood, The *Virgin Among the Virgins*, also called *The Virgin and Saints*, by Gérard David (c 1460-1523), considered to be one of the masterpieces of Flemish Primitive painting.

Besides the Italian Primitives, you can admire works by Guerchin, Giordano, Bronzino and especially Veronese *(St Barnabus Healing the Sick)* and Caravaggio *(The Flagellation of Christ)*. Spanish masters include Velásquez *(Democritus)* and Ribera; Dutch art is represented by Martin de Vos, Van de Velde, N Berchem and Rubens *(The Adoration of the Shepherds)*. France, too, is acknowledged with paintings by François Clouet *(Diane Bathing)*, Louis de Boullogne *(Ceres or Summer)*, Poussin *(Venus Arming Aeneas* and *The Storm)*, Simon Vouet *(The Abduction of St Louis)* and Jouvenet *(The Twelve Apostles)*.

18C Painting – *Second floor of the south wing.* The most noteworthy painters are Lancret *(The Bathers)*, Fragonard *(The Washerwomen)*, Van Loo *(Virgin with Child)* and Traversi *(The Music Lesson)*. Note the charming Napolitan crib with 75 figurines and 15 farm animals, as well as the clay statue of French playwright Pierre Corneille by Caffieri.

19C Painting – This section is unquestionably the highlight of the museum, on account of both its size and the high standard of its collections. Europe's main artistic movements are represented, whether it be **neo-Classicism**, **Impressionism** or **Symbolism**. and the great masters are all here: Ingres *(Beautiful Zelia, Portrait of Madame Aymon)*, Monet *(rue Saint-Denis, Celebrations on 30 June 1878, Doorway of Rouen Cathedral, Grey Skies)*, David, Géricault *(Cavalry Officiers of the Imperial Guard Charging)*, Degas *(Dead Fox, The Underwood)*, Caillebotte *(Café Scene)*, Corot *(Quayside Trade in Rouen)*, Chassériau *(Emperor Augustus Travelling through Spain)*, Millet *(Portrait of Amable Gachot, Naval Officer)*, Moreau *(Diomedes Devoured by his Horses)*, Sisley (*The Church at Moret-sur-Loire, Icy Weather*, 1893), Renoir *(Women with Mirror)*.

In the Salle du Jubé (Rood Screen Room), **Romanticism** is present with a set of five sculptures by David d'Angers (note the original plaster cast made for the memorial to Bonchamp) with stand opposite *Justice of Trajan* by Delacroix and, on the side, *Les Énervés de Jumièges*, a "hyper-realist" painting by Vital-Luminais.

20C Painting – Contemporary painting is represented by Modigliani *(Paul Alexandre at Window)* and Puvis de Chavannes *(Inter Artes et Naturam)*. The sculpture gardens display works by Dufy *(The Seine River)*, Tolmer *(The Blind)*, Bissière *(Tonight Spring is Born)*, Villon *(Camille Renault)* and Grün *(One Friday at the Salon des Artistes)*.

★★ **Musée de la Céramique** ⊘ – The 17C Hôtel d'Hocqueville houses the Ceramics Museum which presents the history of Rouen pottery with outstanding faience collections.

Rouen Faience

The word ceramics covers all aspects of terracotta (baked clay) whereas faience is a type of ceramic made of compound clay covered with a tin-based enamel. White in colour, faience can be decorated. Two types of earth went into the making of Rouen faience: St-Aubin (from the Boos Plateau), clayey and bright red, and earth from Quatre-Mares (between Sotteville and St-Étienne-du-Rouvray), a light, sandy alluvial soil. Mixed in the right proportions – the result was ground, washed, dried, powdered, sifted and placed in decantation containers. When sufficiently consistant the mixture was placed near an oven to finish the evaporation process, and then trodden to extract fermentation gases and add the sand needed for a ceramic compound. Finally there were the different processes of shaping, casting, glazing, painting and curing.

The rich and varied collections make it possible to offer a comprehensive presentation of the Rouen faience production from the mid 14C to the early 19C.

The work of Masséot Abaquesne, the very first faience maker in Rouen, who plied his trade around 1550, is represented by paving flags and portrait vases. After a lull, production resumed thanks to Louis Poterat (1644-1725), whose workshop became famous for its dishes and tiles enhanced with a blue and white decor, inspired by the art of Nevers as well as by Chinese pottery. The colour red made its first appearance around 1670, probably through the influence of Dutch ceramists working with Poterat.

Faience was to enjoy a surge of popularity towards the early 18C: workshops mushroomed all over the region and it became fashionable to conceive decors featuring five colours (starch or yellow ochre ground). In the room devoted to polychrome decoration, note the **celestial globe** by Pierre Chapelle, a masterpiece of faience making; also of note is the fine series of busts illustrating Apollo and the Seasons in the vestibule. After 1721, motifs became more varied. The *style rayonnant* and its arabesques inspired by embroidery and metalwork was succeeded by chinoiseries, in which the drawing is in blue, superimposed on an ochre ground. Subsequently, around the mid 18C, the Rococo style came into fashion, embellished with all manner of floral motifs (rose, carnation, rockery). Two of the most common designs, especially on tureens, were the *décor à la corne* and *décor à la double corne*, featuring ornate horns of plenty spilling over with birds, insects and flowers.

A display of faience pieces coming from other countries or from other regions of France illustrate the impact of these outside influences on the Rouen production.

★★**Musée Le Secq des Tournelles** ⊙ – The Wrought Ironwork Museum is housed in old St Lawrence' Church, a fine Flamboyant building, and is exceptionally rich (3C-19C).

The nave and transept contain large items such as balconies, signs, railings etc and in the display cabinets locks, door knockers and keys. Their evolution can be studied from Gallo-Roman times.

The north aisle includes displays of locks, belts and buckles from the 15C to 19C. In an adjoining room are a stained-glass window taken from St Vincent's Church (15C Last Judgement), 15C statues and a 17C gilt wooden altar.

The south aisle exhibits a large variety of domestic utensils and tools, such as knives, grills, irons spice and coffee mills etc.

The north gallery on the first floor is devoted to accessories such as jewels, clasps, combs, and smoking requisites.

A rare 16C to 19C collection of professional tools is housed in the south gallery, concerning areas as varied as hairdressing, woodwork, watch making, gardening and surgery.

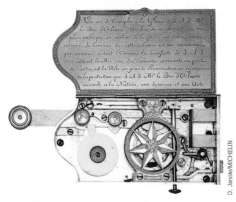

D. Janole/MICHELIN

Model of locks, Musée Le Secq des Tournelles

Musée Jeanne-d'Arc ⊙ – Posters, manuscripts (facsimiles), models, wax museum etc. A vaulted cellar houses a model of the castle where Joan of Arc was imprisoned.

Hôtel de Bourgtheroulde ⊙ – *No 15 place de la Pucelle.* This famous mansion (pronounced Boortrood) inspired simultaneously by Gothic and the first precepts of the Renaissance, was built in the first half of the 16C by Guillaume le Roux, Counsellor to the Exchequer and Lord Bourgtheroulde.

Stand back a little to look at the façade and then enter the justifiably well-known inner court.

The end building is pure Flamboyant, with gable pinnacles and a hexagonal staircase tower. The left gallery is entirely Renaissance with six wide basket handle arches. It is surrounded by friezes: the upper one, disfigured, shows the Triumphs of Petrarch, the lower, the Field of the Cloth of Gold (1520) at which, besides Henry VIII and François I, Abbot Aumale, son of Guillaume le Roux, was also present. It was he who later erected the mansion.

Musée Pierre-Corneille ⊙ – This house where the French playwright **Pierre Corneille** (1606-84) was born and lived for 56 years, contains drawings and engravings recounting the story of his life. Often considered the father of French Classical tragedy he wrote, among others, *Mélite* (1629; first performed in Rouen), *Le Cid, Horace* and *Cinna*.

On the first floor is his writing room; on the second floor the library contains first editions of his works. Also displayed are 17C models and engravings of old Rouen, including the Old Market Square.

Musée Flaubert ⊘ – *Place de la Madeleine*. The Hôtel-Dieu (17C-18C) has a Classical façade. This museum devoted to the history of medicine is set in the home (one of the pavilions) where **Gustave Flaubert** (1821-80) was born. His father worked as a surgeon. On display are souvenirs of Flaubert, 19C surgical instruments and 17C and 18C documents concerning Rouen hospitals.

Tour Jeanne-d'Arc ⊘ – This is the former keep in Philippe Auguste's 13C castle where Joan was subjected to torture on 9 May 1431. A facsimile of the manuscript relating to her trial is displayed on the ground floor from which a spiral staircase leads up to the first floor where models and documents evoke the history of the castle.
The second floor is devoted to the life of Joan of Arc.

★★**Musée des Antiquités de la Seine-Maritime** ⊘ – An old 17C convent houses this museum which displays objects from prehistory to the 19C.
Representing the Middle Ages and the Renaissance are tiles, stained-glass windows, capitals, altarpieces, English alabaster altarpieces (15C), stunning religious gold and silver plate (12C Valasse Cross), 12C to 13C **enamels★**, 5C to 16C **ivories★** (a 14C seated Virgin) as well as a collection of arms and Moorish and Italian majolica. In a long gallery is an interesting series of Gothic and Renaissance **carved façades★** from half-timbered houses in old Rouen. A separate gallery set aside to display tapestries contains the 15C **Winged Deer tapestry★★** and Renaissance furnishings.
There is also an important **Gallo-Roman collection★** noteworthy for its bronzes and glassware. In the centre of the lapidary gallery is the famous **Lillebonne mosaic★★** (4C; restored 19C), the largest signed and illuminated mosaic to be found in France – note especially the scenes depicting the deer hunt.
Near the museum gardens is the large **Fontaine Ste-Marie** by Falguière.

Lycée Corneille – The school is in the former 17C-18C Jesuit college and was attended not only by Corneille but later also by Corot, Flaubert, Maupassant and Maurois.

SIGHTS ON THE OUTSKIRTS

★**Jardin des plantes** – *2.5km/1.5mi. Leave Rouen by avenue de Bretagne, or take bus route no 12 and get off at Dufay or Jardin des Plantes.* In a beautiful 10ha/25-acre park planted with shrubs of flowers and tree species of all kinds, the **tropical hothouses** ⊘ present an outstanding collection of rare varieties (in particular orchids, *bromeliaceae* and *araceae*). The park, originally designed in the 17C, contains around 3 000 plant species inside the greenhouses and a further 5 000 out in the open air. One of the star attractions is the legendary **Victoria Regia**, a giant water lily from the Amazon, whose large, flat leaves can reach a diameter of 1m/3.3ft in summer. When the flowers bloom in the morning, they are white, around noon they turn pink and later on in the day they take on a delicate mauve hue before withering and dying that very evening. Note the **19C greenhouses:** the central tropical hothouse, the orangery and the two side hothouses known as the "Botanical Pavilion" and the "Palmarium" (reserved for ornamental tropical species). In front of the 17C pavilion, covered with ampelopsis vine, seasonal varieties are presented in prettily arranged flower beds. Note the old cider press under a half-timbered building.

Centre Universitaire – *5km/3mi. Leave Rouen by rue Chasselièvre northwest on the plan.* From the road which ends on the Mont-aux-Malades plateau on which the university campus has been built, there is a good **panorama★★** of the city, the port and the curve in the river.

Manoir Pierre-Corneille ⊘ – *In Petit-Couronne, 8km/5mi. From Rouen take avenuë de Bretagne, on the plan; turn right by the first houses of Petit-Couronne onto rue Pierre-Corneille. Leave the car before no 502.*
The "house in the fields" was bought in 1608 by the poet's father. When his father died Corneille inherited the house, in 1639, and continued to stay there. The Norman house is now a museum and evokes the writer's family life with 17C furniture and numerous documents. At the bottom of the garden is a thatched bakery reconstructed to look as it did in the 17C.

Musée industriel de la Corderie Vallois ⊘ – *8km/5mi. Leave Rouen by quai Gaston-Boulet and proceed towards Dieppe and follow N 27 until you reach* **Notre-Dame-de-Bondeville.** In 1822, a spinning-mill was set up on the spot where a paper mill had stood; converted into a rope-making factory in 1880 by Jules Vallois, this factory remained operational until 1978. Recently restored, the building with timber framing has retained a set of 19C machinery in working order. A huge paddle wheel produces the necessary energy to drive the whole complex mechanism. This museum is a remarkable memento of an archaic activity and a telling example of 19C industrial **architecture**. There are demonstrations at set hours.

Forêt Verte – *23km/14mi – about 1hr. Leave Rouen by rue Bouquet (BY).*
The road passes through the forest, a favourite spot with the people of Rouen.

Barentin – *17km/11mi northwest. Leave Rouen by A 15 or N 15.* Visitors entering the town from Mesnil-Roux may be surprised to be greeted by the Statue of Liberty. This was made out of polystyrene for the French film *Le Cerveau (The Brain)*; it measures 13.5m/44ft and weighs 3t. Barentin is an industrial town. One of its best-known features is the brick railway viaduct, 505m/1 657ft long, which carries the Paris-Le Havre railway line across the Austreberthe Valley. The town boasts a large number of works by contemporary sculptors such as Rodin, Janniot, Bourdelle and Gromaire, whose monumental fresco represents peace under the skies of France.

The 19C **church** ⊙ has a number of elegant and well-proportioned modern windows depicting the lives of St Martin, St Helier and St Austreberthe.

★★★**The Corniche** – *10km/6mi – plus 15min sightseeing. Preferably at sunset. Starting from place St-Paul (CZ), drive along rue Henri-Rivière and its continuation rue du Mont-Gargan. Branch right onto rue Annie-de-Pène.*

The road climbs by a hairpin bend to the top of Ste-Catherine Hill, a chalk spur separating the Robec and Seine valleys.

★★★**Côte Ste-Catherine** – Leave the car on a terrace in a sharp bend to the left. There is a strikingly beautiful **panorama** *(viewing table)* over the river bend and the town with all its belfries.

Continue along D 95 which meets N 14bis by a school. Turn left; after 200m turn right before the Café de la Mairie.

★★**Bonsecours** – The neo-Gothic basilica of Bonsecours (1840) which crowns the Mount Thuringe spur is a popular place of pilgrimage and also an excellent belvedere from which to see the shipping on the river and industrial Rouen. From the monument to Joan of Arc located on a terrace there is a **view** that includes Rouen and the Seine Valley.

The bell, the Great Lion, at the cemetery entrance is rung on solemn occasions. From the foot of the Calvary *(viewing table)* there is a **panorama** downstream to the river bend: (left bank) the port and the bridges and (right bank) the cathedral.

Continue on N 14 towards Paris; turn right onto N 14 to return to Rouen.

This is a fine corniche stretch of road.

★**Croisset; Canteleu** – *9km/6mi – plus 15min sightseeing. Leave Rouen by quai Gaston-Boulet (AY), towards Duclair. Turn left onto D 51 towards Croisset.*

Croisset – The **Pavillon Flaubert** ⊙, now a museum, is all that remains of the house in which Gustave Flaubert wrote *Madame Bovary* and *Salammbô*. The museum contains mementoes of the great writer whose library is housed in the town hall.

Return to D 982 and continue west to Canteleu.

★**Canteleu** – There is an interesting but limited **view** of the port and part of the town from the church terrace.

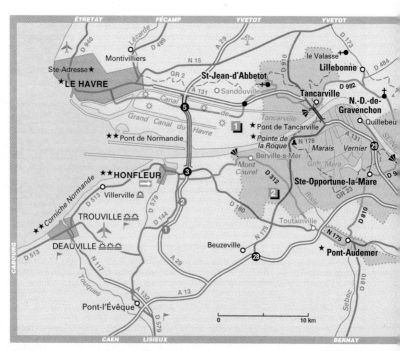

★★★THE LOWER SEINE VALLEY

① From Rouen to Le Havre

109km/68mi – about 4hr 30min

The route offers two attractions; first it is the **abbey road** but it also provides a variety of views of the meanderings of the Lower Seine.

From Rouen take D 982.

A **view**★ of Rouen can be glimpsed to the east through a small valley.

★**Canteleu** – *See Outskirts of Rouen.*

The road *(D 982)* crosses the Forêt de Roumare before emerging near St-Martin-de-Boscherville with a view of the Seine Valley and the old abbey church in the foreground.

★**St-Martin-de-Boscherville** – *See ST-MARTIN-DE-BOSCHERVILLE.*

The road between La Fontaine and Mesnil-sous-Jumièges follows the outer side of the bend for several miles between the river bank and the cliff.

Duclair – *See ST-MARTIN-DE-BOSCHERVILLE.*

West of Duclair bear left onto D 65.

The drive across the end of the Jumièges Promontory is through typically Norman scenery and is at its best at apple blossom time.

There is a succession of elegant houses. The road is part of the picturesque **Route des Fruits**, where blackcurrants, redcurrants, cherries etc are sold directly to the public, and is very popular on summer weekends.

Le Mesnil-sous-Jumièges – It was in the 13C manor house at Mesnil that Agnès Sorel, the favourite of Charles VII, died in 1450.

The road runs past the **country park** and **open-air leisure centre** (windsurfing, canoeing, swimming, tennis, archery, climbing, golf, camping, caravanning), part of the Brotonne Regional Nature Park.

★★★**Abbaye de Jumièges** – *See Abbaye de JUMIÈGES.*

Yainville – The square church tower and nave are 11C. The goldsmiths, Christofle, set up a factory in the town in 1971.

Le Trait – The 16C **parish church** ⊘ of this industrial district includes some delightful alabasters (Adoration of the Magi and Coronation of the Virgin) on the pedestals beneath the statues surrounding the altar. In a recess on the north side there is a 16C restored Entombment.

In Caudebecquet turn right to St-Wandrille.

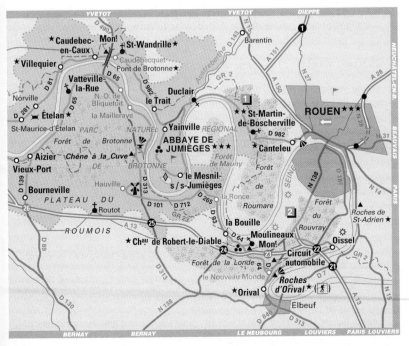

★**St-Wandrille** – *See ST-WANDRILLE.*

Continue west on D 982.

Caudebec-en-Caux – *See CAUDEBEC-EN-CAUX.*

From Caudebec-en-Caux take D 81 and D 281 south and west.

West of Caudebec-en-Caux, the woodland, which has so far dominated the land-scape, gives way to the alluvial lowland along the estuary and industrial sites.

★**Villequier** – *See CAUDEBEC-EN-CAUX.*

★**Château d'Ételan** ⊙ – This remarkable Flamboyant Gothic building dating from 1494, which occupies the site of an old fortress, dominates the valley. An elegant nine-bay staircase turret heralds the "early Normandy Renaissance". The chapel (restored) is decorated with some interesting 16C murals and handsome wood-work. Some of the rooms are furnished and lived in, others are used for tempo-rary exhibitions or for chamber music concerts. The terrace provides a superb **view** (foreground) of the St-Maurice-d'Ételan and Norville marshes and (background) of Brotonne Forest. The boats on the Seine appear to be gliding through the field – an unexpected sight.

Notre-Dame-de-Gravenchon – Interesting modern church with a lead and copper composition on the façade of St George slaying the dragon.

Lillebonne – *See LILLEBONNE.*

The whitish cliffs around Tancarville emerge in the distance; the road bridge comes clearly into view; the alluvial plain widens.

Tancarville – The last chalk cliff on the north bank of the Seine provides a fine view of the river estuary.
The **Pont de Tancarville** ★ (1954-59) is one of the largest suspension bridges in Europe (length 1 400m/4 943ft; deck height above water at high tide 48m/156ft; height of pylons 125m/410ft; central span 608m/1 995ft). Previously all cross-river traffic on the Lower Seine had been carried by ferries so as to allow a clear passage to Rouen for sea-going vessels.
From the bridge *(leave your car at one end)* there is a lovely **view** ★ of the Seine Estuary and Tancarville Canal in the foreground, while in the far distance you can glimpse the recently opened Pont de Normandie, which channels the traffic above the Seine Estuary slightly more downstream.
The feudal **château** dates from the 10C; the only part to survive intact is the Tour de l'Aigle (Eagle Tower) built in the 15C. On the other side of the terrace stands a square 12C tower. This castle was part of a strategic defence commanding the Seine Estuary. In the 11C it received certain privileges granted by William the Conqueror to his tutor, Raoul de Tancarville. Two round towers flank the entrance gate. In the courtyard are the ruins of the living quarters with three pointed arches; the part overlooking the valley has been rebuilt to house a restaurant.
West of Tancarville the road *(D 982)* passes under the north end of the bridge (view of the bridge) and skirts the cliff as far as Le Hode. There is a good view of the south bank of the estuary and of the industrial zone south of the Tancarville Canal.

St-Jean-d'Abbetot – The **church**, which dates from the first half of the 11C, is decorated with frescoes (12C, 13C, 16C); the **finest frescoes** ★ are in the crypt.

Continue west to Le Havre.

Itinerary ② *, see page 235.*

ST-ÉVROULT-NOTRE-DAME-DU-BOIS

Michelin map 60 north of fold 4 or 231 folds 32 and 33

The ruins of this abbey, which was one of the greatest centres of intellectual life in Normandy in the 11C-12C, are set in a lovely landscape. The area where monks once prayed and sang is still propitious for quiet meditation, and the River Charentonne flows through a pretty valley of the same, making the St-Évroult forest a charming place to have a relaxing walk in the woods.

Abbey ruins – Destroyed in the 10C by wars, the Romanesque abbey of Ouche came back to life in the 11C. It was rebuilt in the 13C in the Gothic style, but what remains of it today has little to recognise.
In front of the main entrance, there stands a monument to the memory of Orderic Vital. This monk was a historian who wrote about Normandy (1075-1142) and left an enthusiastic description of the monastery. Without his work, it would be hard to imagine what these ruins once looked like.
Behind the monument, beyond the porch (late 13C) to the left, the remnants of the abbey church are currently being restored.

Where to stay and eat

MODERATE

Le Manoir de Villers – *61550 Villers-en-Ouche – 9km/5.6mi north of St-Évroult via D 230 towards Bocquencé – ☎ 02 33 34 98 00 – http://perso.wanadoo.fr/le.manoir/ – closed Tues, Wed and Thur except the hotel – reservation advisable – 12.20/19.06€.* Amazing place... Housed in a former 17C farm, you will find an equestrian centre, an Italian restaurant and four small rooms. If the thought of home-made noodles makes your mouth water, try the rustic dining room or the owner's table.

THE CHARENTONNE VALLEY

From St-Évroult to Serquigny

The **River Charentonne** is a quick-flowing river, well loved by fishermen. A tributary of the Risle, its north-south course carries it from the St-Évroult Forest to Serquigny. It winds through tall grass of a green and sometimes lonely valley.

65km/41mi – about 2hr30min. Leave St-Évroult by D 31 travelling northeast. After 5km/3mi, take D 14 left. At La Ferté-Frênel, take D 252 and D 33 north.

This tour takes you into the département of Calvados, between Anceins and Notre-Dame-du-Hamel; from Anceins, the road often runs alongside the river. You will glimpse castles and church spires through the greenery.

In Mélicourt, take D 819 left.

St-Denis-d'Augerons – From the war memorial near a beech wood there is an attractive view of the Norman countryside including the two churches of St-Denis-d'Augerons and St-Aquilin.

Return to Mélicourt; take D 33 northward.

Broglie – In the 18C the small town of Chambrais on the River Charentonne changed its name to Broglie (pronounced Broy) when it became the fief of the famous Broglie family from Piedmont. The extensive buildings of the 18C **château** *(private)*, built around a medieval fortress, dominate the scene. The **church** is built of sandstone and hard limestone *(grison)*; the latter was used for the centre of the façade and the lower part of the belfry and also for the massive pillars, on the north side of the interior; these pillars and the chancel are Romanesque; the rest is 15C and 16C. There are 15C and especially 16C statutes in the south aisle.

Jardin aquatique ⊘ – This charming little water garden, irrigated by the River Charentonne, is planted with a variety of floral species coming from exotic countries as well as milder climes.

Ferrières-St-Hilaire – This village once was a metalworking centre; the remains of the forge and the forge master's manor still stand.

St-Quentin-de-Isles – Below the 19C château, there is a textile plant. The dovecote of the old manor house is on a little island.

Bernay – *See BERNAY.*

Take D 144 east along the opposite side of the river.

Menneval – The village lies in one of the most attractive folds in the valley. Its small country church with renovated façade is delightful. The local Brotherhood of Charity, the oldest in the region, dates from 1060.

5km/3mi farther along, cross the bridge over the Charentonne.

Fontaine-l'Abbé – A pretty Norman village with a Louis XIII château and a **church** ⊘ which houses the colourful banners of the local Brotherhood of Charity.

Return to D 133 and continue into Serquigny.

Serquigny – The church has a chequered façade of black flint and white stone pierced by a Romanesque doorway. Inside, are a Renaissance chapel (left) and stained-glass windows from the same period. Four massive round pillars support the belfry. Note also the small pulpit with its carved panels, modern stained-glass windows in the south chapel and the chapel off the chancel and the old wooden statues in the nave.

ST-LÔ

Population 21 546
Michelin map 54 fold 13 or 231 fold 27

In the 6C the Gaulish town of Briovère took the name of its lord, the Bishop of Coutances. In 1944 it acquired the sad title of Capital of Ruins – it was the administrative centre *(préfecture)* of the Manche; on 19 July, the day the town was liberated, only the battered towers of the collegiate church and a few houses in the suburbs remained standing. Since then St-Lô has recovered to become a modern city, proud of its ancient heritage, as well as the stud farm which is one of the largest in France.

The marked itinerary "D-Day-Le Choc" (The Impact), one of several described in the Historical Area of the Battle of Normandy, goes through this town.

HISTORICAL NOTES

Key Town – St-Lô, a vital communications centre, was destined to play a strategic role in the Battle of Normandy. Owing to its position at a crossroads the town underwent heavy bombing from 6 June aimed at dispersing the enemy forces.

The battle for St-Lô began early in July in the middle of the War of the Hedgerows to capture the Lessay-St-Lô road, the base for Operation Cobra.

The town, which was the centre of German resistance, fell on 19 July. A monument (B B), erected in memory of Major Howie of the American Army, recalls a moving episode in the town's liberation. Major Howie had wanted to be one of the first to enter St-Lô but he was killed on the 18 July; in order to fulfil his wish the first Allied troops to enter St-Lô carried his coffin in with them which they set down in the ruins of the belfry of St Cross Church.

A week later, after an unprecedented aerial bombardment – when 5 000t of bombs fell on an area of $11km^2/4.3sq$ mi, the German front broke in the west and the Avranches breakthrough was launched.

Reconstruction – From the ruins, a new town has arisen, planned so that one can now clearly see the outline of the rocky spur, ringed by ramparts and towers, which have become the landmark. The oldest district, the Enclos, in the upper part of the town includes the Préfecture and administrative buildings, which make an interesting post-war architectural group. The extremely modern tower in place du Général-de-Gaulle is an amazing contrast to the former prison porch nearby, now a memorial to Resistance fighters and the victims of Nazism.

St-Lô and the Unicorn

Strolling through the streets of St-Lô, the attentive visitor will glimpse in many places a strange beast indeed... A handsome white horse with a goat's beard, cloven hooves and a narwhal's spiralled horn growing from his forehead... undoubtedly a Unicorn!

In the Middle Ages, unicorns were seen as shy, wary creatures embodying purity, chastity and loyalty, to such an extent that they soon came to symbolise the Virgin Mary. The people of St-Lô being devout Christians, they fervently worshipped the Holy Virgin, which may account for the presence of a Unicorn on the coat of arms of the city.

This splendid mythological beast thus became part of the town's identity: it can be found on administrative correspondence, in rue de la Porte-au-Lait, or even projecting from a stone fountain on the corner of rue Leturc and rue du Neufbourg.

SIGHTS

Église Notre-Dame ⊙ – The west front of the church (13C-17C) and the two towers have been shored up but otherwise left as they were in 1944 as a witness to the ferocity of the bombardment. The unusual plan is clear; an 18C rood beam was supported by two pillars in the middle of the nave which was lit by stained-glass windows including the 15C "Royal Window". In Thomas Becket's Chapel (south aisle) note the large window by Max Ingrand. In the north aisle there is a collection of varied items (statues and sculptures) that were found among the ruins of the church.

There is an outside pulpit against the north wall, level with the chancel.

Belvedere – From the tower overlooking the spur on which the town stands there is a view of the Vire Valley and the *bocage*.

Hôpital-Mémorial France-États-Unis – *By rue de Villedieu to the southwest.* The hospital was built jointly by the two nations and has a Fernand Léger mosaic on one of its façades.

Musée des Beaux-Arts ⊙ – *In the Centre Culturel Jean-Lurçat.* Several rooms explore the history of tapestry from 16C works to contemporary creations by Picart le Doux, Mategot and particularly Jean Lurçat. The rotunda houses *The Loves*

Eating out

MODERATE

Bistrot de Paul et Roger – *42 r. du Neufbourg* – ☎ *02 33 57 19 00* – *closed 22 July to 5 Aug, Mon evening and Sun* – *11.43/18.29€.* The decor is really worth a detour! In the middle of this crazy bric-a-brac of glazed tiles, Louis XVI chairs, old posters and black-and-white photographs, don't miss the incredible collection of old radio sets... Copious cuisine.

Péché Mignon – *84 r. du Mar.-Juin* – ☎ *02 33 72 23 77* – *closed 25 Feb to 8 Mar, 28 July to 15 Aug, 24-31 Dec, Sat lunch, Sun evening and Mon* – *13.57/49.55€.* A friendly stopover. Behind the curtained windows of this restaurant, the owner/chef prepares regional dishes adapted to today's taste. Two dining rooms including a modern one with brightly coloured table cloths. Good value for money.

Where to stay

MODERATE

Armoric Hotel – *15 r. de la Marne* – ☎ *02 33 05 61 32* – 🅿 – *20 rooms: 33.54/44.21€* – 🍽 *4.57€.* This 1950s building is slightly off the town centre yet close to the ramparts and the old town. The rooms are unassuming with their veneer or wicker furniture but well kept.

MID-RANGE

Château de la Roque Bed and Breakfast – *50180 Hébécrevon* – *7.5km/4.6mi west of St-Lô, towards Coutances then Périers via D 900* – ☎ *02 33 57 33 20* – *www.chateau-de-la-roque.fr/* – *16 rooms: 48.78/76.22€* – *meal 17€.* This fine 16C-17C residence stands at the end of an alleyway lined with poplars. You will be welcomed by the owner who will take you for a stroll near the lakes then invite you to have dinner with her before letting you go up to one of the bedrooms, tastefully decorated.

Château d'Agneaux Hotel – *Av. Ste-Marie* – *50180 Hébécrevon* – *2km/1.2mi W of St-Lô towards Coutances via D 972* – ☎ *02 33 57 65 88* – *chateau.agneaux@wanadoo.fr* – *hotel: closed Jan and Feb* – *rest: closed Oct-Apr* – 🅿 – *12 rooms: 62.81/150.92€* – 🍽 *10.06€* – *restaurant 23/55€.* This small 13C castle, standing in a park where deer roam freely, overlooks the Vire Valley. Among its most attractive features are the medieval-style dining room, the stone spiral staircase and the lovely wood panelling of the bedrooms. There are four additional bedrooms, more simply fitted out, in the 16C square tower.

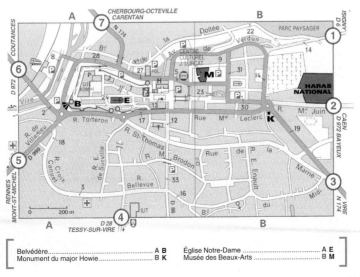

ST-LÔ

of Gombaut and Macée (late 16C or early 17C), a tapestry made up of eight panels providing a lively account of the romance between Gombaut and Macée, as well as an earthy description of the pains and pleasures of country life: each panel is complemented by an explanatory caption and a popular saying in verse.

The museum also has a gallery hung with portraits of the Matignon-Grimaldi princes and an exhibition of 19C French painting: Boudin, Miller and Corot *(Homer and the Shepherds)*. The collections bequeathed by Octave Feuillet (a 19C writer born in St-Lô) include snuffboxes, manuscripts and miniatures.

★Haras national ⊘ – *Rue du Maréchal-Juin in the Bayeux direction.* Destroyed by bombing in 1944, the "new" stud occupies buildings rebuilt to the original designs. The St-Lô stud, the most important of the 23 national studs, specialises in breeds such as Norman cobs, trotters and French saddle-horses. The eight stables, surrounding the main courtyard, house over 100 stallions of seven different breeds: thoroughbreds, Anglo-Arabs, French trotters, French saddle-horses, French and Norman cobs, Percherons, New-Forest and Connemara ponies.

EXCURSIONS

Vallée de la Vire – *20km/12mi southeast of St-Lô by N 174.*

Torigni-sur-Vire – Since the 19C the **Château des Matignon** ⊘ has consisted of only the west wing (restored). The main staircase (17C) leads to the reception rooms which contain a very fine collection of tapestries (early-17C Brussels, 17C and 18C Aubusson), Louis XIII, Louis XV and Louis XVI furniture and works by the wildlife artist Arthur Le Duc. Temporary exhibitions are held in the long gallery. Of the park that once surrounded the château there remain three ponds encircled by shaded paths lined with lime trees which make for a very pleasant stroll. Strangely enough, the largest pool is sheltered from winds by a wall 12m/40ft high and 300m/985ft long. It was commissioned by Jacques de Matignon for his wife Louise de Grimaldi.

From Torini take N 174 north; after 5km/2mi turn left onto D 286.

★★Roches de Ham – *Alt 80m/260ft.*

🔝 From the magnificent escarpment (above the river) there is a **view** of a beautiful bend in the River Vire as it winds through the ancient schists. The lower platform overlooks the deep and peaceful Vire Valley; the upper platform (150m/155yd) provides a more extensive view.

Return downhill; turn right onto D 551 and right again; pass through Troisgots and descend towards La Chapelle-sur-Vire.

La Chapelle-sur-Vire – This small village has been a centre of pilgrimage since the 12C. In the church, flanking the entrance to the chancel, stand to the left a statue of Our Lady of Vire (15C) and to the right an unusual low relief of St Anne, the Virgin and Child. Other 15C low-relief sculptures ornament the high altar; the low-relief sculptures on the tabernacle are of alabaster.

Continue along D 159.

The shady road crosses the River Vire, then follows its course.

At the crossroads with D 511, turn right.

There is a view of the **château de l'Angotière** (not open to the public).

ST-MARTIN-DE-BOSCHERVILLE ★

Population 1 551
Michelin map 54 fold 10 or 231 fold 22

The Benedictine abbey was founded in 1144 by William of Tancarville on the site of a collegiate church built around 1050 by his father Raoul, Grand Chamberlain to William the Conqueror. Raoul of Tancarville had installed a community of Augustinian Canons Regular who were later replaced by Benedictines for St Évroult. No more than 40 monks were ever present and they were driven out during the Revolution.

★★ANCIENNE ABBAYE ST-GEORGES ⊘1hr 15min

Abbey Church – The abbey church, which became St Martin's Parish Church at the time of the Revolution and so was saved from destruction, is now one of the Seine Valley's finest small monuments. The building, which was constructed from 1080 to 1125, apart from the vaulting in the nave and transept which is 13C, possesses a striking unity of style and harmony of proportion.

The façade is plain: the ornaments on the main door archivolts are geometric, in typical Norman Romanesque style; the capitals, carved with remarkable delicacy, are by craftsmen from Île-de-France or the Chartres region.

The nave of eight bays with aisles on either side, has Gothic vaulting and a false triforium in place of galleries. A big open gallery supported by a monolithic round column ends either transept. The low-relief sculptures inlaid in the wall beneath the balustrade illustrate, the Bishop giving his blessing *(left)* and warriors fighting *(right)*. The monumental confessional in the south transept is 18C.

Groined vaulting covers the chancel and side aisles and a heavier version the oven vault over the apse. The black marble pavement stone near the high altar is to Antoine the Red, 19th Abbot of St George's, who died in 1535.

Abbey Buildings – This tour enlightens visitors on the daily realities of monastic life and its development over the centuries.

Chapter-house – The 12C chapter-house surmounted by a 17C building used to open into the cloister (destroyed) by way of three Romanesque arches supported on groups of slender columns with historiated capitals. On the right are statue columns. Inside, a fine frieze of Hispano-Moorish inspiration runs above the place where the monks' stalls once stood.

Excavations in the cloister have uncovered vestiges of Gaulish and Gallo-Roman temples and a Merovingian funerary church; their location is marked by pavings on the surface.

Conventual outbuilding – Erected by the Maurists in 1690 and partly demolished during the French Revolution, then restored in 1994, it has retained its attractive stone vaulting, especially on the first floor.

Chapelle des Chambellans – It was built in the late 13C to serve the Chambellans of Tancarville. A first-floor gallery was set up to enable the lords to attend Mass. A farming outbuilding until 1987, the chapel has now been restored.

Park – From here one can see the north face of the nave, the cornice modillions and the massive lantern dominating the transept crossing. This formal French garden designed in the tradition of Le Nôtre (1680) is currently being redesigned. The Pavillon des Vents, a black flint and white stone lodge crowning the staircase, offers some pretty views of the Seine Valley and the abbey estate.

Abbey church of St-Georges

H. Dewynter/MICHELIN

Every year concerts are organised on the abbey premises during the months of June and September. The pure lines of the architecture, coupled with the excellent standard of acoustics and the choice of programmes, all make for an unforgettable and highly moving experience.

EXCURSION

Duclair – The town is sited at the confluence of the River Austreberthe and the Seine. From the shade of the lime trees on quai de la Libération one can watch the passage of large cargo vessels, incongruous in such a rural setting, or ferries coming and going across the river.

The **Église St-Denis**, which was restored in the 19C, has retained its 12C belfry surmounted by a 16C spire.

Near the entrance note the vaulting in the belfry and a half column of pink marble topped by a capital decorated with acanthus leaves which once belonged to a Gallo-Roman temple; there are six other such half columns in the church. Against the pillars under the belfry and framed by round-headed arches are two late-14C stone panels carved with many small figures. In the north aisle there is a 14C stone statue of an Apostle from Jumièges. In the nave there are 14C wooden statues: the Holy Trinity, the Virgin of the Assumption and St John. The 15C wooden calvary on the belfry wall shows Christ on the cross, the Virgin mourning and St John. Most of the stained-glass windows, including the one depicting the beheading of St Denis, date from the 16C; the one in the chancel and the one illustrating Pentecost (1968) are by Max Ingrand.

FORÊT DE ROUMARE

36km/22.5mi – about 2hr

Oaks, beeches and hornbeams populate the land around the Seine between Rouen and Duclair.

From St-Martin-de-Boscherville take D 982 east towards Canteleu. After 2km/1mi, at the crossroads in Leu, turn right; after 500m/0.5mi turn left.

The road winds through the forest.

At the Treize Chênes crossroads take D 351 through the forest to Sahurs.

Sahurs – The 16C Marbeuf Chapel, part of the manor, was made famous by the vow of Anne of Austria who promised the chapel a silver statue equal in weight to the child she desired. The silver statue (5.5kg/12lb) despatched on the birth of Louis XIV disappeared during the Revolution.

Take D 51 east.

Église de Sahurs – South of the road from Sahurs to Hautot is a shaded lane leading to the church, facing La Bouille *(see p 234)* and the ruins of Robert the Devil's castle on the south bank of the Seine.

Continue northeast on D 51.

Le Val-de-la-Haye – *5km/3mi from Sahurs.* The column on the right, facing the Grand Couronne Ferry at the north end of the village, commemorates the return of Napoleon's body to France.

Return to Sahurs and follow D 51 northwest along the bank of the Seine. Then proceed along its continuation, D 67.

St-Pierre-de-Manneville – As you approach the village, on the left, you will glimpse the **Manoir de Villers**, a small 16C seigniory, surrounded by a lovely park, now used as a private Norman mansion.

Quevillon – The castle of La Rivière-Bourdet, on the left at the entrance to the village, is a sumptuous 17C building converted into a rest home. The monumental dovecote is well preserved.

Take D 67 to return to St-Martin-de-Boscherville.

ST-PIERRE-SUR-DIVES ★

Population 3 993
Michelin map 54 fold 17 or 231 fold 31

St-Pierre-sur-Dives, which developed round a rich Benedictine abbey founded in the 11C, still possesses the remarkable old abbey church. The town is also the major centre for the manufacture of the distinctive boxes in which local cheeses are packed.

★**Église** ⊙ – *30min.* The original church was burnt down during the wars between William the Conqueror's sons. An examination of the west front reveals several successive periods of reconstruction: the Romanesque south tower dates from the 12C; the west front itself and the north tower were rebuilt in the 14C.

The nave is light and harmonious, the upper parts including the triforium bays surmounting each wide arch date back only to the 15C. The fine lantern tower above the transept is 13C, as is the chancel encircled by wide pointed arches. The bases of the columns dividing the chancel from the ambulatory and south tower once formed part of the old 12C church. On the floor of the nave there is a copper strip which starts in the south aisle, crosses the nave near the font and finishes beside the organ. Although it is known as the Meridian it is not in fact the French O grad Paris meridian, which passes slightly to the east. The line shows the position of the rays of the noontide sun, as they pass through a small bronze plaque in one of the windows.

The founder of the abbey, Comtesse Lesceline, is buried in the apsidal chapel. The history of St-Pierre-sur-Dives is illustrated in the modern chancel windows.

Salle capitulaire ⊙ – *Entrance at 23 rue Saint-Benoît.* The early-13C chapter-house has a 13C glazed brick pavement, which was previously in the sanctuary.

★**Halles** ⊙ – The 11C-12C market, which was burnt down in 1944, has been faithfully rebuilt in the original style, even to the use of 290 000 chestnut pegs in its **timber-work**. Not a nail or a screw has been used. The roof tiles are also fixed by pegs.

EXCURSIONS

★**Château de Vendeuvre** – *6km/3.7mi southwest by D 271. See Château de VEN-DEUVRE.*

Château de Canon ⊙ – *12km/8mi southwest of St-Pierre, in Mézidon-Canon, on D 47.* A château was first built on this pleasant site near the River Laizon in the 17C. The present building, of Classical proportions, was started in 1730 and completed in 1768. This was the birthplace of Léonce Élie de Beaumont, a professor at the Collège de France, who collaborated on the production of the first geological map of France on a scale of 1:50 000.

Parks and gardens – The gardens and grounds are a delightful mixture of the formal French style and the picturesque English fashion, embellished with statues and follies. Some points of interest are the *Temple de la Pleureuse* (Temple of the Weeping Woman), a memorial to Mme Élie de Beaumont, the ornamental pond, an unusual Chinese kiosk and the **chartreuse**★, where fruit and flowers are sheltered from the wind.

In one of the outbuildings, the *Salle des Bonnes Gens* (Room of Good People) recalls a festival instituted in 1775 by the lady of the house, and which honoured the Good Daughter, the Good Elder, the Good Mother and Father.

ST-SAUVEUR-LE-VICOMTE

Population 2 257
Michelin map 54 fold 2 or 231 fold 14

St-Sauveur-le-Vicomte, standing on the banks of the Douve in the heart of Cotentin, is closely associated with the 19C writer **Jules Barbey d'Aurevilly** and St Mary Magdalen Postel who founded the Sisters of the Christian Schools of Mercy in the 19C. Today the congregation bears the saint's name.

SIGHTS

Château – The bust at the entrance is of Barbey d'Aurevilly by Rodin. This 12C castle was the ancestral home of two Norman families, the Néels and the Harcourts. The castle has suffered many a siege notably by the English in 1356 and the French in 1375. Louis XIV had the castle transformed into a hospice in 1691. The remaining parts of the original castle are the two entrance towers and the square keep with its flat buttresses.

Église – Only the transept dates from the 13C, the rest of the church was rebuilt in the 15C. There are two interesting works of art at the entrance to the chancel, a 16C *Ecce Homo* (left) and a 15C statue of St James of Compostela (right).

Musée Barbey-d'Aurevilly ⊙ – *Enter the castle precinct (which now contains an old people's home), climb the stairs (left) beyond the vault.* The museum contains mementoes (portraits, statues including a bronze by Rodin, caricatures, manuscripts and beautifully bound books) belonging to the great writer and influential critic Barbey d'Aurevilly (1809-89) who was born in the town and was known as the Lord High Constable of Literature (*Connétable des Lettres*).

Barbey d'Aurevilly is buried in the castle cemetery *(round the castle, along the curtain walls in the moat, and across the large courtyard).*

Abbaye ⊙ – This is the mother house of the congregation of the Sisters of St Mary Magdalen Postel with its co-educational college. The abbey was founded in the 10C by Néel de Néhon, Vicomte de St-Sauveur. The Hundred Years War brought ruin on the abbey and forced the monks into exile. At the Revolution the building was further dismantled. In 1832 it was bought by Mother Mary Magdalen Postel to serve as the mother house of the order, which she had founded in Cherbourg in 1807. The local architect and sculptor, François Halley, was responsible for the restoration work. Although damaged again during the Second World War the abbey was repaired between 1945 and 1950.

Eating out

MODERATE

L'Auberge de l'Ouve – *50360 Les Moitiers-en-Bauptois – 13km/8.1mi east of St-Sauveur-le-Vicomte via D 15 and D 24 – ☏ 02 33 21 16 26 – closed Oct to Mar – ⊟ – 11.50/18.50€.* The road stops on the edge of the Douve, in front of this stone inn covered with a slate roof like the village houses. Arrive by car, by boat or even in a horse-drawn caravan. Simple regional cuisine, generous helpings, no fuss!

Where to stay

MID-RANGE

Château de Beaulieu Bed and Breakfast – *3.5km/2.2mi W of St-Sauveur along D 15, towards Portbail – ☏ 02 33 21 44 26 – chateau.de.beaulieu@wanadoo.fr – closed Jan and Feb – ⊟ – 4 rooms: 44.21/54.88€.* The British owners of this 19C castle have decorated the interior with surprising colour schemes: pink, turquoise, white and gold. Antique furniture and parquet flooring, fine fireplaces and curios in the drawing room. The spacious bedrooms open out to a peaceful wooded park.

Abbatiale – The plain round-headed windows in the south aisle of the abbey church date from the Romanesque period. Under the pointed vaulting of the nave the arches of the blind triforium rest on slender columns. Each transverse arch springs from a column with a foliated capital. Near the entrance is a stone pulpit, the unfinished work of François Halley. He carved his self-portrait on the north pillar in the second bay. In the apse the lovely 15C carved wood altar portrays scenes from the childhood of Christ. The tomb of St Mary Magdalen Postel in the north transept is also the work of François Halley.

Parc – The well-tended park with its fine trees and colourful flower beds is a pleasant place for a stroll. The well restored conventual buildings add an elegant note to this setting.

EXCURSION

Château de Crosville-sur-Douve ⊙ – *Proceed towards Valognes for 5km/3mi and in Rauville-la-Place take D 15 towards Pont-l'Abbé, then follow the signposts.*
This 17C château is one of the most imposing in the Manche *département*. A carriage and postern gate lead to the courtyard surrounded by the main range and outbuildings. The oldest part is the round, machicolated tower with its staircase turret. On the courtyard front the mullioned windows, the twin-dormer windows and the door are all surmounted by triangular pediments. The imposing granite staircase and the remnants of painted decoration in the great hall are two of the more interesting features of the interior.

Château de Crosville-sur-Douve

ST-VAAST-LA-HOUGUE

Population 2 134
Michelin map 54 fold 3 or 231 fold 15

If you travel to this picturesque fishing port, speak like the locals do and call it "Saint Va". Among the good reasons to visit this popular seaside resort with a marina and a mild climate are the delicious oysters. The fortifications protecting the harbour date back to Vauban (17C); they were rebuilt after the French defeat at the naval battle of La Hougue. Offshore lies Tatihou Island, the Îlet Fort, which can be reached at low tide.

The **lighthouse** stands at the end of the granite jetty. The Chapelle des Marins served as a navigational landmark; beside the white apse is a terrace overlooking the sea: (north) Réville Bay; (south) the Hougue Fort attached to the coast by a narrow isthmus; the flat Cotentin coast; on a clear day, St Marcouf Islands (offshore), Grandcamp in Veys Bay, and the cliffs of Port-en-Bessin.

Port de St-Vaast-la-Hougue

The beach, **Grande-Plage** (1.5km/1mi long), is bordered by tamarisk. The breakwater occupies the full width of the isthmus which links the former island of La Hougue to St-Vaast. At the southern end of the beach stands a **fort** with an impressive keep *(military property)*.

Île de Tatihou ⊙ – An amphibious vehicle takes visitors over to Tatihou which means "mound surrounded by water" (*hou* is Norse for water). The **Musée maritime départemental** (Maritime Museum) has sections on the building of the liners and on their crews at the time of the great French Admiral Tourville. Underwater excavations at the site of the Battle of La Hougue (1692) have made it possible to recover hundreds of objects from the wrecks of the *Ambitieux*, the *Foudroyant*, the *Magnifique*, the *Merveilleux* and the *Saint-Philippe*: guns, shoes, bowls, china, pipes, cutlery, part of the upper works and deadeyes which give a good insight into life

Eating out

MODERATE

Le Chasse Marée – 8 pl. du Gén.-de-Gaulle – ☎ 02 33 23 14 08 – closed Sun evening and Mon except July-Aug – 13.42 lunch – 16.77/22.87€. The fresh, well-prepared dishes, with a definite flavour from the sea, are served in the delightful blue-and-white-gloss decor of the dining room. Hanging on the walls, the flags of the most prestigious yacht clubs in the world (mainly British) and old photographs of harbours and sailing ships form an appropriate setting for the refined cuisine.

Lesdos-Allaire – 23 r. des Chantiers – ☎ 02 33 54 42 13 – 3.35/7.62€. Friendly welcome at this stand pervaded by the smell of fresh algae and seafood. Enjoy a few dozen oysters right here, if it is not too crowded; alternatively, take them home or have a picnic...

Where to stay

MODERATE

La Ferme de Cabourg Bed and Breakfast – 50760 Réville – 3km/1.9mi from St-Vaast via D 1 – ☎ 02 33 54 48 42 – ⊐ – 3 rooms: 28.97/38.11€. An alleyway lined with poplars leads to this fortified 15C farm with its elegant double porch. The guestrooms have retained the original loopholes, now glazed, which stand out against the white walls and add to the light provided by the mullioned windows.

Hôtel de France et Fuchsias – ☎ 02 33 54 42 26 – closed 3 Jan to 1 Mar, Mon from mid-Sept to 30 Apr, Mon lunch in May-June and Tues lunch from Nov to Mar – 34 rooms: 34.30/70.89€ – ⊐ 6.86€ – restaurant 21/48€. When the fuchsias are in bloom, their pink bell-shaped flowers cover the walls of this hotel set back from the harbour. Some of the rooms overlook the enclosed shaded garden. Whether in the dining room, on the veranda or the terrace, enjoy a well-preapred meal.

on board one of His Majesty's ships. A nature reserve (20ha/50 acres), covering a combination of moorland, sand dunes and shingle beach, offers many opportunities for birdwatching. In the old fort built by Vauban, there is a bookshop, a cafeteria and a restaurant.

From St-Vaast-la-Hougue take D 1 north towards Réville; after crossing the bridge over the Saire turn right to the Pointe de Saire.

Pointe de Saire – Beyond the hamlet of Jonville, by the sea, is an old blockhouse: good **view**★ of the attractive rock-strewn beaches of Pointe de Saire and of Tatihou Island with St-Vaast in the background.

Continue north on D 1.

Beyond Réville the road passes La Crasvillerie, a delightful 16C manor house. This is market gardening country where they specialise in cabbages. As you approach Barfleur, the countryside becomes more Armorican in character with granite houses, rocky bays and gnarled trees bent by the wind. Gatteville lighthouse stands to the north.

Abbaye de ST-WANDRILLE ★

Population 1 184
Michelin map 54 fold 9 or 231 fold 22

St-Wandrille Abbey and the renascent abbey of Le Bec-Hellouin are a moving testimony to the continuity of the Benedictine Order in Normandy since the earliest times.
Today the monks earn their living mainly from the manufacture of furniture polish and household products.

A PRESTIGIOUS WESTERN MONASTERY

God's Athlete (7C) – King Dagobert's court was celebrating the marriage of the wise and handsome Count Wandrille, who seemed destined to a brilliant career, when, by common accord, the young newlyweds decided to consecrate their lives to God. The bride entered a convent and Wandrille joined a group of hermits. The King ordered Wandrille to return to court but the new hermit placed his cause in the hands of God and, in time, Dagobert was enlightened by a miracle and resigned himself to the loss of his subject. After staying in distant monasteries, Wandrille returned to St Ouen in Rouen where he was ordained. His saintliness and his magnificent physique earned him the nickname of God's True Athlete.

Valley of the Saints (7C-9C) – In 649 Wandrille founded a monastery in the Fontenelle Valley. The monks cleared the forest and planted the first vines. **Fontenelle** library and schools became famous (the abbey had not yet taken the name of its founder). A succession of learned men were appointed as abbots: Einhard, Charlemagne's historian, and Ansegise who organised the first collection of the Emperor's capitulary ordinances. In 831 the *Epic of the Abbots of Fontenelle* appeared – the first history of a western monastery. Fontenelle "where saints flourish like rose trees in a greenhouse" was known locally as the Valley of the Saints and to this day St Wandrille is the only monastery in Christendom to celebrate its own feast of All the Saints of the Monastery.

Benedictine Continuity – In the 10C some monks began to rebuild the ruined abbey, destroyed by the fury of the Northmen. The new abbey, which took the name of its original founder, became one of the most flourishing centres of the Benedictine Order which spread widely throughout Normandy in the 11C. The Wars of Religion brought only a temporary decline; the Maurist Reform sustained its influence but the Revolution led to the dispersal of the monks and the buildings fell into ruin. In the 19C the abbey passed successively into the hands of a textile mill owner and the English peer, the Marquess of Stacpoole. In 1894, the Benedictines returned but seven years later were again dispersed. For several years the author Maurice Maeterlinck lived in the abbey. In 1931, however, Gregorian chant began once more to be heard in the church.

★ABBAYE *45min*

The monumental gateway was erected in the 19C by the Marquess of Stacpoole. The entrance to the abbey is through a 15C door surmounted by a symbolical pelican (the pelican piercing its breast so that its offspring may feed on its blood is the symbol of Christ). The porter's lodge and its twin are 18C; the gate between the two is known as the Jarente Gate.

Porte de Jarente – This imposing 18C gate leads to the main courtyard, accessible on guided tours only. It was built by Abbot Louis-Sexte de Jarente, Bishop of Orléans, after whom it took its name.
At the back of the courtyard are the monks' workshops (woodwork, baking, laundry).

Ruins – The bases of the columns which supported the main arches of the 14C nave can be seen rising out of the grass. The only parts of the abbey church still standing are the tall columns in two groups of massive and slender pillars which stood at the opening of the north transept. The 13C chancel, with six bays, was circled by an ambulatory and 15 chapels.

★**Cloisters** ⊙ – All four galleries of the cloister remain. The 14C south gallery (the only one open to the public), parallel with the nave, was linked to it by a fine door surmounted by a now mutilated tympanum illustrating the Coronation of the Virgin. A niche, in the 13C church wall at right angles, contains the deeply venerated and graceful 14C statue of Our Lady of Fontenelle. On either side lie the tombstones of Jean, bailiff of Fontenelle in the 13C, and Abbot Jean de Brametot; a small lapidary museum has been installed in the south gallery.
In the north gallery *(no access)* is a half Gothic, half Renaissance **lavabo**. Above is a gable decorated with a fretwork of leaves and a blind arcade with six sections each containing a tap. Scenes from the New Testament are illustrated in an exquisitely delicate Flamboyant decoration.

Church ⊙ – The church is an old 13C tithe barn, the Canteloup Barn, which was transported piece by piece in 1969 from La Neuville-du-Bosc in the Eure and re-erected at St-Wandrille by the monks themselves. The beams and uprights of the roof are assembled with dowels and enhanced by discreet lighting.
The Chapel of the Holy Sacrament, characterised by its wooden beams, was originally the barn porch.
To the right of the chapel entrance is a 1970 shrine containing the head of St Wandrille.

Chapelle Notre-Dame-de-Callouville – The chapel was built by the monks in accordance with a vow made by the abbot after a bombing raid in 1944.

CHAPELLE ST-SATURNIN

🔜 *By car, follow the signs; on foot about 45min there and back. On leaving the abbey take the path downhill (right).*

Note the 16C Entombment in a niche.

Skirt the wall for 150m/164yd; go round a field and take the path beside the abbey wall.

Chapelle St-Saturnin – *Not open to the public.* The chapel stands on the edge of the abbey park; it is a small oratory, trefoil in plan, reconstructed in the 10C on probably Merovingian foundations. The façade was remodelled in the 16C but the building has retained the squat shape, with three apses, surmounted by a massive square tower.
The interior, visible through the barred door, has been restored. The tops of three pillars embedded in the base of the tower and decorated with roses, palms and fantastic animals probably come from an earlier construction of the Carolingian period.

STE-MÈRE-ÉGLISE

Population 1 556
Michelin map 54 folds 2 and 3 or 231 fold 15

This town at the centre of the traditional Normandy livestock breeding area entered the news headlines brutally on the night of 5-6 June 1944 when troops from the American 82nd Airborne Division landed to assist the 101st Division in clearing the exits from Utah Beach. The action is commemorated by a monument in the square.
Ste-Mère-Église was liberated on 6 June but fighting continued all around until tanks advanced into the town from Utah Beach the following day.

The marked itinerary "Objectif-Un Port" (Objective-A Harbour), one of several described in the Historical Area of the Battle of Normandy, goes through this town.

SIGHTS

Church – The solid 11C-13C church was damaged particularly during the dislodging of German snipers from the belfry. A dummy at the end of a parachute hangs from the steeple as a reminder of private Steele's alarming experience. Dropped over the area during the night of 6 June 1944, he was caught hanging from the steeple of the church by his parachute. Scared out of his wits by the

Commemoration of Steel's adventures

events happening below him, he pretended to be dead for 2hr, a few feet from a bell which never stopped ringing; he was eventually "unhooked" by the Germans.

The American parachute drop can be seen in the modern glass of the main door.

Borne O de la Voie de la Liberté – *In front of the town hall*. This is the first of the 12 000 symbolic milestones *(bornes)* planted along the "Road of Liberty" followed by General Patton's troops to Metz and Bastogne. From Avranches onwards they recall the rapid advance of the 20th Corps of the American 3rd Army.

Musée des Troupes Aéroportées ⊘ – A parachute-shaped building houses the Airborne Troops' Museum which contains mementos (uniforms, military equipment and a Douglas C 147) of the first fighting on D-Day.

Ferme-Musée du Cotentin ⊘ – Housed in the Beauvais farm (16C), this Cotentin Farm Museum recreates rural life of the early years of the 20C: agricultural implements and tools, furnishings and domestic items are displayed in the gardens and buildings.

Eating out

MODERATE

Le John Steele – *4 r. du Cap-de-Laine* – *50480 Ste-Marie-du-Mont-Village* – ☎ *02 33 41 41 16* – *closed 15 Jan to 11 Feb, Sun evening and Wed except 1 July to 15 Sept* – *12.50/33.54€*. Situated near the regrettably famous church, this inn pays homage to GI Steele. Typically Norman dining room with exposed beams and stone walls. Regional cuisine with the chef's personal touch. A few simple rooms.

Where to stay

MODERATE

Ferme-Musée du Cotentin Bed and Breakfast – *Chemin de Beauvais* – *50480 Ste-Marie-du-Mont-Village* – ☎ *02 33 95 40 20* – *closed Dec and Jan* – *4 rooms: 30/36€*. Sleeping in a museum is an unusual way of discovering regional rural traditions, all the more since the admission fee is waived for the guests. Following local tradition, the rooms are decorated in pastel shades, pale blue, pink and yellow, and have recessed or canopied beds.

STE-SUZANNE

Population 935
Michelin map 60 fold 11 or 232 fold 8

This peaceful village occupies a picturesque **setting★** on the summit of a rocky promontory commanding the north bank of the Erve. In the 11C, the viscounts of Beaumont built on the site one of the most important Maine strong points.

Ste-Suzanne, girt with ramparts, stoutly resisted the attacks of William the Conqueror. William's troops had made their camp at Beugy on the Assé-le-Béranger road. After a siege of three years (1083-86) William abandoned his efforts and, out of respect for his opponent, Hubert II de Beaumont, he returned his lands of Fresnay and Beaumont. During the Hundred Years War the English took possession of Ste-Suzanne (1425) and remained its overlords for 14 years.

SIGHTS

Viewing table – *Via rue du Grenier-à-Sel*. From the top of the tower you look down on the small town nestling round its stout 11C keep, the ramparts, the new town grouped beyond the ramparts and the surrounding countryside.

Promenade de la Poterne – The walk along the ramparts encircling the town starts from the Tour du Guet (Watchtower) in the southwest corner, and passes alongside the castle, which dates from the reign of Henri IV, and the old Porte de Fer (Iron Gate). From time to time there are attractive views of the river below and a water mill, of Tertre Gane (Gane Hill), of the plain and Grande Charnie Forest. The Iron Gate, with its pointed windows, has two gates; the lower gate was defended by a portcullis for which only the grooves remain; the square bastion was defended by artillery. The second half of the walk, which ends at the Porte du Guichet (Wicket Gate) with its 16C cannon-balls, provides distant views (northeast) of the Coëvrons Hills and the white quarry, named La Kabylie after the men from the Kabylie region in Algeria who worked there during the First World War, and (north) of Mont Rochard topped by a television mast and the Butte de Montaigu topped by St Michael's Chapel.

Church – There are several interesting statues, especially the one at the far end of the chancel, a gracious St Suzanne, a 16C polychrome wood statue and in the north transept a 14C stone Virgin and Child. At the north entrance to the sacristy the bust of the Virgin carrying the Infant Jesus is a lovely example of Renaissance religious art.

Dolmen des Erves – *3km/2mi by D 143 or the Assé-le-Béranger road*. Excavations prior to the 1983 restoration revealed that this megalithic monument was built during the 4th millennium BC.

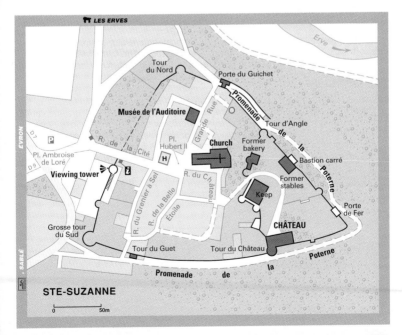

Where to stay

MODERATE

Le Chêne Vert Bed and Breakfast – *6km/3.7mi SW of Ste-Suzanne towards Sablé-sur-Sarthe then Chammes and D 125* – ☏ *02 43 01 41 12 – 10 rooms: 32.01/38.11€ – meal*. The renovated barns of this old cereal-growing farm contain 10 guestrooms. Children are welcome and can play in the garden or have a dip in the swimming pool in summer. Dinner for guests in the evening, served on the terrace weather permitting.

Musée de l'Auditoire ⊙ – The building where court hearings used to be held now houses an exhibition on the medieval town of Ste-Suzanne. The story of its thousand years of history is woven round historical documents, local artefacts and important events, often reconstituted with small figures.

Château ⊙ – The château was built in 1608 by Fouquet de la Varenne, the first French Controller General of the postal services.
On entering the courtyard, note on the left, the former bake house. The château itself, on the far right, has dormer windows with triangular pediments, mullioned windows and a flight of stairs under a slate covered dome.
The rooms on the second floor have an astonishing **timberwork roof** in the form of an upturned keel.

EXCURSION

Forêt de la Grande Charnie

26km/16mi – about 1hr 30min. Leave Ste-Suzanne by D 9 and after 1km/0.5mi turn right onto a small steep road. 700m/766yd further on leave the car at a group of houses.

Tertre Gane Viewpoint – At the woodland picnic area, there is a platform which provides a picturesque view of Ste-Suzanne and the surrounding plain.
Return downhill; turn first right by La Foussillère, an old people's home; east of the crossroads turn right onto an uphill road.

Signal de Viviers – The road ends at the edge of a wooded precipice from which you can see the dense Grande Charnie Forest. A path on the left leads to a rock crowned with a statue of the Sacred-Heart, from which you will get a view between the trees of the Coëvrons Range.
Return downhill to Torcé-Viviers-en-Charnie; turn left and left again onto D 210 going southwest. After 5.5km/3mi turn right onto D 156 and right again onto D 7 to return to Ste-Suzanne.

Saulges – *19km/12mi south by D 125 and D 235.*
The road follows the Erve Valley.

Grottes de Saulges ⊙ – The caves present some interesting geological formations and traces of human habitation: bones and flint tools. The **Grotte à Margot** has some interesting fissures and erosion features. The **Grotte de Rochefort** is hollowed out of the west bank of the Erve; a corridor and ladder lead to a small underground lake at the same level as the river.

Saulges – In the square opposite the parish church stands the **Église St-Pierre**. The 16C **Chapelle St-Sérénède** enshrines the relics of St Serenious or Celerinus, a local 7C evangelist; on the south wall there is a fresco portraying St Serenious (left) and St Anne (right) teaching the Virgin to read. Several steps lead down into a rare Merovingian building, the **Chapelle St-Pierre**, built by St Serenious in the mid 7C.
Take D 554 northwest towards Vaiges; after 1km/0.5mi turn left onto a downhill road to a car park; walk over the footbridge.

Oratoire St-Cénéré – The hermitage is secluded at the foot of a rocky slope, near where the Erve forms a small lake known for its good fishing.

SÉES★

Sées has been the seat of an episcopal see since St Latuin converted the district to Christianity in 400 and became the first bishop. The quiet old cathedral town, with its several religious communities, one institution and two seminaries, has been sensitively restored. It lies northeast of Écouves Forest.

★★CATHÉDRALE ⊙ *15min*

Despite many vicissitudes, the cathedral is one of the finest examples of 13C and 14C Norman Gothic.

Exterior – The west front is pierced by a large porch which is unfortunately disfigured by heavy buttresses; they were added in the 16C when the west front began to lean alarmingly, owing to poor foundations on unstable ground.

Interior – The great arches of the nave are separated by cornerstones adorned with fretted roses; above is a triforium surmounted by a delicate frieze. The organ is by Cavaillé Coll.

In the **chancel★★** and the **transepts★★** the triforium is of a different design. This part of the church, an interesting example of Gothic art, is like an immense clerestory section, lit by magnificent 13C **stained glass★★** and rose windows in the transept.

The double Louis XVI high altar is by Brousseau, the episcopal architect; the gilt bronze low relief facing the nave represents the Entombment; the marble low relief on the chancel side shows the discovery of the bodies of St Gervase and St Protase.

The south transept contains *(left of the altar)* an 18C marble bust of Christ and *(facing the altar)* a 14C marble Virgin, Our Lady of Sées.

ADDITIONAL SIGHTS

Église Notre-Dame-de-la-Place ⊙ – The organ loft is Renaissance and the 12 low-relief sculptures, in groups of three illustrating scenes from the New Testament, are 16C.

Musée départemental d'Art religieux ⊙ – The Museum of Religious Art occupies the former canons' residence and presents a varied collection (12C-19C) of paintings, sculptures, vestments and sacred vessels.

Ancienne abbaye St-Martin – The Old Abbey is now a children's home. Through the great main door with its classical entablature one can see the gracious 18C abbot's lodging.

Ancien évêché – This majestic group of buildings was built for Bishop Argentré in 1778, hence its name Argentré Palace. The court is through a beautiful wrought-iron gate complete with escutcheon and foliated scrolls.

Anciennes halles – This unusual covered market, a rotunda with a peristyle, dates from the 19C. The timber-work roof is supported by columns of stone.

Cathédrale de Sées

SÉES

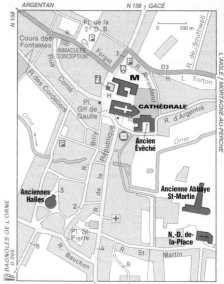

EXCURSIONS

★Château d'O ⊘

8km/5mi northwest by N 158 and a right turn.

The calm water of the moat reflects the graceful composite silhouette of the château which is a highly original example of the imaginative style of early Renaissance Norman architects.

For many years the château belonged to the O family: Jean I d'O, councillor and chamberlain to Charles VIII, his son Charles d'O, his grandson Jean II, Captain of the Scots Guards of François I, and François d'O, Superintendant of Finances and favourite of Henri III.

The château consists of three ranges of buildings framing a courtyard which is open on the north side facing the moat.

The **East Wing** is the oldest part of the château (late 15C). The Gothic core is decorated with the new motifs of the French Renaissance. Wide windows open on to the park. The ornamentation is particularly delicate in the inner courtyard. The many sloping roofs, the slim turrets and the walls patterned in brick and stone make a charming ensemble.

The 16C **South Wing** consists of a floor with large window bays over an arcade divided by slim columns decorated with ermines, the emblem of the house of O.

The **West Wing**, which dates from the reign of Henri IV, is built of brick and stone and decorated with carved medallions. The interior decor was altered in the 18C.

Tour of the Écouves Forest

From Sées to Alençon – 29km17mi – 2hr 15min

This **forest** ⊘ (14 000 ha/37 000 acres) with its deep glades of oak, beech, Norman and woodland pine as well as spruce, covers the eastern promontory of the hills of Basse-Normandie. It is remarkable for the diversity of its woodlands and the layout of its forest tracks converging on star-shaped junctions. There is a continual process of reforestation.

The forest provides pasture for deer and roebuck which are hunted from October to late March, usually on Tuesdays and Saturdays.

🏃 There is a fitness trail at the Chêne-au-Verdier and a nature discovery trail at the Carrefour du Rendez-vous.

Carrefour de la Croix de Médavy – This important crossroads is marked by an old octagonal milestone carved with the old road names.

The tank *Valois*, which had been hit by a *Panzer*, pays tribute to the courage shown by the French 2nd Armoured Division commanded by General Leclerc on 12-13 August 1944 during the Battle of Normandy.

The **Signal d'Écouves** is with the Mont des Avaloirs the joint highest point (417m/1 368ft) in western France. The Écouves Signal Station rises to the left of the Croix de Médavy crossroads.

Eating out

MODERATE

Le Cheval Blanc – *1 pl. St-Pierre* – ☎ *02 33 27 80 48 – closed 2nd and 3rd week of Feb, last 3 weeks of Nov and Fri – 10,52€ lunch – 13,57/38,11€.* "The White Horse" is about as typical a name as you could find for a restaurant in France, and this is indeed a typical French eatery. The half-timbering on the 20C building is attractive, the dishes are time-tested favourites, and the guest rooms are clean and neat.

MID-RANGE

Ferme-auberge de la Motte – *61140 Courtomer – 15km/9.3mi east of Sées via D 3 to Gaprée* – ☎ *02 33 28 40 03 – www.fermeauberge-lamotte.com – closed Wed – ☞ – reservation essential – 17.53/20.58€.* This place conveys all the charm and simplicity of the countryside. Chickens, calves and pigs are bred here and you can enjoy their meat when you stop for a meal. And that is not all... there is also the famous Camembert pie and home-made cider... Beautiful dining room with an imposing fireplace in a 16C tower. Five simple bedrooms.

Where to stay

MODERATE

Ferme Équestre des Tertres Bed and Breakfast – *61500 Chapelle-près-Sées – 4km/2.5mi S of Sées, towards La Ferté-Macé via D 908 then Bouillon via C 14* – ☎ *02 33 27 74 67 – ☞ – 5 rooms: 30/37€ – meal 12€.* This is an address for horse riders: the farm is the starting point of fine rides through the Écouves Forest. Hikers can follow GR paths and others could try a barouche ride. Three stylish bedrooms with solid furniture.

MID-RANGE

Île de Sées Hotel – *61500 Macé – 5.5km/3.4mi NW of Sées towards Argentat via D 303 and D 747* – ☎ *02 33 27 98 65 – closed 15 Jan to 1 Mar, Sun evening and Mon –* **P** *– 16 rooms: 47.26/56.41€ – ☞ 5.79€ – restaurant 17.53/28.97€.* Those who like daydreaming and lazing away will appreciate the peace and quiet of the countryside, in the buildings of a former dairy, in the middle of a park. Dark wood panelling adds warmth to the interior decoration. Pine furniture in the rooms.

Carrefour de la Croix-Madame – This crossroads is marked with an ancient milestone.

🚶 The several attractive walks, which can be made from the crossroads, include the Sapaie Pichon path *(1hr 30min; yellow blazes on the trees)*.
Parts of the forest here are being replanted and firs are being replaced by seedlings. It is hilly country and there are some good glimpses over the wooded countryside.

Take D 204 south.

During the descent there is a beautiful view. Beyond the Chêne-au-Verdier crossroads there are some splendid oaks, beeches and firs.

At the Rochers du Vignage crossroads bear right onto D 26 and again right onto a forest road; park the car.

★ **Rochers du Vignage** – *1hr 45min on foot there and back.*
🚶 The path (marked with yellow blazes) leaves the forest road to turn back, right, to a low rock crest from which there are outstanding views over the forest. The path reaches the Chêne-au-Verdier, then parallels the Aubert forest road for 300m/330yd, then forks right. The path crosses a fitness trail to go downhill again to the forest road and the car.

Take D 26 south to Alençon.

On the edge of the wood at the junction with a forest road, stands a monument to the French 2nd Armoured Division. There is a cemetery 200m/220yd to the south. From the road there are views of the conical Butte Chaumont, of Mont Souprat in the distance and later of the Alençon district backed by Perseigne Forest.

SILLÉ-LE-GUILLAUME

Population 2 583
Michelin map 60 fold 12 or 232 fold 9

The small town of Sillé-le-Guillaume, built in a semicircle on the southern slope of the Coëvrons, had a rich and eventful past since it was one of the strong points, like Ste-Suzanne and Mayenne, which protected northern Maine from Norman invasion.

Château – At the end of the Hundred Years War, the English sacked the fortress which had been built in the 11C at Sillé. In the 15C Antoine de Beauvau built the castle we see today on the ancient ruins. Although considerably restored, the keep built into the living rock and the round towers linked by 16C and 17C buildings, give the old castle a proud air.

Église Notre-Dame – The church stands upon the site of a former Romanesque church of which the **crypt** and the south transept gable remain. A beautiful 13C door restored in the 15C is decorated with a statue of the Virgin and Child under a decorative canopy. Numerous rebuildings have occurred since, but the most recent in 1977 restored the 15C nave to its original aspect with its timber ceiling.

Eating out

MODERATE

La Bretagne – *Pl. Croix-d'Or* – ☎ *02 43 20 10 10 – closed Sun evening –*
12.04/40.40€.
Stagecoaches have long deserted this former coaching inn... The hotel, situated in the town centre, offers rooms decorated in a simple manner. The cuisine is simple too, yet well-prepared and good value for money.

EXCURSIONS

Forêt de Sillé – *42km/26mi – 1hr. From Sillé-le-Guillaume take D 310 northeast.*
🔲 The road rises before entering Sillé Forest which covers the eastern crest of the Coëvrons chain of hills and is well organised for walkers (shelters, signposted footpaths and special riding lanes). The forest was over exploited at the turn of the century and today it is composed of copses, copses under tall stands or plantations of conifers on the poorer soils.

After 4km/2.5mi turn left onto the forest road; after 800m/875yd turn left again onto a forest road which skirts the north end of Defais Pool.

Étang du Defais – This stretch of water, also known as the Lac de Sillé, with its attractive surroundings, is a favourite spot with the local townspeople. There is a good bathing area with facilities for yachting, canoeing, swimming, camping etc.

From the west side of the pool take the road west; at the crossroads turn right onto D 16.

From the northern edge of the forest there is a good view of the Norman *bocage*.

In La Boissière turn left; in St-Pierre-sur-Orthe take D 143 southwest via Vimarcé.

Château de Foulletorte – *Park beside D 143; walk up the avenue which leads to the castle.* The attractive moated château (the water is supplied by the River Erve) was built by Antoine de Vassé at the end of the 16C. The staircase loggia on the entrance front, the projecting cornice on the two wings at right angles, the round-headed or mullioned windows and the tall chimneys are the only decorative notes on this sobre granite building.

Return to St Pierre-sur-Orthe; turn right onto D 35.

After traversing the wooded Coëvrons Ridge, the road descends towards Sillé: attractive view of **La Croix de la Mare** (La Mare Cross) (290m/951ft).

La SUISSE NORMANDE★★

Michelin map 55 folds 11 and 12, 60 fold 1 or 231 folds 29, 30 and 42

This extraordinary name denotes an area in Normandy which has neither mountains nor lakes in the Swiss sense and does not even include Normandy's highest points but is nevertheless an attractive tourist area particularly enjoyed by walkers, canoeists, anglers, hang-gliders and trekking enthusiasts.

The River Orne, as it cuts its way through the ancient rocks of the Armorican Massif, produces a kind of hollow relief of which the most typical elements are a pleasantly winding river course bordered by steep banks surmounted by rock escarpments and occasional isolated high points which provide a view of the rolling, wooded countryside.

★★VALLÉE DE L'ORNE

From Thury-Harcourt to Putanges

99km/61mi – about 3hr – see local map below

Thury-Harcourt – *See THURY-HARCOURT.*

From Thury-Harcourt take D 562 south.

The road drops down into the valley. Ahead is the small Chapelle de la Bonne-Nouvelle, perched on a hillock, followed immediately by Caumont with its abandoned sandstone quarry (left) and St-Rémy and its mining installations.

St-Rémy – The St-Rémy iron mines, where one of the richest ores in Normandy was extracted, were worked from 1875 to 1967.

Fosses d'Enfer: Maison des Ressources Géologiques de Normandie ⊙ – There is a tour of the old mine site, where visitors learn all about the ore and its extraction.

🚶 A footpath offers an interesting itinerary that takes you past the geological site, the open-air working of the mine and the miners' former lodgings.

★Clécy – *See CLÉCY.*

Leave Clécy along D 562, south.

The Rochers de la Houle can be seen on the left. Towards the top of the hill, after a right bend, there is a bird's-eye view of the valley and Clécy, and, on the horizon, the Éminence and Mont Ancre (331m/1 086ft).

In Le Fresne turn left onto D 1.

The road follows the crest of the ridge separating the valleys of the Orne and Noireau and then joins up with the Béron crest. East of the Rendez-vous des Chasseurs (500m/550yd) there is a view north of the Orne Valley and of Parcs Rocks. The downhill stretch before St Roch's Chapel provides a view, on the horizon (right), of the escarpment of the Oëtre Rock.

Chapelle St-Roch – This 16C pilgrimage chapel with modern frescoes by Maurice le Scouèzec is the scene of a *pardon* held on the Sunday after 15 August in full local Norman costume.

Pont-d'Ouilly – The village located at the confluence of the River Orne and River Noireau is a busy tourist centre.

Take D 167 southeast.

Eating out

MODERATE

Au Poisson Vivant – *61790 Pont-Érambourg – 9km/5.6mi west of Pont-d'Ouilly via D 511 towards Caen and Pont-Érambourg –* ☎ *02 31 69 01 58 – closed 15-31 Jan, 3-17 Sept, Sun evening and Mon – reservation advisable Sat-Sun – 13.72/32.01€.* People used to come here to eat and dance. The dance hall has been replaced by a small dining room... decorated in 1930 style (for nostalgia's sake!), lengthened by a veranda.

Auberge de la Rouvre – *In the village centre – 61430 Rouvrou –* ☎ *02 33 65 98 09 – larouvre@wanadoo.fr – closed winter school holidays and Wed – 14.94/17.99€.* This inn, close to the site of the Roche d'Oëtre on a bend in the River Rouvrou, is a convivial stopover. The dining room is a little old-fashioned but you will be warmly greeted by the young owners whose cooking will revive you and enable you to continue on your way.

Where to stay

MODERATE

L'Orangerie Bed and Breakfast – *At the place known as "Le Pont" – 61210 La Forêt-Auvray – 6km/3.7mi southeast of Rouvrou (near the Roche d'Oëtre) via D 301, towards Rabodanges –* ☎ *02 33 64 29 48 – ⌿ – 3 rooms: 30.49/ 38.11€.* Congratulations! You have arrived... Ring the bell for a dog guards this orangerie which once belonged to the castle situated below. The rooms, which all contain antique furniture, have character; ask for the room with the canopied bed... No smokers.

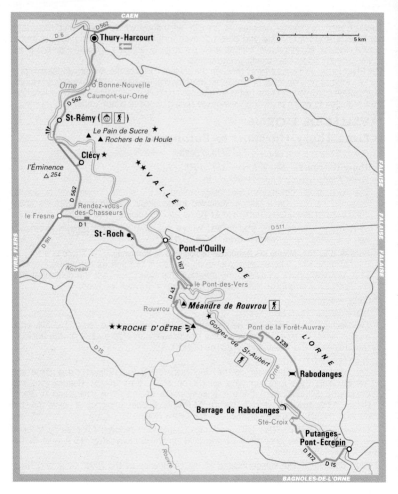

As the road leaves Pont-d'Ouilly it passes at the foot of the rock which in its upper part resembles a lion's head. The road runs beside the Orne to Pont-des-Vers.

Turn right onto D 43.

The road climbs, revealing a view of the Rouvre with its almost geometrically enclosed curves – the most outstanding being the Rouvrou meander.

In Rouvrou, take the road signposted "Site de Saint-Jean", then turn right after the cemetery.

Méandre de Rouvrou – *15min on foot there and back from the war memorial.*

This is the best point from which to view the bend in the river at the narrowest part of the rock ridge, where it is only a few metres wide and the river looks about to break through; the surroundings are pleasantly shaded by pine trees.

Return to the car and follows the signs.

★★**Roche d'Oëtre** – *15min. The belvedere belongs to a café but there is no obligation to buy a drink or souvenirs.*

The rock, in its grandiose **setting** dominating the wild and winding Rouvre Gorges with its steep escarpment, is the most mountainous feature to be found in Suisse Normande. From the viewing table the view of the precipice is quite astonishing. To the right of the viewing table, below the first belvedere, there is a ridge of rock with an almost human profile.

East of the Roche d'Oëtre the road runs along the side of the valley providing views of the Orne Valley and the wild north slopes; the last viewpoint is the bridge in La Forêt-Auvray.

At this point on its course, north of the Argentan region, the Orne flows through a succession of narrow defiles, known as the **Gorges de St-Aubert**★, which are accessible only on foot.

Roche d'Oëtre

N. Hautemanière/SCOPE

Rabodanges – The 17C castle is set in a park overlooking the Orne Valley.

Take the road to the dam.

Barrage de Rabodanges – The dam is of the multi-arch type. The east bank has a belvedere, cafés and a motor boat club. There are fine views of the reservoir, known as Rabodanges Lake, from the road and also from the bridge in Ste-Croix.

In Ste-Croix turn left onto D 872 just before the war memorial.

Putanges-Pont-Écrepin – This little town on the banks of the Orne makes a good starting point for visiting the **Gorges de St-Aubert** – accessible only on foot.

THURY-HARCOURT

Population 1 803
Michelin map 54 fold 15 or 231 fold 29

The town, rebuilt, stands on the banks of the Orne and is now a tourist centre for the Suisse Normande to the south.

Thury adopted the name Harcourt from the Harcourt family which came from the town of Harcourt in the county of Évreux; in 1700 Thury became the Harcourt ancestral seat.

★**Park and gardens of the château** ⊘ – Near the ruins of the family château (once the residence of the governors of Normandy), the park stretches out with 4km/2mi of walkways bordered with trees and shrubs – especially lovely in the spring. On the lower level, the side nearest town is planted with flower beds and grassy paths.

EXCURSION

★**Boucle du Hom**

5km/3mi. Leave Thury-Harcourt on D 6 to the northwest. After 1.5km/1mi take D 212 to the right.

The road follows the west bank of the Orne, skirting the **loop's** steep bank, and offers good viewpoints overlooking the Orne and its green banks.

Turn right at Le Hom where the road leaves the Orne to enter a deep cutting through the rock at the end of the curve's promontory.

Return towards Thury-Harcourt by D 6.

★**Mont Pinçon** – The **Pré-Bocage** is a picturesque rural countryside which borders the Caen plain, the Bessin and the *bocage*.

At the top of the climb of 365m/1 201ft, near a television transmitter, turn left and continue for another 600m/656yd. Leave the car to walk over the heathland *(the rough stony path can be difficult in winter, take care)*; there is a wide-ranging **panorama** of the *bocage*.

Chapelle St-Joseph – The road goes up the Orne Valley. Turn right at Mesnil-Roger to St-Martin-de-Sallen and turn right again here onto a narrow uphill road from which a one-lane road leads off to the right to St Joseph's. From behind the chapel, at a circular viewing table, there is a beautiful **panorama**★ of the Orne Valley and the heights of the Suisse Normande.

Return to St-Martin-de-Sallen and take the next road on the right to rejoin D 6 to Thury.

Eating out

MODERATE

La Roc qui Beu – ⊡ – At La Roque qui Beu – 2km/1.2mi west of Thury via D 6 then D 166 – ☎ 02 31 79 73 08 – closed 20 Dec to 20 Jan and Mon-Fri lunch – ⊐ – reservation advisable – 14.94/28.05€. Children love this chalet on the banks of the River Orne: pedalos, playground and delicious home-made pancakes! Grown-ups will look with amusement at the unusual decor, which draws its inspiration both from the mountain and the countryside, and enjoy the smoked salmon and foie gras. A real relaxing time for everyone.

Le TRÉPORT ⚓

Le Tréport, a small fishing port at the mouth of the Bresle near the border with Picardy, is a seaside resort which is all the more popular for its close proximity to Paris. During the summer lively crowds round the harbour turn the town into a fair. The long shingle beach, backed by tall cliffs, is packed with visitors on weekends.
Mers-les-Bains, on the right bank of the Bresle, is less commercial than Le Tréport and has many devotees, as has Ault, a beach further north.

Le Tréport harbour

SIGHTS

★Calvaire des Terrasses – *Allow 30min on foot there and back; access by car via rue de Paris, rue St-Michel and boulevard du Calvaire.*
A flight of stairs *(378 steps)* leads up from the town hall, a brick and flint building, to the Calvary on the clifftop. From the terrace on which the Cross stands, there is a **view** which extends north beyond the last of the Caux cliffs to Hourdel Point, the Somme estuary and inland, along the Lower Bresle Valley to Eu and over the lower town's slate roofs, beach and harbour.

Église St-Jacques – The church, which stands half way up the hill, dates from the second half of the 16C although it has been extensively restored. The modern porch shelters a Renaissance doorway.

Inside are several interesting 16C features including remarkable hanging keystones, a Pietà in the Chapel of Our Lady of Mercy (north aisle) and a low relief above the altar showing the Virgin encircled by biblical emblems. At the far end of the church, in which the chancel is on a lower level than the nave, is the fine statue of Our Lady of Tréport.

Eating out

MODERATE

La Matelote – *34 quai François-1er* – ☎ *02 35 86 01 13* – *closed Tues evening except July-Aug –⌂ – reservation advisable in summer and Sat-Sun – 12.04/41.16€.* Bluish lighting, a fine view of the harbour and tasty fish and shellfish are the characteristic features of this restaurant opposite the fish auction building... Besides seafood, meat dishes and a variety of other dishes are also on the menu... enough to satisfy every taste.

Le St-Louis – *43 quai François-1er* – ☎ *02 35 86 20 70* – *closed 20 Nov to 15 Dec – 14.48/48.78€.* A fish and seafood restaurant with a view of the harbour. Brasserie-style decor with cubicles and leatherette-upholstered seats under a coloured-glass roof. Covered veranda in front.

Where to stay

MID-RANGE

Le Prieuré Sainte-Croix Bed and Breakfast – *2km/1.2mi east of Le Tréport along D 925 from Abbeville to Dieppe* – ☎ *02 35 86 14 77* – ⌂ – *5 rooms: 39.64/48.78€.* Those who love peace and quiet should not hesitate to go to this farm built during Louis-Philippe's reign. Cattle breeding is still going on there. The guestrooms are located in a separate building. Varied furniture and parquet flooring. Lovely shaded garden and view of the surrounding countryside.

Golf Hôtel – *102 rte de Dieppe* – ☎ *02 27 28 01 52* – *www.treport-hotels.com* – *closed Jan and Feb* – **P** – *10 rooms: 44.52/76.99€* – ☕ *5.95€.* Turn left at the entrance of the camp site. An alleyway lined with trees leads to a fine 19C timber-framed house. The non-smoking rooms are all different and well fitted out. Pleasant welcome. A small, charming hotel charging reasonable prices.

Royal Albion Hotel – *76910 Criel-sur-Mer* – *6km/3.7mi southwest of Le Tréport via D 126E* – ☎ *02 35 86 21 42* – *closed 2-30 Jan* – **P** – *20 rooms: 60.52/105.04€* – ☕ *6.71€.* With its fake colonial-house look, this waterfront hotel offers its guests a pleasant stay. Its park, overlooking the coast and its Directoire-style decor appeal to foreign tourists. Ask for one of the six rooms above the reception area, they are the best.

TROUVILLE-SUR-MER ⚓⚓

Population 5 607
Michelin map 54 fold or 231 fold 19

Trouville is situated on the coast where the cliffs of the Normandy Corniche slope away at the mouth of the River Touques, to be replaced by a wonderful beach of fine golden sand. The town has all the latest amenities and so maintains its reputation; it was the seaside resort which, as long ago as the start of the Second Empire (1852), launched the Fleurie Coast.

As in Deauville, the wooden plank promenade *(planches)* running the full length of the beach is the main gathering place for all holidaymakers. In the right wing of the Casino (opposite the swimming pool) there is a centre providing sea water treatment. The other centre of attraction is the area around the quays.

Owing to the coming and goings of the fishermen and the small resident population, Trouville is still worth visiting out of season.

Corniche – *Make for the corniche road to the north by way of boulevard Aristide-Briand and a left turn.* On the way down there is a magnificent **view** of the Trouville and Deauville beaches and the Côte Fleurie.
From the Calvaire de Bon-Secours *(viewing table)* the view is equally breathtaking.

Aquarium ⊘ – *Seafront promenade.* Different species of fish are displayed in a reconstitution of their natural setting. Fresh and salt water fish together with equatorial forest reptiles provide a colourful and sometimes surprising spectacle.

Musée Villa Montebello ⊘ – This villa is a fine example of seaside architecture patronized by the aristocracy under the Second Empire, reproducing many features of the Renaissance style. Its windows opening onto Seine Bay offer a unique panorama of the beach at Trouville. The museum itself presents collections illustrating the art and history of the area: paintings, drawings and engravings by artists who contributed to making the town famous. One room is devoted to the history of bathing in Trouville, another to André Hambourg, a third to the poster artist **Raymond Savignac**.

Galerie d'exposition ⊘ – *Enter through the tourist office.* This gallery, which is run by the museum, hosts temporary art exhibitions.

EXCURSIONS

The Corniche Normande from Trouville to Honfleur

21km/13mi – See page 162.

The Côte Fleurie from Trouville to Cabourg

19km/11mi See page 162.

VALOGNES ★

Population 7 412
Michelin map 54 fold 2 or 231 fold 14
Local map see Presqu'île du COTENTIN

Valognes is an important road junction at the heart of the Cotentin peninsula; it is the market town for the surrounding agricultural area.

The aristocratic town described by Barbey d'Aurevilly was partially destroyed in June 1944; it has been rebuilt in the modern style and expanded.

Several traces of the past have survived: Gallo-Roman ruins, 11C-18C churches, private mansions built in the 18C when local high society made Valognes the Versailles of Normandy.

The marked itinerary "Objectif-Un Port" (Objective-A Harbour), one of several described in the Historical Area of the Battle of Normandy, goes through this town.

SIGHTS

★**Hôtel de Beaumont** ⊘ – Outstanding on account of its lavish architecture, this noble 18C residence, miraculously spared by the bombings, has a splendid front in dressed stone. A protruding, elegantly curved, runs along the 50m/165ft long façade: the balcony is supported by four engaged columns with Ionic decoration and surmounted by a curved triangular pediment.

Eating out

MODERATE

La Forge d'Yvetot – *At Le Tapotin* – *50700 Yvetot-Bocage* – *2km/1.2mi west of Valognes towards Bricquebec* – ☎ *02 33 40 13 01* – *closed 3 weeks in Mar, 3 weeks in Nov, Mon evening and Tues* – *reservation advisable July and Aug* – *10.37/16.01€.* The locals love this old smithy with its original decor, its wide fireplace and huge bellows. Meat and fish grilled on a wood fire of course but pizzas and pancakes are also on the menu. Sayings and aphorisms written on slates hanging on the walls for your entertainment...

Where to stay

MODERATE

Manoir de Bellaunay Bed and Breakfast – *On D 902* – *50700 Tamerville* – *3km/1.9mi northeast of Valognes towards Quetteville* – ☎ *02 33 40 10 62* – *closed 15 Nov to 15 Mar* – ⊟ – *3 rooms: 34/54€.* A large garden planted with various species of trees extends in front of this 16C manor house flanked by three Romanesque arches and a tower. Beautiful period wood panelling in the breakfast room. The overall impression is one of nearness and the bedroom furniture has character.

Inside, the sweeping flight of steps with its double winding stairwell gives access to the upper floor by a stone arch ending in mid-air. The tour takes you through the ground floor (dining hall, salon and library with Louis XV and Louis XVI furniture), the first floor (bedroom and amusing children's playroom) and a sort of semi-basement (kitchens and servants' quarters).

The back of the building is adorned with a balustrade running along the terraces, tastefully laid out as formal gardens, reinforcing the classical touch of the whole ensemble.

Hôtel de Grandval-Caligny ⊙ – *32 rue des Religieuses.* **Jules Barbey d'Aurevilly** once lived in this handsome 17C-18C mansion; note the staircase with its wrought-iron banister, the Empire ceramic stove in the dining room, the 18C drawing room and alcoved bedrooms.

Musée régional du Cidre et du Calvados ⊙ – *The Regional Museum has been divided and set up in two different locations not too far apart.*

Musée du Cidre – The Cider Museum is set up in the **Maison du Grand Quartier**, the last building from a group of several which housed the premises of a well-known linen manufacturer between the 15C and the 18C. The museum explains the

Hôtel de Beaumont

various stages of cider making in the region. The exhibits include old Cotentin pottery, 16C to 20C apple presses and mills, crushers and stone grinders. Tableaux present traditional scenes of life in Normandy, illustrating the local costumes and solid Cotentin furniture.

Musée du Calvados et des Vieux Métiers – Housed in the **Hôtel de Thieuville** (16C-19C), this museum displays tools, equipment and machinery connected with distillation, stone-masonry, iron and copper work. Eighteen crafts are illustrated in 15 rooms. The collections extend from the 11C to the 20C.
After the visit it is possible to taste and buy regional products.

EXCURSIONS

Bricquebec – *11km/8mi west by D 902*. The town is known for its old castle and its Trappist monastery.
The inner courtyard of the **castle** ⊙ is still enclosed by its fortified wall. The 14C **keep** is a handsome polygonal tower (23m/75ft high); the four floors have collapsed. There is a view of the town and its surroundings from the sentry walk between the keep and the clock tower *(viewing table on top of the keep)*. The **Tour de l'Horloge** houses a small regional museum displaying old furniture, medals, mineral specimens. The south building contains a 13C crypt (restored).
From Bricquebec take D 50 and D 121 north; just before the calvary turn left onto a path.

Abbaye Notre-Dame-de-Grâce ⊙ – The Trappist monastery, which is occupied by a community of Cistercian monks, was founded in 1824 by Abbot Dom Augustin Onfroy, a priest in the small village of Disgoville near Cherbourg. The public may visit the church and the visitor centre which provides information about the monastery.

If you are looking for a pleasant, quiet, well-located hotel anywhere in France, consult The Red Guide, published yearly.

VARENGEVILLE-SUR-MER ⌂

Michelin map 52 fold 4 or 231 fold 10

The resort consists of a series of hamlets linked by deep roads in a charming and typically Norman landscape of hedges and half-timbered houses, favoured by many artists. The **church** is built on an attractive **site**★ overlooking the sea. The porch dates from the 16C. The stained-glass window in the chancel is by Ubac, the one in the south aisle depicting the Tree of Jesse by Georges Braque, who is buried in the graveyard (left of entrance).

★**Parc floral du Bois des Moustiers** ⊙ – In a valley facing the sea, this ornamental and botanical garden (9ha/22 acres) is laid out in the English style, with rare species, a profusion of flowering plants and giant rhododendrons *(in flower from April to June)*. The **house** (1898) was designed by Sir Edwin Luytens, the English architect, known for his country houses and the Viceroy's palace in New Delhi, and the landscape artist Gertrude Jekyll. Earlier in the century, the park welcomed many famous artists: Monet, Pisarro, Vallotton, Braque, Miró, Calder and especially Jean Cocteau, who mentions it in one of his very first books *(Le Potomac)*.
There is more stained glass by Braque in the **Chapelle St-Dominique** ⊙ *(north side of the road to Dieppe)* which also contains a painting by Maurice Denis from Granville.

Eating out

MID-RANGE

La Buissonnière – *Rte du Phare d'Ailly – 76119 Ste-Marguerite-sur-Mer – 2km/1.2mi north of Varengeville via D 75 –* ☎ *02 35 83 17 13 – www.planete-b.fr/labuissoniere – closed Jan, Feb, Sun evening and Mon – reservation essential Sat-Sun – 26.68/37.35€*. Small early-20C house surrounded by one of the most exquisite gardens in the area. Delightful restaurant inside. Whether you choose one of the small dining areas or the terrace, you will enjoy the imaginative cuisine based on fresh produce. Idyllic setting.

EXCURSIONS

Phare d'Ailly – *0.8km/0.5mi on D 75A off D 75.* A modern lighthouse, which can be seen 80km/50mi away, has replaced the two older ones, (18C-19C) which were destroyed in 1944. Look for the signs to the Petit-Ailly and Vastérival gorges. These are typical Norman *valleuses*, small dry valleys that seem to hang above the sea, created by the erosion of the cliffs.

Manoir d'Ango ⊙ – *Follow the signs from D 75 onto a little road, and turn right a bit farther on; a drive bordered with a double row of beech trees leads to the parking area.* This lovely Renaissance home was built between 1535 and 1545 by Italian artists, and was the home of Jean Ango. He welcomed François I here, and much later the house also enchanted the French poets Louis Aragon, André Breton and Jacques Prévert.

The building is designed around a large inner courtyard. The southern part of the building opens on the ground floor into an Italian-style **loggia**, which was originally embellished by frescoes from the Leonardo de Vinci School. The mullion windows are set in walls of sandstone and flint. The decor is typically Renaissance, with many sculpted ornaments forming the shapes of foliage, seashells and medallions.

Château de VENDEUVRE★

Michelin map 54 fold 17 or 231 fold 31 – 5km/3mi southwest of St-Pierre-sur-Dives

The château standing on the banks of the Dives is situated on the borders of the Auge and Falaise regions. In 1750 Alexandre le Forestier d'Osseville, Count of Vendeuvre, commissioned the architect Jacques-François Blondel to build him a summer residence. The château still fulfils this role today.

Alleys on either side of a French style formal garden lead up to the plain entrance front with a pedimented projecting centrepiece.

★★**Musée du Mobilier miniature** ⊙ – The lovely vaulted rooms of the orangery are the setting for an exceptional collection of miniature furniture, models and masterpieces of skilled craftsmen. These small pieces (11-75cm/4-30in tall) are all made of the same wood as the full-size originals. Some were made as a hobby in the craftsman's free time or during his retirement but they are all proof of great skill and craftsmanship. When guilds or associations of craftsmen were common, the companions (*cum + panis* meaning those who shared bread) had to submit a full-size or reduced model as a masterpiece before becoming master craftsmen. About 100 pieces from all over the world, dating from the 16C to the present, are exhibited in the showcases of the three rooms. Meticulous care and attention to detail has been lavished on these jewels of perfection with their ivory inlays, chased bronze and miniature paintings and embroideries. Note in particular a staircase with 12 flights of stairs (19C), the dimensions of which are all a multiple of three; a master craftsman's submitted work (19C): a cupboard containing the carver's

Miniature furniture from the collection in the Château de Vendeuvre

tools; Empress Sissi's 19C gaming table with paintings on alabaster on the door; a 19C revolving library in mahogany; a darkened pearwood cabinet decorated with panels of tinted ivory engraved with hunting scenes; an 18C canopied bed for the cat of Madame Adélaïde, Louis XV's daughter; and a 16C Spanish swing, four-poster bed. Tiny pieces of cutlery and porcelain complete this miniature world.

★**Château** ⊘ – The rooms are attractively furnished. In the dining room, looking out on the evening sunset as was the custom, the table is laid with a linen cloth bearing the family arms and with the rear façade of the château woven into the cloth. The reception room has some lovely carved panelling. Two of the more popular 18C games are on display: tric-trac table and loto. Note the special chair for a woman wearing panniers and in the main bedroom the toiletry set, the pastels in the salon, the study (collection of goose feathers) the smoking room (paraphernalia of an 18C smoker) and the kitchens. Behind the château there is a water garden.

Garden of surprises – Among the trees and the fanciful delights of the garden, the spray of fountains may catch you by surprise. True to the playful spirit that motivated 18C landscape artists, there are many wonders, including a not-to-be-missed grotto made of 200,000 seashells. High kitsch!

VERNEUIL-SUR-AVRE ★

Population 6 446
Michelin map 60 fold 6 or 231 fold 46

Verneuil is composed of three districts, the main streets of which are rue de la Madeleine, rue Gambetta and rue Notre-Dame.
In the past each district was like a mini-town protected by a fortified wall and a moat, just as the whole town was surrounded by an outer wall and moat; the water for the moats was supplied by the River Iton.
Some very fine half-timbered houses and old mansions (restored) have been preserved in the town, which centres on place de la Madeleine.
The jovial and congenial **Jean-Marie Proslier** (1928-97), a popular figure in French cabaret and theatre as well as a prolific television actor, bought a house in this town and set up a "restaurant-cum-grocery" which also served as a venue for performers. He was a dedicated supporter of this region, of which he had grown extremely fond over the years.

A BORDER TOWN

Verneuil was formerly a fortified city created in the 12C by Henry Beauclerk, Duke of Normandy, third son of William the Conqueror. Together with Tillières and Nonancourt it formed the Avre defence line on the Franco-Norman frontier.
As the River Avre flowed through French territory, Henry had a canal dug in order to divert the Iton, about 10km/6mi to the north, to supply Verneuil. The town became French in 1204 under Philippe Auguste, who granted a charter and built the Grise Tower and its defence system.
The town was the object of many battles including the bloody defeat of Charles VII in 1424. The French victory of 1449 was achieved through the guile of miller Jean Bertin who helped the front line troops to enter the town.

SIGHTS

Tour Grise – The sentry walk at the top of this 13C tower commands the town and surrounding countryside. Like the church, it is built of red agglomerate *(grison)*, from which it takes its name.
To the south of the tower cross the small bridge over one of the arms of the Iton to view the building together with a charming little house at its base. The pleasant and relaxing Fougère Park lies near the bridge.

Église St-Jean – This partly ruined church has retained its 15C tower and its Gothic doorway.

Promenades – The term refers to boulevard Casati and its prolongation.
Remains of several of the old outer fortifications are visible: the ruins of the Tour Gelée (boulevard Casati) and Jean Bertin's Mill (boulevard Jean-Bertin). Interesting views of the town can be seen from avenue du Maréchal-Joffre and avenue du Maréchal-Foch.

Old Houses – They are extremely well restored and undeniably add to Verneuil's charm.

Where to stay and eat

MODERATE

Le Moulin des Planches – 28270 Montigny-sur-Avre – 10km/6.2mi east of Verneuil via N 12, D 54 then D 102 – ☎ 02 37 48 25 97 – closed 1 Jan to 1 Feb, Sun evening and Mon – 🅿 – 18 rooms: 36.59/95.28€ – ☑ 7.32€ – restaurant 14.94/29.88€. Been dreaming of a pastoral holiday? Well this remote mill at the heart of the countryside, on the banks of the River Avre, could be the realisation of your dream. Nothing but nature all round and, inside, the warmth and comfort of simple, bright and colourful rooms, tastefully furnished... A gem!

LUXURY

Hostellerie Le Clos – 98 r. Ferté-Vidame – ☎ 02 32 32 21 81 – closed 13 Dec to 20 Jan – 🅿 – 4 rooms: from 114.34€ – ☑ 14.48€ – restaurant 29.73/44.97€. You step into another world when you enter this hotel looking like a large manor house or a small castle with its intricate brickwork façade. Beautifully refined rooms with sloping ceilings, spacious, almost luxurious suites. Everything here is steeped in elegance... for your sole pleasure.

Corner of rue de la Madeleine and rue du Canon – 15C residence with chequered walls and angle turret. The building currently houses the public library.

Rue de la Madeleine – Between rue Canon and rue Thiers stand a number of attractive stone or timbered houses. The 18C Hôtel Bournonville has wrought-iron balconies. Note also the houses at nos 532, 466 and 401. No 532 stands behind a courtyard.

Rue des Tanneries – A Renaissance house stands at no 136, with a carved wooden door surmounted by wooden statues.

Corner of rue Notre-Dame and rue du Pont-aux-Chèvres – A 16C town house with chequered wall and decorated turret.

Place de Verdun, place de la Madeleine, rue de la Poissonnerie – Other picturesque old wooden houses can be seen.

★**Église de la Madeleine** ⊘ – Enter by the south doorway. The **tower**★ abutting the church dates from the late 15C to early 16C; it consists of four tiers with pierced bays decorated on all sides with statues. The third tier is surmounted by a richly ornamented belfry.

The different materials used during successive reconstructions from the 13C to the 15C, particularly during the Gothic period, are clearly visible from the south side. The Renaissance style porch is flanked by mutilated but still beautiful 16C statues of the Virgin and of St Anne.

VERNEUIL-S-AVRE

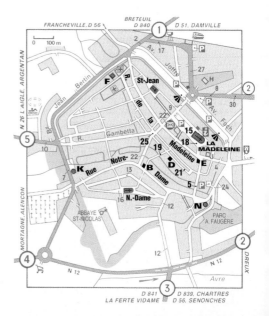

The interior, lit by 15C and 16C stained-glass windows, contains a number of works of art, mostly 15C and 16C: (near the door) St Crispin seated in a shoemaker's workshop; (in the south transept) a 16C St Sepulchre, an early-19C memorial by David d'Angers to the Count of Frotté, and (opposite) a statue of St Theresa of the Child Jesus with a solemn expression; (above the confessional) *Resurrection of Lazarus*, a canvas by JB Van Loo; (in the Holy Sacrament Chapel) a 15C polychrome statue of the Virgin with an apple; (near the font) John the Baptist; (at the end of the south aisle) a 16C Pietà beside the great 18C organ; (in the nave) a handsome wrought-iron pulpit (Louis XVI period). The nave ceiling is vaulted in wood.

Église Notre-Dame – The church, which was built of the red agglomerate stone known as *grison* in the 12C and has been remodelled, possesses a number of 16C **statues★** carved by local sculptors.

1) St Denis (14C)
2) St James the Great
3) St Christopher
4) St Christine
5) St Fiacre
6) St Susanna
7) St Barbara
8) St Francis of Assisi
9) St Benedict
10) Joan of Arc, as a Lorraine country girl
11) Renaissance Pietà
12) St Lawrence
13) St Augustine
14) St Denis with open skull
15) St Louis (17C)
16) Two Prophets (Renaissance woodwork)
17) St Sebastian (17C woodwork)
18) 15C chest and altar base
19) 11C font
20) 14C Trinity (early Norman Renaissance)
21) Virgin at Calvary (13C)
22) St John

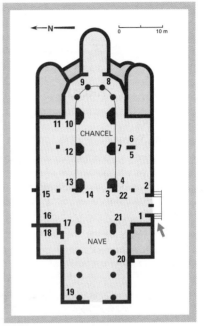

EXCURSION

Francheville – *9km/5mi northwest on D 56*. The village, located in an attractive setting beside the River Iton, has a pretty country church, restored, with interesting folk statues. On the square stands a small **Musée de la Ferronnerie** (Ironwork Museum) ⊘.

VALLÉE DE L'AVRE

From Verneuil-sur-Avre to Nonancourt

20km/12mi – 45 min. From Verneuil take D 839 to the south; turn left onto D 316 which continues as D 102.

The road runs along the pleasantly shaded south bank of the Avre.

Continue via Montigny-sur-Avre and Bérou-la-Mulotière, to Tillières.

Tillières-sur-Avre – Tillières was the first Norman fortified town built (1013) to guard the Avre defence line. The church, with its Romanesque nave and panelled vault was rebuilt in the 16C. Badly damaged by fire in 1969, restoration work has been carried out. Note the carvings on the beautiful pointed arch vaulting of the chancel (16C), the work of the Jean Goujon School. From the garden known as the Grand Parterre there is a fine view of the village and the Avre Valley.

From Tillières-sur-Avre take N 12 east to Nonancourt.

The **Église St-Lubin** *(south of the river in St-Lubin-des-Joncherets)* was rebuilt in the 16C, also in the Flamboyant style; the façade is Renaissance in style. The nave has a panelled ceiling and is flanked by rib vaulted aisles ornamented with Renaissance medallions. The 17C font is decorated with a delightful Nativity. In the south aisle there is a fine marble by Nicolas Coustou of President de Gramont who died in 1658.

Nonancourt – Like Verneuil and Tillières, Nonancourt was a Norman frontier fortress on the Avre defence line facing France. It was built in 1112 by Henry Beauclerk to protect the Duchy of Normandy against the Capetians.

There are several typical half-timbered houses in place Aristide Briand and a fine corbelled house on the corner of the main street.

The Flamboyant-style **Église St-Martin** ⊘ dates from 1511. The belfry dates from 1204. The stained glass in the nave (16C) depicts Holy Week, the Passion and the Ascension of Christ. The Renaissance organ is the most interesting of the furnishings. In the north aisle, near the font, is a 15C statue of St Anne; the Lady Chapel (right) contains a 14C Virgin and Child.

Take N 12 west to return to Verneuil-sur-Avre.

VERNON ★

Population 23 659
Michelin map 55 folds 17 and 18 or 231 fold 36

Vernon, which is close to the forest of the same name, was created by **Rollo**, first Duke of Normandy, in the 9C. It became French during the reign of Philippe Auguste early in the 13C and is now an extremely pleasant residential town.

A STROLL THROUGH TOWN

Park near the Clemenceau bridge (access from boulevard du Maréchal-Leclerc or rue de la Ravine).

Bridge Viewpoint – From the bridge there is a view of Vernon, the wooded islands in the Seine and the ruined piles on which the 12C bridge stood.

On the right bank half-hidden in the trees are the towers of Tourelles Castle which formed part of the defences of the old bridge.

Turn left and walk along the Seine.

The riverside walk takes you by the 18C Bourbon-Penthièvre house, named for the last Duke of Vernon. The street of the same name leads into the **old town**. Notre-Dame Church stands at the end of the pretty street with some half-timbered houses. Notice the 16C façade embellished with Gothic sculptures at no 15.

★**Église Notre-Dame** – This 12C collegiate church was remodelled several times before the Renaissance. The 15C west front has a beautiful rose window flanked by galleries. The nave, also 15C, is higher than the transept and chancel, its triforium and tall windows having considerable beauty of line. The Romanesque arches in the chancel were superimposed by an upper tier in the 16C, the period also of the organ loft and the windows in the second chapel off the south aisle.

To the left of the church, in front of the town hall, the tourist office is lodged in a beautiful half-timbered 15C building, with an over-hanging upper story. It is one of the oldest houses in Vernon. On the corner post, there is a carving of the Annunciation.

Eating out

MID-RANGE

Les Fleurs – *71 r. Carnot* – ☎ *02 32 51 16 80* – *closed 6-13 Mar, 30 July to 21 Aug, Sun evening and Mon* – *19.82/33.54€.* Located in the town centre, this 15C house reveals its cosy, conventional decor and Louis XV furniture, a setting conducive to the appreciation of fine varied cooking.

Le Relais Normand – *11 pl. d'Évreux* – ☎ *02 32 21 16 12* – *closed Sun except holidays* – *19.82/29.73€.* This restaurant of the Hôtel d'Évreux *(see below)* serves traditional fare based on fresh produce in the fine dining room or in the lovely patio as soon as the weather permits.

Where to stay

MODERATE

Hôtel d'Évreux – *11 pl. d'Évreux* – ☎ *02 32 21 16 12* – 🅿 – *14 rooms: 32.01/53.36€* – ☕ *5.34€* – *restaurant 19.82/29.73€.* This 17C house, once the residence of the Earl of Évreux, became a coaching inn before it was converted into a hotel. As a reminder of its former glory, the drawing room has retained its elegant decor and, when the rooms were redecorated, their antique materials were carefully preserved.

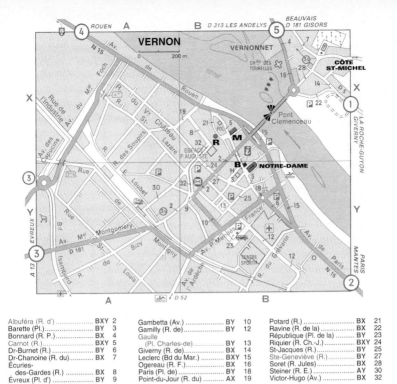

The priests of the old collegiate church live in rue du Chapitre, along the right side of the church; in the same street there is a 17C house (nos 3-5).

There are other interesting old houses in rue Carnot and rue Potard, in particular.

★**Côte St-Michel** – *1hr on foot there and back – depart from Vernonnet, north bank, and take rue J.-Soret as far as the church, turn right and follow the signs.*

From the top of the hill there is a good view of Vernon and the Seine Valley.

SIGHTS

Musée A.-G.-Poulain ⊘ – A wrought-iron door opens onto the courtyard of the museum which is arranged in several buildings dating from the 15C to the 19C. The collections concentrate on prehistory, paintings and drawings and include works by Monet, Rosa Bonheur, Maurice Denis, Pierre Bonnard, Vuillard and Steinlen (1859-1923).

Tour des Archives ⊘ – The tower was the keep of the 12C castle built by Philippe Auguste. The ground floor, first and second floors and the sentry walk are accessible by a spiral staircase. The first floor room has quadripartite vaulting supported by four carved capitals and is decorated with the arms of the four governors of the castle between the 14C and the 17C.

From the sentry walk there is a view over the town and its surroundings.

EXCURSION

★**Giverny** – *See GIVERNY.*

★**Château de Bizy** ⊘ – *4km/2mi west of Vernon by D 181.* The château was begun in 1740 by Coutant d'Ivry for the Maréchal de Belle-Isle, grandson of Fouquet; it was remodelled, except for the stables, by subsequent occupants, the Duc de Penthièvre, King Louis-Philippe and Baron de Schicker.

The Classical architecture presents a handsome front with colonnades and oculi facing the park. The courtyard is bordered by the more austere south front and the outbuildings and the stables, which house a collection of old cars.

The rooms are decorated with beautiful Regency woodwork, 18C tapestries and furniture in the Empire style and souvenirs of Napoleon and the present owners' ancestors, Maréchal Suchet, Maréchal Masséna and Maréchal Davout. Fine carved oak staircase.

Salon of the Château de Bizy

The **park** was laid out in the 18C by Garnier d'Isle and redesigned in the English style by King Louis-Philippe. It has retained some splendid walks lined with lime trees (reaching down to the Seine in some cases) and is decorated with 18C statues (including the sea horses) fountains and ponds. Thanks to recent renovation work, the *chemin d'eau* (waterway) has been restored to its former glory, leading from the Bassin de Gribouille to the footbath in the main courtyard.

Signal des Coutumes – *8km/5mi from Vernon. Take N15 out of town and after 5km/3mi, just before Port-Villez, turn right on D 89.*

Notre-Dame-de-la-Mer – From the look-out point by the chapel, you can gaze out over the river as it flows between Bonnières and Villez.

Carry on along D 89. At the town hall of Jeufosse, make a sharp turn to the left and leave the paved road on the right. Outside the hamlet of Les Coutumes, take a paved road to the right, which leads to the egde of the woods.

Signal des Coutumes – There is a lovely, broad **view**★ over the Bonnières meander from this site.

★★THE VEXIN NORMAND

From Vernon to Rouen

100km/63mi – allow 5hr

The road in the main runs parallel to the right bank of the Seine, sometimes at a distance through the farmlands of the alluvial plain, sometimes between the river bank and the bare escarpment to be found at each hollow bend.

From Vernon take D 313.

Between Pressagny-l'Orgueilleux and Port-Mort, the road crosses a plain ringed by a semicircle of hills. Near the junction with D 10 there is a dolmen *(right)*, known as the Gravier de Gargantua (Gargantua's Pebble), standing in a field.

In Courcelles-sur-Seine cross the river to the south bank.

Gaillon – Gaillon, which became the property of the archbishops of Rouen at the time of Philippe Auguste, was made famous at the end of the 15C by **Georges d'Amboise**, the first of France's great Cardinal-Ministers. After an expedition to Italy, led by Louis XII, the prelate rebuilt Gaillon Castle in the new Italian style (1497-1510), thus launching the Renaissance movement in Normandy. Near the church in the main street stands an attractive 16C wooden house. The vast **château** *(the access roads branch north off N 15 going west to Rouen)*, which is perfectly situated and now belongs to the Fine Arts School, was stripped of its riches during the Revolution. The entrance lodge with its Renaissance-style decoration, is flanked by two towers.

From Gaillon take D 65 north. In Villers-sur-le-Roule turn right onto D 176.

There is a fine **view**★ south of Tosny. A suspension bridge carries the road over the Seine to Les Andelys and Gaillard Castle superbly sited on the cliff.

Eating out

MODERATE

Chez Dédé – *Les Écluses* – *27380 Amfreville-sous-les-Monts* – ☎ *02 32 49 80 06* – *closed 1-15 Jan and Tues* – *13.57/20.58€*. Located on the banks of the Seine, this restaurant organises dancing sessions in the afternoon and popular dancing in the evening, when people waltz or dance the tango to the sounds of the accordion as in the good old days. Simple snacks: mussels and chips or deep fried smelt.

★★Les Andelys – *See Les ANDELYS.*
  From Les Andelys to Muids the road (D 313) runs at the foot of strangely jagged chalk escarpments bordering the river. The outcrop at La Roque has an almost human profile.
  Beyond Muids (D 65) the escarpment is visible on the opposite bank, in accordance with the action of the water flow.
  In Amfreville-sous-les-Monts turn right onto D 20 which climbs rapidly to the top of the hill; park 50m/55yd beyond the TCF viewing table.

★★Côte des Deux-Amants – From a bend in the road there is a magnificent view of the Seine Valley: Amfreville Locks and Dam and the bend in the Seine.
  In the 12C, Marie de France, the first French woman writer, told the touching story of Caliste and Raoul. The King of Pitres did not want to give away his daughter so he decreed that her future husband would have to be strong enough to run non-stop to the top of the nearby hill with Caliste in his arms. Raoul, the son of a count, made an attempt but collapsed and died from exhaustion at the top of the hill and Caliste fell dead beside him; the two young people were buried on the spot and so the hill acquired their name.

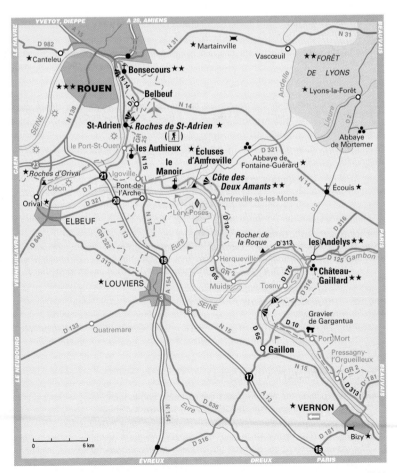

341

★**Écluses d'Amfreville** – The locks together with the Poses Dam constitute the main control of the water flow in the Lower Seine and divide the canalised stretch below Paris from the tidal section which flows into the Channel. The **tour** *(hour)* includes the main lock (220m/722ft long by 17m/56ft wide) which can accommodate 15 boats (38m/125ft in length) and the smaller lock, able to receive six of the same length; the locks are operated by a central control station fitted with a television circuit. Take the footbridge overlooking the locks to see the water pouring over the Poses Dam; go over to the left bank where a recent (1992) mini hydroelectric power station can generate 8 000kW. Along the bank, a spillway specially designed for fish with an observation room shows how the different species make their way upstream... By following the towpath which skirts the village of Poses over a distance of 1.7km/1mi, you will come across the *Fauvette*, a tug built in 1928, and the barge called the *Midway*, which are being converted into a Musée de la Batellerie sur la Seine (River Transport Museum).

Le Manoir – The new church preceded by a detached belfry is a plain, modern building. A vast composition in glass by Barillet makes up the pierced façade which also gives a warm light to the interior.

In Igoville turn right onto N 15 which cuts across the neck of a promontory which points towards Elbeuf on the south bank.

Les Authieux-sur-le-Port-St-Ouen – The church has a fine series of Renaissance stained-glass windows.

Opposite Le Port-St-Ouen on the south bank the first industrial plants on the outskirts of Rouen begin to appear.

North of St-Adrien turn right onto D 7 which climbs up to the plateau at Belbeuf.

Chapelle St-Adrien – Situated 20m/65ft below the road, the 13C chapel is partly built inside the cliff and partly thatched.

🔼 *South of Belbeuf turn sharp right onto rue de Verdun; bear left, then right, cross a forest crossroads and take the first right; park near the housing development; take the path (45min on foot there and back) to the rocks.*

★**Roches St-Adrien** – The bare rock spur provides a very attractive view of the river and of the Rouen conurbation to the north.

Belbeuf – The small church, guarded by its old yew tree, is pleasantly situated. The château dates from the 18C; the park, badly damaged during the war, is being restored.

Turn left onto N 14.

As the road descends below the basilica in Bonsecours, there is a grand **panorama**★★ of green islands in the river and of Rouen and its cathedral.

VILLEDIEU-LES-POÊLES

Population 4 356
Michelin map 59 fold 8 or 231 fold 27

The town occupies a bend in the River Sienne and is an important road junction. It takes part of its name (*poêle* means pot or frying pan) from the making of pots and pans which was a local activity as early as the 12C. At the height of this activity in 1740, there were as many as 139 workshops in the town. From making the great round-bellied copper milk churns *(cannes)* the local factories have converted to the manufacture of copper and aluminium boilers for domestic and industrial use and of souvenirs. Other industries, such as the bell foundry and leather tanning, contribute to Villedieu's reputation.

The town has retained its medieval appearance with many attractive inner courtyards (cour des Trois Rois, cour aux Lys, cour aux Moines), stepped streets and alleys and old houses.

DISCOVERING VILLEDIEU

Take our advice and enjoy a stroll early in the morning, or visit the town out of season – it is a lovely place and attracts big crowds of tourists.

Église Notre-Dame – This 15C church in the Flamboyant Gothic style was built on the site of a 12C church erected by the Brothers of Mercy of St John of Jerusalem. The square transept tower over the crossing is emblazoned with various heraldic emblems.

The Great Coronation and the Knights of Malta

A few years after their creation in the late 12C, the Order of the Hospitallers of St John of Jerusalem established a commandery near Villedieu, on the banks of the River Sienne; it is believed to be the very first one in France. In 1530 they changed their name to the Knights of Malta and renamed the city Villa Dei (Villedieu). In the 17C a priest-commander founded the Brotherhood of the Holy Sacrament (the Great Sacrament or the Eucharist) and introduced the "Great Coronation", another name for Corpus Christi. In 1955 it was decided to re-establish links with the Order of Malta, whose members now take part in the commemorative event. Every four years, on the fourth Sunday after Pentecost, the city is seized with religious fervour and participates in the solemn celebrations. After a dignified welcome in church and High Mass sung in the park of the former commandery, the procession starts at 3pm and slowly advances throughout the town. In each neighbourhood the population make altars of repose devoted to various religious themes. More than 30 000 people attend the Great Coronation; the next edition will take place in the year 2004.

At the entrance the eye is drawn immediately to the chancel: an 18C gilt wooden tabernacle flanked by two Villedieu copper vases and supported by an 18C painting representing the Adoration of the Holy Sacrament.

The church contains various statues: (in the north aisle) a late-15C stone group of Our Lady of Mercy (the figures are not well proportioned), (in the right transept chapel) St Elisabeth of Hungary (17C), St Barbara and St Joachim, father of the Virgin Mary, wearing a turban (17C), polychrome wooden statues.

Atelier du Cuivre ⊘ – Here is the history of copper working in Villedieu: the copper deposits, various techniques of copper working (audio-visual presentation) and a tour of the workshop to see the craftsmen at work embossing, galvanizing, hammering, burnishing or polishing. An explanatory panel describes the making of a ewer from the raw material to the finished product, describing the art of the coppersmith.

Musée de la Poeslerie and Maison de la Dentellière ⊘ – This mansion, now restored to its original appearance, contains a reconstruction of a workshop illustrating the copper-making process in the past and an exhibition of old copperware. The lacemaker's house displays specimens of Villedieu lace, which was very popular in the 18C, old lacemaking frames, bobbins and a collection of lace.

Fonderie de Cloches ⊘ – The foundry was established by the Knights of St John of Jerusalem and this unique workshop has retained a certain charm. The foundry still produces bells for belfries, ships and other public buildings, and they are exported worldwide. The guided tour, conducted by a skilled craftsman, includes the furnaces, moulds made of a refractory substance (mixture of clay, goats' hair and horses' dung) and the deep pits where the moulds are filled with the molten metal and left to cool. The tonality of the bells depends on their weight and diameter.

Maison de l'Étain ⊘ – An exhibition of over 200 moulds and a working potter's workshop illustrate the art of pewter-working in the past.

Royaume de l'Horloge ⊘ – This small but neatly arranged museum cum repair and restoration workshop gives an insight into the Norman clockmaking tradition in the

Fonderie de Cloches

18C. The various clocks and watches demonstrate the progression from lantern clocks to 30-hour timepieces showing an increasing use of iron with brass for the cogs and dials and finally the 8-day clocks with Franche-Comté movements.

C. Havard/Fonderie de Cloches

Eating out

MODERATE

Manoir de l'Acherie – *In L'Acherie, 3.5km/2.2mi E via N 175 bypass and D 554 – 50800 Villedieu-les-Poêles* – ☎ *02 33 51 13 87 – closed 6-22 Nov, Feb school holidays, Sun evening from Nov to Mar and Mon except lunch in July-Aug – 14.48/36.59€.* If you wish to admire at leisure the "Norman bocage" scenery (farmland crisscrossed by lanes and hedges), stop for a moment in this 17C manor house with its colourful garden, the lovely shine of its dark wood and its old stonework. The cuisine is plentiful, with grills sizzling on a wood fire in the fireplace. A few rooms with solid-wood furniture.

Where to stay

MODERATE

La Gaieté Bed and Breakfast – *2 r. St-Georges – 50320 Beauchamps – 10km/6.2mi west of Villedieu-les-Poêles towards Granville* – ☎ *02 33 61 30 42* – ⌷ – *5 rooms: 28.97/33.54€.* This impressive stone house with adjacent garden, situated on the roadside, is adequately soundproof. The recently decorated rooms are accessible up a staircase with lovely old boxwood banisters.

Musée du Meuble normand ⊙ – The first exhibit of this Norman Furniture Museum is a typical rural interior (1750) from the Coutances area. The furniture collection includes pieces from all over Normandy and date from 1680 to 1930 *(see illustration p 47)*. The many diverse items – traditional Norman cupboards, buffets, chests, longcase clocks, a baker's kneading trough and hosiery forms – are regrouped by *département*.

EXCURSIONS

★★Abbaye de Hambye ⊙ – *12km/8mi north of Villedieu by D 9 and D 51.* Beside the River Sienne are the majestic ruins of Hambye Abbey which was founded in about 1145 by Guillaume Paynel, lord of the manor. The **church★** is imposing although it lacks a roof, a west front and the first bay of the nave. The narrow 13C nave was extended in the 14C by three bays. The lack of ornamentation is redeemed by the romantic note supplied by the slender lancet windows.

Above the transept crossing, once capped by rib vaulting, is a square two-storey belfry with twinned, round-headed bays.

The exceptionally large Gothic chancel has pointed arches, an ambulatory and radiating chapels; two tombstones at the centre mark the graves of Jeanne Paynel, the last descendant of the founders of Hambye, and of her husband, Louis d'Estouteville (15C).

The lay brothers' refectory (now used as a conference room) is furnished with 17C Rouen tapestries and a collection of old furniture; the dormitory (above) is used as a repository for liturgical ornaments.

VILLEDIEU-LES-POÊLES

Around the old cloisters are several rooms: the sacristy, a narrow cradle-vaulted chamber containing a 16C painted wood Pietà; the Norman Gothic chapter-house; the Hall of the Dead, a little room decorated with frescoes; the warming room adorned with a handsome 14C wooden crucifix; the kitchen and its vast fireplace. A fine collection of paintings of Hambye is displayed in the stables.

★**Mont Robin** – *13km/8mi north by D 999. 2km/1mi beyond Percy turn right towards Tessy-sur-Vire and right again almost immediately to Mount Robin. Park beside the gate (left); walk across the grass field, to the calvary beside the television relay mast.*

From this point (276m/905ft) there is an expansive **view** east towards the direction of the Suisse Normande. By climbing the rocky mound to the right of the calvary there is another viewpoint from which it is possible to see the spires of Coutances Cathedral. On a clear day it is sometimes possible to see the Channel Islands. Follow the road to the end to see more views of the countryside.

Parc zoologique de Champrepus ⊙ – *8km/5mi west by D 924 to Granville. Picnic area and adventure playground.*

⊚ This modern zoo aims essentially at providing the animals in its care with comfort and a suitable environment. Over 80 species are presented in a pleasantly shaded setting of parkland covering 6ha/15 acres: lions, panthers, tigers, ocelots, zebras, bears, llama, kangaroos, deer, monkeys, emus and exotic birds. There is also an amusement park and various eating establishments open in July and August.

VIMOUTIERS

Population 4 723
Michelin map 55 fold 13 or 231 fold 32

The small town of Vimoutiers is tucked away in the valley of the River Vie between hills covered with apple trees which supply the local cider factories. Vimoutiers has close ties with **Marie Harel**, who gave us the famous Camembert cheese. A statue to her memory, offered by an American cheesemaker, stands on the town hall square.

Musée du Camembert ⊙ – *10 avenue du Général-de-Gaulle in the tourist office.* The exhibition includes the history and different stages in the manufacturing process of Camembert from the arrival of the milk to the dispatching of the final product, with the aid of explanatory documents. Note the impressive collection of Camembert labels.

EXCURSIONS

Camembert – *5km/2mi south by D 246.*

Musée du Camembert ⊙ – Enter through the tourist office. Information on this famous cheese and the place where it is made are presented to visitors through documentation about the village, cheesemaking techniques and the daily use of old-fashioned utensils belonging to the dairy industry.

A few farms can also be visited where cheese is still made in the traditional way.

Prieuré St-Michel de Crouttes ⊙ – *5km/2mi west by D 916 and the third turning to the right.* The origin of this monastic house dates from the 10C when the fief was presented to Jumièges Abbey by the Lord of Crouttes.

The priory is set in the heart of the green and tranquil Auge countryside, half way up the slope, sheltered from the wind and rain; the noble rustic architecture of the buildings is admirably set off by an orchard, gardens and water.

Beyond the 18C dairy, which houses the reception, is the **tithe barn** which dates from the 13C; this majestic building has an impressive roof which rests on an oak timber frame, supported on very low walls which carried the gutters; it is now used for art exhibitions, concerts and summer university courses.

Eating out

MODERATE

La Camembertière – *61120 Camembert – 8km/5mi southwest of Vimoutiers via D 916, D 16 then D 246 –* ☎ *02 33 39 31 87 – closed Jan, Feb and Wed except June-Aug – reservation essential – 12.20/25.92€.* The landscape is sweet like a child's drawing. Here you will taste a choice of camemberts among other carefully matured local cheeses. The owner is a connoisseur and he will give you expert advice. A unique place, not to be missed.

The Making of a Great Cheese

According to the legend, **Marie Harel** (1761-1812), a young girl from the Ferme de Beaumoncel (17C) near Camembert, made cheeses which she sold at the village market. In 1790 she hid a refractory priest from his enemies. In return the grateful clergyman, who was a native of Brie, gave her the secret of his personal cheese recipe and its maturation process: Camembert was born.

In 1863, during the official opening of the Alençon-Paris railway track, one of Marie's descendants offered a slab of her cheese to Emperor Napoleon III. The ruler found it to his taste and insisted that it be served on his dinner table every day from then on. Camembert cheese became wildly popular overnight. The cheese was promptly sent to the capital by train. However, when transported on a bed of straw, it had a tendency to run and therefore could not travel long distances. Until one day the brilliant idea of packing it in a round wooden box was born. Thanks to this ingenious container, Camembert can now be kept fresh for much longer and it can be shipped to countries all over the world.

Some Normandy farms still perpetuate traditional cheesemaking techniques involving milk coming straight from the cow, poured with an old fashioned ladle: the result is a Camembert whose taste and consistency are highly distinctive and succulent beyond comparison!

One can also see the 18C prior's lodging, the chapel (13C) and the bakery, an 18C timber-framed building. The 15C apple press is impressive for the size and shape of its frame.

The old hostelry (14C) houses the **Edgar Chahine Museum**, which is named after a painter-engraver who left a gallery of portraits and scenes from Parisian life in the late 19C.

The most attractive feature of this fine priory are the vegetable and herb gardens, and the rose garden, which contains old varieties of rose tree. The priory houses temporary exhibitions of contemporary sculpture.

VIRE

Michelin map 59 folds 9 and 10 or 231 fold 28

Vire stands on a hillock overlooking the rolling Normandy *bocage*. The town grew up around its castle in the 8C. In the 12C Henry Beauclerc, King of England, strengthened the castle's fortifications and built the keep.

In the 13C the population increased, trade flourished and Vire developed apace. The Wars of Religion were detrimental to the town and it lost its military significance in 1630 when Richelieu dismantled the castle. The 17C and 18C were once again a period of prosperity for Vire when both agriculture and trade flourished.

Vire is an important road junction and as such it was almost annihilated in 1944.

The marked itinerary "L'Affrontement" (The Attack), one of several described in the Historical Area of the Battle of Normandy, goes through this town.

SIGHTS

Église Notre-Dame – This 13C-15C church was erected on the site of a Romanesque chapel built by Henry Beauclerc, Henry I of England. The 13C doorway is flanked by a square turret with a slate roof. The belfry is a square tower with mullioned windows and is crowned by a balustrade.

The five-bay nave has octagonal capitals on its main arches; the triforium has two windows per bay. The chancel, with its slender columns is decorated with a Flamboyant frieze of interlacing. The south transept has a gilt Baroque altarpiece and a Pietà, a wood sculpture by a 19C artist from Lisieux.

Vire Chitterlings

This well-known local speciality *(andouille)* is prepared to a traditional recipe. The stomach and the smaller intestines of the pig are cleaned, chopped, salted and marinated and then stuffed into the larger intestine which is smoked over a beechwood fire for several weeks. The black colour produced by the process is proof of authenticity. The sausage-like chitterlings are then cooked in water and tied off.

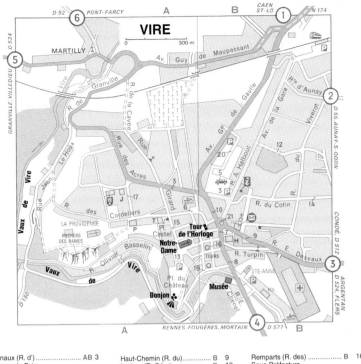

Donjon – The ruins of the square keep of the castle (12C) stand on a promontory, place du Château; there is a view down to the Vaux de Vire (west) and the lock (east). Fireplaces and windows are still visible in the surviving walls.

Vaux de Vire – *Access via rue du Valhérel.* The Vaux de Vire is the name given to the steep-sided Vire and Virenne valleys close to where they meet. Towards the end of the 14C, cloth-workers from Coutances came to live and work in the Vaux. The area became an industrial zone with many fulling mills. *Vaux de Vire* is also the name of the collection of songs of a textile worker, Olivier Basselin, who lived in these parts in the 15C and from which the word *Vaudeville* was later derived.

Eating out

MODERATE

Ferme-auberge La Petite Fosse – *La Petite Fosse – 14500 St-Germain-de-Taillevende – 3km/1.9mi south of Vire towards Mortain then a minor road – ☎ 02 31 67 22 44 – reservation advisable – 11.43/14.48€.* Would you like to be given the opportunity of tasting farm veal and chicken? The owner is happy to oblige and will even offer to serve a good home-made cider with the meal. When you book, don't forget to ask for a table near the fireplace.

Au Vrai Normand – *14 r. A.-Gasté – ☎ 02 31 67 90 99 – michael-wahl@aol.com – closed Sun evening, Tues evening and Wed evening – 10.52€ lunch – 14.94/25.15€.* Situated within easy reach of the main sights of the town, this small restaurant, decorated with pastel shades, has a few tables outside for those who insist on having lunch in the open. The chef uses butter and cream in moderation, a good point for those who are watching their figure!

Where to stay

MODERATE

Le Champ Touillon Bed and Breakfast – *14350 Campeaux 15km/9mi N of Vire via N 174 – ☎ 02 31 68 75 02 – ⇌ – 4 rooms: 25.92/33.54€ – meal 13€.* A pleasant family atmosphere welcomes guests in this old farm. The rooms are fairly plain but the dinner gets full marks: country food, home-made *charcuterie*, poultry and cider from the farm...

Tour de l'Horloge ⊘ – The centrepiece of the main square is the old main gate (13C) to the fortified town, flanked by twin towers and surmounted by a 15C belfry. It took its present name in 1840 when the belfry was added; the stone dome was to serve as a watchtower and house a public clock. The gate bears the arms of Vire – an arrow, point down, flanked by two crenellated towers. A spiral stair climbs to the top; there is a beautiful **view** of the surrounding countryside, the Vaux de Vire *(see below)* and Mount Pinçon topped by a television mast.

South of the clock tower in rue des Remparts are two 13C towers – St-Sauveur and Tour aux Raines – once part of the town's fortifications.

Musée ⊘ – The museum, which is housed in the medieval hospital (Hôtel Dieu), is devoted to the arts and traditions of the locality. The ground floor has a series of workshops: sabot maker, basket maker, saddler, cooper, blacksmith and wheelwright. The history of the town is illustrated by documents, drawings and photographs. On the first floor there is a collection of Norman furniture (cupboards, dressers and a baby's walking frame), headdresses and costumes. On the second floor are drawings, paintings and sculpture; note the drawings and caricatures by **Charles Léandre** (1862-1934), a native of Orne, who illustrated the works of Flaubert and Courteline. There are sculptures by Pompon (1855-1933) and Anne-Marie Profillet (1898-1939). The chapel houses a small French organ; concerts of Baroque music are given during the season.

EXCURSIONS

Plan d'Eau de la Dathée – There is a good general view of the lake (43ha/106 acres) from the dam at the east end; there is also a walk (7km/4mi) round the shore. A water sports centre, a bird reserve and picnic area make the reservoir a popular place for an outing.

Normandy Sweetmeats

Visiting a new region of France also involves discovering its local products and sampling new dishes. Here are a few specialities for those with a sweet tooth.

Deauville-Trouville
Planches de Deauville: small slabs of shortbread shaped as planks

Évreux
Pétales de rose: rose-flavoured dark chocolate sweets
Zouzous: praline pastry coated in chocolate and flavoured with raspberry

Fécamp
Caïques: caramel, almond and hazelnut sweet with Benedictine liqueur coated in dark chocolate
Calettes: hazelnuts coated in dark chocolate

Le Havre
Dominos du pays: domino-shaped plain chocolates

Rouen
Les 100 clochers de Rouen: chocolates filled with baked apples steeped in Calvados and Pommeau
Larmes de Jeanne: roasted almonds, lightly caramelised, coated in chocolate sprinkled with cocoa

Vimoutiers
Étriers normands: chocolates filled with burnt almonds

Mont Orgueil Castle overlooking `Gorey harbour

The Channel Islands

The bailiwicks

For many people the name of the Channel Islands conjures up a northern mini paradise providing a tax haven for the very rich or sun and sand for the carefree holidaymaker. Although the Channel Islands have been associated with the English crown since the Norman conquest, they lie much nearer to the French coast and were largely French-speaking until the 20C. Beneath their apparent Englishness lie 1 000 years of Norman tradition and sturdy independence. Under self-government the Channel Islands have fostered a most attractive relaxed atmosphere.

Owing to their situation and the Gulf Stream, the islands enjoy a mild climate that nurtures spring flowers and semi-tropical plants. Local features echo not only Normandy but also Cornwall; long sandy beaches contrast with rugged cliffs; quiet country lanes meander between traditional granite houses. Tidal currents in the islands are among the strongest in the world; at low water, when the sea may retreat as much as 12m/40ft, huge areas of rocky reefs are exposed, greatly increasing the land mass and making it possible to walk seaward (up to 3km/2mi). All the islands encourage and control tourism, constructing marinas to attract sailors, ensuring clean beaches for surfers and swimmers, and conserving the countryside to the delight of birdwatchers, walkers and cyclists.

Constitution – The Channel Islands are divided into the **Bailiwick of Jersey**, which includes two rocky islets – the Minquiers and the Ecréhou – and the **Bailiwick of Guernsey**, which includes Alderney, Sark and Brecqhou, Herm and Jethou. The original Norman laws and systems enshrined in the first charters granted by King John in the 13C have been renewed by subsequent monarchs, although modifications were introduced this century to separate the judiciary from the legislature.

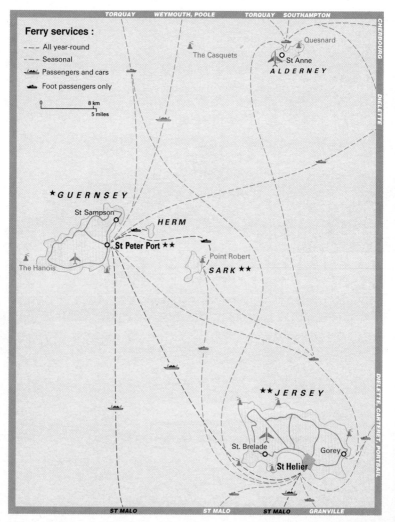

Channel Island stamps

With kind permission from the Post Offices of Jersey and Guernsey

353

Language – English is now the universal language of the islands; the native tongue, a dialect of Norman-French, the language of William the Conqueror, is rarely spoken. In Jersey and Guernsey, societies for its preservation exist which trace the regional variations in vocabulary and pronunciation. In Jersey the dialect is called Jerriais and those who speak it are called Jersiais.

Wrecks and lighthouses – The Channel Islands are surrounded by extensive offshore reefs and rocky islets. The coast, together with strong tides, treacherous currents and fog, make these seas some of the most hazardous in Britain, claiming many ships. Among those documented are a Roman galley which sank off St Peter Port; the *White Ship* carrying the heir to the English throne which foundered on the Casquets in 1119; *HMS Victory*, which went down on the Casquets in 1774 with the loss of 1 000 men; the *Liverpool*, the largest sailing ship wrecked in the Channel Islands, which ran aground off Corblets Bay due to fog in 1902; the *Briseis*, which struck a reef off Vazon Bay in 1937 with 7 000 casks of wine on board; the *Orion*, an oil rig mounted on an ocean-going barge, which ran aground off Grand Rocques in Guernsey in 1978. There are now four lighthouses owned by Trinity House in the Channel Islands.

The earliest to be built was the one marking the **Casquets** (1723); then followed the three towers, known as St Peter, St Thomas and Donjon (30ft high), which were lit by coal fires. In 1770 oil lamps were introduced, and in 1818 revolving lights which had to be wound every 2hr. The main light (37m/120ft above sea-level) now has a range of 27km/17mi in clear weather. The story of the lightkeeper's daughter, who found life on Alderney too noisy, is beautifully told by Swinburne in his poem *Les Casquettes*.

The **Hanois Lighthouse** was built in 1862 on the treacherous Hanois Reef. The first approaches for a light were made to Trinity House in 1816 but 43 years passed before the decision to build was taken. The tower (117ft above sea-level; 32ft in diameter) is constructed of Cornish granite.

Quesnard Light (1912) on Alderney and **Point Robert** (1913) on Sark are sited on land rather than offshore and can be visited. Point Robert is most unusual in that the light is mounted above the buildings for stores and accommodation which cling to the cliff face like a Greek monastery.

JERSEY ★★

Population 85 150
Michelin Atlas p 5 or Map 403

Jersey is the largest of the Channel Islands (116km²/45sq mi; 9x5mi); it lies close to the coast of France (19km/12mi). It is more or less rectangular and slopes gently from the north coast with its dramatic steep pink-granite cliffs (91-122m/300–400ft), opening here and there into a sandy bay or plunging into the sea, to the couth coast with its firm flat sandy beaches interspersed with rocky outcrops.

Victor Hugo, who spent three years in Jersey (1852-55) before moving to Guernsey, was enchanted: "It possesses a unique and exquisite beauty. It is a garden of flowers cradled by the sea. Woods, meadows and gardens seem to mingle with the rocks and reefs in the sea."

The island is ringed by several circular defensive towers, built in the 18C and 19C and similar to the Martello towers on the south coast of England.

In addition to the delights of the beaches and the countryside, visitors to Jersey can enjoy a wide range of more sophisticated pleasures – theatre and cinema, cabaret and floor shows, discotheques and disco-bars.

Economy – Agriculture has long sustained the islanders: wheat and rye, turnips and parsnips, four-horned sheep supplying wool for the famous Jersey stockings and knitwear (17C), apples for cider (18C), table grapes grown under glass and famous Doyenne de Comice pears. The mild climate continues to favour the cultivation of flowers (daffodils, freesias, carnations and lavender) and vegetables for export (potatoes including the famous Jersey Royal, cabbages, broccoli and tomatoes which became more lucrative than apples). Some crops are grown in the open fields, others under glass. Unique to Jersey is the giant cabbage *(Brassica oleracea longata)* which grows up to 3m/10ft tall.

As traditional industries such as boat building, knitting and fishing have dwindled, more lucrative businesses have developed in tourism and financial services, industries which sustain the highly competitive young residents who have benefited from excellent local education.

Historical notes – The tombs and prehistoric monuments found on the island indicate human habitation between 7500 and 2500 BC. The Roman presence was brief, and in the 6C St Helier arrived and established Christianity. The dominant influence is that of the Normans who invaded the islands in the 10C and left a rich heritage of customs and traditions that survive even today.

After 1204, when King John was forced to cede Normandy to France, the French made repeated attempts to recover the Channel Islands: the last attempt occurred in 1781 when Baron de Rullecourt, a soldier of fortune, landed by night in St Clement's Bay in the southeast corner of Jersey. Taken by surprise the Lt Governor surrendered but under Major Peirson, a young man of 24, the militia and British forces engaged the enemy and defeated them in the main square in what came to be known as the **Battle of Jersey**; both leaders were mortally wounded.

Constitution – Jersey is divided into 12 parishes, which together with two groups of islets, the Minquiers to the south and the Ecréhous to the northeast, make up the Bailiwick of Jersey. The Parliament, known as the States of Jersey, is headed by five officers: the Lt Governor, normally a high-ranking military man who represents the Queen; the Bailiff, a senior judge who acts as President of the States; the Attorney-General and the Solicitor-General who contribute to debates in Parliament in a consultative capacity only – these four officers are appointed by the Crown – the fifth officer is the Dean of Jersey, an Anglican clergyman. Together, they preside over 12 Senators, 12 Constables and 29 Deputies, elected to serve for a period of three to six years – all of whom assume different functions on the different committees.

Famous sons and daughters

The most famous name connected with Jersey is **Lillie Langtry** (1853-1929) – the "Jersey Lily" who became an actress and a close friend of Edward VII and captivated British high society with her beauty – she is buried in St Saviour's churchyard.

The fashionable 19C painter, **Sir John Everett Millais** (1829-96) who won acclaim with his painting entitled *Bubbles*, grew up in Jersey and belonged to an old island family. So too did **Elinor Glyn** (1864-1943), who became a novelist and Hollywood scriptwriter.

The well-known French firm which makes Martell brandy was started by **Jean Martell** from St Brelade.

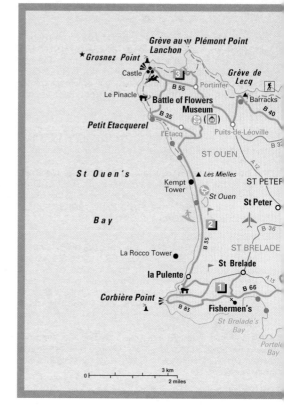

ST HELIER

St Helier is a lively town, the main commercial centre on the island and the seat of government, situated in a sheltered position on the south side of the island. The shops in the pedestrian precinct formed by **King and Queen Streets** are a popular attraction for visitors to the island. English street names have sometimes replaced the more evocative Norman. Church Street was formerly called rue Trousse Cotillon where women had to tuck up their skirts out of the mire.

The town is named after St Helier, one of the first Christian missionaries to land in Jersey, who was murdered by pirates after living as a hermit there for 15 years (c 555). The scant local population was swelled by two waves of refugees fleeing from repercussions of the St Bartholomew Day Massacre (1572) and the Revolution (1789) in France.

Royal Square – The gilded-lead statue of George II, dressed as a Roman emperor, looks down on this charming small square with its spreading chestnut trees; from this point are measured the distances to all the milestones on the island. It was here in the Market Place that malefactors were once exposed in the pillory during market hours and where the Battle of Jersey erupted. Bordering the south side are the granite buildings of the **Royal Court House** ⊙ (**Z J**). The public entrance bears the arms of George II, the Bailiff's entrance the arms of George VI. A plaque records the birth of the Norman poet, **Wace** (1135-74). At the east end of the range of buildings are the **States Chambers** *(entrance round the corner)* where the Jersey Parliament sits in session.

Central Market – The granite building (1882) is furnished with cast-iron grilles at the windows and entrances, and covered with a glass (perspex) roof supported on iron columns. Beneath it open-stall holders proffer local produce to the sound of the fountain, which makes this a lively and colourful scene. The **fish market** is around the corner in Beresford Street.

St Helier Parish Church – The foundation of the present pink-granite church with its square tower pre-dates the Conquest. It was here that Parish business was decided up until 1830 and where the militia cannon was kept until 1844. It

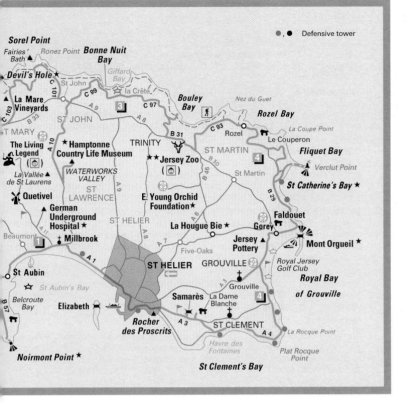

Defensive tower

Sorel Point
Fairies'
Bath
Ronez Point **Bonne Nuit
Bay**
Devil's Hole ★
Giffard
Bay
St John
la Crête
**La Mare
Vineyards**
ST MARY
St JOHN
**Bouley
Bay**
Nez du Guet
Rozel Bay
The Living
Legend
★ **Hamptonne
Country Life Museum**
TRINITY
★★ **Jersey Zoo**
ST MARTIN
La Coupe Point
Le Couperon
Fliquet Bay
La Vallée
de St Laurens
WATERWORKS
VALLEY
ST
LAWRENCE
Rozel
St Martin
Verclut Point
St Catherine's Bay ★
Quetivel
E. Young Orchid
Foundation ★
**German
Underground
Hospital ★**
ST HELIER
Millbrook
La Hougue Bie ★
Gorey
Faldouet
Mont Orgueil ★
Beaumont
Five-Oaks
ST HELIER
GROUVILLE
Jersey
Pottery
Royal Jersey
Golf Club
**Royal Bay
of Grouville**
St Aubin
St Aubin's Bay
Belcroute
Bay
Elizabeth
Samarès
La Dame
Blanche
Grouville
**Rocher
des Proscrits**
ST CLEMENT
La Rocque Point
Havre des
Fontaines
Plat Rocque
Point
Noirmont Point ★
St Clement's Bay

continues to be the seat of the Dean of Jersey – hence the epithet "Cathedral of Jersey". In the south transept hangs a plan of the seating in 1868 showing the names of the pew-holders: the nearer the altar, the higher the rent. The altar cross and candlesticks were a gift from Queen Elizabeth, the Queen Mother.

Museums

Elizabeth Castle ⊙ – *Access on foot by a causeway at low tide (30min); otherwise by amphibious vehicle from West Park Slipway.*

In the 12C William Fitz-Hamon, one of Henry II's courtiers, founded an abbey on St Helier's Isle in St Aubin's Bay. The castle buildings were completed shortly before Sir Walter Ralegh was appointed Governor (1600) and called Fort Isabella Bellissima in honour of Queen Elizabeth I. It was considerably reinforced during the Civil War while occupied by Royalists who, after resisting the repeated assaults from Parliamentary forces on the island, surrendered after a 50-day siege. Contemporary documents confirm that the young Prince of Wales stayed here when fleeing from England in 1646, and again three years later when returning to be proclaimed King Charles II. During the Second World War the Germans added to the fortifications by installing a roving searchlight, bunkers and gun batteries. In 1996 Queen Elizabeth II handed the castle, together with Mont Orgueil, to the islanders. The guard-room displays the various stages in the construction of the castle. The **Militia Museum** contains mementoes of the Royal Jersey Regiment: uniforms, weapons, flags and silver including an unusual snuffbox in the shape of a ram's head.

The Upper Ward encloses the keep, known as the Mount, where the Germans built a concrete fire-control tower surmounted by an anti-aircraft position. There is a fine **view★** of the castle itself and also of St Aubin's Fort across the bay.

South of the castle a breakwater extends past the chapel on the rock where, according to legend, St Helier lived as a hermit *(procession on or about 16 July, St Helier's Day)*.

Eating out

MODERATE

Jersey Pottery Café – *1 Bond St. – JE2 4WH St Helier –* ☏ *01534 725115 – closed evenings and Sun – £3/6*. This is a good place for breakfast or a snack in the centre of St Helier. Run by the owners of the Garden Restaurant in Gorey, this modest yet modern café offers a simple menu: salads, sandwiches and a choice of desserts.

Village Bistro – *JE3 9EP Gorey Village –* ☏ *01534 853429 – closed 3 weeks in Jan or Feb, Tues lunch and Mon – reservation essential – £13.50/28.35*. Look forward to a pleasant meal in the relaxed atmosphere of this family cottage. Specialities include prawn-and-mushroom risotto and orange-flavoured crème brûlée. Lunch menu at attractive price.

Old Court House Inn – *St Aubin Harbour – JE3 8AB St Aubin –* ☏ *01534 746433 – closed 25 Dec – £12/18*. This 15C inn in the harbour has a historic past. You will enjoy its fish and seafood specialities in one of the rooms of the former tribunal or in the reconstructed stern of a galleon. Spacious rooms with a personal touch. Terrace overlooking the harbour.

Le Moulin de Lecq – *JE3 2DT Grève de Lecq –* ☏ *01534 482818 – £8/12*. The paddle wheel of this 12C water mill is still turning! Now converted into a pub with lots of character, the building has retained its mechanism visible in the bar where you can enjoy the local lager or a simple dish. In summer, barbecue in the garden. Playground for children.

Frère de Mer – *Le Mont de Rozel – JG3 GAN Rozel Bay –* ☏ *01534 861000 – closed Mon – £8.95/12.95*. This "brother" is very much in demand! His secret? A menu to satisfy every taste, reasonable prices and a splendid terrace with a view of the sea and the French coast, the latter in fine weather only.

MID-RANGE

Suma's – *Gorey – JE3 6ET Gorey Hill –* ☏ *01534 853291 – closed 23 Dec to end of Jan, Sun evening – reservation essential – £19.50/33.20*. This elegant restaurant is sought after by locals and tourists alike. The bright interior is decorated with works by local artists. In fine weather, you can sit on the terrace and enjoy the view of Mont-Orgueil Castle and of the harbour.

Green Islet – *JE2 GLS St Clement –* ☏ *01534 857787 – closed Sun evening and Mon – £18.95/24.40*. This place is popular with tourists and islanders because of its reasonable prices and its menu based on the availability of fresh produce. Relaxed atmosphere in the dining room with its nautical decor.

Where to stay

MODERATE

La Bonne Vie Bed and Breakfast – *Roseville St. – JE2 4PL St Helier –* ☏ *01534 735955 – 10 rooms: £28/56*. Situated close to the beach and the town centre, this flower-decked Victorian house is meticulously looked after. Warm welcome in these guest rooms which are exquisite with their flowery eiderdowns, curtains and cushions.

Champ Colin Bed and Breakfast – *Rue du Champ-Colin, Hougue Bie – JE2 7UN St Saviour –* ☏ *01534 851877 – closed three weeks at Christmas and New Year's Day – 3 rooms: £35/50*. Peace and quiet are guaranteed in these pleasant guest rooms housed in a 19C farm building. Antique furniture and curios add to the charm of the place. Olde worlde atmosphere in the lovely breakfast room.

MID-RANGE

Elmdale Farm – *Ville Emphrie – JE3 1EF St Lawrence – 4.8km/3mi north of St-Helier –* ☏ *01534 734779 –* 🅿 *– 19 rooms: £39.50/79 – restaurant £8.95/14.95*. This old farm, situated right out in the country, has a renowned restaurant. The guest rooms, located in recently built cottages, are decorated without fuss and have pine furniture. The garden and heated swimming pool call for relaxation in summer.

Moorings – *JE3 6EW Gorey Pier –* ☏ *01534 853633 – 15 rooms: £49/98 – restaurant £14.25/30*. The location of this small unpretentious hotel, just below Mont-Orgueil castle and facing the harbour, will certainly appeal to you. The rooms are well-fitted out and you will receive a warm welcome.

Apollo – *9 St Saviour's Rd – JE2 4GJ St Helier –* ☏ *01534 725441 – www.huggler.com –* 🅿 *– 85 rooms: £51.50/103 – restaurant £7.5/14.8*. A good place for a family holiday. Renovated in 1998, this hotel may look slightly austere but the rooms are spacious and well fitted out. Those who are keen on sport will appreciate the two swimming pools (a covered one and an open-air one with a slide) and the fitness room.

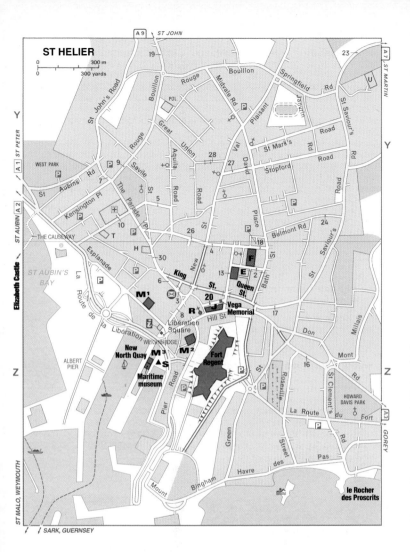

ST HELIER

In this guide town plans show the main streets and the way to the sights;
local maps show the main roads and the roads o the recommended tour.

★**Jersey Museum** ⊘ – Housed in a former merchant's house and adjoining warehouse belonging to Philippe Nicolle (1769-1835) is the local museum which tells the story of the island, its traditions and its industries.

The **ground-floor** area is shared by temporary exhibitions and films about Jersey. The treadmill, which was turned by 12 men and operated a pepper mill, was used in St Helier prison during the 19C. By the stairs is displayed a number of silver toilet articles from the set which accompanied Lillie Langtry on her travels.

On the **first floor**, the history of the island from the Stone Age to the present is unfurled as a series of tableaux: artefacts excavated at La Cotte; archive photographs and interactive screens complemented by historic tools and implements to illustrate traditional farming and fishing practices; the development of Jersey as a Victorian resort and as a centre offering off-shore banking and other financial services.

The **second floor** displays the Barreau-Le Maistre collection of fine art with paintings, drawings and watercolours by local artists or of topographical interest: Sir John Everett Millais PRA (1829-96), PJ Ouless (1817-85), "the Jersey Turner" J Le Capelain (1812-48) and the illustrator Edmund Blampied (1886-1966). Works by **Sir Francis Cook** (1907-78) bequeathed to the Jersey Heritage Trust are on permanent display in their own gallery, a converted Methodist Chapel, in Augrès *(A 8, Route de Trinité)*.

The **third floor** rooms recreate domestic interiors (1861) typical of a middle-class Jersey family.

New North Quay – The most prominent landmark is the world's largest **steam clock** (36ft tall), modelled on a traditional paddle steamer of a type that once shuttled between the islands and Southampton. It was inaugurated in August 1997 as part of the development of the St Helier waterfront.

Maritime Museum and Jersey Occupation Tapestry ⊘ – Installed in converted 19C warehouses, the Jersey **Maritime Museum** is dedicated to celebrating the importance of the sea with changing displays relating to the fishing, ship-building and trading industries and to piracy.

The **Jersey Occupation Tapestry** comprises 12 panels (6x3ft) illustrating the story of the Occupation of Jersey from the outbreak of war to the Liberation: each scene, based on archive photographs and contemporary film footage, has been embroidered by a separate Parish. An audio-visual presentation provides additional background information.

St Clements: Liberation, Jersey Occupation Tapestry

Fort Regent ⊘ – *Access by escalators in Pier Road.*
◉ The massive fortifications of Fort Regent were built to protect Jersey from invasion by Napoleon. Within, topped by a shallow white dome, is a modern leisure centre providing a variety of sports facilities and entertainment: swimming pool, badminton, squash, table tennis, snooker, play area for children, puppet theatre, exhibitions, aquarium, and audio-visual shows on the history and culture of the island. It is also home to the Jersey Signal Station. The rampart walk provides splendid **views**★ of the town and St Aubin's Bay *(west)*.

Island Fortress Occupation Museum ⊘ – A limited collection of military uniforms, flak sheds, weaponry and equipment evoke the five-year German occupation (1940-45). A video tells of the anguish endured and of the relief of the eventual liberation.

Asking the way

Jersey has a number of **cycling routes**, marked by blue signs with white writing, and a network of tree-lined lanes, known as **green lanes**, where walkers, cyclists and horse-riders have priority over the car (maximum speed 15mph/24kmph). There are also long stretches of **coastal footpath**. Most of the principal tourist sites are flagged by brown signs with white writing.

When local Jersey people give directions, they tend to refer to the roads by name rather than number; it is therefore well worth obtaining a Perry's Pathfinder map, which marks footpaths, car parks and refreshment facilities, or the Town and Island Map, which contains information on green lanes, coastal footpaths, sites of special interest, heritage sights and Second World War sites; it is produced by Jersey Tourism which also publishes a cycling and walking guide.

EXCURSIONS INLAND

★★Jersey Zoo

From St Helier take A 8 north to Mont de la Trinité; rue Asplet turn right onto B 31 towards Trinity Church; this road soon becomes rue des Picots passing in front of the zoo (right).

Jersey Zoo ⊘ – *2-3hr*. The Durrell Wildlife Conservation Trust, with its headquarters at Jersey Zoo (Les Augrès Manor), was founded by the naturalist **Gerald Durrell** in 1963 as a unique centre for research and breeding of rare and endangered species. The high rate of success in this prime objective has led to exchanges with other zoos (Bristol, Newquay, Paignton, Dublin, Washington) and the reintroduction of a number of threatened species into native habitats. The symbol of the Trust is the dodo, the great non-flying bird of Mauritius which was first identified in 1599 and was extinct by 1693.

The undulating park (10 acres) is dedicated to providing compatible environments for some 1 000 animals in cages, temperate housing, landscaped enclosures or open garden and woodland. Exotic species of plants are grown to provide the animals with both food and natural cover – their controlled diets being otherwise supplemented with locally produced organic meat, fruit and vegetables.

Residents include babirusas from Indonesia; spectacled bears from the forest uplands of Bolivia and Peru (the only bear indigenous to South America); snow leopards and cheetahs; a long list of birds includes the St Lucia parrot, the Mexican thick-billed parrot, the white-eared pheasant from China, the pink pigeon from Mauritius, the white-naped crane native of Japan and Korea, the Rothschild mynah bird, the Chilean flamingo and the Waldrapp Ibis.

The most popular animals, however, are probably the primates: a dynasty of lowland gorillas descended from the silverback "Jambo" (1961-92); orangutans from Sumatra and the less extrovert lemurs from Madagascar, marmosets and tamarins from Brazil, some of which roam freely in the thick shrubbery.

Tortoises, terrapins, snakes, frogs, toads and lizards, happy to lounge in their warmed enclosures among sprigs of flowering orchids, thrive in the **Gaherty Reptile Breeding Centre**. A special unit enables visitors to observe the activities of rare fruit bats and the intriguingly named aye-aye by subdued artificial light.

★**Eric Young Orchid Foundation** ⊘ – *Victoria Village, Trinity. 1hr. Signs in Victoria village, but the Orchid Foundation is difficult to find.*

J. Morgan/DWCT Photo library

Ring-tailed Lemur

A fabulous show of prize plants appealing to both amateur and professional growers of orchids is presented here in a Display House. The mission of the Foundation is to "promote orchid improvement for all" – it therefore collaborates on a conservation and research basis with the Royal Horticultural Society and the Royal Botanic Gardens at Kew, and other passionate growers ever fascinated by variations in colour and form achieved by hybridisation. Displays are regularly reorganised to ensure constant shows of species, the groups arranged to allow close study of their distinctive blooms. The five adjacent growing houses *(open but roped off)* are dedicated to the genera Cymbidium, Paphiopedilium or slipper orchids, Cattleya, Phalaenopsis or moth orchids, Odontoglossum or butterfly orchids (including Miltonias or pansy orchids).

5km/3mi west. Leave St Helier on the St Aubin road, at Bel Royal, turn right.

★**German Underground Hospital** ⊙ – This large complex of tunnels is kept as a compelling memorial to the forced labourers (Spaniards, Moroccans, Alsatian Jews, Poles, Frenchmen, Russians) who worked on its construction for three and a half years under the severest conditions. Note that some visitors may find the visit rather harrowing, others may suffer from claustrophobia.
Hohlgangsanlagen 8 was intended as a secure, bomb-proof artillery barracks, complete with accommodation and a storage facility for ammunition. In January 1944, still incomplete, it was converted into a hospital equipped with an operating theatre, five 100-bed wards, X-ray room, mortuary, stores, kitchen, staff quarters etc. On entering the long dark galleries hewn deep into the solid rock, the temperature drops, the air is damp, the sound of footsteps is amplified through the concrete emptiness. Wartime films, archive photographs, newspaper cuttings, letters and memorabilia document the personal suffering and trauma of those caught up in the events.
The **Occupation Walk** up onto high ground opposite the complex leads to an area fortified by genuine anti-aircraft gun positions, crawl trenches, barbed wire entanglements and personnel shelters *(leaflet available from the Visitor Centre)*.

Moulin de Quétivel ⊙ – The **mill** (pre-1309), on a bend in St Peter's Valley, is one of several which was operated by the stream until they were made obsolete by steam power. During the German Occupation the machinery was restored for temporary service before being largely destroyed by fire (1969). Since 1979, re-equipped with parts from other disused Jersey mills, Quétivel has been in operation grinding locally grown grain and producing stone-ground flour for sale.
From the mill pond the water is channelled by the mill leat down through the wood (inhabited by red squirrels and woodpeckers) to the mill wheel, a pitch-back overshot wheel. The tour shows each stage of the process from the arrival of the grain by hoist in the loft to the production of stone-ground flour for sale on the ground floor. Most of the grinding stones are made of French burr, quarried near Orly Airport south of Paris; these are composed of segments set with plaster of Paris and last 100 years. A pair of stones will produce 25t of flour before needing to be dressed, when the grooves are recut to the required depth using a tool called a "bill" – this process can take a miller about a week.

Living Legend ⊙ – Inside the granite buildings unfurls the entertaining multi-sensory experience that relates the history and myths of Jersey. The time-travellers explore a labyrinth of mysterious chambers, make their way through castle towers and across the decks of a Victorian paddle steamer to discover the lives of past islanders and stories told of heroes and villains. The atmosphere is enhanced by visual and sound effects (holograms, lasers, wind machines...).

St Peter's Village

Jersey Motor Museum ⊙ – This collection of veteran and vintage vehicles, all in working order and appearing at rallies in Jersey and elsewhere, includes the 1936 Rolls-Royce Phantom III, used by General Montgomery in 1944 during D-Day preparations, and the 1964 Hillman Husky which belonged to Sir Winston Churchill. Cars by Ford, Austin, Talbot, Triumph, Bentley and Jaguar contrast with Allied and German military vehicles, bicycles (c 1869 Boneshaker) and motorbikes. Other items include several period brass lamps, classic pedal- and petrol-driven children's cars, toys, an old AA callbox and a car from the Jersey steam railway.
On the opposite side of the square is an underground bunker built by the German Organization Todt in 1942, strategically placed so as to keep surveillance over the airport and access roads to the west of the island.

St Peter's Church – The parish church has a remarkable steeple (124ft high) which by chance escaped from being faced with cement; at its apex is a red navigation light used by aircraft coming in to land at the airport nearby. Behind the altar is a reredos by George Tinworth, commissioned in the 1880s from Royal Doulton.

★La Hougue Bie ⊙

From St Helier take either A 6 (Route Bagatelle) or A 7 (St Saviour's Hill) north-west; at Five Oaks take A 7 (Princes Tower Road) to the entrance to La Hougue Bie (left).

The tiny park, encircled by trees, is dominated by a high circular mound. Its name may be derived from the Old Norse word *haugr* (meaning barrow) and *bie*, a shorthand for Hambye, a Norman lord who in the Middle Ages came to rid Jersey of a dragon that stalked St Lawrence marsh. During the German occupation, the site was heavily fortified, as it provides an excellent **view** over outlying countryside.

Archeology and Geology Museum – Artefacts displayed were brought to light by local excavations – notably from La Cotte de St Brelade, a sea cave in the Ouaisné headland and the Belle Hougue caves on the north coast: remains of mammoths, polished stone axes, flint tools, stone querns for grinding corn (belonging to Neolithic settlers who were farmers), pottery, ornaments; Bronze Age metal objects found in St Lawrence etc. The geology section presents samples of the various rocks and minerals found on the island: shales (south), volcanic lavas (north), pink and grey granites and diorites (northwest and southwest), Rozel conglomerates or puddingstone.

★**Neolithic Tomb** – The cruciform passage burial chamber, long suspected by archeologists but excavated only in 1924, dates from 3500 BC. Similar tombs have been discovered in England and Brittany. The grave was originally built above ground with upright stones and roofed with granite slabs before being covered by a mound of earth and rubble (12m/40ft). A passage (10m/33ft long) leads to the funeral chamber (3m/10ftx9m/30ft), which is covered with huge capstones (the heaviest weighing 25t); this central space opens into three smaller chambers. The central granite pillar is a modern addition to support the large capstones which were found to be cracked.

Chapels – The mound is surmounted by two medieval chapels: the **Chapel of Our Lady of the Dawn** (Notre-Dame-de-la-Clarté) dates from the 12C; the altar (Late Medieval) came from Mont-Orgueil Castle. The abutting **Jerusalem Chapel** was built in 1520 by Dean Richard Mabon after a pilgrimage to Jerusalem. The interior bears traces of frescoes of two archangels.

German Occupation Museum – A German bunker, built in 1942 as a communications centre, houses radio equipment, weapons, medals, original documents (orders and propaganda) and photographs of the period.

TOUR OF THE ISLAND

① From St Helier to Corbière
18km/10mi – about 2hr

From St Helier take A 1 (Route de St Aubin) west.

Millbrook – The Villa Millbrook was once home to Sir Jesse Boot, the first Baron Trent of Nottingham and founder of Boots the Chemists, who is buried at St Brelade.

St Matthew's Church ⊙ – The **Glass Church**, as it is also known, was unexceptional until 1934 when **René Lalique** (1860-1945), the French specialist in moulded glass, was invited

Jersey Museum Service

Sadie with visitors, Hamptonne Country Life Museum

by Lord Trent's widow to redecorate the interior with distinctive **glasswork**★: the entrance doors are made of panels presenting a row of four angels guarding another behind the main altar. The other decorative element is the flowering lily which appears in the windows, screens and in the Lady Chapel. The luminescent, ethereal quality is most apparent at dusk when the lights are switched on.

Follow the main road (Route de La Haule) and then A 1 (Route de La Neuve).

Lalique angel, Millbrook

St Aubin – The little town, which faces east across St Aubin's Bay, is particularly picturesque with its long sandy beach, fishermen's cottages and tall granite merchants' houses lining steep, narrow streets or clinging to the cliffs along the shore. The name is auspicious as St Aubin, besides being Bishop of Angers (d AD 550) during the lifetime of St Helier, was invoked as protector against pirates.

The local church (1892) has a fine stained-glass window made by William Morris & Co.

St Aubin's Fort on the island *(access at low tide)* was built in the reign of Henry VIII to protect the town which enjoyed considerable prosperity during the 17C.

The Corbière Walk from St Helier to Corbière follows the line of the old **Jersey Railway** which opened in 1870 and ran from St Helier to St Aubin before being extended.

Turn left off the main road onto B 57 (Route de Noirmont) for access to the promontory and Portelet Bay.

★Noirmont Point – The local saying warns of the onset of gales from the southwest:

> *"Quand Nièrmont met san bonnet,*
> *Ch'est signe de plyie."*
> *("When Noirmont [Black Hill] dons his cap,*
> *It is a sign of rain.")*

Beyond the pebble beach nestling in **Belcroute** stretches the headland, still scarred by the remains of substantial German fortifications (1941 and 1943-44) including the **Command Bunker** ⊘ – a post for the naval coastal artillery battery. The most advanced bastion gives fine views of the rocks immediately below and round westwards to the Île au Guerdain, surmounted by a defensive tower, in the centre of Portelet Bay.

The southernmost parts of the promontory have revealed an important Bronze Age burial ground, not far from the site of the famous cave of La Cotte de St Brelade.

Return to the main road A 13 (Route des Genets) and then fork left down B 66 (Mont Sohier).

Noirmont Point

St Brelade – This favourite seaside resort is situated in a sheltered bay; its sandy beaches and usually safe waters *(certain areas can be tricky)* are ideal for swimming and water-skiing. A waterfall tumbles over the rocks on the wooded slopes of the **Winston Churchill Memorial Park** which backs the bay.

At the western end of the beach, behind a screen of trees, the parish church and detached medieval chapel are surrounded by a graveyard. At one time this was the resting place of 337 German servicemen who were on the islands as prisoners during the First World War or on active duty during the Occupation: they were reinterred in 1961 at Mont de Huisnes at St Malo.

Parish Church – *Light switch inside on the left of entrance.* The cherished church of St Brelade is built of granite from the cliffs of La Moye (meaning rocky headland). The earliest parts of the structure – the chancel, nave and belfry – date from the 11C. In the 12C the church became cruciform with the addition of a transept; the aisles were added later.

The altar is a solid slab of stone, marked with five crosses representing the five wounds of the Crucifixion. The 15C font is made of granite from the Chausey Islands, which lie south of Jersey and belong to France.

Fishermen's Chapel – *Light switch inside on the left of entrance.* The family chapel, which is built of the same granite as the church, is decorated in the interior with delicate medieval **frescoes★**. At the east end is an Annunciation – dated as c 1375 from the medieval attire of the donors at prayer; the other paintings are from a second phase of work c 1425: the south wall (right of the altar) shows Adam and Eve followed by The Annunciation and The Adoration of the Magi, the west wall bears The Last Judgement, on north wall fragments have been deciphered as Scenes from the Passion. The survival of the paintings is largely due to the fact that from c 1550 to the mid 19C the chapel was used as an armoury, housing the parochial cannon, and as a carpenter's shop. The windows, by a local craftsman HT Bosdet (1857-1934), narrate the story of St Brendan, who set sail from the west coast of Ireland in the 6C and is thought to have reached the American continent.

Behind the chapel a short flight of steps leads to a path through the churchyard to the beach; this is the only surviving example of a *perquage*: once commonplace in medieval Europe, these paths were intended as escape routes from a chapel or church traditionally a place of sanctuary to the shore and away out to sea.

Continue along the road back into town; turn left onto A 13 (Route Orange); bear left down B 83 (Route du Sud) to Corbière.

Corbière – All that remains of the terminus of the Jersey Railway is the concrete platform. As the road descends, a magnificent view is steadily revealed of the rock-strewn point and the white lighthouse rising from its islet: a good place to watch the sun set over the Atlantic. Before the lighthouse *(access on foot at low tide but closed to the public)* was built in 1874, this was a perilous stretch of water where a number of ships foundered, lost to the tide; in clear weather the electric beam carries 28km/17mi.

② From Corbière to Petit Étacquerel *13km/8mi– 1hr*

Follow the road round to the junction with B 35 (rue de Sergente); turn left towards the coast.

St Ouen's Bay – The major part of this coastline is taken up with this magnificent, open stretch of sand (5mi) backed by sand dunes. The deep surf which rolls into the bay makes it a favourite spot for experienced surfboard and windsurf enthusiasts. The firm sand attracts motor and motorcycle racing fans.

In the middle of the bay sits **La Rocco Tower**, the last round tower to be built in Jersey (1800); having been severely damaged during the war, the tower was finally restored during the 1970s.

Beyond the beach, the landscape is wild and uncultivated, the vegetation sparse. **La Pulente** used to be the main centre for gathering seaweed *(vraic)* which was traditionally used as fertiliser. **La Sergenté**, also known as the Beehive Hut, is another important Neolithic tomb near to which a large hoard of coins from Brittany was found. The **St Ouen Pond** on the right of the road is also known as La Mare du Seigneur as it once belonged to the Seigneur of St Ouen (the most senior of the island seigneurs resident in St Ouen's Manor). This stretch of fresh water is a haven for birds and wild flowers, notably the Jersey or lax-flowered orchid. The three upright stones, Les Trois Rocques, are presumed to be part of a dolmen.

Kempt Tower ⊘ – This defensive tower has been converted into an Interpretation Centre with maps, photographs and pamphlets about the region: geological features, archeological remains, flora and fauna. The area around it has been made into a nature reserve called **Les Mielles** (the Jersey dialect word for sand dunes) to monitor and protect indigenous plants, birds and butterflies.

Follow B 35 (Route des Laveurs); turn left onto C 114 (Mont des Corvées).

Birds to be seen around Les Mielles

Besides such common birds as blackbirds, thrushes, wrens, robins and tits, the sand dunes harbour colonies of kestrels and skylarks and attract such migrants as willow warblers, stonechats and wheatears. Stretches of fresh open water and reed-beds provide popular habitats for moorhens, coots, ducks (mallard, tufted, shoveler), kingfishers, sandpipers, lapwings, herons and snipe. Please show consideration by not disturbing pairs or fledgelings through the nesting and breeding season (April to July).

During the summer, the coastal footpath from Plemont to Grève de Lecq affords good sightings of seabirds: fulmars (May to September), puffins and razorbills – notably early morning and early evening. In winter, Brent geese, plovers, redshanks, turnstones, dunlin, bar-tailed godwits, curlews, oystercatchers, teal, snipe, lapwings and herons may be seen feeding on an incoming tide.

Battle of Flowers Museum ⊘ – ⌧ The **Battle of Flowers**, held on the second Thursday in August along Victoria Avenue in St Helier, was started in 1902 to celebrate the coronation of Edward VII. Traditionally, the floats were broken up after the parade and the crowd pelted one another with the flowers, then mostly hydrangeas. Today, a collection of floats which over the years have been entered in the wild flower category, is here presented by their creator. The tableaux are made up of different grasses and concentrate on animal subjects.

Return to the coastal road; bear right onto B 35 (Route de l'Étacq).

Petit Étacquerel – A defensive tower guards the point which marks the northern end of St Ouen's Bay. It is here that in 1651 Admiral Blake landed with the Parliamentary forces which forced the Royalists to surrender.

③ From Grosnez Point to Rozel Bay *27km/17mi – 2hr 30min*

The northern coast of the island is less densely populated than other parts as steep rocky cliffs alternate with small sandy bays. Cliff paths, which stretch from Plémont Bay to Sorel Point and beyond, provide spectacular views of the uneven coastline and the open sea to France, Guernsey and Alderney (although they say that a clear view of Alderney heralds rain). Early crop potatoes are grown on the steeply sloping hillsides *(côtils)*.

Continue north by bearing left onto B 55 (Route de l'Ouest): bear left again to reach the car park and look-out point at Grosnez.

★**Grosnez Point** – An area of desolate heathland, covered with gorse and heather and known as Les Landes, extends from Étacquerel to Grosnez Point. Southwest of the racecourse sits **Le Pinacle**, a strange yet impressive rock that has been found to be associated with pagan rituals since Neolithic, Bronze Age, Iron Age, even Roman times.

Dramatically positioned overlooking the sea are the ruins of a medieval stronghold which must have provided a place of temporary refuge against invasion. Little remains of **Grosnez Castle** (c 1373-1540) besides the curtain wall with ditch, gateway and drawbridge; however it enjoys magnificent views out to sea, of Sark and the other islands *(northwest)*.

Return to B 55; in Portinfer turn left onto C 105 (Route de Plémont); fork left to Grève au Lançon; eventually the road skirts the holiday village to end in a car park from where a footpath runs along the coast to Grève de Lecq.

Steep cliffs containing caves shelter this attractive small bay, **Grève au Lanchon**, which has a sandy beach at low tide. The rocky promontory **Plémont Point** projects into the sea giving a fine view of the cliffs.

Return along C 105 (Route de Plémont); turn left onto B 55 (Route de Vinchelez) from Grosnez, which leads to Leoville in the parish of St Mary. Turn left onto B 65 (Mont de la Grève de Lecq).

Grève de Lecq – This charming sandy bay with its stream and mill was defended against invasion most recently by the Germans, in the Second World War, and earlier against the French in the 18C-19C. The defensive tower was built in 1780 although the conical hill behind it is from an Iron Age fortification.

The **barracks** ⊘ were built between 1810 and 1815 to accommodate the 150 British soldiers who manned the gun batteries on the slopes around the bay – although blocks were built at Bonne Nuit Bay, Rozel Bay and St Peter's Parish, these here are the only ones to survive. There were two blocks, each consisting of four rooms for the soldiers and two for the NCOs; the central building was for the officers. Behind stood the ablutions block and two prison cells; to the south was the stabling. In spring and early summer the area is abloom with wild flowers: gorse, daffodils, bluebells, foxgloves.

The water's edge is broken by jagged rocks locally known as **Paternoster Rocks** after the many prayers uttered through time by passing fishermen, remembering colleagues who perished there. Far out to sea is the French coast.

From Grève de Lecq continue along B 40 (Mont de Ste-Marie); turn left onto B 33 (La Verte Rue) and left again before the West View Hotel onto C 103.

La Mare Vineyards ⊘ – The estate of an 18C farmhouse has been planted with the only vineyards and cider orchard in Jersey. An introductory video film, describing its history, the vineyards, the harvest and the wine-making process, adds to the interest of touring the vineyards and the gleaming modern vintry, where German-style white wines are produced and may be tasted: Clos de la Mare, Clos de Seyval and Blayney Special Reserve.

Continue along C 103 to the Priory Inn.

★**Devil's Hole** – *Park by the inn and take the concrete path down to the cliff.* The blow hole is an impressive sight dramatised by the amplified thunder of the sea entering the cave below. The name is thought to derive from the old French Creux de Vis meaning screwhole, although other stories tell of the wreck of a French ship in 1871, whose figurehead resembled a devil.

Minor roads run east to St John's Parish and north to the coast.

Sorel Point – The section of road named **Route du Nord** is dedicated to the islanders who suffered during the German Occupation (stone in the car park). It runs from Sorel Point where a mysterious pool (7.3m/24ft wide by 4.6m/15ft deep) is revealed in the rocks at low tide: disputes continue as to whether it is a natural or man-made phenomenon; the pool is known as the Fairies' Bath (Lavoir des Dames). To the east is Ronez Point, a headland scarred by granite quarries.

Drive through St John; turn left onto A 9 (Route des Issues); after the Jersey Pearl Centre fork left again onto B 67 (Route de Mont Mado). Turn left onto C 99, a minor road to Bonne Nuit Bay and Giffard Bay.

Bonne Nuit Bay – This bay, which may well have been haunted by smugglers and pirates in the past, is a favourite place for swimming and sailing. Charles II is supposed to have returned from exile to England from this attractive bay where a stone jetty shelters the tiny harbour. The fort, La Crête, at the east end was built in 1835.

From here a footpath follows the coast to Bouley Bay; to reach Bouley Bay by car, take C 98, B 63, C 97 (rue des Platons).

Bouley Bay – In the 19C it was proposed that the deep sandy bay protected by a jetty and backed by high granite cliffs should be transformed into a sheltered harbour. Today it is a safe, popular place for swimming.

Return towards Trinity; turn left onto B 31 (rue ès Picots) past Jersey Zoo before turning sharp left onto C 93 (rue du Rocquier) to Rozel Bay.

Rozel Bay – Part of the bay is taken up with a fishing port where the boats go aground at low tide. Above the bay, at the northern end, traces of a great earth rampart survive from the Castel de Rozel, an Iron Age settlement. Many coins from different eras have also been recovered from the area. At the opposite end, sits **Le Couperon**, a Neolithic passage grave (2500 BC). Below it, at the water's edge among the rocks at low tide, are a profusion of pools inhabited by small crustacea making it a wonderful place for amateur zoologists and children to explore.

④ **From Rozel Bay to St Helier** *8km/13mi – 1hr 30min*

The road turns inland before returning to the coast above Fliquet Bay and finally meandering down to the water line: a submarine cable runs from the Martello Tower to France.

Fliquet Bay is a rocky bay between La Coupe and Verclut Points: an ideal place for deciphering the volcanic evolution of the island.

Either follow the road to St Martin or make a detour to explore the country roads – B 38 (Grande Route de Rozel), B 91 (rue des Pelles), B 91 (Route du Villot), B 29 (Mont des Ormes) to Verclut Point (left) and to Gorey Harbour (right).

★**St Catherine's Bay** – The long breakwater (0.8km/0.5mi), which protects the bay to the north, was part of a British government scheme (1847-55) to create a huge naval "harbour of refuge" as the French developed coastal stations around Cherbourg: work to build a second breakwater was abandoned in 1852 as relations with Napoleon III improved. From the lighthouse at the end there is a magnificent **view**★★ of sandy bays alternating with rocky promontories along the coast southwards. Out to sea lie the Ecréhou islets administered by St Martin's Parish – once a favoured trading bank for smugglers and now a popular spot for a Sunday picnic.

Eating out

MID-RANGE

Jersey Pottery Garden Restaurant and Brasserie – *JE3 9EP Gorey Village –* ☎ *01534 851119 – closed 23 Dec to end of Jan, evenings and Sun – £21.25/32.25.*
This restaurant, adjacent to the pottery workshop, looks like a hot house: green plants and vines creep along the dining room, from floor to ceiling. Connoisseurs will enjoy the local seafood. Those on a low budget will prefer to have lunch at the brasserie, a self-service area with a good choice of sandwiches, salads and desserts.

Royal Jersey Golf Club – The local golf course enjoys a particularly picturesque position; founded in 1878, it was granted its Royal Charter by Queen Victoria.

Grouville Church – Originally dedicated to St Martin of Tours, the church has an unusual 15C granite font and a number of early examples of locally made church plate.

St Clement's – St Clement is Jersey's smallest parish, named after the church dedicated to Clement I, the third Pope (AD 68-78); it was here that Hugo wrote two volumes of poetry: *Les Châtiments* and *Les Contemplations*, before departing to Guernsey...
The dolmen at Mont Ubé, the 3.4m/11ft menhir known as **La Dame Blanche**, and a tall granite outcrop called Rocqueberg suggest that this section of the island was inhabited by Neolithic man. The earliest priory on the site belonged to the Abbey of Mont-St-Michel.
The oldest extant parts of the present church date from the 12C; the wall paintings from the 15C (*St Michael slaying the Dragon;* the legend of the *Three Living and Three Dead Kings*).

St Clement's Bay – This sandy bay stretches from Plat Rocque Point, past Le Hocq Point, marked by a defensive tower, to Le Nez Point *(3.2km/2mi)*. Out to sea strong tides sweep through, continually churning the water. In 1781 Baron de Rullecourt landed with 600 French troops at the eastern end of the bay in the last French attempt to capture Jersey.
From A 4 (Grande Route de St Clement) turn onto B 48 (rue du Pontille), which leads onto A 5 (St Clement's Road), to reach Samarès Manor (right).

Samarès Manor ⊘ – The name Samarès is probably derived from the Norman *salse marais*, the salt pans which provided the lord of the manor with a significant part of his revenue.
The history of the estate began in the 11C when William Rufus granted the Samarès fief to his faithful servant Rodolph of St Hilaire. In the 17C Philippe Dumaresq decided to give the estate a new look; he drained the marsh by building a canal to St Helier and imported trees and vines from France. The gardens were landscaped and largely replanted by Sir James Knott who acquired the property in 1924; the herb garden is later still. Of particular interest in the grounds is the rare 11C dovecot; in the house there is the Norman undercroft or manor chapel crypt and the walnut-panelled dining room.

Where to stay

MID-RANGE

Samarès Manor Farmhouse Apartments – *JE2 6QW St Clement –* ☎ *01534 870551 – closed Nov to Feb – reservation advisable in season – 4 apartments, £490/565 per week for 1 to 4 persons.* Prolong your visit of Samarès by staying in one of the comfortable apartments housed in the farm, close to the manor. This will enable you to explore the numerous attractions (crafts, animals, plants) the site has to offer.

Continue west on A 4 (the coast road) to Dicq Corner; see plan of St Helier.

Le Rocher des Proscrits – *Small plaque facing the road.* On the east side of the White Horse Inn, a slipway descends to the beach and a group of rocks, Le Rocher des Proscrits (The Rock of the Exiles), where **Victor Hugo** *(see p 372)* used to meet regularly with fellow exiles.

Faldouet Dolmen – *Bear right off the coast road (Route d'Anne Port).* A tree-lined path leads to this dolmen, which is 15m/49ft long and dates from 2500 BC. The funeral chamber (6m/20ft wide) is covered by a block of granite weighing 25t. Excavation has revealed a number of vases, stone pendants and polished stone axes.

Mont Orgueil, Gorey

Gorey – This charming little port at the northern end of Grouville Bay is dominated by the proud walls of Mont Orgueil Castle set on its rocky promontory. Attractive old houses line the quay where yachts add colour to the scene in summer. In the days of the Jersey Eastern Railway (1873-1929) there was a steamship service from Gorey to Normandy.

★**Mont-Orgueil Castle** ⊘ – *45min.* Gorey Castle received its present name in 1468 from Henry V's brother, Thomas, Duke of Clarence, who was so impressed by the castle's position and its defensive strength that he called it Mount Pride (Mont Orgueil in French). Over the centuries the castle has served as a residence to the lords and governors of the island, including Sir Walter Ralegh (1600-03), a prison for English political prisoners, and a refuge for a spy-network during the French Revolution.

The earliest buildings date back to the 13C when King John lost control of Normandy and built a castle to defend the island from invasion; new fortifications were added over the years as assaults from bows and arrows evolved into mortar attack and cannon fire. It was subsequently used as a prison and eventually ceded by the Crown to the States of Jersey in 1907; in 1996 Queen Elizabeth II handed the castle to the islanders.

The castle is built on a concentric plan, each system of defence being independent of the other. The solid walls founded on the granite rocks are a formidable obstacle. It is like threading a maze to walk up the complex network of passages and steps to the summit. The **view**★★ from the top is extensive: down into Port Gorey, south over the broad sweep of Grouville Bay, north to the rocks of Petit Portelet and west to the French coast.

A series of waxwork tableaux in the rooms of the castle illustrates significant events in the history of Mont Orgueil including one of Charles II during his exile in Jersey as the guest of the Governor George de Carteret, to whom he granted the land in Virginia that became New Jersey.

Take A 3 (Gorey Coast Road) along the waterfront.

Royal Bay of Grouville – The rarish of Grouville is graced with Jersey's finest bay, a magnificent crescent of sand stretching from Gorey harbour to La Rocque Point. The skyline is punctuated by a series of Martello towers and forts which were constructed during the Napoleonic Wars: of these the Seymour and Icho towers (1811) may be reached on foot at low tide.

Jersey Pottery ⊘ – *45min.* A paved garden, hung with baskets of flowers and refreshed by fountains, surrounds the workshops where the distinctive pottery is produced. Each stage in the process is explained on large panels and the visitor can stand and watch the craftsmen at work at their various skills. The show room displays the full range of products for sale.

GUERNSEY ★

Population 58 867
Michelin Atlas p 5 or Map 403

Guernsey is the second largest of the Channel Islands (63km²/24sq mi): less sophisticated than its larger neighbour, it has its own particular charm: a slower tempo, the Regency elegance of the capital St Peter Port, the proximity of other islands – Sark, Herm and Jethou. Since the Second World War its main sources of income have been tourism, offshore finance, insurance, and tomatoes.

Guernsey is shaped like a right-angled triangle; the west coast forms the hypotenuse, the south coast the base and the east coast the perpendicular. From the air the whole island seems to be covered with small fields and dwellings, and many glass-houses, linked by a network of narrow lanes. There is little open country – L'Ancresse Common at the north end and a narrow strip of wild country along the southern cliffs where flowers abound in spring. The **water lane**, where a stream runs in a channel down the side of the road, is a special feature of Guernsey, as through Moulin Huet Valley and Petit Bot Valley.

Victor Hugo's Exile

★**Hauteville House** ⊙ – *38 Hauteville*. **Victor Hugo** was exiled from his native France for political reasons in 1851. After a year in Brussels and three in Jersey, from which he was expelled because a fellow exile made disparaging remarks about Queen Victoria, he came to Guernsey. He bought this great white house – supposedly haunted – in 1856 for a derisory sum.

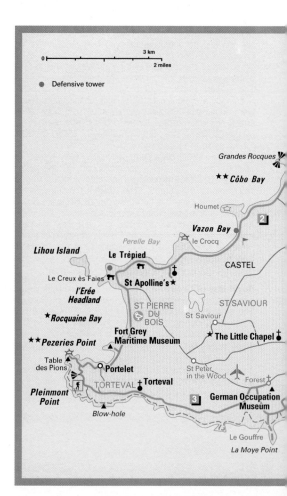

Set back from the street, the plain façade gives no hint of the incongruous and eccentric decor inside. During his 14 years' residence Hugo redecorated the interior, doing much of the work himself: every inch of wall and ceiling is covered with wood carvings or tiles (from Delft or Rouen), tapestries or silk fabric. In the dining room a soup tureen serves as a finger bowl and iron stands are incorporated into the "ancestors' armchair" to give it a Gothic look; in the Red Drawing Room the torches of liberty held by the negro slaves are simply upturned candlesticks supporting copper scale pans. Mottoes and inscriptions abound and mirrors are placed so as to enhance the effect of various features. Hugo used to work on his poems and novels standing at a small table in the **Glass Room** on the third floor overlooking the sea about which he wrote: "there is nothing more peaceful than this creek in calm weather, nothing more tumultuous in a heavy sea. There were ends of branches perpetually wet from the foam. In the spring, it was full of flowers, nests, scents, birds, butterflies and bees." Regularly, he would take a break from his work by going down to Havelet Bay to swim.

From the **Look out** where he sometimes slept, he could see the house up the road (La Fallue at 1 Beauregard Lane) into which his faithful mistress, Juliette Drouot, settled in November 1856. In April 1864 she moved down the road (no 20 Hauteville).

Candie Gardens – A dramatic statue of the French Romantic poet and novelist Victor Hugo looks out over the sloping lawn. Splendid gardens extend below the museum and the Priaulx Library (formerly Candie House); these were laid out in 1898 as public pleasure gardens with exotic plants (maidenhair tree), replacing the walled orchard and vegetable garden. In the Lower Garden are preserved two glasshouses – the first heated glasshouses to be erected in Guernsey (1792).

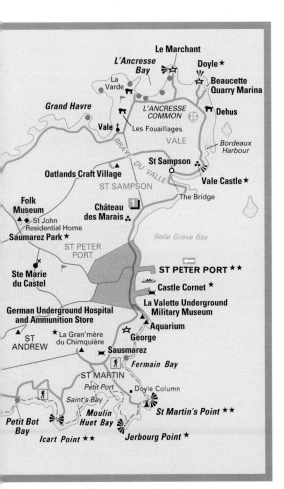

Eating out

MODERATE

Le Nautique – *Quay Steps – GY1 2LE St Peter Port –* ☎ *01481 721714 – closed Sat lunch and Sun – £11.50/20*. The oars hanging on the walls of this restaurant contribute to the maritime atmosphere as does the view of the harbour with its constant comings and goings. Seafood is omnipresent on the menus with a French slant.

Fleur du Jardin – *GY5 7JT Kings Mills – 5km/3mi from St Peter Port towards Vazon Bay –* ☎ *01481 57996 – £14.95/22.95*. In view of its pleasant garden, the name of this 15C house is certainly very appropriate. In the evening, you can enjoy dishes adapted to today's tastes in the rustic dining room with its granite fireplace. Lunch is served at the bar. Spacious and smart bedrooms.

Christies – *Le Pollet – GY1 1WH St Peter Port –* ☎ *01481 726624 – £9.50/16.95*. If you are in a hurry, you will prefer the fast service of the lively bistro. If you can take your time, all the better... ask for a table on the terrace of the more peaceful restaurant, conveniently situated in the town centre.

MID-RANGE

Auberge du Val – *GY7 9FX St Saviour –* ☎ *01481 263862 – closed 25 Dec, Sun evening and Mon – reservation essential – £20/40*. This entirely white 19C farm is situated below the church of St Saviour. Its botanical garden gives off fragrances which you will recognise in the cuisine based on fresh produce. Summer terrace in the park. Rooms available.

The Absolute End – *Longstore – GY1 2BG St Peter Port – north of St Peter Port via St George's Esplanade –* ☎ *01481 723822 – closed Jan and Sun – £16.70/27.60*. Situated at the north end of town, this restaurant is sought after by the locals for its seafood and warm welcome. Interesting lunch menu. Comfortable bar upstairs.

Where to stay

MODERATE

Tudor Lodge Deer Farm Bed and Breakfast – *Forest Road – GY8 0AG Forest – 9.6km/6mi west of St Peter Port –* ☎ *01481 237849 – closed Oct to Mar – ⊭ – 5 rooms: £35/60*. A warm welcome awaits you in this 19C guesthouse. The rooms are spacious. Self-catering accommodation available in the cottage. Cold meals based on vegetables and fruit from the garden.

Maison Bel Air Bed and Breakfast – *Le Chêne – GY8 0AL Forest – 9.6km/6mi west of St Peter Port –* ☎ *01481 238503 – ⊭ – 4 rooms: £30/50*. This smart Victorian guesthouse overlooks Petit Bot Bay accessible on foot. Restful large south-facing garden. Spacious rooms. No smokers.

Résidence Del Mar Court – *Le Varclin – GY4 6AL St Martin –* ☎ *01481 237491 –* **P** *– 21 apartments: £175/540 per week*. Situated close to the cliffs dotted with wild flowers, this peaceful residence between the sea and St Peter Port is ideal for a family holiday; all the apartments open on to the swimming pool (heated in summer).

Bordeaux Guest House – *GY3 5LX Bordeaux Bay – 5.5km/3.5mi northeast of St Peter Port –* ☎ *01481 247461 – closed Oct to Mar – 8 rooms: £37/54 – meal £10*. A warm family atmosphere pervades this smart traditional house, painted white all over. The well-kept rooms have a personal touch. In the evening, guests meet to enjoy the food lovingly prepared by the owner. Garden.

MID-RANGE

Moore's Central – *Le Pollet – GY1 1WH St Peter Port –* ☎ *01481 724452 – 49 rooms: £54/108 – restaurant £15/20*. This granite-built hotel is located in the French district, right in the centre of town. Two dining rooms. The greedy can indulge in Austrian-style cakes and soft sandwiches in the cake shop. Flower-decked terrace in season.

LUXURY

Les Piques Country Hotel – *Rue des Piques – GY7 9FW St Saviour –* ☎ *01481 264515 – closed in winter –* **P** *– 17 rooms: from £70 – restaurant £15.95*. This 15C farm has retained its thick granite walls and exposed beams. The rooms are bright and spacious. Some of them on the ground floor open on to a terrace in the colourful garden. Dining room near the large fireplace and cosy bar.

DISCOVERING THE ISLAND

★★St Peter Port

The island capital is built on a most attractive site on a hillside on the east coast overlooking a safe anchorage protected from high seas by Herm and Sark. The medieval town by the shore was rebuilt after bombardment during the Civil War. Another building boom, financed by the profits earned from privateering in the late 18C, produced a delightful Regency town of a variety of local granite embellished by elegant garden railings. Guernsey's popularity as a tourist destination in the Victorian era was assured by a visit made by Queen Victoria in 1846, commemorated two years later by the 100ft Victoria Tower designed by William Collings.

Market Halls – On the right is the first covered market to be built comprising Les Halles with the Assembly Rooms above, completed in 1782. Opposite is the single-storey Doric-style meat market (1822). "Les Arcades, 1830" *(on the left)* is very handsome despite the loss of the final bay. The Fish Market, with its row of round windows like great portholes was finished in 1877. Finally, the Vegetable Market was constructed in 1879. All stand on the site of the Rectory Garden.

Harbour – The large modern harbour is a scene of constant activity bustling with car and passenger ferries to the mainland and neighbouring islands, fishing boats and private yachts. The north pier was added in the 18C to the original 13C pier to form the Old Harbour. The Castle Pier and St Julian's Pier out to White Rock were built between 1835 and 1909; the Jetty was added in the 1920s. The North Marina provides more accommodation for private craft.

It is worth strolling out to White Rock or visiting the castle for a fine **view** of the town, the harbour and the neighbouring islands.

★St Peter's – The Town Church, as it is known, was begun by William the Conqueror in 1048, and completed around 1475. The nave and west door are part of the original Norman structure. In those days it doubled as a fort and in the past it has housed the guns of the artillery, the fire engine, and the flower market on wet days. The interior is furnished with an interesting range of stained glass and a handsome collection of memorials and monuments commemorating famous Guernseymen.

Elizabeth College was founded as a grammar school in 1563 by Elizabeth I. The pseudo-Tudor style building by John Wilson dates from 1826-29.

SIGHTS

★Castle Cornet ⊙ – *2hr*. The castle suffered its greatest misfortune not in war but in a storm in 1672 when a lightning strike ignited the gunpowder store in the old tower keep. The explosion decapitated the castle, destroying not only the tower but the medieval banqueting hall and the Governor's house, and killed his wife and daughter.

History – The original castle (c 1206) was reinforced under Elizabeth I and again under Victoria. The **Prisoners' Walk** is the original barbican – an unusual and most effective piece of defence work. The castle was superseded as principal defensive stronghold when Fort George was built shortly after the outbreak of the French Revolution. During the 20C, the citadel was fitted with two 12-pounder quick-firing guns and equipped with searchlights: these were fitted so as to monitor defences at water level. An exhibition in the Main Guard graphically relates the **Story of Castle Cornet** from prehistoric to present times.

Firing the Noonday Gun, Castle Cornet

Th. Juillier/PHOTONONSTOP

In the guard-room at the entrance of the castle, built in Victorian times, is a display relating to the history of **201 Guernsey's Own Squadron**.

On the Saluting Platform in the outer bailey the ceremony of the **noonday gun** is performed by two men dressed in the Guernsey Militia uniform; one trains a telescope on the town clock and the other fires the cannon (beware of the extremely loud bang!).

From the Citadel there is a fine **view★** of the harbour and town *(west)*, St Sampson, Vale Castle and Alderney *(35km22mi north)*, Herm, Sark and the French coast *(east)* and Jersey *(south)*.

The **Maritime Museum** relates the island's maritime history from the Gallo-Roman period to the present day. Exhibitions centre on the harbour, Roman and medieval trade, fish and fishing, smuggling, privateering and the Royal Navy; there is a gallery of marine art, a carpenter's workshop, displays on shipbuilding and cross-Channel steamers, divers and lifeboats. A **Militia Museum**, housed in the Hospital Building (1746), contains two collections: the Spencer Collection *(lower floor)* of uniforms and insignia of the Channel Islands militias, and on the upper floor, regimental silver, musical instruments and mementoes of the Royal Guernsey Militia which was disbanded in 1939. Collections of weapons used by the militia and other regiments connected with Guernsey – Civil War armaments – are housed in the **Armoury**.

Guernsey Museum ⊙ – A cluster of modern octagonal structures arranged alongside a former Victorian bandstand (now a tearoom), houses the Lukis archeological collection of artefacts retrieved from La Varde chambered tomb in 1811 and the Wilfred Carey Collection of paintings, prints and ceramics. The re-creation of a Victorian domestic interior features the pioneer archeologist and eclectic antiquarian collector Frederick Corbin Lukis and his daughter Mary Anne. Certain items were assembled by Wilfred Carey who served several years as a diplomat in the Far East.

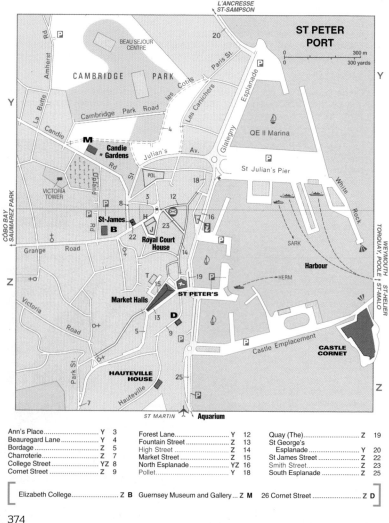

An excellent display traces the chronological development of Guernsey complete with geological, archeological and natural history exhibits from the earliest settlers, through the ages to the modern day – the broad range of information given is further supplemented by touch screens.

Also of Interest – The elegant neo-Classical church of **St James'** ⊘, designed by John Wilson in 1818 for services held in English for the British garrison, is now a concert hall. The law courts and the States of Deliberation hold their sittings in the elegant **Royal Court House** ⊘ (1792); its archives go back 400 years. **26 Cornet Street** ⊘, a Victorian shop, complete with period reeded shutters in the bay windows, carefully recreates a sweetshop and parlour as it would have been in 1900. It also serves as the headquarters of the National Trust for Guernsey.

Based on historic records, efforts have been made to recreate **gardens** from the 16C (Sutler's Garden outside the resident keeper's house), 17C (Lambert Garden created by Sir John Lambert, "The Knight of the Golden Tulip", one of Cromwell's favourites, who won acclaim growing tulips in Wimbledon) and 18C (Governor's Garden and Master Gunner's Garden as laid out in 1735).

EXCURSIONS

★Saumarez Park

From St Peter Port take the main road (St Julian's Avenue) uphill opposite the harbour; continue straight past the St Pierre Park Hotel on the left, and straight over at the crossroads with Rectory Hill (left) and rue du Friquet (right). Follow the one-way system by bearing left, turning right and immediately left (sign) on route de Côbo. From the car park walk back parallel with the main road to reach the museum.

The trees and shrubs of this beautiful park are matched by the formal rose gardens; the pond is alive with wildfowl. The **Battle of Flowers** is held here every year on the fourth Thursday in August; most of the floats which compete in the different classes are now made of paper flowers, although real flowers grown locally are still used in some areas and for small floats.

The house **(St John's Residential Home)** dates from 1721 and was the home of Admiral Lord James de Saumarez.

★Guernsey Folk Museum ⊘ – Inside the farmstead buildings of Saumarez House are recreated a series of Victorian interiors: downstairs, the kitchen and parlour, heated by a great open fireplace fuelled by seaweed, dung or furze, were known as *la tchuisaene* which, in dialect, alludes to it being the heart of the family home; upstairs are the bedrooms and nursery. Carefully selected period furniture and furnishings are complemented by the fascinating and unusual, old-fashioned accoutrements (kettles, cauldrons) and toys. Elsewhere are displayed a selection of clothes and textiles retrieved in excellent condition from grandmothers' attic chests. Across the courtyard, additional outbuildings display items from the **Langlois Collection of Agricultural Implements** used to furnish a washroom, dairy, cider barn, plough shed – with illustrations and explanations of the different harvesting methods applied to gathering parsnips, potatoes, wheat and corn given in the room above. Other traditional tools common to the quarrymen, tin-smith, blacksmith, cooper, wheelwright and carpenter are also preserved.

Castel

From St Peter Port take the main road (St Julian's Avenue) uphill opposite the harbour; continue straight past the St Pierre Park Hotel on the left, and turn left down Castle Hill/Les Rohais de Haut. The church is on the right before the crossroads.

Parish Church – Early documents list the church of St Mary of the castle (**Ste-Marie-du-Castel** or Our Lady of Deliverance) as belonging to the abbey of Mont-St-Michel in 1155; before then, the site may have had a pre-Christian sanctuary and Roman fort, hence its rectangular churchyard.

The 12C church contains 13C frescoes of *The Last Supper* and of the fable of *The Three Living Kings and The Three Dead* – represented by three men hawking on horseback and three skeletal figures *(timed light switch next to the organ).*

Outside the church entrance stands a granite statue menhir found beneath the chancel in 1878. It represents a female figure, probably the mother-goddess of the Neolithic and Bronze Age cults; the stone seats were probably used at the former medieval court of Fief St Michael.

Fine **views** extend to the coast and across to Vale Church.

St Andrew

From St Peter Port take the main road (St Julian's Avenue) uphill opposite the harbour; bear left onto Queen's Road and continue straight on to Mount Row/Le Vauquiedor/ Mauxmarquis Road, after passing the church (left) turn left to the German Underground Hospital (sign).

German Underground Hospital and Ammunition Store ⏱ – *La Vassalerie. 20min*. This is the most extensive project undertaken by the Germans during their occupation of Guernsey: it took nearly three and a half years to build and consists of a series of tunnels, covering an area of 6 968m²/75 000sq ft, excavated from 13.7-22.9m/45-75ft down into the granite bedrock. Upon completion, the 500-bed hospital section was used for only nine months to treat French casualties wounded in action against the Liberating Forces. Today the miles of hollow corridors and interlocking wards echo with dripping water, one's own footsteps and silent thoughts: ducts from the central heating and air-conditioning units rust in the confined emptiness, rows of narrow hospital beds furnish the odd ward, signs identify each department: operating theatre, X-ray room, and laboratory (9); dispensary (2); staff sleeping quarters; store rooms; cinema (15); mortuary (16)...

Return to the main road, turn left and drive west; as the road descends, turn right (sign) to the Little Chapel and Guernsey Clockmakers.

The Little Chapel

★**Little Chapel** – *Les Vauxbelets. 20min*. Nestling in a shrubbery, "The Unknown Little Jewel" is a unique model of the grotto and shrine at Lourdes. It was the third in fact to be built in 1925 by Brother Deodat, a Salesian monk from Les Vauxbelets College. Its clinker walls are faced, within and without, with a brilliant mosaic of shells, fragments of glass and bone china: much of which flooded to the site following an article in *The Daily Mirror*.

TOUR OF THE ISLAND

① Clos du Valle: St Peter Port to Vale Church

8km/5mi – Half a day

Until 1806 the northern part of Guernsey, known as Clos du Valle, was cut off by the Braye du Valle – a tidal channel of mudflats and salt-marsh, now protected as a nature reserve, which runs from St Sampson to Le Grand Havre.

The channel was crossed by a bridge in St Sampson and by a causeway at low water near Vale Church. For reasons of military security it was filled in by Sir John Doyle; the area of reclaimed salt pans and mudflats (300 acres) is now covered with glasshouses. The Clos du Valle is densely populated owing to the many quarries which were worked in the area in the 19C.

Leave St Peter Port by the coast road (Glategny Esplanade) north towards St Sampson. Turn left in Belle Greve Bay onto Le Grand Bouet and then second right.

Château des Marais – The ruined medieval **Castle in the Marshes** crowns a low knoll: it was first used in the Bronze Age, protected by the surrounding marshy ground. An outer wall encloses a ditch and inner fortification. Excavations in 1975-77 uncovered 13C coins in a chapel dedicated to Our Lady of the Marshes. The castle was refortified in the 18C and was later known as Ivy Castle owing to the creeper which covered it.

St Sampson – Guernsey's second port, which has taken all bulk cargoes since 1964, lies at the eastern end of the Braye du Valle *(see below)*. Shipbuilding in the 18C was eclipsed as the main industry in the 19C by the export of granite for road building; the first of the handsome granite quays was built in 1820. The harbour and its environs feature in Hugo's novel *The Toilers of the Sea* as La Durande.

The first **bridge** originally spanned the Braye du Valle *(see below)*: when it became blocked in 1806, it was faced with stone to form a mooring.

St Sampson, the oldest church in Guernsey, was allegedly built where the saint came ashore (c 550), either from Llantwit Major in South Wales or from Dol in Brittany. The oldest section is the Early Norman saddleback tower. Its attractive churchyard overlooks the disused Longue Hougue Quarry.

From the bridge take Vale Avenue north and bear left onto the main road (Route du Braye). Oatlands Craft Centre is located opposite a garden centre in Gigandis Road.

Oatlands Craft Centre ⊙ – *Braye Road, St Sampson*. An old brick farmstead and its thatched outbuildings arranged around a courtyard house a craft centre where craftsmen exercise their skills in cheesemaking, goldsmithing, silversmithing and engraving. The two distinctive kilns were later used from 1800 to the 1930s to produce bricks for fortifications, chimneys and boiler pits for heating glasshouses, and clay pots for tomatoes.

Vale Castle – The medieval castle, now in ruins, was built on the site of an Iron Age hillfort (c 600 BC) on the only high point in Clos du Valle, overlooking St Sampson harbour. Most of the extant masonry dates from work undertaken after the American War of Independence, when France ratified her alliance with the independent American colonies and it was considered necessary to consolidate artillery defences and provide additional barracks. These were used by the Island's Militia and by Russian troops evacuated from Holland at the end of the 18C.

There is a fine **view** inland, along the east coast and out to sea to the reef, Alderney *(north)*, Herm and Sark *(west)*, and Jersey *(south)*.

Defensive towers

In 1778-79 the shoreline of Guernsey was reinforced by a chain of 15 loopholed granite towers (9m/30ft high, 6m/20ft in diameter, with walls 1.22m/4ft thick). The 12 that survive, numbered in an anticlockwise sequence, illustrate how advanced they were for their period – an adapted design was later used when similar towers were built in Jersey. The ground level was used for storage; entrance to the first floor was by a retractable wooden ladder and gave access to two levels of accommodation loopholed for musketry defence; the open roof was subsequently altered to make room for a 12-pounder gun. The shortcomings of the design, however, were soon realised by Royal Engineers who advocated a different format for the Martello Towers built at Fort Saumarez, Fort Grey and Fort Hommet (1804), in keeping with those being constructed on the south coast of England.

Detached magazines were built alongside in which kegs or barrels of black powder would be stored protected from the damp sea winds and where muskets could be serviced.

Bordeaux Harbour provides mooring for fishing boats; the sheltered bay, which provides the only safe swimming in the area, is described by Victor Hugo in his novel *The Toilers of the Sea*.

Follow the main road north; as it curves gently left, turn right onto the minor road; bear left; park by the dilapidated glasshouses (right) opposite the passage tomb.

Dehus Dolmen ⊙ – *Light switch on left inside the entrance*. This, the second largest passage grave in Guernsey, has four side-chambers covered by seven capstones: crouch down to see Le Gardien du Tombeau, the figure of an archer *(switch for spotlight)*. It was first excavated in 1837 by Lukis whose finds are in the Guernsey Museum in St Peter Port.

Several minor roads meander northwards to the coast.

Beaucette Quarry Marina – A breach was blasted in the side of this old diorite quarry to turn it into a sheltered marina. Even at high tide only the tops of the masts can be seen.

★**Fort Doyle** – From the fort there is an excellent **view** of the Casquets reef and Alderney *(north)*, the French coast, Herm and Sark *(west)*.

Fort Le Marchant – This promontory is the most northerly point in Guernsey. The fort is named after the founder of the Royal Military College at Sandhurst in England. Fine view, particularly of L'Ancresse Bay and L'Ancresse Common.

Golfing on L'Ancresse Common

L'Ancresse Bay – The bay is very popular for bathing and surfing particularly at the western end near Fort Pembroke.

L'Ancresse Common – This is the only extensive open space on the island and is much used for strolling, walking the dog, horse racing, cattle grazing, kite flying and as a golf course. The area is rich in archeological sites: **La Varde Dolmen** is the largest passage grave in Guernsey; human bones and limpet shells were found beneath the six capstones. **Les Fouaillages** burial ground is 7 000 years old; excavations as recent as 1978-81 produced very interesting material. The coastline is well defended by forts and seven defensive towers.

Vale Church – St-Michel-du-Valle was consecrated in 1117 on the site of an earlier chapel dedicated to St Magloire, who with St Sampson brought Christianity to Guernsey in the 6C. The curious will note that the church is irregular in alignment, suggesting that it was built in stages by Benedictine monks from Mont-St-Michel who had founded a priory nearby in 968; the priory was in ruins by 1406 and finally demolished in 1928.

☐ West Coast: Le Grand Havre to Pezeries Point

15km/10mi – About half a day

The **Grand Havre**, an ample inlet at the west end of the Braye du Valle, is best admired from the Rousse headland with its tower and jetty. A more extensive horizon, including the many sandy bays which scallop the west coast in both directions, is visible from the German gun battery strategically situated on the granite headland, the **Grandes Rocques**.

★★**Côbo Bay** – The bay is a charming combination of sand for swimming and surfing, and rocks for exploring marine life.

Vazon Bay – The huge beach between Fort Houmet *(north)* and Fort le Crocq *(south)* is excellent for swimming, sunbathing, surfing, horse riding and motor and motorcycle racing. Beneath the sands lie the remains of a submerged forest; at dusk, the rocks assume animal-like shapes such as lions and camels.

★**St Apolline's Chapel** – In 1394 a charter was granted for a chantry chapel which is decorated with a **fresco** *(light switch)* of *The Last Supper*. The original dedication to Ste Marie de la Perelle was changed in 1452 to St Apolline (or St Apollonia), whose cult became very popular in Europe at that time. She was an elderly deaconess who was burned to death in an anti-Christian riot in Alexandria in 249; as she was first struck repeatedly in the face and lost many teeth she is invoked against toothache; she is often represented bearing forceps.

After the Reformation the chapel was used as a barn; it was restored in 1978.

Le Trépied Dolmen – This burial chamber at the southern end of Perelle Bay was excavated in 1840 by Frederic Lukis, whose finds are in the Guernsey Museum. In past centuries the site was used for witches' Sabbaths on Friday nights.

L'Erée Headland – The tall defensive tower on the headland is called Fort Saumarez. To the south stands **Le Creux ès Faies Dolmen**, a passage grave said locally to be the entrance to Fairyland; other local myths talk of it being a meeting place for witches. Excavation has produced items dating from 2000 BC to 1800 BC.

Lihou island – *Accessible by causeway at low tide; check tide tables before setting out and take note of the time for returning to the main island.* The semi-detached character of the island is inviting to those seeking the contemplative life. In 1114 a priory was founded and dedicated to Our Lady of the Rock (now in ruins). Earlier this century there was a burst of activity from a factory making iodine from seaweed. The predecessor of the present lonely farmhouse was used by the Germans for target practice. On the west coast a 30m/100ft rock pool provides excellent bathing.

★**Rocquaine Bay** – The grand sweep of the bay, which is protected from erosion by a high sea wall, is interrupted by the Cup and Saucer, originally a medieval fort to which a defensive tower was added in 1804. It is painted white as a navigation mark.

Fort Grey Maritime Museum ⊙ – The tower presently accommodates a small museum on two floors dedicated to the history of the fort, and to the many shipwrecks in Guernsey waters, the Hanois Reef and Lighthouse; displays also include artefacts salvaged by marine archeologists from 100 ships which have run aground along the west coast between 1750 and 1978 – a video explains the disaster involving the loss of the *Orion* and the ensuing difficult rescue operation.

Portelet – The picturesque harbour full of fishing boats is backed by the houses of the Hanois Lighthouse keepers. Nearby is the **Table des Pions**, a circle of turf surrounded by a ditch and a ring of stones, where the *pions* or footmen of the Chevauchée de St Michel ate their lunch sitting at the grass table with their feet in the trench.

La Chevauchée de St Michel

Until 1837 this medieval ceremony, which probably originated in pagan Normandy, took place every three years just before the Feast of Corpus Christi with its procession of the blessed sacrament. The cavalcade *(chevauchée)* consisted of the Crown Officers and the officials of the feudal court of St Michel du Valle who made a tour of inspection of the island highways; they were dressed in costume and mounted on horseback, armed with a sword and attended by one or two footmen *(pions)*. The *pions* were usually handsome bachelors and it was their privilege to kiss any young women they met. They lunched at Pezeries; dinner was provided out of the fines levied on the owners of any obstructions; Le Perron du Roi near to the Forest Church served as a mounting block for dignitaries.

★★**Pezeries Point** – This is the most westerly point in all the Channel Islands, a remote and unfrequented place. The fort was built in the Napoleonic era.

③ Southern Cliffs: Pleinmont Point to St Peter Port

26km/16mi – Half a day

These cliffs which extend along the south coast and round to St Peter Port provide some of the most wild and dramatic scenery in the island *(beware of the cliff face which can be unstable and dangerous)*; a footpath runs from the western end to the town, following the contours up and down the valleys and bays.

Pleinmont Point – The headland which is crowned by TV masts provides an extensive **view**: along the southern cliffs *(east)*, out to the Hanois Lighthouse and its surrounding reefs *(west)*, across Rocquaine Bay to Lihou Island *(north)*. The headland is still dominated by a coastal artillery direction-finding tower with wide observation openings, imposed by the Germans upon an existing Martello Tower; others were constructed at Fort Saumarez, Chouet, La Corbière and L'Angle.

From here to La Moye Point the cliffs are bare and rugged, indented by small bays and inlets and pierced by many caves. A footpath stretches all along the clifftops through National Trust land, past all the watch houses before coming out by the Aquarium in St Peter Port.

The roof of a cave in La Forge Bay has fallen in to form a **blow-hole** *(souffleur)*; the best time to see and hear it in action is about 2hr after low tide.

La Moye Point, the smallest of the three promontories on the south coast, is wild and beautiful. Le Gouffre, a charming steep valley, flanks it on the west. On the east side precipitous steps lead down to a three-tiered mooring for fishing boats in the shelter of the headland.

German Occupation Museum ⊙ – *1hr*. This museum has grown out of a private collection of artefacts from the Nazi occupation of the Channel Islands. A short video *(7min)* serves as an introduction to the period of occupation. A series of rooms displays various aspects of life at that time: military hardware (weaponry, radio telephones); vehicles; clothing, uniforms and associated paraphernalia (badges, buttons, mending kits); a field kitchen, food parcels, food substitutes and rationing; personal mementoes of German soldiers and forced labourers, newspapers and posters; video of the occupation and the liberation. All vehicles and mechanical artefacts are carefully maintained in working order – hence the smell of motor oil!

Petit Bot Bay – This attractive bay which has good bathing and sand at low water lies at the foot of a green valley guarded by a defensive tower (1780). The stream used to turn a corn and a paper mill but they and two hotels were destroyed by the Germans after a British Commando raid in July 1940.

Return uphill to the main road; turn right down rue de la Villette, which turns inland to rejoin the valley leading down to Moulin Huet Bay.

★★**Icart Point** – This is the highest and most southerly headland with very fine **views** of the coast. The view west reveals a string of quiet sandy beaches, some difficult to access, curving round to La Moye Point. On the east side is **Saint's Bay**, a favourite mooring for fishermen.

Moulin Huet Bay – A water lane runs down the valley, one of the most beautiful in Guernsey, to the bay where the stream plunges down the cliff face to the sea. This is where the French Impressionist painter **Renoir** used to come (1883), fascinated by the rocks that glow pink in the setting sun. Both this bay and its eastern neighbour are good for bathing but the sandy beach at **Petit Port** is superior.

Renoir in Guernsey

The French Impressionist painter spent a month in Guernsey late in 1883, during which time he painted some 15 canvases with views of the bay and beach of Moulin Huet – heralded in contemporary guidebooks as the island's finest scenic attraction. Little is known of the reasons why Renoir visited the island – which Hugo later described as having "the singular attraction of combining a climate made for leisure with a population made for toil". For the Victorian Englishman, the place provided idyllic holiday conditions blessed with a gentle climate and exotic vegetation including the sweetest grapes, ripened under glass and harvested from July to September. For the French, Guernsey was a secluded retreat from the bustle of the Brittany coastal resorts.

St Martin – The parish occupies the southeast section of Guernsey and is principally residential, well-served by former military roads to its jagged coastline.

★★**St Martin's Point** – There is a magnificent **view** down to the lighthouse on the point, north up the coast to St Peter Port and seaward to the other islands.

★**Jerbourg Point** – From the Pea Stacks rising from the sea just off the point the view swings northwest into the broad sweep of Moulin Huet Bay. The Jerbourg peninsula is Guernsey's southeastern extremity: excavations have revealed that it was inhabited in Neolithic times, that earthern ramparts and ditches were reinforced during the Bronze Age and that a defensive castle, the Château de Jerbourg, was built here to shelter islanders through troubles in the Middle Ages when the French occupied Castle Cornet.

Fermain Bay – *Access on foot from the car park or cliff path from Jerbourg.* This charming bay with its pebbled cove, backed by densely wooded cliffs and an 18C defensive tower, offers a sandy beach and good bathing at low tide. The pepper-pot tower is a Napoleonic sentry box. At low spring tides the remains of German anti-landing barriers can be discerned.

Continue east on the main road; on a left-hand curve, turn left beyond main gate into the shaded car park.

Sausmarez Manor ⊙ – *1hr.* The elegant Queen Anne house was built in 1714-18 by Sir Edmund Andros, the Seigneur of Sausmarez and former Governor of New York. The roof-top "widow's walk" is a traditional East Coast American feature implemented to provide a view far out to sea. The later Regency additions at the rear were largely rebuilt in the 1870s by General George de Sausmarez who served with the East India Company.

The welcoming interior displays portraits and souvenirs of 750 years of occupation by the Seigneurs of Sausmarez: fine antique tapestries hang in the dark and cosy dining room; handsome family furniture and objects are scattered through the spacious drawing room and larger dining room; the log of the round-the-world voyage of *HMS Centurion* in which Philip Saumarez served is kept with the Inca silver from a captured Spanish treasure ship which was turned into coin of the realm in the great beamed hall...

In an outbuilding are displayed a **collection of dolls' houses** ⊙, several of which meticulously recreate typical Guernsey household interiors.

The wooded **grounds** are planted with various strains of tall bamboo and camellias. The **sculpture park** displays a beautiful and comprehensive range of work by artists from many countries – to be admired, enjoyed and purchased; works may also be commissioned.

The park gates, with sculptures by Sir Henry Cheere, celebrate the return of the Manor to the De Sausmarez branch of the family in 1748.

Fort George – This modern luxury housing estate occupies the site of the British garrison, Fort George, built from 1782 to 1812 and destroyed by Allied bombers the day before D-Day, having been adapted by the Germans to serve as the wartime headquarters of the Luftwaffe early warning service. The garrison troops used to bathe in the sea below, hence the name Soldiers' Bay. The military cemetery on the clifftop below the fort harbours the only German war graves still on the island.

★ **La Gran'mère du Chimquière** – At the gate into St Martin's churchyard stands a Stone Age menhir carved to represent a female figure; her facial features were chiselled later. Known as the Grandmother of the Cemetery, she is supposed to guarantee fertility and receives gifts of coins and flowers. The statue was broken in two in the 19C by an over-zealous churchwarden but re-erected by the parishioners. The church itself dates from 1225 to 1250; the south porch was added in the 1520s. Inside, it has a pre-Reformation font; the lectern and oak pulpit are worked in the Breton style and date from 1657.

Return to the main road; turn right to Jerbourg.

The road passes the **Doyle Column** which commemorates Sir John Doyle, Lt Governor (1803-15); plaque showing distances to other islands.

La Valette Underground Military Museum ⊙ – The museum occupies five tunnels that were excavated to hold fuel tanks *(Höhlgang)* for refuelling U-boats: one tunnel was never completed. The four metal containers in situ at the end of the occupation were manufactured in Bremen, and had a capacity of 30 000gal; on examination they were found to contain a kind of oil extracted from coal. Today the area has been adapted to accommodate displays of uniforms and apparel belonging to the Guernsey Militia (officially constituted in 1203), German artefacts and mementoes of the occupation.

Guernsey Aquarium ⊙ – Installed in a disused tunnel is a series of water tanks housing a variety of aquatic creatures: tropical and indigenous fish, conger eels, sharks, lobsters, reptiles and amphibians. The tunnel housing them was excavated in 1860 to carry a tramway south along the coast; work was abandoned after a rock fall; the Germans extended it from 1940 to 1945.

SARK ★★

Population 550
Michelin Atlas p 5 or Map 403

Sark, the last feudal fief in Europe and also the smallest independent state in the Commonwealth, offers peace and tranquillity and a traditional way of life without cars. It is located at the very heart of the Channel Islands (12km/7.5mi east of Guernsey, 30.4km/19mi south of Alderney, 19.2km/12mi northwest of Jersey). Its two parts – Great Sark and Little Sark – are linked by La Coupée, a high narrow neck of land which inspired Turner, Swinburne and Mervyn Peake, who set the closing scenes of his novel *Mr Pye* here.

The island (5.6km/3.5mi long by 2.4km/1.5mi wide) consists of a green plateau bounded by high granite cliffs dropping sheer into the sea or flanking sheltered bays and sandy beaches. Many walks give access to the spectacular coastal scenery. Sark is a haven for wildlife – marine creatures in the rock pools and caves; a wide range of bird species; wild flowers in spring and summer.

Constitution – At its head is the hereditary Lord (seigneur) who holds the fief of Sark; the present holder is Michael Beaumont, grandson of Sybil Hathaway, the Dame of Sark, whose long reign from 1927 to 1974 saw the island through difficult and changing times. The Seigneur of Sark has retained a number of privileges from the feudal period: the right to keep pigeons and to own a bitch. He also receives one-thirteenth of the sale price of all island property.

Sark has its own Parliament, the Chief Pleas, composed of the 40 tenants and 12 deputies elected for three years. The Seneschal is responsible for justice, together with the Clerk of the Court (Greffier) and the Sheriff (Prévôt). Law and order are upheld by the Constable assisted by the Vingtenier. A person under arrest is held in the tiny prison (two cells) for 48hr. In summer the local force is supplemented by a policeman from Guernsey. Serious cases are heard by the Guernsey courts.

History – In the middle of the 6C St Magloire, the nephew of St Sampson, landed in Sark from Brittany with 62 companions and founded a monastery. In the 9C the island was prey to Viking raids but little is known of the island's history before it became part of the Duchy of Normandy. In 1042 Sark was given to the abbey of Mont-St-

Visiting Sark

Michel by William the Conqueror, the Duke of Normandy. A few years later the island was attached to the diocese of Coutances. In 1336 Sark was invaded by a party of Scotsmen under David Bruce, a king in exile. Two years later Sark was attacked by Frenchmen. In 1349 the monks abandoned the island and for several years it was a lawless place, the haunt of pirates. The French regained it in 1549 but were thrown out by an Anglo-Dutch force which returned it to England.

In 1565 Elizabeth I granted Sark to Helier de Carteret, Lord of the Manor of St Ouen in Jersey, on condition that he establish a colony of 40 settlers prepared to defend the island. Helier became the first Lord of Sark who set about dividing the land into 40 holdings, attributing one to each of the 40 families who had accompanied him from Jersey, on condition that each tenant build and maintain a house and provide an armed man to defend the island. The number of holdings has not changed since then.

The island of Brecqhou (just off the west coast across the Gouliot Passage) has been a dependent of the fiefdom of Sark since 1565; it is now on perpetual lease to the reclusive multi-millionaire Barclay twins who have built a massive neo-Gothic mansion, which they rarely visit.

TOUR OF THE ISLAND *One day*

Great Sark

Maseline Harbour – The lighthouse (1912) looks down over the harbour from the cliffs on Point Robert as the boat docks inside the modern concrete jetty, which was inaugurated in 1949 by the Duke of Edinburgh when he and the then Princess Elizabeth visited Sark.

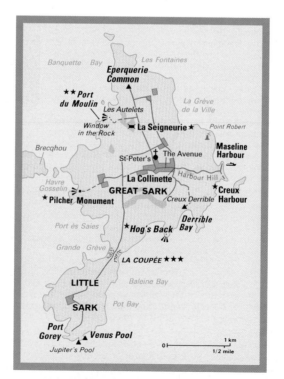

Eating out

MID-RANGE

La Sablonnerie – *Little Sark – GY9 0SD Sark –* ☎ *01481 832061 – closed mid-Oct to Easter – £23.80/25.80.* A country lane leads to this restaurant located in a beautifully renovated 16C farm. The wood furniture and the fire burning in the fireplace contribute to the genuine rural atmosphere. Spacious, comfortable rooms.

Where to stay

MID-RANGE

Dixcart – *GY9 0SD Sark –* ☎ *01481 832015 – 15 rooms: £45/90 – restaurant £15/25.75.* This 16C farm houses the oldest hotel on the island. Exposed beams, antique furniture, fireplaces and stone walls add to the warmth of the place which is ideal for a restful stay in the area. Restaurant with terrace overlooking the gardens.

★**Creux Harbour** – Opposite the tunnel to Maseline Harbour is a second tunnel to Creux Harbour, an older and picturesque little harbour, which is dry at low tide.

La Collinette – A short tunnel leads to Harbour Hill *(0.8km/0.5mi)*; at the top is the crossroads called La Collinette.
Straight ahead stretches **The Avenue**, once the drive to the original manor house and lined with trees but now the main street lined with shops. The small barrel-roofed building on the left at the far end is the island prison built in 1856.
Beyond is **Le Manoir**, built by the first Seigneur and bearing the De Carteret arms, where in 1581 his son presided over the first meeting of the islanders and created the Sark court of law and legislature.
St Peter's Church dates from the 19C. The embroidered hassocks are the work of the island women; the designs incorporate the motifs and some of the names of the landholdings with which the seats are traditionally associated.

★**La Seigneurie** – The present beautiful stone and granite manor house, the residence of the Seigneur of Sark, stands on the site of St Magloire's 6C monastery, after which the house is named, La Moinerie. Begun in 1565, it was considerably enlarged in 1730 by the Le Pelley family who then held the fief of Sark. The square tower, which provides a splendid view of the island, was built as a signalling tower in 1860.
The house is sheltered from the wind by a screen of trees and high walls. The **gardens** ⊙, on which the Dame of Sark lavished so much attention, are luxuriant with flowers and shrubs, some brought from foreign parts, and maintained with undiminished care.

★★**Port du Moulin** – A road along the north side of the Seigneurie grounds soon turns onto a path following the windings of the clifftop. The sign "Window and Bay" marks the way to the **Window in the Rock**, which the Rev William Collings had made in the 1850s to provide an impressive **view** of Port du Moulin. *Return to the fork in the path and take the other branch to Port du Moulin.*
The bay, which is popular with bathers in summer, is flanked by stark rocks in strange shapes; at low tide huge arches in the rock appear. On the right stand **Les Autelets**, three granite columns accessible as the sea retreats.

Derrible Bay – At Petit Dixcart turn left onto a stony path, then right onto a path beside a field; a left fork leads down through the trees to Derrible Bay which a retreating tide will reveal to contain a large sandy beach.
Part way down, a turning to the right leads to the **Creux Derrible**, an enormous hole in the granite cliffs *(take care in poor light)*.
Return to the first fork and bear left, for at the seaward end of this high ridge known as the **Hog's Back★** stands an ancient cannon, from which there is a magnificent **view**: to the left Derrible Bay and Derrible Point; to the right Dixcart Bay with La Coupée and Little Sark in the background.

Pilcher Monument★

This granite column was raised in memory of a London merchant, F Pilcher, who died at sea in 1868 with three companions while returning to Guernsey. From the plinth there is a fine **view** of the west coast and of Brecqhou, Herm, Jethou and Guernsey. A path runs down to Havre Gosselin where yachts moor in the summer months.

★★★ **La Coupée** – The concrete roadway and the guard rails were constructed in 1945 by German prisoners of war working under the direction of the Royal Engineers. The narrow isthmus joining the two parts of Sark is uniquely impressive, as on either side steep cliffs drop some 79m/260ft into the sea. The view is magnificent: to the right lie Brecqhou, Jethou, Herm and Guernsey; to the left the coast of Jersey can be made out before the more distant shadow of the French coast. At the foot of the cliff is Grande Grève Bay, a good place for bathing.

Grande Grève Bay

Little Sark

On the southern headland are the chimneys of the old silver mines, now overgrown, which were started in the 19C but had to close because of the infiltration of water into the workings. A footpath to the left of the old mine chimney runs down to **Venus Pool**, a circular pool under the cliffs, formed by the sea and visible at low tide.

At low tide *(to avoid being stranded, check the time of high tide)*, visitors can walk from the Venus Pool westward round the headland via **Jupiter's Pool**, several caves and the rocks in Plat Rue Bay, to **Port Gorey** which served the silver mines.

The clifftop path is always open and provides a fine view down into Port Gorey.

ALDERNEY

Population 2 297
Michelin Atlas p 5 or Map 403

Alderney is the most northerly of the Channel Islands and lies west (12km/8mi) of the tip of the Cherbourg Peninsula in Normandy, separated from the Cap de la Hague headland by the treacherous tidal current known to sailors as the **Alderney Race**. The island (5.6km/3.5mi long by 2.4km/1.5mi wide) slopes gently from a plateau (296ft/90m) of farmland, skirted by high cliffs in the southwest, to a tongue of low-lying land in the northeast, fringed by rocky spits and sandy bays, and bristling with redundant fortifications.

There is one main settlement, St Anne, also known as The Town, which extends north towards the coast and the harbour; there are a few outlying dwellings, some in former military forts.

Alderney is a haven for nature lovers. The flora includes wild broom, thrift, sea campion, ox-eye daisies, wild orchids and the bastard toadflax (thesium humifusum); among the fauna are black rabbits and blonde hedgehogs. Birdwatchers have much to choose from – hoopoes and golden orioles, birds of prey and the occasional white stork or purple heron, and the seabirds, fulmars, guillemots and kittiwakes, especially the colonies of gannets and puffins. At low tide the rock pools reveal a variety of marine life; anemones, corals and ormers.

Constitution – Alderney is part of the Bailiwick of Guernsey. Since the introduction of the new constitution on 1 January 1949, the budget and other financial matters have to be approved by the States of Guernsey. Otherwise all island business is decided by the Committees of the States of Alderney, which consists of 10 elected members and an elected President, who serve for four years. The Court consists of six Jurats under a Chairman, who are appointed by the Home Office.

The pre-1949 constitution which had evolved down the centuries included two other bodies, the Douzaine, an assembly of 12 heads of families, and the Court of Chief Pleas. All offices were then elective. The feudal system under a seigneur was never established in Alderney; later Governors, appointed by the Crown from the 16C to the 19C, often met with opposition from the independent-minded islanders.

Where to stay

MODERATE

Bonjour Guest House – *16 High St. – GY9 3UG St Anne –* ☎ *01481 822152 – 3 rooms: £50.* This "Bonjour" heralds a charming welcome in this guesthouse. Situated in an old picturesque street of St Anne, it has well-kept rooms with a personal touch. Good value for money on this island.

Historical notes – Owing to its key position, nearest to England, France and the Channel shipping lanes, Alderney has frequently been fortified. The Romans seem to have used it as a naval base; there are traces of a late-Roman fort at the Nunnery. The first English fortifications date from the reign of Henry VIII who started to construct a fort on the hill south of Longis Bay. Faced with the threat of invasion in the Napoleonic period, the British Government strengthened the existing defences and sent a garrison of 300 to assist the local militia.

The most impressive fortifications were built between 1847 and 1858. Alarmed by the development of a French naval base at Cherbourg, the British Government decided to create a safe harbour at Braye, by constructing a huge breakwater, and to defend the island, by building a chain of 10 forts along the north coast from Clonque in the west round to Longis Bay in the east. There was also a plan to build another harbour at Longis and link it to Braye with a canal, thus strengthening the defence of the northeastern sector and providing a safe harbour whatever the wind. The forts were constructed of local stone with white quoins and dressings; several stood offshore and were reached by causeways at low tide.

In June 1940 almost all the population left the island and the livestock was evacuated to Guernsey. During their five-year occupation the Germans re-fortified most of the Victorian forts and built masses of ugly concrete fortifications. When the islanders began to return late in 1945 they found their possessions gone and the houses derelict or destroyed. It took 10 years and substantial government aid to make good the damage.

ST ANNE

The charm of St Anne lies in its cobbled streets and smart whitewashed granite houses; its appearance is reminiscent of villages in Cornwall and Normandy. The Town, as it is called by the islanders, lies about half a mile from the north coast on the edge of the best agricultural land, known as La Blaye.

The original medieval settlement of farmhouses was centred on **Marais Square** which was then unpaved and had a stream running through it where the washing was done. As in ancient times, narrow lanes or *venelles* lead out to the un-enclosed fields divided into *riages*, each consisting of a number of strips: Alderney is one of the few places in the British Isles still to operate this archaic system of managing open agricultural land, although electric fencing is occasionally used.

Another settlement grew up at **Le Huret**, where the people gathered to decide when to gather the seaweed *(vraic)* used to fertilise the land. In the 15C more houses were built to the east of the square, to accommodate settlers from Guernsey, and the Blaye was extended to support a population of 700. In the 18C the huge profits made from privateering led to a building boom; thatch was replaced by tiles, the first Court House was built and the Governor spent money on improving the communal buildings as well as his own residence. The northern part of the town – **Queen Elizabeth II Street, Victoria Street and Ollivier Street** – developed in the early Victorian era when the population of the island trebled with the introduction of a military garrison and many immigrant labourers brought in to build the harbour. Utilitarian workmen's cottages were built of local sandstone at Newtown and elsewhere. Many attractive houses and gardens line the green lanes, such as La Vallée, which run from St Anne down to the north coast.

St Anne's – The church, consecrated in 1850, was designed by Sir Gilbert Scott in the transitional style from Norman to Early English cruciform and built in local granite dressed with white Caen stone. The cost was borne by Revd Canon John Le Mesurier, son of the last hereditary governor of Alderney, in memory of his parents. The church is unexpectedly large as it was intended to hold not only the local population, then swollen by immigrant labourers, but also the military garrison.

English was then replacing Norman French as the local language; the lectern holds two Bibles, and the texts in the apse and near the door appear in both languages. Below the west window, which shows children of all races, are six brass plaques commemorating the Le Mesurier family who governed the island from 1721 to 1825. Queen Elizabeth II's visit to Alderney in 1957 is recorded in the window in the Lady Chapel.

During the war the church was damaged by being used as a store and the bells were removed; two were recovered on the island and the other four were found in Cherbourg. The churchyard gates in Victoria Street, erected as a memorial to Prince Albert, were removed by the Germans but replaced by a local resident.

Museum ⊙ – The Alderney Society's Museum presents a comprehensive view of the island: geology; flora and fauna; archeology, particularly finds from the Iron Age Settlement at Les Hughettes; domestic and military history, including the Victorian fortifications and the German Occupation.

The collections are displayed in the **old school** which was endowed in 1790 by the Governor *(inscription over the gate)*.

The **Clock Tower** (1767) standing nearby is all that remains of the old church which was pulled down when the present one was built. The original dedication to St Mary, and the name of the town too, was changed to St Anne early in the 17C.

Royal Connaught Square – This elegant square, which was renamed in 1905 on the occasion of a visit by the Duke of Connaught, was the centre of the town in the 18C.

Island Hall *(north side)*, a handsome granite building which is now a community centre and library, was enlarged in 1763 by John Le Mesurier to become Government House. The first house on the site was built by Captain Nicholas Ling, who was appointed Lt Governor in 1657 and lived there until his death in 1679. **Mouriaux House** was completed in 1779 by the Governor as his private residence.

Court House ⊙ – The present building in Queen Elizabeth II Street (formerly New Street) dates from 1850. Both the Court and the States of Alderney hold their sessions in the first-floor Court Room which was restored in 1955.

Victoria Street – This, the main shopping street, runs north past the church gates and the war memorial, which records the dead of both World Wars. Its name was changed from rue du Grosnez to celebrate Queen Victoria's visit in 1854.

Butes – The recreation ground, formerly the Butts, provides fine views of Braye Bay *(northeast)*, across Crabby Bay and the Swinge to the Casquets *(northwest)* and the English Channel.

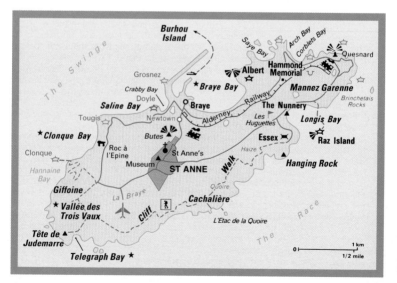

TOUR OF THE ISLAND *14km/9mi; one day*

⬛ *It is possible to walk round the island following the cliff-top footpath or to drive round making detours on foot to places of interest.*

Braye – The harbour is protected by Fort Grosnez (1853) which was built at the same time as the massive **breakwater** (1 000yd long plus another 600yd submerged) by the British Government in 1847, just as the French were consolidating their defences at Cherbourg. As with St Catherine's Bay in Jersey, the ambitious plans for harbours of refuge were never completely realised. The first quay, the Old Jetty, was built in 1736 by the Governor to provide a safe landing-stage for the privateers and smugglers he "protected". The modern concrete jetty dates from the turn of the century.

★ **Braye Bay** – The largest bay on the island offers a sandy beach with good bathing and a fine view of the ferries, yachts and fishing boats in the harbour. Skirting the beach is a strip of grass, Le Banquage, where the seaweed *(vraic)* was left to dry.

Fort Albert – Mount Touraille, at the east end of Braye Bay, is crowned by Fort Albert (1853), the most impressive element in the Victorian chain of forts and German fortifications. From the seaward side there is a fine **view** inland to St Anne, westwards across Braye Bay to Fort Grosnez and the breakwater with Fort Tourgis in the background, and eastwards over the northern end of the island.

Hammond Memorial – *At the fork in the road east of Fort Albert.* The labourers of the Todt Organisation – paid volunteers from Vichy France, political refugees from Franco's Spain, Ukraine, Russia and North Africa who worked under duress on the fortifications during the Nazi Occupation are commemorated in a series of plaques inscribed in the languages of the prisoners. There were three camps on Alderney, each holding 1 500 men.

North Coast – Three excellent sandy bathing bays cluster round the most northerly headland beneath the walls of Fort Château à l'Étoc (1854), now converted into private flats: **Saye Bay**, nearly symmetrical in shape; **Arch Bay**, named after the tunnel through which the carts collecting seaweed reached the shore; **Corblets Bay**, overlooked by Fort Corblets (1855), now a private house with a splendid view.

Mannez Garenne – The low-lying northern end of the island, known as Mannez Garenne (Warren) is dominated by the remains of a German observation tower on the edge of the quarry.

Quesnard Lighthouse ⊙ – Built in 1912, it stands 121ft high and casts its beam nearly 17 miles. From the lantern platform there is a magnificent **view**★ of the coast and the Race and, on a clear day, of the nuclear power station on the French coast. Many ships have come to grief on this rocky coast where the strong currents of the Swinge and the Race (Raz) meet. The most famous was the *Liverpool*, which ran aground due to fog in February 1902.

Three forts command the coastline: Les Homeaux Florains (1858), now in ruins, was approached by a causeway; Fort Quesnard, on the east side of Cats Bay, and Fort Houmet Herbe, another offshore fort reached by a causeway, were built in 1853.

Longis Bay – The retreating tide reveals a broad stretch of sand backed by a German tank trap which provides excellent shelter for sunbathing. The shallow bay was the island's natural harbour from prehistoric times until it silted up early in the 18C. Traces of an Iron Age settlement were discovered at **Les Huguettes** in 1968 when the golf course was being laid out on Longis Common; the finds are displayed in the museum. Various relics (coins, tiles, pottery and brickwork) indicate the existence of a Roman naval base protected by a fort (c 2C-4C AD).

Raz Island – A causeway, which is covered at high tide, runs out to the island in the centre of Longis Bay. The fort (1853) has been partially restored and there is a fine **view** of Essex Castle and Hanging Rock *(southwest)*.

The Nunnery – This building, which is thought to be the oldest on the island, stands on a rectangular site enclosed within a wall (16ft high). John Chamberlain converted it to his use when he became Governor in 1584. Its name was supplied by the British soldiers who were garrisoned there in the late 18C. It is now private dwellings owned by the States of Alderney.

Essex Castle – The first fort on Essex Hill overlooking Longis Bay was begun in 1546 by Henry VIII but abandoned in 1553. It consisted of an outer bailey, to hold the islanders and their flocks, around a central fort divided into four keeps. All but the north and west sides of the outer wall were razed in 1840 when the present structure was built, to be used first as a barracks and then as a military hospital; it is now private property. The pepper-pot gazebo was added by the Governor, John Le Mesurier, who started a farm to feed the garrison at the nunnery and called it Essex Farm; the name ascended the hill to the castle. At this point, the coastline to the west and south becomes ruggedly rocky.

Hanging Rock – The tilt of the 50ft column of rock projecting from the cliff face is said to have been caused by the people of Guernsey hitching a rope to the rock and trying to tow Alderney away.

Cliff Walk

 From Haize round to Giffoine there is a magnificent cliff walk served by frequent paths running inland back to St Anne. The cliff edge is indented by a series of small valleys sloping seaward and a few narrow bays, difficult or impossible to access; bathing is not advisable owing to the swiftly flowing currents in the Race. The view of the steep cliffs plunging into the rock-strewn sea is magnificent.

Cachalière – A path leads down past the old quarry to a pier, built early this century for loading granite but abandoned owing to the dangerous offshore currents. The name derives from Chicago where the Alderney man who paid for the pier had made his fortune. From here the rocks of **L'Étac de la Quoire** can be reached at low water.

★**Telegraph Bay** – *Access by a path and steps, which are not recommended as they are steep and difficult; beware of being cut off from the base of the steps by the rising tide.* The Telegraph Tower (1811), which provided communication with Jersey and Guernsey via a repeating telegraph signal on Sark, has given its name to the bay below. Except at high tide there is excellent bathing, sheltered from all but a south wind, and a fine view of La Nache and Fourquie rocks.

Tête de Judemarre – The headland provides a fine **view** of the rock-bound coast and of the islands of Guernsey, Herm and Sark.

★**Vallée des Trois Vaux** – This deep cleft is in fact three valleys meeting on a shingle beach.

Giffoine – From the cliff it is possible to see the birds on their nests in the gannet colony on Les Étacs. The remains of a German coastal battery crown the headland above Hannaine Bay, where sandy spits between the rocks provide reasonable bathing. Fine **view** of Burhou, Ortac and the Casquets *(north)*.

★**Clonque Bay** – A zigzag path descends the gorse and heather-clad slope above the attractive sweep of the bay. A causeway runs out to Fort Clonque (1855) which was designed by Captain William Jervois, the same military architect as for most of the other forts on Alderney, now converted into flats belonging to the Landmark Trust. Seaweed from Clonque was highly prized as fertiliser and two causeways enabled the *"vraicing"* carts to descend to the beds of seaweed.

Just south of Fort Tourgis (1855), now largely derelict, at the northern end of the bay, is the best preserved burial chamber on the island, **Roc à l'Épine**, which consists of a capstone supported on two upright stones. Alderney was once rich in such megaliths but all the others seem to have been destroyed when the Victorian fortifications were built.

Saline Bay – The shore, which is exposed to heavy seas so that bathing can be hazardous, is commanded by a gun battery and Fort Doyle, now a youth centre; beyond lies **Crabby Bay** in the lee of Fort Grosnez.

BURHOU ISLAND ⊙

The island, which lies northwest across The Swinge (about 2km/1.2mi), is extensively riddled with rabbit warrens and supports large colonies of puffins, razorbills, gannets and storm petrels as well as other seabirds. A hut provides simple accommodation for an overnight stay for birdwatching.

HERM

Population 97

Michelin Atlas p 5 or Map 403

Herm (2.4km/1.5mi long by 0.8km/0.5mi wide) lies halfway between Guernsey and Sark. The broad sandy beaches on its north coast contrast with the steep cliffs at the southern end of the island. Herm is a haven of tranquillity having neither roads nor cars; walking is the only way to enjoy the profusion of wild flowers, the dunes, the trees and cliffs. The deep fringe of rocks which lies offshore is most impressive at low tide.

Southwest of Herm, across a narrow channel, the islet of Jethou *(private property leased from the British Crown)* rises like a hillock in the sea, the home of many seabirds.

Historical notes – Prehistoric tombs made of granite slabs found in the north of the island are evidence of human settlement in 2000 BC; little remains, however, of a Roman presence other than a few coins and some pottery. In the 6C Christianity was introduced by St Magloire who founded monasteries in Sark and Jersey. The monks of Sark built a small chapel on a reef between Herm and Jethou, but this was engulfed in the 8C during a violent storm which separated the two islands. In the 17C pirates used the island as a base from which to prey on the many shipwrecks in the area; it was later deserted until the 19C when, for a brief period, granite was quarried for export.

As Crown property the island has been leased to various tenants: in 1890 a German prince, Blucher von Wahlstatt, built the manor house and planted the pine and eucalyptus trees; in 1920 Sir Compton Mackenzie settled there and wrote several novels on and about the island, including *Fairy Gold*, before finally settling on Jethou.

Where to stay

MID-RANGE

White House – *GY1 3HR Herm –* ☎ *01481 722159 – closed Oct to Mar – 39 rooms, half board: £70/166.* This hotel will seduce you with its splendid view of the island's scenery, its small harbour and its beach. Choice of rooms in the main house or in the cottages. Traditional or informal meals depending on which dining room you choose. Garden with summer swimming pool.

During the Second World War the island was occasionally occupied by German troops and appeared in a German propaganda film called *The Invasion of the Isle of Wight;* in February 1943 the British mounted a commando raid. In 1947 Herm was sold by the Crown to the States of Guernsey and in 1949 Major Peter Wood and his wife became tenant. In 1987 the lease was transferred to their family company to enable their daughter Pennie and her husband Adrian Heyworth to become the guardians of the island. During the 50 years of family tenancy the island has been carefully developed for the needs of tourism while at the same time the peacefulness and outstanding natural beauty have been maintained. There is a small permanent community of 10 families living and working on Herm throughout the year.

TOUR OF THE ISLAND

Le Manoir Village – A surfaced road climbs up to the farm and the handful of cottages which make up the hamlet next to the 18C manor house with its square tower.

St Tugual's Chapel was built of island granite in the 11C when Robert the Magnificent was Duke of Normandy. There is a handsome stained-glass window depicting Christ stilling the Tempest.

The Common – The northern end of the island is composed of sand dunes, known as the Common, covered by prickly vegetation and fringed by sandy beaches which are very popular in summer (Bear's Beach, Mousonnière Beach, **Shell Beach** so called because it is composed of millions of shells deposited by the tides and currents from the Gulf Stream).

Halfway along the north coast stands a stone obelisk which replaces the menhir that mariners once used as a landmark.

★ **Le Grand Monceau** – From this hillock there is a splendid panoramic **view** of the sands, the rocks and the islands. North on the horizon lies Alderney; to the east the French coast. **Le Petit Monceau** beyond is a smaller hillock, overlooking the Bear's Beach.

The Cliffs – In contrast with the low land in the north, the southern end of the island is composed of steep granite cliffs dropping sheer into the sea. In **Belvoir Bay** nestles a small sheltered beach, good for bathing. The southern headland, **Sauzebourge Point**, provides a view of Jethou *(southwest)* with Guernsey in the background *(west)* and Sark *(southeast).*

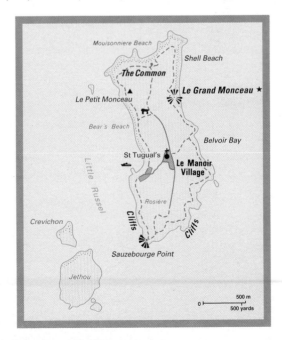

Trouville

Practical Information

Planning your trip

Formalities

Passport – Nationals of countries within the European Union entering France need only a national identity card. Nationals of other countries must be in possession of a valid national **passport**. In case of loss or theft report to the embassy or consulate and the local police.

Visa – An **entry visa** is required for Canadian and US citizens (for a stay of more than three months) and for Australian and New Zealand citizens. Apply to the French Consulate (visa issued same day; delay if request submitted by mail).

US citizens should obtain the booklet *Safe Trip Abroad* ($1), which provides useful information on visa requirements, customs regulations, medical care etc for international travellers. Published by the Government Printing Office, it can be ordered by phone – ☎ (202) 512-1800 – or consulted on-line (www. access.gpo.gov).

Customs – Apply to the Customs Office (UK) for a leaflet on customs regulations and the full range of "duty free" allowances; available from HM Customs and Excise, Dorset House, Stamford Street, London SE1 9PS, ☎ 0171 928 3344. The US Customs Service offers a publication *Know before you go* for US citizens: for the office nearest you, consult the phone book, Federal Government, US Treasury (www.customs.ustreas.gov).

There are no customs formalities for holidaymakers bringing their caravans into France for a stay of less than six months. No customs document is necessary for pleasure boats and outboard motors for a stay of less than six months but the registration certificate should be kept on board.

Americans can bring home, tax-free, up to US$400 worth of goods; Canadians up to CND$300; Australians up to AUS$400 and New Zealanders up to NZ$700. Persons living in a Member State of the European Union are not restricted in regard to purchasing goods for private use, but the recommended allowances for alcoholic beverages and tobacco are as follows:

Spirits (whisky, gin, vodka etc)	10l	Cigarettes	800
Fortified wines (vermouth, ports etc)	20l	Cigarillos	400
Wine (not more than 60 sparkling)	90l	Cigars	200
Beer	110l	Smoking tobacco	1kg

Embassies and consulates

Australia	Embassy 4, rue Jean-Rey, 75015 Paris; ☎ 01 40 59 33 00; Fax 01 40 59 33 10
Canada	Embassy 35, avenue Montaigne, 75008 Paris; ☎ 01.44 43 29 00; Fax 01 44 43 29 99
Eire	Embassy 4, rue Rude, 75016 Paris; ☎ 01 44 17 67 00; Fax 01 45 00 84 17
New Zealand	Embassy 7 ter, rue Léonard-de-Vinci, 75016 Paris; ☎ 01 45 01 43 43; Fax 01 45 01 43 44
UK	Embassy 35, rue du Faubourg-St-Honoré, 75008 Paris; ☎ 01 42 66 91 42; Fax 01 42 66 95 90
	Consulate 16, rue d'Anjou, 75008 Paris; ☎ 01 42 66 06 68 (visas)
USA	Embassy 2, avenue Gabriel, 75008 Paris; ☎ 01 43 12 22 22; Fax 01 42 66 97 83
	Consulate 2 , rue St-Florentin, 75001 Paris; ☎ 01 42 96 14 88.

French tourist offices abroad

For information, brochures, maps and assistance in planning a trip to France travellers should apply to the official French Tourist Office or Maison de la France in their own country:

Australia – New Zealand
Sydney – BNP Building, 12 Castlereagh Street
Sydney, New South Wales 2000
☎ (61) 2 231 52 44, fax: (61) 2 221 86 82.

Canada
Toronto – 30 St Patrick's Street, Suite 700, Toronto, ONT M5T 3A3,
☎ (416) 593 4723
Montreal – 1981 McGill College Avenue, Suite 490,
Montreal PQ H3A 2W9
☎ (514) 288-4264, fax: (514) 845 48 68.

Eire
Dublin – 38 Lower Abbey St, Dublin 1
☎ (1) 703 40 46, fax: (1) 874 73 24.

United Kingdom
London – 179 Piccadilly, London WIJ 9AL
☎ 09068 244 123, fax: (020) 793 6594.

United States
East Coast: New York – 444 Madison Avenue, NY 10022
☎ 212-838-7800, fax: (212) 838 7855.
Midwest: Chicago – 676 North Michigan Avenue, Suite 3360
Chicago, IL 60611
☎ (312) 751 7800, fax: (312) 337 6339.
West Coast: Los Angeles – 9454 Wilshire Boulevard, Suite 715
Beverly Hills, CA 90212.
☎ (310) 271 2693, fax: (310) 276 2835.

Cyberspace
www.info.france-usa.org
The French Embassy's web site provides basic information (geography,
demographics, history), a news digest and business-related information. It offers
special pages for children, and pages devoted to culture, language study and travel,
and you can reach other selected French sites (regions, cities, ministries) with a
hypertext link.

www.ottowa.ambafrance.org
The Cultural Service of the French Embassy in Ottawa has a bright and varied site with
many links to other sites for French literature, news updates, E-texts in both French
and English.

www.fr-holidaystore.co.uk
The new Travel Centre in London has gone on-line with this service, providing
information on all of the regions of France, including updated special travel offers and
details on available accommodation.

www.visiteurope.com
The European Travel Commission provides useful information on travelling to and
around 27 European countries, and includes links to some commercial booking services
(ie vehicle hire), rail schedules, weather reports and more.

Local tourist offices

Regional Tourist Offices – Comité Régional de Tourisme de Normandie, 14, rue
Charles-Corbeau, 27000 Evreux. ☎ 02 32 33 79 00.

Departmental Tourist Offices – Fédération Nationale des Comités Départmentaux de
Tourisme, 2 rue Linois, 75015 Paris. ☎ 01 45 75 62 16.
Calvados: Comité Départemental de Tourisme du Calvados, place du Canada, 14000
Caen. ☎ 02 31 86 53 30. Fax 02 31 79 39 41.
Eure: Comité Départemental de Tourisme de l'Eure, bd George-Chauvin, BP 367,
27003 Evreux Cedex. ☎ 02 32 31 51 51. Fax 02 32 31 05 98.
Manche: Office Départemental de Tourisme de la Manche, Maison du Département,
Route de Villedieu, 50008 Saint-Lô Cedex. ☎ 02 33 05 98 70.
Orne: Comité Départemental de Tourisme de l'Orne, 88 rue Saint-Blaise, BP 50, 61002
Alençon Cedex. ☎ 02 33 28 88 71.
Seine-Maritime: Comité Départemental de Tourisme de Seine-Maritime, 6, rue Couronné,
BP 60, 76420 Bihorel-lès-Rouen Cedex. ☎ 02 35 59 26 26.

Tourist Information Centres (🚹) – See the Admission Times and Charges for the
addresses and telephone numbers of the Local Tourist Information Offices *(Syndicats
d'Initiative)*; they provide information on craft courses and itineraries with special
themes – wine tours, history tours, artistic tours.

Tourist Pass: 100 sights for 42.69€

This pass gives unrestricted access to more than one hundred historic buildings
managed by the Caisse Nationale des Monuments Historiques et des Sites
(CNMHS). It is valid for one year throughout France as of the date of purchase.
It is available at the ticket windows of major monuments and some musuems.

When to go

The most pleasant season is July to September although the mildness of the coastal climate makes it possible to visit Normandy at any time of the year. In spring, the blossoming of the apple trees in April and May transforms the Normandy countryside. Apples flower last, after the Gaillon cherries and the Domfront pears. Apple blossom time is really without equal, and this would, therefore, be the ideal time to explore the countryside by driving through the Pays d'Auge and along the Seine valley.

In summer, the hot weather comes earlier inland than on the coast, and the beach season does not begin before June, when the last storms have died away. From Le Tréport to the Mont-St-Michel, the coast is taken over by the people in search of sea air, relaxation and amusement. The sky remains hazy, the sunshine has a special quality. The inevitable changes in the weather are felt most inland.

The autumn months are the wettest of the year but as soon as November approaches there are many magnificent days. It is the time of year to enjoy the wonderful changing colours of the forest trees. The light is incomparably soft, making some stone buildings appear all the more substantial. It is never very cold.

Mean Temperatures					
January	February	March	April	May	June
min max °F					
33° 44°	35° 46°	37° 51°	41° 55°	46° 62°	50° 68°
min max °C					
1° 7°	1° 8°	3° 11°	5° 13°	8° 17°	10° 20°
July	August	September	October	November	December
min max °F					
53° 71°	53° 71°	51° 68°	40° 59°	40° 51°	35° 46°
min max °C					
12° 22°	12° 22°	11° 20°	7° 15°	4° 11°	2° 8°

Precipitation					
January	February	March	April	May	June
Average monthly fall					
68mm	55mm	44mm	47mm	54mm	43mm
July	August	September	October	November	December
Average monthly fall					
50mm	57mm	65mm	72mm	75mm	60mm

Getting there

By air

The various international and other independent airlines operate services to **Paris** (Roissy-Charles de Gaulle and Orly airports), and the main provincial airports: Caen, Cherbourg, Le Havre and Rouen. Check with your travel agent, however, before booking direct flights, as it is sometimes cheaper to travel via Paris.

Contact airline companies and travel agents for details of package tour flights with a rail or coach link-up as well as Fly-Drive schemes.

Arriving by sea from the UK or Ireland

There are numerous **cross-Channel services** (passenger and car ferries, hovercraft) from the United Kingdom and Ireland and also the rail Shuttle through the Channel Tunnel (**Le Shuttle-Eurotunnel**, ☎ 0990 353-535). To choose the most suitable route between your port of arrival and your destination use the Michelin Tourist and Motoring Atlas France, Michelin map 911 (which gives travel times and mileages) or Michelin maps from the 1:200,000 series (with the yellow cover). For details apply to travel agencies or to:

P & O Stena Line Ferries	Channel House, Channel View Road, Dover CT17 9JT, ☎ 0990 980 980 or 01304 863 000 (Switchboard)
Hoverspeed	International Hoverport, Marine Parade, Dover, Kent CT17 9TG, ☎ 0990 240 241, fax 01304 240088 www.hoverspeed.co.uk
Brittany Ferries	Millbay Docks; Plymouth, Devon. PL1 3EW. ☎ 0990 360 360
Portsmouth Commercial Port (and ferry information)	George Byng Way, Portsmouth, Hampshire PO2 8SP, ☎ 01705 297391, fax 01705 861165.
Irish Ferries	50 West Norland Street, Dublin 2. ☎ (353) 1-6-610-511.
Seafrance	Eastern Docks, Dover, Kent, CT16 1JA ☎ 01304 212696, fax 01304 240033.

By rail

Eurostar runs via the Channel Tunnel between **London** (Waterloo) and **Paris** (Gare du Nord) in 3hr (bookings and information ☏ 0345 303 030 in the UK; b 1-888-EUROSTAR in the US). In Paris it links to the high-speed rail network (TGV) which covers most of France.

Eurailpass, Flexipass and **Saverpass** are travel passes which may be purchased in the US. Contact your travel agent or: **Rail Europe** 2100 Central Ave. Boulder, CO, 80301, ☏ 1-800-4-EURAIL and in the UK 179 Piccadilly London W1V OBA, ☏ 0990 848 848; **Europrail International** ☏ 1-888-667-9731. Information on schedules can be obtained on web sites for these agencies and the **SNCF**, respectively: www.raileurop.com.us, www.eurail.on.ca, www.sncf.fr

Tickets bought in France must be validated *(composter)* by using the orange automatic date-stamping machines at the platform entrance (failure to do so may result in a fine).

The French railway company SNCF operates a telephone information, reservation and prepayment service in English from 7am to 10pm (French time). In France call ☏ 08 36 35 35 39 (when calling from outside France, drop the initial 0).

By coach

Regular coach services operate from London to Paris and to large provincial towns:

Eurolines (London), 4 Cardiff Road, Luton, Bedfordshire, L41 1PP ☏ 0990 143219, fax 01582 400694 welcome@eurolinesuk.com and www.eurolines.co.uk

Eurolines (Paris), 28 avenue du Général-de-Gaulle, 93541 Bagnolet; ☏ 08 36 69 52 52

Travellers with special needs

The sights described in this guide which are easily accessible to people of reduced mobility are indicated in the Admission times and charges section by the symbol ♿.

Useful information on transportation, holidaymaking and sports associations for the disabled is available from the *Comité National Français de Liaison pour la Réadaptation des Handicapés* (CNRH), 236 bis rue de Tolbiac, 75013 Paris. Call their international information number ☏ 01 53 80 66 44, or write to request a catalogue of publications. Web-surfers can find information for slow walkers, mature travellers and others with special needs at www.access-able.com and www.handitel.org. For information on museum access for the disabled contact La Direction, *Les Musées de France, Service Accueil des Publics Spécifiques*, 6 rue des Pyramides, 75041 Paris Cedex 1, ☏ 01 40 15 35 88.

The Red Guide France and the **Michelin Camping Caravaning France Guide** indicate hotels and camp sites with facilities suitable for physically handicapped people.

Motoring in France

Planning your route – The area covered in this guide is easily reached by main motorways and national routes. **Michelin map 911** indicates the main itineraries as well as alternate routes for avoiding heavy traffic during busy holiday periods, and gives estimated travel times. **Michelin map 914** is a detailed atlas of French motorways, indicating tolls, rest areas and services along the route; it includes a table for calculating distances and times. The latest Michelin route-planning service is available on Internet, **www.ViaMichelin.com**. Travellers can calculate a precise route using such options as shortest route, route avoiding toll roads, Michelin-recommended route and gain access to tourist information (hotels, restaurants, attractions). The service is available on a pay-per-route basis or by subscription.

The roads are very busy during the holiday period (particularly weekends in July and August), and to avoid traffic congestion it is advisable to follow the recommended secondary routes (signposted as *Bison Futé – itinéraires bis*). The motorway network-includes rest areas *(aires)* and petrol stations, usually with restaurant and shopping complexes attached, about every 40km/25mi, so that long-distance drivers have no excuse not to stop for a rest every now and then.

Documents – Travellers from other European Union countries and North America can drive in France with a valid national or home-state **driving licence**. An **international driving licence** is useful because the information on it appears in nine languages (keep in mind that traffic officers are empowered to fine motorists). A permit is available (US$10) from the National Automobile Club (visit their Web site or call 650-294-7000); or contact your local branch of the American Automobile Association. For the vehicle it is necessary to have the registration papers (logbook) and a nationality plate of the approved size.

Insurance – Certain motoring organisations (AAA, AA, RAC) offer accident insurance and breakdown service schemes for members. Check with your current insurance company in regard to coverage while abroad. If you plan to hire a car using your credit card, check with the company, which may provide liability insurance automatically (and thus save you having to pay the cost for optimum coverage).

Highway Code – The minimum driving age is 18. Traffic drives on the right. It is compulsory for the front-seat passengers to wear **seat belts** and it is also compulsory for the back-seat passengers when the car is fitted with them. Children under the age of 10 must travel on the back seat of the vehicle. Full or dipped headlights must be switched on in poor visibility and at night; use side-lights only when the vehicle is stationary.

In the case of a **breakdown** a red warning triangle or hazard warning lights are obligatory. In the absence of stop signs at intersections, cars must **yield to the right**. Traffic on main roads outside built-up areas (priority indicated by a yellow diamond sign) and on roundabouts has right of way. Vehicles must stop when the lights turn red at road junctions and may filter to the right only when indicated by an amber arrow.

The regulations on **drinking and driving** (limited to 0.50g/l) and **speeding** are strictly enforced – usually by an on-the-spot fine and/or confiscation of the vehicle.

Speed limits – Although liable to modification, these are as follows:
– toll motorways *(péage)* 130kph/80mph (110kph/68mph when raining);
– dual carriageways and motorways without tolls 110kph/68mph (100kph/62mph when raining);
– other roads 90kph/56mph (80kph/50mph when raining) and in towns 50kph/31mph;
– outside lane on motorways during daylight, on level ground and with good visibility – minimum speed limit of 80kph/50mph.

 Parking Regulations – In town there are zones where parking is either restricted or subject to a fee; tickets should be obtained from the ticket machines (*horodateurs* – small change necessary) and displayed inside the windscreen on the driver's side; failure to display may result in a fine, or towing and impoundment. In some towns you may find blue parking zones *(zone bleue)* marked by a blue line on the pavement or road and a blue signpost with a P and a small square underneath. In this case you have to display a cardboard disc with various times indicated on it. This will enable you to stay for 1hr 30min (2hr 30min over lunch time) free. Discs are available in supermarkets or petrol stations (ask for a *disque de stationnement*); they are sometimes given away free.

Tolls – In France, most motorway sections are subject to a toll *(péage)*. You can pay in cash or with a credit card (Visa, Mastercard).

Car Rental

There are car rental agencies at airports, railway stations and in all large towns throughout France. European cars have manual transmission; automatic cars are available in larger cities only if an advance reservation is made. Drivers must be over 21; between ages 21-25, drivers are required to pay an extra daily fee of 50-100F; some companies allow drivers under 23 only if the reservation has been made through a travel agent.

It is relatively expensive to hire a car in France; Americans in particular will notice the difference and should make arrangements before leaving, take advantage of fly-drive offers, or seek advice from a travel agent, specifying requirements.

Central Reservation in France:

Avis: ☎08 02 05 05 05
Budget France: 08 00 10 00 01
SIXT-Eurorent: 01 44 38 55 55
Baron's Limousine and Driver: 01 45 30 21 21

Europcar: ☎08 03 352 352
Hertz France: ☎08 03 861 861
National-CITER: 01 44 38 61 61

Overseas Motorhome Tours, Inc organises escorted tours and individual rental of recreational vehicles: in the US ☎ 800-322-2127; outside the US ☎ 1-310-543-2590; Internet www.omtinc.com

Petrol (US: gas) – French service stations dispense: *sans plomb 98* (super unleaded 98), *sans plomb 95* (super unleaded 95) and *diesel/gazole* (diesel). Petrol is considerably more expensive in France than in the USA. Prices are listed on signboards on the motorways; it is usually cheaper to fill up after leaving the motorway, check the large hypermarkets on the outskirts of town.

Accommodation

The **Places to stay map** indicates recommended places for overnight stops and can be used in conjunction with the current **Michelin Red Guide France**, which lists a selection of hotels and restaurants.

Loisirs Accueil is a booking service that has offices in most French *départements*: contact the tourist offices listed above for further information, or Réservation Loisirs Accueil, 280, boulevard St-Germain, 75007 Paris, ☎ 01 44 11 10 44 (www.resinfrance.com for internet booking).

A guide to good-value, family-run hotels, **Logis et Auberges de France**, is available from the French Tourist Office, as are lists of other kinds of accommodation such as hotel-châteaux, bed-and-breakfasts etc. **Relais et châteaux** provides information on booking in luxury hotels with character: 15 , rue Galvani, 75017 Paris, ☎ 01 45 72 90 00.

Economy Chain Hotels – If you need a place to stop en route, these can be useful, as they are inexpensive (30-45€ for a double room) and generally located near the main road. While breakfast is available, there may not be a restaurant; rooms are small, with a television and bathroom. Central reservation numbers:
– **B&B** ☎ 0 803 00 29 29 from abroad, dial (0) 2 98 33 75 00
– **Etap Hôtel** ☎ in France, 08 92 68 89 00
– **Mister Bed** ☎ 01 46 14 38 00
– **Villages Hôtel** ☎ 03 80 60 92 70
The hotels listed below are slightly more expensive (from 45€), and offer a few more amenities and services. Central reservation numbers:
– **Campanile** ☎ 01 64 62 46 46
– **Kyriad** ☎ 01 64 62 51 96
– **Ibis** ☎ 0 803 88 22 22

Rural accommodation

Self-catering accommodation – The **Maison des Gîtes de France** is an information service on self-catering accommodation in the regions of France. *Gîtes* usually take the form of a cottage or apartment decorated in the local style where visitors can make themselves at home.

Contact the Gîtes de France office in Paris: 59 , rue St-Lazare, 75439 Paris Cedex 09, ☎ 01 49 70 75 75, or their representative, in the UK, **Brittany Ferries** *(address above)*. The web site is quite complete and has an excellent English version (www.gites-de-france.fr).

Gîtes de France, Springfield Books Ltd and FHG Publications/World Leisure Marketing all publish listings of *gîtes* in France with details of how to book. Try contacting the local tourist offices as they also publish lists of available properties.

Bed and Breakfast – Gîtes de France *(see above)* publishes a booklet on bed and breakfast accommodation *(chambres d'hôtes)* which include a room and breakfast at a reasonable price. You can also contact:
Bed & Breakfast (France), International reservations centre, PO Box 66, Henley-on-Thames, Oxon RG9 1XS, ☎ (01491) 578 803, Fax (01491) 410 806.

Youth Hostels

There are two main youth hostel *(auberge de jeunesse)* associations in France.
– **Ligue Française pour les Auberges de Jeunesse**, 38, boulevard Raspail, 75007 Paris, ☎ 01 45 48 69 84, Fax 01 45 44 57 47
– **Fédération Unie des Auberges de Jeunesse**, 27, rue Pajol, 75012 Paris, ☎ 01 44 89 87 27, Fax 01 44 89 87 10, www.Fuaj.org.
Holders of an International Youth Hostel Federation card should contact the IYHF in their own country for information and membership applications (US ☎ 202 783 6161; UK ☎ 1727 855215; Canada ☎ 613-273 7884; Australia ☎ 61-2-9565-1669; internet www.iyhf.org).

Camping

There are numerous officially graded sites with varying standards of facilities throughout the region; the **Michelin Guide Camping Caravaning France** lists a selection of the best camp sites. An International Camping Carnet for caravans is useful but not compulsory; it can be obtained from the motoring organisations or the Camping and Caravanning Club (Greenfield House, Westwood Way, Coventry CV4 8JH; ☎ (01203) 694-995).

The Fédération Française des Stations Vertes de Vacances, Hôtel du Département de la Côte d'Or, BP 1601, 21035 Dijon Cedex, ☎ 03 80 49 97 80, publishes two guides (no charge), *Guide des stations vertes de vacances* and *Guide des villages de neige*, which list accommodation, leisure facilities and natural attractions in rural locations.

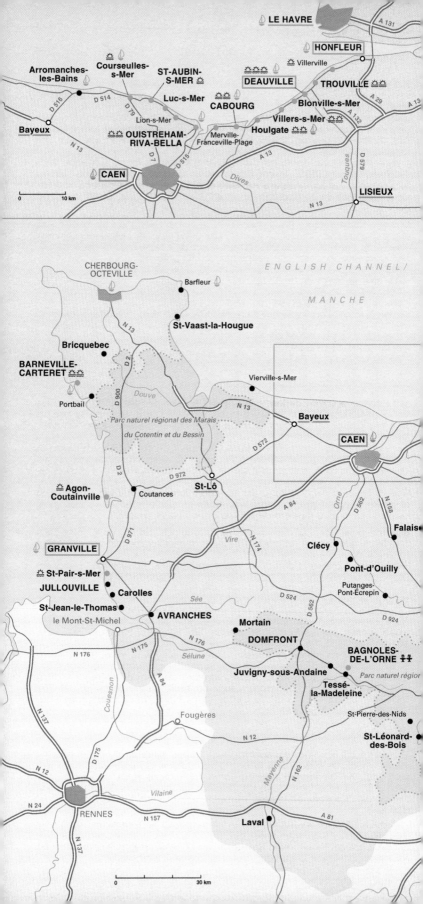

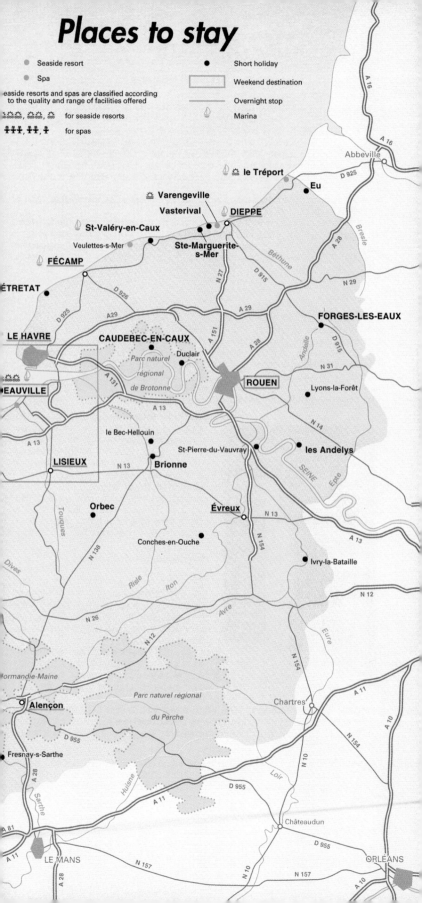

Places to stay

Seaside resort
Spa

Seaside resorts and spas are classified according to the quality and range of facilities offered

for seaside resorts

for spas

Short holiday

Weekend destination

Overnight stop

Marina

le Tréport

Eu

Varengeville

Vasterival

DIEPPE

St-Valéry-en-Caux

Ste-Marguerite-s-Mer

Veulettes-s-Mer

FÉCAMP

FORGES-LES-EAUX

ÉTRETAT

CAUDEBEC-EN-CAUX

LE HAVRE

Parc naturel régional de Brotonne

Duclair

ROUEN

Lyons-la-Forêt

EAUVILLE

le Bec-Hellouin

LISIEUX

Brionne

St-Pierre-du-Vauvray

les Andelys

Orbec

Évreux

Conches-en-Ouche

Ivry-la-Bataille

Normandie-Maine

Parc naturel régional du Perche

Chartres

Alençon

Fresnay-s-Sarthe

Châteaudun

LE MANS

ORLÉANS

Basic information

Medical treatment

First aid, medical advice and chemists' night service rota are available from chemists (*pharmacie* – green cross sign). Prescription drugs should be clearly labelled and tourists are advised to carry a copy of prescriptions.

It is advisable to take out comprehensive insurance cover as medical treatment in French hospitals or clinics must be paid for by the recipient. Nationals of non-EU countries should check with their insurance companies about policy limitations. Reimbursement can then be negotiated with the insurance company according to the terms of the policy held.

American Express offers insurance policies for card-holders for any medical, legal or personal emergency. Contact the company for details.

British citizens should apply to the Department of Health and Social Security for **Form E 111**, which entitles the holder to urgent treatment for accident or unexpected illness in EU countries. A refund of part of the costs of treatment can be obtained on application in person or by post to the local Social Security Offices (Caisse Primaire d'Assurance Maladie).

Currency

There are no restrictions on the amount of currency visitors can take into France, however, the amount of cash you may take out of France is subject to a limit, so visitors carrying a lot of cash should complete a currency declaration form on arrival.

The European Union's currency unit, the **euro**, is in use in France. French francs (notes and coins) can be exchanged in banks until the end of June 2002, but only the euro is accepted in transactions.

During the introduction of the euro, some prices quoted in this book may be approximate conversions from the former currency.

A. EM/MICHELIN

Tipping – Since a service charge is automatically included in the prices of meals and accommodation in France, it is not necessary to tip in restaurants and hotels. However if the service in a restaurant is especially good or if you have enjoyed a fine meal, an extra tip (this is the *pourboire*, rather than the *service*) is a well-appreciated gesture. Usually 2 or 3 euro is enough, but if the bill is big (a large party or a luxury restaurant), it is not uncommon to leave 7 euro or more.

Banks

Banks are usually open from 9am to noon and 2pm to 5pm and are closed on Mondays or Saturdays (except on market days); some branches open for limited transactions on Saturdays. Banks close early on the day before a bank holiday.

A passport is necessary as identification when cashing cheques in banks. Commission charges vary and hotels usually charge more than banks for cashing cheques for non-residents.

Most banks have **cash dispensers** (ATM) which accept international credit or debit cards and are easily recognised by the logo showing a hand holding a card. American Express cards can be used only in dispensers operated by the Crédit Lyonnais Bank or by American Express.

Credit cards – American Express, Visa (Carte Bleue), Mastercard/Eurocard and Diners Club are widely accepted in shops, hotels and restaurants and petrol stations. If your card is lost or stolen while you are in France, call one of the following 24-hour numbers:

American Express	☎ 01 47 77 72 00	**Visa**	☎ 08 36 69 08 80
Mastercard/Eurocard	☎ 01 45 67 84 84	**Diners Club**	☎ 01 49 06 17 50

Such loss or theft must also be reported to the local police who will issue a certificate to show to the credit card company.

Public holidays

Public services, museums and other monuments may be closed or may vary their hours of admission on the following public holidays:

1 January	New Year's Day *(Jour de l'An)*
Easter Day and Easter Monday *(Pâques)*	
1 May	May Day
8 May	VE Day
40 days after Easter	Ascension Day *(Ascension)*
7th Sun after Easter	Whitsun *(Pentecôte)*
14 July	France's National Day (Bastille Day)
15 August	Assumption *(Assomption)*
1 November	All Saint's Day *(Toussaint)*
11 November	Armistice Day
25 December	Christmas Day *(Noël)*

National museums and art galleries are closed on Tuesdays; municipal museums are generally closed on Mondays. In addition to the usual school holidays at Christmas and in the spring and summer, there are long mid-term breaks (10 days to a fortnight) in February and early November.

Post and telephone

Post offices open Mondays to Fridays, 8am to 7pm, Saturdays, 8am to noon. Smaller branch post offices often close at lunchtime between noon and 2pm and in the afternoon at 4pm.
Postage via air mail to
– UK letter (20g) 0.46€
– North America letter (20g) 0.67€
– North America postcard 0.63€
– Australia and New Zealand letter (20g) 0.79€
Stamps are also available from newsagents and tobacconists.
Stamp collectors should ask for *timbres de collection* in any post office.
Poste Restante (General Delivery) mail should be addressed as follows: Name, Poste Restante, Poste Centrale, postal code of the *département* followed by town name, France. The *Michelin Red Guide France* gives local postal codes.

Public Telephones – Most public phones in France use prepaid phone cards *(télécartes)*, rather than coins. Some telephone booths accept credit cards (Visa, Mastercard/Eurocard). *Télécartes* (50 or 120 units) can be bought in post offices, branches of France Télécom, *bureaux de tabac* (cafés that sell cigarettes) and newsagents and can be used to make calls in France and abroad. Calls can be received at phone boxes where the blue bell sign is shown; the phone will not ring, so keep your eye on the little message screen.

National calls – French telephone numbers have 10 digits. Paris and Paris region numbers begin with 01; 02 in northwest France; 03 in northeast France; 04 in southeast France and Corsica; 05 in southwest France. Numbers beginning with 08 (special rates) cannot be called from outside France.

International calls – To call France from abroad, dial the country code (33) + 9-digit number (omit the initial 0). When calling abroad from France dial 00, then dial the country code followed by the area code and number of your correspondent.

International dialling codes (00 + code):

Australia	☎ 61	New Zealand	☎ 64
Canada	☎ 1	United Kingdom	☎ 44
Eire	☎ 353	United States	☎ 1

Conversion Tables

Weights and measures

1 kilogram (kg)	2.2 pounds (lb)	2.2 pounds
1 metric ton (tn)	1.1 tons	1.1 tons

to convert kilograms to pounds, multiply by 2.2

1 litre (l)	2.1 pints (pt)	1.8 pints
1 litre	0.3 gallon (gal)	0.2 gallon

to convert litres to gallons, multiply by 0.26 (US) or 0.22 (UK)

1 hectare (ha)	2.5 acres	2.5 acres
1 square kilometre (km²)	0.4 square miles (sq mi)	0.4 square miles

to convert hectares to acres, multiply by 2.4

1 centimetre (cm)	0.4 inches (in)	0.4 inches
1 metre (m)	3.3 feet (ft) - 39.4 inches - 1.1 yards (yd)	
1 kilometre (km)	0.6 miles (mi)	0.6 miles

to convert metres to feet, multiply by 3.28 . kilometres to miles, multiply by 0.6

Clothing

Women								Men
	35	4	2½		40	7½	7	
	36	5	3½		41	8½	8	
	37	6	4½		42	9½	9	
Shoes	38	7	5½		43	10½	10	**Shoes**
	39	8	6½		44	11½	11	
	40	9	7½		45	12½	12	
	41	10	8½		46	13½	13	
	36	4	8		46	36	36	
	38	6	10		48	38	38	
Dresses &	40	8	12		50	40	40	**Suits**
Suits	42	12	14		52	42	42	
	44	14	16		54	44	44	
	46	16	18		56	46	48	
	36	08	30		37	14½	14,5	
	38	10	32		38	15	15	
Blouses &	40	12	14		39	15½	15½	**Shirts**
sweaters	42	14	36		40	15¾	15¾	
	44	16	38		41	16	16	
	46	18	40		42	16½	16½	

Sizes often vary depending on the designer. These equivalents are given for guidance only.

Speed

kph	10	30	50	70	80	90	100	110	120	130
mph	6	19	31	43	50	56	62	68	75	81

Temperature

Celsius (°C)	0°	5°	10°	15°	20°	25°	30°	40°	60°	80°	100°
Fahrenheit (°F)	32°	41°	50°	59°	68°	77°	86°	104°	140°	176°	212°

To convert Celsius into Fahrenheit, multiply °C by 9, divide by 5, and add 32.
To convert Fahrenheit into Celsius, subtract 32 from °F, multiply by 5, and divide by 9.

To use your **personal calling card** dial:

AT&T . . . ☏ 0-800 99 00 11   Sprint . . . . ☏ 0-800 99 00 87
MCI . . . . ☏ 0-800 99 00 19   Canada Direct . . . . ☏ 0-800 99 00 16

International Information, US/Canada: 00 33 12 11
International operator: 00 33 12 + country code
Local directory assistance: 12
Toll-free numbers in France begin with 0 800.

Emergency numbers:			
Police:	17	**"SAMU"** (Paramedics):	15
Fire (Pompiers):	18		

Minitel – France Télécom operates a system offering directory enquiries (free of charge up to 3min), travel and entertainment reservations, and other services (cost varies between 0.37F – 5.57F/min). These small computer-like terminals can be found in some post offices, hotels and France Télécom agencies and in many French homes. 3614 PAGES E is the code for **directory assistance in English** (turn on the unit, dial 3614, hit the *connexion* button when you get the tone, type in "PAGES E", and follow the instructions on the screen).

Cellular phones in France have numbers which begin with 06. Two-watt (lighter, shorter reach) and eight-watt models are on the market, using the Itinéris (France Télécom) or SFR network. *Mobicartes* are prepaid phone cards that fit into mobile units. Cell phone rentals (delivery or airport pickup provided):

A.L.T. Rent A Phone   ☏ 01 48 00 06 60, e-mail altloc@jre.fr
Rent a Cell Express   ☏ 01 53 93 78 00, fax 01 53 93 78 09
Cell' Force   ☏ 01 44 40 02 80, fax 01 44 40 02 88

Shopping

The big stores and larger shops are open Mondays to Saturdays from 9am to 6.30 or 7.30pm. Smaller, individual shops may close during the lunch hour. Food shops – grocers, wine merchants and bakeries – are open from 7am to 6.30 or 7.30pm; some open on Sunday mornings. Many food shops close between noon and 2pm and on Mondays. Hypermarkets usually open until 9pm or 11pm.

People travelling to the USA cannot import plant products or fresh food, including fruit, cheeses and nuts. It is alright to carry tinned products or preserves.

VAT refunds are available to visitors from outside the EU only if purchases exceed US$ 200 per store, but repeat visits to a store can be combined. The value-added tax on goods varies between 4.8 and 18.6% of the sale price, so it can be worth your while to recover it. The system works in large stores which cater to tourists, in luxury stores and other shops advertising "Duty Free". Show your passport, and the store will complete a form which is to be stamped (at the airport) by a European customs agents. The sum due can be collected at the airport or by mailing the forms from home. The most practical form of reimbursement is one made directly to your credit card account.

Electricity

The electric current is 220 volts. Circular two pin plugs are the rule – an electrical adaptor may be necessary. US appliances (hairdryers, shavers) will not work without one. Adapters are on sale in electronics stores and also at international airports.

Time

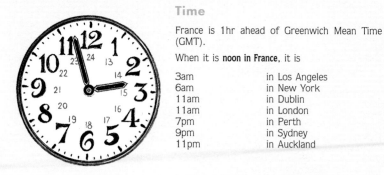

France is 1hr ahead of Greenwich Mean Time (GMT).

When it is **noon in France**, it is

3am	in Los Angeles
6am	in New York
11am	in Dublin
11am	in London
7pm	in Perth
9pm	in Sydney
11pm	in Auckland

In France "am" and "pm" are not used but the 24-hour clock is widely applied.

Sport and recreation

Normandy's long coastline has many impressive headlands and rocky foreshores punctuated by sandy beaches; this variety makes it suitable for many maritime sports.

Weather – For any outdoor activity on sea or land, it is useful to have reliable weather forecasts. For coastal weather reports, ☏ 08 36 65 08 followed by the number of the *département* and for general weather reports, ☏ 08 36 68 02 followed by the number of the *département*:

Caen	☏ 08 36 68 08 14	☏ 08 36 68 02 14
Cherbourg	☏ 08 36 68 08 50	☏ 08 36 38 02 50
Le Havre	☏ 08 36 68 08 76	☏ 08 36 68 02 76.

The Minitel service 36 15 METEO gives weather forecasts for the next five days, tides, wind forces *(see the Beaufort scale below)* etc.

Cruises along the River Seine – A number of boats able to accommodate between 80 and 350 passengers visit the main harbours (Le Havre, Honfleur, Rouen). Trips can take half a day or a whole day, including meals on board. Groups of 50 people or more can book luxury cruises between Paris and Honfleur. The following list features the most popular boats offering this type of excursion: the *Salamandre* (cruises stopping at Villequier, Caudebec-en-Caux and Rouen, tour of Rouen harbour and bay); the *Bali* (barge offering cruises leaving from Conflans-Ste-Honorine); the *Normandie* (residential boat travelling between Paris and Honfleur from mid-April to end of Oct); the *Château-Gaillard*; the *Guillaume-le-Conquérant* (Rouen, Elbeuf, Les Andelys); the *Chateaubriand* (restaurant-barge leaving from Rouen and heading for Caudebec-en-Caux or La Bouille or Duclair).

Parks and gardens – In the Haute-Normandie, the gentle, rolling countryside has always been an incentive for man to tame nature and produce beautiful gardens which are the perfect setting for a leisurely stroll or even a spot of quiet meditation. Thanks to the imagination and creativity of both gardeners and enlightened landlords, the parks and gardens of Normandy have become one of the area's most appreciated features and most visited sights. There follows a list of the main parks described in this guide:

Park of the **Château d'Acquigny** *(see p 254)*
Park of the **Château de Beaumesnil** *(see p 101)*
Park of the Bois des Moutiers in **Varengeville-sur-Mer** *(see p 333)*
Jardins de **Bosmelet** *(see p 143)*
Parc Zoologique de **Clères** *(see p 142)*
Jardins de Claude Monet in **Giverny** *(see p 215)*
Park of the **Château de Launay** *(see p 104)*
Jardin des Plantes in **Rouen** *(see p 305)*
Park of the Château du **Champ de Bataille** *(see p 133)*
Park of the **Château de Miromesnil** *(see p 69)*

Further information about Normandy's parks and gardens can be obtained from the **Agence Régionale de l'Environnement de Haute-Normandie**, Le Cloître des Pénitents, 8 allée Daniel-Lavallé, 76000 Rouen, ☏ 02 35 15 78 00. You can also contact the **Comité Régional du Tourisme de Normandie**, Le Doyenné, 14 rue Charles-Corbeau, 27000 **Évreux**, ☏ 02 32 33 79 00, which publishes a free guide presenting around 30 parks and gardens open to the public (generally between May and October).

Swimming – The first thing to do is become acquainted with the rhythm of the tides which alternate from high tide to low tide every 6hr. It is usually safer and warmer to bathe on an incoming tide. On steeply sloping shingle beaches high tide can be dangerous as children are rapidly out of their depth. Low tide on the other hand is often impatiently awaited by a happy group with nets for shrimping or forks and spades to dig for bait or pails for gathering mussels and crabs.
Guarded beaches have a system of flags to warn bathers of possible risks: green – safe bathing; orange – be careful; red – bathing prohibited.

Every year a number of seaside resorts are awarded a "Pavillon Bleu d'Europe" label on account of the excellence of their beaches or sailing harbours. The criteria for inclusion are extremely rigorous and apply to the cleanliness of the water, the extent of swimming and sporting facilities, safety measures, waste management and public awareness campaigns focusing on the environment.
The "Pavillon Bleu d'Europe" scheme is a hallmark of quality for the 18 European countries taking part in the operation.
Details from the Fondation pour l'Éducation et l'Environnement Europe (FEEE), 6 avenue du Maine, 75015 Paris, ☏ 01 45 49 40 50.

The Secrets of the Tide

This curious phenomenon, which manifests itself quite spectacularly in the English Channel, is due to the influence of the moon and, to a lesser extent, to that of the sun.

When the moon passes over the sea, it attracts the water and the water level rises as a result, creating a **high tide**.

Six hours later, after the earth has accomplished a quarter of a turn, the moon is no longer above the sea and its influence wanes: the water level drops, causing a **low tide**.

Every fortnight, when the tide-generating force of the sun acts in the same direction as that of the moon, it causes the greatest difference in tidal level – the **spring tide** – which occurs either at new moon or full moon.

When the tide-generating forces of the sun and the moon oppose each other, they produce the smallest difference in tidal level – the **neap tide** – which occurs at the first or last quarter of the moon.

In France, the highest spring tides, known as **equinoctial springs**, occur at the equinoxes, in March and September.

The difference in the water level between the high and low tide is called the **tidal range**. In France, this phenomenon is at its most striking in Granville, where the water is known to rise 16m/53ft during spring tides!

Sailing – A few old ships, restored or rebuilt after the original plans, can be seen cruising along the Channel coast. One of the most famous is *La Granvillaise* (its sister ship in Brittany is *La Cancalaise*) whose route goes through Granville Bay, the Îles Chausey, Mont-St-Michel Bay and the Channel Islands. For information and reservations apply to the Associations des Vieux Gréements Granvillais, boulevard des Amiraux, BP 614, 50406 Granville Cedex, ☎ 02 33 90 07 51.

The main moorings and marinas for visiting yachtsmen are indicated on the **Places to stay map** in the Introduction. They usually provide fuelling facilities, convenient water stands for drinking water and electricity points, WCs, showers and sometimes laundry facilities, handling equipment and repair facilties and a 24-hour guard. Many sailing clubs offer instruction. In season it is possible to hire boats with or without crew; apply to **the Fédération Française de Voile**: 55, avenue Kléber, 75784 Paris Cedex 16, ☎ 01 44 05 81 00.

A new French law requires foreigners who own or want to rent a boat (with an engine of more than 6hp) in France to take a compulsory test in sailing skills *(carte mer)*.

Spas – There exist in Nomandy several centres for thalassotherapy and water cures aimed at preventing or treating certain ailments. In addition to the bracing climate and vivifying sea air, they rely on the curative virtues of the local waters, mud and algae. The Normandy coast offers two establishments of this type, which also offer accommodation:

Cures Marines de Trouville, promenade des Planches, 14360 Trouville, ☎ 02 31 88 10 35. Recommended for those suffering from rheumatism, lymphatism, neurovegetative disorders and gynecological problems.

Thalasso-Deauville, boulevard de la Mer, BP 94, 14800 Deauville, ☎ 02 31 87 72 00. For cellulite, obesity, muscular re-education and heat treatment.

Bisquine "La Granvillaise"

Windsurfing – This sport, which is permitted on lakes and in sports and leisure centres, is subject to certain rules. Apply to sailing clubs. Boards may be hired on all major beaches.

Land sailing – The great stretches of sandy beach on the Calvados and Cotentin coasts are ideal for land sailing, an exhilarating sport performed on a three-wheeled cart equipped with a sail that can reach a speed of 100kph/63mph. A new, similar sport has recently seen the light of day: **speed sailing**, a form of wind-surfing on wheels. Further information may be obtained from the following addresses:
Fédération Française de Char à Voile, BP 165, 62605 Berck-sur-Mer Cedex, ☎ 03 21 84 27 69;
Aéroplage-Club du Havre, 16 rue de la Résidence, 76310 Ste-Adresse, ☎ 02 35 44 78 40.

Wind skating – For wind skating on skateboards, the best surface is concrete or tarmac or even grass. Some of the more enthusiastic train on the lawns of boulevard de Verdun in Dieppe.

Skin diving – The right conditions for deep-sea diving are to be found between Dieppe and Le Havre and between Barfleur and Avranches on the Cotentin coast. Further information can be obtained from the **Fédération Française d'Étude et de Sports Sous-Marins**, 24 quai de Rive-Neuve, 13007 Marseille, ☎ 04 91 33 99 31; Caen ☎ 02 31 86 04 12; Courseulles ☎ 02 31 37 93 96; Cherbourg ☎ 02 33 93 06 77; Coutances ☎ 02 33 07 51 40; St-Lô ☎ 02 33 57 04 93; Alençon ☎ 02 33 28 10 92.

Fishing – For those interested in freshwater fishing, it is necessary to know the dates of the *saison de la pêche*: all over France, the second Saturday in March heralds the start of the fishing season for rivers belonging to the first category *(première catégorie)*, ending on the third Sunday in September. In the case of second category rivers *(deuxième catégorie)*, fishing is permitted all year round, except for pike, which can be usually caught between July and January, depending on the area.
Normandy, well known for its luxuriant countrysides, is also dotted with a great many lakes, rivers and ponds of astounding variety. This particular type of topography makes it one of France's most treasured regions for fishing.
The fast-flowing rivers are peopled with fario trout, a local variety, and rainbow trout, brought over from America, whereas the various lakes and ponds are the favourite haunt of carnivorous species such as pike, pikeperch and salmon. The most popular rivers among anglers are believed to be the **Risle** (fario trout, carnivores); the **Iton** (pike, rainbow trout); the **Charentonne** (fario trout); the **Huisne** (grayling, fario trout); the **Touques** (fario trout); the **Yères** (fario trout); the **Bresle** (sea trout); the **Béthune** (trout); the **Arques** (salmon and sea trout); the **Durdent** (fario trout and sea trout).
Wherever you choose to go fishing, make sure you obey the current legislation on angling and apply for details from the relevant federations and associations. You have to become a member (for the year in progress) of an affiliated angling association in the *département* of your choice, pay the annual angling tax or buy a day card, and obtain permission from the landowner if you wish to fish on private land.
Fédération Départementale des AAPPMA de l'Eure, BP 411, 27504 Pont-Audemer Cedex, ☎ 02 32 57 10 73 or **Fédération Départementale des APP de Seine-Maritime**, 10 rue d'Harcourt, 76000 Rouen, ☎ 02 35 07 57 28.
A leaflet with a map and information called *La Pêche en France* (Fishing in France) is available from the **Conseil Supérieur de la Pêche**, 134 avenue de Malakoff, 75016 Paris, ☎ 01 45 02 20 20.
It is also possible to take up sea fishing, both along the coast or on board one of the boats leaving from Trouville, Honfleur, Fécamp, Dieppe, Le Tréport or St-Valery-en-Caux. The waters near Dieppe are believed to be teeming with fish and anglers who settle near the piers often see their patience rewarded by landing mackerel, pollock, sole or bass. Details are available from regional tourist offices.

Anglers are expected to comply with the present legislation on fishing, in particular concerning the size of their catch. They are expected to throw back certain fish into rivers if their length does not meet the required standards (40cm/16in in the case of pike; 23cm/9.2in in the case of trout).

Canoeing – Normandy's many rivers, lakes and reservoirs are ideal for this sport. The fast-flowing rivers in the Suisse Normande are particularly good for canoes and kayaks. Apply to the **Comité Départemental de Canoë-Kayak Calvados**, Stade Nautique, avenue Albert-Sorel, 14016 Caen, the **Fédération Française de Canoë-Kayak**, 87 quai de la Marne, BP 58, 94340 Joinville-le-Pont, ☎ 01 48 89 39 89 or the **Comité Départemental de Canoë-Kayak de la Manche**, 4 rue Charles-Péguy, appt 15, 50100 Cherbourg.

Ramblers on Cap de la Hague

Rambling – Walking is one of the best ways of discovering the countryside – the superb beech forests and the occasional manor houses on well-kept farms. Throughout the region there are short, medium and long distance footpaths marked with red and white lined posts. Detailed topographical guides are available showing the routes of the long-distance footpaths (*sentiers de grande randonnée* – GR) and giving good advice to walkers. The Topo-guides are published by the **Fédération Française de la Randonnée Pédestre** – Comité National des Sentiers de Grande Randonnée and are on sale at 64 rue de Gergovie 75014 Paris, ☎ 01 45 45 31 02.

Several of these well marked footpaths cross Normandy.

The **GR 2** follows the north bank of the Seine and crosses the Londe and Roumare forests.

The **GR 21** runs up the Lézarde Valley to meet the coast at Étretat and then continues to Le Tréport.

The **GR 211** crosses Maulévrier Forest in its path from the Seine Valley northwards to the coast at Conteville.

The **GR 22** from Paris to Mont-St-Michel crosses the Parc Naturel Régional Normandie-Maine in the southern part of Normandy.

The **GR 22A** and **22B** run westwards through the Orne, Calvados and Manche *départements*.

The **GR 221** passes through the Suisse Normande and then the Cotentin.

The **GR 222** starts in the Yvelines *département* and then winds its way across the Eure and Calvados *départements* to reach the Côte de Nacre at Deauville.

The **GR 223** follows the contours of the north and west coasts of the Cotentin peninsula.

The **GR 225** passes from the Vexin to the Forest of Lyons and then the Pays de Bray before reaching the sea at Dieppe.

The **GR 23** runs along the south bank of the Seine and through Brotonne Forest.

The **GR 25** makes a large loop around Rouen.

Regional parks are a popular destination for ramblers and nature lovers alike since they provide countless opportunities for a wide range of open-air activities. In these highly protected areas, extensive facilities have been set up to introduce visitors to local flora and fauna and to increase their awareness of environmental concerns. There are a great many sports in which to indulge, depending on the time of year. *For more details, read about the Regional nature parks described in this guide: the parks of BROTONNE, Perche (see MORTAGNE), Normandie-Maine (see ALENÇON) and Marais du Cotentin et du Bessin (see COTENTIN).*

Cycling – Good cycling country is found in the Brotonne Forest, Lyons Forest, Eure Valley, Seine Valley and along the Caux coast; there are steeper gradients in the Suisse Normande and the Cotentin peninsula.

The **Fédération Française de Cyclotourisme:** 8 rue Jean-Marie-Jégo, 75013 Paris, ☎ 01 44 16 88 88 supplies itineraries covering most of France, mentioning mileage, difficult routes and sights to see. **Bicy-Club de France**: 8 place de la Porte Champerret, 75017 Paris.

Comité Départemental de Cyclotourisme et VTT, Randonnée de l'Eure, 6 Le Clos Tiger, 27170 Beaumontel, ☎ 02 32 45 35 06.

Lists of cycle hire businesses are available from Tourist Information Centres.

Climbing – Climbers are attracted to the steep rocky slopes of the Alpes Mancelles and Suisse Normande, particularly the vertical walls of the Rochers du Parc near Clécy. For information apply to Tourist Information Centres or to the **Club Alpin-Français**, 92 rue de Géôle, 1400 Caen, ☎ 02 31 86 29 55 or to the **Comité Départemental d'Esca-lade et Varappe**, Le Château, 61150 Rânes, ☎ 02 33 36 24 63 or at Clécy, ☎ 02 31 69 72 82.

Riding and Pony Trekking – In such a well-known horse-breeding region many riding clubs and centres organise around 200 rides on the many miles of bridle-paths through the woodlands or exhilarating canters along the shore as well as pony-trekking holidays. There are many local gymkhanas and equestrian events and race-goers are spoilt for choice for a day at the races.
Information is available from:
Confédération Nationale des Usagers des Loisirs Équestres (CNULE), Maison de Tourisme de la Gironde, 21 cours de l'Intendance, 33000 Bordeaux, ☎ 05 56 09 01 93.
Délégation Nationale au Tourisme Équestre de la Fédération Française d'Équitation (A.N.T.E.), 30 avenue d'Iéna, 75116 Paris, ☎ 01 53 67 44 44;
Ligue de Normandie des Sports Équestres, 10 place de la Demi-Lune, BP 2018, 14089 Caen Cedex 6, ☎ 02 31 84 61 87, Fax 02 31 84 61 91.

Horse-drawn caravans – In the Orne and Calvados *départements* one can hire a horse-drawn caravan *(roulotte)*. Information on holidays in a horse-drawn caravan is available from Tourist Information Centres.

Hunting – For all enquiries apply to **Saint-Hubert Club de France**, 10 rue de Lisbonne, 75008 Paris, ☎ 01 45 22 38 90 or the **Union Nationale des Fédérations Départementales des Chasseurs**, 48 rue d'Alésia, 75014 Paris, ☎ 01 43 27 85 76.

Golf – Dedicated golf adepts will be able to indulge in all forms of their favourite sport (bunker, practice, training, putting-green, clubhouse) by applying to the **Ligue de Golf de Normandie**, 94 rue St-Jacques, 76600 Le Havre, ☎ 02 35 42 71 19. or the **Fédération Française de Golf**, 69 avenue Victor-Hugo, 75783 Paris Cedex 16, ☎ 01 44 17 63 00. The guide called *Golf, les Parcours Français*, based on Michelin map no 989 and published by Éditions Plein Sud, 65 rue Danton, 92300 Levallois-Perret, ☎ 01 47 48 03 03, provides comprehensive information about most French golf courses, including full addresses and telephone numbers.
It is always advisable to book first. Although some golf clubs are private, most of them welcome non-members but conditions for joining may vary from club to club.

Holidays on a theme

Heritage trails – To help tourists discover France's national heritage in its historical context, local municipalities all over the country have set up a number of routes focusing on a given theme. Each itinerary is clearly signposted by panels laid out along the French roads and is described in leaflets available from regional tourist offices.
Route des Maisons d'Écrivains – A literary tour leaving from Île-de-France and wending its way to Haute-Normandie via the Eure and Seine-Maritime *départements* will show you round a dozen houses that were once lived in by famous writers.
Château de Vascœuil, rue Jules-Michelet, 27910 Vascœuil, ☎ 02 35 23 62 35.
Route Normandie-Vexin – Discover the most striking sights and landscapes lying between Paris and Rouen: Giverny, Bizy, Mortemer, Château-Gaillard...
Madame Vergé, Présidente de la Route, 6 avenue Pierre-1er-de-Serbie, 75116 Paris, ☎ 01 47 20 51 71 or Château de Bizy, 27000 Vernon, ☎ 02 32 51 00 82.
Route du Val de Seine et des Abbayes – This route takes you on a tour of six abbeys situated between Rouen and Le Havre, including those of Jumièges, St-Wandrille and St-Martin-de-Boscherville.
Madame Cayron, Office de Tourisme de Rouen, BP 666, 76008 Rouen Cedex.
Route du Verre – In the Bresle Valley, from Le Tréport to Aumale, enjoy the sight of traditional glass-making, which has always produced fine articles of outstanding quality.
Monsieur Vialaret, Président de la Route, Mairie, 76430 Blangy-sur-Bresle, ☎ 02 35 93 50 05.
Route des Ducs de Normandie – A retrospective of 10 centuries of Normandy architecture featuring some of the area's most prestigious monuments and sites: Canapville, St-Germain-de-Livet, and Crèvecœur-en-Auge.
Monsieur de Ceunynck, Président, Château de Crèvecœur-en-Auge, 14340 Crèvecoeur-en-Auge, ☎ 02 31 63 02 45.
Route de l'Ivoire et des Épices – This itinerary takes you back to the Middle Ages, when the commerce of ivory and spices thrived, concentrating on the harbours of Eu and Le Havre, with a few glimpses inland (Valmont, Cany-Barville, Bailleul).

Route de l'Ivoire et des Épices, 110 rue Alexandre-le-Grand, 76400 Fécamp, ☎ 02 35 10 26 10.

Route du Patrimoine Cultural Québécois – This long route has been conceived especially for French Canadians arriving in France in an attempt to familiarise them with the lands of their ancestors..
Comité Chomedey de Maisonneuve, 33 rue Victor-Hugo, 10190 Estissac, ☎ 03 25 40 40 62.

Route de Guillaume le Conquérant – Learn all about the life and achievements of William, Duke of Normandy, by embarking on this historical trail of the legendary French statesman.
Madame la Présidente de la Route, 1 boulevard de Clichy, 75009 Paris, ☎ 01 42 81 04 59.

Thematic itineraries – An alternative series of routes devoted to traditional aspects of Normandy are also available to tourists visiting the area.
Three circuits, each representing around 30km/18mi, have been mapped out and are jointly referred to as *Goûtez à la Ferme en Pays de Caux*. They will delight amateur architects interested in half-timbered houses as well as gourmets with a soft spot for apple pie, cheese, jam and cider.
Visitors may also be tempted by the following tours:

Route des Colombiers Cauchois – Visit Normandy's famous dovecots nestling along the valleys of the Durdent, Valmont or Gonzeville.

Route du Fromage de Neufchâtel – The Pays de Bray will hold no more secrets for you after following this route from Mesnières-en-Bray to Forges-les-Eaux. Points of sale of Neufchâtel cheese are clearly signposted on the way.

Route de la Pomme et du Cidre – The countryside stretching from the Pays de Caux and the Pays de Bray is dotted with *cour-masures* planted with venerable apple trees. Leaflets about apples and cider making are available from local tourists offices.

Traditional markets – These provincial-style markets are usually held in the morning.

Calvados – Beuvron-en-Auge (Saturday afternoons); **Dives-sur-Mer** (Tuesdays); **Honfleur** (Saturdays); **St-Pierre-sur-Dives** (Mondays); **Trouville** (Wednesdays and Sundays).

Eure – Les Andelys (Saturdays); **Bernay** (Saturdays); **Évreux** (Wednesdays and Saturdays); **Gisors** (Mondays); **Louviers** (Saturdays); **Lyons-la-Forêt** (Thursdays); **Le Neubourg** (Wednesdays); **Pont-Audemer** (Mondays); **Verneuil-sur-Avre** (Saturdays).

Seine-Maritime – Caudebec-en-Caux (Saturdays); **Dieppe** (Saturdays); **Étretat** (Thursdays); **Eu** (Fridays); **Fécamp** (Saturdays); **Forges-les-Eaux** (Thursdays); **Harfleur** (Sundays); **Yvetot** (Wednesdays).

There are also markets specialised in regional products:

Calvados – Deauville (fish market every day in summer); **Honfleur** (antiques); **Lisieux** (country products on Wednesdays in July and August); **Pont-l'Évêque** (country products on Sunday mornings in July and August); **Trouville-sur-Mer** (covered fish market every day).

Eure – Bernay (foie gras in June); **Cormeilles** (country fare on Sundays in July and August); **Le Neubourg** (foie gras in October, November and December).

Orne – L'Aigle (travelling market on Tuesday mornings); **La Perrière** (traditional fare 14 July and 15 August); **Longny-au-Perche** (Wednesdays).

Seine-Maritime – Forges-les-Eaux (farmer's market on Sunday afternoons in July and August).

The **Caisse Nationale des Monuments Historiques et des Sites (CNMHS)** issues a pass that provides free, unlimited access to over 100 monuments and other sights belonging to France's national heritage, as well as to the temporary exhibitions staged at these venues. The pass is valid for the whole of France: it lasts for one year and costs 280F. The two abbeys included in the pass which are described in this guide are the Abbaye de Jumièges and the Abbaye du Bec-Hellouin.

Strolling Through the Beautiful Gardens of Basse-Normandie – Route Historique des Parcs et Jardins de Basse-Normandie, le Prieuré Saint-Michel, 61120 Crouttes, ☎ 02 33 39 15 15.
Here is a selection of gardens which are described in this guide:
Jardin des Plantes in **Caen** *(see p 1191)*
Park and gardens of the **Château de Canon** *(see p 315)*
Gardens of the **Château de Brécy** *(see p 94)*
Park and gardens of **Thury-Harcourt** *(see p 329)*
Botanical garden in **Vauville** *(see p 152)*
Parc Emmanuel-Liais and its greenhouses in **Cherbourg** *(see p 136)*
Jardin des Plantes Quesnel-Morinière in **Coutances** *(see p 153)*
Jardin Christian-Dior in **Granville** *(see p 217)*
Park of the Château de **Nacqueville** *(see p 149)*
Gardens of the **Château d'O** *(see p 1491)*
Gardens and terraces of the **Château de Sassy** *(see p 67)*

Visiting Mont-St-Michel Bay

The bay surrounding Mont-St-Michel, which features on UNESCO's list of World Nature and Culture Heritage Sites, is also an exceptional place on account of its tidal range – the greatest in continental Europe. During spring tides, the sea level can rise up to 14m/46ft between low and high tide. The water recedes 15km/9.5mi from the coast, then rushes back, accelerating its pace towards the end.

Throughout the year the two "**Maisons de la Baie**" in Genêts and Courtils welcome tourists, provide information and stage exhibitions and all sorts of other activities aimed at promoting the nature, culture and population of the bay.

Visits, crossings (5-6hr), walks, rambles (2hr 15min-4hr) and even bicycle tours are regularly organised. Placed under the supervision of specialised guides and lecturers, they are devoted to a number of different themes: pilgrimages, history, literature, geology, ornithology, the silting of the bay, spring tides etc. The *balades gourmandes* (a 25-30km/15.5-18.5mi cycling tour including a meal) is an excellent opportunity to enjoy the lush countryside as well as sample local gastronomy *(mountain bikes can be hired)*.

To obtain further information, including the programme of events, or to make reservations (essential), apply to:

Maison de la Baie du Mont-St-Michel, Relais des **Genêts**, place de la Mairie, 50530 Genêts, ☎ 02 33 70 86 46.

Maison de la Baie du Mont-St-Michel, Relais de **Courtils**, route de Roche Torin, 50220 Courtils, ☎ 02 33 60 11 01.

These *relais* are open daily from 15 April to 30 October. A manned telephone line is open to the public all year.

Historical Area of the Battle of Normandy – This itinerary was inaugurated in 1994 to celebrate the 50th anniversary of the Battle of Normandy. The waymarked itineraries take in the sites, museums and memorials relating to the events of June 1944. Eight themed itineraries help visitors to follow the events in a chronological order. The symbol is a sea gull.

Overlord-L'Assaut (70km/43.5mi) – from Pegasus Bridge to Bayeux via Sword, Juno and Gold beaches.

D-Day-Le Choc (130km/81mi) – from Bayeux to Carentan taking in Omaha Beach and St-Lô.

Objectif-Un Port (95km/59mi) – from Carentan to Cherbourg via Ste-Mère-Église and Valogne.

L'Affrontement (207km/129mi) – this itinerary completes the Overlord-L'Assaut one and carries on from Bénouville to Vire coming back by Caen.

Cobra-La Percée (155km/96mi) – from Cherbourg to Avranches by Coutances.

La Contre-Attaque (162km/100mi) – from Avranches to Alençon via Mortain. **L'Encerclement** (145km/90mi) – from Alençon to L'Aigle via Chambois and Montormel.

Le Dénouement (122km/76mi) – from Caen to L'Aigle by Montormel and Vimoutiers.

A passport (30F) valid for a year, and a book of coupons with reductions for the 25 museums belonging to the Historical Area are on sale.

The Channel Islands

Entry regulations

Passports are not required by British subjects. The same requirements apply for other tourists as in France *(see Planning your trip p xxx)*.

Travel

By air – There are flights from **Paris** to **Jersey** or **Guernsey** operated by Jersey European Airways. From **Dinard** and from **Cherbourg** by Aurigny Air Services.

By sea – From **Carteret** in 35min with Emeraude Lines (fast catamaran *Trident*), arrival at Gorey; apply to Emeraude Lines, 22 place de l'Église, 50270 Barneville-Carteret, ☎ 02 33 53 87 21.
– From **Granville** in 70min with Emeraude Lines (fast catamaran *Trident*), arrival at St Helier; apply to Emeraude Lines, 1 rue Lecampion, 50400 Granville, ☎ 02 33 50 16 36 or ☎ 02 33 50 77 45 *(Jersey only)*.
For **Sark**, **Herm** and **Alderney**, sea links are available leaving from Jersey.

Currency

The local currency issued by the banks of Jersey and Guernsey is not legal tender outside the islands. All the British clearing banks have branches in the Channel Islands.

Aurigny Air Service

Accommodation

There is a wide range of hotels and guesthouses: see **The Michelin Red Guide Great Britain and Ireland.**
Caravans are forbidden and there are therefore no caravan sites.
There are camp sites in Jersey at St Aubin and St Brelade; in Guernsey at Torteval, Vale, Castel, St Sampson's and St Peter Port; in Alderney at Saye Bay; in Herm at the Mermaid Site and the Little Seagull Camp Site.

Tourist Information Centres

Jersey

In **Paris** – Office de Tourisme de Jersey *(no address)*, ☎ 01 48 04 86 06.

In **Jersey** – Office de Tourisme, Liberation Square, St Helier, Jersey, Channel Islands JEI 1BB, ☎ 00 44 1534 878 000.

In **London** – Jersey Tourism Office, 35 Dover Street, London WIX 3RB, ☎ 00 40 11171 493 52 78.

Guernsey

In **Paris** – Maison de la Grande-Bretagne, 19 rue des Mathurins, 75009 Paris, ☎ 01 44 51 56 20.

In **Guernsey** – Tourism Offices, PO Box 23, St-Peter Port, Channel Islands JYI 3AN, ☎ 00 44 1481 723 552.

Alderney

In **Alderney** – Tourist Information Centre, Victoria Street, Alderney, Channel Islands, ☎ 00 01 48 1822 994.

Calendar of events

1st fortnight in March

Rouen................... International Nordic Festival ☎ 02 35 98 28 46

3rd weekend in March

Mortagne-au-Perche ...... "Foire au Boudin": Pudding Festival ☎ 02 33 83 76 76

April to October

Le Havre................ International Regattas

Mid-March

Caen .... "Aspects des Musiques d'Aujourd'hui"
☎ 02 31 50 05 64

From the preceding Sunday to Shrove Tuesday

Granville .... Carnival ☎ 02 33 91 30 03

In spring

Haras national du Pin ..... Horse-riding competition

30 April to 1 May

Rouen................... 24-hour boat race: international competition reunited
100 motor boats around Île Lacroix ☎ 02 32 08 32 40

1 May

Le Marais Vernier........ Branding of cows ☎ 02 32 57 61 62

May to September

Montivilliers .... "Les Concerts de l'Abbaye" Music Festival
☎ 02 35 22 68 70

In May

Mont-Saint-Michel....... Spring Festival of St Michael: folklore festivities and
Brothers of Charity procession

Château d'O............. Exhibition and sale of vintage cars

Whit Sunday and Whit Monday

Honfleur .... Seamen's Festival – Sunday: Blessing of the sea; Monday
morning: Seamen's Pilgrimage ☎ 02 31 89 23 30

Whit Monday

Bernay .... Pilgrimage to Notre-Dame-de-Couture

Sunday nearest 30 May, except Whit Sunday

Rouen................... Joan of Arc Festival. Fêtes de Rouen: films, medieval
market ☎ 02 32 08 13 90

Last Sunday in May

Mont de Cerisi .... Rhododendron Fair ☎ 02 33 66 52 62

Ascension Week

Coutances .... Jazz Festival; ☎ 02 33 76 78 50

Early June to mid-September

Lisieux .... Son et lumière "Des Vikings à Thérèse" at the Cathédrale
St-Pierre every evening at 9.45pm except Sundays
☎ 02 31 62 08 41

1st weekend in June

Cabourg................ Cabourg Film Festival – "Journées Romantiques"
☎ 02 31 91 01 09

6 June

Ste-Marie-du-Mont .... Commemoration of the airborne landing of 6 June 1944
at Utah Beach ☎ 02 33 71 58 00

2nd or 3rd Sunday in June *(next edition in 2000)*

Villedieu-les-Poêles .... The Great Coronation: Procession attended by members
of the Order of Malta *(every four years)*
☎ 02 33 61 00 16

*(1) For those places not mentioned in the guide, we have indicated the number of the
Michelin map at a 1/200 000 scale and the number of the fold.*

Deauville . . . . American Film Festival ☎ 02 31 14 14 14

Quillebeuf . . . . Branding of cows ☎ 02 35 37 23 16

Haras national du Pin . . . . . Horse racing events; special Percheron Competition, prestigious cross-country race and procession of carriages and stallions in the evening ☎ 02 33 39 92 01

Alençon, Argentan . . . . Septembre Musical de l'Orne:

Bagnoles-de-l'Orne, Bellême, Ceton, Château d'O, Carrouges, Mortrée, Sées . Music Festival ☎ 02 33 26 11 36 (Alençon) or 02 33 28 88 71 (Haras national du Pin)

Lessay . . . . "Foire de la Sainte-Croix": Holy Cross Fair, the largest and most typical fair in Normandy; amusements, Horse and Dog Fair on the moor ☎ 02 33 46 46 18

St-Lô . . . . "Nuits Foraines": Circus and Performing Arts Festival ☎ 02 33 05 02 09

Dieppe . . . . Every even year. International Kite Meeting ☎ 02 35 84 11 77

Le Havre . . . . Euromasters Sailing Competition ☎ 02 35 42 41 21

Mont-St-Michel . . . . Feast of the Archangel Michael: Mass in the abbey church in the presence of the bishops of Bayeux and Coutances ☎ 02 33 60 14 30

Lisieux . . . . St Thérèse Festival – On Saturday evening and Sunday; procession with shrine containing the saint's relics ☎ 02 31 48 55 08

Bellême . . . . "Mycologiades Internationales": Mushroom Festival ☎ 02 33 73 09 69

Dieppe-Le Havre-Rouen . . . "Octobre en Normandie": Music and Danse Festival ☎ 02 35 70 04 07

Biville . . . . Pilgrimage to the tomb of Thomas Hélye ☎ 02 33 52 72 98

Calvados . . . . "Equi' Days": Horseriding events ☎ 02 31 86 53 30

Essay 60 fold 3 *(1)*. . . . . "Foire au Boudin Blanc". White Pudding Fair ☎ 02 33 28 40 52

Sées . . . . Turkey Fair ☎ 02 33 28 74 79

Dreux . . . . "Les Flambarts" Carnival ☎ 02 37 46 01 73

St-Hilaire-du Harcouët . . . . Nativity Play ☎ 02 33 49 10 06

Gastronomic Fairs

Every year a number of fairs and events are held throughout Normandy in connection with local specialities. The following list features the most important ones.

March
International Pudding Festival in **Mortagne-au-Perche**

May
Mussels Fair in **Le Tréport**

June
Cherry Fair in **Vernon**

August
Seafood and Mackerel Fair in **Le Tréport**
Cheese Fair in **Livarot**

September
Cheese Fair in **Neufchâtel-en-Bray**

October
Food Market in **Beuvron-en-Auge**
Sheep and Horse Fair in **Veules-les-Roses**
Prawn Festival in **Honfleur**

November
Herring Fair in **Dieppe** and **St-Valery-en-Caux**

Quite often, these lively events are enhanced by a musical accompaniment provided by one of the many traditional folk groups that continue to perform in local villages.

The Channel Islands

In March
Jersey. . . . . Jersey Jazz Weekend

Late May
Jersey. . . . . Gastronomic Fair

In July
Guernsey . . . . Round Table Harbour Festival; Rocquaine regattas

Late July to early August
Sark . . . . Water Carnival

1st to 2nd Saturday in August
Alderney . . . . Carnival Week

2nd Thursday in August
Jersey. . . . . Jersey Battle of Flowers

3rd to 4th Thursday in August
Guernsey . . . . Battle of Flowers in Saumarez Park

Early September
Guernsey and Jersey . . . . . . Commemoration of the Battle of England (Battle of Britain Air)

3rd week in September
Jersey. . . . . International Folk and Blues Festival

P. Roy/EXPLORER

Books, videos and cassettes

Normandy by Nesta Roberts *(Collins, 1986)*

Six Armies in Normandy by Keegan *(Penguin)*

The Bayeux Tapestry by DM Wilson *(Thames and Hudson, 1985)*

Normandy, Brittany and the Loire Valley: Blue Guide *(AC Black and WW Norton, 1978)*

Norman Achievement by R Cassady *(Sidgwick & Jackson)*

The Archaeology of Brittany, Normandy and the Channel Islands by Bender *(Faber & Faber)*

The Normans and the Norman Conquest by R Allen Brown *(Boydell & Brewer, 1986)*

Access to Channel Ports and Access in Jersey (Holiday guides for the disabled). Obtainable from Access Project, 39 Bradley Gardens, (PHSP) London WI3 8HE.

A Holiday History of France by Ronald Hamilton *(Chatto and Windus)*

Claude Monet: Life at Giverny by Joyes *(Thames and Hudson)*

The Impressionists by William Gaunt *(Thames and Hudson)*

Food Lover's Guide to France by Patricia Wells *(Eyre and Spottiswoode)*

Normandy, Picardy and Pas de Calais by Barbara Eperon *(Christopher Helm)*

The Second World War (6 volumes) by Winston Churchill *(Penguin)*

The Normans and their Myth by RHC Davis *(Thames and Hudson)*

A Concise History of France by Roger Price *(Cambridge University Press)*

On the Battle of Normandy:

The D-Day Encyclopedia edited by DG Chandler and J Lawton *(Helicon, 1994)*

D-Day: 6th June 1944 – The Climactic Battle of World War II by S Ambrose *(Simon & Schuster, 1994)*

D-Day: 1944 Voices from Normandy by R Neillands and R de Normann *(Orion, 1994)*

The Penguin Atlas of D-Day and the Normandy Campaign by D Man *(Penguin, 1994)*

One Night in June – The Story of Operation Tonga by K Shannon and S Wright *(Air Life, 1994)*

The Lonely Leader: Monty 1944-45 by A Horne and D Montgomery *(Macmillan, 1994)*

Nothing Less than Victory: The Oral History of D-Day by R Miller *(Penguin, 1994)*

Overlord-D-Day and the Battle of Normandy, 1944 by M Hastings *(Michael Joseph)*

Brightly Shone the Dawn – Some Experiences of the Invasion of Normandy by G Johnson and C Dunphie *(Frederick Warne Ltd, 1980)*

Six Armies in Normandy by Keegan *(Penguin)*

Overlord: Normandy 1944 by WGF Jackson *(1994)*

D-Day by A Grimshaw *(1988)*

The Battle of Normandy by Belfield and Essame *(Pan, 1967)*

Flames in the Field: The Story of Four SOE Agents in Occupied France by R Kramer *(Michael Joseph, 1984)*

Codebreakers: The Inside Story of Bletchley Park edited by FH Hinsley and A Stripp *(Oxford University Press, 1993)*

Videos:

Dunkirk MGM/UA, PG, 1958 – Sombre portrait of the Dunkirk evacuation.

The Longest Day Fox Video, PG, 1962 – Re-creation of the Normandy landings.

Target for Tonight DD (50min) – The heroes of Bomber Command and some of their most dangerous missions.

The World at War Thames (4 volumes) – Historians and journalists give a detailed presentation of World War II.

VE Day Remembered Castle (60min) – VE Day is vividly recalled.

Cassettes or CDs:

D-Day A Commemoration in Sound – An essential collection of songs and music from the war years *(Conifer Records, 1994)*.

416

Admission times and charges

As times and charges for admission are liable to alteration, the information below is given for guidance only. Every sight for which there are times and charges is indicated by the symbol ⊙ in the main part of the guide. During the transition to the euro, some prices given are conversions of prices reported to our services in francs. Sometimes no prices were reported to our service, but this does not necessarily mean the attraction is free of charge.

Order: The information is listed in the same order as the entries in the alphabetical section of the guide.

Dates: Dates given are inclusive.

Last admission: Ticket offices usually shut 30min before closing time; exceptions only are mentioned below.

Charge: The charge is for an individual adult; where appropriate the charge for a child is given.

Disabled tourists: Sights which have comprehensive facilities for disabled tourists are indicated by the symbol ♿ below.

Guided tours: The departure time of the last tour of the morning or afternoon will be up to 1hr before the actual closing time. Most tours are conducted by French speaking guides but in some cases the term "guided tours" may cover group visiting with recorded commentaries; some of the larger and more frequented sights may offer guided tours in other languages. Enquire at the ticket office or bookstall. Other aids commonly available for the foreign tourist are notes, pamphlets or audio-guides.

Lecture tours: These are regularly organised during the tourist season in towns of special interest. The information is given under the appropriate heading. In towns labelled "Villes d'Art et d'Histoire" and "Villes d'Art" A, tours are conducted by lecturers/guides approved by the "Caisse Nationale des Monuments Historiques et des Sites."

Churches: Admission times are indicated if the interior is of special interest. Churches are usually closed from noon to 2pm. Visitors should refrain from walking about during services. Visitors to chapels are accompanied by the person who keeps the keys. A donation is welcome.

Tourist Information Centres: The addresses and telephone numbers are given for the local Tourist Information Centres, which provide information on local market days, early closing days etc.

A

L'AIGLE
🛈 Pl. Fulbert-de-Bejna, 61300, ☎ 02 33 24 12 40.

Musée Marcel-Angot – Daily except Sat-Sun 2.30-5pm (Fri 4.30pm). Closed public holidays. No charge. ☎ 02 33 84 16 16.

Musée "Juin 1944: bataille de Normandie" – ♿ May to mid-Sept: 9.30am-6.30pm; mid-Sept to end Apr: 10am-12.30pm, 2-6pm. Closed from mid to end of Jan, 1 Jan, 25 Dec. 5.18€. ☎ 02 31 51 46 90.

Aube:Musée de la Comtesse de Ségur – Mid-June to mid-Sept: guided tours (45min) daily except Tues 2-6pm; Oct to mid-June: Mon to Fri (call for information). 3.81€. ☎ 02 33 24 60 09.

Musée de la Grosse Forge d'Aube – Mid-June to mid-Sept: audio-visual show (45min) daily except Tues 2-6pm, Wed; Oct to mid-June: Mon to Fri (call for information). 3.81€. ☎ 02 33 34 14 93.

ALENÇON
🛈 Maison d'Ozé, pl. Lamagdelaine, 61003 cedex, ☎ 02 33 26 11 36.

Musée des Beaux-Arts et de la Dentelle – ♿ Daily except Mon 10am-noon, 2-6pm. Closed 1 Jan, 1 May, 25 Dec. 2.74€. ☎ 02 33 32 40 07.

Musée de la Dentelle "au point d'Alençon" et Musée du Général-Leclerc – Daily except Sun 10am-noon, 2-6pm. Closed public holidays. 4.6€ (ticket gives access to both museums). 3€ (musée de la Dentelle), 2.30€ (musée Leclerc). ☎ 02 33 26 27 26.

Église Notre-Dame – Summer: guided tours available, ask at the tourist office.

Église St-Léonard – Apply to the presbytery to visit. ☎ 02 33 26 20 89.

Chapelle Ste-Thérèse – June to Sept: guided tours (30min) 9am-noon, 2-6pm; Oct to May: daily except Tues 9.30am-noon, 2.30-5pm. Closed in Jan. No charge. ☎ 02 33 26 09 87.

Les ANDELYS 🛈 24 r. Philippe-Auguste, 27700, ☎ 02 32 54 41 93.

Château-Gaillard – Mid-Mar to mid-Nov: daily except Tues 8.30am-noon, 2-6pm, Wed 2-6pm. Closed 1 May. 2.74€. ☎ 02 32 54 04 16.

Musée Normandie-Niémen – June to mid-Sept: daily except Tues 10am-noon, 2-6pm: mid-Sept to end of May: daily except Tues 2-6pm. Closed 1 Jan, 1May, 24, 25 and 31Dec. 3.05€. ☎ 02 32 54 49 76.

ARGENTAN 🛈 Chapelle Saint-Nicolas, pl. du Marché, 61202, ☎ 02 33 67 12 48.

Église St-Germain – Mid-June to mid-Sept: weekdays 2.30-6pm.

Église St-Martin – July to end of Aug: during religious services or by appointment ☎ 02 33 67 12 48.

Le "Point d'Argentan" – ♿ Daily except Sun 2.30-4pm. Closed public holidays. 1.52€. ☎ 02 33 67 12 01.

Excursions

Écouché: Church – Mid-July to mid-Sept: daily 2.30-5.30pm.

Mémorial de Montormel – ♿ May to Sept: guided tours (1hr) 9am-6pm; Oct to Apr: Wed, Sat-Sun 10am-5pm. Closed mid-Dec to mid-Jan. 4.12€. ☎ 02 33 67 38 61.

Médavy: Château – Mid-July to mid-Sept: Guided tours (30min) 10am-noon, 2-6.30pm. 4.57€. ☎ 02 33 35 34 54.

ARQUES-LA-BATAILLE 🛈 Pl. Desceliers, 76880, ☎ 02 35 04 43 95.

Château – Closed for safety reasons. Free admission to the château grounds. ☎ 02 35 04 43 95.

Excursions

Château de Miromesnil – May to mid-Oct: guided tours (1hr15min) daily except Tues 2-6pm. 5.34€. ☎ 02 35 85 02 80.

ARROMANCHES-LES-BAINS 🛈 4, r. Maréchal Joffre, 14117, ☎ 02 31 21 47 56.

Musée du Débarquement – ♿ May to Aug: 9am-7pm (last admission 30min before closing); May: 10am-7pm); Sept: 9am-6pm, Sun 10am-6pm; Oct to Apr: 9.30am-12.30pm, 1.30-5.30pm (Oct to Dec and Feb: 10am-12.30pm, 1.30-5pm; Apr: 6pm). Closed in Jan and during Christmas school holidays. 5.34€. ☎ 02 31 22 34 31.

Arromanches 360 – ♿ June to Aug: 9.40am-6.40pm; Apr, May, Sept and Oct: 10.10am-5.40pm (Mid to end of May: 6.40pm); Mar and Nov: 10.10am-5.10pm; Feb and Dec: 10.10am-4.40pm. Closed in Jan. 3.65€. ☎ 02 31 22 30 30.

PAYS D'AUGE

Clermont-en-Auge: Chapel – Easter to 1 Nov: 10am-6pm.

Pierrefitte-en-Auge: Church – Contact the town hall. ☎ 02 31 64 07 41.

Coquainvilliers: Distillerie du Moulin de la Foulonnerie – ♿ Apr to Oct: 10am-6pm; Nov to Mar: daily except Sun 11am-4pm. 3.05€. ☎ 02 31 48 24 01.

Ouilly-le-Vicomte: Church – Apply to the town hall to visit. ☎ 02 31 61 12 64.

Pont-l'Évêque: La Belle Époque de l'Automobile – ♿ July and Aug: 10am-7pm; Apr to June and Sept: 10am-12.30pm, 1.30-7pm; Oct to mid-Nov: 2-6pm. 5.34€ (children: 3.05€). ☎ 02 31 65 05 02.

Canapville: Manoir des Évêques de Lisieux – July and Aug: guided tours (30min) daily except Tues 2-7pm. 5€ (children under 10: no charge). ☎ 02 31 65 24 75.

Touques: Église St-Pierre – ♿ Apr to Sept: 2-6pm, Sat-Sun and public holidays 11am-1pm, 3-7pm (July and Aug: 11am-1pm, 3-7pm). No charge. ☎ 02 31 88 70 93.

AVRANCHES 🛈 2, r. Général-de-Gaulle, 50300, ☎ 02 33 58 00 22.

Musée – Mid-May to mid-Oct: 9.30am-noon, 2-6pm (May and Oct: closed Tues). 2.29€. ☎ 02 33 58 25 15.

Town hall library: Manuscrits du Mont-Saint-Michel – ♿ July and Aug: 10am-6pm; June and Sept: 10am-noon, 2-6pm. 3.05€, 4.57€ (ticket combined with the museum and the treasury). ☎ 02 33 68 33 18.

Le Val-St-Père: Musée de la Seconde Guerre mondiale – Mid-Mar to mid-Nov: 10am-noon, 2-6pm (July and Aug: 9am-6pm; Sept: 10am-12.30pm, 2-6pm); mid-Nov to mid-Mar: Sun and school holidays 10am-noon, 2-6pm. 6.86€. ☎ 02 33 60 36 99.

Sightseeing flights over the Bay of Mont-St-Michel – Contact the Aéro-club des Grèves du Mont St-Michel, aérodrome d'Avranches, 50300 Le Val-St-Père. ☎ 02 33 58 02 91.

B

BAGNOLES-DE-L'ORNE   🖪 Pl. du Marché, 61140, ☎ 02 33 37 85 66.

Le Roc au Chien – May to mid-Sept: tours by tourist train Sat-Sun and public holidays 3-6pm (July and Aug: 3-5pm). 3.05€. ☎ 02 33 30 73 73 or ☎ 02 33 30 72 70.

Musée départemental des Sapeurs-Pompiers de l'Orne – ♿ Apr to end of Oct: 2-6pm. 3.75€. ☎ 02 33 38 10 34.

Excursion

La Ferté-Macé: Musée du Jouet – Apr to end of Oct: Sat-Sun and public holidays 3-6pm (July and Aug: daily). 3.05€ (children: 1.52€). ☎ 02 33 37 47 00 or ☎ 02 33 37 04 08.

Château de BALLEROY

Intérieur, Musée des Ballons and park – Mid-Mar to mid-Oct: unaccompanied visits of the museum, guided tours (45min) of the château daily except Tues 9am-noon, 2-6pm (July and Aug: daily 10am-6pm). 6.87€ (Museum: 4.27€, Château: 5.34€). ☎ 02 31 21 60 61.

BARFLEUR   🖪 2 quai Henri-Chardon, 50760, ☎ 02 33 54 02 48.

Maison de Julie Postel – June to Sept: 10am-7pm; Oct to Apr: 10am-5pm. No charge. ☎ 02 33 54 02 17.

Pointe de Barfleur: Phare – 10am-noon, 2-4pm (Apr to Sept: 7pm). Closed in Jan and from mid-Nov to mid-Dec, 1 May, 25 Dec and if winds are too high. 2€. ☎ 02 33 23 17 97.

BARNEVILLE-CARTERET   🖪 10 r. des Écoles, BP 101, 5070, ☎ 02 33 04 90 58.

Excursion

Portbail: Église Notre-Dame – July to end of Aug: 10am-noon, 2-6.30pm. ☎ 02 33 04 03 07.

Baptistère – July to end of Aug: 10am-noon, 3-7pm, Sun 3-7pm. 1.52€. ☎ 02 33 04 03 07.

BAYEUX   🖪 Pont St-Jean, BP 343, 14403, ☎ 02 31 51 28 28.

Centre Guillaume-le-Conquérant: "Queen Matilda's Tapestry" – ♿ Mid-Mar to early Nov: 9am-6.30pm (May to Aug: 9am-7pm); beginning Nov to mid-Mar: 9.30am-12.30pm, 2-6pm. Closed 1 and 2 Jan (morning), 25 and 26 Dec (morning). 6.25€ (ticket combined with the Baron-Gérard Museum and the Museum of Religious Art). ☎ 02 31 51 25 50.

Hôtel du Doyen, Museum of Diocesan Religious Art and the Academy of Lace – 10am-12.30pm, 2-6pm (July and Aug: closing time: 7pm). Closed 1 Jan and 25 Dec. 6.25€ (ticket combined with the Bayeux Tapestry Museum and Baron-Gérard Museum). ☎ 02 31 51 60 50.

Musée Baron-Gérard – June to mid-Sept: 9am-7pm; mid-Sept to end of May: 10am-12.30pm, 2-6pm. Closed 1 Jan and 25 Dec. 6.25€ (ticket combined with the Bayeux Tapestry Museum and the Museum of Religious Art).

☎ 02 31 51 60 50.

Mémorial de la Bataille de Normandie – ♿ May to mid-Sept: 9.30am-6.30pm; mid-Sept to end Apr: 10am-12.30pm, 2-6pm. Closed from mid to end of Jan, 1 Jan, 25 Dec. 5.18€. ☎ 02 31 51 46 90.

Mémorial Charles-de-Gaulle – Mid-Mar to mid-Nov: 9.30am-12.30pm, 2-6.30pm. 3.05€. ☎ 02 31 92 45 55.

Excursions

Le Molay-Littry: Musée de la Mine – ♿ 10am-noon, 2-6pm. Closed in Jan. 5.34€ (children: 3.05€). ☎ 02 31 22 89 10.

Abbaye de Mondaye – Mid-June to end of Aug: guided tours (1hr) at 3pm, 4pm and 5pm. Sept to mid-June: Sun and public holidays at 3pm and 4pm. 3.05€. ☎ 02 31 92 58 11.

Creully: Château – July to end of Aug: guided tours (45min) Tues to Fri 10am-noon, 3-6pm. 2.29€. ☎ 02 31 80 18 65.

Château de Lantheuil – Guided tours (1hr) 2-6pm by appointment. 4.57€ (children under 12: no charge). ☎ 02 31 80 14 00.

Ancien prieuré de St-Gabriel – Unaccompanied visits daily 8am-7pm. No charge. ☎ 02 31 80 10 20.

Château de Brécy – Easter to 1 Nov: Tues, Thur, Sun and public holidays 2.30-6.30pm (June: Sat only). 5€ (children under 12: no charge). ☎ 02 31 80 11 48.

Le BEC-HELLOUIN

Abbaye – June to Sept: guided tours (1hr) daily except Tues at 10.30am, 3pm, 4pm, 5pm, Sat at 10.30am, 3pm, 4pm, Sun and public holidays at noon, 3pm, 4pm; Oct to May: daily except Tues at 10.30am, 3pm, 4pm, Sun and public holidays at noon, 3pm, 4pm, contact Mr. Watson. 3.96.€. ☎ 02 32 43 72 60.

Touring suggestion

Écaquelon: Church – To visit, make an appointment with the Maison paroissiale (vicarage) de Montfort, 14 r. Saint-Pierre, 27290 Montfort-sur-Risle. ☎ 02 32 56 10 81.

BELLÊME
🛈 Bd. Bansard-des-Bois, 61130, ☎ 02 33 73 09 69.

The Perche Normand

Hameau de Ste-Gauburge: Musée départemental des Arts et Traditions populaires du Perche – Apr to Sept: daily except Tues 2-6.30pm (Oct to Mar: daily except Tues 2-6pm. Closed 1 Jan, 24, 25 and 31 Dec. 3.81€. ☎ 02 33 73 48 06.

BERNAY
🛈 29 r. Thiers, 27300, ☎ 02 32 43 32 08.

Ancienne église abbatiale – As for the municipal museum.

Musée municipal – July and Aug: daily except Tues 10am-noon, 2-7pm, Sun and public holidays 10am-noon, 3-7pm; Sept to June: daily except Tues 10am-noon, 2-5.30pm, Sun and public holidays 3-5.30pm. Closed 1 Jan, 1 May, 25 Dec (ticket combined with the abbey church). 3.05€, no charge Wed and 1st Sunday in the month. ☎ 02 32 46 63 23.

Basilique Notre-Dame-de-la-Couture – Ask at the presbytery, 12 r. Alexendre, ☎ 02 32 43 06 82.

Excursion

Château de Beaumesnil– July and Aug: daily except Tues 10am-noon, 2-6pm: Apr to June and Sept to Oct: Fri to Mon 2-6pm. 5.34€. ☎ 02 32 44 40 09.

BLAINVILLE-CREVON

Church – June to Sept: Sat-Sun 2pm-6.30pm; Oct to May: contact the town hall. ☎ 02 35 34 01 60.

Château – Mid-Mar to spring and autumn: visits possible during weekends when workers present; from 22 to end of June: weekend open days; rest of the year by appointment, ☎ 01 42 88 95 29.

Excursions

Ry: Musée d'Automates – July and Aug: 3-6pm; from Easter to June then Sept and Oct: Mon, Sat-Sun and public holidays 11am-noon, 2-7pm. 4.57€. ☎ 02 35 23 61 44.

Martainville: Château – Daily except Tues 10am-12.30pm, 2-5pm, Sun 2-5.30pm (Apr to Sept: 6pm, Sun 6.30pm). Closed 1 Jan, 1 May, 1 and 11 Nov, 25 Dec. 3.05€. ☎ 02 35 23 44 70.

BRIONNE
🛈 1 r. du Gén. de Gaulle, 27800, ☎ 02 32 45 70 51.

Tour of the Lieuvin region

Château de Launay – Unaccompanied visits to the dovecote, the commons and park.

Forêt de BROTONNE
🛈 Maison du Parc, 76940 Forêt de BROTONNE, ☎ 02 35 37 23 16.

La Haye-de-Routot:Church – Guided tours Sat-Sun 2-6pm.
Bread oven – ♿ July and Aug: 1.30-6.30pm; May, June and Sept: Sun and public holidays 2-6.30pm; Oct, Nov and Apr: Sun and public holidays 2-6pm; Mar: Sun. 2-6pm. 1.52€. ☎ 02 32 57 07 99.
Musée du Sabot – ♿ July and Aug: 1.30-6.30pm; May, June and Sept: Sun and public holidays 2-6.30pm; Apr, Oct and Nov: Sun and public holidays 2-6pm. 1.83€. ☎ 02 32 57 59 67.

St-Nicolas-de-Bliquetuit: Maison du Parc de Brotonne – ♿ ♿ Apr to Oct: 9am-6pm (July and Aug: 6.30pm, Sat-Sun and public holidays 10am-6.30pm; Apr, Sept and Oct: Sat-Sun 2pm-6pm; May to June: Sat-Sun 10am-6pm); Nov to Mar: daily except Sat-Sun and public holidays 9am-6pm; No charge. ☎ 02 35 37 23 16.

C

🛈 Jardins du Casino, 14390, ☎ 02 31 91 20 00.

Excursion

Merville-Franceville-Plage: Musée des Batteries – Apr to end of Sept: daily 10am-6pm; mid to end of Mar and Oct to mid-Nov: Mon, Wed, Sat-Sun and public holidays. 3.35€. ☎ 02 31 24 21 83.

CAEN 🛈 Hôtel d'Escoville, pl. St-Pierre, 14000, ☎ 02 31 27 14 14.

Guided tours of the town 🅰 – Caen, which is listed as a "Town of Art and history", offers discovery tours conducted by guide-lecturers approved by the Ministry of Culture and Communication. Information at the tourist office or on www.vpah.culture.fr

Monastery buildings of the Abbaye-aux-Hommes – Guided tours (1hr15min) at 9.30am, 11am, 2.30pm and 4pm. Closed 1 Jan, 1 May, 25 Dec. 1.52€. ☎ 02 31 30 42 81.

Conventual buildings of the Abbaye-aux-Dames – ♿ Guided tours (1hr15min) at 2.30pm and 4pm. Closed 1 Jan, 1 May and 25 Dec. No charge. ☎ 02 31 06 98 98.

Musée des Beaux-Arts – ♿ Daily except Tues 9.30am-6pm. Closed 1 Jan, Easter Sunday, 1 May, Ascension, 1 Nov, 25 Dec. 3.81€ (exhibition periods), 3.05€ (other periods), no charge Wed. (children under 18: no charge). ☎ 02 31 30 47 70.

Musée de Normandie – Daily except Tues 9.30am-12.30pm, 2-6pm Closed 1 Jan, Easter, 1 May, Ascension, 1 Nov, 25 Dec. 1.5€, no charge Wed. ☎ 02 31 30 47 60.

Le Mémorial – ♿ Beginning of July to mid-Aug: 9am-8pm; beginning of Feb to beginning of July, mid-Aug to beginning of Nov and mid to end of Dec: daily 9am-7pm (last admission 1hr15min before closing); beginning of Nov to mid-Dec and mid-Jan to beginning of Feb: daily 9am-6pm. Closed beginning Jan to mid-Jan, 25 Dec. 11.59€. ☎ 02 31 06 06 44. Bookshop and multimedia collection, ☎ 02 31 06 06 52, www.memorial.fr.

Église et cimetière St-Nicolas – Closed to the public for restoration work. Cemetery: 8am-6pm (winter: 8am-5pm). No charge.

Église St-Julien – By request at the presbytery. ☎ 02 31 85 44 53.

Excursions

Norrey-en-Bessin: Church – Contact the town hall. The keys are available at "L'Estaminet" (bar) opposite the church. ☎ 02 31 80 01 99.

Fontaine-Étoupefour: Château – Beginning of July to end of Sept: guided tours (1hr) Sun to Tues 2.30-6pm. Closed public holidays. 5.34€. ☎ 02 31 26 73 20.

🛈 Pl. Leveneur, 61320 CARROUGES, ☎ 02 33 27 40 62.

Château – Beginning of Apr to mid-June and Sept: guided tours (45min, last departure 45min before closing time) 9.30am-noon, 2-6pm; mid-June to end of Aug: 6.30pm; Oct to Mar: 10am-noon, 2-5pm. Closed 1 Jan, 1 May, 1 and 11 Nov, 25 Dec. 5.49€. ☎ 02 33 27 20 32.

Maison des Métiers du Parc naturel régional Normandie-Maine – July, Aug and Dec: temporary exhibitions of handicrafts. ☎ 02 33 81 75 75.

CAUDEBEC-EN-CAUX 🛈 Pl. du Gén.-de-Gaulle, 76490 CAUDEBEC-EN-CAUX, ☎ 02 35 96 20 65.

Église Notre-Dame – Guided tours available, ask at the tourist office.

Maisons des Templiers – Apr to Oct: Sat-Sun 2.30-6.30pm and by appointment ☎ 02 35 95 90 12 (July to Sept: daily except Mon 3-6pm) 2.29€. ☎ 02 35 96 95 91.

Musée de la Marine de Seine – Daily except Tues 2-6.30pm (July and Aug: daily). Closed 1 Jan and 25 Dec. 3.05€. ☎ 02 35 95 90 13.

Around Barre-y-Va

Villequier: Musée Victor-Hugo – Apr to Sept: daily except Tues 10am-12.30pm, 2-6pm, Sun. 2-6.30pm; Oct to Mar: daily except Tues 10am-12.30pm, 2-5pm, Sun 2-5.30pm. Closed 1 Jan, 1 May, 1 and 11 Nov, 25 Dec. 3.05€. ☎ 02 35 56 78 31.

Barre-y-Va: Chapel – Daily except Tues 2-6.30pm (July and Aug: daily).

Around Yvetot

Allouville-Bellefosse: Musée de la Nature – Wed to Sat 9am-noon, 2-6pm, Sun and public holidays 10am-noon, 2-6pm (Mid-Mar to mid-Oct and school holidays: 9am-noon, 2-7pm, Sun and public holidays 10am-noon, 2-7pm). 3.05€. ☎ 02 35 96 06 54.

Pays de CAUX

Ermenouville: Château du Mesnil-Geoffroy – May to end of Sept: guided tours (45min) Fri, Sat-Sun and public holidays 2.30-6pm. 4.58€ (children: 3.05€). ☎ 02 35 57 12 77.

Paluel: Centre nucléaire de production d'électricité – Information centre: May to Sept: 10am-1pm, 2-7pm, Sun and public holidays 2-7pm; Oct to Apr: 10am-noon, 2-6pm, Sat-Sun and public holidays 2-6pm. Guided tours of the machine room (2hrs) by appointment 24hrs in advance. Closed 1 Jan, 1 May and 25 Dec. No charge. ☎ 02 35 57 69 99.

Cany-Barville:
Écomusee des Arts et Traditions populaires – &. Apr to end of Oct: weekdays and 1ˢᵗ Sun in the month: 2-7pm. 3.81€. ☎ 02 35 97 59 71.
Church –For a guided tour, ask at the Tourist Office.

Château de Cany: July to end of Aug: guided tours (45min) daily except Fri. 10am-noon, 3-6pm. Closed last Sun in July. 4I.57€ (children: 2I.44€). ☎ 02 35 97 87 36.

CERISY-LA-FORÊT

Église abbatiale and Bâtiments conventuels – Easter to Sept: guided tours (45min) 10.30am-12.30pm, 2.30-6.30pm; Oct to mid-Nov: Sat-Sun and public holidays 10.30am-noon, 2.30-6pm. 3.05€. ☎ 02 33 57 34 63.

Château du CHAMP DE BATAILLE

Mar to end of Nov: guided tours (1hr) Sat-Sun and public holidays 2-6pm (May to Sept: daily 2-6pm). Closed Dec to end of Feb. 12.20€ (children: 5.35€). ☎ 02 32 34 84 34.

Excursion

Château d'Harcourt – Mar to mid-Nov: daily except Tues 2-6pm (mid-June to mid-Sept: daily 10.30am-6.30pm). 3.81€. ☎ 02 32 46 29 70.
Arboretum – &. <HP> Same as for the château.

CHERBOURG

🖪 2, quai Alexandre-III, 50100, ☎ 02 33 93 52 02.

Musée Thomas-Henry – &. Daily except Mon 9am-noon, 2-6pm. 2.29€, no charge Sun. ☎ 02 33 23 02 23.

Musée d'Ethnographie, d'Histoire naturelle et d'Archéologie – Daily except Mon and Sun mornings 10am-noon, 2-5pm. 1.52€, no charge Sun. ☎ 02 33 53 51 61.

Navy base (Arsenal) – &. July to end of Aug: daily except Sat-Sun 10am, 11am, 2pm, 3pm and 4pm. Closed public holidays. Photography prohibited. French identity card required. No charge. ☎ 02 33 95 65 30.

Tours of the harbour aboard the "Vega" – Apr to Sept: departures at 2pm, 3.30pm and 5pm; July and Aug: additional departure at 10.30am. From 6.56€ to 8.38€ depending on the circuit. ☎ 02 33 93 75 27.

Musée de la Libération – &. Summer: 10am-6pm; winter: daily except Mon 9.30am-noon, 2-5.30pm. 3.05€, no charge Sun. ☎ 02 33 20 14 12.

Excursion

Tourlaville:Parc du château – .June to Aug: 8am-7.30pm; Apr to May and Sept: 8am-7pm; Mar and Oct: 8am-6pm; Jan: 8.30am-5.30pm; Feb: 8.15am-6pm; Nov: 8am-5.30pm; Dec: 8.30am-5pm. No charge. ☎ 02 33 87 88 98.
Musée maritime Chantereyne – Guided tours (1hr30min) Sun and public holidays 2.30-5.30pm (July and Aug: daily). 3I05<EURO>. ☎ 02 33 43 27 00.

CLÉCY

🖪 Pl. de la Mairie, 14570, ☎ 02 31 69 79 95.

Musée du Chemin de fer miniature – &. Easter to Sept: guided tours (30min) 10am-noon, 2-6pm; Mar to Easter: Sun and public holidays 2-5.30pm; Oct, Nov, autumn half-term: 2-5pm. Closed Dec to Feb. 3.81€. ☎ 02 31 69 07 13.

Excursion

Château de Pontécoulant – Mid-Apr to end of Sept: guided tours (45min) daily except Tues 10am-noon, 2.30-6pm; beginning to mid-Nov: daily except Tues 10am-noon, 2.30-6.30pm; mid-Nov to mid-Apr: daily except Mon and Tues 2.30-6.30pm. Closed in Oct. 1.52€. ☎ 02 31 69 62 54.

CLÈRES
🛈 59 av. du Parc, 76690, ☎ 02 35 33 38 64.

Parc zoologique de Clères-Jean-Delacour – From the 1st Sat-Sun in Mar to end of Nov: (last admission 1hr before closing) 9.30am-noon, 1.30-6pm (Easter to autumn: 9.30am-6.30pm, Sun and public holidays 9.30am-7pm); Nov: 9.30am-noon, 1.30-5pm. 4.57€ (3-16 years: 3.05€). ☎ 02 35 33 23 08.

Excursions

Parc du Bocasse – ♿ Apr to Sept: for opening days and times, ask at the park (end of June to beginning of Sept: daily). High season: 7.62€, low season: 7.01€. ☎ 02 35 33 22 25.

Montville: Musée des Sapeurs-pompiers de France – ♿ Sat-Sun and public holidays 1-6pm (Apr to Oct: daily). Closed 1 Jan, 1 May, 25 Dec. 3.80€. ☎ 02 35 33 13 51.

CONCHES-EN-OUCHE
🛈 Pl. A. Briand, 27190, ☎ 02 32 30 76 42.

Musee du Livre, du Verre et de la Pierre – July to mid-Sept: daily except Mon 10am-12.30pm, 2-6pm, Tues 2-6pm, Sun 10am-noon. Closed public holidays. 2.29€. ☎ 02 32 30 90 41.

Presqu'île du COTENTIN

Utah Beach: Musée du Débarquement – June to Sept: 10am-12.30pm, 2-6pm; Apr and May: 9.30am-7pm; Feb and Mar: 10am-12.30pm, 2-5.30pm; Oct to mid-Nov: 10am-12.30pm, 2-5.30pm; mid-Nov to end of Mar: Sat-Sun, public and school holidays 10am-12.30pm, 2-5.30pm. Closed 1 Jan and 25 Dec. 4.12€. ☎ 02 33 71 53 35.

Quinéville: Musée de la Liberté – ♿ Mid-Mar to mid-Nov: 10am-6pm (June to Sept: 9.30am-7.30pm). 5.5€ (children: 4€). ☎ 02 33 21 40 44.

Équeurdreville-Hainneville: Hôtel de ville – ♿ Daily except Sat-Sun 9am-noon, 2-5.30pm. Closed public holidays. No charge. ☎ 02 33 53 96 45.

Château et parc de Nacqueville – Easter to end of Sept: guided tours (1hr) daily except Tues (except public holidays) at 2pm, 3pm, 4pm and 5pm. 4.57€ (children: 1.52€). ☎ 02 33 03 21 12.

Omonville-la-Petite: Maison Prévert – June to Sept: 11am-6pm (July and Aug: 7pm); Apr, May and Oct: 1-6pm; Mar: Sun 1-6pm; school holidays 1-6pm. 4€. ☎ 02 33 52 72 38.

Vauville: Botanical Garden – ♿ May to end of Sept: guided tours (1hr) Tues and Sun 2-6pm (July and Aug: daily). 4.57€. ☎ 02 33 10 00 00.

Flamanville: Centre nucléaire de production d'électricité – Guided tours (3hrs) by appointment 2 weeks in advance. A valid identity document will be requested. No charge. ☎ 02 33 04 12 99.

COUTANCES
🛈 Pl. Georges-Leclerc, 50200, ☎ 02 33 45 17 79.

Guided tours of the town – Coutance, which is listed as a "Town of Art and history", offers discovery tours conducted by guide-lecturers approved by the Ministry of Culture and Communication. Information at the tourist office or on www.vpah.culture.fr

Cathedral: Upper storeys – July and Aug: guided tours (1hr.30min) daily except Sat and Sun morning 10.30am, 2.30pm and 4pm; end of May-June and mid-Sept: daily except Sat and Sun morning 2.30pm. 5.34€. ☎ 02 33 19 08 10.

Jardin des plantes – ♿ Apr to Oct: 9am-8pm (July and Aug: 9am-11.30pm); Oct to Mar: 9am-5pm. No charge. ☎ 02 33 19 08 10.

Musée Quesnel-Morinière – Daily except Tues and Sun mornings 10am-noon, 2-5pm (July and Aug: closing time: 6pm). Closed public holidays. 1.52€, no charge Sun afternoon from Sept to June. ☎ 02 33 45 11 92.

From Coutances to the coast

Château de Gratot – 10am-7pm. 2.29€. ☎ 02 31 27 97 40.

Regnéville-sur-Mer: Musée du Littoral et de la Chaux – June to Sept: 11am-7pm; school holidays, Apr, May and Oct: 1-6pm; Mar: Sun. 1-6pm. 3.81€. ☎ 02 33 46 82 18.

Château de CRÈVECŒUR-EN-AUGE

Apr to end of Oct: daily except Tues 11am-6pm (July and Aug: daily 11am-7pm; Oct: Sat-Sun and public holidays 2-6pm) 4.88€. ☎ 02 31 63 02 45.

D

DEAUVILLE
🛈 Pl. de la Mairie BP 79, 14800, ☎ 02 31 14 40 00.

Visite guidée de la ville – Contact the tourist office.

A tourist train makes a tour of the town with commentaries (35min). Departure from in front of the town hall 10.30am-6.30pm from Easter to end of Sept 4.60€.

Excursions

Villers-Sur-Mer: Musée paléontologique – ♿ Mar to Oct: 10am-12.30pm, 2.30-5pm (July and Aug: 9am-7pm); May, June and Sept: 9.30am-12.30pm, 2.30-6pm. Closed 1 Jan and 25 Dec. No charge. ☎ 02 31 87 01 18.

The Normandy Beaches

Bénouville: Château – End of June to mid-Sept: daily except Tues 2-6pm. 1.52€. ☎ 02 31 57 10 30.

Douvres-la-Délivrande: Musée-Radar – July and Aug: 10am-12.30pm, 1.30-6.30pm; June: daily except Mon and Tues 10am-12.30pm, 2-6pm. 5.18€. ☎ 02 31 06 06 45.

Courseulles-sur-Mer: Maison de la Mer – ♿ July and Aug: 9am-7pm; May to June: 9am-1pm, 2-7pm; Sept to Apr: 10am-noon, 2-6pm (Oct to Apr: daily except Mon). 6€. ☎ 02 31 37 92 58.

Château de Colombières – July and Aug: guided tours (45min) daily except Sat-Sun 2.30-6pm; Sept: Sat-Sun and public holidays 2.30-6pm. 4.57€. ☎ 02 31 22 51 65.

Abbaye Ste-Marie – Easter to 1 Nov: Thur 2-6pm (July and beginning to mid-Sept: daily except Sun). 1.52€. Closed public holidays. ☎ 02 31 21 78 41.

DIEPPE
🛈 Quai du Carénage - BP 152, 76204, ☎ 02 32 14 40 60.

Guided tours of the town 🄰 – Contact "Dieppe, ville d'Art et d'Histoire", hôtel de ville, VP 226 - 76203 Dieppe Cedex.

Museum – Daily except Tues (last admission 30min before closing time) 10am-noon, 2-5pm, Sun and public holidays 10am-noon, 2-6pm (June to Sept: daily 10am-noon, 2-6pm). Closed 1 Jan, 1 May, 1 Nov, 25 Dec. 2.29€. ☎ 02 35 84 19 76.

Estran-Cité de la Mer – ♿ 10am-noon, 2-6pm. 4.27€ (children: 2.44€). ☎ 02 35 06 93 20.

DOMFRONT
🛈 R. St-Julien, BP 7, 61700, ☎ 02 33 38 53 97.

Hôtel de ville (Salle Charles-Léandre) – ♿ Guided tours (1hr) daily except Sun 9am-noon, 2-4pm, Mon 2-4pm, Sat 9am-noon. Closed public holidays. No charge. ☎ 02 33 30 60 60.

DREUX
🛈 4 Porte Chartraine, 28100, ☎ 02 37 46 01 73.

Beffroi – Closed for renovation work.

Église St-Pierre – Guided tours available, ask at the tourist office.

Chapelle royale St-Louis – Apr to end of Sept: daily except Tues 9.30am-noon, 2-6pm (July and Aug: daily except Tues 9.30am-noon, 1.30-6.30pm). 5.33€. ☎ 02 37 46 07 06.

Musée d'Art et d'Histoire Marcel-Dessal – Daily except Tues, 2-6pm, Sat-Sun and public holidays 10am-noon, 2-6pm. Closed 1 Jan and 25 Dec. 1.98€, no charge Sun. ☎ 02 37 50 18 61.

Excursion

Château d'Anet and Chapelle Diane de Poitiers– Feb to end of Nov: guided tours (45min) daily except Tues 2-5pm (Apr to Oct: daily except Tues 2-6.30pm). 5.95€ (children: 3.81€). ☎ 02 37 41 90 07.

E

ÉCOUIS

Collégiale Notre-Dame – To visit, make an appointment at the presbytery. ☎ 02 32 69 43 08.

Excursion

Abbaye de Fontaine-Guérard – ♿ Apr to end of Oct: daily except Mon 2-6pm. 3.81€. ☎ 02 32 49 03 82.

ELBEUF
🛈 28 r. Henry, 76500, ☎ 02 35 77 03 78.

Musée municipal d'Elbeuf – Summer school holidays: Daily except Mon and Sun. 2.30-5.30pm: winter school holidays: daily except Mon 2.30-5.30pm; during school term: Wed, Sat-Sun 2.30-5.30pm. Closed public holidays. No charge. ☎ 02 32 96 90 15.

Église St-Jean – To visit, make an appointment at the presbytery or the town hall.

Église St-Étienne – Guided tours by appointment. Paroisse d'Elbeuf, 7, pl. de la Liberté, 76500 Elbeuf.

Excursions

St-Ouen-de-Pontcheuil: Moulin Amour – May to end of Sept: Sun and public holidays 2.30-6.30pm (July and Aug: daily except Mon). 3.04€. ☎ 02 32 35 80 27.

Château de Robert le Diable: Musée des Vikings – Mar to Aug: 9am-7pm; Sept: daily except Mon 10am-6pm, Sat-Sun and public holidays 9am-7pm; Oct to mid-Nov: daily except Mon 10am-5pm. 3.35€. ☎ 02 35 18 02 36.

ÉTRETAT

🛈 Pl. Maurice-Guillard, 76790, ☎ 02 35 27 05 21.

Musée Nungesser-et-Coli – Mid-June to mid-Sept: 10am-noon, 2-6pm; Easter to mid-June: Sat-Sun 10am-noon, 2-6pm. 0.91€. ☎ 02 35 27 07 47.

Le Clos Lupin – Apr to Sept: guided tours (45min) 10am-7pm; Oct to Mar: Fri, Sat-Sun and school holidays 11am-5pm. 5.33€. ☎ 02 35 10 59 53.

EU

🛈 41 r. Paul-Bignon, 76260, ☎ 02 35 86 04 68.

Guided tours of the town – Contact the tourist office.

Crypte de la collégiale Notre-Dame-et-Saint-Laurent – 9am-noon, 2-5pm, Sun and public holidays 10.30am-12.30pm, 2-5pm (Apr to Oct: 6pm). No charge. ☎ 02 35 86 27 11.

Musée Louis-Philippe – Closed for renovation work. Documentary video and shop only. ☎ 02 35 86 44 00.

Musee des Traditions verrières – ♿ June to end of Aug: Tues, Sat-Sun and public holidays 2.30-6pm; Mid-Apr to end of May: Sat-Sun and public holidays 2.30-6pm. 2.3€. ☎ 02 35 86 04 68

ÉVREUX

🛈 3 pl. du Général-de-Gaulle, 27000, ☎ 02 32 24 04 43.

Museum – ♿ Daily except Mon 10am-noon, 2-6pm. Closed 1 Jan, 1 May, 1 and 11 Nov, 25 Dec. No charge. ☎ 02 32 31 81 90.

ÉVRON

Excursions

Château du Rocher – Mid-June to mid-Sept: unaccompanied tours of the outside 10am-noon, 3-6pm. No charge.

Château de la Roche-Pichemer – July to mid-Aug: tours of the garden only 2-6pm. No charge. ☎ 02 43 90 00 41.

F

FALAISE

🛈 Le Forum, bd de la Libération, 14700, ☎ 02 31 90 17 26.

Château Guillaume-le-Conquérant – Mar to Sept: 10am-6pm. Rest of the year, call for information. 4.57€. ☎ 02 31 41 61 44.

Musée Août 1944: La Bataille de la Poche de Falaise – ♿ Beginning of Apr to mid-Nov: daily except Tues 10am-noon, 2-6pm (June to Aug: daily). 5€ (children: 2€). ☎ 02 31 90 37 19.

Automates Avenue – ♿ Apr to Sept: 10am-12.30pm, 1.30-6pm; Oct to Mar: school holidays, Sat-Sun and public holidays 10am-12.30pm, 1.30-6pm. Closed from the second week in Jan to the first week in Feb, 1 Jan, 25 Dec. 4.57€ (children: 3.05€). ☎ 02 31 90 02 43.

FÉCAMP

🛈 113 r. Alexandre-le-Grand BP 112, 76400, ☎ 02 35 28 51 01.

Guided tours of the town 🅰 – Contact the 'Service Animation du Patrimoine' (Heritage Dept). ☎ 02 35 28 84 39.

Musée des Arts et de l'Enfance – Daily except Tues 10am-noon, 2-5.30pm (July and Aug: daily 10am-noon, 2-6.30pm). Closed 1 Jan, 1May, 25 Dec. 3.05€ ticket combined with the Musée des Terre-Neuvas et de la pêche. ☎ 02 35 28 31 99.

Palais Bénédictine – Mid-July to end of Aug: (guided tours (1hr), last admission 1hr before closing time) 10am-7.30pm; end of Mar to mid-July and Sept: 10am-1pm, 2-6.30pm; Feb to end of Mar and Oct to end of Dec: 10am-12.15pm, 2-6pm. Closed in Jan and 25 Dec. 5€. ☎ 02 35 10 26 10.

Musée des Terre-Neuvas et de la Pêche – ♿ Daily except Tues 10am-noon, 2-5.30pm (July and Aug: daily 10am-7pm) Closed 1 Jan, 1 May, 25 Dec. 3.05€ (ticket combined with the Musée des Arts et de l'Enfance). ☎ 02 35 28 31 99.

Excursion

Valmont:Abbey – Undergoing restoration.

Château – July and Aug: 9am-noon, 2-5pm.

FLERS 🛈 Pl. du Général-de-Gaulle, 61100, ☎ 02 33 65 06 75.

Musée du Château – Easter to mid-Oct: daily except Sat morning 10am-noon, 2-6pm. Closed 1 May. 2.44€. ☎ 02 33 64 66 49.

Tour around Mont de Cerisy

Mont de Cerisy – Mid-Jan to mid-Dec: 10am-7pm. 3.20€ (admission and car park). ☎ 02 33 66 52 62.

Château de FONTAINE-HENRY

Easter to beginning of Nov: guided tours (1hr30min) Sat-Sun and public holidays 2.30-6.30pm (mid-June to mid-Sept: daily except Tues). Closed 1 Jan and 25 Dec. 5.34€ (children under 16: 3.05€). ☎ 02 31 80 00 42.

FORGES-LES-EAUX 🛈 R. Albert Bochet, 76440, ☎ 02 35 90 52 10.

Musée de la Faïence de Forges – Tours by appointment, contact the tourist office. 1.83€. ☎ 02 35 90 52 10.

FRESNAY-SUR-SARTHE 🛈 19 av. du Dr-Riant, 72130, ☎ 02 43 33 28 04.

Église Notre-Dame – July to end of Aug: 3.30-6pm.

Musée des Coiffes – Easter to end of Sept: 11am-noon, 2.30-6pm. 2€. ☎ 02 43 97 22 20.

Cave du Lion – July to end of Aug: daily except Mon 4.15-7.15pm, Sat-Sun and public holidays 10.30am-12.30pm, 4.15-7.15pm. No charge. ☎ 02 43 33 64 42.

G

GISORS 🛈 4 r. du Gén. de Gaulle, 27140, ☎ 02 32 27 60 63.

Château fort – Apr to Sept: guided tours (1hr) daily except Tues at 10am, 11am, 2.30pm, 3.45pm and 5pm, Sat-Sun and public holidays at 10am, 11am, 2.30pm, 3.15pm, 4pm and 5pm; Oct to Mar: Sat-Sun and public holidays at 10.30am, 2.30pm and 4pm. Closed Dec, Jan, 1 May. 3.81€. ☎ 02 32 27 60 63.

Excursions

Château de Boury-en-Vexin – Easter to 1 Nov: guided tours (45min) Sat-Sun 2.30-6.30pm (July and Aug: daily except Tues). 6€. ☎ 01 32 55 15 10.

Dangu: Church – Closed for renovation work.

GIVERNY

Maison de Claude Monet – Apr to 1 Nov: daily except Mon 10am-6pm. 5.34€. ☎ 02 32 51 28 21.

Musée d'Art américain Giverny – ♿ Apr to end of Oct: daily except Mon 10am-6pm (last admission 30min before closing); Nov: Sat-Sun and public holidays 10am-6pm. 5.34€. ☎ 02 32 51 94 65.

GRANVILLE 🛈 4, cours Jonville, 50400 GRANVILLE, ☎ 02 33 91 30 03.

Jardin public Christian-Dior – End of May to end of Sept: 10am-12.30pm, 2.30-6.30pm. 3.81€. ☎ 02 33 61 48 21.

Musée Richard-Anacréon – June to Sept: daily except Tues 11am-6pm; Oct to May: daily except Mon and Tues. 2-6pm. Closed 1 Jan, 1 Nov, 25 Dec. 2.3.€. ☎ 02 33 51 02 94.

Musée de la Mer et Musée de la Terre – Apr to Sept: 9.30am-noon, 2-7pm (last admission 1hr before closing). 6.71€ (children: 3.35€). ☎ 02 33 50 19 83.

Musée du Vieux Granville – July to Sept: daily except Tues 10am-noon, 2-6pm; Apr to June: daily except Mon and Tues 10am-noon, 2-6pm; Oct to Mar: Wed, Sat-Sun and public holidays 2-6pm. Closed between Christmas and New Year's Day, 1 May, 1 and 11 Nov. 1.52€. ☎ 02 33 50 44 10.

H

Le HAVRE

🆔 186 bd Clemenceau, 76059, ☎ 02 32 74 04 04.

Boat tours of Le Havre harbour – Guided tour (1hr15min). Contact the tourist office or "Visite du Port du Havre", quai de la Marine, BP 1086 – 76062 Le Havre Cedex ☎ 02 35 42 01 31.

Musée des Beaux-Arts André-Malraux – ♿ Daily except Tues 11am-6pm (Sat-Sun 11am-7pm). Closed 1 Jan, 1 and 8 May, 14 July, 11 Nov, 25 Dec. 3.81€. ☎ 02 35 19 62 62.

Muséum d'Histoire naturelle – Daily except Tues 2.30-5.30pm, Wed, Sat-Sun and public holidays 10-11.30am, 2.30-5.30pm. No charge. ☎ 02 35 41 37 28.

Musée de l'Ancien Havre – Daily except Mon and Tues 10am-noon, 2-6pm. Closed public holidays. 1.52€. ☎ 02 35 42 27 90.

Espace maritime et portuaire des Docks Vauban – ♿ Tues, Wed, Sat-Sun 2.30-6pm. Closed public holidays. 3.81€. ☎ 02 35 24 51 00.

Sights nearby

Musée du Prieuré de Graville – Daily except Mon and Tues 10am-noon, 2-6pm. Closed public holidays. 1.52€. ☎ 02 35 47 14 01.

Harfleur: Église St-Martin – 9am-12.30pm.

Château d'Orcher – ♿ Beginning of July to mid-Aug: Guided tours (30min) 2-6pm. 5€.

Château de Filières – May to end of Sept: guided tours (30min) Wed, Sat-Sun and public holidays 2-6pm (July and Aug: daily). 5€ (children: 2€). ☎ 02 35 20 53 30.

HONFLEUR

🆔 Pl. Arthur Boudin, 14602, ☎ 02 31 89 23 30.

Guided tours of the town – Contact the tourist office.

Greniers à sel – Open during temporary exhibitions. Tourist office ☎ 02 31 89 04 40.

Clocher de St-Catherine – Apr to end of Sept: daily except Tues 10am-noon, 2-6pm. Closed 1 May and 14 July. 1.52€. ☎ 02 31 89 54 00.

Musée Eugène-Boudin – Mid-Mar to end of Sept: daily except Tues 10am-noon, 2-6pm: Oct to mid-Mar: daily except Tues 2.30-5pm, Sat-Sun and public holidays 10am-noon, 2.30-5pm. Closed Jan to mid-Feb, 1 May, 14 July, 25 Dec. 4.57€ (summer). ☎ 02 31 89 54 00.

Musée de la Marine – ♿ Same as for the Musée d'Ethnographie et d'Art Populaire. 2.29€.

Musée d'Ethnographie et d'Art populaire – Apr to Sept: daily except Mon 10am-noon, 2-6pm (July and Aug: daily 10am-1pm, 2-6.30pm); mid-Feb to end of Mar and Oct to mid-Nov: daily except Mon 2-5.30pm, Sat-Sun 10am-noon, 2-5.30pm. Closed 1 May. 2.29€. ☎ 02 31 89 14 12.

Maison Satie – May to Sept: daily except Tues 10am-7pm; Oct to Apr: daily except Tues 10.30am-6pm. Closed beginning Jan to mid-Feb, 1 May, 14 July. 4.57€. ☎ 02 31 89 11 11.

Sights nearby

Bourneville: Maison des Métiers – May to mid-Sept: daily except Tues 2-6.30pm (May: Sat-Sun and public holidays). 2.29€. ☎ 02 32 57 40 41.

Moulin d'Hauville – July and Aug: 2-7pm; May, June and Sept: Sat-Sun and public holidays 2-6.30pm; Mar, Apr and Oct: Sun and public holidays 2-6pm. 2.29€. ☎ 02 32 56 57 32.

Moulineaux: Church – Apply to the town hall to visit. ☎ 02 35 18 02 45.

J

Ville romaine de JUBLAINS

Musée départemental d'Archéologie et Forteresse gallo-romaine – ♿ May to Sept: 9am-12.30pm, 1.30-6pm; Oct to Apr: daily except Mon 9.30am-12.30pm, 1.30-5.30pm. Closed in Feb, 1 Jan, 25 Dec. 3.81€. ☎ 02 43 04 30 16.

Public baths – Entry permitted during museum opening times.

Temple and theatre – ♿ Literature available at the museum.

Abbaye de JUMIÈGES

Abbaye: Mid-Apr to mid-Sept: 9.30am-7pm; mid-Sept to mid-Apr: 9.30am-1pm, 2.30-5.30pm. Closed 1 Jan, 1 May, 1 and 11 Nov, 25 Dec. 3.96€. ☎ 02 35 37 24 02.

Église paroissiale St-Valentin – July and Aug: tours by appointment with the Parish Association, Mr Paul Lecerf ☎ 02 35 37 24 32.

L

LASSAY-LES-CHÂTEAUX 🖪 8 r. du Château, BP 42, 53110, ☎ 02 43 04 74 33.

Château – June to Sept: guided tours (1hr) 2.30-6.30pm; Easter to Ascension: Sat-Sun and public holidays 2.30-6.30pm. 3.66€. ☎ 02 43 04 71 22.

LAVAL 🖪 1 allée du Vieux-Saint-Louis, BP 614, 53006, ☎ 02 43 49 46 46.

Guided tours of the town 🅰 – Laval, which is listed as a "Town of Art and history", offers discovery tours conducted by guide-lecturers approved by the Ministry of Culture and Communication. Information at the tourist office or on www.vpah.culture.fr

Le St-Julien – July to end of Aug: daily except Mon 10am-noon, 2-5.45pm. Closed public holidays. No charge. ☎ 02 43 53 39 89.

Vieux château – Guided tours (1hr, last departure 5pm) daily except Mon 10am-noon, 2-6pm. Closed public holidays. 2.90€ (ticket gives access to the Museum of Naive Art), no charge Wed except in July and Aug ☎ 02 43 53 39 89.

Musée d'Art naïf – Same as for old château but visits are unaccompanied.

Musée des Sciences – Daily except Mon 10am-noon, 2-6pm. Closed public holidays. 1.52€, no charge 1st Sunday in the month. ☎ 02 43 49 47 81.

Ancienne église du Pritz – Thur 10am-1pm.

Excursions

Abbaye de Clermont – Beginning of Apr to mid-Sept: 9.30am-6pm: mid-Sept to end of May: 10am-4pm; Jan to mid-Apr: daily except Sun morning. 3.05€. ☎ 02 43 02 11 96.

Entrammes: Gallo Romain baths – ♿ Beginning Apr to mid-Oct: guided tours (1hr) Sun and public holidays 2-7pm (end of June to beginning of Sept: daily 2-7pm; mid-July to mid-Aug: daily 10am-noon, 2-7pm). 2.6€. ☎ 02 43 98 00 25.

LILLEBONNE 🖪 1 r. du Hauzay, 76170, ☎ 02 35 38 08 45.

Théâtre-Amphithéâtre romain – Guided tours by appointment only. ☎ 02 35 71 78 78.

Musée municipal – May to Oct: 10am-noon, 2.30-6.30pm; Nov to Apr: daily except Tues 2.30-6.30pm. 0.94€. ☎ 02 35 38 53 73.

Excursions

Le Mesnil-sous-Lillebonne: église – May to end of Oct: 2.30-6.30pm; Nov to Apr: by appointment. 0.94€. ☎ 02 35 38 30 52.

Abbaye du Valasse – Tours of the abbey have been suspended but the grounds are still open to the public. ☎ 02 35 39 03 75.

LISIEUX 🖪 11 r. d'Alençon, 14100, ☎ 02 31 48 18 10.

Les Buissonnets – Palm Sunday to Sept: audio tours (15min) 9am-noon, 2-6pm; Feb to Mar and Oct: 10am-noon, 2-5pm; Nov to Dec: 10am-noon, 2-4pm; Jan: on request. No charge. ☎ 02 31 48 55 08.

Exposition "Le Carmel de Ste-Thérèse" – ♿ May to end of Sept: 10.30am-12.30pm, 2-5pm. No charge. ☎ 02 31 48 55 08.

Surrounding area

Norolles: Musée vivant de la Basse-cour – ♿ Apr to end of Sept: 10am-6pm. 7.62€ (children under 9: 4.60€). ☎ 02 31 62 78 78.

Hermival-les-Vaux: Zoo – CERZA – Apr to Sept: 9.30am-6.30pm; winter: 10am-4pm. Closed Dec and Jan. 10.67€ (children: 5.33€). ☎ 02 31 62 15 76.

Fervaques: Château Le Kinnor – Guided tours (1hr30min) by appointment (15 days in advance). 4.57€ ☎ 02 31 32 33 96.

Château de St-Germain-de-Livet – Guided tours (1hr) daily except Tues 10am-noon, 2-5pm (Apr to Sept: 7pm). Closed from beginning to mid-Oct, Dec and Jan, 1 May. 5.64€ (children: no charge). ☎ 02 31 31 00 03.

🚊 10 r. du Maréchal-Foch, 27400, ☎ 02 32 40 04 41.

Musée municipal – ♿ Daily except Tues 10am-noon, 2-6pm. No charge. ☎ 02 32 09 58 55

Excursion

La Croix-St-Leufroy: **Church** – Sun. 9am-noon.

Abbaye de LUCERNE

Eglise abbatiale – Easter to Oct: 10am-noon, 2-6.30pm; Nov to Easter: 10am-noon, 2-5.30pm; Feb and Mar: daily except Tues. Closed from Jan to February School holidays. 3.80€. ☎ 02 33 48 83 56.

LYONS-LA-FORÊT 🚊 20 pl. de l'Hôtel de Ville, 27480, ☎ 02 32 49 31 65.

Église St-Denis – Sun at 11.30am.

Abbaye de Mortemer – Easter to 1 Nov: guided tours of the museum (45min) 2-6.30pm, park 11am-6.30pm; 1 Nov to Easter: museum, Sat-Sun and public holidays 2-6pm, park daily. 6.10€. ☎ 02 32 49 54 34.

Beauficel-en-Lyons: Church – Guided tours by appointment with Mr. Dufour, 1, rte de Fleury. ☎ 02 32 49 62 51.

Château de Fleury-la-Forêt – Guided tours (45min) Sun and public holidays 2-6pm (May to Aug: daily, closing time: 6.30pm). Closed Dec and Jan. 6.10€ (children: 3.81€). ☎ 02 32 49 54 34.

Bosquentin: Musée de la Ferme et des Vieux Métiers – Easter to 1 Nov: guided tours (1hr15min) Sat-Sun and public holidays 2.15-6.30pm. 4.57€ (children: 2.29€). ☎ 02 32 48 07 22.

Vascœuil:

Centre régional d'Art et d'Histoire et Musée Michelet – Mid-Apr to mid-Oct: 2.30-6.30pm (July and Aug: 11.30am-7pm). 6€. ☎ 02 35 23 62 35.

Église St-Martial – Open during religious services only.

M

MAYENNE 🚊 Quai de Waiblingen, 53100, ☎ 02 43 04 19 37.

Église St-Martin – ♿ Beginning Apr to mid-Oct: guided tours (1hr) Sun and public holidays 2-7pm (end of June to beginning of Sept: daily 2-7pm; mid-July to mid-Aug: daily 10am-noon, 2-7pm). 2.6€. ☎ 02 43 98 00 25.

MONT-ST-MICHEL 🚊 Corps de garde des Bourgeois, 50116, ☎ 02 33 60 14 30.

Notice boards at car park entrances – Notice boards at car park entrances are updated daily with information on times of high tides and any possible risks. Be careful to observe the instructions given on the spot. 2.29€.

Les Imaginaires du Mont-Saint-Michel – May to Aug: walk (1hr, last departure midnight) to the accompaniment of music, silence, shadows and light, daily except Sun in season. Low season: during school holidays (except Sun).

Abbey gardens – Open in high season only, contact the abbey ticket office.

Archéoscope – Beginning of Feb to mid-Nov and Christmas school holidays: 9am-5.30pm; (July and Aug: 7pm). 6.86€ (children: 4.57€). ☎ 02 33 48 09 37.

Logis Tiphaine – Closed for an undetermined period of time.

Abbey – May to Sept: 9am-6.30pm (last admission 1hr before closing); Oct to Apr: 9.30am-5.30pm, school holidays 9.30am-6pm. Closed 1 Jan, 1 May, 1 and 11 Nov, 25 Dec. 6.40€, 9.91€ (lecture tours by appointment), no charge 1st Sun of the month from Oct to May. ☎ 02 33 60 14 14.

MORTAGNE-AU-PERCHE 🚊 Pl. du Général-de-Gaulle, 61400, ☎ 02 33 85 11 18.

Musée Percheron – Mid-June to mid-Sept: daily except Mon 3-6pm. Closed public holidays. No charge.

Musée Alain – Daily except Mon and Sun. 3-6pm, Wed 10am-noon, 2-6pm, Sat 10am-noon, 2-5pm. Closed between Christmas and New Years Day and public holidays. No charge. ☎ 02 33 25 25 87.

Fôret domaniale du Perche et de la Trappe

Abbaye de la Trappe – ♿ Audio-visual presentation 8.30am-8pm. No charge. ☎ 02 33 84 17 00.

Manoir de la Vove – Tours of the outside Mon and Sat 2-5pm. No charge. Car park facilities outside the park.

MORTAIN
🛈 R. du Bourglopin, 50140, ☎ 02 33 59 19 74.

Abbaye Blanche – July to end of Sept: daily except Tues 9am-noon, 2.30-5pm, Sat 9-11.30am, 2.30-6pm, Sun and public holidays 2.30-6pm. No charge. ☎ 02 33 79 47 47.

Église St-Évroult: Treasury – July and Aug: guided tours (1hr30min) Tues and Thur at 3pm; Sept to June: contact the town hall. No charge ☎ 02 33 79 30 30.

Vallée de la Sée

Brouains: Moulin de la Sée - Écomusée de la Vallée de Brouains – ♿ Mid-June to mid-Sept: 11am-7pm; mid-Sept to mid-June: daily except Tues 2-6pm. Closed Jan,Feb, 25 Dec. 3.75€. ☎ 02 33 59 20 50.

St-Michel-de-Montjoie: Musée du Granit – Mid-June to mid-Sept: 2-6pm. 4€. ☎ 02 33 59 02 22.

Village enchanté de Bellefontaine – Apr to end of Sept: 10am-6pm (July and Aug: closing time, 7pm), Sat-Sun 10am-7pm. 5.34€. ☎ 02 33 59 01 93.

Ste-Opportune-la-Mare: Maison de la Pomme et de la Poire – Apr to end of Sept: 9.30am-12.30pm, 2-7pm. 3.81€. ☎ 02 33 59 56 22.

N

NEUFCHÂTEL-EN-BRAY
🛈 6 pl. Notre-Dame, 76270, ☎ 02 35 93 22 96.

Musée J.-B.-Mathon-A.-Durand – Guided tours (1hr) Sat-Sun 3-6pm (July and Aug: daily except Mon). 2.29€. ☎ 02 35 93 06 55.

The Northern Pays de Bray

Bures-en-Bray: Church – If closed contact Mrs. Jourdain. ☎ 02 35 93 29 28.

Château de Mesnières-en-Bray – Easter to 1 Nov: guided tours (45min) Sat-Sun and public holidays 2.30-6.30pm (July and Aug: daily). 3.81€. ☎ 02 35 93 10 04.

NOGENT-LE-ROTROU
🛈 44 r. Villette-Gate, 28400, ☎ 02 37 29 68 86.

Musée du Perche – Daily except Tues 10am-noon, 2-5pm (May to Oct: 6pm). Closed 1 Jan, 1 May, 1 Nov, 25 Dec. 2.21€. ☎ 02 37 52 18 02.

Église St-Laurent – Wed 3-6pm, the keys are available from Mr Claude Houlle, 4 r. de Lattre de Tassigny, 28400 Nogent le Rotrou.

O – P

OMAHA BEACH

Musée Omaha 6 juin 1944 – ♿ Mid-May to end of Sept: 9.30am-7pm (July and Aug: 7.30pm); mid-Mar to mid-May and Oct to mid-Nov: 9.30am-6.30pm; mid-Feb to mid-Mar: 10am-12.30pm, 2.30-6pm. Closed mid-Nov to mid-Feb. 4.57€. ☎ 02 31 21 97 44.

ORBEC
🛈 R. Guillonnière, 14290, ☎ 02 31 61 12 35.

Musée municipal – Apr to Dec: Sat-Sun and public holidays 10am-noon, 2pm-5pm (June and Aug: daily except Tues 10am-noon, 2-5pm) No charge. ☎ 02 31 61 12 35.

OUISTREHAM-RIVA-BELLA
🛈 Jardins du Casino, 14150, ☎ 02 31 97 18 63.

Lighthouse – Apr, mid-July to end of Aug: Tues, Thur, Sat-Sun and public holidays from 3pm; May: Sat-Sun and public holidays from 3pm. No charge. ☎ 02 31 96 95 14.

Big Bunker – Feb to mid-Nov: 10am-6pm (Apr to Sept: 9am-7pm). 6.09€. ☎ 02 31 97 28 69.

Musée du Débarquement "n°4 Commando" – ♿ Apr to end of Oct: 10.30am-6pm. 3.81€. ☎ 02 31 96 63 10.

Haras du Pin national stud farm

♿ Apr to mid-Oct: guided tours (1hr) 9.30am-6pm; mid-Oct to end Mar: 2-5pm (school holidays 10.30am-noon, 2-5pm). Closed 1 Jan and 25 Dec. 3.8€. ☎ 02 33 36 68 68.

Excursions

St-Germain-de-Clairefeuille: Church – Guided tours available by appointment with Mr Guérin. ☎ 02 33 36 15 01.

Manoir d'Argentelles – Mid-Apr to mid-Oct: Sun. 2.30-6pm; mid-Oct to mid-Apr: guided tours by request 3.30-6pm. No charge. ☎ 02 33 39 93 70.

Château de PIROU

Easter to Oct: 10am-noon, 2-6.30pm; Nov to Easter: daily except Tues 10am-noon, 2-5.30pm. Closed from Jan to February school holidays. 3.80.€. ☎ 02 33 46 34 71.

PONT-AUDEMER
🛈 Pl. Maubert, 27500, ☎ 02 32 41 08 15.

Église St-Germain – Sat 9am-7pm by appointment. Presbytery. ☎ 02 32 41 12 88.

Excursions

Corneville-sur-Risle: Carillon – Daily except Mon 10-11.30am, 6-7pm, Sun 3.30-5.30pm. Closed Jan and Feb. 2.28€. ☎ 02 32 57 01 04.

Beaumont-le-Roger: Église St-Nicolas – If closed ask for the key at the cake shop, Mrs Mérieux, pl. de l'Église ☎ 02 32 45 86 50 or ☎ 02 32 45 22 24.

PONTMAIN

Musée des Missions – ♿ Wed, Sun and public holidays 2.30-6pm; Mon, Tues, Thur, Sat: on request. No charge. ☎ 02 43 30 26 46.

PONTORSON
🛈 Pl. de la Mairie, 50170, ☎ 02 33 60 20 25.

Excursion

St-James: Cimetière américain et Mémorial de Bretagne – ♿ 9am-5pm. No charge. ☎ 02 33 89 24 90.

Q – R

QUILLEBEUF

Réserve naturelle de Mannevilles – Guided tours (2hrs30min) daily except Sat-Sun 9am-6pm. Prices and information are available at the reserve's office in Ste-Opportune-la-Mare. ☎ 02 32 20 27 10.

ROUEN
🛈 25 pl. de la Cathédrale, 76000, ☎ 02 32 08 32 40.

The RouenPass, valid for 1 year, entitles visitors to a free tour of Rouen and a number of reductions or free admission to several museums. Subject to certain conditions, reductions are granted in some hotels. 9.15€.

Guided tours of the town 🅰 – Contact the tourist office.

Crypte, déambulatoire and chapelle de la Vierge – ♿ Guided tours (45min) 10.30am-7pm, Sun and public holidays 1-6pm. Closed 1 Jan, 1 May, 11 Nov. Price information not provided. ☎ 02 35 07 40 23.

Musée national de l'Éducation – Reopening planned for end 2001. Information: ☎ 02 32 82 95 95.

Main courtyard of the Palais de Justice – Contact the tourist office.

Gros-Horloge: Belfry – Closed for renovation.

Église St-Ouen – Mid-Mar to end of Oct: daily except Tues 10am-12.30pm, 2-6pm; mid-Jan to mid-Mar and beginning Nov to mid-Dec: Wed, Sat-Sun 10am-12.30pm, 2-4.30pm. Closed mid-Dec to mid-Jan. ☎ 02 32 08 13 90.

Église St-Godard – Unaccompanied tours Sat 2-7pm.

Église St-Patrice – Sat 3-5pm.

Musée des Beaux-Arts – ♿ Daily except Tues 10am-6pm. Closed public holidays. 3.05€. ☎ 02 35 71 28 40 or ☎ 02 35 52 00 62.

Musée de la Céramique – Daily except Tues 10am-1pm, 2-6pm. 2.29€. ☎ 02 35 07 31 74 or ☎ 02 35 52 00 62.

Musée Le Secq des Tournelles – Daily except Tues 10am-1pm, 2-6pm. Closed public holidays. 2.29€. ☎ 02 35 88 42 92 or ☎ 02 35 52 00 62.

Musée Jeanne-d'Arc – 10am-noon, 2-6.30pm (Mid-Apr to end of Sept: 9.30am-7pm). Closed Christmas and New Year's Day. 3.80€. ☎ 02 35 88 02 70.

Hôtel de Bourgtheroulde – Unaccompanied tours daily except Sun 9am-12.30pm, 1.30-6pm, Sat 2-6pm. Closed public holidays. No charge. ☎ 02 32 08 32 40.

Musée Pierre-Corneille – Guided tours (30min) 10am-noon, 2-6pm Tues and Wed 2-6pm. 0.76€, no charge 1 Apr ☎ 02 35 71 63 92.

Musée Flaubert et d'Histoire de la Médecine – Daily except Sun and Mon 10am-noon, 2-6pm, Tues 10am-6pm. Closed public holidays. 1.83€. ☎ 02 35 15 59 95.

Musée des Antiquités de la Seine-Maritime – Daily except Tues 10am-12.15pm, 1.30-5.30pm, Sun 2-6pm. Closed 1 Jan, 1 May, 1 and 11 Nov, 25 Dec. 3.05€. ☎ 02 35 98 55 10.

Sights on the outskirts

Jardin des plantes – Daily except Sat-Sun 8-11am, 1.30-4.45 by appointment (2 weeks in advance). Closed public holidays. No charge. ☎ 02 32 18 21 30.

Petit-Couronne: Manoir Pierre-Corneille – Daily except Tues 10am-12.30pm, 2-5pm, Sun 2-5.30pm (Apr to Sept: 2-6pm, Sun 6.30pm). 3.05€. ☎ 02 35 68 13 89.

Notre-Dame-de-Bondeville: Musée industriel de la Corderie Vallois – ♿ Guided tours (1hr15min) 1.30-6pm. Closed 1 Jan, 1 May, 1 and 11 Nov, 25 Dec. 3.05€. ☎ 02 35 74 35 35.

Barentin: Church – Weekdays: 9am-6pm.

Croisset: Pavillon Flaubert – Guided tours (15min) 10am-noon, 2-6pm Tues and Wed 2-6pm. 0.76€, no charge 1 Apr ☎ 02 35 36 43 91.

The Lower Seine Valley

Le Trait: Church – Open only on Sat evenings and Sun during religious services.

Château d'Ételan – Mid-July to end of Aug: daily except Tues 10.30am-12.30pm, 2.30-6.30pm. 3.81€. ☎ 02 35 39 91 27.

S

ST-ÉVROULT-NOTRE-DAME-DU-BOIS

The Charentonne Valley

Broglie: Jardin aquatique – Apr to Sept: 8.30am-8pm; Oct to Mar: 9am-5.30pm. No charge. ☎ 02 32 46 27 52.

Fontaine-l'Abbé: Church – Closed except for religious services.

ST-LÔ   🛈 Pl. du Général-de-Gaulle, 50000, ☎ 02 33 05 02 09.

Église Notre-Dame – 9am-6pm; possibility of guided tours. Contact the presbytery. ☎ 02 33 57 14 73.

Musée des Beaux-Arts – ♿ Daily except Tues 10am-noon, 2-6pm. Closed 1 Jan, Easter, 1 May. Ascension, 1 Nov, 25 Dec. 1.52€. ☎ 02 33 72 52 55.

Haras national – ♿ June to end of Sept: guided tours (1hr) 2-5.30pm (July and Aug: additional tour at 11am). Free admission to the "Jeudis du haras" (presentation of stallions at 3pm every Thursday during the month of August). Closed 1 Jan and 25 Dec. 3.81€. ☎ 02 33 55 29 09.

Excursion

Torigni-sur-Vire: Château des Matignon – Mid-June to mid-Sept: guided tours (45min) Sat-Sun and public holidays 2.30-6pm (July and Aug: daily). 2.28€. ☎ 02 33 56 71 44.

ST-MARTIN-DE-BOSCHERVILLE

Ancienne abbaye St Georges – June to Sept: 9am-7pm; Apr and May: 9.30am-noon, 2-7pm; Oct to Mar: 2-5pm. Closed 1 Jan and 25 Dec. 3.18€. ☎ 02 35 32 10 82.

ST-PIERRE-SUR-DIVES   🛈 R. Saint-Benoît, 14170, ☎ 02 31 20 97 90.

Church – July and Aug: Mon at 5pm and Thur at 11am. Guided tours available, ask at the tourist office. ☎ 02 31 20 97 90

Salle capitulaire – May to Oct: daily except Sun 9.30am-12.30pm, 1.30-6pm, Sat 10am-noon, 2-5pm; Nov to Apr: 9.30am-12.30pm, 1.30-5.30pm, Sat 10am-noon. Closed 1 May. No charge. ☏ 02 31 20 97 90.

Halles (covered market) – ♿ 8am-7pm. No charge. ☏ 02 31 20 97 90.

Excursion

Château de Canon – ♿ July to Sept: daily except Tues 2-7pm; Easter to end of June: Sat-Sun and public holidays 2-6pm. 4.57€. ☏ 02 31 20 71 50.

ST-SAUVEUR-LE-VICOMTE 🛈 Pl. Auguste-Cousin, 50390, ☏ 02 33 21 50 44.

Musée Barbey-d'Aurevilly – Mid-May to mid-Sept: daily except Tues 10am-noon, 3-6pm; Mid-Sept to mid-May: Sat-Sun 3-5pm. Closed 1 Jan, 25 Dec. 2.29€. ☏ 02 33 41 65 18.

Abbaye – 10am-noon, 2-6pm. No charge. ☏ 02 33 21 63 29.

Excursion

Château de Crosville-sur-Douve – Easter to end of Sept: 2-6pm. 3.81€ (children: no charge). ☏ 02 33 41 67 25.

ST-VAAST-LA-HOUGUE 🛈 1 pl. du Gén. de Gaulle, 50550, ☏ 02 33 23 19 32.

Île de Tatihou – Crossing (10min) every 30min (high tide) and every hour (low tide). Easter to Sept: 10am-4.30pm; Oct to Easter: Sat-Sun 2-4.30pm. Numbers of visitors limited to 500 persons per day, it is advisable to book. 7.62€ Return fare (visit of the museum and the Tour Vauban). ☏ 02 33 23 19 92.

Abbaye de ST-WANDRILLE

Abbey cloisters – Guided tours (45min) daily except Mon at 3.30pm, Sat-Sun and public holidays 11.30am and 3.30pm. 3€. ☏ 02 35 96 23 11.

Church – Mass conducted in Gregorian chant at 9.45am weekdays, Sun and public holidays at 10am. Vespers at 5.30pm (Thur at 6.45pm), Sun and public holidays at 5pm.

STE-MÈRE-ÉGLISE 🛈 Pl. du Gén. de Gaulle, 50480, ☏ 02 33 21 53 91.

Musée des Troupes aéroportées – ♿ Feb to end of Nov: 9.30am-noon, 2-6pm (Apr to Sept: 9am-6.45pm). 4.57€. ☏ 02 33 41 41 35.

Ferme-Musée du Cotentin – ♿ June to Sept: 11am-7pm; school holidays, Apr, May and Oct: 1-6pm; Mar: Sun. 1-6pm. 3.81€ (children: 1.52€). ☏ 02 33 95 40 20.

STE-SUZANNE 🛈 13 r. de la Cité, 53270, ☏ 02 43 01 43 60.

Musée de l'Auditoire – Apr to Sept: 2-6pm (mid-June to end of Aug: 6.30pm); Mar and Oct: Sun. 2-5.30pm. 3.08€. ☏ 02 43 01 42 65.

Château – Beginning of Apr to end of Sept: 9.30am-12.30pm, 1.30-5.30pm (May to end of Sept: 9am-6pm). Closed in Feb, 1 Jan, 25 Dec. 3.05€. ☏ 02 43 01 40 77.

Excursion

Grottes de Saulges – Mid-Feb to mid-Nov: guided tours (45min) daily. Price information not provided. ☏ 02 43 90 51 30.

SÉES 🛈 Pl. du Gén.-de-Gaulle, 61500, ☏ 02 33 28 74 79.

Cathédrale – Guided tours available, ask at the tourist office.

Église Notre-Dame-de-la-Place – Closed for an unspecified period of time. ☏ 02 33 27 36 05.

Musée départemental d'Art religieux – July to end of Sept: daily except Tues 10am-6pm. 1.52€. ☏ 02 33 81 23 00.

Excursions

Château d'O – Call for information on ☏ 02 33 35 30 81 (Mortrée town hall).

Forêt d'Écouves – Guided tours on foot or on horseback through the forest massifs (Écouves, Andaines, Bellême and Perche-Trappe, Réno-Valdieu, Moulins-Bonsmoulins) are available on request to the Office National des Forêts (National Forestry Commission), 36 r. St-Blaise, Alençon. ☏ 02 33 82 55 00.

La SUISSE NORMANDE 🛈 Pl. de la Mairie, 14570 CLÉCY, ☏ 02 31 69 79 95.

St-Rémy: Les Fosses d'Enfer – June to Sept: 10am-6.30pm; Mar to May: daily except Tues 10am-noon, 2-6pm; Oct to Feb: daily except Tues 2-6pm. Closed 1 Jan and 25 Dec. 4.57€ (children: 2.28€). ☏ 02 31 69 67 77.

T

THURY-HARCOURT

🖪 2 pl. St-Sauveur, 14220, ☎ 02 31 79 70 45.

Park and gardens of the château – May to Sept: 2.30-6.30pm; Apr and Oct: Sun and public holidays 2.30-6.30pm. 3.96€ summer, 3.51€ winter. ☎ 02 31 79 72 05.

TROUVILLE-SUR-MER

🖪 32 bd. F.-Moureaux, 14360, ☎ 02 31 14 60 70.

Aquarium – ♿ Easter to Oct: 10am-noon, 2-6.30pm (July and Aug: 10am-7.30pm); Nov to Easter: 2-6.30pm. Closed 25 Dec. 5.79€. ☎ 02 31 88 46 04.

Musée Villa Montebello – Apr to Sept: daily except Tues 2-6.30pm. 1.52€, no charge Wed. ☎ 02 31 88 52 33.

Gallerie d'exposition – ♿ July to Sept and school holidays: daily except Tues 10am-noon, 2-6pm: Oct to June: daily except Tues 2-5.30pm, Sat-Sun and public holidays 10am-noon, 2-5.30pm. Closed in Jan. No charge. ☎ 02 31 88 52 33.

V

VALOGNES

🖪 Pl. du Château, 50700, ☎ 02 33 40 11 55.

Guided tours of the town – Valognes, which is listed as a "Town of Art and history", offers discovery tours conducted by guide-lecturers approved by the Ministry of Culture and Communication. Information available at the Maison du Patrimoine (Heritage Dept.) or on www.vpah.culture.fr

Hôtel de Beaumont – July to mid-Sept: guided tours (1hr) 2.30pm-6.30pm and Tues 10.30am-noon. 4.3€. ☎ 02 33 40 12 30.

Hôtel de Grandval-Caligny – Aug: guided tours (45min) 2-6pm, Sat 11am-noon; June and Sept: by appointment. 4€. ☎ 02 33 40 01 75.

Musée régional du Cidre et du Calvados – Apr to end of Sept: daily except Tues 10am-noon, 2-6pm, Sun and public holidays 2-6pm (July and Aug: daily). 3.05€. ☎ 02 33 40 22 73.

Excursions

Bricquebec:Castle – July to Sept: guided tours (1hr) daily except Tues 2.30-6.30pm; June: daily except Tues 2-6.30pm. 1.83€. ☎ 02 33 87 22 50.

Abbaye Notre-Dame-de-Grâce – The abbey is not open for visits but it is possible to attend services, watch an audio-visual presentation and purchase items produced in the monastery. Information is available to visitors throughout the year. ☎ 02 33 87 56 10.

VARENGEVILLE-SUR-MER

Parc floral du Bois des Moutiers – Mid-Mar to mid-Nov: 10am-noon, 2-6pm. Walks in the park permitted from May to end of Sept. 5.34€/6.10€ (children: 2.29€. ☎ 02 35 85 10 02.

Chapelle St-Dominique – Easter to end of Sept: 9am-6pm. ☎ 02 35 85 12 14.

Manoir d'Ango – Mid-Mar to mid-Nov: daily 10am-12.30pm, 2-6.30pm. 4.57€. ☎ 02 35 85 14 80.

Château de VENDEUVRE

Château, garden and Musée du Mobilier miniature – ♿ May to Sept: 10am-6pm; Mar, Apr and Oct to 11 Nov: Sun and public holidays 2-6pm; Easter and Nov school holidays: 2-6pm. 7.62€ (children: 6.10€) ticket includes château, gardens, miniature furniture exhibition and kitchens. ☎ 02 31 40 93 83.

VERNEUIL-SUR-AVRE

🖪 Pl. de la Madeleine, 27130, ☎ 02 32 32 17 17.

Église de la Madeleine – Ascent of the tower 1st Sun in the month.

Excursions

Francheville: Musée de la Ferronnerie – ♿ Mid-Mar to mid-Nov: Sun and public holidays 3-6pm (mid-June to mid-Sept: Sat-Sun and public holidays 3pm-7pm) 1.52€. ☎ 02 32 32 61 71.

Nonancourt: Église St-Martin – Closed for renovation work.

VERNON

🖪 36 r. Carnot, 27200, ☎ 02 32 51 39 60.

Musée A.-G.-Poulain – Apr to Oct: daily except Mon 11am-1pm, 2-6pm, Sat-Sun and public holidays 2-6pm. 2.29€. ☎ 02 32 21 28 09.

Tours des Archives – Contact the tourist office. ☎ 02 32 51 39 60.

Excursion

Château de Bizy – ♿ Feb to end of Nov: guided tours of the interior (45min) Sat-Sun and public holidays 2-5pm (Apr to Oct: daily except Mon 10am-noon, 2-6pm). 6€. ☎ 02 32 51 00 82.

VILLEDIEU-LES-POÊLES
🖪 Pl. des Costils, 50800, ☎ 02 33 61 05 69.

The "Théopolitain" tourist train takes visitors on tours of the town every day in July and Aug 10am-noon and 2-6.30pm. The train leaves from in front of the tourist office. 2.30€ (children: 1.50€).

Atelier du Cuivre – Daily except Sun 9am-noon, 1.30-5.30pm, Sat 9am-noon, 2.30-5.30pm (mid-July to end of Aug: daily 10am-noon, 2.30-5.30pm). 3€. ☎ 02 33 51 31 85.

Musée du cuivre et Maison de la Dentellière – Easter to 1 Nov: 10am-noon, 2-6.30pm, Tues 2-6.30pm (July and Aug: 10am-6.30pm). 3.35€. ☎ 02 33 61 11 78.

Fonderie de Cloches – ♿ Beginning of Feb to beginning of Nov: daily except Mon 10am-noon, 1.30-5.30 (July and Aug: 8am-5.30pm). Closed mid-Nov to mid-Feb. 3.36€. ☎ 02 33 61 00 56.

Maison de l'Étain – Apr to Oct: daily except Sun and Mon 10am-noon, 2-5.30pm (mid-July to end of Aug: daily except Sun 10am-noon, 2.30-5.30pm); Nov to Dec: daily except Sun and Mon 2-5.30pm. 3€. ☎ 02 33 51 05 08.

Royaume de l'Horloge – ♿ July and Aug: daily except Mon 9am-12.30pm, 2-6.30pm, Sun and public holidays 2.30-6.30pm; low season: Daily except Mon and Sun. 9am-12.30pm, 2-6.30pm. 4€. ☎ 02 33 90 95 38.

Musée du Meuble normand – Easter to 1 Nov: 10am-noon, 2-6.30pm, Tues 2-6.30pm (July and Aug: daily 10am-6.30pm). 3.35€. ☎ 02 33 61 11 78.

Excursions

Abbaye de Hambye: Convent buildings – Apr to end of Oct: guided tours (1hr, last departures at 11.30am and 5.30pm) daily except Tues 10am-noon, 2-6pm. 4€. ☎ 02 33 61 76 92.

Parc zoologique de Champrepus – ♿ Feb to 11 Nov: 1.30-6pm (Apr to Aug: 10am-7pm). 8.38€ (children: 4.57€). ☎ 02 33 61 30 74.

VIMOUTIERS
🖪 10 av. du Général-de-Gaulle, 61120, ☎ 02 33 39 30 29.

Musée du Camembert – Apr to Oct: guided tours (30min) 9am-noon, 2-6pm, Mon 2-6pm, Sun and public holidays 10am-noon, 2.30-6pm; Nov to Mar: daily except Sun and public holidays 10am-noon, 2-5.30pm, Mon 2-5.30pm. 2.28€. ☎ 02 33 39 30 29.

Excursions

Camembert: Maison du camembert – Apr to Oct: 10.30am-6.30pm (10am-7pm Sun). 2.5€. ☎ 02 33 39 43 35.

Prieuré St-Michel de Crouttes – May to June: Sat-Sun and public holidays 2-6pm; July and Aug: Fri and Sat-Sun 2-6pm; Sept: first three weekends 2pm-6pm. 4.57€ (children under 10: 3.81€). ☎ 02 33 39 15 15.

VIRE
🖪 Square de la Résistance, 14500, ☎ 02 31 68 00 05.

Tour de l'Horloge – July to mid-Sept: daily except Sun 2.30-6.30pm. Closed 14 July and 15 Aug. 1.52€. ☎ 02 31 66 28 50.

Musée – Daily except Tues 10am-noon, 2-6pm. Closed 1 Jan and 25 Dec. 3.81€. ☎ 02 31 68 10 49.

The Channel Islands

Abbreviations: EH = *English Heritage*; NACF = *National Art Collections Fund*; RSPB = *Royal Society for the Protection of Birds*; NT = *The National Trust*; NTJ = *The National Trust for Jersey*; NTG = *The National Trust for Guernsey*

ALDERNEY

▣ Victoria Street, St Anne – ☎ 01481 823 737 – Fax 01481 822 436

Alderney Taxis – Taxis can be hired from the following companies. ☎ 01481 823 760 (ABC Taxis); ☎ 01481 822 611 or 822 992 (Alderney Taxis); ☎ 01481 823 823 (Island Taxis); ☎ 01481 823 181 (JS Taxis).

Riduna Buses – Operate from Butes car park via Victoria Street taxi rank, the Harbour, Campsite (Arch & corblets & Lighthouse) to Longis Bay (Nunnery) late-July to early-Sept, at 10am, 11am, midday, 1.40pm, 4pm 5pm and 5.30pm; also at 7pm during August. ☎ 01481 823 760.

Alderney Guided Tour – Operate from the Taxi rank in Victoria Street, daily, 2-4pm. £5. Bookings at The Alderney Gift Box (next to the post office) or at Selections, Victoria Street; ☎ 01481 823 760 (Riduna Buses/AABC Taxis).

Alderney Vehicle Hire – Self-drive hire cars with unlimited mileage allowance are offered by the following companies. Valid driving licence required. Parking discs are provided and must be displayed. ☎ 01481 823 738 (Braye Hire Cars); ☎ 01481 823 352 (Alderney Fuel Services: Cars, Jeep and Buggies); ☎ 01481 822 971 (Central Car Hire - summer months only); ☎ 01481 823 352 (Alderney Moped Hire); ☎ 01841 822 086; Fax 822 087 (Mermaid Rent-a-Car).

Alderney Cycle Hire – Bicycles for adults and children are offered by the following companies. ☎ 01481 822 286 or 824 377 (Pedal Power, Les Rocquettes); ☎ 01481 822 294 (J Cycle, Val Reuter Garages); ☎ 01481 822 000 (Top Gear, Le Banquage); ☎ 01481 823 725 (Puffin Cycles).

Alderney Railway – Operates Easter–Sept, Sat, Sun and bank holiday Mon, at 2pm, 3pm (also 4pm in the high season). Extra trains on Wed, July and Aug and during Alderney Week. Diesel train and Wickham train. Return £2 (child £1). ☎ 822 980 or 822 643.

Forts Tour – Victorian and German forts tour (approx 3hr; minimum 6 people) by appointment. £5. ☎ 01481 823 270.

Voyager Boat Trips – Operate round the island (2hr 30min) or by charter to Sark, Herm or France. For bookings on Voyager apply to McAllister's Fish Shop, Victoria Street, St Anne's, Alderney; ☎ 01481 823 666.

Lady Maris Boat trips – Operate round the island (2hr 30min) or by charter to Sark, Herm or France. For bookings on Lady Maris apply to The Alderney Gift Box, Victoria Street, St Anne's, Alderney; ☎ 01481 823 532.

Alderney Museum – ♿ Open Easter–Oct, daily, 10am–noon and Mon–Fri, 2pm–4pm. £1 (free for child under 18). ☎ 01481 823 222 or 822 655 (Administrator).

Court House – Open all year, Mon–Fri, 9.30am–12.30pm and 2-4pm, with permission from the Clerk of the Court. ☎ 01481 822 811.

Quesnard Lighthouse – Guided tour (weather permitting) Good Friday-Easter Monday, May Day and Spring Bank Holiday weekend–Sept, Sat–Sun, at 2.30pm and 3.30pm. £1.50 (child under 16 £1). Steep steps; people less than 1m in height are not permitted to ascend. ☎ 01481 824 309 (Lighthouse attendant).

Burhou Island – Open all year (except during the breeding season, mid-Mar to mid-July). Apply for permission to stay overnight (£10 per night; take drinking water) from the Harbour Office (Open in summer, daily, 8am–6pm; winter, Mon–Fri, 8am–5pm); ☎ 01481 822 620; Fax 01481 823 699.

GUERNSEY

▣ White Rock, St Peter Port – ☎ 01481 723 552 – Fax 01481 714 951

Guernseybus – North and west coast tour (K-route) by open-top bus operates (weather permitting) at 10.45am or 2pm (also 10.15am and 1.15pm in the high season); £7 (child £3.50). Also scenic tours (choice of eight); Rover Ticket valid for 1, 3, 5 or 7 days (£4.50-£29); Monthly Ticket valid for 31 days (£28-£52 according to zone; £34 park-and-ride); 10-journey voucher (£5.50-£10 according to zone). ☎ 01481 724 677; guernseybus@gtonline.net; www.gtonline.net/business/guernseybus

Hauteville House – Guided tour (15 max) Apr–Sept, Mon–Sat, 10am–11.45am and 2pm–4.45pm. Closed Sun and bank holiday Mon. £4 (concession £2), children free of charge. ☎ 01481 721 911; Fax 01481 715 913.

Castle Cornet – Open Apr–Oct, daily, 10am–5pm. Noonday gun fired daily. £4.00; joint ticket with Guernsey Museum and Fort Grey £6. Guided tour (1hr) morning and afternoon. Parking nearby. Refreshments. ☎ 01481 721 657 (Castle); 01481 726 518; Fax 01481 715 177 (Guernsey Museum).

Guernsey Museum – ♿ Open all year, daily, 10am–5pm (4pm Nov-Mar). Closed 25 Dec to 1 Jan. £2.50 (senior £1.25), children and students free of charge; joint ticket with Castle Cornet and Fort Grey £6. Refreshments. ☎ 01481 726 518; Fax 01481 715 177; admin@museum.guernsey.net; www.museum.guernsey.net

26 Cornet Street – Open late-Mar to mid-Oct, Tues–Thur and Sat, 10am–4pm; also for 3 weeks before Christmas. ☎ 01481 728 451.

St James' – Box Office: Open all year, Mon–Fri, 9am–2pm, Sat, 10am–12pm. ☎ 01481 711 361.

Royal Court House – Jan–Dec during sessions (except in Aug), last Wed and Thurs of the month (second Wed in Dec), 10am to close of business. Details of debates available from the Greffe. ☎ 01481 725 277.

Guernsey Folk Museum – Open late-Mar to late-Oct, daily, 10am–5.30pm (4pm in winter). Last admission 30min before closing. £2.50 (concession £1). Parking. ☎ 01481 255 384.

German Underground Hospital – Open May–Sept, daily, 10am–noon and 2–4pm; Apr and Oct, daily, 2–4pm; Mar and Nov, Sun and Thur, 2–3pm. £2.50 (child 60p). ☎ 01481 239 100.

Oatlands Craft Centre – ♿ Open all year, daily, 9.30am–5pm (reduced hours in winter). Parking. Refreshments. ☎ 01481 244 282.

Dehus Dolmen – Open all year, daily, sunrise–sunset. ☎ 01481 717 000 (Secretary of Heritage Committee).

Fort Grey Maritime Museum – Open Apr–Oct, daily, 10am–5pm. £2 (senior £1), children and students free of charge; joint ticket with Guernsey Museum and Castle Cornet £6. Parking. ☎ 01481 265 036 (museum); 01481 726 518; Fax 01481 715 177 (Guernsey Museum).

German Occupation Museum – ♿ Open all year (except Jan), daily, 10am–5pm (1pm in winter). £2.75 (child £1.25). Parking. Refreshments. ☎ 01481 238 205.

Sausmarez Manor – ♿ Garden: all year, daily, 10am–5pm. Subtropical Gardens: Feb–Dec, daily, 10.30am–5pm. Art park sculpture garden: Mar-Jan, daily, 10.30am-5.30pm. House: Guided tour June–Sept, Mon-Wed, 10.30am, 11.30am, 2pm and 3pm, Thur, 10.30am, 11.30am, Thurs, 2pm with complimentary glass of wine; Mar–May and Oct, Mon-Thurs, 10.30am and 11.30am. Dolls' House Collection: Mar–Oct, daily, 10am–5pm. Petland: Apr-Oct, daily, 10.30am (2pm Wed) to 5pm. Garden no charge; Art park £2.50; House £4.90; Subtropical garden £2.50; Dolls' House £1.95; Petland £5 (family ticket); season ticket £13 (10 visits inc activities), £20 (A+C); £7 (5 visits inc activities), £12 (A+C). Pitch and putt; putting green. Play areas. Parking. Tearooms. ☎ 01481 235 571 (Estate Office); Fax 01481 235 572. ☎ 01481 235 904 (Dolls' House).

La Valette Underground Military Hospital – Open daily, 10am–5pm. £2.75 (child £1) and £2.25 for senior citizens. ☎ 01481 722 300.

Aquarium – ♿ Open all year, daily, 10am–sunset. Closed 25–26 Dec. £2.50 (child £1.65), £1.85 for senior citizens and £2.10 for students. ☎ 01481 723 301.

JERSEY

🛈 Liberation Square, St Helier, – JE1 1BB – ☎ 01534 500 777 – Fax 01534 500 899

Royal Court House – Open all year during sessions (except Aug), alternate Tues, 9.30am to close of business; also Fri, 2.30pm for public property purchases hearings. ☎ 01534 502 101.

Elizabeth Castle – Open late-Mar to Oct, daily, 9.30am to 6pm (5pm last admission). £3.50 (concession £2.50). Special Discount Ticket £7 (also valid for 2 other Jersey Heritage sites: Jersey Museum, Jersey Maritime, La Hougue Bie, Hamptonne, Mont Orgueil). Guided tour (1hr 30min). Restaurant. ☎ 01534 823 971 (Castle), 01534 633 300 (Jersey Heritage Trust); Fax 01534 633 301; museum@jerseyheritagetrust.org; www.jerseyheritagetrust.org

Jersey Museum – ♿ Open all year, daily, 10am–5pm (4pm winter). Closed 25 Dec. £3.50 (concession £2.50); Special Discount Ticket £7 (also valid at 2 other Jersey Heritage Trust sites: Jersey Maritime, Elizabeth Castle, La Hougue Bie, Hamptonne, Mont Orgueil). Guided tour by appointment. ☎ 01534 633 300 (Museum and Jersey Heritage Trust); Fax 01534 633 301; museum@jerseyheritagetrust.org; www.jerseyheritagetrust.org

Jersey Maritime Museum – ♿ Open daily, 10am–5pm (4pm Nov-Mar). Closed 1 Jan, 25 Dec. £3.50, £2.50 (reduction); Special Discount Ticket £7 (also valid at 2 other Jersey Heritage Trust sites : Jersey Museum, Elizabeth Castle, La Hougue Bie, Hamptonne, Mont Orgueil). ☎ 01534 811 043 (Museum), 01534 633 300 (Jersey Heritage Trust); Fax 01534 633 301; museum@jerseyheritagetrust.org; www.jerseyheritagetrust.org.

Fort Regent – ♿ Open daily; telephone for times and charges. Parking. Refreshments. ☎ 01534 500 200; Fax 01534 500 225; www.jersey.gov.uk/slr

Island Fortress Occupation Museum – ♿ Open all year, daily, 9.30am (10am Nov–Mar) to 10pm (6.30pm Fri-Sat; earlier Nov–Mar). £3 (child 8-16 £1.50) and £2 for seniors/students. ☎ 01534 734 306; Fax 01534 877 693.

Jersey Zoo – ♿ Open all year, daily, 9.30am to 6pm/sunset (4pm last admission). Closed 25 Dec. £8 (child £5.50) and £6.50 for seniors. Guided tour (1hr) by arrangement. Parking. Refreshments. ☎ 01534 860 000; Fax 01534 860 001; jersey.zoo@durrell.org; www.jersey.co.uk/jwpt

Eric Young Orchid Foundation – ♿ Closed for redevelopment until early in 2001. Previously open all year, Thur–Sat, 10am–4pm. Closed 1 Jan, 25–26 Dec. £2.50 (child £1.00) and concession £1.50. ☎ 01534 861 963; Fax 01534 863 293.

German Underground Hospital – ♿ Closed for refurbishment Nov-Dec 2000. Open early-Mar to early-Nov, daily, 9.30am–5pm (4.15pm last admission); Nov–Dec, Sun and Thur, 2pm–5pm (4.15pm last admission). £5.20 (child £2.60). Parking. Cafe. ☎ 01534 863 442; Fax 01534 865 970.

Moulin de Quétivel – (NTJ) Open mid-May to mid-Oct, Tues–Thurs, 10am–4pm. £1.50 (child over 10 50p) and concession £1. Parking. ☎ 01534 745 408 (mill); 01534 483 193 (NT office).

Living Legend – ♿ Open Apr–Oct, daily, 9.30am–5.30pm; Mar and Nov, Sat–Wed, 10am–5pm. Narrative (French, German, Norwegian, Swedish). Show £5.35, £3.25 (child), £4.95 (senior citizen), £3.90 (student), £4 (disabled). Adventure golf, £4.10, £3 (child). Parking. Refreshments. Shops. ☎ 01534 485 496; Fax 01534 485 855; gerard@livinglegend.freeserve.co.uk

Jersey Motor Museum – (♿) Open end-Mar to late-Oct, daily, 10am–5pm. £2.50 (child £1.20) and free for the disabled. Parking. ☎ 01534 482 966.

La Hougue Bie Museums – ♿ Open late-Mar to Oct, daily, 10am–5pm. £3.50, £2.50 (reduction). Special Discount Ticket £7 (also valid for 2 other Jersey Heritage Trust sites : Jersey Museum, Jersey Maritime, Elizabeth Castle, Hamptonne, Mont Orgueil). Parking. ☎ 01534 853 823 (La Hougue Bie), 01534 633 301 (Jersey Heritage Trust); Fax 01534 633 301; museum@jerseyheritagetrust.org; www.jersey-heritagetrust.org

Hamptonne Country Life Museum – ♿ Open late-Mar to Oct, daily, 10am–5pm. £3.50 (concession £2.50). Special Discount Ticket £7 (also valid for 2 other Jersey Heritage Trust sites: Jersey Museum, Jersey Maritime, Elizabeth Castle, La Hougue Bie, Mont Orgueil). ☎ 01534 863 955 (Hamptonne Museum), 01534 633 300 (Jersey Heritage Trust); Fax 01534 633 301; museum@jerseyjeritagetrust.org; www.jerseyheritagetrust.org

St Matthew's Church (Glass Church) – Open all year, Mon–Fri, 9am–6pm (4.30pm Oct–Mar), Sat–Sun, for services only. Guide book (French). Parking. ☎/Fax 01534 502 864.

Command Bunker – Open June–Aug, Thur, 7pm–9.30pm; Sept, Mon, 10am to midday. Parking (£1). Further details from the Channel Island Occupation Society, The Chateau, Five Mile Road, St Ouen.

Kempt Tower – Open May–Sept, daily, 2pm–5pm. No charge. Free guided nature walk (1hr 30min): May–June, Thur, at 2.30pm. Parking. ☎ 01534 483 140.

Battle of Flowers Museum – (♿) Open Easter to mid-Nov, daily, 10am–5pm. £2.50 (child 70p) and concession £2.25. Parking. ☎ 01534 482 408.

Greve de Lecq Barracks (North Coast Visitor Centre) – (NTJ) ♿ Open May to mid-Oct, Tues–Sun, 11am (2pm Sun) to 5pm. Donation. Parking. ☎ 01534 482 238 (barracks); 01534 483 193 (NT office).

La Mare Vineyards – ♿ Open mid-Apr to mid-Oct, Mon–Sat, 10am–5.30pm. £3.85 (child 12-18 £1) and free for under 12s. Free wine tasting. Parking. Refreshments. ☎ 01534 481 178; Fax 01534 485 210; timcrowley@lamarejersey.com; www.lamarejersey.com

Mont Orgueil Castle – Open daily, 9.30am–6pm (sunset in winter); last admission 1hr before closing. £3.50 (concession £2.50). Special Discount Ticket £7 (also valid for 2 other Jersey Heritage Trust sites: Jersey Museum, Jersey Maritime, Elizabeth Castle, La Hougue Bie, Hamptonne). ☎ 01534 853 292 (Castle), Jersey Heritage Trust 01534 633 300; Fax 01534 633 301; museum@jerseyheritagetrust.org; www.jerseyheritagetrust.org

Jersey Pottery – ♿ Open all year, daily, 9am (10am Sun) to 5.30pm. Closed Christmas to New Year. No charge. Parking. Licensed restaurant. Shop. Museum. ☎ 01534 851 119; Fax 01534 856 403; jsypot@itl.net; www.jerseypottery.com

Samarés Manor – ♿ Garden: Apr–Oct, daily, 10am–5pm. House: guided tour (40min) Apr–Oct, Mon–Sat, at 11.45am, 12.30pm. Gardens £3.90 (child over 5 £1.90) and £3.25 for senior citizens; house £1.80. Herb talks: Mon–Fri, at 2.30pm. Parking. Refreshments. ☎ 01534 870 551; Fax 01534 768 949.

SARK

▣ ☎ 01481 832 345

La Seigneurie Gardens – ♿ Open Easter to mid-Oct, Mon–Fri, 10am–5pm; also July–Aug, Sat (for charity). £1 (child 50p). ☎ 01481 832 345 (Sark Tourism); www.sark-tourism.com

Useful French words and phrases

ARCHITECTURAL TERMS

See the ABC of Architecture in the Introduction

SIGHTS

abbey	abbaye	lock (canal)	écluse
belfry	beffroi	market	marché
bridge	pont	monastery	monastère
castle	château	museum	musée
cemetery	cimetière	park	parc
chapel	chapelle	port/harbour	port
church	église	quay	quai
cloisters	cloître	ramparts	remparts
convent	couvent	statue	statue
courtyard	cour	street	rue
covered market	halle	tower	tour
fountain	fontaine	square	place
garden	jardin	town hall	mairie
gateway	porte	windmill	moulin
house	maison		

NATURAL SITES

beach	plage	pass	col
beacon	signal	river	rivière
cave	grotte	source	spring
chasm	abîme	stream	ruisseau
coast, hillside	côte	swallow-hole	aven
dam	barrage	valley	vallée
forest	forêt	waterfall	cascade
lake	lac	viewpoint	belvédère
scenic road	corniche		

ON THE ROAD

car park	parking	petrol/gas station	station essence
driving licence	permis de conduire	right	droite
east	Est	south	Sud
garage (for repairs)	garage	toll	péage
left	gauche	traffic lights	feu tricolore
motorway/highway	autoroute	tyre	pneu
north	Nord	west	Ouest
parking meter	horodateur	wheel clamp	sabot
petrol/gas	essence	zebra crossing	passage clouté

TIME

today	aujourd'hui	week	semaine
tomorrow	demain	Monday	lundi
yesterday	hier	Tuesday	mardi
		Wednesday	mercredi
autunm/fall	automne	Thursday	jeudi
winter	hiver	Friday	vendredi
spring	printemps	Saturday	samedi
summer	été	Sunday	dimanche

NUMBERS

0	zéro	10	dix	20	vingt
1	un	11	onze	30	trente
2	deux	12	douze	40	quarante
3	trois	13	treize	50	cinquante
4	quatre	14	quatorze	60	soixante
5	cinq	15	quinze	70	soixante-dix
6	six	16	seize	80	quatre-vingts
7	sept	17	dix-sept	90	quatre-vingt-dix
8	huit	18	dix-huit	100	cent
9	neuf	19	dix-neuf	1000	mille

SHOPPING

bank	banque	fishmonger's	poissonnerie
baker's	boulangerie	grocer's	épicerie
big	grand	newsagent, bookshop	librairie
butcher's	boucherie	open	ouvert
chemist's	pharmacie	post office	poste
closed	fermé	push	pousser
cough mixture	sirop pour la toux	pull	tirer
cough sweets	cachets pour la gorge	shop	magasin
entrance	entrée	small	petit
exit	sortie	stamps	timbres

FOOD AND DRINK

beef	bœuf	lamb	agneau
beer	bière	lunch	déjeuner
butter	beurre	lettuce salad	salade
bread	pain	meat	viande
breakfast	petit-déjeuner	mineral water	eau minérale
cheese	fromage	mixed salad	salade composée
chicken	poulet	orange juice	jus d'orange
dessert	dessert	plate	assiette
dinner	dîner	pork	porc
fish	poisson	restaurant	restaurant
fork	fourchette	red wine	vin rouge
fruit	fruits	salt	sel
sugar	sucre	spoon	cuillère
glass	verre	vegetables	légumes
ice cream	glace	water	de l'eau
ice cubes	glaçons	white wine	vin blanc
ham	jambon	yoghurt	yaourt
knife	couteau		

PERSONAL DOCUMENTS AND TRAVEL

airport	aéroport	railway station	gare
credit card	carte de crédit	shuttle	navette
customs	douane	suitcase	valise
passport	passeport	train/plane ticket	billet de train/d'avion
platform	voie	wallet	portefeuille

CLOTHING

coat	manteau	socks	chaussettes
jumper	pull	stockings	bas
raincoat	imperméable	suit	costume
shirt	chemise	tights	collants
shoes	chaussures	trousers	pantalons

USEFUL PHRASES

goodbye	au revoir	yes/no	oui/non
hello/good morning	bonjour	I am sorry	pardon
how	comment	why	pourquoi
excuse me	excusez-moi	when	quand
thank you	merci	please	s'il vous plaît

Do you speak English?	Parlez-vous anglais?
I don't understand	Je ne comprend pas
Talk slowly	Parlez lentement
Where's...?	Où est...?
When does the ... leave?	A quelle heure part...?
When does the ... arrive?	A quelle heure arrive...?
When does the museum open?	A quelle heure ouvre le musée?
When is the show?	A quelle heure est la représentation?
When is breakfast served?	A quelle heure sert-on le petit-déjeuner?
What does it cost?	Combien cela coûte?
Where can I buy a newspaper in English?	Où puis-je acheter un journal en anglais?
Where is the nearest petrol/gas station?	Où se trouve la station essence la plus proche?
Where can I change traveller's cheques?	Où puis-je échanger des traveller's cheques?
Where are the toilets?	Où sont les toilettes?
Do you accept credit cards?	Acceptez-voous les cartes de crédit?

Index

A

Notes

Notes

Notes